Handbook of Research on Transforming Teachers' Online Pedagogical Reasoning for Engaging K–12 Students in Virtual Learning

Margaret L. Niess
Oregon State University, USA

Henry Gillow-Wiles
Oregon State University, USA

Volume I

A volume in the Advances in Mobile and Distance Learning (AMDL) Book Series

Published in the United States of America by
IGI Global
Information Science Reference (an imprint of IGI Global)
701 E. Chocolate Avenue
Hershey PA, USA 17033
Tel: 717-533-8845
Fax: 717-533-8661
E-mail: cust@igi-global.com
Web site: http://www.igi-global.com

Copyright © 2021 by IGI Global. All rights reserved. No part of this publication may be reproduced, stored or distributed in any form or by any means, electronic or mechanical, including photocopying, without written permission from the publisher. Product or company names used in this set are for identification purposes only. Inclusion of the names of the products or companies does not indicate a claim of ownership by IGI Global of the trademark or registered trademark.
Library of Congress Cataloging-in-Publication Data

Names: Niess, Margaret, editor. | Gillow-Wiles, Henry, 1957- editor.
Title: Handbook of research on transforming teachers' online pedagogical
   reasoning for engaging K-12 students in virtual learning /
   Margaret L. Niess, and Henry Gillow-Wiles, Editors.
Description: Hershey, PA : Information Science Reference, [2021] | Includes
   bibliographical references and index. | Summary: "This book presents
   actual best practices and pedagogical reasoning for designing online
   strategies that work for K-12 virtual learning suggesting ways to think
   about teaching in virtual environments that can be used to guide
   instructional strategy choices and ultimate decisions"-- Provided by
   publisher.
Identifiers: LCCN 2021015990 (print) | LCCN 2021015991 (ebook) | ISBN
   9781799872221 (hardcover) | ISBN 9781799872245 (ebook)
Subjects: LCSH: Web-based instruction--Design. | Computer-assisted
   instruction. | Critical pedagogy. | Internet in education.
Classification: LCC LB1044.87 .T736 2021 (print) | LCC LB1044.87 (ebook)
   | DDC 371.33/4--dc23
LC record available at https://lccn.loc.gov/2021015990
LC ebook record available at https://lccn.loc.gov/2021015991

This book is published in the IGI Global book series Advances in Mobile and Distance Learning (AMDL) (ISSN: 2327-1892; eISSN: 2327-1906)

British Cataloguing in Publication Data
A Cataloguing in Publication record for this book is available from the British Library.

All work contributed to this book is new, previously-unpublished material. The views expressed in this book are those of the authors, but not necessarily of the publisher.

For electronic access to this publication, please contact: eresources@igi-global.com.

Advances in Mobile and Distance Learning (AMDL) Book Series

Patricia Ordóñez de Pablos
Universidad de Oviedo, Spain

ISSN:2327-1892
EISSN:2327-1906

Mission

Private and public institutions have made great strides in the fields of mobile and distance learning in recent years, providing greater learning opportunities outside of a traditional classroom setting. While the online learning revolution has allowed for greater learning opportunities, it has also presented numerous challenges for students and educators alike. As research advances, online educational settings can continue to develop and advance the technologies available for learners of all ages.

The **Advances in Mobile and Distance Learning** (AMDL) Book Series publishes research encompassing a variety of topics related to all facets of mobile and distance learning. This series aims to be an essential resource for the timeliest research to help advance the development of new educational technologies and pedagogy for use in online classrooms.

Coverage

- Economics of Distance and M-Learning
- Ethical Considerations
- Course Design
- Student-Teacher Interaction
- Tablets and Education
- Lifelong Learning
- Ubiquitous and Pervasive Learning
- Mobile Learning
- Online Class Management
- Student Achievement and Satisfaction

IGI Global is currently accepting manuscripts for publication within this series. To submit a proposal for a volume in this series, please contact our Acquisition Editors at Acquisitions@igi-global.com or visit: http://www.igi-global.com/publish/.

The Advances in Mobile and Distance Learning (AMDL) Book Series (ISSN 2327-1892) is published by IGI Global, 701 E. Chocolate Avenue, Hershey, PA 17033-1240, USA, www.igi-global.com. This series is composed of titles available for purchase individually; each title is edited to be contextually exclusive from any other title within the series. For pricing and ordering information please visit http://www.igi-global.com/book-series/advances-mobile-distance-learning/37162. Postmaster: Send all address changes to above address. © © 2021 IGI Global. All rights, including translation in other languages reserved by the publisher. No part of this series may be reproduced or used in any form or by any means – graphics, electronic, or mechanical, including photocopying, recording, taping, or information and retrieval systems – without written permission from the publisher, except for non commercial, educational use, including classroom teaching purposes. The views expressed in this series are those of the authors, but not necessarily of IGI Global.

Titles in this Series

For a list of additional titles in this series, please visit: www.igi-global.com/book-series

Educational Recovery for PK-12 Education During and After a Pndemic
Penelope D. Keough (National University, USA)
Information Science Reference • © 2021 • 283pp • H/C (ISBN: 9781799869528) • US $195.00

The Black Experience and Navigating Higher Education Through a Virtual World
Kimetta R. Hairston (Bowie State University, USA) Wendy M. Edmonds (Bowie State University, USA) and Shanetia P. Clark (Salisbury University, USA)
Information Science Reference • © 2021 • 282pp • H/C (ISBN: 9781799875376) • US $195.00

Curriculum Development and Online Instruction for the 21st Century
Tamara Phillips Fudge (Purdue University Global, USA) and Susan Shepherd Ferebee (Purdue University Global, USA)
Information Science Reference • © 2021 • 335pp • H/C (ISBN: 9781799876533) • US $195.00

Enhancing Human Rights Law Learning With Mobile Technologies
Joan Lu (University of Hudderseld, UK) and Stuart Toddington (University of Manchester, UK)
Information Science Reference • © 2021 • 330pp • H/C (ISBN: 9781799879756) • US $195.00

Handbook of Research on Lessons Learned From Transitioning to Virtual Classrooms During a Pandemic
Amy W. Thornburg (Queens University of Charlotte, USA) Robert J. Ceglie (Queens University of Charlotte, USA) and Dixie F. Abernathy (Queens University of Charlotte, USA)
Information Science Reference • © 2021 • 457pp • H/C (ISBN: 9781799865575) • US $245.00

Handbook of Research on Inequities in Online Education During Global Crises
Lydia Kyei-Blankson (Illinois State University, USA) Joseph Blankson (Ohio Northern University, USA) and Esther Ntuli (Idaho State University, USA)
Information Science Reference • © 2021 • 640pp • H/C (ISBN: 9781799865339) • US $245.00

Designing Effective Distance and Blended Learning Environments in K-12
Thomas F. Driscoll III (Bristol Warren Regional School District, USA)
Information Science Reference • © 2021 • 330pp • H/C (ISBN: 9781799868293) • US $195.00

Handbook of Research on K-12 Blended and Virtual Learning Through the i²Flex Classroom Model
Maria D. Avgerinou (American Community Schools (ACS), Athens, Greece) and Peggy Pelonis (American Community Schools (ACS), Athens, Greece)
Information Science Reference • © 2021 • 710pp • H/C (ISBN: 9781799877608) • US $245.00

701 East Chocolate Avenue, Hershey, PA 17033, USA
Tel: 717-533-8845 x100 • Fax: 717-533-8661
E-Mail: cust@igi-global.com • www.igi-global.com

We wish to dedicate this book in memory of
Professor Göran Fransson, University of Gävle, Sweden

In the process of producing this handbook, we were saddened with the passing of Professor Fransson as he was co-authoring a chapter titled *An Interactional and Aligned Educational Design Framework to Support Teachers' Pedagogical Reasoning* with Assistant Professor Jörgen Holmberg. Göran was a Professor in Curriculum Studies and an Associate Professor of Education at the Faculty of Education and Business Studies, University of Gävle, Sweden. His research centered on digital technologies in educational contexts, teacher commitment, teachers' professional development and induction and mentoring in different professions, with a primary focus on teachers. Göran was a true humanist and is admired for his commitment to supporting free speech and press, fighting injustices of all kinds, and the importance of caring for the environment. He absolutely believed that the world could be made a better place through education. That belief was what drove him throughout many late nights. He was convinced that when we understand each other better, and when we (through science) understand more about the world that we inhabit together, we will treat each other and our world with an increased respect and make more informed decisions. He was a true scholar, mentor and friend who will truly be missed both personally and professionally.

Editorial Advisory Board

Andrea C. Burrows, *University of Wyoming, USA*
Dawn Hathaway, *George Mason University, USA*
Yi Jin, *Kennesaw State University, USA*
John K. Lee, *North Carolina State University, USA*
Irina Lyublinskaya, *Teachers College, Columbia University , USA*
Tia C. Madkins, *The University of Texas at Austin, USA*
S. Asli Özgün-Koca, *Wayne State University, USA*
Keryn Pratt, *University of Otago, New Zealand*
David K. Pugalee, *University of North Carolina at Charlotte, USA*
Stephen I. Tucker, *University of Queensland, Australia*
Joke Voogt, *University of Amsterdam, The Netherlands*
Janet M. Walker, *Indiana University of Pennsylvania, USA*

List of Contributors

Acuña, Kym / *Midwestern State University, USA* 194
Albert, Jennifer / *The Citadel, USA* 359
Andrews, Ashley Ray / *The Citadel, USA* 359
Baker, Courtney K. / *George Mason University, USA* 470
Balcerzak, Phyllis / *University of Missouri, St. Louis, USA* 379
Barrios, Amy M. / *Texas A&M University, San Antonio, USA* 583
Bengtson, Douglas W. / *Battle Creek STEM Academy, USA* 446
Beschorner, Beth / *Minnesota State University, Mankato, USA* 109
Blanton, Melanie / *The Citadel, USA* 359
Broderick, Maggie / *Northcentral University, USA* 212
Bullock, Emma / *Sam Houston State University, USA* 561
Carey, Lisa Beth / *Kennedy Krieger Institute, USA* 42
Choucair, Mona / *Baylor University, USA* 604
Cory, Beth / *Sam Houston State University, USA* 561
Driskell, Shannon O. / *University of Dayton, USA* 494
Du, Xiaoxue / *Teachers College, Columbia University, USA* 534
Fletcher, Nicole / *Fairfield University, USA* 402
Fransson, Göran / *University of Gävle, Sweden* 516
Galanti, Terrie McLaughlin / *University of North Florida, USA* 470
Gallagher-Immenschuh, Charlotte Kristyn / *Northcentral University, USA* 212
Gillow-Wiles, Henry / *Oregon State University, USA* 1, 643
Golden, John / *Grand Valley State University, USA* 446
Gupta, Dittika / *Midwestern State University, USA* 194
Herron, Julie / *Augusta University, USA* 561
Hodges, Tracey S. / *University of Alabama, USA* 318
Hodge-Zickerman, Angie / *Northern Arizona University, USA* 278
Holmberg, Jörgen / *University of Gävle, Sweden* 516
Janakiraman, Shamila / *Purdue University, USA* 236
Jocius, Robin / *University of Texas at Arlington, USA* 359
Johnston, Eleanor M. / *York University, Canada* 335
Joshi, Deepti / *The Citadel, USA* 359
Joswick, Candace / *The University of Texas at Arlington, USA* 402
Kasmer, Lisa A. / *Grand Valley State University, USA* 446
Khazanchi, Pankaj / *Cobb County School District, USA & Liberty University, USA* 19
Khazanchi, Rashmi / *Mitchell County School System, USA & Open University of the
    Netherlands, Heerlen, Netherlands* 19
Kohler, Karen L. / *Texas A&M University, San Antonio, USA* 583

Kouo, Jennifer Lee / *Towson University, USA* 42
Kraft, Tammy / *George Mason University, USA* 470
Labissiere, Tiffany / *Literacy Network, USA* 297
Lawrence, Salika A. / *The College of New Jersey, USA* 297
Lee, Victor R. / *Stanford University, USA* 624
Lyublinskaya, Irina / *Teachers College, Columbia University, USA* 534
Malhotra, Taru / *York University, Canada* 335
Mardi, Fatemeh / *University of Missouri, St. Louis, USA* 379
Meador, Audrey / *West Texas A&M, USA* 402
Medellin, Kelly / *Midwestern State University, USA* 194
Meier, Ellen B. / *Teachers College, Columbia University, USA* 86
Mellman, Letha / *University of Wyoming, USA* 149
Mineo, Caron / *Teachers College, Columbia University, USA* 86
Morrison, Mia L. / *University of Maine, Orono, USA* 170
Morrow-Leong, Kimberly / *George Mason University, USA* 470
Niess, Margaret L. / *Oregon State University, USA* 1, 643
Parrish, Andrea Harkins / *Johns Hopkins University, USA* 42
Pinnell, Margaret F. / *University of Dayton, USA* 494
Randhawa, Simran / *Assessments Mentoring and Impact, India* 19
Ray, Amy / *Sam Houston State University, USA* 561
Rigelman, Nicole / *Portland State University, USA & The Math Learning Center, USA* 423
Sableski, Mary-Kate / *University of Dayton, USA* 494
Saxton, Emily / *The Math Learning Center, USA* 423
Singh, Jason Anthony / *University of Toronto, Canada* 259
Slykhuis, David A. / *University of Northern Colorado, USA* 149
Smith, Jess / *Baylor University, USA* 604
Southerton, Emily / *Stanford University, USA* 624
Stade, Eric / *University of Colorado, Boulder, USA* 278
Stone, Monique C. / *Literacy Network, USA* 297
Swallow, Meredith J. C. / *University of Maine, Farmington, USA* 170
Swanson, Christopher / *Johns Hopkins University, USA* 42
Talbert, Sandra / *Baylor University, USA* 604
Terlop, Rachel E. / *George Mason University, USA* 67
Thomas, Sarah M. / *Battle Creek STEM Academy, USA* 446
Vargas-Ewing, James / *New York City Public Schools, USA* 67
Vennebush, Patrick / *The Math Learning Center, USA* 423
Walsh-Rock, Elizabeth / *Ferguson-Florissant R-II School District, USA* 379
Webb, C. Lorraine / *Texas A&M University, San Antonio, USA* 583
Williams, Mia Kim / *University of Wyoming, USA* 149
Woodward, Lindsay / *Drake University, USA* 109
Worwood, Matthew / *University of Connecticut, USA* 126
York, Cindy S. / *Northern Illinois University, USA* 278
Yu, Paul Woo Dong / *Grand Valley State University, USA* 446

Table of Contents

Preface xxvi

Acknowledgment xxxiv

Volume I

Section 1
Foundation Knowledge For Transforming Teachers' Online Pedagogical Reasoning For Virtual Learning Environments

Chapter 1
Is There Recess on Mars? Developing a Sense of Belonging in Online Learning 1
    Henry Gillow-Wiles, Oregon State University, USA
    Margaret L. Niess, Oregon State University, USA

Chapter 2
Teaching Students With Learning Disabilities in a Virtual Learning Environment 19
    Pankaj Khazanchi, Cobb County School District, USA & Liberty University, USA
    Rashmi Khazanchi, Mitchell County School System, USA & Open University of the
        Netherlands, Heerlen, Netherlands
    Simran Randhawa, Assessments Mentoring and Impact, India

Chapter 3
Implementing Universal Design for Learning in the Virtual Learning Environment 42
    Andrea Harkins Parrish, Johns Hopkins University, USA
    Jennifer Lee Kouo, Towson University, USA
    Lisa Beth Carey, Kennedy Krieger Institute, USA
    Christopher Swanson, Johns Hopkins University, USA

Chapter 4
Choosing Culturally, Linguistically, and Cognitively Distance Learning Platforms: Correlations
Across Early Childhood Professional Standards to Promote Inclusion 67
    Rachel E. Terlop, George Mason University, USA
    James Vargas-Ewing, New York City Public Schools, USA

Chapter 5
Pedagogical Challenges During COVID: Opportunities for Transformative Shifts 86
    Ellen B. Meier, Teachers College, Columbia University, USA
    Caron Mineo, Teachers College, Columbia University, USA

Chapter 6
Using the Technology Integration Planning Cycle to Select Digital Tools for Virtual Instruction 109
    Lindsay Woodward, Drake University, USA
    Beth Beschorner, Minnesota State University, Mankato, USA

Chapter 7
Four Steps to Promote Teacher Creativity When Making the Transition to Virtual Learning
Experiences 126
    Matthew Worwood, University of Connecticut, USA

Section 2
Best Practices And Pedagogical Reasoning In K-12 Grade Levels

Chapter 8
Using Generation Z's Learning Approaches to Create Meaningful Online Learning 149
    Letha Mellman, University of Wyoming, USA
    Mia Kim Williams, University of Wyoming, USA
    David A. Slykhuis, University of Northern Colorado, USA

Chapter 9
Intersections of Micro-Level Contextual Factors and Technological Pedagogical Knowledge 170
    Meredith J. C. Swallow, University of Maine, Farmington, USA
    Mia L. Morrison, University of Maine, Orono, USA

Chapter 10
Teaching Strategies During a Pandemic: Learnings and Reflections 194
    Kelly Medellin, Midwestern State University, USA
    Dittika Gupta, Midwestern State University, USA
    Kym Acuña, Midwestern State University, USA

Chapter 11
Crystallizing Moments: Teacher-Student Interaction and Engagement in Online Primary Grades
Education 212
    Charlotte Kristyn Gallagher-Immenschuh, Northcentral University, USA
    Maggie Broderick, Northcentral University, USA

Chapter 12
Using Digital Games in Virtual Classrooms to Make Attitudinal Learning Motivating and
Engaging 236
    Shamila Janakiraman, Purdue University, USA

Chapter 13
Building Community in Online Learning Environments: Strategies for High School Teachers 259
    Jason Anthony Singh, University of Toronto, Canada

Chapter 14
TACTivities: A Way to Promote Hands-On, Minds-On Learning in a Virtual Learning
Environment 278
    Angie Hodge-Zickerman, Northern Arizona University, USA
    Eric Stade, University of Colorado, Boulder, USA
    Cindy S. York, Northern Illinois University, USA

Chapter 15
The 4Cs of Academic Language and Literacy: Facilitating Structured Discussions in Remote
Classrooms 297
    Salika A. Lawrence, The College of New Jersey, USA
    Tiffany Labissiere, Literacy Network, USA
    Monique C. Stone, Literacy Network, USA

Volume II

Section 3
Best Practices And Pedagogical Reasoning In K-12 Content Areas

Chapter 16
How Foundational Writing Informs Early Decoding Skills in Virtual Instruction 318
    Tracey S. Hodges, University of Alabama, USA

Chapter 17
Examining Digital Pedagogy of Teachers Using Engeström's Activity Theory 335
    Taru Malhotra, York University, Canada
    Eleanor M. Johnston, York University, Canada

Chapter 18
Computational Thinking and Making in Virtual Elementary Classrooms 359
    Robin Jocius, University of Texas at Arlington, USA
    Melanie Blanton, The Citadel, USA
    Jennifer Albert, The Citadel, USA
    Deepti Joshi, The Citadel, USA
    Ashley Ray Andrews, The Citadel, USA

Chapter 19
Designing Virtual Collaborations in Case-Based Science Learning: Using Google Slides, Padlet,
and FlipGrid 379
    Fatemeh Mardi, University of Missouri, St. Louis, USA
    Elizabeth Walsh-Rock, Ferguson-Florissant R-II School District, USA
    Phyllis Balcerzak, University of Missouri, St. Louis, USA

Chapter 20
Transforming K-12 Mathematics Classroom Teacher Pedagogy Through Virtual Number Talks 402
Candace Joswick, The University of Texas at Arlington, USA
Nicole Fletcher, Fairfield University, USA
Audrey Meador, West Texas A&M, USA

Chapter 21
Using Technology-Enhanced Activities to Transform K–5 Mathematics Planning, Teaching, and Learning 423
Nicole Rigelman, Portland State University, USA & The Math Learning Center, USA
Patrick Vennebush, The Math Learning Center, USA
Emily Saxton, The Math Learning Center, USA

Chapter 22
Mathematics, Social Structure, and Technology: A Categorical Framework to Support Online Middle School Mathematics Teaching 446
Douglas W. Bengtson, Battle Creek STEM Academy, USA
John Golden, Grand Valley State University, USA
Lisa A. Kasmer, Grand Valley State University, USA
Sarah M. Thomas, Battle Creek STEM Academy, USA
Paul Woo Dong Yu, Grand Valley State University, USA

Chapter 23
Using Mathematics Digital Interactive Notebooks as Authentic Integrated Online Assessments 470
Terrie McLaughlin Galanti, University of North Florida, USA
Courtney K. Baker, George Mason University, USA
Tammy Kraft, George Mason University, USA
Kimberly Morrow-Leong, George Mason University, USA

Chapter 24
Virtual STEM Stories: Blending STEM and Literacy in a Virtual Environment 494
Shannon O. Driskell, University of Dayton, USA
Margaret F. Pinnell, University of Dayton, USA
Mary-Kate Sableski, University of Dayton, USA

Section 4
Transforming Teachers Knowledge for Teaching in Virtual Environments – Pre-service, In-service and Professional Development

Chapter 25
An Interactional and Aligned Educational Design Framework to Support Teachers' Pedagogical Reasoning 516
Jörgen Holmberg, University of Gävle, Sweden
Göran Fransson, University of Gävle, Sweden

Chapter 26
Transforming Teaching for Virtual Environments: Developing Preservice Teachers' Online TPACK 534
 Irina Lyublinskaya, Teachers College, Columbia University, USA
 Xiaoxue Du, Teachers College, Columbia University, USA

Chapter 27
Promoting Higher Student Mathematics Achievement in Online Settings: Introducing PHiSMAOS 561
 Emma Bullock, Sam Houston State University, USA
 Amy Ray, Sam Houston State University, USA
 Beth Cory, Sam Houston State University, USA
 Julie Herron, Augusta University, USA

Chapter 28
Classroom Management, Lesson Planning, and Technology Integration . . . Oh My! Ways to Cope With Online Pedagogical Practices 583
 C. Lorraine Webb, Texas A&M University, San Antonio, USA
 Amy M. Barrios, Texas A&M University, San Antonio, USA
 Karen L. Kohler, Texas A&M University, San Antonio, USA

Chapter 29
What Now? Online Pedagogical Reasoning of Student Teaching Secondary ELAR in Virtual Learning Environments 604
 Jess Smith, Baylor University, USA
 Sandra Talbert, Baylor University, USA
 Mona Choucair, Baylor University, USA

Chapter 30
Current Approaches in Teacher Learning on Digital Social Platforms 624
 Emily Southerton, Stanford University, USA
 Victor R. Lee, Stanford University, USA

Section 5

Chapter 31
Developing Teachers' Knowledge for Teaching in Virtual Contexts: Lessons From the Pandemic of 2020-2021 643
 Margaret L. Niess, Oregon State University, USA
 Henry Gillow-Wiles, Oregon State University, USA

Compilation of References xxxvi

About the Contributors cxiv

Index cxxix

Detailed Table of Contents

Preface xxvi

Acknowledgment xxxiv

Volume I

Section 1
Foundation Knowledge For Transforming Teachers' Online Pedagogical Reasoning For Virtual Learning Environments

Chapter 1
Is There Recess on Mars? Developing a Sense of Belonging in Online Learning 1
    Henry Gillow-Wiles, Oregon State University, USA
    Margaret L. Niess, Oregon State University, USA

The pandemic of 2019 created a multitude of challenges for teachers and students alike. The urgency with which education was forced to transition to a fully online delivery paradigm necessitated a triage and curate process to decide where efforts were to be placed. Teachers, forced to move quickly, leveraged existing research in designing their courses and activities. However, little research exists concerning how to meaningfully create online learning environments for K-12 students. This chapter explores the importance of recess, where children have free-play, self-constructed interactions essential for developing a sense of belonging. Through exploring the sense of belonging construct in the context of how it is formed, its importance for developing social skills, and the connection between a sense of belonging and successful online learning, the authors present critical gaps in research and suggest directions for research.

Chapter 2
Teaching Students With Learning Disabilities in a Virtual Learning Environment 19
    Pankaj Khazanchi, Cobb County School District, USA & Liberty University, USA
    Rashmi Khazanchi, Mitchell County School System, USA & Open University of the
        Netherlands, Heerlen, Netherlands
    Simran Randhawa, Assessments Mentoring and Impact, India

COVID-19 brought unprecedented changes in the education sector at all levels globally. These rapid changes have transformed the way teachers are transacting the curriculum in K-12 classrooms. Teachers have had to adapt and depend on a virtual mode to reach students and facilitate student engagement and subsequent learning. In the absence of professional development support, such overnight changes and giant leaps from traditional face-to-face interaction with students have been extremely challenging for teachers and equally stressful for students and their parents. Many teachers describe their helplessness with growing absenteeism and delayed submission of student assignments. It is even more difficult for students with a learning disability to engage virtually for a longer time in front of a computer screen. They often need intensive, one-on-one support from the parent. This chapter aims to highlight the challenges faced by professionals to teach students with specific learning disabilities effectively in a virtual learning environment and identify effective solutions.

Chapter 3
Implementing Universal Design for Learning in the Virtual Learning Environment 42
    Andrea Harkins Parrish, Johns Hopkins University, USA
    Jennifer Lee Kouo, Towson University, USA
    Lisa Beth Carey, Kennedy Krieger Institute, USA
    Christopher Swanson, Johns Hopkins University, USA

This chapter presents an overview of learner variability and addresses how the Universal Design for Learning framework can be applied to meet the diverse needs of all students in a virtual learning environment. Emphasis is placed on how educational professionals at multiple levels can apply their current knowledge to design and implement effective and universally designed instruction through multiple means of engagement, representation, and action and expression. It also addresses the importance of providing specialized instruction, including how educators can provide federally protected educational supports in virtual learning environments. The authors provide directions for further examination of virtual learning and the implications of this instructional delivery model for meeting the needs of all learners in light of recent trends.

Chapter 4
Choosing Culturally, Linguistically, and Cognitively Distance Learning Platforms: Correlations Across Early Childhood Professional Standards to Promote Inclusion 67
    Rachel E. Terlop, George Mason University, USA
    James Vargas-Ewing, New York City Public Schools, USA

Upon completion of their educator preparation program, a study done by Archambault found that teachers felt most prepared in the areas of pedagogy, content, and pedagogical content. However, the same teachers reported feeling least prepared in the areas of technology and technology integration. With instruction shifting to an online space during COVID-19, the consideration of how to teach virtually was no longer abstract. This chapter highlights the journey of a teacher working to find supportive technology for their class, evaluating existing resources, connecting the tools to teaching standards, and ensuring platforms are inclusive and relevant for the culturally, linguistically, and cognitively diverse (CLCD) learners who utilize augmentative and alternative communication (AAC) devices. This chapter is rooted in early childhood education, social constructivism, and disability critical race theory (DisCrit) and seeks to serve as a critical guide, or model, for intentional and inclusive educators, researchers, practitioners, and learners.

Chapter 5
Pedagogical Challenges During COVID: Opportunities for Transformative Shifts 86
    Ellen B. Meier, Teachers College, Columbia University, USA
    Caron Mineo, Teachers College, Columbia University, USA

Educators could not have predicted the degree of disruption that COVID-19 could cause until schools closed and forced teachers to move to online teaching. This chapter describes the use of a research-based model, Innovating Instruction, to support teachers in their transition to remote learning. Grounded in a concern for greater equity and social justice for all students, the model prepares teachers to design inquiry-based, culturally relevant projects. The development of the model is based on a critique that technology has largely failed to impact pedagogical change because of a limited sense of the scope of the change needed. Instructional Innovation brings together key aspects of a systems change effort, thus contributing to an emerging educational theory for the catalytic use of technology to promote pedagogical practices that are culturally responsive, rigorous, and engaging.

Chapter 6
Using the Technology Integration Planning Cycle to Select Digital Tools for Virtual Instruction.... 109
Lindsay Woodward, Drake University, USA
Beth Beschorner, Minnesota State University, Mankato, USA

This chapter explores the use of the Technology Integration Planning Cycle (TIPC) for supporting teachers' decision-making as they plan virtual instruction. The TIPC is designed to support teachers in evaluating the possible contributions of digital tools to instruction that facilitates meeting specific learning goals. The use of the TIPC to support pre-service teachers, in-service teachers, and in professional development settings is discussed. Then, examples of a teacher using the TIPC as she plans virtual reading and writing instruction illustrate the potential of the TIPC to support effective virtual instruction. Finally, issues of access, equity, and safety related to use the TIPC are discussed.

Chapter 7
Four Steps to Promote Teacher Creativity When Making the Transition to Virtual Learning
Experiences 126
Matthew Worwood, University of Connecticut, USA

This chapter presents four steps for teacher creativity as part of a design-based approach to problem-solving pedagogical challenges using virtual learning environments. Building on existing practices found in creative problem-solving and design thinking methodology, these steps explore change as a journey that begins with an intent to produce an outcome that improves a specific aspect of the learning experience. Glaveanu's five-A framework provides a sociocultural perspective to support the concept of teacher creativity in the classroom, while Kaufman and Beghetto's 4-C model serves as a developmental approach to evaluating outcomes based on the impact they have in the environment. Future opportunities for study, including integrating learning analytics and situating the different stages of creative problem-solving in education, are also discussed.

Section 2
Best Practices And Pedagogical Reasoning In K-12 Grade Levels

Chapter 8
Using Generation Z's Learning Approaches to Create Meaningful Online Learning 149
Letha Mellman, University of Wyoming, USA
Mia Kim Williams, University of Wyoming, USA
David A. Slykhuis, University of Northern Colorado, USA

This chapter presents findings from an eDelphi research study through which participant experts of Generation Z established learning approaches for online environments. Experts were members of this generation all being born in 2001 or 2002 who have participated in informal or formal pre-pandemic online learning. Background on Generation Z, description of the eDelphi research method, and implications of the learning approaches provide insight to different pedagogical practices that support successful online teaching and learning aligned with the learning approaches established by Generation Z. This generation bridges the bulk of K12 and undergraduate learners. As educators re-vision classrooms necessitated by the current educational climate, understanding the learning approaches of students provides a critical foundation on which educators can make pedagogical decisions that engage learners in online contexts.

Chapter 9
Intersections of Micro-Level Contextual Factors and Technological Pedagogical Knowledge 170
Meredith J. C. Swallow, University of Maine, Farmington, USA
Mia L. Morrison, University of Maine, Orono, USA

Context is an essential component of educator knowledge development and practice. When K-12 learning environments shifted from traditional schools and classrooms to remote learning, teacher knowledge of context was challenged as students were situated in varied and unpredictable settings. In this chapter, researchers examine the ways in which purposeful attention to technological pedagogical knowledge in teacher development and practice can influence the impact of fluctuations in micro level teaching contexts in remote learning environments. To provide direction in enhancing knowledge across contexts, the authors focus on the cross curricular learning skills of critical thinking, communication, collaboration, and creativity. Particular attention is given to learning activities that can span across contexts, grade levels, and subject areas.

Chapter 10
Teaching Strategies During a Pandemic: Learnings and Reflections 194
Kelly Medellin, Midwestern State University, USA
Dittika Gupta, Midwestern State University, USA
Kym Acuña, Midwestern State University, USA

Due to the COVID-19 pandemic, teachers were faced with the insurmountable task of changing teaching methods to virtual online pedagogy, practically overnight, that continued to provide students with quality instruction using best practices. Action research was employed to help seek the answers to the question: During a pandemic with school online and students socially distanced in person simultaneously, how could teachers still provide cooperative learning experiences that give students opportunities to collaborate in class while continuing to use best practices like the 4Cs (communication, collaboration, critical thinking, and creativity)? Through completely online and synchronous (online and face-to-face) instruction, Jamboard, Padlet, Mentimeter, Flipgrid, and Bitmoji Classroom were implemented to support student learning through the 4Cs of 21st century learning. In this chapter, the rationale, implementation, successes, and challenges will be revealed from self-examined action research.

Chapter 11
Crystallizing Moments: Teacher-Student Interaction and Engagement in Online Primary Grades Education 212
Charlotte Kristyn Gallagher-Immenschuh, Northcentral University, USA
Maggie Broderick, Northcentral University, USA

The COVID-19 pandemic has forced K-12 teachers to think differently about their teaching methods. Primary grade teachers must especially consider how to make online learning engaging, motivating, and as hands-on and developmentally appropriate as possible for young learners. This chapter provides insight into purposely created and child-centered crystallizing moments, in which research-based strategies can enhance teacher-student interaction and engagement. Examples from real-world teaching practice are included.

Chapter 12
Using Digital Games in Virtual Classrooms to Make Attitudinal Learning Motivating and Engaging 236
> *Shamila Janakiraman, Purdue University, USA*

The COVID-19 global pandemic has made it difficult for schools to conduct in-person learning, pushing educators to think innovatively to create digital classrooms and engage K-12 learners. This chapter will provide best practices and pedagogical reasoning into the use of digital game-based learning (DGBL) for attitudinal instruction in virtual classrooms of middle and high school students. When it comes to teaching socio-scientific topics, providing cognitive knowledge is not the only goal of education. Young learners need to develop appropriate attitudes and behaviors to ensure the holistic development of their personality. This is where DGBL has been found to be an effective instructional activity. Although the focus of this chapter is on using DGBL in environmental sustainability education, it provides implications that are applicable to other socio-scientific topics as well.

Chapter 13
Building Community in Online Learning Environments: Strategies for High School Teachers 259
> *Jason Anthony Singh, University of Toronto, Canada*

This self-study assesses the impact on classroom communities using distance learning activities. Five activities used in the author's high school science classes during the COVID-19 pandemic are analyzed based on a bilateral framework interweaving transactional distance (student-teacher interactions) and social interaction (student-student interaction). A reflective narration of activity development leads to a discussion of the effects of activity design on student-teacher and student-student interactions. The intersection between these interactions serves as a foundation for analyzing their impact on the classroom community. A predominant theme is the psychological separation students face when learning remotely and how activity design can intensify or diminish this perceived detachment. This chapter provides an exemplar for other educators to consider how transactional distance and social interaction play a role in the development of their own classroom communities.

Chapter 14
TACTivities: A Way to Promote Hands-On, Minds-On Learning in a Virtual Learning Environment.. 278
> *Angie Hodge-Zickerman, Northern Arizona University, USA*
> *Eric Stade, University of Colorado, Boulder, USA*
> *Cindy S. York, Northern Illinois University, USA*

The need to keep students engaged is particularly acute in virtual environments. In this chapter, the authors describe TACTivities (learning activities with tactile components), designed to help encourage student participation, collaboration, and communication. Originally developed for in-person instruction,

TACTivities are readily adaptable to online learning environments. TACTivities are intended to foster a sense of play, creative problem-solving, and exploration among the students who undertake to complete these tasks, and also among the teachers who design them. Unlike other tactile learning ventures, which may involve various kinds of physical props, TACTivities entail only moveable pieces of paper, or electronic equivalents. This feature means that TACTivities are quite portable, and they are easily implemented, shared, and modified (particularly in remote settings). Further, TACTivities allow for inclusion of discipline-specific content, language, and formalism, while still cultivating physical engagement in problem-solving and critical thinking in any subject area.

Chapter 15
The 4Cs of Academic Language and Literacy: Facilitating Structured Discussions in Remote Classrooms 297
    Salika A. Lawrence, The College of New Jersey, USA
    Tiffany Labissiere, Literacy Network, USA
    Monique C. Stone, Literacy Network, USA

This chapter describes how teachers have used structured discussions and digital tools to transition from traditional classrooms to remote, online instruction during the COVID-19 pandemic. With emphasis on culturally and linguistically diverse students, the chapter includes examples of how teachers reinforce literacy while supporting 21st century skills such as collaboration, communication, critical thinking, and creativity. Tools and strategies are presented along with examples teachers can use to facilitate student learning across content areas in virtual classrooms.

Volume II

Section 3
Best Practices And Pedagogical Reasoning In K-12 Content Areas

Chapter 16
How Foundational Writing Informs Early Decoding Skills in Virtual Instruction 318
    Tracey S. Hodges, University of Alabama, USA

How do you teach a child to read in a virtual classroom? Answering this question can feel like a daunting task – the new kindergartener, five-years-old, may not be able to navigate the virtual classroom because they do not yet possess the skill of reading. When the act of teaching reading takes up the majority of instructional time in the early elementary classroom, this task can seem impossible in online learning environments. This chapter presents methods and approaches for teaching early reading and writing virtually. Specifically, the chapter covers developmental levels for reading and writing, technological frameworks for engaging students in virtual instruction, and applications of virtual instruction to early literacy instruction. The chapter serves as a practical toolkit for teachers to help set students up for success without hindering their knowledge of skills that will be essential to their learning in the future.

Chapter 17
Examining Digital Pedagogy of Teachers Using Engeström's Activity Theory 335
    Taru Malhotra, York University, Canada
    Eleanor M. Johnston, York University, Canada

This chapter proposes that Engeström's activity triangles in tandem with direct attention to the 4Cs—collaboration, communication, critical thinking, and creativity—can help teachers and researchers identify effective teaching practices in online environments. The authors illustrate this technique using data from two studies on teachers' technology use in brick-and-mortar classrooms. Focusing on literacy and music in the elementary classroom, the authors suggest ways teachers can reflect upon and design their online activities considering students' use of the 4Cs. They demonstrate the process using an exemplar online activity. Apart from individual pedagogical concerns, the chapter also discusses more significant issues around policy, access, professional development, and the 4Cs and offers implications to research and practice.

Chapter 18
Computational Thinking and Making in Virtual Elementary Classrooms 359
    Robin Jocius, University of Texas at Arlington, USA
    Melanie Blanton, The Citadel, USA
    Jennifer Albert, The Citadel, USA
    Deepti Joshi, The Citadel, USA
    Ashley Ray Andrews, The Citadel, USA

This chapter documents findings from the Making CT (Computational Thinking) project, a collaborative effort between project team members and elementary teachers that aims to reimagine interdisciplinary, computational thinking-infused making lessons for a virtual format. Virtual making CT lessons were grounded in four design principles: standards-based practices, clear and explicit expectations, multiple means of engagement, and opportunities for collaboration. Drawing on data from virtual teacher professional development sessions, lesson implementation, and teacher interviews, this chapter illustrates how teachers were able to engage in the difficult work of reconceptualizing CT-infused making lessons for the virtual classroom. These principles can be used to support the design of other interdisciplinary activities to support P-5 students' development of creative and authentic problem-solving in virtual learning environments.

Chapter 19
Designing Virtual Collaborations in Case-Based Science Learning: Using Google Slides, Padlet, and FlipGrid 379
    Fatemeh Mardi, University of Missouri, St. Louis, USA
    Elizabeth Walsh-Rock, Ferguson-Florissant R-II School District, USA
    Phyllis Balcerzak, University of Missouri, St. Louis, USA

This chapter focuses on the design components and layout of digitally engaging high school students in high level thinking activities during virtual synchronous science sessions. By integrating digital tools and applying case-based lessons that target "engaging in argument from evidence," learning experiences that engage all students in an online setting are described. Two virtual experiences from a high school anatomy class related to making a diagnosis and justifying it using evidence are presented in this chapter. In the bell ringer and summative case study diagnosis activities, Zoom breakout room, Google Slides, and Google Docs are used. From a biomedical science course, two other learning experiences are described which utilize career-oriented role play and cases studies to have students collaborate and authentically apply their content knowledge. In the contact tracing and genetic counseling activities, Padlet and FlipGrid are used respectively. The related pedagogical reasoning, successes, and challenges follow the explanations of the four experiences.

Chapter 20

Transforming K-12 Mathematics Classroom Teacher Pedagogy Through Virtual Number Talks..... 402

    Candace Joswick, The University of Texas at Arlington, USA
    Nicole Fletcher, Fairfield University, USA
    Audrey Meador, West Texas A&M, USA

Number Talks is a popular K-12 mathematics routine utilized in classrooms across the United States. Number Talks allows teachers to elicit and respond to students' mathematical thinking through the development of an encouraging classroom community and provide opportunities for students to engage in critical thinking, collaboration, communication, and creativity. In this chapter, the authors report their "virtualization" of the Number Talks routine and the development of a teacher learning cycle that supports implementation of this practice. The virtualization of Number Talks is illustrated through the pedagogical transformation of one teacher, who begins the teacher learning cycle skeptical of the value of Number Talks and ends with an innovative Virtual Number Talks practice that benefited both students and teachers in her school. This teacher's implementation of Virtual Number Talks and engagement in the "4C" of 21st century learning demonstrate a transformation of pedagogy that uses technology to create rich online mathematics learning experiences.

Chapter 21

Using Technology-Enhanced Activities to Transform K–5 Mathematics Planning, Teaching, and Learning..423

    Nicole Rigelman, Portland State University, USA & The Math Learning Center, USA
    Patrick Vennebush, The Math Learning Center, USA
    Emily Saxton, The Math Learning Center, USA

In this chapter, the authors describe the technology-enhanced activities intended to transform the ways elementary mathematics teachers provide instruction to their students during a time of distance learning and potentially beyond. Recognizing instruction would take place in a variety of formats, The Math Learning Center supported teachers by providing resources that allow them to continue to engage students in the 4Cs—critical thinking, creative thinking, communicating, and collaborating—even in distance-learning environments. More specifically, the authors describe the alignment between the design of the technology-enhanced activities (TEAs) and the 4Cs as well as how the flexibility built into the TEAs provides opportunities for teachers to employ their technological pedagogical content knowledge as they make decisions for implementation in their specific contexts. Results from surveys and teacher interviews influenced the organization's plans for future research and development opportunities.

Chapter 22

Mathematics, Social Structure, and Technology: A Categorical Framework to Support Online Middle School Mathematics Teaching..446

    Douglas W. Bengtson, Battle Creek STEM Academy, USA
    John Golden, Grand Valley State University, USA
    Lisa A. Kasmer, Grand Valley State University, USA
    Sarah M. Thomas, Battle Creek STEM Academy, USA
    Paul Woo Dong Yu, Grand Valley State University, USA

This chapter provides insights gained from a collaborative action research project with university and middle school mathematics faculty. A categorical framework that considers the relationship between technology, mathematics content, and social interaction was used by the researchers to more deeply examine the varied uses and types of technology related to online teaching. In particular was the use of a relatively new category of software, Interactive Mathematics Classroom Builders, which integrates powerful mathematics tools with highly interactive classroom management features. The teachers found opportunities to try several novel uses of technology in their online lessons, advancing their teaching and the student experience, while learning lessons about teaching with technology that may apply to both remote teaching and the face-to-face classroom.

Chapter 23
Using Mathematics Digital Interactive Notebooks as Authentic Integrated Online Assessments 470
    Terrie McLaughlin Galanti, University of North Florida, USA
    Courtney K. Baker, George Mason University, USA
    Tammy Kraft, George Mason University, USA
    Kimberly Morrow-Leong, George Mason University, USA

In response to the global health crisis, K-12 mathematics teachers were forced to rapidly transition to online learning and assessment. The mathematics teacher educators in this study identified an unprecedented opportunity to design and facilitate more equitable assessments that leveraged emergent collaborative technologies. They replaced traditional written reflections with a digital interactive notebook (dINB) in a graduate synchronous online geometry and measurement course for practicing teachers. This prototype of an authentic integrated online assessment model emphasized cycles of reflection and revision based on instructor and peer feedback. While the K-12 teachers enrolled in this course valued the dINB as evaluative of their own progress toward content mastery, they faced challenges in realizing the full potential of this model to integrate formative, summative, and ipsative assessment functions in their own classrooms. Implications for the development of K-12 teachers' TPACK (Technological Pedagogical Content Knowledge) and their readiness to use more innovative forms of assessment in virtual learning are presented.

Chapter 24
Virtual STEM Stories: Blending STEM and Literacy in a Virtual Environment 494
    Shannon O. Driskell, University of Dayton, USA
    Margaret F. Pinnell, University of Dayton, USA
    Mary-Kate Sableski, University of Dayton, USA

Literacy is critical for success in other areas, including science and engineering. As teachers responded to the demands of remote learning because of the COVID-19 pandemic, they developed innovative methods to teach both reading and STEM (Science, Technology, Engineering, Mathematics) subjects in virtual environments. This chapter describes how one team of teachers adapted face-to-face STEM and literacy modules for a virtual environment. The authors describe the face-to-face modules and the process the teachers followed to transition them to a virtual environment. The Analyze, Design, Develop, Implement, and Evaluate (ADDIE) framework—an approach to designing online learning—was used as a lens to analyze the process and the product of the virtual modules. Implications and recommendations for teachers seeking to adapt face-to-face lessons to a virtual environment are presented.

Section 4
Transforming Teachers Knowledge for Teaching in Virtual Environments – Pre-service, In-service and Professional Development

Chapter 25
An Interactional and Aligned Educational Design Framework to Support Teachers' Pedagogical Reasoning.. 516
    Jörgen Holmberg, University of Gävle, Sweden
    Göran Fransson, University of Gävle, Sweden

This chapter presents and problematizes a theoretical design framework for understanding and supporting teachers' pedagogical reasoning in online contexts. The framework synthesizes existing educational theories to illustrate how digital technologies can be used to create interactional and aligned educational designs and is therefore referred to as the IAED framework. The IAED framework can be used in teacher education and development programs, and by teachers, researchers, educational designers, and others. In the chapter, empirical examples and analysis are provided to illustrate and discuss how the IAED framework can be used to (1) support teachers' pedagogical reasoning and educational design practices, (2) evaluate existing educational designs and design practices, and (3) study educational designs and design practices, as well as (changes in) teachers' pedagogical reasoning.

Chapter 26
Transforming Teaching for Virtual Environments: Developing Preservice Teachers' Online TPACK.. 534
    Irina Lyublinskaya, Teachers College, Columbia University, USA
    Xiaoxue Du, Teachers College, Columbia University, USA

This chapter describes pedagogical practices and teaching strategies with instructional technology used in an online summer course with preservice K-12 teachers. The course provided preservice teachers (PSTs) with experiences in using technology in K-12 classrooms from both students' and teachers' perspectives, engaged PSTs in active explorations of various K-12 curriculum topics using technology that could enhance high-impact teaching strategies, and supported PSTs in development of virtual lessons using instructional technology. The study identified effective practices with instructional technology to support preservice teachers' development of Technological Pedagogical Content Knowledge (TPACK) for their own online teaching. Study findings suggest that online immersive experience created a virtual student-centered space to nurture collaborative inquiry and that contributed to the growth of PST's TPACK. However, this experience also brought challenges and concerns for sustaining and transforming teaching and learning with instructional technology to an online environment.

Chapter 27
Promoting Higher Student Mathematics Achievement in Online Settings: Introducing PHiSMAOS.. 561
    Emma Bullock, Sam Houston State University, USA
    Amy Ray, Sam Houston State University, USA
    Beth Cory, Sam Houston State University, USA
    Julie Herron, Augusta University, USA

This chapter describes how the authors structured effective online mathematics content courses for preservice teachers (PSTs) using the promoting higher student mathematics achievement in online settings (PHiSMAOS) conceptual framework. This framework focuses on the mathematics teacher educator (MTE) view from which they are using their technological content knowledge (TCK) to develop their PSTs' own technological knowledge (TK), content knowledge (CK), and TCK when in an online mathematics classroom setting. The PHiSMAOS conceptual framework then wraps this reality in the concepts of growth mindset and productive struggle, providing a pragmatic way for MTEs to productively promote growth mindset in PSTs' mathematics content classrooms in online settings. This framework was developed using grounded theory research techniques from data consisting of exit cards, video-recorded discussions, assignments, and test scores across seven semesters of the authors' courses. Implications for MTEs, use in K-12 settings, and further research are also discussed.

Chapter 28
Classroom Management, Lesson Planning, and Technology Integration . . . Oh My! Ways to Cope With Online Pedagogical Practices... 583
C. Lorraine Webb, Texas A&M University, San Antonio, USA
Amy M. Barrios, Texas A&M University, San Antonio, USA
Karen L. Kohler, Texas A&M University, San Antonio, USA

This chapter aims to share the results of a study of faculty in teacher preparation programs across the state of Texas to identify ways educator preparation has shifted its instruction as a result of COVID-19. Both quantitative and qualitative data results are shared, along with implications. The research provides some clarity regarding how future educator preparation programs and K-12 classroom teachers can adjust instructional practices as the shift to a virtual learning environment continues. The authors offer suggestions for best practices in virtual instruction for lesson planning, classroom management, and technology integration for K-12 teachers, as well as recommendations for teacher preparation programs to prepare pre-service teachers for successful implementation in those three areas while teaching in a virtual environment.

Chapter 29
What Now? Online Pedagogical Reasoning of Student Teaching Secondary ELAR in Virtual Learning Environments.. 604
Jess Smith, Baylor University, USA
Sandra Talbert, Baylor University, USA
Mona Choucair, Baylor University, USA

This descriptive case study centers the experiences of 12 preservice secondary English Language Arts (ELAR) teachers in their final two years of study as they navigate changing school environments in light of COVID-19 restrictions. The preservice teachers discuss successes and challenges with regard to their preparedness to teaching in online or hybrid modalities, their struggles to build learner engagement with social distancing restrictions within the classroom and some students who never log into class live, and similar struggles with intentional relationship building. From these emergent themes, the authors make recommendations on praxis for pre- and inservice teachers, teacher educators, and teacher education programs.

Chapter 30
Current Approaches in Teacher Learning on Digital Social Platforms 624
Emily Southerton, Stanford University, USA
Victor R. Lee, Stanford University, USA

Within digital ecologies, teachers routinely find an abundance of information related to their teaching. While many teachers pursue brute force searches for online ideas and resources, during the COVID-19 pandemic, teachers had to address pressing new challenges in online teaching in the most efficient ways possible. This chapter reports on an ongoing study of 16 teachers and how they relied upon digital social platforms to make the move to online teaching. Analysis revolves around socially-distanced video-recorded interviews with these teachers. Given their limited time, teachers had to be selective about what they deemed useful and relevant to their immediate needs. Strategic uses of digital social platforms served to address some of those needs. Specific strategies observed in the data regarding the development of pedagogy included joining teacher collectives, accessing expert-like spaces, and finding pedagogical inspiration within posts by teacher-influencers.

Section 5

Chapter 31
Developing Teachers' Knowledge for Teaching in Virtual Contexts: Lessons From the Pandemic of 2020-2021 643
Margaret L. Niess, Oregon State University, USA
Henry Gillow-Wiles, Oregon State University, USA

The 2020 worldwide pandemic signaled the COVID-19 crisis as a real threat and forced K-12 schools to move teaching and learning from face-to-face classrooms to online virtual classrooms. Educators searched for a silver lining amid the hardships created by the virtual teaching and learning environments. This chapter answers an important question: How has the knowledge that teachers need for teaching changed as a result of School Lockdown 2020-2021? Analysis of the chapters in this book in addition to extensive qualitative observations of two middle school virtual computer science classrooms over six months identified two important lessons needing consideration when requiring K-12 virtual instruction: (1) teachers' knowledge for teaching requires developing their technological pedagogical content knowledge for teaching in both face-to-face and virtual contexts, and (2) teaching virtually relies on a social presence that assures students' sense of belonging to engage in virtual learning experiences.

Compilation of References xxxvi

About the Contributors cxiv

Index cxxix

Preface

On March 11, 2020, the World Health Organization declared a global pandemic. The responses to the pandemic forced educators worldwide to rethink teaching and learning as it currently existed, where the majority of students learned through face-to-face classrooms. With little warning, K-12 teachers were challenged to redesign their curriculum and instruction and quickly transition to online virtual classrooms to protect students and teachers from the deadly virus. Nevertheless, teachers were still expected to guide students in learning the 4Cs - communication, collaboration, critical thinking (and problem solving), and creativity – in a society far more globally connected through technology than that of the twentieth century (Partnership for 21st Century Learning, 2015; Thoughtful Learning Organization, 2016). Thankfully, the twenty-first century had resulted in the expansion and development of more advanced technologies – technologies that supported virtual communications for the social interactions needed for a virtual classroom where students were to collaborate virtually as they explored new ideas and engaged in critical thinking.

THE CHALLENGES

Many challenges, however, were clearly present. The teachers had not been prepared for designing and managing instruction virtually. In fact, their education in preparation for teaching had been within the context of face-to-face instructional environments. Their elementary, secondary and college education had primarily been in face-to-face environments. Their teacher preparation programs had primarily focused on curriculum and instruction in face-to-face environments as they developed an initial Technological Pedagogical Content Knowledge (TPACK) – their knowledge for teaching with the enhanced technologies that emerged in the twenty-first century (Angeli & Valanides, 2005; Margerum-Leys & Marx, 2002; Mishra & Koehler, 2006; Niess, 2005; Pierson, 2001; Zhao, 2003). Could this knowledge adequately support them as they transition their instruction to virtual online classrooms? However, this rapid shift to online education on 2020 left teachers and parents lacking in confidence that students would receive the proper education as they were engaged in the new virtual environments.

Time for professional development would help in supporting teachers in incorporating the technological advancements of the new century clearly would be useful for the move to online instruction. There simply was not adequate time and support for teachers to develop the pedagogical knowledge, reasoning and skills for engaging students in the unfamiliar virtual context. Superficial observations of the features and organizations for online classrooms revealed a lack of key elements for guiding students in developing the called-for K-12 educational goals like the 4Cs. Many questioned whether K-12 students could learn in virtual environments citing that many elementary children were just now learning to read and write. How could they possibly gain these skills virtually? Were there other problems for students in the different K-12 levels – elementary, middle and high school?

SEARCHING FOR SOLUTIONS

In response to the many challenges and concerns, educators quickly searched for a silver lining amid the perceived weaknesses of adequately meeting K-12 student needs through virtual learning environments. The *Handbook of Research on Transforming Teachers' Online Pedagogical Reasoning for Engaging K-12 Students in Virtual Learning* was undertaken to gather and present actual best practices and pedagogical reasoning to guide the design of online teaching and learning strategies that would work for K-12 virtual learning. Thus, the goal for this book was to identify best practices in order to take advantage of the features of virtual environments, demonstrating researched results that provide teachers with the means to create effective learning experiences. These chapters provide ways to think about and plan for teaching and learning in virtual environments, to guide instructional strategy choices that also present effective online pedagogical reasoning for the redesign and implementation of K-12 learning in virtual classrooms. Moreover, these chapters suggest ideas that might even be implemented with a return to face-to-face instruction to more adequately engage students' engagement with the 4Cs.

To guide thinking about which best practices and pedagogical reasoning are supportive of virtual instruction, this book is divided into five sections. The initial section provides foundations for transforming teachers' online pedagogical reasoning in designing engaging virtual learning environments that leverage the unique strengths and opportunities while avoiding the weaknesses and threats of the online world. This section asks the question: What are the underlying factors that will impact the transition to a virtual learning environment? The second and third sections provide chapters that describe the pedagogical reasoning and multiple instructional strategies for teaching virtually. The second section focuses thinking about multiple K-12 grade levels and the third section considers these ideas through multiple content areas. Each of these sections describes the best practices that work and why they work as well as the teachers' pedagogical reasoning that supports the online implementations. The fourth section then considers models and programs for transforming teachers' knowledge and pedagogical reasoning for constructing engaging virtual learning experiences. The final section is a single chapter that not only summarizes the results of the lessons learned from the previous sections but highlights the lessons learned from the global pandemic lockdown 2020-2021. The chapter ends this handbook with recommendations for future action and research needed to adjust to the ever-changing landscape of education launched by the initial challenges that were revealed when dealing with the global pandemic.

In sum, the impact of the chapters is to provide a foundation for building a knowledgebase for teaching online through the collection of clear directions and implications as teachers are faced with the redesign of their instruction for virtual classroom instruction and then return to face-to-face instruction. The question is whether the lessons learned from the lockdown 2020-2021 will provide new knowledge for teaching in more normal face-to-face classroom environments. The directions and ideas in this book hopefully provide directions for not only teachers, but also for educational designers and developers who are currently faced with supporting and encouraging teachers in the shift to online virtual instruction to effectively influence student learning. Hopefully, what has been learned helps to shape the future of education - both face-to-face and online instruction. As teachers learn to take advantage of the affordances and strengths of the multiple technologies available for virtual classroom instruction, their instruction, both in online and face-to-face, will impact what and how students learn in the twenty-first century.

The following paragraphs describe each of the chapters in the five sections. An important feature of these chapters presents the scholarly work that the authors have completed in the identification of the best practices and pedagogical reasoning. The challenge for the readers is to imagine and consider how these ideas might be implemented in not only K-12 educational environments but also in teacher education programs to better prepare teachers with the robust knowledge needed for actively engaging students in learning – in either face-to-face or virtual classroom environments.

ORGANIZATION OF THE BOOK

This book is organized into five sections, each containing multiple chapters. A brief description of each of the chapters in each section follows:

Section 1. Foundation Knowledge for Transforming Teachers' Online Pedagogical Reasoning for Virtual Learning Environments

These chapters highlight the diversity of challenges teachers and students face when in virtual learning environments. Research-based frameworks and models highlight key features and considerations for guiding teachers' thinking and reasoning in the design of virtual learning experiences that meet the learning needs of the diversity of all K-12 students - from learning disabilities to culturally, linguistically, and cognitively diverse students. Specific attention highlights the challenge of gaining students' sense of belonging when engaged in online learning.

In Chapter 1, Gillow-Wiles and Niess rely on the importance of elementary school recess as a key to students' engagement in learning. Recess engages students in free-play, self-constructed interactions that build their sense of belonging in their elementary learning. Attending to this sense of belonging in online learning suggests directions for research needed for establishing meaningfully online learning environments for K-12 students.

In Chapter 2, Khazanchi, Khazanchi, and Randhawa identify the challenges of teaching students with learning disabilities in virtual learning experiences. This chapter highlights effective educational practices for teaching students with specific learning disabilities in an online learning environment, offering technology-based solutions for challenges faced by students in reading, writing, and mathematics.

In Chapter 3, Parish, Kouo, Carey, and Swanson introduce the Universal Design for Learning framework for meeting diverse needs of all K-12 students in a virtual learning environment. They address how its application attends to the design of instruction through engagement, representation, and action and expression that meets the needs of all learners.

In Chapter 4, Terlop and Vargas-Ewing consider how early childhood education, social constructivism, and disability critical race guides educators and researchers. The chapter highlights a teacher's journey in finding supportive technology for the classes relevant for the culturally, linguistically, and cognitively diverse (CLCD) learners who utilize augmentative and alternative communication devices.

In Chapter 5, Meier and Mineo describe Innovating Instruction as a research-based model that supports teachers as they transition to virtual learning, designing inquiry-based, culturally relevant projects that support equity and social justice for all students. This model contributes to an emerging education

Preface

theory for the catalytic use of technology in promoting pedagogical practices that are culturally responsive, rigorous, and engaging.

In Chapter 6, Woodward and Beschorner explore the use of the Technology Integration Planning Cycle (TIPC) for supporting teachers' decision-making as they plan virtual instruction with digital tools that meets specific learning goals. The chapter provides an example of using TIPC when planning virtual reading and writing instruction with a consideration of issue of access, equity and safety.

In Chapter 7, Worwood promotes teacher creativity as an important part in the design of virtual learning experiences. The chapter presents four steps for teacher creativity, exploring change as a journey that begins with an intention to provide a creative outcome that ultimately improves the virtual learning experience.

Section 2. Best Practices and Pedagogical Reasoning in K-12 Grade Levels

These chapters present research-based best practices and pedagogical reasoning approaches for multiple K-12 grade level virtual environments. In recognition of the nature of K-12 students (Generation Z), the chapters provide virtual best practices for all grades, highlighting technologies that engage students in discussions as well as learning with digital games, hands-on and minds-on activities. Specific recognition is given to how the context of virtual instruction influences teachers' TPACK as they engage multiple technologies to incorporate the 4Cs.

In Chapter 8, Mellman, Williams, and Slykhuis introduce Generation Z (Gen Z) as individuals born between 1997-2012 (the bulk of students in K-12 in 2020). Their research provides insights to the different pedagogical practices that support successful online teaching and learning aligned with the learning approaches established by Gen Z for meaningful online teaching and learning.

In Chapter 9, Swallow and Morrison identify the importance of Context in the TPACK model and examine attention to technological pedagogical knowledge (TPK) in teacher development and practice influence remote learning environments. The chapter focuses on the co-construction of learning through the interplay of teachers' TPK and ConteXtual knowledge when considering factors of space, resources, and interactions with learning activities.

In Chapter 10, Medellin, Gupta, and Acuña use action research in identifying online teaching strategies that provide cooperative learning experiences that give students opportunities to collaborate in class using best practices like the 4Cs. The research results unveil the rationale, implementation, success and challenges with five key technologies for engaging online students in the 4Cs: Jamboard, Padlet, Mentimeter, Flipgrid, and Bitmoji Classroom.

In Chapter 11, Gallaher-Immenschuh and Broderick describe online teaching methods for primary grades teacher-student interaction and engagement. The chapter provides research-based insights into purposely created and child-centered Crystallizing Moments in online learning through activities that are motivating, hands-on and developmentally appropriate for young learners.

In Chapter 12, Janakiraman identifies best practices and pedagogical reasoning with digital game-based attitudinal instruction that reduces zoom fatigue and allows for discovery learning, creativity and critical thinking. Through research about environmental sustainability issues, the author identifies that digital games provide cognitive knowledge but also engaged learners emotionally and allowed them to test behaviors by examining consequences instantly.

In Chapter 13, Singh considers the psychological separation high school science students face when learning remotely and how activity design can intensify or diminish their perceived detachment. Using a reflection narration of activity development, the author discusses the effects of activity design on student-teacher and student-student interactions.

In Chapter 14, Hodge-Zickerman, Stade, and York promote hands-on, minds-on learning in virtual learning environments through TACTivities that incorporate tactile components designed to encourage student participation and engagement in creative solutions with little or no directions. The research identifies best practices that make learning more playful while fostering creativity in both teachers and students, fitting learning objectives, students' interests, grade-band, and subject matter.

In Chapter 15, Lawrence, Labissiere, and Stone tackle the challenge of engaging online K-12 students across content areas in structured discussions using digital tools. Their research provides best practice examples of classroom discussions that facilitate opportunities where students engage in the 4Cs of academic language and literacy in virtual classrooms.

Section 3. Best Practices and Pedagogical Reasoning in K-12 Content Areas

These chapters reveal best practices and pedagogical reasoning approaches for teaching and learning in virtual learning environments in K-12 content areas, including reading and writing in kindergarten, elementary computational thinking, as well as mathematics, science, and STEM content areas. Multiple collaborative research groups consider the impact of the virtual context on teachers' TPACK as they examine multiple technologies to support specific instructional strategies to incorporate the 4Cs.

In Chapter 16, Hodges confronts the challenge of teaching kindergarten children reading and writing in virtual environments. The chapter identifies best practices as a practical toolkit for teachers to set students up for success in virtual learning environments without hindering their knowledge of skills provides a solid foundation for long-term academic success.

In Chapter 17, Malhotra and Johnston use Engeström's activity triangles for planning lessons that support students in using the 4Cs in virtual environments. Beginning with face-to-face Canadian elementary schools, the authors adapt elementary literacy and music activities in the elementary classroom to virtual activities using Engeström's activity theory.

In Chapter 18, Jocius, Blanton, Albert, Joshi, and Andrews reimagine interdisciplinary, computational thinking-infused (CT) Making lessons for elementary students learning in a virtual format. Four design principles (standards-based practices, clear and explicit expectations, multiple means of engagement, and opportunities for collaboration) support the design of interdisciplinary activities that support primary to grade 5 students' development of creative and authentic problem-solving in virtual learning environments.

In Chapter 19, Mardi, Walsh-Rock, and Balcerzak design virtual collaboration for high school case-based science learning. Using Google Slides, Padlet and FlipGrid the authors describe learning experiences related to making a diagnosis and justifying them using evidence. The students were overall more engaged in learning content through the story-telling and problem-solving aspects of the activity and secondly, were able to share thoughts and interact with their peers on social platforms supporting social and emotional well-being while still providing an academic focus.

In Chapter 20, Joswick, Fletcher, and Meador re-envisioned K-12 mathematics Number Talks into Virtual Number Talk practices that benefit sixth grade teachers and students in virtual classrooms, demonstrating the transformation of one teacher's pedagogy to Virtual Number Talk practice that benefited all Grade 6 teachers and students in her school. Relying on a teacher learning cycle, the common classroom routine engages students in the 4C's—solving problems, generating discussion strategies with classmates.

Preface

In Chapter 21, Rigelman, Vennebush, and Saxton use technology-enhanced activities to transform K–5 mathematics planning, teaching, and learning in virtual environments. The authors describe how these activities that draw from a suite of virtual manipulatives, digital display materials, the new additions of "Digital Work Place are aligned with the four C's and provide opportunities for teachers to employ their technological pedagogical content knowledge as they make decision for implementing specific contexts.

In Chapter 22, Bengtson, Golden, Kasmer, Thomas, and Yu use a collaborative action research project with university and middle school mathematics faculty to consider the relationship between technology, mathematics content, and social interaction, examining the varied uses, and types of technology for online teaching. The teachers identify opportunities for trying novel uses of technology in their online lessons, advancing their teaching and the student experience, while learning lessons about teaching with technology in virtual classrooms.

In Chapter 23, Galanti, Baker, Kraft, and Morrow-Leong integrated ipsative assessments in the development of using mathematics digital interactive notebooks for authentic integrated online assessments. Their prototype of an Authentic Integrated Online Assessment model emphasizes cycles of reflection and revision based on instructor and peer feedback. The chapter reveals the K-12 teachers' challenges in realizing the full potential of this model to integrate formative, summative, and ipsative assessment functions in their own classrooms.

In Chapter 24, Driskell, Pinnell, and Sableski blend project-based Science, Technology, Engineering, and Mathematics (STEM) with Reading Literacy producing STEM Stories modules for virtual environments. Five teachers adapted five National Science Foundation face-to-face modules to virtual modules using an Analyze, Design, Develop, Implement, and Evaluate (ADDIE) instructional design process. The results identified best practices and instructional strategies that better support elementary students in virtual strategies and activities using multiple technologies in understanding STEM and literacy skills.

Section 4. Transforming Teacher Knowledge for Teaching in Virtual Environments: Pre-Service, In-Service, and Professional Development

These chapters focus on models/frameworks/programs for transforming teachers' knowledge and pedagogical reasoning for transforming their knowledge for teaching in online virtual learning environments. Specifically, the authors provide frameworks and consider paths for pre-service, in-service and professional development mechanisms for guiding teachers in developing the knowledge for teaching in online virtual environments.

In Chapter 25, Holmberg and Fransson formalize a theoretical design framework for online contexts, illustrating how digital technologies can be used to create interactional and aligned educational designs for online learning. The chapter discusses how the framework can be used to: (a) support teachers' pedagogical reasoning and educational design practices, (b) evaluate existing educational designs and design practices, and (c) study educational designs and design practices, as well as (changes in) teachers' pedagogical reasoning.

In Chapter 26, Lyublinskaya and Du designed a course to transform pre-service teachers' knowledge for teaching in virtual environments, developing pedagogical practices and teaching strategies with instructional technology. The results suggest that the online immersive experience creates a virtual student-centered space to nurture collaborative inquiry and that contributed to the growth of their TPACK.

In Chapter 27, Bullock, Ray, Cory, and Herron developed an online mathematics content course for pre-service teachers through a conceptual framework that uses mathematics teacher educator views of key subsets of TPACK knowledge. Grounded theory research techniques were used to incorporate exit cards, video-recorded discussions, assignments, and test scores across seven semesters to inform the framework for online course content.

In Chapter 28, Webb, Barrios, and Kohler investigate teacher preparation programs to identify ways to better prepared educators for virtual instruction. The authors offer suggestions for best practices in virtual instruction for lesson planning, classroom management, and technology integration for K-12 teachers, as well as recommendations for teacher preparation programs to prepare pre-service teachers for successful implementation in those three areas while teaching in a virtual environment.

In Chapter 29, Smith, Talbert, and Choucair use a descriptive case study to describe secondary pre-service teachers successes and challenges with regard to their preparedness for teaching in online or hybrid modalities, their struggles to build learner engagement with social distancing restrictions within the classroom and some students who never log into class live, and similar struggles with intentional relationship building. The authors make recommendations on praxis for pre- and in-service teachers, teacher educators, and teacher education programs.

In Chapter 30, Southerton and Lee report on their ongoing study of sixteen teachers and how digital social platforms support teacher professional development for moving to online teaching. They indicate that teachers are able to self-direct their professional learning by way of participation in various online teaching communities to develop new practices and pedagogies for teaching effectively in emergency or other rapidly changing situations.

Section 5. Lessons Learned From the Move to Online Virtual Learning With Recommendations for Transforming Teachers' Pedagogical Knowledge for Designing and Implementing Virtual Learning Environments

This section contains one chapter with the intent of capturing the lessons learned from the Lockdown of 2020-2021. The multiple research efforts revealed in this book worked to identify best practices and pedagogical reasoning approaches for teaching and learning in various K-12 virtual learning environments.

In Chapter 31, Niess and Gillow-Wiles answer an important question: How has the knowledge that teachers need for teaching changed as a result of School Lockdown 2020-2021? Analysis of the chapters in this book in addition to extensive qualitative observations of two middle school virtual computer science classrooms over six months identified two important lessons needing consideration when requiring K-12 virtual instruction: (1) Teachers' knowledge for teaching requires developing their Technological Pedagogical Content Knowledge for teaching in both face-to-face and virtual contexts; (2) Teaching virtually relies on a social presence that assures students' sense of belonging to engage in virtual learning experiences.

CONCLUSION

March 2020 marked the immediate requirement for moving students and their teachers into unfamiliar learning environments that relied on a massive technological infrastructure for communication. Suddenly teachers' knowledge for teaching was shifted to a significantly different context – one in which most were unfamiliar as to how to guide students' learning. Teachers swiftly adapted as best they could

Preface

while many scholars, educators and researchers scrambled to identify the best practices and pedagogical strategies for adequately engaging students.

This handbook provides some of what has been learned from throughout the School Lockdown 2020-2021. Interestingly, the majority of the studies have been collaborative ones – collaborations of teachers, faculties of education and educational businesses. The results have identified how the twenty-first century technologies have supported communication and collaboration in unique educational ways. The question is whether the lessons learned will be considered in the return to face-to-face learning where the social presence educational considerations are better attended to for reestablishing the students' sense of belonging to engage in learning that incorporates the best practices identified in this past year.

Margaret L. Niess
Oregon State University, USA

Henry Gillow-Wiles
Oregon State University, USA

REFERENCES

Angeli, C., & Valanides, N. (2005). Preservice teachers as ICT designers: An instructional design model based on an expanded view of pedagogical content knowledge. *Journal of Computer Assisted Learning*, *21*(4), 292–302. doi:10.1111/j.1365-2729.2005.00135.x

Margerum-Leys, J., & Marx, R. W. (2002). Teacher knowledge of educational technology: A study of student teacher/mentor teacher pairs. *Journal of Educational Computing Research*, *26*(4), 427–462. doi:10.2190/JXBR-2G0G-1E4T-7T4M

Mishra, P., & Koehler, M. J. (2006). Technological pedagogical content knowledge: A framework for integrating technology in teacher knowledge. *Teachers College Record*, *108*(6), 1017–1054. doi:10.1111/j.1467-9620.2006.00684.x

Niess, M. L. (2005). Preparing teachers to teach science and mathematics with technology: Developing a technology pedagogical content knowledge. *Teaching and Teacher Education*, *21*(5), 509–523. doi:10.1016/j.tate.2005.03.006

Partnership for 21st Century Learning. (2015). Retrieved from https://www.P21.org//our-work/p21-framework

Pierson, M. E. (2001). Technology integration practices as function of pedagogical expertise. *Journal of Research on Computing in Education*, *33*(4), 413–429. doi:10.1080/08886504.2001.10782325

Thoughtful Learning Organization. (2016). Retrieved from https://k12.toughtfullearning.com/FAQ/what-are-learning-skills

Zhao, Y. (2003). *What teachers should know about technology? Perspectives and practices*. Information Age Publishing.

Acknowledgment

Deciding to take on the ask of editing a new publication is a difficult decision. Add to that the recognition and realization that health issues were worldwide and in everyone's mind. Early in 2020, who knew what the next stage of the pandemic was. Yet, soon the realization was that education had to change. It was not going to be safe to continue with face-to-face classroom learning. What would the shift to online virtual learning accommodate the educational needs throughout the world? The opportunity to engage in this publication provided an opportunity to examine the impact of this unknown as the world moved into what is now referred to as the virtual school lockdown for health safety.

Throughout this process, the preparation and publication of this book has truly been a collaborative effort among the authors, the editors, the editorial advisory board, and IGI Global. During these difficult times, we have received proposals for chapters from throughout the world and we were challenged with completing the book within a one-year timespan. As difficult as that timeline was, the most difficult time was the unexpected passing of one of the chapter authors, Professor Göran Fransson, University of Gävle, Sweden. We have dedicated this book in his memory.

We have been fortunate to have a tremendous Editorial Advisory Board. They have provided thoughtful comments and suggestions in search of the best prospects for identifying important lessons as a result of the sudden shifting to remote virtual learning. The Board members have provided key reviews when the chapters were received. They assisted us in making decisions as to which chapters provided important direction for when the world returned to the traditional educational venue. Their knowledge and efforts have assured the quality of the chapters presented in this book.

Without a doubt, the chapter authors have provided the direction for proceeding beyond School Lookdown 2002-2021. The communication of their research has provided important understandings and lessons learned from the truly unusual school environment as a result of the global pandemic. Their research now provides important understandings for scholars, researchers, and teacher educators as they examine, design, and redesign programs, courses, workshops, and additional professional development ways for guiding teachers in transforming their teacher knowledge teaching in this increasingly digital age. Throughout the process these authors have not only prepared their chapters, but they have also completed multiple chapter reviews; their solid understanding of the challenges in writing a chapter for this book resulted in detailed and important recommendations for the improvement of quality, coherence, and content presentation of chapters.

Acknowledgment

We also want to express our sincere appreciation for the IGI Global vision, organization and, support throughout the publication process. Without their efforts, this book would not have been possible. We are proud of this book and feel that the chapters contained herein provide an important, worldwide view of current research and scholarly work in teacher preparation for this digital age.

Margaret L. Niess
Oregon State University, USA

Henry Gillow-Wiles
Oregon State University, USA

Section 1
Foundation Knowledge For Transforming Teachers' Online Pedagogical Reasoning For Virtual Learning Environments

Chapter 1
Is There Recess on Mars?
Developing a Sense of Belonging in Online Learning

Henry Gillow-Wiles
Oregon State University, USA

Margaret L. Niess
https://orcid.org/0000-0002-1673-0978
Oregon State University, USA

ABSTRACT

The pandemic of 2019 created a multitude of challenges for teachers and students alike. The urgency with which education was forced to transition to a fully online delivery paradigm necessitated a triage and curate process to decide where efforts were to be placed. Teachers, forced to move quickly, leveraged existing research in designing their courses and activities. However, little research exists concerning how to meaningfully create online learning environments for K-12 students. This chapter explores the importance of recess, where children have free-play, self-constructed interactions essential for developing a sense of belonging. Through exploring the sense of belonging construct in the context of how it is formed, its importance for developing social skills, and the connection between a sense of belonging and successful online learning, the authors present critical gaps in research and suggest directions for research.

INTRODUCTION

Ernie loved school. Ok, maybe not all of third grade, but he really enjoyed being with his friends as they played during recess. When one of them did well in kick-ball or four-square, the others yelled and cheered. They were not just there for him in the good times, either. He remembered when his mom was really sick and how his circle of friends helped him stay hopeful for her recovery. Having a tight-knit group of friends even helped him doing school stuff. History is not his best subject but working with his friends on the big project really helped him learn about the pyramids as well as to better understand

DOI: 10.4018/978-1-7998-7222-1.ch001

how to make sense of history in general. He felt safe in his community to show that he did not know something and to ask for help.

The time spent at school consumes a significant portion of most students' days and provides the primary avenue for interaction with peers. Through developing an awareness of how they fit in with others and of how their actions impact the relationships they have with their peer group, children develop a *sense of belonging* (Hagerty et al., 1992; Lambert et al., 2013; St-Amand et al., 2017). This sense of belonging is what gave Ernie comfort and support as he navigated the oft-times challenging world of third grade.

In March 2020, the need for developing knowledge and understanding for teaching and learning in an online context increased exponentially when the Center for Disease Control (CDC) announced that the world-wide COVID-19 infection rate indicated the existence of a pandemic. As a response to this announcement and the CDC recommendations, education transitioned from a face-to-face environment to one where distance learning was the sole delivery method. In one broad stroke, it was as if all the students in the world were magically teleported to Mars, where everyone lived in their own isolating bubble, cut off from the world they knew. For Ernie, it was like he was transported to Mars with all his friends, but it was impossible for them to be together at all, much less to hang out during recess like they were used to doing. Even though they saw each other every day during the Zoom based classes, he never felt so alone. Not being able to see his teacher, be in the familiar classroom surroundings, or even eat the terrible cafeteria food at lunch just added to his sense of isolation. All the video classes did was to remind him of how much he missed recess and being with his friends. That sense of belonging Ernie felt when he was with his friends was gone and Ernie felt like he was out in space, alone in a strange and potentially hostile environment.

For elementary students in particular, the shift to online classes was a trying experience. Being deprived of the ability to physically interact with their peer groups took away one of the primary avenues through which they learned how to be social beings. As immature learners, children do not have the emotional resources needed to be self-regulated enough to navigate online learning alone. Their success (or more often failure) depends on the amount of support they can get from both the teacher and their peer group. Part of this support comes from the aforementioned sense of belonging and originates in peer group interactions. Other support comes from the teacher, who, through directed actions, has a substantial impact on academic success. As well-meaning and proactive a teacher may be, the fact that student-teacher interactions are constructed and framed by the teacher mean that these interactions are ineffective and possible counter-productive in helping children develop peer-based social skills. This ineffectiveness results in a schism, where students might be able to learn how to academically engage through instructor actions, but they will be challenged to develop the kinds of social skills that come from child constructed and directed activities.

This chapter unpacks several concepts and constructs to more deeply explore what a sense of belonging means to children and how this belonging is integrated into and frames their online school experiences. The authors begin by borrowing from health science literature in describing a sense of belonging. Following this background development, the authors again return to health science literature to explore the social lives of children, how and where they interact, and how they develop social skills. Included in this discussion is the impact of family on a child's sense of belonging. After this, the transition to a sense of belonging in an academic context (sense of belonging at school) is described, including a differentiation of a sense of belonging from social presence. Finally, the authors suggest best practices for helping students develop a sense of belonging in an online environment.

To investigate the impact of moving to an online learning context on the development of a sense of belonging for children and what it means in terms of academic success, this chapter focuses on: 1) what a sense of belonging is and how students develop a sense of belonging, 2) importance of developing a sense of belonging as a precursor to successful distance learning, 3) the challenges of K-12 online education for creating spaces where students can develop a sense of belonging, and 4) suggestions for helping online students develop a sense of belonging.

SENSE OF BELONGING

A sense of belonging is about feeling included and valued. Hagerty et al., (1992) extending the work of Anant (1966), described a sense of belonging as "a personal involvement in a social system so that the persons feel themselves to be an indispensable and integral part of the system" (p. 170). Hagerty detailed two dimensions of sense of belonging: (1) valued involvement: the experience of feeling valued, needed, and accepted; and (2) fit as the persons' perceptions that their characteristics articulate with or complement the system or environment. Building on the idea of *person-ness* (St-Amand et al., 2017), Sung & Mayer (2012) found that the concept that a sense of belonging centers on friendship, group commitment, and group caring.

Borrowing from health care research, a sense of belonging can be effectively characterized as having five elements: 1) subjectivity, 2) groundedness, 3) reciprocity, 4) dynamism, and 5) self-determination (Mahar et al., 2013). In this construct, these five elements are intertwined to create a sense of belonging. The first element, *subjectivity* reflects how a sense of belonging is unique to an individual, where even though each member feels part of a group or groups, how membership is realized is particular to each individual. *Groundedness* refers to the need to belong *to* something. Here, groundedness suggests the requirement for a referent group for belonging to, as an anchor for the individual feelings described by the subjectivity element. *Reciprocity* describes an important element, the sense of relatedness shared by the individual and the referent group(s). This relatedness goes beyond identifying group member characteristics to include shared experiences, understandings, and beliefs, all necessary in cementing a person's feelings of connectedness and creating a sense of belonging. *Dynamism* focuses on contexts, both social and physical, that have an impact on a person's sense of belonging. This element describes the interplay between enablers and barriers that mediate the development of a sense of belonging. The effects of these factors may be transitory or permanent. The final element, *self-determination*, describes the right of individuals to select how they interact with members of the referent group. This idea of choice suggests that individuals have control over which referent group they belong to and the ability to create meaningfully reciprocal relationships, the foundation for a sense of belonging. Individuals who feel powerless to belong due to factors associated with the dynamism element, but otherwise have the necessary identifying characteristic for referent group membership, may never achieve a satisfying sense of belonging.

THE IMPORTANCE OF RECESS IN DEVELOPING A SENSE OF BELONGING

Children spend the majority of their time in an adult run world and have little opportunity to interact in spaces of their own making. Giving children opportunities to create their own activities is an important component of developing a sense of belonging. Framing their work with the lens of the cognitive immaturity hypothesis (Bjorklund & Green, 1992), Pellegrini investigated the role recess plays in children's cognitive performance (Pellegrini & Bjorklund, 1997; Pellegrini & Bohn, 2005). The cognitive immaturity hypothesis posits that rather than being a hindrance, children's propensity to be unrealistically confident in their cognitive abilities and social status is part of learning new skills and behaviors. It is this confidence allows children to persist with high expectations of success in the face of failure, leading to self-perceived competence that helps in learning complicated skills and strategies.

Beyond learning new skills, the point of view of the cognitive immaturity hypothesis suggests that during social play, children often enact roles and behaviors that are, at some level, not attainable in real life. Building on the idea that children's social skills increase as they enact different social roles, Pellegrini and Bohn (2005) found that in the process of these interactions, children learn to take other children's "perspectives, comprehend and produce social signals, and inhibit their aggressions" (p. 14). They concluded that the free play, child-directed exchanges most common during recess are significant in fostering cognitive performance and more general adjustment to school. The importance of free, unstructured play was reinforced through the work of the American Academy of Pediatrics, where they describe peer interactions during recess as supporting communication, cooperation, and problem solving, complementing the classroom experience. They concluded that unstructured play gives children the opportunity to "develop important social and emotional skills, essential to a well-rounded education" (Ramstetter & Murray, 2017, p. 18).

Not only are children's activities most often adult driven, the spaces in which children exist are also adult created and controlled. Recalling Mahar's five elements of a sense of belonging, *dynamism*, or the context in which children are interacting, is an important driver for developing a sense of belonging. The playground is a combination of adult and child mediated spaces. Rasmussen (2004) describes this distinction as *places for children* and *children's places*. Playgrounds, with their adult designed structures and adult designed uses, are *places for children*, where the target audience is children, but the space is designed and facilitated by adults. Even though these spaces are designed by adults for the use of children in ways determined by adults, children will often discover or create their own spaces within these larger spaces. These child created spaces are *children's places*, created and facilitated by children for their own, self-directed purposes. Even though teachers plan recess games and often use recess as an extension of the classroom, children will find unintended spaces and create their own micro-worlds where they can act out events and situations of their own making. These discovered spaces are where children do the work of building social skills through self-guided play activities.

Using this conception of a sense of belonging as a lens can bring understanding to Ernie's experiences with social isolation. When quarantining and social distancing policies were introduced, Ernie's world was upended. It did not take him long to realize that he probably was not going to be able to play games with his friends for a long time. While he missed doing some of the school related stuff, it was recess time with his friends that he missed the most. In his new Mars like virtual learning life, the isolating context dramatically affected the dynamism component of his sense of belonging and became the driving force in determining his feelings of connectedness. Rather than having social interactions with his peers, his teacher tried to get students to work together in the Zoom classes. However, Ernie was often grouped with classmates he did not know that well and did not feel connected with them. On top of that, Ernie felt like he never got to just do stuff. It seemed to him like everything was going to be graded, even how well he worked with his group mates. He lost all decision making power in how he engaged with his friends and other classmates, both in and out of school. The much more restrictive environment in which he found himself all but eliminated his self-determination, the ability for choosing how he engaged with his social group. This increase in the influence of the context and the reduction of subjectivity and self-determination put Ernie in danger of losing that sense of belonging he felt when he was able to be with his social group during recess and after school.

The emerging themes around a sense of belonging suggest that it is a multifaceted, complex feeling governed by the position and relationships one has with a community, both in terms of individual relationships and with the group as a whole. This acceptance by the group along with the social capitol of the individual together create the foundations for building a sense of belonging. The focus on the dynamic interplay between the actions of the individual and the actions of the group is at the heart of a sense of belonging. Living in a Mars like world of isolation changed how Ernie was able to be with his friends and impacted the supportive relationships he had with his teacher and the other students in his class. The change in context eliminated a critical component needed for Ernie to develop a sense of belonging. Moving to a digital environment meant Ernie was going to have to develop his social group all over again, without being able to physically be with anyone. His world was even more dominated by adult created spaces and activities and he was going to have to rely on his teachers for help in creating the communities needed for learning how to be a social being. This reliance on his teacher and other aspects of a school environment points to the need to contextualize a sense of belonging in an academic context. Having a conception of what a sense of belonging in an academic environment encompasses provides a foundation for understanding the challenges faced by the Ernie's of the world.

A SENSE OF BELONGING AT SCHOOL

The nature of K-12 classrooms and students present unique challenges for effective distance learning. Student success in a distance learning environment requires students to be highly self-regulated and motivated (Garrison et al., 1999; Garrison & Cleveland-Innes, 2005). However, younger students often have not sufficiently matured to have the skills to navigate the distance learning environment without support. While literature describes children as having the potential to learn how to initiate, cease, and modulate behaviors with support from cultural and social models (Post et al., 2006), they have not reached the developmental level of older, more mature learners. Combining the need to form productive relationships as a foundational skill required for developing a community of learners that supports meaningful discourse (Kahn et al., 2017; Oh et al., 2018) with the positively correlated relationship between effective communication and increased social cooperation and social independence (Atabey, 2018), implies that children, with their lack of maturity, are a work in progress as it comes to transitioning to a distance model of school (Niess & Gillow-Wiles, 2013; Bolliger & Martin, 2018; Kinsel et al., 2005).

Conceptualizing a sense of belonging as an essential component of academic success grew from ideas around student involvement, characterized as the amount of "physical and psychological energy a student devotes to the academic experience" (Astin, 1984, p. 297). Astin's work combined the Freudian belief that people invest psychological energy in objects and persons outside themselves with what learning theorists refer to as *vigilance* or *time-on-task* to describe the relationship between involvement and academic success. This interweaving of student energy investment and persistence grew into a more encompassing concept described as an academic sense of belonging. As this idea evolved, the connection between a sense of belonging and student academic success became more apparent, detailing how a students' experience of acceptance impacts their perceptions and behaviors (Osterman, 2000).

A sense of belonging being intimately connected with student academic success begs the question of how to think about a sense of belonging as it applies to teaching and learning. One answer is to present a *sense of belonging at school* that is contextualized to an academic environment. Goodenow (1993) described a sense of belonging at school as

being accepted, valued, encouraged, and included by teachers and peers in the academic classroom, and of feeling oneself to be an importance part of the life and activity of the class. More than simple perceived liking or warmth, it also involves support and respect for personal autonomy and for the student as an individual. (p. 23)

Other researchers have focused on other aspects when characterizing a sense of belonging at school. Recall how Ernie felt about being part of a friend group. The critical nature of friend groups was explored when St-Amand et al. (2017) focused on social relationships and found that student friendships were an essential component of belonging.

The critical distinction between young children developing a personal, general sense of belonging and developing a sense of belonging at school lies in the underlying goals of each. In the process of developing a personal sense of belonging, a child learns emotional and social skills, builds relationships, and begins to create an understanding of how to navigate a complex world. On the other hand, building a sense of belonging at school is much more about learning how to work with others towards a common goal through developing a community identity and membership. In this case, while personal growth and development is desired, it is not the primary outcome.

While this definition preserves the aspects of feeling an important part of the community, several critical distinctions require more research and thought. The distinction between a sense of belonging at school and a more general personal sense of belonging results from contextualizing the development of the relationships that drive a sense of belonging. Returning to the five elements of a sense of belonging presented by Mahar et al. (2013) discussed earlier, several elements are no longer under the control of the individual. In a sense of belonging at school, the ways students engage with the group are no longer individual, students cannot choose their desired referent group or how they interact with the group, and the contexts are predefined and highly structured. These differences call in to question the characterization of the sense of belonging at school as a sense of belonging in the more traditional sense. A path to understanding for resolving these apparent distinctions might lie in that, in an online context, there is alignment between the themes of a sense of belonging at school and social presence (Garrison et al., 1999), with the distinction being a matter of emphasis more than focusing on different aspects of community identity development.

SOCIAL PRESENCE AND ONLINE SENSE OF BELONGING AT SCHOOL

The Community of Inquiry (CoI) construct, introduced by Garrison et al. (1999), identified three interrelated concepts (social presence, cognitive presence, teaching presence), describing the interplay between them to characterize the online educational learning experience. In the CoI construct, social presence is the degree to which participants in an online community feel affectively connected to one another. Developing and supporting social presence leads to meaningful community member participation, the development and support of a community of learners, and educational experiences that result in meaningful learning (Garrison & Cleveland-Innes, 2005; Hill et al., 2009; Kinsel et al., 2005; Swan, & Shih 2005).

As knowledge around online learning evolved, other researchers began to investigate CoI and develop their own conceptions of social presence. To bring a sense of consistency to how social presence is conceptualized in literature, Lowenthal and Snelson, (2017) used a literature review process to investigate how researchers define social presence and how that definition has evolved.

In general, these definitions all revolve around one or more of the following elements:

- Being there
  - the degree of salience between two communicators
- Being real
  - the degree to which a person is perceived as 'real' in mediated communications
- Projecting
  - the ability to project oneself socially and effectively in a community of inquiry
- Connecting
  - the degree of feeling and reaction of being connected on computer mediated communications to another entity
- Belonging
  - a student's sense of being in and belonging in a course and the ability to interact with other students and an instructor. (p. 3)

The thrust of social presence is to support individuals as they work to be seen as authentic group members. This relationship is much like the idea of identity or what it means to be a "certain kind of person" (Gee, 2001, p. 100) in terms of how to think, act and speak as a member of a group. The focus on relationships an individual has with other group members and how this relationship affords individual learning is at the heart of social presence. Looking at an online student sense of belonging at school from an identity perspective, Garrison et al. (2004) described several expectations beyond those that are more typically a part of being an effective online learner. In addition to technological ability, distance learners need to be comfortable with new modes of communication and have increased levels of self-direction, self-regulation, and self-motivation. Taking role identity adjustment as being "acquired in, and facilitated by, the online community" (Garrison et al., 2004, p. 65), the iterative comparison of one's own behavior to others is core to role identity adjustment.

In the main, literature around an online sense of belonging at school has focused on extending the social presence construct. As related as they are, a sense of belonging and a social presence are fundamentally different. An important distinction between a sense of belonging and social presence centers on what is at the root of each. A sense of belonging is all about finding a place in a community where one feels both a fully accepted member of a community as well as being supported and valued by that community. It is this *Reciprocity* element, or how the individual and the community are intertwined, that forms the basis for developing important social skills and social capitol, where actions on the part of the individual elicit responses from the community that in turn guide and inform future member actions. This iterative action/reaction cycle creates a pathway for community membership building reciprocal trust and a sense of intimacy that provide meaning and perceptions of value.

This focus is in contrast with social presence, where the desired endpoint is having group members recognize the 'realness' of an individual in a computer mediated context in such a way that relationships supporting a community of inquiry are made possible. In social presence, the focus in not so much on developing deep relationships where community members find an enhanced meaning in life, as it is on transcending the inherent limits of technology mediated communications. In the social presence construct, trust, value, and support all have importance, but if one is not seen as a *real person*, these relationship elements are very difficult to foster. This focus can be seen in how researchers view social presence as presented earlier. Three of the five defining elements are based on one's ability to be seen as real and the ability to project that realness in a community of inquiry.

Another distinction between the two constructs is in how they are developed. For the most part, a sense of belonging has its formative roots in unstructured peer group activities, situated in informally found or created spaces. A sense of belonging grows out of individually driven interactions where relationships are negotiated, behaviors are trialed, and bonds are made and broken. As people engage with others in this context, they are finding their place in a group where they share common experiences, thinking, and beliefs (Healy & Richardson, 2017; Mahar et al., 2013; Sedgwick & Yonge, 2008). The process of developing a sense of belonging is most effectively driven by participants. In children, this sense of belonging is most often and most effectively developed when children are in self-constructed spaces and are engaged in self-constructed activities. Adult interaction shifts the locus of control from child participant to outside facilitator, resulting in a feeling of losing ownership and relevance on the part of the children (Ballam & Cosgriff, 2018; Harrison, 2018; Pellegrini & Bohn, 2005). The overarching theme from this line of research is that a sense of belonging comes from iterative group/individual interactions where the difficult social cognitive work necessary to sustain peer interaction is done.

In comparison, social presence is developed through targeted actions on the part of instructors who guide students through activities where the students have opportunities to meaningfully engage with each other and with course content. The dominate theme from best practices literature is that social presence development is primarily the result of purposeful instructor actions, designed to help students see others as real people and to develop useful student-student, student-instructor, and student-content relationships (Aldheleai et al., 2020; Dikkers et al., 2013; Garrison et al., 2010; Lowenthal & Snelson, 2017; Oh et al., 2018; Whiteside, 2015). Setting role identity adjustment as part of online community membership, Garrison and Cleveland-Innes (2005) place deliberate actions on the part of instructors as an essential component for students to transition into effective distance learners. Effective instructor actions that lead to student social presence center on managing student expectations, asking for feedback, and being friendly and empathic (Aldheleai et al., 2020; Valenzuela et al., 2013).

In spite of these fundamental differences, there are similarities between an online sense of belonging at school and social presence. In general, both have elements of group membership development and identity construction. Additionally, just as in developing a social presence, developing an online sense of belonging at school revolves around the actions of the instructor and the relationships with students these actions foster (Peacock et al., 2020). Discussing the importance of the actions of instructors in supporting an online sense of belonging at school (Chiu et al., 2016) suggest that while classmate relationships are linked to students' sense of belonging, instructor elements such as teacher-student relationships and teacher support have the greatest mediating impact.

This tension between an online sense of belonging at school and social presence described the uncomfortableness Ernie felt as his teachers tried so hard to make school fun and engaging. It seemed to him like even though he had lots of group engagement, it did not fill the loneliness he was feeling. In every interaction there seemed like there was a right answer for everything he did. He did not have a chance to just try and do things with the same kind of freedom he had when he was able to have recess.

A SENSE OF BELONGING AT SCHOOL AND ONLINE LEARNING SUCCESS

To investigate the importance of a sense of belonging at school has for successful online learning, Peacock and Cowan (2016) re-envisioned the three presences of the CoI construct; social, cognitive, and teaching, to better represent elements of a sense of belonging at school and the relationships between the elements. In their conception, Peacock and Cowan rename teaching presence as tutoring presence to be more compatible with student-centered learning (see Figure 1).

Figure 1. An adapted version of the CoI framework (Peacock & Cowan, 2016)

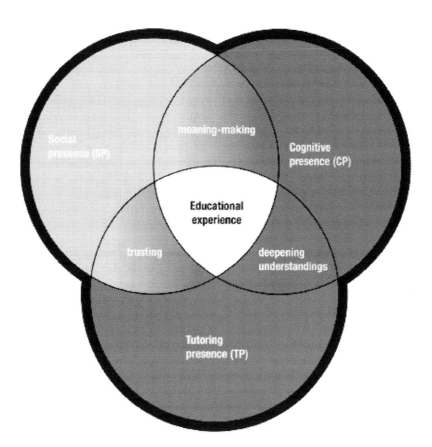

Here, they define *tutor* as "a staff member appointed to both support the creating planning of a course before learning commences, and in the facilitation of learning during the course" (Peacock & Cowan, 2019, p.68). The role of the tutor is to facilitate student engagement without directing specific actions taken by learners. This focus on student engagement without active direction is the primary realignment of the CoI construct that reflects an essential element of sense of belonging development understanding.

Retaining the underlying elements of social and cognitive presence that are part of the CoI construct, Peacock and Cowan (2019) describe tutoring presences as the support given by a "caring, trusted and engaged tutor" (p. 71). In their version, the goal of a tutor is to help create and enhance the development of interpersonal relationships and a sense of belonging through the design and facilitation of social and cognitive presences. Their work suggests that it is the trusting relationship between students and tutors that is at the heart of promoting a sense of belonging in an online learning environment. Further work by Peacock et al., (2020) identified tutors as being pivotal to the development of students' sense of belonging, where tutors were thought of as "the glue that brings it together" (p. 25).

Just as in the CoI construct, a sense of belonging at school has been shown to be an important component to online learning success. In an exploration of the importance of a sense of belonging at school for online learners, Peacock et al. (2020) identified three overarching themes:

- interaction/engagement - learner involvement and interaction;
- a culture of learning - sharing the challenges and anxieties as learners;
- and support - peer interaction assisting in resolving learning difficulties.

They found that when these themes were attended to, students felt a stronger sense of belonging that translated to more meaningful group and peer interactions, and hence greater student academic achievement. This result was in alignment with earlier studies showing that an online environment where participants share common goals and feel that their ideas and views are welcomed brings about high quality online education (Chiu et al., 2016; Hagerty et al., 2002; Heinisch, 2018; O'Keefe, 2013; Post et al., 2006). Much like social presence in a CoI, developing a sense of belonging at school supports online learning primarily through creating a structured space where students and tutors are able to collectively and collaboratively negotiate successful pathways leading to deep understanding.

DISCUSSION

This section presents a discussion of the challenges facing developing a sense of belonging for younger children in an online environment. Like putting together a jigsaw puzzle, the authors assembled concepts and ideas from a variety of areas of research to build a picture of a children's sense of belonging. This construct illustrates how shifting to online learning creates challenges for children and their social development that may not be sufficiently negotiated by applying current understanding.

Elementary Students and an Online Sense of Belonging

When Ernie ended up on what felt like Mars, he lost access to his referent group as well as to the children's places he and his friend had constructed. This loss made it all but impossible for Ernie to feel connected with his peers in the same ways as when they were all together in their familiar environment. Online classes gave him access to help, but not always when or from whom he needed it. Additionally, he almost never got to have his teacher's full attention. With a class of 30 students, Ernie's teacher could not individually check in with each student the way he did in the classroom. Although the teacher used the breakout room feature of Zoom, Ernie often did not know what he was supposed to be doing or how to ask for help. The other students in the breakout room were usually not very helpful and Ernie did not know them well enough to ask them for help without feeling stupid for not knowing.

When Ernie and all his friends felt like they were teleported to Mars, the teachers were under extraordinary pressure to make the transition to fully online teaching. Responding to the sense of urgency in the process, the focus was rightly put on content delivery, in which research has created a significant body of knowledge. While not forgotten, the more affective elements of an elementary level classroom, such as social development, were back-grounded to make space for meeting academic performance goals. Attempts to reconfigure social presence development understanding to serve as a beginning construct in developing a sense of belonging left out critical aspects of what it means to feel like one belongs to a community. The need for children to be together to develop social skills did not change when they could no longer be in a physical school setting.

Through the previous sections, the authors have established the nature of a sense of belonging, how younger children create and nurture their sense of belonging, and the nature of the world in which children live. Additionally, the authors have described current literature around a sense of belonging in an online learning environment and the importance of fostering a sense of belonging at school. Synthesizing these ideas, it becomes apparent that the importance of a sense of belonging in both personal development and online academic success, combined with the relocation of classrooms from a face-to-face to a virtual environment creates challenges for younger students such as those in K-12 grades.

With few exceptions, research into the importance of developing a sense of belonging in an online learning context leverages ideas and concepts coming from some form of the CoI construct and is situated in college or adult learning. In particular, the thinking that a sense of belonging at school is fostered by purposeful, directive actions on the part of the instructor or tutor who drives most best practices recommendations. Additionally, and just as important for the thrust of this chapter, the majority of this research in question has been situated in a post-secondary context, with college level or adult learners as study populations.

The focus on more mature learners comes with a subtle assumption of a sufficient level of self-regulation and motivation to navigate online learning. These assumptions hide the challenges younger children face when they are put into cognitively challenging situations without their accustomed support groups. Additionally, this focus on older students assumes a certain developmental level of social skills and a personal sense of belonging. From this perspective, with already having a referent group membership, the online sense of belonging at school construct is sufficient for older students to feel connected with their peers and the tutor. However, when applied to younger K-12 children, this perspective omits the fact that this group is still learning the necessary social skills for building a personal sense of belonging.

The Open Question

Without reducing the importance of that research, the authors suggest that an important question has been overlooked. Namely, is there enough underlying commonality between a sense of belonging in the general sense and an online sense of belonging at school for younger children to develop important social skills that come from free-form, play-based interactions? A sense of belonging has, at its root, an element of an individually constructed set of relationships and world view. Transitioning the environment to a virtual space, controlled by others, removes a significant portion of that individuality and shifts the locus of control to the instructor. If one accepts the importance of children developing a sense of belonging through self-directed peer interactions, then the way a sense of belonging at school in online learning is described presents challenges. Namely, how can the self-directed, free-from play experiences be replicated in an online environment, the experiences that are critical for younger students in developing a sense of belonging, both in general and at school?

When K-12 education transitioned to being fully online, quite a bit of the learning experience was forced to take a different form. Some of the face-to-face elements of these experiences had online analogues that retained the essential components. Other elements were enhanced by the integration of technologies. Finally, some elements had no online representations and were lost all together. This chapter presents the idea that recess is an element of the learning experience that has no online representation and thus was a causality of the pandemic. The trend to marginalize recess as important in the face of increasing budget reductions and community demand for higher academic standards meant that losing recess was not much of a concern (Bauml et al., 2020).

The importance of child-directed free play in social development, combined with the apparent impossibility of creating these play experiences in online education begs the question of where to go from here. How do educators create online experiences where children can create their own spaces and interactions in such ways as to support their developing social skills and a true sense of belonging? Emerging technologies might prove useful, but the underlying constraints of digitally mediated interactions put up large roadblocks.

Possible Best Practices for Developing an Online Sense of Belonging at School

St-Amand et al. (2017) presented a series of recommendations for building a sense of belonging that leads to student academic success. These recommendations suggest that teachers learn to decode and give importance to student's emotional well-being, make certain that each student has a role in a team and feels accepted, and give students opportunities to find and develop common interests with their team/group members in the classroom. A distinguishing element of the work of St-Amand et al. (2017) lay in the recommendations that focus on student interactions outside the classroom or in ways that are not strictly academically focused. For example, they suggest that students be encouraged to participate in extra-curricular activities where they can find common interests outside the classroom. More to the focus of this chapter, St-Amand et al. recommends social competence programs early in a students' school career. These programs would include learning cooperative play skills, language and communication skills, emotional regulation, and aggression control. Recalling the self-directed play activities discussed previously concerning recess, social competence programs promote the same kinds of social development learning that happens organically during unstructured recess play time.

There is little room in the online school day for a virtual recess analogue, making outside of school time an important resource where students and their families might work to build social confidence and interpersonal relationship skills. Similar to Peacock and Cowan's *tutor,* other people in a child's life can play an important part in helping develop a sense of belonging. Through acting as a mentor, or someone in the capacity of a confidant, guide, or counselor, family members can actively provide support to help the child develop social skills and learn how to navigate social interactions. When the mentor really cares for and looks out for the well-being of the child, the latter is more inclined to open up and accept a relationship based on trust (Drolet & Arcand, 2013). This trust relationship is similar to that formed in peer groups through processes discussed earlier and serves a similar purpose. It is in these trust relationships where children can experiment with behaviors with minimal consequences.

In all cases, best practices for helping children develop the social skills necessary for building a sense of belonging recognize that every interaction with adults and peers is contributive. Teachers, parents, and peers are the referent groups with which a child forms close relationships. These relationships are shaping factors in how children learn to interact with and form groups with other people (Uslu & Gizir, 2017).

Ernie really missed his friends. He missed being able to be his authentic self and he missed doing what he wanted instead of what others wanted. For all that he was longing for, he did find happiness in the extra attention he was receiving from his family. He knew it was because of being stuck on Mars, but that did not matter to him. His dad spent time with him doing stuff his dad liked and he included him in new activities, like baking cookies. He seemed happy to have Ernie's help and did not get mad with spilling the flour. He just helped clean it up and laughed at the flour in his hair. Additionally, his dad joined Ernie in activities he liked. Playing ball, exploring outside, building forts and riding bikes with his dad helped Ernie see his dad as a trusted companion, with whom he could discuss important matters. His mom was doing the same things, having Ernie help with the things she was doing, like fixing the car and spending time doing what Ernie liked. Ernie did not know much about how cars worked, but he really liked how his mom spent time teaching him and did not get mad when he got bored and wanted to go do something else. She also helped him when he was having trouble putting together a model of the Millennium Falcon. She did not take over; she just did what he asked her to do. These interactions with his parents made Ernie feel supported, valued, and confident, much like how he felt when he was with his friends. While being with his family would never replace being with his friends, it did help him feel less isolated and alone.

FUTURE RESEARCH

At the time this chapter was written, there has been some relief in the impacts of the pandemic. People are getting vaccinated, businesses are finding ways to re-open, and most importantly, schools are moving back to in-class learning. This return to a new normal does not make the discussion around an online sense of belonging moot. Even though students are returning to the classroom and the playground, there remains a need for enhancing and extending understanding of the importance of a sense of belonging and the need for children to feel like they are part of a caring, supportive community, where their thoughts matter and they have value. The ideas and constructs presented in this chapter provide a foundational understanding of how children grow and learn, both socially and academically. This underpinning can provide a base upon which future research might build knowledge around ways to construct virtual spaces where children have the freedom to do the work necessary to create social skills that help them be successful and find meaning throughout their lives.

REFERENCES

Al-dheleai, Y., Tasir, Z., Al-Rahmi, W., Al-Sharafi, M., & Mydin, A. (2020). Modeling of Students Online Social Presence on Social Networking Sites and Academic Performance. *International Journal of Emerging Technologies in Learning, 15*(12), 56–71. doi:10.3991/ijet.v15i12.12599

Anant, S. S. (1966). Need to belong. *Canada's Mental Health, 14*(2), 21–27.

Astin, A. W. (1984). Student involvement: A developmental theory for higher education. *Student Involvement: A Developmental Theory for Higher Education, 25*(4), 297–308.

Atabey, D. (2018). A Study into the Effective Communication and Social Skills of Preschool Children Derya. Alanya Alaaddin Keykubat University, 19, 185–199. doi:10.17679/inuefd.323598

Ballam, N., & Cosgriff, M. (2018). Enabling ability and growing talent: The contribution of self, place, and belonging. *Australasian Journal of Gifted Education, 27*(1), 21–30. doi:10.21505/ajge.2018.0003

Bauml, M., Patton, M. M., & Rhea, D. (2020). A Qualitative Study of Teachers' Perceptions of Increased Recess Time on Teaching, Learning, and Behavior. *Journal of Research in Childhood Education, 34*(4), 506–520. doi:10.1080/02568543.2020.1718808

Bjorklund, D. F., & Green, B. L. (1992). The adaptive nature of cognitive immaturity. *The American Psychologist, 47*(1), 46–54. doi:10.1037/0003-066X.47.1.46

Bolliger, D. U., & Martin, F. (2018). Instructor and student perceptions of online student engagement strategies. *Distance Education, 39*(4), 568–583. doi:10.1080/01587919.2018.1520041

Chiu, M. M., Chow, B. W. Y., McBride, C., & Mol, S. T. (2016). Students' Sense of Belonging at School in 41 Countries: Cross-Cultural Variability. *Journal of Cross-Cultural Psychology, 47*(2), 175–196. doi:10.1177/0022022115617031

Dikkers, A., Whiteside, A., & Lewis, S. (2013). Virtual high school teacher and student reactions to the social presence model. *Journal of Interactive Online Learning, 12*(3).

Drolet, M., & Arcand, I. (2013). Positive development, sense of belonging, and support of peers among early adolescents: Perspectives of different actors. *International Education Studies, 6*(4), 29–38. doi:10.5539/ies.v6n4p29

Garrison, D. R., Anderson, T., & Archer, W. (1999). Critical thinking and computer conferencing: A model and tool to assess cognitive presence. *American Journal of Distance Education, 15*(1), 7–23. doi:10.1080/08923640109527071

Garrison, D. R., & Cleveland-Innes, M. (2005). Facilitating cognitive presence in online learning: Interaction is not enough. *American Journal of Distance Education, 19*(3), 133–148. doi:10.120715389286ajde1903_2

Garrison, D. R., Cleveland-Innes, M., & Fung, T. (2004). Student role adjustment in online communities of inquiry: Model and instrument validation. *Journal of Asynchronous Learning Networks, 8*(2), 61–74. doi:10.24059/olj.v8i2.1828

Garrison, D. R., Cleveland-Innes, M., & Fung, T. S. (2010). Exploring causal relationships among teaching, cognitive and social presence: Student perceptions of the community of inquiry framework. *The internet and higher education, 13*(1-2), 31–36. doi:10.1016/j.iheduc.2009.10.002

Gee, J. P. (2001). Education identity as an analytic lens for research. *Review of Research in Education, 25*, 99–125.

Goodenow, C. (1993). Classroom Belonging among Early Adolescent Students: Relationships to Motivation and Achievement. *The Journal of Early Adolescence, 13*(1), 21–43. doi:10.1177/0272431693013001002

Hagerty, B. M., Williams, R. A., & Oe, H. (2002). Childhood antecedents of adult sense of belonging. *Journal of Clinical Psychology, 58*(7), 793–801. doi:10.1002/jclp.2007 PMID:12205719

Hagerty, B. M. K., Lynch-Sauer, J., Patusky, K. L., Bouwsema, M., & Collier, P. (1992). Sense of belonging: A vital mental health concept. *Archives of Psychiatric Nursing*, *6*(3), 172–177. doi:10.1016/0883-9417(92)90028-H PMID:1622293

Harrison, M. (2018). Space as a tool for analysis: Examining digital learning spaces. *Open Praxis*, *10*(1), 17. doi:10.5944/openpraxis.10.1.782

Healy, M., & Richardson, M. (2017). Images and identity: Children constructing a sense of belonging to Europe. *European Educational Research Journal*, *16*(4), 440–454. doi:10.1177/1474904116674015

Heinisch, B. P. (2018). *DigitalCommons@University of Nebraska-Lincoln Rural Students' Sense of Belonging at a Large Public University*. https://digitalcommons.unl.edu/cehsedaddiss/291

Hill, J., Song, L., & West, R. (2009). Social Learning Theory and Web-Based Learning Environments: A Review of Research and Discussion of Implications. *American Journal of Distance Education*, *23*(2), 88–103. doi:10.1080/08923640902857713

Kahn, P., Everington, L., Kelm, K., Reid, I., & Watkins, F. (2017). Understanding student engagement in online learning environments: The role of reflexivity. *Educational Technology Research and Development*, *65*(1), 203–218. doi:10.100711423-016-9484-z

Kinsel, E., Cleveland-Innes, M., & Garrison, D. R. (2005). *Student Role Adjustment in Online Environments: From the Mouths of Online Babes*. uwex.edu

Lowenthal, P. R., & Snelson, C. (2017). In search of a better understanding of social presence: An investigation into how researchers define social presence. *Distance Education*, *38*(2), 141–159. doi:10.1080/01587919.2017.1324727

Mahar, A. L., Cobigo, V., & Stuart, H. (2013). Conceptualizing belonging. *Disability and Rehabilitation*, *35*(12), 1026–1032. doi:10.3109/09638288.2012.717584 PMID:23020179

Maslow, A. H. (1962). *Toward a psychology of being*. Van Nostrand. doi:10.1037/10793-000

O'Keefe, P. (2013). a Sense of Belonging: Improving Student Retention. *College Student Journal*, *47*(4), 605–613. http://proxygsu-col1.galileo.usg.edu/login?url=http://search.ebscohost.com/login.aspx?direct=true&db=slh&AN=93813989&site=eds-live&scope=site

Oh, C. S., Bailenson, J. N., & Welch, G. F. (2018). A systematic review of social presence: Definition, antecedents, and implications. *Frontiers in Robotics and AI*, *5*(OCT), 1–35. doi:10.3389/frobt.2018.00114 PMID:33500993

Osterman, K. F. (2000). Students' need for belonging in the school community. *Review of Educational Research*, *70*(3), 323–367. doi:10.3102/00346543070003323

Peacock, S., & Cowan, J. (2016). From Presences to Linked Influences Within Communities of Inquiry. *International Review of Research in Open and Distributed Learning*, *17*(5), 267–286. doi:10.19173/irrodl.v17i5.2602

Peacock, S., & Cowan, J. (2019). Promoting sense of belonging in online learning communities of inquiry in accredited courses. *Online Learning Journal*, *23*(2), 67–81. doi:10.24059/olj.v23i2.1488

Peacock, S., Cowan, J., Irvine, L., & Williams, J. (2020). An Exploration Into the Importance of a Sense of Belonging for Online Learners. *International Review of Research in Open and Distributed Learning, 21*(2), 18–35. doi:10.19173/irrodl.v20i5.4539

Pellegrini, A. D., & Bjorklund, D. F. (1997). The role of recess in children's cognitive performance. *Educational Psychologist, 32*(1), 35–40. doi:10.120715326985ep3201_3

Pellegrini, A. D., & Bohn, C. M. (2005). The Role of Recess in Children's Cognitive Performance and School Adjustment. *Educational Researcher, 34*(1), 13–19. doi:10.3102/0013189X034001013

Post, Y., Boyer, W., & Brett, L. (2006). A historical examination of self-regulation: Helping children now and in the future. *Early Childhood Education Journal, 34*(1), 5–14. doi:10.100710643-006-0107-x

Poston, B. (2009). An Exercise in Personal Exploration: Maslow's Hierarchy of Needs. *The Surgical Technologist, 41*(8), 347–353. http://www.ast.org/pdf/308.pdf

Ramstetter, C., & Murray, R. (2017). Time to Play: Recognizing the Benefits of Recess. *American Educator, 41*(1), 17.

Rasmussen, K. (2004). Places for children - Children's places. *Childhood, 11*(2), 155–173. doi:10.1177/0907568204043053

Sedgwick, M. G., & Yonge, O. (2008). "We're it", "we're a team", "we're family" means a sense of belonging. *Rural and Remote Health, 8*(3), 1021. PMID:18771338

St-Amand, J., Girard, S., & Smith, J. (2017). Sense of Belonging at School: Defining Attributes, Determinants, and Sustaining Strategies. *IAFOR Journal of Education, 5*(2), 105–119. doi:10.22492/ije.5.2.05

Sung, E., & Mayer, R. E. (2012). Five facets of social presence in online distance education. *Computers in Human Behavior, 28*(5), 1738–1747. doi:10.1016/j.chb.2012.04.014

Swan, K. (2005). A constructivist model for thinking about learning online. *Elements of Quality Online Education: Engaging Communities, 6*, 13–30.

Swan, K., & Shih, L. F. (2005). On the nature and development of social presence in online course discussions. *Journal of Asynchronous Learning Networks, 9*(3), 115–136.

Uslu, F., & Gizir, S. (2017). School belonging of adolescents: The role of teacher–student relationships, peer relationships and family involvement. *Kuram ve Uygulamada Egitim Bilimleri, 17*(1), 63–82. doi:10.12738/estp.2017.1.0104

Valenzuela, F. R., Fisher, J., Whale, S., & Adapa, S. (2013). Developing and evaluating social presence in the online learning environment. *International Proceedings of Economics Development and Research, 60*, 95.

Walker, L., & Avant, K. C. (2011). *Strategies for theory construction* (5th ed.). Prentice Hall.

Whiteside, A. L. (2015). Introducing the social presence model to explore online and blended learning experiences. *Online Learning, 19*(2), n2. doi:10.24059/olj.v19i2.453

ADDITIONAL READING

Chiu, M. M., Chow, B. W. Y., McBride, C., & Mol, S. T. (2016). Students' Sense of Belonging at School in 41 Countries: Cross-Cultural Variability. *Journal of Cross-Cultural Psychology, 47*(2), 175–196. doi:10.1177/0022022115617031

Davis, G. M., Hanzsek-Brill, M. B., Petzold, M. C., & Robinson, D. H. (2019). Students' Sense of Belonging: The Development of a Predictive Retention Model. *The Journal of Scholarship of Teaching and Learning, 19*(1), 117–127. doi:10.14434/josotl.v19i1.26787

Fong Lam, U., Chen, W. W., Zhang, J., & Liang, T. (2015). It feels good to learn where I belong: School belonging, academic emotions, and academic achievement in adolescents. *School Psychology International, 36*(4), 393–409. doi:10.1177/0143034315589649

Hagerty, B. M., Williams, R. A., & Oe, H. (2002). Childhood antecedents of adult sense of belonging. *Journal of Clinical Psychology, 58*(7), 793–801. doi:10.1002/jclp.2007 PMID:12205719

Hagerty, B. M. K., & Patusky, K. (1995). Developing a measure of sense of belonging. *Nursing Research, 44*(1), 9–13. doi:10.1097/00006199-199501000-00003 PMID:7862549

Healy, M., & Richardson, M. (2017). Images and identity: Children constructing a sense of belonging to Europe. *European Educational Research Journal, 16*(4), 440–454. doi:10.1177/1474904116674015

Lambert, N. M., Stillman, T. F., Hicks, J. A., Kamble, S., Baumeister, R. F., & Fincham, F. D. (2013). To Belong Is to Matter: Sense of Belonging Enhances Meaning in Life. *Personality and Social Psychology Bulletin, 39*(11), 1418–1427. doi:10.1177/0146167213499186 PMID:23950557

Pendergast, D., Allen, J., McGregor, G., & Ronksley-Pavia, M. (2018). Engaging marginalized, "at-risk" middle-level students: A focus on the importance of a sense of belonging at school. *Education Sciences, 8*(3), 138. Advance online publication. doi:10.3390/educsci8030138

Sancho, M., & Cline, T. (2012). Fostering a sense of belonging and community as children start a new school. *Educational and Child Psychology, 29*(1), 64–74.

van Herpen, S. G. A., Meeuwisse, M., Hofman, W. H. A., & Severiens, S. E. (2020). A head start in higher education: The effect of a transition intervention on interaction, sense of belonging, and academic performance. *Studies in Higher Education, 45*(4), 862–877. doi:10.1080/03075079.2019.1572088

KEY TERMS AND DEFINITIONS

Community of Inquiry: A group of individuals who collaboratively engage in purposeful critical discourse and reflection to construct personal meaning and confirm mutual understanding.

Deepening Understandings: The influence linking tutor presence and cognitive presence. The worthwhile deepening of the accumulating understandings that are developing in Social Presence and Cognitive Presence. Such deepening covers the subject matter in hand, and also the ongoing use and development of the abilities, cognitive and interpersonal, that facilitate such learning, individually and within the community.

Influences: The interwoven areas in the modified Community of Inquiry model that serve to combine presences in a community's purposeful pursuit of the desired educational experience.

Meaning-Making: The influence linking social presence and cognitive presence, the monitoring of co-cognition, and learners' joint management of opportunities for and impediments to cognition, supported through social communications online.

Referent Group: The group to which a person belongs when developing a sense of belonging. In education, referent groups might include schools or institutes of higher learning, peer groups, classrooms or an entire campus community.

Sense of Belonging: The psychological feeling of belonging or connectedness to a social, spatial, cultural, professional, or other type of group or a community.

Trusting: The influence linking tutor presence and social presence. The foundation upon which the key behaviors are founded is trust among the community and with the tutor.

Tutor Presence: The support given by a caring, trusted and engaged tutor in an online learning environment.

Chapter 2
Teaching Students With Learning Disabilities in a Virtual Learning Environment

Pankaj Khazanchi
https://orcid.org/0000-0002-1854-7384
Cobb County School District, USA & Liberty University, USA

Rashmi Khazanchi
https://orcid.org/0000-0001-8601-4144
Mitchell County School System, USA & Open University of the Netherlands, Heerlen, Netherlands

Simran Randhawa
Assessments Mentoring and Impact, India

ABSTRACT

COVID-19 brought unprecedented changes in the education sector at all levels globally. These rapid changes have transformed the way teachers are transacting the curriculum in K-12 classrooms. Teachers have had to adapt and depend on a virtual mode to reach students and facilitate student engagement and subsequent learning. In the absence of professional development support, such overnight changes and giant leaps from traditional face-to-face interaction with students have been extremely challenging for teachers and equally stressful for students and their parents. Many teachers describe their helplessness with growing absenteeism and delayed submission of student assignments. It is even more difficult for students with a learning disability to engage virtually for a longer time in front of a computer screen. They often need intensive, one-on-one support from the parent. This chapter aims to highlight the challenges faced by professionals to teach students with specific learning disabilities effectively in a virtual learning environment and identify effective solutions.

DOI: 10.4018/978-1-7998-7222-1.ch002

INTRODUCTION

Since the onset in the spring of 2020, the COVID-19 pandemic has resulted in complete or partial lockdowns, social distancing, and social isolation to curb the virus or at least keep it at bay. As reported by John Hopkins University (2021), globally, COVID-19 has infected more than 111 million people worldwide and has led to almost 2.5 million deaths. In the United States, the pandemic situation is quite grim, with more than 33 million people infected and 605,000 lives lost forever (John Hopkins University, 2021). Disasters create havoc in the lives of people (Di Pietro, 2017). The pandemic has disrupted lives at every level - economically, financially, and socially. The temporary school closures may have a psychological impact on students' health and may worsen the wellbeing of the most vulnerable student populations, such as students with disabilities (Colao et al., 2020).

The field of education is equally impacted by the pandemic and has witnessed drastic measures. Millions of students at the primary, middle, and high school levels got affected due to the pandemic causing worldwide school closures over health and safety uncertainty (Quezada et al., 2020). With these COVID-related school closures, many countries have turned to online instruction to ensure continuity of learning. However, online learning focuses on how many learners with disabilities are left behind as social distancing is not conducive to learning. Many students with disabilities require the exact opposite: face-to-face teaching, and a strong, close-knit network of educators, parents, and significant others, often supporting complex and multiple learning needs. Viewing the pandemic's current scenario and no sight of its ending soon, most of the student population had shifted to remote/virtual learning to maintain their continuity of education.

The transition to remote teaching-learning has been smooth for students with access to technology and internet at home. However, the lack of support and no accessibility to the internet, software, and learning materials, may leave some students no choice but to rely on a paper-pencil mode of learning. The new way of schooling restricted to the home environment has created a burden for students, families, and schools. Many students and teachers would probably face psychological problems during these times - like stress, fear, anxiety, depression, and insomnia, leading to a lack of focus and concentration. Therefore, in the time of COVID-19 crisis, implementing educational practices that promote Social-Emotional Learning (SEL) skills in classrooms are crucial. Students with SEL skills are more likely to manage stress and anxiety, make appropriate decisions, and are more likely to succeed in life (Khazanchi et al., 2021).

Working parents need to adapt and plan to adequately meet the SEL and other educational needs of their children during unprecedented time. Most of the parents face concerns with the education of their children due to unavailability of insufficient/updated devices and a fast-speed internet. Parents' responsibilities have increased manifold, especially for those with children at the elementary school level or those with special needs children. Also, students taking advanced placement courses at high school often find it difficult to manage their studies when learning is restricted to an online mode only. Both students with and without disabilities are struggling in an online virtual environment. Regardless of age and ability levels, all students deserve equal access to learning opportunities, both in a face-to-face and virtual classroom environment.

Students with specific learning disabilities (SLDs) show difficulties with learning problems, such as acquisition, retention, and organization of skills and poor comprehension of directions, even though they have an average to above-average intelligence quotient (Dominguez, 2020). There is a high prevalence of SLDs in school-going students diagnosed with learning problems in elementary schools. It is important to provide continuing education to students with SLDs as a break in learning/education often widens the learning/achievement gap. Often general education teachers, special educators, and related service providers deliver services to students with SLDs. Students with SLDs need intensive, explicit individualized intervention to develop appropriate academic skills (Grigorenko et al.,2020), and the COVID-19 pandemic has resulted in reduced learning opportunities for these students.

This book chapter explores the challenges faced by professionals to teach students with SLDs in a virtual learning environment. This chapter highlights effective educational practices for teaching students with SLDs in an online learning environment. It offers technology-based solutions for challenges faced by students in reading, writing, and mathematics.

BACKGROUND

Learning disabilities are complex neurodevelopmental disorders manifested by difficulties in listening, speaking, reading, writing, reasoning, and mathematics (Oxford, 1990). SLD is defined by the Individuals with Disabilities Education Improvement Act (IDEIA, 2004) as a disorder involving one or more basic psychological processes in comprehending and using spoken or written language, which may manifest itself in the imperfect ability to listen, think, speak, read, write, spell, or do mathematical calculations. "SLD does not include learning problems that are primarily the result of a visual, hearing, or motor disabilities, of intellectual disability, of emotional disturbance, or environmental, cultural, or economic disadvantage" (IDEIA, 2004, p.3). Students with SLDs show difficulties using metacognitive strategies, such as planning, observing, evaluating, and decision-making, to control their learning (Khasawneh et al., 2020). It becomes difficult for students with SLDs to effectively adapt and improve their understanding of their learning abilities, tasks, and strategies (Firat & Ergül, 2020).

Within reading, students with SLDs show difficulties with reading comprehension, recalling details, comprehending printed materials, story retelling, and may demonstrate an inability to connect ideas with the text presented (Gersten et al., 2001; Wade et al., 2010). Students at a high-risk for reading-related difficulties benefit from high-quality instructions involved in reading and writing. Rice (2017) demonstrated that the instructional materials in several online environments were not designed to support students with disabilities' comprehension that affected their reading. The lack of high-quality instruction increases the educational performance gap between students with SLDs and their typically developing peers. Students with learning difficulties experience low self-esteem and decreased motivation to complete their academic tasks, show disruptive behaviors, and frustration, resulting in incomplete target tasks (Shamir & Dushnitzky, 2019).

Who are Students with Learning Disabilities?

Learning is a multidimensional experience that everyone goes through since birth. These experiences also include scholastic experiences, that rely on learners' characteristics and abilities, which contribute positively or adversely to some learners' educational performance. For some individuals, these experiences become adverse due to a lack of integration and a breakdown in the levels of the psychological processes required for learning, namely: sensation, attention, perception, imagery, symbolization, and conceptualization; its inter-relationship with learning has been frequently cited in research (Kavale & Forness, 2000). The construct of Learning Disabilities (LDs) represents unique and heterogeneous groups of individuals who demonstrate significant difficulties in one or more educational performance areas. SLD is one of the 13 disability categories in which students may qualify for special services under the Individuals with Disabilities Education Improvement Act (IDEIA, 2004).

According to IDEIA (2004), individuals with SLDs show underachievement in eight areas: oral expression, listening comprehension, mathematical calculations, mathematics problem solving, written expression, basic reading skills, reading fluency skills, and reading comprehension (see Figure 1). Individuals with LDs may exhibit certain overlapping characteristics with individuals with other disabilities (Beckeman & Minnaert, 2018). However, the defining characteristic of LDs are that the cognitive processes influence learning which underline the educational difficulties that the learner with LDs experiences (Swanson,1991). "LDs are neurobiologically based, involve cognitive processes, and affect learning" (Gartland & Strosnider, 2018, p.195). They are pervasive (Adelman,1992) as nearly 40% of the students who have been found eligible for special education programs under IDEIA are served under the SLD category (Horowitz et al., 2017). LDs persist in various forms across the life span (Engel,1997), most often with precursors of language delays or language deficits in early childhood that emerge before formal schooling and continue into adulthood (National Joint Committee for Learning Disabilities, 2008).

Figure 1. Students with Learning Disabilities show challenges in eight areas

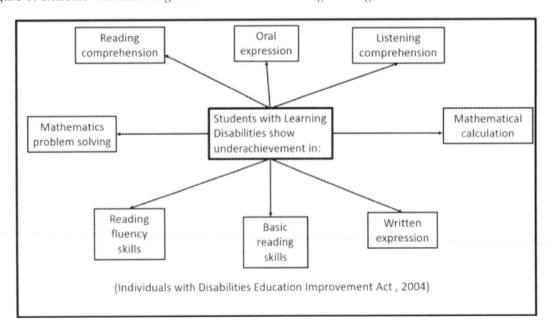

Learning Challenges Faced by Students with Learning Disabilities

Students with LDs may show learning challenges, such as a) short attention span, poor concentration, and may display hyperactivity; b) poor gross motor coordination leading to general awkwardness and clumsiness; (c) slow processing and interpreting visual and auditory information; (d) difficulty recognizing phoneme sounds in spoken language; (e) poor organizational skills; (f) inability to decode single words; (g) difficulty in oral reading, reading comprehension, and word recognition skill; (h) weakened memory skills, as well as difficulties with executive functioning and cognitive skills; (i) higher risk of having socio-emotional problems in comparison to their non-disabled peers resulting in low self-esteem and self-concept, anxiety issues, peer rejection, external locus of control, depression, and learned helplessness (Beckeman & Minnaert, 2018; Elbaum & Vaughn, 2003; Galway & Metsala, 2011; Graham et al., 2017; Swanson, 1993; Swanson et al., 2013; Trainin & Swanson, 2005).

There is a variation in the functional impact of LDs across the lifespan due to changing environments, contexts, demands of learning, and support. Each student with LD has a unique pattern of strengths (Shaywitz, 2003) and needs, which determine the extent to which LD interferes with learning and success at educational outcomes. Based on the pattern of characteristics that an individual exhibits, LDs are classified into subtypes of Dyslexia (reading difficulties), Dysgraphia (written expression disorder: difficulties in written expression, spelling, & handwriting), Dyscalculia (mathematical difficulties- students struggle in mathematics and show difficulties, with computation, place value, problem-solving, and number operations), and Non-Verbal LD (visuospatial and social difficulties) (Bouck et al., 2018).

Mental Health Implications Of COVID-19 On Students with Learning Disabilities

The world suddenly underwent a major and abrupt change with the advent of COVID-19, which forced many school districts to switch to an online learning environment with less preparation. The uncertainty about the personal and global effects of COVID-19 is creating great concern in addition to the specific psychological effects of quarantine (Brooks et al.,2020). Many families have lost their loved ones to the COVID-19, and many more people suffered from job loss and pay cuts, among other changes. With schools being suspended since March 2020 worldwide in 189 countries (UNICEF, 2020), the impact is evident with schools and colleges shifting classes online and work from home becoming a way of life worldwide (Patel, 2020).

It is already evident that the direct and indirect psychological and social effects of the COVID-19 pandemic are pervasive and could affect mental health now and in the future (Holmes et al., 2020). Even though the human population worldwide is affected by this situation, people with learning difficulties and neurodevelopmental disorders might be affected by changes and disruption to routines, isolation, loneliness, and support systems (Holmes et al., 2020). Routines generally lend a sense of structure and order to daily lives, which is important for an individual's emotional and psychological development (Patel, 2020). Children may struggle with significant adjustments to their routines, which may interfere with their sense of structure, predictability, and security. A few international organizations and researchers measured school closures' effect on students' learning and found a measurable loss in the acquisition of basic skills, especially of the most disadvantaged students (Cattaneo et al., 2017; Quinn et al., 2016). Even a relatively short period of missed school will have consequences for skill growth (Burgess & Sievertsen, 2020; Goldstein, 2020). As accommodation for the COVID-19 pandemic, the circumstances regarding education rapidly transitioned over the past two years from teaching in person to virtual learning, negatively impacting students with disabilities and their families. This rushed shift towards online learning rendered schools unprepared to properly teach students, especially those with disabilities. Still, despite these harmful consequences of virtual learning which disproportionately affect students with disabilities, virtual learning will most likely continue for an extended period of time (National Center for Learning Disabilities, 2020).

The United States has seven million children between 3 and 21 years of age who have received special education classes at school (National Center for Education Statistics, 2020). It is evident from the literature that students with disabilities and their families are likely to be at higher risk of experiencing poor mental health and being under substantially greater pressure than less vulnerable families during COVID-19 (Asbury et al., 2020). A lot of students require and benefit most from skilled, in person, evidence-based, and individualized instruction at school. With the switch to virtual learning, many of these students' parents are forced to be the providers of such instruction in place of specialized teachers, oftentimes proving arduous for these families to handle as they already typically face more stressors than those with neurotypical children (Asbury et al., 2020; Hills, 2020; Mc Stay et al., 2014). Such stressors can negatively influence the quality of family relationships, making patient and empathic parenting challenging (Osborne et al., 2008) which may impact students' development with SLDs, amongst other disabilities. Learning under stress may significantly affects motivation, cognition, engagement, retention, and participation (Meo et al., 2020; Patel, 2020). These repercussions derived from virtual learning lead us to grasp the significant impact of the pandemic on students with SLDs and, consequently, the urgent need to design educational responses emphasizing integrated social, emotional, cognitive, and academic development.

Role of Technology to Engage Students with Learning Disabilities

Integrating technology into the education system has helped build a strong foundation for students' learning environments. Even before COVID-19, many teachers integrated technology into their classrooms. With the COVID-19 school closure, all K-12 teachers were required to implement some form of technology to supplement virtual learning for their students their students. Technology has the potential to improve the learning outcomes of at-risk students (Darling-Hammond et al., 2014). Electronic devices, including desktops, laptops, smartphones, and tablets, are increasingly being used in K-12 classrooms to provide students with instructional opportunities in virtual learning environments (Ok et al., 2016). Many teachers integrate technology, such as Seesaw, Zoom, Microsoft 365, Schoology, EdPuzzle, Google classrooms, to teach students with and without disabilities (Peterson et al., 2020). Based on the Universal Design of Learning (UDL) principles, students with disabilities need various ways to express their learning, which can be achieved by integrating the right technology in K-12 classrooms (Khazanchi & Khazanchi, 2020). UDL is a set of principles that applies to a universal curriculum and instruction to give all students an equal opportunity to learn and grow (Black et al., 2015). Several educational technologies provide differentiated learning through multiple pathways and alternative content presentations, thus encouraging multiple means of representation, multiple means of action and expression, and multiple means of engagement.

1. **Seesaw:** This digital platform is designed for students to share their portfolio, available through several browsers, including Google Chrome, Firefox, Safari, and mobile devices, such as smartphones and iPads. Seesaw allows students to create their work in multiple formats, including texts, drawings, photos, videos, and links. Teachers may evaluate and create immediate feedback based on students' diverse interests and needs with audio, video, and text annotations (Moorehouse, 2019). In Figure 2, students wrote on the worksheet using the label tool in seesaw and added pictures by doing a google search. When completing this task, the students were highly engaged, linked words with the pictures, thus learning the vocabulary words meaningfully. Teachers may record themselves reading aloud and use draw tools to solve math problems and convert them into a video. Students

with LD may use this video lesson to review and practice (see Figure 3). Students could use the drag and move tool to manipulate the objects when counting and adding numbers (see Figure 4).

Figure 2. Students worked on writing activities using the Seesaw app

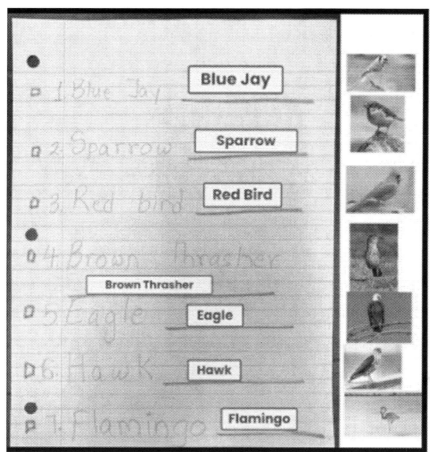

2. **Zoom.** COVID-19 pandemic has increased the reliance on virtual technology like Zoom. It is one of the live video conferencing platforms that allows users to screen share and interact with users. Both teachers and students can share their screens and interact with each other. The breakout room feature allows teachers to assign small group discussion projects. The chat feature allows students to interact with short answers. The whiteboard and annotation feature allows students to engage with the activity. Teachers may use the text, draw, stamp, and arrow features of the whiteboard to help students interact during the synchronous zoom sessions (see Figure 5). The life captions capability of Zoom can help students with dyslexia focus on their learning.

Figure 3. Seesaw allows to record voice and convert it into video

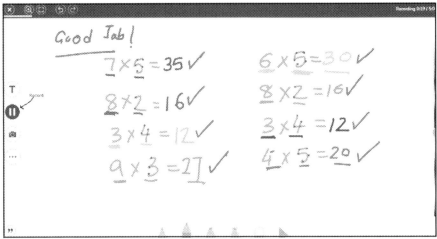

Figure 4. Interactive math lesson on Seesaw

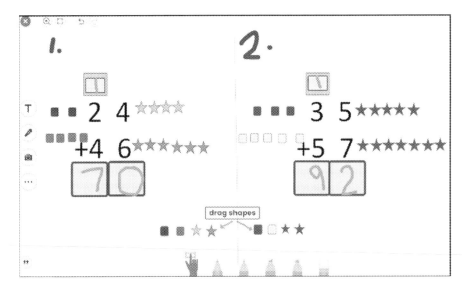

3. **Microsoft Office365:** Microsoft learning tools in Office and Edge provide learners with a list of accessibility features, such as enhanced dictation (improves authoring text), immersive reading (helps in comprehension and improves attention, see Figure 6), read aloud (reads aloud and highlights the words), adjustable line and font spacing (addresses "visual crowding' thus improving reading speed), parts of speech (improves writing quality by supporting writing instruction), syllabification (improves word recognition), picture dictionary (shows pictures on clicking certain words), comprehension mode (improves comprehension), and line focus (improves learning speed by sustaining focus). Advanced immersive reader features in Office provide math assistant (step-by-step directions to solve equations), page colors (changes the background color to make reading easier), and translator (converts word and pages into various language).

Figure 5. Students interacting with whiteboard and annotation features to learn to decode the words

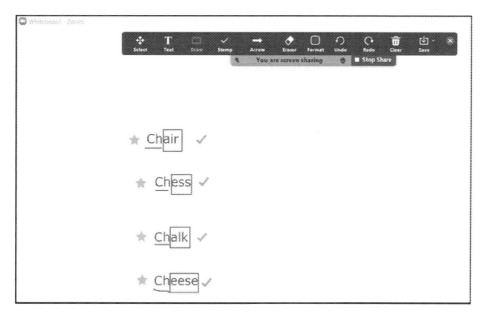

Figure 6. Students used spell checker and immersive reader on OneNote

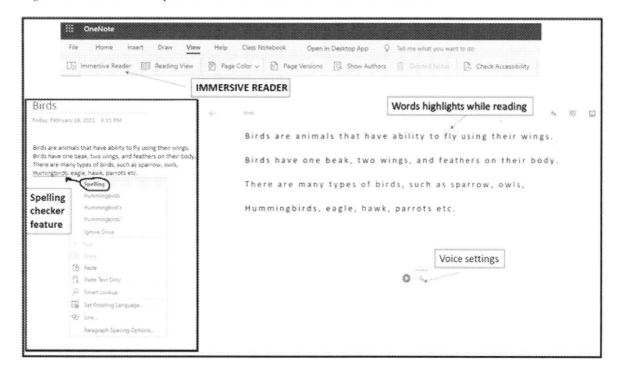

Teaching Inclusively in a Virtual Learning Environment

Students both with and without disabilities are learning in a virtual learning environment during the global pandemic. Virtual learning environments are called by several names, such as virtual education, virtual classroom, online classes, online sessions, distance learning, remote learning, remote teaching, and cyber classes. Virtual learning is defined as instruction in an online environment, where teachers and students interact with the learning content using the internet and videoconferencing platforms, such as Google Meet, Microsoft Teams, WebEx, Cisco, Gotomeeting, and Zoom. Students need lots of adaptation when transitioning to a virtual learning environment. In a virtual learning environment, teachers and students interact using electronic devices, such as desktops, laptops, iPads, and mobile phones, to complete the learning process (Joan, 2018). In an inclusive virtual environment, the focus should be to provide all students access to high-quality materials (Rice & Ortiz, 2020). The virtual learning environment must provide visual and auditory stimuli that provide a virtual space where students interact with high-quality learning materials.

Teaching inclusively involves serving all students' needs by accommodating their different learning and ability levels (An & Carr, 2017). Inclusive teaching practices are based on the principles of the Universal Design of Learning (UDL). Teachers need to provide all students in virtual learning environments equal opportunities to access meaningful curriculum and maximize their involvement. For students' active participation, teachers must promote class discussions and provide interactive lessons to all students with varying degrees of difficulty. When teachers provide a positive learning environment, students maximize their learning. Students with LDs need a personalized learning environment, and a flexible curriculum, through multiple modes of implementation.

Teachers must provide extra time and teach individual lessons to students who need different strategies. Teachers must make students feel part of the virtual learning environment and encourage student participation by valuing and rewarding students' efforts. Teachers and school administrators need to provide all students access to reliable devices, technology, and a strong network connection. Smart technologies incorporate the principles of UDL and have the potential to adapt to the diversity and unique needs of all learners (Martiniello et al., 2021). When teaching virtually, teachers may need more time to plan for their lessons. School administrators must provide extra planning time to teachers.

Technology-based classrooms can bring more inclusivity in the virtual learning environment, providing more transparency and equality to teaching (Jain et al., 2021). Studies have shown that students with LDs achieve higher grades when educated in inclusive settings than in pull-out programs (Rea et al., 2002). In a face-to-face session, teachers provide accommodations, such as reading a section aloud, peer reading, word bank, enlarged text, and/or extended time. Teachers can provide adequate support and accommodation and modifications in an inclusive virtual learning environment. Students with LDs benefit from the customized and systematic self-paced curriculum offered in virtual learning settings. Given the higher number of students with LDs in inclusive K-12 classrooms, all-digital experiences across the curriculum must be inclusive and accessible for all students.

Software Applications to Support Students with Learning Disabilities in Virtual Learning Environment

Students with LDs may benefit from software applications that help improve reading, writing, and math skills (see Figure 7).

1. **Reading**: Students with LDs may show challenges in reading because of poor phonological skills, processing abilities, and cognitive skills. They show less motivation to read and avoid participation in reading activities. Teachers in a virtual classroom environment need to provide each student with reading activities at their independent reading level. Assigning students with reading software will help in the curriculum. Screen reader on devices helps to transmit text audibly (Agee, 2019). Reading applications, such as Reading Horizon, RAZ kids, and ReadON.ai, provide differentiated reading instructions based on students' individualized reading levels (Khazanchi & Khazanchi, 2019). ReadON.ai software created by Orange Neurosciences in Ontario, Canada, developed game-based software reading intervention program for students with LDs. ReadON provides Software-as-a-Service based cognitive solutions to solve their struggle with reading fluency and comprehension, thus improving students' working memory and executive functioning skills (OrangeNeurosciences, 2021). Raz Kids online program provides students with the curriculum at different reading levels. It has the feature for word audio playback, continuous audio play, and interactive flip-book pages. Programs like TumbleBooks, RazKids, and BookFlix allow students to choose reading material based on their interests and reading level (Schott, 2017).
2. **Mathematics**: Students with LDs may show difficulties in recalling basic arithmetic facts, poor number sense, challenges in working memory, and solving math problems. Teachers may provide students with online calculators, graphing tools, equation-solving tools, manipulatives, number lines, and number frames in a virtual learning environment. Online tools, such as Popplet, Khan Academy, MathTalk, Plicker, Microsoft Mathematics, and Wolfram Alpha, help students with LDs compute math problems and double-check their answers (Dyscalculia, 2021). Teachers have used online educational programs, like IXL, Mathletics, and coolmathgames, giving students with LDs more opportunities for additional math practice.
3. **Writing**: Students with LDs often show challenges in initiating writing tasks, complete writing assignments, avoid writing, and share their writing with others (Roitsch et al., 2021). Word processing software has spell check functions, dictionary tools, word prediction, and checking for grammatical errors. Dragon Professional Voice Recognition Software recognizes students' voices and converts it into text or reads the text with ease. Graphic organizers provide support with organizing and connecting ideas, thus promoting writing. Grammarly allows students to check for grammatical errors, punctuation, and spellings errors instantly. Inspiration Maps is a mind mapping software, which allows students with LDs to brainstorm and take notes by organizing materials.

Evidence-Based Practices to Engage Students with Learning Disabilities in a Virtual Learning Environment

Digital technologies can provide an authenticated online learning that can enhance collaboration and facilitate interdependence between students. Students benefit from online learning, as they can access the curriculum and assignments at any time from anywhere. To make learning optimal for all students, teachers may follow multiple strategies to empower students learning.

1. When giving individualized lessons, adapt the font of the reading material to students with LDs. Most students with SLDs prefer easy-to-read fonts, with less information on a page.
2. Students must have access to text-to-speech, speech-to-text, and word prediction software in a virtual learning environment.

Figure 7. Online resources to overcome challenges in reading, writing, and mathematics

Reading	Mathematics	Writing
• Poor Phonological skills • Poor processing abilities • Deficit in cognitive skills • Less motivation to read • Poor reading comprehension	• Deficit in recalling basic arithmetic facts • Poor number sense • Challenges in working memory • Difficulty in solving math problems • Difficulty in interpreting math symbols	• Difficulty initiating writing tasks • Avoid writing • Incomplete assignments • Difficulty in sharing their writing work • Spelling errors
Online Resources	**Online Resources**	**Online Resources**
• RAZ kids (https://www.raz-kids.com/) • ReadON.ai (https://readon.ai/) • Reading Horizon (https://www.readinghorizons.com/) • Tumble Books (www.tumblebooklibrary.com) • Book Flix (http://teacher.scholastic.com/products/bookflix)	• Online calculators • Graphing tools • Equation solving tools • Popplet (https://www.popplet.com/) • Khan Academy (https://www.khanacademy.org/) • MathTalk (https://mathtalk.com) • Plicker (https://www.plickers.com) • Microsoft Mathematics • Wolfram Alpha (https://www.wolframalpha.com) • IXL (https://www.ixl.com) • Mathletics (https://www.mathletics.com) • Coolmathgames (https://www.coolmathgames.com)	• Spell check function • Dictionary tools • Word prediction • Dragon Professional • Voice Recognition software • Graphic Organizer • Inspiration Maps

3. Encourage students to interact using chat features, helping students with LDs interact with other students in their classroom.
4. Collaborate with the Assistive Technology team to help students with LDs access the right devices, software applications, and tools that assist in reading, writing, and mathematics.
5. Educate students on the accessibility features of smart devices, such as iPads and iPhones. The speak features allow students to look at the highlighted words and listen to the text simultaneously.
6. Prioritize social-emotional well-being and encourage positive online conversations to make students feel comfortable and relaxed in a virtual learning environment (Peterson et al., 2020)
7. Differentiate content meeting the needs of students with LD. Develop content that is explicit, systematic, sequential, and includes more repetitions opportunities (Dickman, 2018).
8. Customize the virtual learning environment and accommodate and modify the grade-level content based on students' individualized educational plans (Stetter, 2018).
9. Provide accessible resources to students with LDs matching their learning needs.

Challenges Faced by Teachers in Teaching Students with Learning Disabilities during COVID-19 Time

Online learning can customize learning to meet the needs of students with disabilities. Educational institutions and educators unwilling to change traditional pedagogical methods of teaching had to shift to virtual teaching. In the context of K-12 classrooms, the teachers faced significant challenges during this transition, including how to continue with their instructions, adapting to virtual teaching, supporting students' learning, assess student's learning, providing feedback, and communicate with students and parents (Hamilton et al., 2020; König et al., 2020). Various teachers reported that they were not prepared for virtual teaching and had to modify their teaching methodology. The teachers also reported that most of their students did not even log in to complete the assigned task. During the early phase of the pandemic, nearly half of the teachers introduced new concepts less frequently, lowered their expectations for quality assignments, reduced the number of assignments and tests, and instead chose the pass/fail model for the spring semester (Johnson et al., 2020).

Teachers have been presented with the challenge of assessing student performance during the COVID -19 time. Student learning and hence their performance may have been suffered by anxiety, stress, being forces to learn in a virtual environment, and the fear of falling behind due to inadequate access to technology, the internet, lack of quiet space, or sharing devices (Conn et al., 2020; Zughoul, 2018). Assessing students in the current situation is different as the teachers may have to change the scores. The classroom-based formal and informal assessments drive the instructions. If assessment scores indicate excessive construct-irrelevant variance, the assessment scores may not paint a clear picture, therefore, may not be useful in planning instruction (Middleton, 2020).

Role of Parents in Teaching Students with Learning Disabilities in a Virtual Learning Environment

The disruption caused by the COVID –19 crisis prompted the school districts to employ remote learning plans, including academic instructions, general educational resources, assignments, and progress monitoring. Stakeholders distributed digital devices to students who were in need and provided adequate support to students with disabilities.

Students with LDs may face many challenges in the virtual environment. In a virtual environment, all instructions, assignments, and directions are presented in a written format rather than verbal. Parents played an important role in providing support to students during the virtual learning environment. Parents, siblings, and other household family members helped students complete homework, projects, reading texts, and keeping things organized (Armstrong, 2020).

Parents may struggle to provide their children with the needed accommodations and modifications in a virtual learning environment (Stetter, 2018). Parents need more training and support from the school district. Teachers must involve parents when making the educational decision of a student. When students get older, they strive to become more independent and may not want parent support in their homework. Teachers and stakeholders' collaboration with parents and family members will support students with LDs in the virtual learning environment.

Barriers and Challenges in Teaching Students with Learning Disabilities during the COVID-19 Pandemic

Students with LDs show unique difficulties, struggle to process visual and auditory inputs and show challenges in engaging in the virtual learning environment. Many online learning programs available for K-12 education may not be adequately designed to make them accessible for students with disabilities. Congress amended section 508 of the Rehabilitation Act of 1973 in 1988 to ensure that technology (hardware and software) purchased by the federal government are accessible and usable to students with disabilities. Section 504 (amended in 2017) of the Rehabilitation Act of 1973 requires reasonable accommodation for students with disabilities (Shaheen & Watulak, 2019). Efforts have been made to create an accessible print material version both by government agencies and private entities. For instance, National Instructional Materials Access Center (NIMAC), Learning Ally, and Bookshare are creating Accessible Instructional Material (AIM) for students with disabilities (Hashey & Stahl, 2014).

Many teachers struggle to create an online learning environment for students with LDs. When the learning environment creates a distraction and disorganized stimuli, it may prevent students from learning (Ok et al., 2016). The virtual learning environment needs to integrate multimedia and provide immediate feedback on students' strengths and preferences (Mayer, 2019). The virtual learning environment has its challenges. Students may quickly disengage from virtual learning, turn the video function, mute the microphone, and close the learning platform. Virtual learning may leave students and teachers with a feeling of isolation and a sense of disconnect, impacting student engagement (Kennedy & Ferdig, 2018). Students with LDs may show difficulty in engaging in academic lessons. If the activities are not interesting, the students show the least motivation to participate. Students who are motivated remain more engaged in the lesson (Reyes et al., 2012). Motivating students to participate in classroom tasks becomes challenging for some teachers (Wei et al., 2021).

Students with LDs may face difficulty managing multiple zoom classes and struggle to connect with teachers and classmates. Students may get distracted and face difficulty when asked to multi-task in the virtual learning environment (Hauge, 2020). Teachers need to show students with LDs how to use the program applications successfully. The online platform's architecture may not be best suited to meet the learning needs of diverse students.

SOLUTIONS AND RECOMMENDATIONS

School districts and school administrators need to equip teachers with appropriate educational technology tools to support and engage all learners, including students with LDs. Teachers need to collaborate to identify innovative ways to empower students with LDs by integrating technology. Providing too many online resources and technological tools to students with LDs can make them anxious, nervous, upset, and overwhelmed. Teachers need to find ways to provide balanced resources matching the individual needs of their students. Students with LDs may lack confidence and have poor self-esteem. Students must have access to online resources on SEL activities, which will help them develop their confidence and self-esteem.

Teaching in a virtual learning environment needs careful planning, design, and execution (Terry, 2019). Publishers need to provide accessible digital versions of textbooks for students to use. Today's technology comes with customizable input and outputs that can efficiently improve students learning and facilitate communication. Though students come to virtual classrooms more familiar with technology, students with LDs may need support to access and organize the online resources. Students who face challenges in reading, listening, and organizational skills may benefit from personalized assessments using technology-enabled strategies.

In the aftermath of the pandemic, stakeholders need to analyze the effectiveness of the virtual learning environment. Dhawan (2020) suggests the SWOC Analysis for gathering the Strengths, Weaknesses, Opportunities, and Challenges of online learning during the crisis (see Figure 8). SWOC analysis identifies the strengths, weaknesses, opportunities, and challenges specific to teaching in the virtual learning environment. The synthesis of weaknesses and challenges helps in the strategic management of virtual learning educational services in the perspective of their effectiveness and students' learning. SWOC analysis focuses more on the students and how to adequately teach them in a virtual learning environment. SWOC analysis helps address the weaknesses and deter the challenges (Dhawan, 2020; Shahabadkar et al., 2019).

Figure 8. SWOC analysis identifies the strengths, weaknesses, opportunities, and challenges of educational services

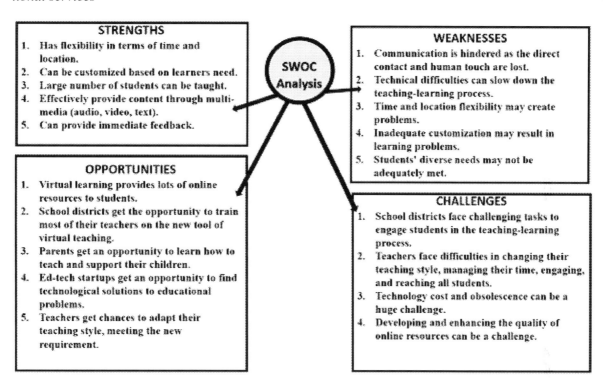

FUTURE RESEARCH DIRECTIONS

More research is needed to understand students with LDs learning needs in a virtual learning environment. Teachers' challenges in reaching the needs of all students in an inclusive virtual environment require further research. Future work needs to study how successfully teachers can implement accommodations and modifications in virtual classroom settings.

Studies on student engagement in a virtual learning environment will provide more insight into online resources' effectiveness. Future studies are needed to determine how online reading programs impact student's reading skills. Teachers, parents, school administrators, and stakeholders, including students with disabilities, need to develop new technologies and future research studies (Fichten et al., 2020). Further research is required to study the efficacy of new innovative tools, techniques, and educational technology.

CONCLUSION

COVID-19 pandemic presented a tremendous challenge to stakeholders and educational researchers. Globally, the post-COVID world will likely adapt and accelerate new ways of teaching and learning because of the experience. Online educational technology will have an immense impact on the education of students with LDs. This pandemic has taught everyone to adapt to new challenges. Despite the challenges to teachers, parents, and students, the experiences have opened a new teaching and learning method - online learning. The teachers can reach all the parents and students in no time through online services. School districts have struggled to build online learning platforms and provide professional learning opportunities for all their teachers. Teachers taught and supported each other to achieve a successful integration of technology in their classrooms.

Some of what has been learned for future applications of online learning was that school districts need to collaborate with tech support teams and technology companies to develop their own or adapt their existing integrated learning system to teach their students successfully. Online tools like Seesaw, Office365, Google Classroom, NearPod, EdPuzzle, Zoom, Google Meet, and Microsoft Teams all come in handy to support teachers and students with LDs in the virtual learning environment. When planning online resources for students with LDs, teachers need to collaborate and plan to provide appropriate online educational resources, meeting diverse students' needs. Text-to-speech devices, read-aloud tools, graphic organizers, and computer applications are beneficial for students with LDs.

Social interaction takes on a different dimension since a virtual interface has replaced the human element. What was once related to educational support has become the primary mode of interaction in the teaching-learning diad. The virtual learning environment has enabled students who live miles apart to work collaboratively on school projects. Yet not all software is equally useful and may not have been carefully evaluated. The pandemic has made educators worldwide think of novel, creative and compatible ways to impart instruction. It has challenged educators worldwide to use and create technology-based tools to facilitate teaching and learning – for all students. As a result, the pandemic has brought more awareness of various technologies and teaching methods needed to engage students with LDs in learning.

REFERENCES

Adelman, H. S. (1992). LD: The next 25 years. *Journal of Learning Disabilities*, *25*(1), 17–22. doi:10.1177/002221949202500103 PMID:1740634

Agee, S. (2019). Equal access+equal opportunity=success for all learners. *Knowledge Quest*, *48*(2), 24–29. https://files.eric.ed.gov/fulltext/EJ1233107.pdf

An, D., & Carr, M. (2017). Learning styles theory fails to explain learning and achievement: Recommendations for alternative approaches. *Personality and Individual Differences*, *116*, 410–416. doi:10.1016/j.paid.2017.04.050

Armstrong, A. (2020). Emergent technological practices of middle school students with mathematics learning disabilities. *General Report*. https://doi.org/ doi:10.5206/eei.v30i1.10912

Asbury, K., Fox, L., Deniz, E., Code, A., & Toseeb, U. (2020). How is COVID-19 Affecting the Mental Health of Children with Special Educational Needs and Disabilities and Their Families? *Journal of Autism and Developmental Disorders*, 1–9. doi:10.31234/osf.ioevyd PMID:32737668

Asbury, K., Fox, L., Deniz, E., Code, A., & Toseeb, U. (2020). How is COVID-19 affecting the mental health of children with special educational needs and disabilities and their families? *Journal of Autism and Developmental Disorders*, 1–9. doi:10.100710803-020-04577-2 PMID:32737668

Beckmann, E., & Minnaert, A. (2018). Non-cognitive characteristics of gifted students with learning disabilities: An in-depth systematic review. *Frontiers in Psychology*, 9, 504. doi:10.3389/fpsyg.2018.00504 PMID:29731728

Black, R. D., Weinberg, L. A., & Brodwin, M. G. (2015). Universal design for learning and instruction: Perspectives of students with disabilities in higher education. *Exceptionality Education International*, 25(2). Advance online publication. doi:10.5206/eei.v25i2.7723

Brooks, S. K., Webster, R. K., Smith, L. E., Woodland, L., Wessely, S., Greenberg, N., & Rubin, G. J. (2020). The psychological impact of quarantine and how to reduce it: Rapid review of the evidence. *Lancet*, 395(10227), 912–920. doi:10.1016/S0140-6736(20)30460-8 PMID:32112714

Burgess, S., & Sievertsen, H. H. (2020). *Schools, skills, and learning: The impact of COVID-19 on education*. https://voxeu.org/article/impact-covid-19-education

Colao, A., Piscitelli, P., Pulimeno, M., Colazzo, S., Miani, A., & Giannini, S. (2020). Rethinking the role of the school after COVID-19. *The Lancet Public Health*, 5(7), e370. PMID:32464100

Conn, C. A., Bohan, K. J., Pieper, S. L., & Musumeci, M. (2020). Validity inquiry process: Practical guidance for examining performance assessments and building a validity argument. *Studies in Educational Evaluation*, 65, 100843. doi:10.1016/j.stueduc.2020.100843

Cortiella, C., & Horowitz, S. H. (2014). The state of learning disabilities: Facts, trends, and emerging issues. *National Center for Learning Disabilities*, 25, 2-45. https://www.ncld.org/wp-content/uploads/2014/11/2014-State-of-LD.pdf

Dhawan, S. (2020). Online learning: A panacea in the time of COVID-19 crisis. *Journal of Educational Technology Systems*, 49(1), 5–22. doi:10.1177/0047239520934018

Di Pietro, G. (2018). The academic impact of natural disasters: Evidence from L'Aquila earthquake. *Education Economics*, 26(1), 62–77. doi:10.1080/09645292.2017.1394984

Dickman, G. (2018). Ladder of reading infographic. *Examiner*, 7(3). https://dyslexiaida.org

Dominguez, O., & Carugno, P. (2020). Learning Disability. StatPearls Publishing.

Dyscalculia. (2021). *Best tools*. https://www.dyscalculia.org/math-tools

Elbaum, B., & Vaughn, S. (2003). For which students with learning disabilities are self-concept interventions effective? *Journal of Learning Disabilities*, 36(2), 101–108. doi:10.1177/002221940303600203 PMID:15493426

Engel, R. (1997). Instrument for locating students with suspected learning disabilities: A quantitative approach. *International Journal of Rehabilitation Research. Internationale Zeitschrift fur Rehabilitationsforschung. Revue Internationale de Recherches de Readaptation, 20*, 169–181. doi:10.1097/00004356-199706000-00006 PMID:9226500

Fichten, C., Olenik-Shemesh, D., Asuncion, J., Jorgensen, M., & Colwell, C. (2020). Higher education, information and communication technologies and students with disabilities: An overview of the current situation. *Improving accessible digital practices in higher education*, 21-44. https://doi.org/doi:10.1007/978-3-030-37125-8_2

Fırat, T., & Ergül, C. (2020). The effect of TWA strategy instruction on students with learning disabilities developing cognitive and metacognitive strategies. *Kastamonu Education Journal, 28*(3), 1390–1406.

Galway, T. M., & Metsala, J. L. (2011). Social cognition and its relation to psychosocial adjustment in children with nonverbal learning disabilities. *Journal of Learning Disabilities, 44*(1), 33–49. doi:10.1177/0022219410371680 PMID:20574062

Gartland, D., & Strosnider, R. (2018). Learning Disabilities: Implications for Policy Regarding Research and Practice: A Report by the National Joint Committee on Learning Disabilities. *Learning Disability Quarterly, 41*(4), 195–199. doi:10.1177/0731948718789994

Gersten, R., Fuchs, L. S., Williams, J. P., & Baker, S. (2001). Teaching reading comprehension strategies to students with learning disabilities: A review of research. *Review of Educational Research, 21*, 279–320. doi:10.3102/00346543071002279

Goldstein, D. (2020). Research shows students falling months behind during virus disruptions. *The New York Times, 5*. https://www.nytimes.com/2020/06/05/us/coronavirus-education-lost-learning.html?smid=tw-share

Graham, S., Collins, A. A., & Rigby-Wills, H. (2017). Writing characteristics of students with learning disabilities and typically achieving peers: A meta-analysis. *Exceptional Children, 83*(2), 199–218. doi:10.1177/0014402916664070

Grigorenko, E. L., Compton, D. L., Fuchs, L. S., Wagner, R. K., Willcutt, E. G., & Fletcher, J. M. (2020). Understanding, educating, and supporting children with specific learning disabilities: 50 Years of science and practice. *The American Psychologist, 75*(1), 37. doi:10.1037/amp0000452 PMID:31081650

Hamilton, L. S., Grant, D., Kaufman, J. H., Diliberti, M., Schwartz, H. L., Hunter, G. P., Claude, M. S., & Young, C. J. (2020). *COVID-19 and the State of K-12 Schools: Results and Technical Documentation from the Spring 2020 American Educator Panels COVID-19 Surveys*. RAND Corporation. doi:10.7249/RRA168-1

Hashey, A. I., & Stahl, S. (2014). Making online learning accessible for students with disabilities. *Teaching Exceptional Children, 46*(5), 70–78.

Hauge, C. (2020). Agency with virtual learning: Prioritizing children's social emotional health in the pandemic. *Childhood Education, 96*(6), 54–59. doi:10.1080/00094056.2020.1846391

Hill, F. (2020). The pandemic is a crisis for students with special needs. *The Atlantic*. https://www.theatlantic.com/education/archive/2020/04/special-education-goes-remote-covid-19-pandemic/610231/

Holmes, E. A., O'Connor, R. C., Perry, V. H., Tracey, I., Wessely, S., Arseneault, L., Ballard, C., Christensen, H., Cohen Silver, R., Everall, I., Ford, T., John, A., Kabir, T., King, K., Madan, I., Michie, S., Przybylski, A. K., Shafran, R., Sweeney, A., ... Bullmore, E. (2020). Multidisciplinary research priorities for the COVID-19 pandemic: A call for action for mental health science. *The Lancet Psychiatry*, *7*(6), 547–560. doi:10.1016/S2215-0366(20)30168-1 PMID:32304649

Horowitz, S. H., Rawe, J., & Whittaker, M. C. (2017). *The state of learning disabilities: Understanding the 1 in 5*. National Center for Learning Disabilities.

Individuals With Disabilities Education Improvement Act. (2004). Public Law 105-17 (20 U. S. C. § 1400 et seq.).

Jain, S., Lall, M., & Singh, A. (2021). Teachers' voices on the impact of COVID-19 on school education. Are ed-tech companies really the panacea? *Contemporary Education Dialogue*, *18*(1), 58–89. doi:10.1177/0973184920976433

Joan, D. R. R. (2018). Virtual Classroom: A gift for disabled children. *I-Manager's Journal on School Educational Technology*, *14*(2), 7. http://doi. doi:10.26634/jsch.14.2.15100

John Hopkins University. (2021, February). CoronaVirus Resource Center. *CoronaVirus*. https://coronavirus.jhu.edu/

Johnson, N., Veletsianos, G., & Seaman, J. (2020). US Faculty and Administrators' Experiences and Approaches in the Early Weeks of the COVID-19 Pandemic. *Online Learning*, *24*(2), 6–21. doi:10.24059/olj.v24i2.2285

Kavale, K. A., & Forness, S. R. (2000). What definitions of learning disability say and don't say: A critical analysis. *Journal of Learning Disabilities*, *33*, 239–256. http://ldx.sagepub.com/ PMID:15505963

Kennedy, K., & Ferdig, R. E. (Eds.). (2018). *Handbook of Research of K12 Online and Blended Learning* (2nd ed.). Carnegie Mellon University: ETC Press.

Khasawneh, M., Alkhawaldeh, M., & Al-Khasawneh, F. (2020). The levels of metacognitive thinking among students with learning disabilities. *International Journal of English Linguistics*, *10*(5). Advance online publication. doi:10.5539/ijel.v10n5p343

Khazanchi, P., & Khazanchi, R. (2019). Hands-On Activities to Keep Students With Disabilities Engaged in K-12 Classrooms. In Handmade Teaching Materials for Students With Disabilities (pp. 185-211). IGI Global.

Khazanchi, R., & Khazanchi, P. (2020). Effective Pedagogical Practices in Inclusive Classrooms for Students with Disabilities. In *Special Education Design and Development Tools for School Rehabilitation Professionals* (pp. 38–60). IGI Global. doi:10.4018/978-1-7998-1431-3.ch003

Khazanchi, R., Khazanchi, P., Mehta, V., & Tuli, N. (2021). Incorporating Social–Emotional Learning to Build Positive Behaviors. *Kappa Delta Pi Record*, *57*(1), 11–17.

King, K., Madan, I., Michie, S., Przybylski, A. K., Shafran, R., Sweeney, A., Worthman, C. M., & Bullmore, E. (2020). Multidisciplinary research priorities for the COVID-19 pandemic: A call for action for mental health science. *The Lancet. Psychiatry*, 7(6), 547–560. doi:10.1016/S2215-0366(20)30168-1 PMID:32304649

König, J., Jäger-Biela, D. J., & Glutsch, N. (2020). Adapting to online teaching during COVID-19 school closure: Teacher education and teacher competence effects among early career teachers in Germany. *European Journal of Teacher Education*, 43(4), 608–622. doi:10.1080/02619768.2020.1809650

Mayer, R. E. (2019). How multimedia can improve learning and instruction. In J. Dunlosky & K. A. Rawson (Eds.), *The Cambridge handbook of cognition and education* (pp. 460–479). Cambridge University Press. doi:10.1017/9781108235631.019

Meo, S. A., Abukhalaf, D. A. A., Alomar, A. A., Sattar, K., & Klonoff, D. C. (2020). COVID-19 pandemic: Impact of quarantine on Medical Students' mental wellbeing and learning behaviors. *Pakistan Journal of Medical Sciences*, 36(S4), S43–S48. doi:10.12669/pjms.36.COVID19-S4.2809 PMID:32582313

Middleton, K. V. (2020). The longer-term impact of COVID-19 on K–12 student learning and assessment. *Educational Measurement: Issues and Practice*, 39(3), 41–44. doi:10.1111/emip.12368

Moorhouse, B. L. (2019). Seesaw. *RELC Journal*, 50(3), 493-496. https://doi.org/doi:10.1177/0033688218781976

Morrison, G. M., & Cosden, M. A. (1997). Risk, resilience, and adjustment of individuals with learning disabilities. *Learning Disability Quarterly*, 20(1), 43–60. doi:10.2307/1511092

National Center for Education Statistics. (2020). *Children and Youth with Disabilities.* https://nces.ed.gov/programs/coe/indicator_cgg.asp

National Center for Learning Disabilities. (2020). *Exploring intersectionality: Understanding student identity to promote equitable social, emotional, cognitive, and academic development during and beyond the covid-19 pandemic.* https://www.ncld.org/wp-content/uploads/2020/11/2020-SEL_Exploring-Intersectionality-Guide_FINAL.pdf

National Commission on Social, Emotional, and Academic Development. (2019). From a nation at risk to a nation at hope. *The Aspen Institute.* https://www.aspeninstitute.org/programs/national-commission-on-social-emotional-and-academic-development

National Joint Committee on Learning Disabilities. (2008). Adolescent literacy and older students with learning disabilities: A report from the National Joint Committee on Learning Disabilities. *Learning Disability Quarterly*, 211–218. doi:10.2307/25474653

Ok, M. W., Kim, M. K., Kang, E. Y., & Bryant, B. R. (2016). How to find good Apps: An evaluation rubric for instructional apps for teaching students with learning disabilities. *Intervention in School and Clinic*, 51(4), 244–252. doi:10.1177/1053451215589179

Oxford, R. L. (1990). Language learning strategies: What every teacher should Know. Newbury House, Harper Collins.

Patel, K. (2020). Mental health implications of COVID-19 on children with disabilities. *Asian Journal of Psychiatry*, *54*, 102273. doi:10.1016/j.ajp.2020.102273 PMID:32653852

Peterson, L., Scharber, C., Thuesen, A., & Baskin, K. (2020). A rapid response to COVID-19: One district's pivot from technology integration to distance learning. *Information and Learning Science*, *121*(5/6), 461–469. doi:10.1108/ILS-04-2020-0131

Quezada, R. L., Talbot, C., & Quezada-Parker, K. B. (2020). From bricks and mortar to remote teaching: A teacher education program 's response to COVID-19. *Journal of Education for Teaching*, 1–12. doi: 10.1080/02607476.2020.1801330

Rea, P. J., McLuaghlin, V. L., & Walter-Thomas, C. (2002). Outcomes for students with learning disabilities in inclusive and pullout programs. *Exceptional Children*, *68*(2), 203–222. doi:10.1177/001440290206800204

Reyes, M. R., Brackett, M. A., Rivers, S. E., White, M., & Salovey, P. (2012). Classroom emotional climate, student engagement, and academic achievement. *Journal of Educational Psychology*, *104*(3), 700-712. https://doi:10.1037/a0027268

Rice, M., & Dykman, B. (2018). The emerging research base for online learning and students with disabilities. Handbook of research on K-12 online and blended learning, 189-206.

Rice & Ortiz. (2020). Perceptions of accessibility in online course materials: A survey of teachers from six virtual schools. *Journal of Online Learning Research*, *6*(3), 245–254. https://www.learntechlib.org/primary/p/217628/paper_217628.pdf

Roitsch, J., Gumpert, M., Springle, A., & Raymer, A. M. (2021). 2020;). Writing instruction for students with learning disabilities: Quality appraisal of systematic reviews and meta-analyses. *Reading & Writing Quarterly*, *37*(1), 32–44. doi:10.1080/10573569.2019.1708221

Schott, M. C. (2017). Technology reading programs and their impact on listening comprehension. *Technology*. https://core.ac.uk/download/pdf/233575767.pdf

Shahabadkar, P., Joshi, A., & Nandurkar, K. (2019, February). Developing IT enabled mechanism for SWOC analysis: A case study. In *Proc. of the 2nd International Conference on Manufacturing Excellence (ICMAX-2019)* (pp. 158-164). Academic Press.

Shaheen, N. L., & Lohnes, W. S. (2019). Bringing disability into the discussion: Examining technology accessibility as an equity concern in the field of instructional technology. *Journal of Research on Technology in Education*, *51*(2), 187–201.

Shamir, A., & Dushnitzky, G. (2019). Metacognitive Intervention with e-Books to Promote Vocabulary and Story Comprehension Among Children at Risk for Learning Disabilities. In *Reading in the Digital Age: Young Children's Experiences with E-books* (pp. 237–257). Springer. doi:10.1007/978-3-030-20077-0_13

Shaywitz, S. (2003). *Overcoming dyslexia: A new and complete science-based program for reading problems at any level*. Random House.

Stetter, M. E. (2018). The use of technology to assist school-aged students with high incidence special needs in reading. *Education in Science*, *8*(2), 61. doi:10.3390/educsci8020061

Swanson, H. L. (1991). Operational definitions and learning disabilities: An overview. *Learning Disability Quarterly*, *14*(4), 242–254. doi:10.2307/1510661

Swanson, H. L. (1993). Working memory in learning disability subgroups. *Journal of Experimental Child Psychology*, *56*(1), 87–114. doi:10.1006/jecp.1993.1027 PMID:8366327

Swanson, H. L., Christie, L., & Rubadeau, R. J. (1993). The relationship between metacognition and analogical reasoning in mentally retarded, learning disabled, average, and gifted children. *Learning Disabilities Research & Practice*, *8*, 70–81.

Swanson, L., Harris, K. R., & Graham, S. (2013). *Handbook of Learning Disabilities* (2nd ed.).

Terry, R., Taylor, J., & Davies, M. (2019). Successful teaching in virtual classrooms. In *Learning and Teaching in Higher Education*. Edward Elgar Publishing.

Trainin, G., & Swanson, H. L. (2005). Cognition, metacognition, and achievement of college students with learning disabilities. *Learning Disability Quarterly*, *28*, 261–272. doi:10.2307/4126965

UNICEF. (2020). *Leaving no child behind during the pandemic: Children with disabilities and COVID-19*. https://data.unicef.org/topic/child-disability/covid-19/

Van der Sande, L., Henick, X., Marloes, M. H. G., Boor-Klip, H. J., & Mainhard, T. (2018). Learning disabilities and low social status: The role of peer academic reputation and peer reputation of teacher liking. *Journal of Learning Disabilities*, *51*(3), 211–222. doi:10.1177/0022219417708172 PMID:28470105

Wade, E., Boon, R. T., & Spencer, V. G. (2010). Use of kidspiration software to enhance the reading comprehension of story grammar components for elementary-age students with specific learning disabilities. *Learning Disabilities (Weston, Mass.)*, *8*, 31–41.

Wei, Y., Spear-Swerling, L., & Mercurio, M. (2021). Motivating students with learning disabilities to read. *Intervention in School and Clinic*, *56*(3), 155–162. doi:10.1177/1053451220928956

Zughoul, O., Momani, F., Almasri, O. H., Zaidan, A. A., Zaidan, B. B., Alsalem, M. A., Albahri, O. S., Albhar, A. S., & Hashim, M. (2018). Comprehensive insights into the criteria of student performance in various educational domains. *IEEE Access : Practical Innovations, Open Solutions*, *6*, 73245–73264. doi:10.1109/ACCESS.2018.2881282

ADDITIONAL READING

Chamberlain, L., Lacina, J., Bintz, W. P., Jimerson, J. B., Payne, K., & Zingale, R. (2020). Literacy in lockdown: Learning and teaching during COVID-19 school closures. *The Reading Teacher*, *74*(3), 243–253. doi:10.1002/trtr.1961 PMID:33362300

Eapen, V., Hiscock, H., & Williams, K. (2021). Adaptive innovations to provide services to children with developmental disabilities during the COVID-19 pandemic. *Journal of Paediatrics and Child Health*, *57*(1), 9–11. doi:10.1111/jpc.15224 PMID:33159396

McDowell, M. (2018). Specific learning disability. *Journal of Paediatrics and Child Health, 54*(10), 1077–1083. doi:10.1111/jpc.14168 PMID:30294983

Minkos, M. L., & Gelbar, N. W. (2021). Considerations for educators in supporting student learning in the midst of COVID-19. *Psychology in the Schools, 58*(2), 416–426. doi:10.1002/pits.22454 PMID:33362299

Narvekar, H. (2020). Educational concerns of children with disabilities during COVID-19 pandemic. *Indian Journal of Psychiatry, 62*(5), 603–604. doi:10.4103/psychiatry.IndianJPsychiatry_585_20 PMID:33678855

Penney, C. G. (2018). Rethinking the concept of learning disability. *Canadian Psychology = Psychologie Canadienne, 59*(2), 197-202. https://doi.org/ doi:10.1037/cap0000128

Toquero, C. M. D. (2020). Inclusion of people with disabilities amid COVID-19: Laws, interventions, recommendations. *Multidisciplinary Journal of Educational Research, 10*(2), 158–177. doi:10.17583/remie.2020.5877

KEY TERMS AND DEFINITIONS

COVID-19: A new type of coronavirus (COVID-19) is a novel emerging infectious disease caused by SARS-CoV-2, which has led to a worldwide pandemic.

Educational Technology: Educational technology relates to various electronic devices and applications that help deliver learning resources and support students' learning process in K-12 classrooms and higher education.

Evidence-Based Practices: Evidence-based practices are strategies based on the best empirical evidence appropriate for students learning and proven effective based on the research.

Inclusion Classrooms: Inclusion classrooms are defined as general education classrooms, where both students with disabilities and students without disabilities' learning needs are appropriately met.

Learning Disability: Learning disability is defined as a neurological processing disorder that involves challenges in understanding or using language causing problems with listening comprehension, oral expression, reading, writing, or math, and the problems are not due primarily with vision or hearing, motor deficits, an intellectual disability, or emotional disturbance.

SWOC Analysis: SWOC analysis is an analytic tool that helps in strategic planning by identifying strengths, weaknesses, opportunities, and challenges in a program.

Teacher Challenges: Teacher challenges are the barriers and hardships teachers face in successfully teaching students in their classrooms.

Universal Design of Learning: Universal Design of Learning is a scientific framework based on three primary principles- multiple means of representation of information, multiple means of student action and expression, and multiple means of student engagement.

Virtual Learning Environment: Virtual Learning Environment is defined as asynchronous or/and synchronous facilitation of learning and teaching delivered over the internet or intranet using digital gadgets, such as desktops, laptops, tablets, and smartphones.

Chapter 3
Implementing Universal Design for Learning in the Virtual Learning Environment

Andrea Harkins Parrish
Johns Hopkins University, USA

Jennifer Lee Kouo
https://orcid.org/0000-0002-4609-8555
Towson University, USA

Lisa Beth Carey
Kennedy Krieger Institute, USA

Christopher Swanson
Johns Hopkins University, USA

ABSTRACT

This chapter presents an overview of learner variability and addresses how the Universal Design for Learning framework can be applied to meet the diverse needs of all students in a virtual learning environment. Emphasis is placed on how educational professionals at multiple levels can apply their current knowledge to design and implement effective and universally designed instruction through multiple means of engagement, representation, and action and expression. It also addresses the importance of providing specialized instruction, including how educators can provide federally protected educational supports in virtual learning environments. The authors provide directions for further examination of virtual learning and the implications of this instructional delivery model for meeting the needs of all learners in light of recent trends.

DOI: 10.4018/978-1-7998-7222-1.ch003

Implementing Universal Design for Learning in the Virtual Learning Environment

INTRODUCTION

Sam sits outside a local restaurant and watches people on a bustling city street. He notices a wheelchair user navigating a curb cut (the ramp-like transition from sidewalk to street) to cross the busy street and make his way back to the sidewalk again. Not too far behind, a family traverses the same curb cut. The parents push a stroller, a child rides a scooter, and another child rides a bicycle. All of them transition seamlessly using the same curb cut. Separately, an older couple uses their phone to take a picture of the menu. They pinch and zoom the image to enlarge the text. At another table teenagers use the same built-in functionality to view an item before purchasing it online. The use of real-life ubiquitous accommodations, accessed by many for varying purposes, happen constantly in spontaneous ways within our communities. Common curb cuts, the ability to zoom, and other technological features aim to universally remove barriers and increase accessibility for all people. While these features were originally developed to address the needs of specific individuals, in practicality, these features are beneficial to a wide variety of people in ways sometimes never imagined.

As many veteran educators will attest, the concept of the "average" learner is a myth, despite traditionally held ideas that equip the majority of educators to teach to the *middle* of the classroom. Thankfully, there has been a growing recognition of learner variability within the classroom, and a professional shift to view each learner's unique abilities, interests, and experiences, as assets (Meyer et al., 2014). The development of the Universal Design for Learning (UDL) guidelines has led to changes in how educators design instruction to pro-actively address learner variability through incorporated flexible accommodations, supports, and challenges. Providing options that enable all learners to fully participate enables the entire class to benefit and grow in the same way the benefits from curb cuts are experienced by far more than wheelchair users. These opportunities provide responsive options to students typically excluded from traditional instructional design, including students with disabilities (SWD), English learners (ELs), and students identified as gifted and talented. Just as with curb cuts, by proactively designing for the needs of those who have been previously excluded, educators can provide all students with rich, meaningful learning experiences.

Digital technologies offer rich and varied ways to create flexible instructional design options. The use of instructional technologies alone, however, does not guarantee accessible and equitable instructional design. Educators instructing in virtual learning environments (VLEs), or supporting, monitoring, or researching those who do, benefit from instructional frameworks that support their design thinking, such as the UDL guidelines, as they seek to meet the needs of all learners. According to the International Society for Technology in Education (ISTE, 2021), VLEs are learning experiences provided using a digital platform. These experiences may be self-directed or led by an instructor and can be synchronous, asynchronous, or a combination of both. This chapter aims to equip educators of varying experience levels with practical considerations for implementing instruction within VLEs to address learner variability; establish a foundational understanding for leaders and policymakers on the implications and considerations of virtual learning for students of varying abilities and needs; and provide recommendations for future research and practice.

KNOWLEDGE LEVELS

The teaching profession includes all levels of professionals – from the first-year teacher to the 30-year veteran. These individuals are often given the same fundamental job duties and expected to perform at the same level. Ironically, when it comes to comfort in VLEs, the ladder of professional experience may be inverted as the degree of familiarity rests with those who have less applied experience in accommodating a wide range of students' abilities, needs, and backgrounds. Overall, this situation makes for both an exciting and sometimes daunting period for those in the educational field. What helps is identifying one's own comfort and knowledge level with virtual learning in general, and then the constructs for instructional planning, to know the types of supports and experience needed for each individual's professional learning journey.

Just Getting Started

Thrust into the VLE, Sam has limited experience and training on transferring traditional classroom practices to the virtual environment. As a recent graduate of an elementary education program, Sam did not have any internship experiences that involved teaching in VLEs. He is feeling very uncertain about navigating this new modality and is in need of professional learning opportunities. Sam also remembers completing a course on instructional and assistive technology and a framework called Universal Design for Learning (UDL). He wonders whether what he learned will be helpful in transitioning to virtual teaching.

Advancing Your Craft

Abby has taken several online courses through her graduate program. She feels less nervous about transforming her lessons for the VLE but still finds the task daunting. She recalls her graduate program professors modeling best practices for virtual instruction. They utilized a variety of technologies and mindfully structured their courses to support all learners. Abby believes that what she has experienced and observed in these online courses may be translated to her high school classroom. She also recalls her instructors talking about the importance of UDL and how the framework helped them guide their own instruction.

Teaching Others

Tamara is responsible for providing professional learning in a public school district. She understands that the educators she supports, some of whom have taught for over a decade, may suddenly feel as if they are new educators beginning their first year. Providing professional learning to over 140 educators in her school district has been made even more challenging with the shift to the VLE. Tamara knows that her fellow educators are struggling with engaging learners, transforming their lessons to work within this new modality and effectively assessing student learning. Tamara is also an adjunct professor and teaches an online course on UDL and technology. She realizes that what she teaches and models in her course can certainly help the educators she supports in her district.

The Universal Design for Learning Framework

A constant challenge for educators in the consideration of the full range of learners within classrooms. Sam, Abby, and Tamara are drawn to the potential impact of UDL in VLEs and to address learner variability. Beginning from a belief that learner variability is an asset, UDL principles, guidelines, and checkpoints provide a scientifically valid framework that provides guidance for designing learning activities that address the full spectrum of the classroom (Meyer & Rose, 2005).

Pioneered in the mid-1990s by the Center for Applied Special Technology (CAST), UDL takes inspiration from universal design in architecture, just like the curb cuts mentioned above. Research from the fields of education, educational psychology, the cognitive sciences, and neuropsychology were used to generate a framework that aims to help educators consider ways to minimize barriers and maximize accessibility at the onset of instructional planning. Educators are encouraged to consider how they engage and challenge learners through instructional design. With UDL, flexibility and choice are critical components to any lesson. Ultimately, UDL is a "framework for understanding how to create curricula" and is designed to accommodate learner differences from the beginning while also ensuring high expectations (CAST, 2011, p. 4).

The UDL guidelines include neuropsychological and cognitive sciences research regarding learning and thinking. This research has identified three key neural networks for learning: the affective network (the "why" of learning), the recognition network (the "what" of learning), and the strategic network (the "how" of learning) (Rose & Meyer, 2002). UDL uses these three networks to organize the guidelines into three distinct principles, which are presented vertically in Figure 1. The three distinct principles include: provide multiple means of engagement, provide multiple means of representation, and provide multiple means of action and expression.

The first principle of UDL is multiple means of engagement and this idea focuses on the "why" of learning. This principle emphasizes the importance of emotional connections to learning (Posey, 2019). Emotional connection between the learner and the content helps an individual to focus and persist when tasks are difficult. This principle encourages educators to offer options to learners to encourage emotional connections between the lesson and the learners' lives and interests.

The second principle, multiple means of representation, focuses on the "what" of learning. This principle highlights the ways in which educators may support learners to perceive and comprehend presented information. This principle encourages the offering of information in multiple formats, including text, audio, and video.

Lastly, the third principle of UDL focuses on the "how" of learning. By providing multiple means of action and expression, educators optimally help learners to navigate the learning environment and express what they know. This principle encourages educators to identify different options that allow learners to interact with content materials and to show that they have learned. For instance, different assessment strategies could include a traditional test or a podcast or a newsletter. This principle asks educators to consider how learners physically and mentally engage with learning activities as well as express what they are learning and have mastered.

Each UDL principle is divided into three guidelines, with a total of nine guidelines for driving universally designed learning environments. Each guideline includes checkpoints to provide further guidance to educators. The checkpoints are supported by multiple, peer-reviewed studies from education, educational psychology, and neuropsychological research (CAST, 2018). To the far left of Figure 1, there are three tabs that identify each row under the UDL principles. Horizontally, "the 'access' row includes the

Implementing Universal Design for Learning in the Virtual Learning Environment

guidelines that suggest ways to increase access to the learning goal by recruiting interest and by offering options for perception and physical action. The 'build' row includes the guidelines that suggest ways to develop effort and persistence, language and symbols, and expression and communication. Finally, the 'internalize' row includes the guidelines that suggest ways to empower learners through self-regulation, comprehension, and executive function" (CAST, 2018).

Figure 1. The Universal Design for Learning Guidelines (Source: CAST, (2018)

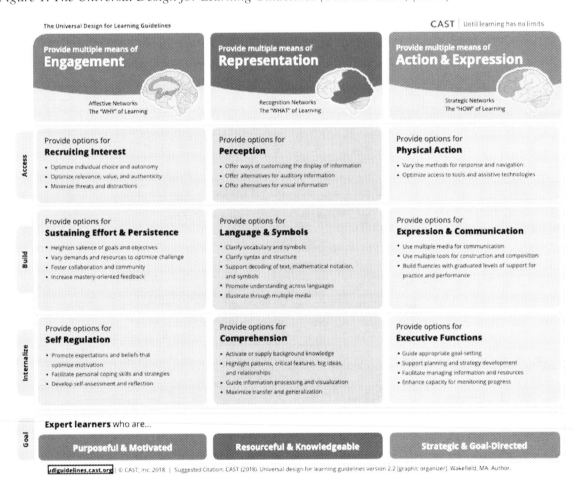

Identifying Current Knowledge Levels

This chapter is designed to address the needs of various audiences, including teachers, administrators, researchers and teacher educators. Professionals are likely at varying levels of knowledge with regard to UDL, teaching online, and applying these principles. Therefore, the section that follows provides recommendations to individuals at various starting points to utilize the information contained in this chapter.

How to Climb Mount Everest: Find the Starting Point

Sometimes, learning to teach effectively in a VLE can feel like climbing Mount Everest! The ever-changing nature of technologies means there is a great deal to learn, regardless of one's role. Embarking on this Everest trek requires a commitment to continuous learning. In order to begin this climb, it is important to first assess one's current knowledge of the basic principles of UDL and the best practices for teaching in a VLE. That said, continuous professional learning is critical so there may be "many mountains" in one's career.

Figure 2. A commitment to continuous learning can be supported through a community of learners (Source: Shutterstock, Inc. 1084870109)

Models for improving teacher practice are well established in educational technology research. Overall, research in this area supports the notion that change is a process, not an event. Change in practice is achieved not by a school district or by an institution, but by individuals. The act of change is highly personalized and is based on our individualized experiences and knowledge. Facilitating change requires us to examine perceptions, the resources available, and the context (Rogers, 2003). It is also important to examine teachers' concerns related to an innovation and their levels of use, or the actions teachers engage in as they become more knowledgeable and skilled in that area (Hall & Hord, 1987). When each individual assesses their current level of understanding, this evaluation serves as a map that helps to identify one's current location and then craft a plan to move onward. This chapter presents three knowledge levels to assist the reader in identifying their starting point. These levels, depicted in Figure 3, are categorized as: (1) *Just Getting Started*, (2) *Advancing Your Craft*, and (3) *Teaching Others*.

Figure 3. Knowledge levels for implementing UDL in virtual learning environments

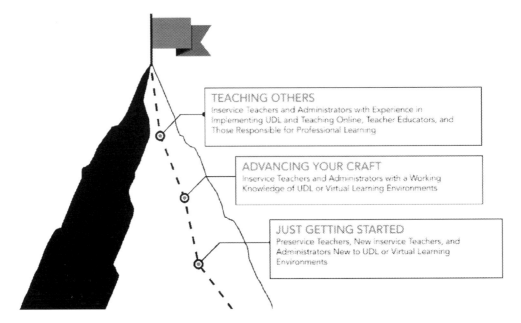

Just Getting Started

This first level likely includes preservice teachers, inservice teachers who are new to the field, or educators and administrators who are building an awareness of the concepts of UDL and how to teach in a VLE. This applies to Sam, who was discussed earlier. It is recommended that these practitioners focus on gaining knowledge about UDL and learner variability in their care, and that they increase their awareness of digital tools that can be used to apply UDL in a VLE. For these practitioners, the focus is on reducing uncertainty by learning all that they can, including the advantages and disadvantages of various approaches. At this stage, it is important for teachers to identify their own perceptions about these concepts and engage in multiple opportunities for new professional learning.

For these educators, coaching and mentoring is also an important part of professional learning. Educators in this stage may be advised to reach out to colleagues informally or to request support from their administrator. An advantage afforded by virtual learning is inherent functionality of the platforms used to record sessions, enabling review and reflection by the teacher afterward. This reflection is encouraged for all educators, but particularly for those *Just Getting Started*. It is advised that they share these recordings to solicit constructive feedback from their mentors. It is not uncommon to find new teachers even sharing examples of lesson plans across larger peer networks via social media to garner this same type of crowd-sourced guidance and validation. However, in doing so, educators are reminded not to share any images or other identifiable information about students unless given express permission by the learner's family and the district – and even then, it is best practice to ensure anonymity by removing or blurring any identifiable information.

Advancing Your Craft

Like Abby, those who are advancing their craft are inservice teachers or administrators with a working knowledge of UDL and teaching in a VLE. For these professionals, the focus is on gaining "how-to" knowledge and expanding what they know. Practitioners at this stage are advised to apply what they know and seek support regarding their implementation decisions. This application can be accomplished by seeking new and continued opportunities for professional learning, such as reading chapters like this one, implementing its resources, and applying other related resources for implementing UDL, such as those provided by the CAST. Implementation tools, such as instructional planning tools, teaching checklists, lesson planning guides, lesson sharing sites, and structured reflection guides can be useful in these endeavors. Those who seek to advance their craft are likely to gain insight and refine their practice of UDL in VLEs by taking steps to evaluate the impact of their practices on student learning and by collaborating with others to share successes and challenges. In each of these exercises, it is critical for teachers to be reflective. This reflection is often accomplished by sharing and learning from others who share a commitment to implementing UDL effectively.

For those in the *Advancing Your Craft* stage, a foundational familiarity with both the medium of virtual learning and the applied constructs of UDL empowers individuals to be more experimental. In this stage, educators may move away from a traditionally didactic approach to engaging students in self-identified strategies that work for them individually. Often, this type of individualization feels like a loss of control, but within a learning environment where the UDL principles have been applied, it is actually the ultimate reflection of classroom management– establishing that the students have been given an understanding of their choices, taught to recognize their own preferences that maximize their learning and performance, and educated on the tools at their disposal to accomplish these tasks. In this way, the teacher has controlled the setting of expectation but has empowered students to take responsibility for meeting that expectation. The promise of this type of classroom is that it mirrors what employers are most likely to expect of students after graduation. Figure 4 depicts these knowledge levels.

Figure 4. Knowledge levels associated with applying UDL in virtual learning environments

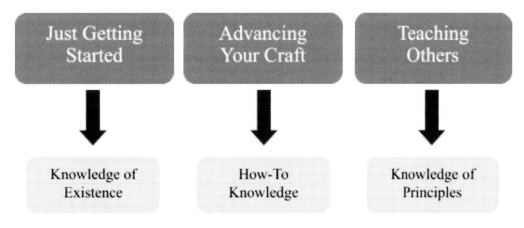

Teaching Others

This final knowledge level represents the most advanced professionals, which likely includes inservice teachers and school or district-level administrators with various levels of experience in implementing UDL and teaching in VLEs. Like Tamara, it may also include teacher educators and those responsible for designing and delivering professional learning related to these concepts. These professionals are focused on the principles of knowledge; specifically, those who seek to gain or refine their intrinsic understanding of the functionality of UDL, namely, how and why it works. The goal for individuals at this level is to assist others who are in earlier stages to define and appreciate the principles of UDL. This goal can be achieved through an organization's professional learning communities (Berquist, 2017) or Communities of Practice (Carey et al., 2021) as well as working with individual teachers to guide reflection and offer coaching. Those responsible for teaching others may find it helpful to incorporate Looi and Wu's (2015) four stages of reflection: familiarization, production, evaluation and post-task reflection. These stages of reflection serve as prompts for designing meaningful professional learning and coaching both new and experienced educators.

Additionally, professionals at this stage can support practitioners by offering targeted feedback, using objective instructional data to point out impacts on student learning, and providing ongoing coaching. Finally, those responsible for teaching others may find it useful to use the Concerns-Based Adoption Model, or CBAM, to assess practitioners' concerns and then match their coaching interventions to address these concerns (Hall & Hord, 1987). Table 1, adapted from Roberts (2015), provides practical suggestions for matching coaching approaches to teachers' present concerns.

Table 1. Coaching interventions aligned with teachers' concerns (Roberts, 2015). Source: Adapted from Roberts (2015)

Concern or Area of Focus	Coaching Approach
(0) Awareness "I am not concerned."	Involve teachers in discussion and decisions.
(1) Informational "I would like to know more."	Provide clear and accurate information. Relate changes to current practice.
(2) Personal "How will this affect me?"	Address personal concerns directly. Implement changes progressively over time.
(3) Management "How will I have time to do this"?	Answer specific "how to" questions.
(4) Consequence "How will this affect my students?"	Provide positive feedback and needed support. Provide opportunities for teachers to share knowledge and skills.
(5) Collaboration "How can I relate what I am doing to what others are doing?"	Provide opportunities to develop skills needed to work collaboratively. Arrange schedules so that people can collaborate.
(6) Refocusing "How can I incorporate my ideas to make this work even better?"	Respect and encourages teachers' interests. Channel teachers' ideas and energies; act on their concerns.

When educators reach the level of *Teaching Others*, they are achieving a professional pinnacle that recognizes their own mastery in application, but also the capability to refine and improve upon the underlying pedagogical models. This is not a time for stagnation. UDL, by design, accounts for variability, and every learner who is before that teacher brings novelty in experience, background, and need. As technology continues to evolve at a rapid pace, staying familiar with the tools in order to understand their possibilities and limitations is a continuous effort.

Applying Knowledge to Climb the Mountain

These three knowledge levels are fluid. At times, several may be relevant, based on professional circumstances. For instance, an educator in the middle stage may find themselves with an opportunity to support and coach others. Nevertheless, to streamline the experience for readers, these knowledge levels are represented as three stages in order to share useful and practical examples that support the reader. Educators in various roles may benefit from incorporating the Learning Forward Standards. These standards emphasize the importance of learning communities, effective integration of resources, learning designs, outcomes, leadership capacity, data usage, and evidence-based implementation practices to support professional learning (Learning Forward, 2021). Those designing professional learning experiences may find it useful to reference Guskey's research on teacher change. Guskey has evaluated the relationship between professional learning and improvement in student learning, focusing on how professional learning efforts can be critically evaluated and assessed in order to promote teacher change (Guskey, 2000; Guskey & Yoon, 2009).

Growing and ultimately changing practice is a journey, not a destination. But through a commitment to assessing one's personal level of knowledge and working to advance that knowledge over time, all individuals can achieve their own personal vision of climbing the mountain, as depicted in Figure 5, and demonstrate increased competency in teaching effectively in VLEs.

Figure 5. Achieving your vision requires a commitment to continuous learning (Source: Shutterstock, Inc. 1677153871)

USING UDL TO DESIGN VIRTUAL LEARNING ENVIRONMENTS

The learning environment includes the physical or VLE, learning tools and materials, content and curriculum, and instructional practices (Meyer et al., 2014). Rather than designing a VLE, only to later retrofit it to meet unanticipated learner needs, the UDL guidelines assist educators in designing with learner variability in mind from the start. UDL is a proactive framework that assists in the design of all learning environments. It is particularly helpful when designing VLEs in which the instructor has a limited ability to observe their learners and make retrofitted adjustments in real-time.

The UDL Virtual Learning Environment

The context of the environment has an impact on learning and a learner's ability to utilize and demonstrate skills with mastery (Fischer et al., 1993). An orderly and calm learning space is much more conductive to learning and skill development than a chaotic, disorganized space where learners are unsure of what to do; or worse, feel unwelcome or threatened. Just like a physical classroom, the instructional design of the VLE should be carefully considered. With in-person learning, the space in which educators organize tools and materials and engage in activities with learners is typically the physical classroom. In virtual learning, this space is typically provided within a learning management system (LMS). This VLE may be part of a robust LMS established by the school or school system (e.g., Coursera, Blackboard, Schoology, Moodle), or a smaller, classroom-level system (e.g., Google Classroom).

As with a physical classroom, a VLE may have some limitations based on the general architecture of the space. But, for the most part, an educator can design a digital space to make it suitable for the variability of learners. Think back to the three principles of UDL described earlier in the chapter; these principles apply to VLEs as much as physical ones (Coy et al., 2014).

Providing Multiple Means of Engagement in the Virtual Learning Environment

To begin designing a universally design VLE, first consider the engagement principle and affective network. This UDL principle emphasizes that learning is emotional work and learners benefit from emotional connections to their curriculum and learning community. Using the UDL engagement principle can enhance virtual learning experiences (Chen et al., 2018). Consider how the VLE engages learners. Is it welcoming? Does it signal that all learners are valued and respected within the learning community? Are there multiple supports for learners who become frustrated or overwhelmed?

The following are considerations for engaging learners within the VLE:

- Provide digital areas (such as discussion boards) in which learners can share information about themselves that is not specific to the class. Use this opportunity to foster classroom community.
- In order to support frustrated learners who are separated from the instructor by time and space, consider creating a Frequently Asked Questions-style section of "What to do if I…" -style section. Use guiding questions similar to what a learner might ask themselves, such as "What to do if I . . ."
- Create shared expectations for behavior and interactions within the VLE and post them. Refer to this posted set of expectations often during instruction.

Providing Multiple Means of Representation in the Virtual Learning Environment

Next, consider the representation principle, which emphasizes that learners are variable in the ways that they perceive and make sense of information. The first step in perceiving information in a VLE is digital accessibility. The VLE must be easy to navigate, be compatible with assistive technologies, and include multiple forms of representation to assist all learners (Coy et al., 2014). For example, an educator may have a weekly schedule for their learners that includes which software and/or apps they will need to use each day. In doing so, include both text and images with alternative text to assist all learners in using the schedule efficiently and minimizing any unnecessary barriers.

The following are considerations for how to best represent content in a VLE:

- Provide videos to students that include accurate captioning.
- Accompany online text with read-aloud options.
- Use images to support narrative text.
- Accompany directions with consistent icons.
- Support learners' understanding of key terms and symbols through access to a virtual "word wall" that includes images and videos.
- Provide general, guiding questions within the VLE that are not tied to specific content.

Providing Multiple Means of Action and Expression in the Virtual Learning Environment

Finally, the action and expression principle reminds educators that learners must have options for navigating and interacting within the VLE. It is vital to consider how learners navigate the various pieces of content, learning tools, and submission portals. Multimedia can create increased cognitive load on learners that negatively impacts learning but using UDL to avoid creating virtual spaces that are too difficult, confusing, or digitally inaccessible, can prevent these barriers (Kennedy et al., 2014).

The following are considerations for incorporating the UDL principle of action and expression within VLEs:

- Consider posting keyboard shortcuts (as an alternative for mouse navigation) within the LMS.
- Consider where the portals for work submission will be housed within the VLE.
- Avoid folder pathways that require multiple mouse clicks.
- Provide instructions and reminders for saving, storing, and labeling saved work.

Using UDL to Select Learning Tools and Materials

The VLE is typically housed within an LMS. The software, apps, and multimedia content selected to fill a VLE is very important to how learners will engage with content. A frequent misconception regarding UDL is that educators must find the perfect tool that addresses the needs of all learners. The UDL guidelines, however, emphasize that due to learner variability, finding such a tool will be difficult (or nearly impossible). Instead, time should be spent finding meaningful options so that all learners may select tools and materials that work best for them. For example, when asking learners to respond to a prompt, a UDL practitioner may provide tools for voice and/or video recording, as well as creating a written response, which can be crafted by typing or dictating using speech-to-text tools. UDL is a pedagogy that values all learners and their variability. Therefore, human representation within learning materials matters. The UDL practitioner takes great care in selecting multimedia, to ensure that individuals within these materials authentically represent various races, ethnicities, abilities/disabilities, and cultures.

Instructional Planning and Implementation

A UDL approach to lesson planning asks educators to consider themselves as the designers of learning experiences. This design approach is vital within a VLE. Virtual instruction can take place synchronously (at the same time) or asynchronously (learners working at different times). To begin to plan, an educator must determine which pieces of content are best suited for each delivery method. For example, a UDL practitioner should consider what barriers might be created if learners are presented with new mathematics skills asynchronously. The UDL guidelines can help educators to think through the potential barriers that might arise. When planning a lesson using UDL, educators may ask themselves several questions based upon the guidelines:

- What options can be offered so that all learners can engage with the content?
- How can options be provided so that all learners can perceive and make sense of the content?
- What options can support all learners to actively participate and demonstrate their learning?

When providing options, if there is a "correct choice" in mind, the teacher has created a trap, not a choice. True choice in the learning environment means that regardless of what option learners select, they will be engaged in a rigorous, robust, and meaningful way. Remember to focus on the expectation and identify the knowledge or skill to be demonstrated in the end. Then, allow students to best choose the path that achieves that goal. Many times, particularly when either the students or the teacher are in the *Just Getting Started* stage, there is a comfort in providing example pathways or options. That is okay – in fact – it is great teaching, but then the teacher must be impartial and weight a student's performance in terms of the evidence, no matter how the facts are presented.

Learner Executive Function and Self-Regulation

UDL is a collection of evidence-based practices organized into an instructional design framework. It is not critical (or even appropriate) to try and address every guideline and checkpoint at once, rather instructional design should incorporate the parts of the framework that best support the learning goal(s).

A learning environment can either create barriers to learning or support learner acquisition and expression of skills (Myers et al., 2014). There is strong evidence that suggests using computers and other digital devices places a greater burden on learner self-regulation and executive function skills (Islam & Gronlund, 2016; Kay & Schellenberg, 2017; Lei & Zhao, 2008; Durak & Saritepeci, 2017; Tallvid, 2016; Tallvid et al., 2015). This situation may be because of the risk of added distractions, the dynamic nature of software, or the need to keep in mind multiple chunks of information when navigating software, all the while simultaneously engaging with new instructional content. Environments which place a greater strain on learner executive function and self-regulation make it difficult for students to engage with those skills (Denckla, 2019; Jacobson & Mahone, 2012). This situation means the VLE may create barriers for learners with weaker executive function and self-regulation.

Implementing Universal Design for Learning in the Virtual Learning Environment

How do UDL practitioners address this potential increase in self-regulation and executive function demand? First, assess the learning environment and reduce the demands on learner executive function and self-regulation when possible. Second, build in flexible supports for these important skills (Carey, 2020). In order to accomplish this, it is necessary to take a deeper look at executive function and self-regulation.

Executive function and self-regulation are strongly linked. In fact, some neuropsychological models do not separate the two concepts (Nigg, 2016). Executive functions are a set of cognitive control skills used to engage in tasks that are not automatic or rehearsed (Diamond, 2013). Consider the difference between the cognitive control needed to drive a new route to work (or to use a new LMS) before it becomes rehearsed, as compared to the cognitive load required when these tasks become more automatic. Since most formal learning environments strive to constantly present new content and skills, students are required to use their executive function skills to complete learning tasks. Therefore, bolstering executive function skills is a critical factor in designing a supportive learning environment.

Self-regulation refers to an individual's ability to purposefully monitor and regulate their emotional state. For example, a learner may become anxious about a writing task, and purposefully engage in a mindfulness breathing activity to calm down. Like executive functions, self-regulation skills are necessary for completing tasks, such as learning new material, or completing an assessment.

Learner executive function and self-regulation skills are variable and dependent on context. It is helpful to teach learners how to notice the signs that they are struggling. This self-knowledge can assist learners in seeking out the supports available. The behavioral signs that a person is struggling with executive function and/or self-regulation (Gioia et al., 2015) include: impulsivity, distractibility, difficulty with complex task completion, difficulty transitioning between activities, and difficulty shifting patterns of thought.

Executive function and self-regulation inhabit the same level of the UDL framework to demonstrate their important link. Blair (2016) refers to the relationship between executive function and self-regulation as a "bidirectional… adaptive feedback loop" (p. 417). These skillsets support one other as an individual engages in activities. Heightened feelings like stress, anxiety, and fear can negatively impact executive function. So too can low feelings such as boredom, sadness, and depression. Being able to regulate emotions can assist in using executive function skills to their fullest potential. Likewise, executive function skills such as inhibiting, planning, and problem-solving can be used to support a learner's self-regulation of emotions. These two skillsets are critical to success in the VLE and ample support for executive function and self-regulation must be present if learners are to succeed.

SPECIALIZED INSTRUCTION IN VIRTUAL LEARNING ENVIRONMENTS

Think back to the vignette about curb cuts. The curb cuts made crossing the street easier for the family with the stroller and children with the bike and scooter. But the curb cuts also made crossing the street possible for the wheelchair user. While UDL assists educators in removing barriers, it does not remove the need for legally protected individualized instruction, accommodations, or modifications. It is important to consider; therefore, how to address the needs of learners who require special education or additional supports.

RESPONSE TO INTERVENTION AND MULTI-TIERED SYSTEMS OF SUPPORT

When planning and delivering instruction in VLEs, the basic tenets of high-quality instruction should be applied for all students. Response to Intervention (RTI) and Multi-Tiered System of Supports (MTSS) are two models which provide a framework for the delivery of highly effective instruction for students and can be applied in VLEs. UDL can and should be infused at each level of the RTI or MTSS model.

RTI is a tiered approach that uses data-driven procedures for analyzing learner needs and providing appropriate levels of academic support. Initially designed to prevent the overidentification of SWD, the approach emphasizes systematic and increasingly intense levels of support based on a learner's academic needs (Friend & Bursuck, 2012). Multi-Tiered System of Supports (MTSS) is a framework that grew from the RTI model but was expanded to address both academic and behavioral support strategies. Both models emphasize a three-tiered approach to instruction, beginning with high-quality and scientifically based instruction for all students (National Center for Learning Disabilities, 2021). Struggling learners are provided increasing intensities of instruction and intervention based on their needs.

UDL and RTI/MTSS have intersections, but the concepts differ. "RTI and UDL differ in that RTI is a process for making educational decisions based on an at-risk learner's success or failure during specialized intervention, while UDL is a process for making curriculum design decisions to maximize success in the general curriculum" (Sacks, 2018, p. 77). RTI and UDL recognize that a lack of student achievement does not necessarily reflect disability but may be the result of ineffective instruction (Sacks, 2018). Regardless of the type of intervention a learner receives, the principles of UDL apply. Practitioners should provide multiple means of representation, action and expression, and engagement to support students in all tiers. Figure 6 provides an overview of these, with emphasis on the application of UDL.

Figure 6. Application of UDL to RTI and MTSS models

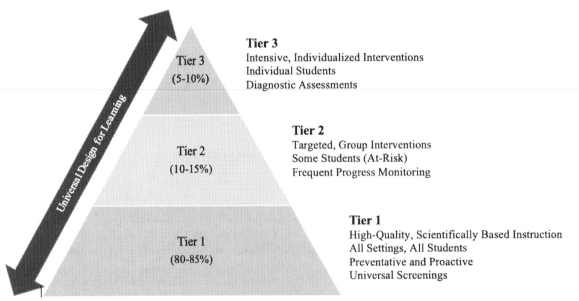

UDL and Legally Protected Education Supports

Students who require additional support in a VLE include: (a) students with a physical or mental impairment who receive services under Section 504 of the Rehabilitation Act of 1873, (b) ELs, or (c) students with an educational disability who receive special education services under the Individuals with Disabilities Education Act (IDEA). Students with a 504 Plan, EL Accommodations Plan, or an IEP who are receiving instruction in a VLE are entitled to receive these services and schools cannot opt out of providing them (USDE, 2020). The concept of learner variability still applies to these groups of learners. However, in addition to creating flexible options for engagement, representation, and action and expression educators must also ensure that the prescribed individualized instruction, accommodations, and modifications are in place.

Students Receiving Services Under Section 504

The Rehabilitation Act of 1973 protects children and adults from discrimination due to disability (Gargiulo & Bouck, 2018). Section 504 of this act requires schools to provide *reasonable accommodations* so that students can participate. Students are eligible to receive supports if they have a record of an existing "physical or mental impairment that substantially limits one or more major life activities" (Gargiulo & Bouck, 2018, p. 52). Students who qualify for support under Section 504 have an Accommodations Plan, commonly referred to as a 504 Plan. Rather than considering 504 accommodations plans as being outside the scope of UDL, educators can use 504 plans as the starting point for planning options within their learning environment.

Students Receiving Special Education Services Under the Individuals with Disabilities Education Act

The IDEA is the federal law governing the eligibility and provision of special education services (Gargiulo & Bouck, 2018. Students are eligible to receive special education services under IDEA if they have an existing impairment that creates adverse educational impact and necessitates specialized instruction delivered (IDEA, 2004). Individualized Education Programs (IEPs) can also be used as an instructional design tool to ensure that the VLE is accessible to all. For example, text-to-speech software may be a required accommodation on one learners' IEP, but by making this software available within the VLE, an educator can increase options for all learners.

English Learners

ELs are defined as those whose primary language is not English and have demonstrated limited English proficiency. Based on an assessment of their English proficiency, ELs may qualify for instructional services and have a plan outlining their needs. The plan for each learner provides documentation regarding the necessary language-related supports they require in order access the general curriculum.

Supporting Students with Disabilities in the Virtual Learning Environment

Some accommodations and modifications typically used in the traditional classroom may need to be adapted for delivery in a VLE. The sections that follow address the necessary considerations for ensuring that students have access to instruction and can learn effectively in VLEs.

Digital Accessibility

UDL focuses on the removal of barriers to learning for all students. For many SWD, digital accessibility is a key component to the removal of barriers. Materials created or curated as part of virtual instruction are sometimes inaccessible to students who are Blind/low-vision, Deaf or Hard of Hearing, or students with limited physical mobility. In order for a resource to be fully accessible, all students need to be able to engage with it, perceive it, understand it, and navigate it. There is no magic technology that will meet the needs of all learners; therefore, digital accessibility must include options.

Section 508 of the Rehabilitation Act of 1973 requires that hardware and software meet standards for ensuring individuals with disabilities have access to technology (Hashey & Stahl, 2014; Smith & Basham, 2014). Additionally, the World Wide Web Consortium (W3C) has developed the Web Content Accessibility Guidelines (WCAG) 2.0. These accessibility standards emphasize that online content must be perceivable, operable, understandable, and robust for individuals with disabilities (Smith & Basham, 2014). The Office of Civil Rights (OCR) also provided guidance in 2011 to indicate that digital curricular resources for students be designed to provide equal opportunity and that curriculum developers have an obligation to make necessary accommodations and modifications to content to guard against disability-based discrimination (Center on Online Learning and Students with Disabilities, 2016).

OCR guidance does not restrict educational systems from acquiring inaccessible resources (Hashey & Stahl, 2014), so ensuring accessibility is a task that often falls to schools and educators. Overall, it is far more efficient and cost effective to ensure that curricular resources are fully accessible from the outset, as modifying resources can be a timely endeavor (Hashey & Strahl, 2014). Voluntary Product Accessibility Template (VPAT) tools can be useful for determining the accessibility of a digital tool. For instance, the VPAT tool created by the Center on Online Learning and SWD (COLSWD) can be used to identify how a device or software may be utilized by students with visual impairments, hearing impairments, or limited physical mobility (Hashey & Strahl, 2014). Practitioners should select digital resources that have the widest range of accessible features to ensure that curated content is usable by all students and VPAT tools can assist educators in making these decisions.

Accommodations and Modifications

Accommodations are practices and procedures that provide a learner with equitable access to content. They are intended to remove barriers to learning, without lowering academic or behavioral expectations. For some learners, access to documented accommodations is a legally protected right. A review of the UDL guidelines will show clear connection between this common accommodation and the guidelines and checkpoints of the framework. Legally protected accommodations may be embedded as option within the VLE and used as a starting point of proactive UDL-based instructional design.

The following is a list of instructional accommodations that could be implemented to support SWD in the VLE:

- Add captions to videos using a captioning service.
- Incorporate softwares, such as audio books, word prediction, text-to-speech, speech-to-text, and screen readers.
- Provide access to digital math tools, such as a ruler, number chart, number line, calculator, math clock, or other virtual math manipulatives.
- Provide access to augmentative alternative communication (AAC) devices.
- Teach students to use spelling and grammar features within word processing software.
- Use web tools to provide digital graphic organizers.
- Show and refer to background visuals during on-camera teacher time.
- Encourage students and families to turn off alerts, notifications, or eliminate other distracting elements on the student's learning device.
- Provide a customized schedule, a visual schedule, or activity schedules to signify the structure of learning.

Modifications are practices that change, lower, or reduce learning expectations for students. While these practices may be necessary to support students with more extensive disabilities, they should be applied with caution because they risk increasing the gap between the achievement of SWD and expectations for grade level proficiency. However, for students with significant learning needs, these practices may be necessary in order to ensure their access to the general education curriculum.

The following is a list of modifications that could be used to support SWD in a VLE:

- Meet with the student to discuss modifications to assignments and deadlines.
- Provide a customized assignment description, scoring rubric, and list of due dates.
- Abbreviate concepts in texts by adapting readability or adding visual supports, such as picture symbols or photos.
- Convert complex online text to a simpler format.
- Provide visual information to accompany assessment items.

Supporting English Learners in a Virtual Learning Environment

ELs may benefit from the use of instructional accommodations to support their receptive and expressive language capabilities in the VLE (WIDA, 2021). The degree to which ELs can access instruction in the VLE is directly related to their level of English proficiency; therefore, educators should review relevant diagnostic criteria for ELs whom they are teaching. However, many ELs can benefit from accommodations which reduce the linguistic load necessary to access content. This reduction allows teachers to measure a learner's true understanding.

It is a widely accepted practice to provide accommodations that allow ELs to access content, but not to change the composition of the content itself. The instructional goal should remain the same for all learners. The pathways (how students emotionally connect, perceive, actively participate, and show what they know) may be variable.

Educators may find it useful to apply the following accommodations to support ELs in VLEs:

1. Provide one-on-one or small group synchronous instruction, whenever possible. Provide linguistic support, such as verbatim oral reading, visuals and digital resources which allow for word study, and extended time.
2. Incorporate digital technologies, such as the use of audio materials, text-to-speech software, or links to web tools that allow students to explore definitions of words and concepts, summaries of text, or relevant background information provided through close-captioned video.
3. Offer explanations to students using direct and concise oral and written language.
4. Incorporate visual and nonverbal cues during synchronous, on-camera teacher time.
5. Highlight and explicitly teach core vocabulary and content-specific terminology.
6. Use a digital system that allows students to develop and maintain a bilingual dictionary that is readily access during instruction.
7. Support students' global understanding through the use of digital graphic organizers, visual aids, and digital word/concept webs.

ANOTHER MOUNTAIN TREK IN ONE'S CAREER

After reading this chapter, Sam, Abby, and Tamara are now ready for the process of change. Each is preparing to embark on another mountain trek as they remain committed to continuous learning and reflection. Based on individualized experiences and knowledge the journey will look different for each of these three educators.

Just Getting Started

Sam will begin his journey by growing his knowledge about UDL and learner variability. He will work to increase his awareness of digital tools and reflect upon how such tools may have an impact on his instructional design and his students. This may be a daunting task, and Sam will certainly reach out to others like Tamara, to engage in professional learning communities and solicit constructive feedback.

Advancing Your Craft

With great excitement, Abby is ready to stretch and explore. With continued reflection and refinement of her application of UDL in VLEs, she will apply new learning tools and materials. Like Sam, Abby will be seeking out opportunities for professional learning and will engage in these communities of practice by sharing with and learning from others. Abby will also work to provide meaningful options and true choice to her students, thus empowering them to become motivated and strategic learners in the VLE.

Teaching Others

Tamara will commence her climb by bringing educators together through professional learning communities. She hopes to work individually with educators to provide coaching, prompting, and guided reflections. Similar to Abby, she is committed to exploring and understanding the capabilities of new technologies, so that she may pass that knowledge to other educators. Tamara is further challenging herself by researching and developing professional developments focused on learner self-regulation and executive function skills. Additionally, she hopes to collaborate with other educators to develop additional training on how to support students with a 504 Plan, EL Accommodations Plan, or an IEP.

DIRECTIONS FOR FURTHER EXAMINATION

The future is now. COVID-19 has showed the world that virtual learning was not only viable, but at times, vital. While some students have struggled in a completely VLE, others have thrived. As such, the often touted but never fully realized promise of personalized learning – taking the concept of UDL to its pinnacle beyond differentiation of presentation and demonstration of learning to allowing students to make choices within the entire learning experience – is likely to continue even in the absence of a pandemic. Already, similar models of instruction are employed in numerous K-12 settings, such as through one-to-one technology initiatives and combinations of in-person learning and virtual programming. Intentionality in policy, instructional planning, and overall implementation are keys to ensuring technology does not become a glorified accessory or another mechanism to further the divides of inequities that affect too many children.

In this chapter, three profiles of educators were presented: those *Just Getting Started*; *Advancing Your Craft*; and those who are *Teaching Others*. These stages are defined by the dimension of familiarity with VLEs and the application of UDL principles, but these stages are fluid as both technology and students are constantly changing and individually unique. The common need for teachers and administrators at any stage is to stay engaged in the latest technology capabilities and the factors that influence students' lives.

The past few decades have seen large advances in the interdisciplinary field of the science of learning (Fischer et al., 2007). The interactions between learning theory, biology, specific technology capabilities and individual contexts will be a continued area of focus for effective educators in the 21st century (Carey et al., 2020). Better understanding of these interactions requires a continuous vigilance to examine the factors that shape students collectively and individually. For example, natural disasters can rock the foundational infrastructure necessary for students to be access VLEs, so ensuring online and offline methods for learning becomes not only sound UDL in action, but critically necessary planning for ensuring continuity of learning. Students who are housing or food insecure, who are dealing with trauma, who are living in fear and uncertainty are as equally disenfranchised for learning in virtual environments as they are in physical ones, but teachers have the advantage of proximity in face-to-face learning to read body language and other non-verbal cues that may be missed in the virtual learning. Building in the mechanisms to plug in to students' lives, establishing even stronger communication channels between the family and school, and being vigilant to the signs of disengagement and withdraw are even more critical in the VLE.

The impact on schooling by COVID-19 has created a mass educational experiment in the benefits, effects, and limitations of VLEs, the results of which may not be known for some time. Future research needs to quantify the social-emotional effects of virtual learning, both by educator level and student type. Researchers must address whether there are characteristic markers that determine which groups thrive and which do not and determine if there are implementation models that allow for stratification between virtual and physical environments. At the same time, the field must determine what benefits are enabled by virtual learning for previously marginalized student populations. When using UDL to approach virtual learning instruction, are students empowered to see more the application of learning to their own experience? Using UDL, there is greater opportunity for students to make connections to their own cultural perspective by harnessing the power of technology. The developers of the UDL framework have initiated a community-driven process to update the UDL guidelines to address issues of cultural bias and social injustice as barriers to learning (CAST, 2020). This announcement is an excellent reminder that the ways the field conceptualizes and addresses barriers to learning is constantly evolving. When these updates to the guidelines are made, their application to VLEs should be studied further.

As mentioned, the adverse childhood experiences that too many children suffer still exist, regardless of the medium of instruction. Those who apply UDL to VLEs must be cognizant of barriers, such as the lack of consistent internet access; learner circumstances that make meaningful engagement and access difficult; and the challenge of building core relationships from a distance. This is why the UDL principles– the why, what, and how of learning – need to be considered *before* the medium of learning is decided. The considerations to achieve these three aims will help to create the ultimate goals of the learning in many ways that will be enhanced for some students via virtual learning but should not be constrained by the use of virtual learning. Educational leaders have a responsibility to advocate for systemic support through affordable and effective universal high-speed internet across all communities and two-generational device provisions for students and families. Associated training is also needed so that home-school connections are strengthened and provide stronger social-safety supports that ensure no child or family fall through the cracks if face-to-face schooling is less prominent.

CONCLUSION

The principles of UDL are beneficial regardless of the learning environment, but there is a risk of assumption by educators that VLEs inherently enable benefits. UDL remains a reflection of intentionality; purposefully designed instruction that meets students where they are and allows them to find the path that best fits their experiences, preferences, and abilities in order to engage with instruction and demonstrate their learning. VLEs afford greater opportunity for some students and teachers to accomplish this vision, but there is a need for caution that the VLE is onto itself a choice that may not be the best mode for all students. Ultimately, when a virtual learning mode is employed, it should incorporate the UDL principles so that the variable needs of all students are met.

REFERENCES

Berquist, E. (2017). *UDL: Moving from exploration to integration*. CAST Publishing.

Blair, C. (2016). The development of executive functions and self-regulation: A bidirectional psychological model. In K. D. Vohs & R. F. Baumeister (Eds.), *Handbook of self-regulation* (3rd ed., pp. 417–440). The Guilford Press.

Carey, L. B. (2020). *Executive function and online learning: Linking research to classroom*. https://www.kennedykrieger.org/stories/linking-research-classrooms-blog/executive-function-and-online-learning

Carey, L. B., Schmidt, J., Dommestrup, A. K., Pritchard, A. E., van Stone, M., Grasmick, N., ... Jacobson, L. A. (2020). Beyond learning about the brain: A situated approach to training teachers in mind, brain, and education. *Mind, Brain and Education: the Official Journal of the International Mind, Brain, and Education Society*, *14*(3), 200–208. doi:10.1111/mbe.12238

Carey, L. B., Sadera, W. A., Cai, Q., & Filipiak. (2020). Creating a community of practice for educators forced to transition to remote teaching. *Teaching, Technology, and Teacher Education during the COVID-19 Pandemic: Stories from the Field*, 251-255. https://www.learntechlib.org/p/216903/

Center for Applied Special Technology (CAST). (2011). *Universal Design for Learning guidelines version 2.0*. http://www.udlcenter.org/aboutudl/udlguidelines

Center for Applied Special Technology (CAST). (2018). *Universal design for learning guidelines version 2.2*. https://udlguidelines.cast.org

Center for Applied Special Technology (CAST). (2020). *CAST announces a community-driven process to update UDL guidelines.* https://www.cast.org/news/2020/community-driven-process-update-udl-guidelines

Center on Online Learning and Students with Disabilities (COLSWD). (2016). *Equity matters: Digital & online learning for students with disabilities*. Lawrence, KS: Author. http://www.centerononlinelearning.res.ku.edu/equity-matters-2016-digital-and-online-learning-for-students-with-disabilities/

Chen, B., Bastedo, K., & Howard, W. (2018). Exploring Design Elements for Online STEM Courses: Active Learning, Engagement & Assessment Design. *Online Learning*, *22*(2), 59–75. doi:10.24059/olj.v22i2.1369

Coy, K., Marino, M. T., & Serianni, B. (2014). Using universal design for learning in synchronous online instruction. *Journal of Special Education Technology*, *29*(1), 63–74. doi:10.1177/016264341402900105

Denckla, M. B. (2018). *Understanding learning and related disabilities: Inconvenient brains*. Routledge. doi:10.4324/9780429425981

Diamond, A. (2013). Executive functions. *Annual Review of Psychology*, *64*(1), 135–168. doi:10.1146/annurev-psych-113011-143750 PMID:23020641

Durak, H., & Saritepeci, M. (2017). Investigating the effect of technology use in education on classroom management within the scope of the FATİH project. *Çukurova Üniversitesi Eğitim Fakültesi Dergisi*, *46*(2), 441-457. doi:10.14812/cufej.303511

Fischer, K. W., Bullock, D., Rotenberg, E. J., & Raya, P. (1993). The dynamics of competence: How context contributes directly to skill. *Development in Context: Acting and Thinking in Specific Environments*, *1*, 93–117.

Fischer, K. W., Daniel, D. B., Immordino-Yang, M. H., Stern, E., Battro, A., & Koizumi, H. (2007). Why mind, brain, and education? Why now? *Mind, Brain and Education: the Official Journal of the International Mind, Brain, and Education Society*, *1*(1), 1–2. doi:10.1111/j.1751-228X.2007.00006.x

Friend, M., & Bursuck, W. D. (2012). *Including students with special needs: A practical guide for classroom teachers* (6th ed.). Pearson.

Gargiulo, R. M., & Bouck, E. C. (2018). *Special education in contemporary society: An introduction to exceptionality* (6th ed.). Sage.

Gioia, G. A., Isquith, P. K., Guy, S. C., & Kenworthy, L. (2015). *BRIEF: Behavior rating inventory of executive function*. Psychological Assessment Resources.

Guskey, T. R. (2000). *Evaluating professional development*. Corwin Press.

Guskey, T. R., & Yoon, K. S. (2009). What works in professional development? *Phi Delta Kappan, 90*(7), 495–500. doi:10.1177/003172170909000709

Hall, G. E., & Hord, S. M. (1987). *Change in schools: Facilitating the process*. State University of New York Press.

Hashey, A. J., & Stahl, S. (2014). Making online learning accessible for students with disabilities. *Teaching Exceptional Children, 46*(5), 70–78. doi:10.1177/0040059914528329

Individuals with Disabilities Education Act, 20 U.S.C. § 1400 (2004).

International Society for Technology in Education. (2021). *Online learning: Creating transformational learning experiences online*. https://www.iste.org/learn/online-learning

Islam, M. S., & Grönlund, Å. (2016). An international literature review of 1: 1 computing in schools. *Journal of Educational Change, 17*(2), 191–222. doi:10.100710833-016-9271-y

Jacobson, L. A., & Mahone, E. M. (2012). Educational implications of executive dysfunction. *Executive Function and Dysfunction*, 232-246. doi:10.1017/CBO9780511977954.021

Kay, R., & Schellenberg, D. (2017, June). Integrating a BYOD program in high school English: Advantage or distraction? In EdMedia+ Innovate Learning (pp. 12-16). Association for the Advancement of Computing in Education (AACE).

Kennedy, M. J., Thomas, C. N., Meyer, J. P., Alves, K. D., & Lloyd, J. W. (2014). Using evidence-based multimedia to improve vocabulary performance of adolescents with LD: A UDL approach. *Learning Disability Quarterly, 37*(2), 71–86. doi:10.1177/0731948713507262

Learning Forward. (2021). *Standards for professional learning*. https://learningforward.org/standards-for-professional-learning/

Lei, J., & Zhao, Y. (2008). One-to-one computing: What does it bring to schools? *Journal of Educational Computing Research, 39*(2), 97–122. doi:10.2190/EC.39.2.a

Looi, C. K., & Wu, L. (2015). *Reflection and preflection prompts and scaffolding*. SAGE.

Meyer, A., & Rose, D. H. (2005). The future is in the margins: The role of technology and disability in educational reform. In D. H. Rose, A. Meyer, & C. Hitchcock (Eds.), *The universally designed classroom: Accessible curriculum and digital technologies* (pp. 13–35). Harvard Education Press.

Meyer, A., Rose, D. H., & Gordon, D. T. (2014). *Universal design for learning: Theory and practice*. CAST Professional Publishing.

National Center for Learning Disabilities. (2021). *What is MTSS?* https://www.pbisrewards.com/blog/what-is-mtss/

Nigg, J. T. (2017). Annual research review: On the relations among self-regulation, self-control, executive functioning, effortful control, cognitive control, impulsivity, risk-taking, and inhibition for developmental psychopathology. *Journal of Child Psychology and Psychiatry, and Allied Disciplines, 58*(4), 361–383. doi:10.1111/jcpp.12675 PMID:28035675

Posey, A. (2019). *Engage the brain: How to design for learning that taps into the power of emotions.* Association for Supervision & Curriculum Development.

Roberts, K. (2015, November 2-4). *Theories of change: Concerns-based adoption model.* 2015 USAID Global Education Summit, Washington, DC. https://2012-2017.usaid.gov/sites/default/files/documents/1865/Roberts.pdf

Rogers, E. M. (2003). *Diffusion of innovations* (4th ed.). Free Press.

Rose, D. H., & Meyer, A. (2002). *Teaching every student in the digital age: Universal design for learning.* Association for Supervision & Curriculum Development.

Sacks, A. (2018). *Special education: A reference book for policy and curriculum development.* Grey House.

Smith, S. J., & Basham, J. D. (2014). Designing online learning opportunities for students with disabilities. *Teaching Exceptional Children, 46*(5), 127–137. doi:10.1177/0040059914530102

Tallvid, M. (2016). Understanding teachers' reluctance to the pedagogical use of ICT in the 1:1 classroom. *Education and Information Technologies, 21*(3), 503–519. doi:10.100710639-014-9335-7

Tallvid, M., Lundin, J., Svensson, L., & Lindström, B. (2015). Exploring the relationship between sanctioned and unsanctioned laptop use in a 1:1 classroom. *Journal of Educational Technology & Society, 18*(1), 237–249. https://www.jstor.org/stable/jeductechsoci.18.1.237

United States Department of Education (USDE). (2020). *Supplemental fact sheet: Addressing the risk of COVID-19 in preschool, elementary and secondary schools while serving children with disabilities.* https://www2.ed.gov/about/offices/list/ocr/frontpage/faq/rr/policyguidance/Supple%20Fact%20Sheet%203.21.20%20FINAL.pdf

World-Class Instructional Design and Assessment (WIDA). (2021). *Distance teaching and learning: Supporting all multilingual learners during COVID-19.* https://wida.wisc.edu/teach/distance-teaching-learning

ADDITIONAL READING

Center for Applied Special Technology (CAST). (2018). *Universal design for learning guidelines version 2.2.* Retrieved from http://udlguidelines.cast.org

Meyer, A., Rose, D. H., & Gordon, D. T. (2014). *Universal design for learning: Theory and practice.* CAST Professional Publishing.

Smith, S. J., & Basham, J. D. (2014). Designing online learning opportunities for students with disabilities. *Teaching Exceptional Children, 46*(5), 127–137. doi:10.1177/0040059914530102

KEY TERMS AND DEFINITIONS

Accommodation: A practice or procedure that provides a student with equitable access to content and is intended to reduce or eliminate the effects of a disability, without lowering academic or behavioral expectations.

Executive Function: A set of cognitive control skills that individuals use to engage in tasks that are not automatic or rehearsed.

Learner Variability: The recognition that there is no average or "typical" learner. Rather, those in a learning environment bring a dynamic mix of strengths, challenges, preferences, interests, and experiences.

Modification: An instructional or assessment practice that changes, lowers, or reduces the learning expectations for students with specialized needs.

Self-Regulation: An individual's ability to purposefully monitor and regulate their emotional state.

Universal Design for Learning: A framework based on scientific research that addresses the variability of all learners and optimizes the teaching and learning experience by providing multiple means of engagement, representation, and action and expression.

Chapter 4
Choosing Culturally, Linguistically, and Cognitively Distance Learning Platforms:
Correlations Across Early Childhood Professional Standards to Promote Inclusion

Rachel E. Terlop
George Mason University, USA

James Vargas-Ewing
New York City Public Schools, USA

ABSTRACT

Upon completion of their educator preparation program, a study done by Archambault found that teachers felt most prepared in the areas of pedagogy, content, and pedagogical content. However, the same teachers reported feeling least prepared in the areas of technology and technology integration. With instruction shifting to an online space during COVID-19, the consideration of how to teach virtually was no longer abstract. This chapter highlights the journey of a teacher working to find supportive technology for their class, evaluating existing resources, connecting the tools to teaching standards, and ensuring platforms are inclusive and relevant for the culturally, linguistically, and cognitively diverse (CLCD) learners who utilize augmentative and alternative communication (AAC) devices. This chapter is rooted in early childhood education, social constructivism, and disability critical race theory (DisCrit) and seeks to serve as a critical guide, or model, for intentional and inclusive educators, researchers, practitioners, and learners.

DOI: 10.4018/978-1-7998-7222-1.ch004

INTRODUCTION

Upon completion of their educator preparation program, a study done by Archambault (2011) found that teachers felt most prepared in the areas of subject-based content and pedagogical content knowledge. However, the same teachers reported feeling least prepared in the areas of technology and technology integration (Archambault, 2011). Articulating personal strengths and areas for growth shows evidence of a reflective practice. To support the ever expanding literature base in education research, districts offer professional development to ensure teachers are up-to-date on best practices. Oftentimes, districts issue mandatory professional development in addition to embedding participation in professional learning communities within district requirements for employment. The Archambault (2011) study emphasizes that identifying areas for growth and development can benefit educators, but only when there is time provided for self-directed learning and professional development based on choice or personal need.

When the instructional practices shifted during the COVID-19 pandemic, the space of grappling of how to teach online in the abstract was no longer optional. Teachers who still felt uncomfortable integrating or utilizing technology were no longer able to avoid learning. While educators of all ages were scrambling to digitize instruction and navigate a new classroom reality, student teachers were pushed as well. Student teachers were impacted because they were required to begin building an additional toolbox for themselves if they did not already have experience participating in, or leading online instruction. A forced outcome for the teachers-in-training who had their student teaching placement in the time of COVID-19, is the opportunity to get their 'toes wet' in the digital world of education. They entered the field with valuable experience that came from forced, traumatic, on-demand training. For any educator that is navigating online instructional spaces, this chapter serves as a navigational tool for exploring the newest educational frontier.

As an idealist interested in qualitative research, Social Constructivism, and Disability Critical Race Theory (DisCrit) in education, the ability to communicate is the most important part of the human experience. This became more apparent during the COVID-19 pandemic while the author was teaching first grade via Google Classroom to students who primarily spoke a language other than English, at home. The challenge to communicate with students, families, and colleagues was impeded in a new way due to varying levels of access and understanding of current technology. The experiences students have at school are captured in their drawings, their conversations, their work samples, and their notes. If technology use was not already part of daily routine, moving to virtual learning during the pandemic removed a great deal of ability to capture understanding, share thinking, and learn from one another. For students who communicate non-verbally, the inability to approach or utilize proximity with a teacher to request or show created an immense barrier to communication and instruction.

Human experiences preserved, beheld, spoken, heard, and written down are what our world is designed around. The sharing of experience is what allows everyone to feel seen, heard, and validated. Ancient texts and images are studied to derive meaning for today, so society can create again, tomorrow. All humans are a part of and contribute to the collective narrative, and this chapter seeks to showcase the impact intentionality can make for culturally, linguistically, and cognitively diverse learners who are working to communicate with or without their voice.

In this chapter focused primarily on Early Childhood Education, the social constructivist theory and DisCrit theory are outlined with the intent of providing a unique lens for those interested in transforming teachers' online pedagogical reasoning for teaching K-12 students in a virtual learning environment. The author created the standards for teaching and learning tables compiled in the chapter, from a variety of organizations and experts in early childhood education and education research. Each of these standards have been presented to the author in her eight years of teaching, at time of writing, and have impacted her practice. The online learning platforms showcased in the chapter are all spaces the author has utilized with her students in Pre-K-3 classrooms that supported the learning of culturally, linguistically, and cognitively diverse students.

THEORETICAL CONSTRUCT

Online learning is not touted as the first professional development opportunity on the docket because online educators indicate a lack of confidence in their ability to promote trust and a sense of community (Wilkens et al., 2014). Preservice teachers and student teachers struggle to motivate their online students in addition to the other components of instruction that are being developed in their pedagogical practice (Graziano & Feher, 2016). However, with schools opting for a hybrid model of instruction, or 100% digital learning due to COVID-19, there is no option for lack of, or avoidance of training. Preparing veteran teachers, as well as those just entering the profession, with the skills and pedagogy for effective online practice is now mandatory. The United States' emphasis on elementary classroom design consisting of socially-constructed learning experiences became the newest challenge in the field of education as of March 2020, because now instruction was online.

The challenge of overcoming obstacles and barriers in order to provide inclusive and accessible instruction is not a new concept for teachers. The No Child Left Behind Act (2001) mandates standards-based accountability for all students enrolled in K-12 classrooms in the United States (Odowd, 2010). 'Standards based accountability' is a three word phrase with a plethora of layers and implications embedded within it. In order for students to effectively and orally communicate information, they must have availability and access to the relevant linguistic and content knowledge as schema, or through immediate feedback and modeling (Gablasova, 2014). With increased fluency of oral communication and a smaller number of pauses, restarts, fillers, and reformulations, more information can be communicated (Gablasova, 2014). Fluency of speech allows students to move through periods of disequilibrium with greater ease. Disequilibrium, rooted in Social Constructivism, is described as the time period when humans are taking in new information, but it does not align to any information already learned. Within a state of disequilibrium, no existing schema is available to reinforce what is being learned (Branscombe, 2013). In order for students to show what they know in terms of the standards, there is a requirement of auditory comprehension, time for students to process the information, and then formulate a verbal, visual, or written response. For students with limited exposure to social or academic language in the language of instruction (LOI) it is a heavy cognitive load to translate from the LOI into the student's first language (L1), and then translating the thought back into the LOI. Research suggests that fluency of speech and dialogue around content material in the K-12 classroom is often then regarded as an indicator of good subject-related discourse competence (Gablasova, 2014).

Pause for a moment now to reflect on the ableist implications that are embedded within the notion that fluency of speech lies in direct correlation to 'good' subject-related discourse competence. As teachers view their students as culturally, linguistically, and cognitively diverse learners, the response to No Child Left Behind has developed into a national conversation around best practices in content instruction for English learners (ELs), scaffolding for students with individualized education programs (IEPs), and how to support students who participate in the classroom experiencing trauma. These social and cultural facets combine to make up each learner's positionality in the classroom; positionality that invites critical reflection of our country's definition of 'success' and what that looks like in the K-12 classroom. Ecological Systems Theory (EST), a theory put forth by Bronfenbrenner (1979), considers a person as being at the center of nested structures of the ecological environment: the micro-, meso-, exo-, and macrosystems (Boonpleng et al, 2013). Each person has a unique ecological environment that involves their immediate family, the people they are physically and emotionally closest to (microsystem), their place of employment or study (mesosystem), the city and town they are physically living in (exosystem), along with the rules of the city, town, county, state, or country of residence (macrosystem). In order to deeply know and support students in the classroom, EST suggests collecting individualized data on the patterns and interconnectedness between these multiple layers of a learner's social structure (Bronfenbrenner, 1979).

Understanding EST and collecting data on each student's individual ecosystems through ecological assessment is paramount for continuing dialogue around how to support culturally, linguistically, and cognitively diverse (CLCD) students in the classroom. Disability Critical Race Theory in Education (DisCrit) is a framework that fosters a critical perspective of inclusion education in postcolonial countries (Elder, 2020). The DisCrit framework comes from Critical Race Theory (CRT) and Disability Studies (DS) combining for a theoretical framework that incorporates a dual analysis of race and ability. Globally, inclusive education has been recognized as one of the best principles to address issues of equity and diversity. Previously, Universal Design for Learning was the standard.

Universal Design for Learning (UDL) is a framework designed by the Center for Applied Special Technology (CAST) intended to improve teaching pedagogy and learning outcomes for all learners (Moore et al., 2018). The UDL framework, although rooted in special education practices, was designed with a socio-cultrual lens for general education professionals to provide instruction in an engaging and accessible manner to support the diverse needs of all learners (Edyburn et al., 2017). Creating lessons that are 'universally designed' speaks to the intention and thoughtfulness in planning that allows for the widest possible range of students to access the information. Using the three main principles of the UDL framework to provide multiple options for (1) representation, (2) action and expression, and (3) engagement, reduces barriers to comprehension, scaffolds lessons, and maintains high expectations for all students (Edyburn, 2017). UDL is seen as the pinnacle of service provision for all children particularly those with disabilities (Ainscow et al., 2006; Elder, 2020). Inclusive education has the ability to lay the foundation for a just and non-discriminatory world, benefitting all children, all while being mindful of cost efficiency and effectiveness (Peters, 2003). The DisCrit framework and theory in education has seven components that expand upon UDL's three.

First, DisCrit theory highlights how racism and ableism are interdependent and normalized within society (Elder, 2020). Ableism and racism appear in schools where special education classrooms are separate from other students in their own hallway, and in academic institutions where departments of Special Education can sometimes be found detached from the educational schools of Curriculum and Instruction (Annamma et al., 2013). Systemic social constructs and interpersonal biases are often unspoken and invisible yet are upheld and reinforced in order to restrict notions of normalcy or to marginalize those perceived as 'different' in society, as well as in schools (Elder, 2020). As soon as a child is 'identified' and perceived as different from the social or cultural 'norm,' the narrative constructed is that they are less capable in academics and behavior.

Secondly, DisCrit values multidimensional identities. DisCrit as a theory is inclusive of all systemic constructs such as class, gender, sexuality, religious affiliation, etc. (Annamma et al., 2013). As students come to a learning environment from their unique microsystem, the mesosystem could be a space for grappling and working through disequilibrium. If a student's microsystem reinforces that gender is a binary construct (male and female are the only two acceptable genders), and the classroom microsystem reinforces that gender is fluid and malleable, the interaction between these two spaces in a student's mesosystem can lead to questioning and disequilibrium. This space of grappling is where critical conversation enters and is the exact reason why ecological assessment is such a valuable tool for educators. With knowledge that a student could be, or is, working through this phase of disequilibrium, educators can provide resources, literature, attention, and opportunities for discussion. Without knowledge of a student's microsystem, opportunities for learning are missed.

A third tenant of disability critical race theory is the understanding that the social construction of disability has been exposed and highlighting the ableist and deficit oriented perspectives of disability are the first steps in navigating and reforming the educational system (Elder, 2020). Keeping in mind that the definition of 'intellectual disability' has been changed numerous times since the 1900's. The AAMD (American Association of Mental Deficiency) revised the definition of mental retardation in 1973; the definition went from those individuals with measured IQ score of 85 being considered to be 'mentally retarded,' to an IQ score of 70 (Annamma et al., 2013). The moment this definition and policy changed, many people who had been unfairly carrying the label of 'mentally retarded' were instantly 'cured.' This change was a result of special education services in public schools being criticized for the optics of over-representation of black, indigenous, people of color (BIPOC) in programs for special needs (Annamma et al., 2013). The educational or medical deficit mindset of 'lesser than' is also upheld in film and media, publications on dis/ability, as well as in sports and recreation. How members of each child's micro-, meso-, exo-, and macro-system talk about and treat those who are perceived to be differently-abled matters. Ecological assessment of learning space provides a lens for educators to notice where different abilities are being embraced or stifled. Are resources and time allocated to scaffolding and supporting, or are different abilities viewed as cumbersome, intrusive, or slowing the pace of learning? Differently abled does not mean lesser than, and learners at the outlier position of bell-curves still hold the same weight and take up as much space as those in the center.

The fourth and fifth tenants of DisCrit revolve around the promotion the voices of oppressed and marginalized populations, and requirement that educators consider how, historically and legally, whiteness and ability have been used to deny rights to those who have had their ethnicity, race, ability, or any other social choice used against them in an attempt to discredit their personhood and lived experience as lesser than or disabled (Elder, 2020; Valencia, 1997). The sixth tenant of DisCrit recognizes whiteness, as well as the ability and privilege that come with being born into that. Over 75% of the world's population has had their lives impacted by colonialism, with the other 25% being the colonizers; power and privilege are abundant features of a life for someone white, or lighter skin (Elder, 2020). This imbalance of representation and power contributes to a dominant culture that is not reflective of global society. Conducting an ecological assessment is the first act of initiating conversations in which educators are forced to confront the power and privilege of systemic structures being embedded in whiteness and colonial culture.

Finally, DisCrit requires activism and supports resistance to the continuation of colonialist practices. Ecological assessment provides teachers with a first step in assessing what was reinforced to them and taught in their teacher educator training. The realization and recognition of systemic oppression, as well as the social construction of 'differences' from the 'norm,' leads to advocacy for change. Teaching is an active process because every single day teachers make decisions to dismantle oppressive systems, or reinforce them, with what they say, do, read, and how they teach. There is nothing more active than searching for or creating methods to teach content that is accessible and equitable to culturally, linguistically, and cognitively diverse students. The goal of being an active educator is to ensure the classroom does not perpetuate socially constructed systemic racism and ableism. Educators have the power to disrupt the cycle of marginalization and oppression and by working to serve as an observational data collector when conducting Ecological Assessments, educators can begin to understand the circumstances that impact their children and their whole development as a human first, then address their needs as a learner.

Ecological assessment with a DisCrit lens as a teaching practice begins the conversation of "Who is represented? Who is not?" and "Is this the message I want my students to receive?" The amount of time, attention, and energy that educators put into their craft does not go unnoticed by the people who are being represented, validated, and celebrated.

Teaching is an active process; every single day teachers make decisions to dismantle oppressive systems, or reinforce them, with what they say, do, read, and how they teach. There is nothing more active than searching for or creating methods to teach content that is accessible and equitable to culturally, linguistically, and cognitively diverse students. Every human is disabled in some aspect of their life in the sense that other humans can do things we cannot, and significant limitations of pursuing major life events exist due to the social constructs in society (Cureton & Hill, 2018). The goal of being an active educator is to ensure the classroom does not perpetuate socially constructed systemic racism and ableism. Educators have the power to disrupt the cycle.

The standards and recommended practices set in place for early childhood educators serve as a guide for educators in knowing the most important considerations for educational practice. The National Association for the Education of Young Children (NAEYC) position statements, Interstate Teacher Assessment and Support Consortium (InTASC) standards, the Council for Exceptional Children's (CEC) Division of Early Childhood (DEC) recommended practices and the National Board for Professional Teaching Standards (NBPTS) are examples of early childhood educator standards. These materials share developmentally appropriate commonalities, and by incorporating the National Standards for Online Learning, *Table 1* highlights the core components of early childhood educational pedagogy for synchronous and asynchronous digital instruction. The seven commonalities are organized by (1) continued learning for educators, (2) classroom environment and social emotional learning (SEL), (3) knowledge of students and developmentally appropriate practice (DAP), (4) assessment, (5) pedagogy, (6) instructional design and/or digital learning platforms, (7) reflection and feedback. *Table 1* highlights the commonalities across the resources.

The internet has a plethora of materials available for educators to utilize during distance learning; the aim is to maintain best practice and teaching content using technology as a facilitation tool for learning and never a replacement for instruction. *Table 2* offers a variety of learning platforms, tried and tested by educators, that can be used to facilitate learning in a digital instructional setting. Each learning platform, or digital tool, is offered across the top of the chart. The column below the identified tool offers information on how each of the seven considerations for best practice are featured within this facilitation tool.

As educators learn to facilitate instruction using these virtual learning platforms and tools, it is important to note that the work does not end here. Finding a tool that is developmentally appropriate, conducive to learning, and is accessible by all learners is just the beginning. Once a tool is identified, then the work of embedding collaborative opportunities, social engagement, and scaffolds begins.

Table 1. Correlations across early childhood professional standards

Elements of Learning	InTASC Educator Standards	NBPTS	National Standards for Online Teaching	NAEYC: Professional Standards	NAEYC: Technology	NAEYC: Advancing Equity	DEC Recommended Practices
Continued Learning	Standard 9: Professional Learning and Ethical Practice; Standard 10: Leadership and Collaboration	Standard X Exemplifying Professionalism and Contributing to the Profession	Standard A: Professional Responsibilities (A3)	STANDARD 4: Developmentally, Culturally, and Linguistically Appropriate Teaching Practices	"Technology tools for communication, collaboration, social networking, and user-generated content have transformed mainstream culture," p. 2	Build awareness and understanding of your culture, personal beliefs, values, and biases.	Teaming and Collaboration RPs; Transition RPs
Classroom Environment and SEL	Standard 3: Learning Environments	Standard VI Managing the Environment for Development and Learning	Standard C: Community Building; Standard E: Digital Citizenship	STANDARD 2: Family–Teacher Partnerships and Community Connections	"Educators are positioned to improve program quality by intentionally leveraging the potential of technology and media for the benefit of every child." p.1	Take responsibility for biased actions, even if unintended, and actively work to repair the harm	Environment RPs; Interaction RPs
Knowledge of Students/DAP	Standard 1: Learner Development; Standard 2: Learning Differences	Standard I Using Knowledge of Child Development to Understand the Whole Child	Standard F: Diverse Instruction	STANDARD 1: Child Development and Learning in Context	"Noninteractive technology and screen media not be used in early childhood programs and that there be no screen time for infants and toddlers," p.2	Recognize the power and benefits of diversity and inclusivity.	Family RPs
Assessment	Standard 6: Assessment	Standard V Assessing Children's Development and Learning	Standard G: Assessment and Measurement	STANDARD 3: Child Observation, Documentation, and Assessment	"Technology integration has been successful when the use of technology and media supports the goals of educators and programs for children, provides children with digital tools for learning and communicating, and helps improve child outcomes (Edutopia 2007)."	Acknowledge and seek to understand structural inequities and their impact over time.	Assessment RPs A4, A5, A6, A9
Strategies and Pedagogy	Standard 8: Instructional Strategies	Standard VIII Implementing Instruction for Development and Learning	Standard B: Digital Pedagogy; Standard D: Learner Engagement	STANDARD 4: Developmentally, Culturally, and Linguistically Appropriate Teaching Practices	"The appeal of technology and the steady stream of new devices may lead some educators to use technology for technology's sake, rather than as a means to an end," p.3	View your commitment to cultural responsiveness as an ongoing process.	Transition RPs
Digital Learning Platforms and Resources	Standard 7: Planning for Instruction	Standard II Partnering with Families and Communities; Standard VIII Implementing Instruction for Development and Learning; Standard VI Managing the Environment for Development and Learning	Standard H: Instructional Design	STANDARD 5: Knowledge, Application, and Integration of Academic Content in the Early Childhood Curriculum	"All screens are not created equal," p.3	Recognize that the professional knowledge base is changing.	Instruction and Family RPs
Daily Reflection and Feedback	Standard 10: Leadership and Collaboration	Standard IX Reflecting on Teaching Young Children	Standard A: Professional Responsibilities (A2)	STANDARD 6: Professionalism as an Early Childhood Educator	"Early childhood educators have an opportunity to provide leadership in assuring equitable access to technology tools and interactive media experiences for the children, parents, and families in their care," p. 4	All of the above	Teaming and Collaboration RPs

Table 2. Correlations of educational tools and elements of learning

	Nearpod	GooseChase	FlipGrid	PearDeck	Edpuzzle	Prezi	WeVideo
COST	**Silver (S):** Free **Gold (G):** $10/month **Platinum (PL):** $29/month **Premium (PR):** Contact for pricing	**Basic:** Free **Educator Plus:** $49/year **Educator Premium:** $199/year	**Basic:** Free	**Basic:** Free **Individual Premium (IP):** $49.99/year	**Basic:** Free **Pro Teacher:** $11.50/month	**Basic:** Free **Plus:** $15/month **Premium:** $59/month	**Free:** 30 day trial **Power:** $4.99/month **Unlimited:** $7.99/month **Professional:** $17.99/month **Classroom:** $299/year
Continued Learning	**All levels:** 8,500+ pre-made interactive lessons, videos, and professional development opportunities **PR Subscription:** unlocks curriculum mapping, personalized training and 21st century premium content	**All levels:** Ability to share their games, and make copies of any games that educators have made sharable	Creating a FlipGrid platform for your professional learning community invites the potential for sharing of understanding and resources in video format Weekly professional development opportunities	**All levels:** 'The Orchard' available with premade lessons, and professional development opportunities	**All levels:** Access to more than 5 million videos as demonstrations in how to create, lessons for personal growth, and pre-made lessons for students	Templates for presentation designs, infographics, and social media posts.	'WeVideo Academy' professional development mini-lessons
Classroom Environment and SEL	**All levels:** Zoom connection available when sharing screen	Program gamifies the way students interact with content as a teacher-created scavenger hunt experience Promotes collaboration, healthy competition, timeliness, and brevity	Video recording and playback allows for repeated attempts to convey a thought Video recording allows to hear change in vocal tone, and witness non-verbals if student chooses to be on camera	**Basic and IP:** Work seamlessly with powerful classroom tools from Google and Microsoft	**All levels:** Create your own interactive video lessons Add questions, audio and notes	Convert PowerPoints, PDFs, and documents into presentations.	Convert PowerPoints, PDFs, and documents into elements of a video presentation
Knowledge of Students/ DAP	**All levels:** Flex between school and home learning with 3 teaching modes: Student-Paced, Live Participation	Provides multiple opportunities for participation - structured answer, unstructured answer, fill in the blank, photo, or video.	Students do not have to show their face during recording. This could look like covering face with emoji, or covering camera lens	**Basic and IP:** Control the pace of class and project student answers anonymously	**All levels:** When creating videos, teachers can use videos that connect to the culture of students in the class	**All levels:** Unlimited visual content; images, backgrounds, and icons Voiceover capability	**All levels:** Visual content; images, backgrounds, and icons Voiceover capability
Assessment	**All levels:** 20+ formative assessments and interactive features	Student submissions within the scavenger hunt are arranged by question and downloadable in all formats; written answer, photo, or video	Video recording of understanding used as verbal explanation of understanding	**Basic and IP:** Design brilliant lessons with interactive questions, polls, quizzes, formative assessments	**All levels:** See detailed analytics on your students' results	*Not Applicable*	*Not Applicable*
Strategies and Pedagogy	**All levels:** Make existing PowerPoints, Google Slides, YouTube videos, or video files interactive	Multiple opportunities for participation mode	Vocal participation option to contribute versus a solely typed or written participation	**Individual Premium:** Add Audio to Slides	Using existing Youtube videos, or teacher owned videos to teach and assess content via use of questioning	**All levels:** Prezi Video and Prezi Design	**All levels:** Create videos **Unlimited Level and Up:** Record screen and webcam together
Digital Learning Platforms and Resources	**All levels:** Platform connections with YouTube, Google Slides, PowerPoint, and Zoom Accessible through computer, tablet, phone, or app	Accessible through computer or app	Accessible through computer or app	**Basic and IP:** Ready-to-teach templates designed by educators **All levels:** Easily accessible through computer, and accessible, but not recommended, through tablet/phone	Accessible through computer	**All levels:** PowerPoint converter	**All levels:** editing features on desktop, iOS and Android Viewing available on any digital platform where link is accessible
Daily Reflection and Feedback	**All levels:** Teacher view organized student participation by tiling images drawn for whole class viewing, providing graphs, and polling results	Digital record of student understanding allows for review of student lesson contributions	Re-playing of videos allows teachers to analyze trends of response in vocal contribution	**Individual Premium:** Provide feedback to individual students during a lesson with Teacher Feedback	Collection of student response in written form as evaluation	*Not Applicable*	*Not Applicable*

IMPLEMENTATION FOR EDUCATOR DEVELOPMENT

The United States Department of Education has offered the following advice when moving forward with instruction during the COVID-19 pandemic. In the published piece, Addressing the Risk of COVID-19 in Preschool, Elementary and Secondary Schools While Serving Children with Disabilities (2020), the US Department of Education through the Office of Civil rights states that it is "important to emphasize that federal disability law allows for flexibility in determining how to meet the individual needs of students with disabilities" (p. 2) and that "ensuring compliance with the Individuals with Disabilities Education Act (IDEA), Section 504 of the Rehabilitation Act (Section 504), and Title II of the Americans with Disabilities Act should not prevent any school from offering educational programs through distance instruction" (p. 1). How services are met, and students are to be supported is not clear, and is ultimately up to the district, school, and individual education provider. Leaving this legislative wording as a vague suggestion created a burden to educators. While educators collect ecological data on each student based on their ability to access and participate in lessons from afar, learn new platforms for instruction, and grapple with through their own disequilibrium or social and emotional trauma due to a pandemic, there is limited bandwidth to fully grapple with how to differentiate based on CLCD learner needs.

In the US Department of Education's Addressing the Risk of COVID-19 While Serving Migratory Children piece, published in May 2020, indicates that under Title I, Part C, Migrant Education Program (MEP) education, services, and activities should continue with support from technology (video conference) and social distancing (2020, p. 1). In the US Department of Education's Fact Sheet, Impact of COVID-19 on Assessments and Accountability Under the Elementary and Secondary Education Act, Federal Acts are cited as guidance for states, districts, and superintendents.

Section 8401 of the ESEA (20 U.S.C. § 7861) permits the Secretary to grant waivers of certain ESEA requirements and, thus, allows the Department to provide some flexibility to schools, districts, and States that may be necessary due to the impact of COVID-19 on the provision of educational services. (2020)

Within two months of publishing, the US Department of education published *Providing Services to English Learners During the COVID-19 Outbreak* (2020), in which yearly assessments went from mandatory and requiring 'some flexibility,' to being fully cancelled.

With respect to assessments specifically, the Secretary invited requests to waive the requirements in Section 1111(b)(2) of ESEA, including the requirement in Section 1111(b)(2)(G) of ESEA to administer an ELP assessment in the school year 2019-2020. All SEAs [State Educational Agencies] have requested and been granted this waiver for the 2019-2020 school year.

The waiver of yearly assessments allowed educators to remove one stressor from their workload and turn their attention to the student's individual learning needs.

Ms. Shannon: A Vignette of First Grade Teacher Teaching Remotely

Consider the following vignette about a first grade teacher (Ms. Shannon) who has been asked to teach from home. She works at a Title 1 Elementary school where 80% of her class speaks a language other than English, and the COVID-19 pandemic just shut down her school. A few weeks into distance learning, a new student is added to her roster. The student has diagnosed Autism Spectrum Disorder (ASD) and communicates nonverbally. The student communicates non-verbally with an image based alternative/augmentative communication device (AAC).

Ms. Shannon, an early childhood educator, took courses in her University Master's Program to gain knowledge on how to better serve students with special educational needs. At one point, her professor explained that she would be utilizing an image based system to encourage students to communicate their needs and desires in the early childhood special education inclusion setting. As Ms. Shannon had never taken a formal class in assistive technology (AT) and/or alternative or augmentative communication (AAC); she turned to the internet to learn more.

Searching the internet for YouTube videos before contacting her Special Education Co-Teacher, Ms. Shannon found videos that showcased a binder with velcro strips on the outside, as well as on the inside. Small 2" x 2" images were cut, laminated, and velcroed within the binder. The educator in the video chose four images to be placed on the outside of the binder and explained these were the options for students to 'mand,' or ask, for. Ms. Shannon thought this looked like something she could make and deliver safely while still observing COVID-19 protocol, and she continued to search for more information on how to create and implement this AAC system.

When critically reviewing videos on Youtube and the protocol being used, Ms. Shannon noticed the images being used did not match the students' ethnicity, home-language, or the physical elements of the classroom environment. She felt like the students had an innate desire to communicate with each other, and the tool they were using was not a reflection of themselves. She was left wondering, was this lack of representation contributing to educational disequilibrium?

Choosing a Tool Supportive to Learner Needs

For parents, caregivers, and educators who are looking to implement picture-based communication within the realm of their classroom, therapy, or home, there are a plethora of materials available for purchase in the app store, or available for download in order to implement alternative and augmentative communication (AAC) systems with an image-based communication practice. For convenience of use, a variety of low technology, digital, and app-based resources are available to support students who are non-speaking or communicate non-verbally. As part of the evaluation process, educators are tasked with finding a tool to support students in order to communicate needs, interests, and insights. It can be overwhelming, cumbersome, and expensive for educational team members to determine how to ensure evidence-based practices are being used, while utilizing technology that appropriately aligns with the learner's goals and is inclusive of the learner's language and culture. This article offers guidance grounded in Disability Critical Race Theory to support educational practitioners when considering what tool would be best suited for their culturally diverse student population. This article aims to improve communication competencies for children with learning disabilities in early education settings by ensuring students are fully *represented* when using their Assistive Technology (AT) tool.

Inclusion and AAC

An absence of studies addressing culturally and linguistically diverse populations has allowed the educational system to reinforce and maintain Eurocentric ideals which is the dominant structure of the educational research base (Kulkarni & Parmar, 2017). Analyzing the image based AAC materials available in the app store, the direct transfer and application of experiences and knowledge produced in the context of English speaking nations to the rest of the world is problematic (Elder, 2020). Many applications have not been adapted to both local historical and cultural contexts of the users (Singal & Muthukrishna, 2014). In order to support families that have a home language other than English, educators and practitioners look to technology to support communication. Thus, the inclusion of technology is often reaffirmed in its value, being seen as an innovative or appealing intervention technique for linguistically diverse students because it also promotes engagement in the classroom setting (Edyburn et al., 2017).

Ms. Shannon turned to her University's digital library, researching possible communication systems through professional organizations. Ms. Shannon was astonished with the myriad of digital AAC tools available and relatively affordable to the teachers. While her low-tech protocol could have been appropriate, Ms. Shannon wondered if digital AAC tools allowing for easy customization were ever considered?

Avoiding Assistive Technology Abandonment

Assistive Technology (AT) in terms of AAC has developed into an essential conversation within special educational environments since the passing of the Technology-Related Assistance for Individuals with Disabilities Act in 1988 (Weng, 2015). When beginning to consider which communicative tool would be best for classroom, therapy, or home-based communication support, all members of the educational team are making contributions to the conversation in the best interest of the learner based on personal and team developed goals for the student.

As of 2009, 3-5% of students with an Individualized Education Plan (IEP) had AAC tools designated (Vue et al., 2015). As of 2017, 10.1% of students, or 5 million students in the United States are English language learners (ELL), with the most common languages spoken as L1 being Spanish, Arabic, Chinese, Vietnamese, Somali, Russian, Portuguese, Haitian, and Hmong (NCES, 2020). In 2014, approximately 665,000 English language learning students were also identified as students with disabilities, representing 13.8% of the total ELL population in the United States (Ramirez-Chase, 2018). With the growing overlap of students who identify as ELL and have AAC written into their IEP, it is vital to investigate what cultures are represented, and which are not.

Considerations when choosing a tool may be influenced by the participants in the conversation; parents, educators, practitioners, and service providers. When choosing an AAC tool, a common barrier to developmental or academic success is abandonment. If the needs of the learner expand or change over time, a stagnant tool would only meet the needs of the present level of the user, causing abandonment. When a tool is not developmentally appropriate for a child, does not fit the needs of the learner, lacks social acceptance (Weng, 2015), or does not represent the learner's uniqueness, it can lead to users and practitioners abandoning the tool.

As Ms. Shannon began to explore what AAC could support the culturally, linguistically, and cognitively diverse students in her classroom, she came across dozens of apps that touted their ability to use a variety of images as a tool for communication. Being able to easily upload the images representative of her diverse learners would hopefully make students more interested in engaging in a conversation. Ms. Shannon has decided to try a few different apps to explore her student's reactions before discussing these innovative options with the education team. She immediately noticed that there was an increase in the amount of times her students were communicating with her and the decrease in inappropriate behaviors among the students.

Culturally, Linguistically, and Cognitively Diverse Learners

Student bilingualism or multilingualism in the classroom is a foundational element of their experience in the world, and a key for unlocking the abstract nature of classroom encounters that occur in a language other than their first (Brevik et al., 2016). Additionally, the honoring and integration of first language, bilingualism, or multilingualism offers psychological and social benefits for students and families (Goldenberg et al., 2013). Research conducted by Gorlewski (2012) indicates that if children's first experiences with content is in their first language, and that language differs from the language of instruction, then it is most appropriate for students to write and discuss this content in their first language. As students are developing their understanding of academic content knowledge and the expressive vocabulary to expand upon their thoughts, the use of a first language can help express full understanding. For example, if a student has learned a math concept in their first language, they do not need to relearn the concept; instead, it is needed for the student to learn the academic vocabulary in the language of instruction (August, 2018). This understanding grounds practitioners in the mindset that although a child may not be able to verbally articulate clearly in the language of instruction, it does not mean that the concept or content is not understood. Rather, students are developing their disciplinary linguistic knowledge (DLK) (Turkan, 2016). This knowledge transfers to students using AAC devices to communicate. The process of choosing an appropriate AAC tool requires the understanding that any tool being introduced and implemented is a form of language and consists of rules that need to be taught and nurtured just like any other language (Kempka Wagner, 2018). Holding that working knowledge at the front of the mind, if an AAC user has a first language (L1) and a separate language of instruction, or second language (L2), this means the AAC device becomes the third language (L3) (Kempka Wagner, 2018). An early childhood-aged student is already striving to effectively communicate clearly in their L1 and is introduced to a language of instruction (LOI) that is different from their L1, the process of developing a social and academic vocabulary of the L2 begins (Booth, 2020). Add in the L3 of AAC, and early childhood students are asked to mentally process three language systems; a heavy cognitive load.

Thus, the app to support learners must be an image based AAC system, provide multiple languages of images to support bilingual families and practitioners, and ideally be able to utilize uploads of user created images. If an app allows for the submission and integration of user created and uploaded images, the library of images not only grows with the learner's content knowledge, but with L1's cultural knowledge base, and L2 LOI development. An image-based AAC app that has the ability of uploading user content allows for the elimination of abandonment as a barrier to implementation.

Reflecting on the initial system, Ms. Shannon realized that the images were of Caucasian children with labels in English (the student's L2), while her students spoke Spanish, Malayalam, and Tegulu in their variety of L1s. Thus, those images were not culturally or linguistically relevant to the students. In addition, Ms. Shannon did not realize that using AAC (low-tech or high-tech) was like teaching an entirely new language to the students (L3). Finally, Ms. Shannon wondered if offering an AAC option that could support other languages would result in the increased use of the device at home. The continuity of use would enhance her students' experiences.

ALIGNED LEARNING

With the increasing pressure in the United States to meet the needs of culturally, linguistically, and developmentally diverse learners (Moore et al., 2018), the Council for Exceptional Children (CEC), a national non-profit, was created to support students with educational differences and exceptionalities. The CEC has a specified division, the Division of Early Childhood (DEC) that promotes best practices for early childhood aged students, birth to five years of age. The DEC Recommended Practices (RPs), released in 2014, have correlating non-disability specific recommended practices that the CEC and DEC have compiled based on the National Association for the Education of Young Children's (NAEYC) position statements, in addition to research, and evidence based interventions. Each recommended practice is observable and promotes learning in all environments.

In consideration of students who are culturally and linguistically diverse, the DEC RP's section on family offers guidance:

Practitioners provide the family of a young child who has or is at risk for developmental delay/disability, and who is a dual language learner, with information about the benefits of learning in multiple languages for the child's growth and development. (Division for Early Childhood, 2014)

Similarly, the researchers in the field of AAC encourage educators to consider "how AAC devices are utilized and perceived by individuals from culturally and linguistically diverse (CLD) backgrounds and their families." (Kulkarni & Parmar, 2017, p. 170). This consideration invites practitioners, educators, and families to critique image based communication programs and apps with an even more scrutinous lens: Is individual language and culture incorporated into apps?

DIRECTIONS FOR FUTURE EXAMINATION

The student's family is one of the foundational elements of choosing an AAC tool (James et al., 2018). A language-related dilemma for families is the uncertainty over whether using the L1, or using L1 and L2 interchangeably at home, might overwhelm the child. Many parents expressed the feeling of "being a lonely fighter,' (Pickl, 2011) in this realm because of any stigma about bilingualism or being an English language learner. In a study done by Kulkarnia and Palmer (2017), family members supporting a learner using AAC shared the challenges of being bilingual and using AAC devices. The study found that AAC professionals predominantly spoke English and users found it to be difficult to find Spanish-speaking support with the tool.

Pickl's (2011) study showcases why caregivers and family should be instrumental in every step of the decision process including assessment and developing goals (Booth, 2020). When considering apps, inquiring about the family's linguistic needs will ensure an app's accessibility and support while everyone on the learner's decision making team learns AAC as an L3. Although caregivers and parents may speak the same L1 and L2 of a student, the goal is full and functional communication. If a parent identifies as bilingual, it means they have the capability to communicate in either of their languages with relative ease; students and families deserve that same option using AAC AT. This essential option is especially true when developing the understanding of an app based AAC tool as an L3. The goal of providing a student with an AAC tool is to allow ease of communication, not provide ease of communication in only the language of instruction. Table 1 offers recommendations of apps that support multilingual learners (Waxenfelter et al., 2013).

After testing a few apps that fit the unique cultural and language needs of her learners, Ms. Shannon shared the implementation data with the education team and the parents. As a result, the best option was chosen to support learners in the classroom and incorporate home language into communications.

Table 3. Bilingual image based communication apps

App Name	Setting for Use	Languages	User Upload Capability	System Requirements	Cost
LessonPix	Functional Communication	Any language available through Google Translate	Yes	Website based	$36/year
SmallTalk Intensive Care	Medical	English	No	iPhone, iPad, iPod Touch. Requires iOS 3.0 or later	Free
Phrase Board	Medical	French, Spanish, German, Italian, Arabic and Swedish versions available through an in-app purchase	Partially - there is a free hand drawing feature	iPad. Requires iOS 3.2 or later	$2.99
Sign4Me	Functional Communication	Signed English, ASL, and English	Partially - users can type the word they need finger spelled and the app animates this word	iPhone, iPod Touch, iPad. Requires iOS 3.0 or later	$9.99
TalkForMe	Functional Communication	More than 30 languages	Yes - the app allows the user add an unlimited number of pictures and phrases, sort them into relevant groups, and then play the phrase aloud	Android, iPhone, iPod Touch, iPad. Requires iOS 3.2 or later	$5.99
Yes/No Bilingual	Functional Communication	English/Spanish	No	iPhone, iPod Touch, iPad. Requires iOS 3.1.3 or later	$1.99
TapSpeak Choice	Functional Communication	Arabic, Flemish (Belgian Dutch), Brazilian, British English, French Canadian, Czech, Danish, Dutch, Finnish, French, German, Greek, Italian, Norwegian, Polish, Portuguese, Russian, Spanish, Swedish, Turkish, US English, US Spanish	Yes - users can upload images from their photo library and add text	iPad	$149.00
My Talk	Social Communication	Arabic, Catalan, Chinese Mandarin, Czech, Danish, Dutch (B), Dutch (NL), English (Australia), English (India), English (UK), English, Finnish, French, French (Canadian), German, Greek, Italian, Japanese, Korean, Norwegian, Polish, Portuguese, Portuguese (Brazil), Russian: Alyona (F), Spanish, Spanish (North America), Swedish, Swedish (Finland), Turkish	Yes - Users can upload images straight from the Internet to personalize the phrases that they want to speak	iPhone, iPod Touch, iPad. Requires iOS 3.2 or later	$99.99, but with a free 30-day trial period. Additional languages for $39.99
Pictello	Social Communication	English, Dutch, French, German, Spanish, Turkish	Yes - all images must come from the device, so this app requires pre-planning	iPhone, iPad, iPod touch, iOS 5.1 or higher	$14.99

Although Table 3 focuses mainly on image-based AAC apps, low-tech tools are still available and creatable. It is suggested that if working with a bilingual client, clinicians can provide multiple methods for communication; either by creating a physical low-tech communication board with Spanish and English labeled images (Booth, 2020), or by using a bilingual app (Table 1; Waxenfelter et al., 2013). As little research exists around whether or not a particular image based communication system, or symbol set, is culturally relevant across interventions outside the dominant culture, educators, practitioners, and caregivers are advised to utilize a tool that will allow for all languages of the individual and their family to be represented (Booth, 2020).

CONCLUSION

For culturally, linguistically, and cognitively diverse (CLCD) learners, the goal is access and equity. As an educator rooted in social constructivism, the author sees the value in having Table 1 and Table 2 because it provides multiple lenses of how the offering of these tools may be interpreted. The financial investment, as well as each theme highlighted in the Early Childhood Education standards for professionals are valuable elements for consideration. However, future qualitative research could focus on which of these areas is most important to educators in designing a classroom that promotes expression of comprehension, engagement, and peer interaction. In terms of specific facilitation tools (Peardeck, Nearpod, etc.) future qualitative and quantitative research focused on student perceptions of educational success, ease of communication, and accessibility would benefit the field of digital learning.

Consulting Table 3, of the top ten more common L1 spoken by students in the United States Spanish, Arabic, Portuguese, Russian, Chinese (Mandarin) are represented in the realm of AAC apps. What exists to support students whose L1 is Vietnamese, Somali, Haitian, Hmong, or any language not showcased in the top ten? Suggestion for future innovation lies in creating tools that allow for L1 and L2 images to be uploaded into AAC programs and providing extensive language translation functions. Suggestion for future research would be around how student self-perception in social or academic settings is connected to using an app that incorporates both L1 and L2. After all, the end goal is communication, not enculturation.

REFERENCES

Ainscow, M., Booth, T., & Dyson, A. (2006). *Improving schools, developing inclusion?* Routledge., doi:10.4324/9780203967157

Allen, I. E., & Seaman, J. (2013). *Changing Course: Ten Years of Tracking Online Education in the United States.* Sloan Consortium. https://search.ebscohost.com/login.aspx?direct=true&AuthType=ip,shib&db=eric&AN=ED541571&site=ehost-live&scope=site&authtype=ip,shib&custid=s3555202

Annamma, S., & Morrison, D. (2018). DisCrit Classroom Ecology: Using praxis to dismantle dysfunctional education ecologies. *Teaching and Teacher Education, 73,* 70–80. doi:10.1016/j.tate.2018.03.008

Annamma, S. A., Connor, D., & Ferri, B. (2013). Dis/ability critical race studies (DisCrit): Theorizing at the intersections of race and dis/ability. *Race, Ethnicity and Education, 16*(1), 1–31. doi:10.1080/13 613324.2012.730511

Arbaugh, F., Ball, D. L., Grossman, P., Heller, D. E., & Monk, D. (2015). Deans' Corner: Views on the state of teacher education in 2015. *Journal of Teacher Education, 66*(5), 435–445. doi:10.1177/0022487115602314

Archambault, L. (2011). The practitioner's perspective on teacher education: Preparing for the K-12 online classroom. *Journal of Technology and Teacher Education, 19*(1), 73–91.

August, D. (2018). Educating English language learners: A review of the latest research. *American Educator, 42*(3), 4–9.

August, D. (n.d.). *A Review of the Latest Research Educating ELLs*. Academic Press.

Baffoe, J. (2020). Subini Ancy Annamma: The pedagogy of pathologization: Dis/abled girls of color in the school-prison nexus. *Journal of Youth and Adolescence, 49*(2), 565–568. doi:10.100710964-019-01169-x

Boonpleng, W., Park, C., Gallo, A., Corte, C., McCreary, L., & Bergren, M. (2013). Ecological Influences of Early Childhood Obesity: A Multilevel Analysis. *Western Journal of Nursing Research, 35*(6), 742–759. doi:10.1177/0193945913480275 PMID:23493675

Booth, T. (2020, January 29). *Bilingual Augmentative and Alternative Communication (AAC) Users*. Retrieved August 03, 2020, from https://hespinterpretation.com/2019/10/07/bilingual-augmentative-and-alternative-communication-aac-users/comment-page-1/

Branscombe, N. A., Castle, K., Surbeck, E., & Burcham, J. G. (2013). *Early Childhood Curriculum: A Constructivist Perspective* (2nd ed.). Routledge., doi:10.4324/9780203808849

Brevik, L. M., Olsen, R. V., & Hellekjær, G. O. (2016). The complexity of second language reading: Investigating the L1-L2 relationship. *Reading in a Foreign Language, 28*(2), 161–182.

Cureton, A., & Hill, T. (2018). Disability in Practice: Attitudes, Policies, and Relationships. In *Disability in Practice*. Oxford University Press. doi:10.1093/oso/9780198812876.001.0001

Dawley, L. K., Rice, E. D. G. & Hinck. (2010). *The Status of Professional Development and Unique Needs of K-12 Online Teachers November, 2010*. Academic Press.

DEC Recommended Practices. (2015). DEC Recommended Practices. *Young Exceptional Children, 18*(3), 54–54. doi:10.1177/1096250615605690

Department of Education (ED), O. for C. R. (OCR) & Office of Special Education and Rehabilitative Services, (ED). (2020b). *Supplemental Fact Sheet: Addressing the Risk of COVID-19 in Preschool, Elementary and Secondary Schools While Serving Children with Disabilities* (Office for Civil Rights, US Department of Education). Office for Civil Rights, US Department of Education.

Digital, R., Rowan, W., Works, D. & Elder, B. (2020). *Decolonizing inclusive education: A collection of practical inclusive CDS-and DisCrit-informed teaching practices implemented in the global South* (Vol. 7). Academic Press.

Edyburn, D. L. (2013). Critical issues in advancing the special education technology evidence base. *Exceptional Children, 80*(1), 7–24. doi:10.1177/001440291308000107

Elaine, Amanda, Burcham, Gunnels, Castle, & Surbeck. (2013). The Aims of Constructivist Curriculum. Routledge.

Elder, B. C., & Migliarini, V. (2020). Decolonizing inclusive education: A collection of practical inclusive CDS and DisCrit-informed teaching practices implemented in the global South. *Disability and the Global South, 7*(1), 1852–1872.

Fact Sheet: Impact of COVID-19 on Assessments and Accountability under the Elementary and Secondary Education Act. (2020). Academic Press.

Gablasova, D. (2014). Issues in the assessment of bilingually educated students: Expressing subject knowledge through L1 and L2. *Language Learning Journal, 42*(2), 151–164. doi:10.1080/09571736.2014.891396

Goldenberg, C., Hicks, J., & Lit, I. (2013). Dual language learners: Effective instruction in early childhood. *American Educator, 37*(2), 26–29.

Gorlewski, J., Meyer, T., Young, M., & Lieberstein-Solera, F. (2012). Research for the classroom: Lost in translation: Assessing writing of English language learners. *English Journal, 101*(5), 93–96.

Graziano, K. J., & Feher, L. (2016). A dual placement approach to online student teaching. *Contemporary Issues in Technology & Teacher Education, 16*(4), 495–513.

Gregg, K. (2011). A document analysis of the National Association for the Education of Young Children's Developmentally Appropriate Practice Position Statement: What does it tell us about supporting children with disabilities? *Contemporary Issues in Early Childhood, 12*(2), 175–186. doi:10.2304/ciec.2011.12.2.175

Hansel, L. (n.d.). Embracing anti-bias education. *YC Young Children, 5*(4–5).

Impact of COVID-19 on assessments and accountability under the Elementary and Secondary Education Act. (2020). Department of Education.

Kempka-Wagner, D. (2018). Building Augmentative Communication Skills in Homes Where English and Spanish Are Spoken: Perspectives of an Evaluator/Interventionist. *Perspectives of the ASHA Special Interest Groups, 3*(12), 172–185. doi:10.1044/persp3.sig12.172

Kulkarni, S., & Parmar, J. (2017). Culturally and linguistically diverse student and family perspectives of AAC. *Augmentative and Alternative Communication, 33*(3), 170–180. https://doi.org/10.1080/07434618.2017.1346706

Meyer, T., Young, M., & Lieberstein-Solera, F. (2012). *Research for the Classroom: Lost in Translation--Assessing Writing of English Language Learners. 101*(5), 93–96. https://search.ebscohost.com/login.aspx?direct=true&AuthType=ip,shib&db=eric&AN=EJ998954&site=ehost-live&scope=site&authtype=ip,shib&custid=s3555202 http://www.ncte.org/journals/ej/issues/v101-5

Moore, E. J. (2018). Voices From the Field: Implementing and Scaling-Up Universal Design for Learning in Teacher Preparation Programs. *Journal of Special Education Technology, 33*(1), 40–53.

National Association for the Education of Y. C. (2009). Developmentally Appropriate Practice in Early Childhood Programs Serving Children from Birth through *Age 8*. Author.

Odowd, E. (2010). The development of linguistic complexity: A functional continuum. *Language Teaching, 45*(3), 329–346. doi:10.10170261444810000510

Peters, L. L., Robledo, R. F., Bult, C. J., Churchill, G. A., Paigen, B. J., & Svenson, K. L. (2007). The mouse as a model for human biology: A resource guide for complex trait analysis. *Nature Reviews. Genetics, 8*(1), 58–69. https://doi.org/10.1038/nrg2025

Pickl, G. (2011). Communication intervention in children with severe disabilities and multilingual backgrounds: Perceptions of pedagogues and parents. *Augmentative and Alternative Communication, 27*, 229–244. doi:10.3109/07434618.2011.630021

Pricing. (n.d.). Retrieved July 14, 2020, from https://www.goosechase.com/edu/pricing/

Ramirez-Chase, M. (2018, March 6). *Earlywood Educational Services / Homepage*. Retrieved August 03, 2020, from https://www.earlywood.org/site/default.aspx?PageType=3

Rice, K., & Dawley, L. (2007). *Going virtual! The status of professional development for K–12 online teachers*. Retrieved from https://edtech.boisestate.edu/goingvirtual/goingvirtual.htm

Scott, I. (2020). Education during COVID-19: Pivots and consequences. *The Clinical Teacher, 17*(4), 443–444. https://doi.org/10.1111/tct.13225

Singal, N., & Muthukrishna, N. (2014). Introduction: Education, childhood and disability in countries of the South: Repositioning the debates. *Childhood, 21*(3), 293–307.

Skylar, A. A., Fitzpatrick, M. & Brown, M. R. (2008). *Assistive Technology Associate Editor's Column Assistive Technology Access and Use: Considerations for Culturally and Linguistically Diverse Students and Their Families* (Vol. 23). Academic Press.

Southern Regional Education Board (SREB). (2009). *Guidelines of professional development for online teachers*. Retrieved from https://www.sreb.org/sites/main/files/file-attachments/09t01_guide_profdev_online_teach.pdf

Svenson, K. L., Churchill, G. A., Peters, L. L., Bult, C. J., Paigen, B. J., & Robledo, R. F. (2007). *The mouse as a model for human biology: a resource guide for complex trait analysis*. doi:10.1038/nrg2025

Teaching Tolerance Anti-Bias Framework. (n.d.). Retrieved July 14, 2020, from https://www.tolerance.org/sites/default/files/general/TT%20anti%20bias%20framework%20pamphlet_final.pdf

Thompson, S. D., & Raisor, J. M. (2013, May). *Meeting the sensory needs of young children*. Retrieved February 18, 2017, from https://www.naeyc.org/yc/files/yc/file/201305/Meeting_Sensory_Needs_Thompson_0513.pdf

Turkan, S. (2016). In-service teachers' reasoning about scenarios of teaching mathematics to English language learners. *The Mathematics Enthusiast, 13*(1), 130–148.

United States Department of Education, Office for Civil Rights. (2020). *Addressing the risk of COVID-19 in preschool, elementary and secondary schools while serving children with disabilities.* Author.

United States Department of Education, Office of Elementary and Secondary Education. (2020a). *Addressing the risk of COVID-19 while serving migratory children.* Author.

United States Department of Education, Office of Elementary and Secondary Education. (2020b) *Providing services to English learners during the COVID-19 outbreak.* Author.

Valencia, R. R. (1997). Conceptualizing the notion of deficit thinking. In R. R. Valencia (Ed.), *The evolution of deficit thinking: Educational thought and practice* (pp. 113–131). Routledge Falmer.

Virginia Department of Education (VDOE). (2020). *School Reopening Frequently Asked Questions – Updated August 10, 2020.* Retrieved August 12, 2020, from https://www.doe.virginia.gov/support/health_medical/office/covid-19-faq-reopening.shtml

Vue, G., Hall, T. E., Robinson, K., Ganley, P., Elizalde, E., & Graham, S. (2015). Informing understanding of young students' writing challenges and opportunities. *Learning Disability Quarterly, 39*(2), 83–94. doi:10.1177/0731948715604571

Waxenfelter, A., Watson, C., & Harry, J. (2013). *Bilingual AAC Apps.* https://www.pdx.edu/multicultural-topics-communication-sciences-disorders/bilingual-aac-apps

Weng, P.-L. (2015). Developing an app evaluation rubric for practitioners in special education. *Journal of Special Education Technology, 30*(1), 43–58.

WIDA Screener. (n.d.). Retrieved from https://wida.wisc.edu/assess/screener

Wilkens, C., Eckdahl, K., Morone, M., Cook, V., Giblin, T., & Coon, J. (2014). Communication, community, and disconnection: Pre-Service teachers in virtual school field experiences. *Journal of Educational Technology Systems, 43*(2), 143–157. https://doi.org/10.2190/ET.43.2.c

Wong, H. K., & Wong, R. T. (2009). *The first days of school: how to be an effective teacher.* Harry K. Wong Publications. Print

Yarmosky, A. (n.d.). *Governor Northam Orders Statewide Closure of Certain Non-Essential Businesses, K-12 Schools.* Retrieved August 12, 2020, from https://www.governor.virginia.gov/newsroom/all-releases/2020/march/headline-855292-en.html

Yilmaz, K. (2008). Constructivism: Its theoretical underpinnings, variations, and implications for classroom instruction. *Educational Horizons, 86*(3), 161–172.

Chapter 5
Pedagogical Challenges During COVID:
Opportunities for Transformative Shifts

Ellen B. Meier
Teachers College, Columbia University, USA

Caron Mineo
Teachers College, Columbia University, USA

ABSTRACT

Educators could not have predicted the degree of disruption that COVID-19 could cause until schools closed and forced teachers to move to online teaching. This chapter describes the use of a research-based model, Innovating Instruction, to support teachers in their transition to remote learning. Grounded in a concern for greater equity and social justice for all students, the model prepares teachers to design inquiry-based, culturally relevant projects. The development of the model is based on a critique that technology has largely failed to impact pedagogical change because of a limited sense of the scope of the change needed. Instructional Innovation brings together key aspects of a systems change effort, thus contributing to an emerging educational theory for the catalytic use of technology to promote pedagogical practices that are culturally responsive, rigorous, and engaging.

INTRODUCTION

The COVID-19 virus touched off a pandemic more pervasive and deadly than any plague in modern history. It filled the hospitals and mortuaries, separated families, and ushered in a new era of mask-wearing and social distancing. A major consequence of this global disaster has been its long-lasting disruptive impact on schools.

The shift to online teaching has been an enormous challenge for teachers and administrators alike. While implementing remote learning, teachers have had to establish relationships with students they see only in little boxes on screens. Teachers have had to scramble to transfer their instructional material to

DOI: 10.4018/978-1-7998-7222-1.ch005

online settings while anxiously measuring student progress against pacing calendars which, even when adjusted to account for the pandemic, reflect student progress that falls short of what might otherwise be expected (Kamenetz, 2020).

The disruption was even more severe for teachers and students in underserved urban areas. School district officials scoured the schools to provide tens of thousands of devices for students and pressed internet providers to secure broadband access for students who had none (Zimmerman & Gould, 2020). While principals struggled to support their teachers and locate students, teachers struggled to find new ways of reaching students and keeping them engaged.

Teachers often had little to go on to guide them to make the transition to online learning, except perhaps a collection of vague remote-learning "techniques." These superficial online learning strategies, often introduced without a pedagogical rationale or design support, left teachers with little choice but to begin putting existing materials online, unable to take advantage of the creative potential of the tools because, by and large, they were essentially unprepared to use the tools or design online learning environments (Adams, 2020).

Given the seriousness of the situation, the urgency for linking theory and practice has never been greater. Educators at every level are looking for theory-based guidance for deepening online teacher practice during COVID. The *Innovating Instruction* model uses a configuration of theoretical frameworks to prepare teachers to use inquiry-based design practices and technology tools for engaging students in knowledge-building practices.

The model was designed and implemented over a period of several years by a research and development center at Teachers College, Columbia University, the Center for Technology and School Change, through design-based research and later, mixed methods research The model features close collaboration between the Center and the administrators at the school to develop shared meaning around the need for inquiry learning, framed by a project-based approach and the thoughtful use of technology. The Center facilitators initiate collaboration with teachers. They introduce teachers to the pedagogical reasoning and the foundational skills needed to design inquiry-based projects. And they work with them through the co-design process to ensure that the projects meet the particular cultural and academic interests and needs of their students, in the context of their school and community. Work with the teachers and administrators continues through the implementation of the projects in the classroom, including a reflection on the overall process.

This chapter describes the foundational rationale behind the *Innovating Instruction* approach, which is designed to be a more concrete and comprehensive model for supporting teachers in learning to use technology tools to make the pedagogical shifts associated with twenty-first century learning. The educational field now knows more about the pedagogical practices that embody advancements in the learning sciences (Darling-Hammond et al., 2020; Bransford et al., 2000; National Academies of Sciences, Engineering, and Medicine, 2018). Building on the growing understanding of how children learn, in the context of the forced dependence on technology during the pandemic, this chapter also describes the opportunity to meet the needs of teachers by aligning their technology challenges with new teaching and learning practices.

BACKGROUND

The mission of *Innovating Instruction* is to provide teachers with the pedagogical reasoning and design skills to support a shift in their instructional practices away from didactic practices toward inquiry learning with the goal of deepening student understanding. Technology is used as a catalyst for this transition. The Center has recently adapted this model for both online professional development, and for online K-12 teaching. Teachers learn to design inquiry-oriented projects, using the affordances of technology to facilitate student engagement and understanding.

A backward design process provides teachers with concrete steps they can take to create an environment in which students explore questions and solve problems together, while considering the needs of the whole child (Darling-Hammond et al., 2020). As researchers continue to learn about pedagogical practices that best support this kind of classroom learning, educators are still learning how best to prepare teachers to make changes that embrace these advancements.

The pandemic, as tragic as it has been, has forced teacher involvement with technology tools that, in many cases, they might have avoided earlier. It is clear that the use of technology, by itself, does not bring about teacher shifts in pedagogy (Cuban, 2013; Meier, 2020). Teachers also need an introduction to design practices to shift the teaching and learning paradigm from transmission of information to inquiry practices, with a focus on developing student understanding. If teachers are not introduced to pedagogical changes as they begin to use technology more extensively, it is likely that teachers will try to appropriate the technology for "business as usual" teaching (Blundell et al., 2020; Meier, 2015). The COVID-19 crisis can be seen as a disaster-driven opportunity to help teachers learn to use technology in service of student understanding. The challenge is to identify and introduce successful models for helping teachers with these transitions and scale up the models to reach larger numbers of educators.

The development of the framework described in this chapter is fundamentally motivated by a concern for greater equity and social justice for all students, particularly marginalized students. Ladson-Billings (2014), Paris (2012), and others challenge the institutionalized deficit-thinking paradigm that often surrounds students in underserved schools. Teachers need the design skills and the pedagogical thinking to engage students in rigorous standards-based projects, designed around learners' interests and needs. Students need the opportunity to explore topics, and actively engage in inquiry learning and problem-solving. Agency is built for both teachers and students through this empowering process.

During the pandemic, when underserved schools had the immediate challenge of equipping students, and ensuring access to the internet, administrative support was needed to help teachers quickly become more fluent with technology. The Center provided synchronous, online professional development that essentially embedded technology training for online instruction with the rapid co-development of projects that teachers could use immediately to engage students in meaningful online learning experiences.

A REVIEW OF THE LITERATURE

Theoretical frameworks are often a critical step in developing a comprehensive theory for a field (Benbunan-Fich et al., 2005, p. 18). The broader goal of *Innovating Instruction* is to contribute to an emerging educational theory for technology integration. Such a theory would embrace a systems perspective to embrace the inter-relatedness of different aspects of the major educational shift needed to move instructional practice to more student-centered, inquiry-based learning with technology. Educational efforts to date have been too fragmented, too limited, and lack the holistic vision needed to realize the potential for using technology wisely.

The frameworks used in the *Innovating Instruction* model address key aspects of a system change effort for school improvement. The five frameworks include: learning theories to ground the use of technology, curriculum design approaches to guide teacher interactions with students, professional development theories to support appropriate engagement with teachers and building leaders, school change theories to guide overall systemic shifts, and the moral imperative that drives the overall shift to student-centered learning: equity and social justice. The literatures that relate to each of the frameworks and contribute to the development of this comprehensive approach are briefly summarized below.

Learning Theories and Technology

Scientific knowledge about the learning process is growing as the learning sciences contribute to the evolving understanding of what it is to "educate" (Bransford et al., 2000; Darling-Hammond et al., 2020; National Academies of Sciences, Engineering, and Medicine, 2018; Sawyer, 2014). The learning sciences capture a growing consensus around the key elements for learning and emphasize the transition to "deep learning" that can result when there is a movement away from memorizing, for instance, to a practice of having students "look for patterns and underlying principles" (Sawyer, 2014, p. 5).

Key elements of the learning process cited by Bransford et al. (2000), include the need to understand students' preconceptions, the need to build students' conceptual knowledge in ways they can retrieve and apply that knowledge, and the need for students to reflect on their learning and take ownership of it (pp. 14-18).

The learning sciences provide general guidance for learning that can transcend learning modalities (Meier, 2018). For instance, providing opportunities for students to reflect on their learning may help them become more self-directed and deepen the learning environment for them (Bransford et al., 2000). This can happen in many different ways though: through video reflections, podcasts, written reflections, or even art forms such as drawings or dance. Darling-Hammond et al.'s (2020) list of "productive instructional strategies" provides more specificity:

Meaningful work that builds on students' prior knowledge and experiences and actively engages them in rich, engaging tasks that help them achieve conceptual understanding and transferable knowledge and skills; inquiry as a major learning strategy, thoughtfully interwoven with explicit instruction and well-scaffolded opportunities to practice and apply learning; well-designed collaborative learning opportunities that encourage students to question, explain, and elaborate their thoughts and co-construct solutions; ongoing diagnostic assessments and opportunities to receive timely and helpful feedback, develop and exhibit competence, and revise work to improve; and opportunities to develop metacognitive skills through planning and management of complex tasks, self- and peer-assessment, and reflection on learning. (p. 100)

Inquiry is a powerful learning strategy and project-based learning offers a way to operationalize inquiry-oriented learning opportunities for students. Inquiry learning is premised on the idea that learning is basically driven by questions (Edelson et al., 1999); project-based learning typically starts with an essential or a driving question, and allows students to "learn by doing, apply ideas, and to solve problems" (Krajcik & Shin, 2014, p. 275). Project-based learning also provides students with the opportunity to build knowledge, both online and offline (National Academies of Sciences, Engineering, and Medicine, 2018) in ways that are relevant to the student. "We saw that many kinds of learning are promoted when the learner engages actively rather than passively, by developing her own models, for example [...]. We saw that learning is predicated on learners' understanding and adopting the learning goal" (National Academies of Sciences, Engineering, and Medicine, 2018, p. 67).

Whether explicitly recognized or not, learning theories often implicitly guide the development and use of technology. For instance, Dede (2008), outlines three learning theories and links specific technologies with the different theories (e.g., behaviorism is linked with drill and practice software). As early as 2005, Wenglinsky identified the "wise" use of technology with constructivism (p. 6).

Scardamalia and Bereiter (2014) position students as "knowledge-builders" for society—not just their classroom—and use technology extensively to connect students to each other and to experts to develop that knowledge. Some feel that Scardamalia and Bereiter have created another learning theory for this century (Harasim, 2012). Harasim (2012) also advances a related concept, the Online Collaborative Learning theory, or OCL, to capture this learning, explaining:

OCL theory provides a model of learning in which students are encouraged and supported to work together to create knowledge to invent, to explore ways to innovate, and by so doing, to seek the conceptual knowledge needed to solve problems rather than recite what they think is the right answer. (p. 90)

Others, however, such as Downes (2004) and Siemens (2005), argue that a totally new learning theory is needed to take advantage of the affordances offered by the technology. They use the term "connectivism" to describe the collective development of knowledge through online communication. Emerging learning theories will undoubtedly continue to proliferate with the growth of global technology networks.

The assumption that learning theories can be easily linked to technology use is not universally accepted. Lowyck (2014) contends that, "The proposition that a science of learning is fundamental to educational technology has been broadly accepted, but it is unclear how bridging both fields can be realized" (p. 12). She provides multiple examples of various definitions of constructivist theories, and concludes that it is the very "lack of precision in interpretations of constructivism, [...] a lack of precision in defining principles for instructional interventions [that] make new prescriptions highly probabilistic" (p. 14). Importantly, she identifies instructional design as a transition science that can link the two fields.

Design Approaches

Curriculum design processes for teachers have been described and operationalized in numerous ways. Early in the development of *Innovating Instruction*, the decision was made to use a "backward design" approach with teachers because of its familiarity, and its focus on student understanding. In particular, Wiggins and McTighe (2005) describe a conceptual framework that provides "a way to design or redesign *any* curriculum to make student understanding (and desired results generally) more likely" (p. 7), and this approach is typically used by the Center. Although different blueprints are used in various renditions of backward design, in a typical "backward design" process, teachers would: 1) identify the desired student understandings, 2) determine how students can demonstrate these understandings, and 3) design the project-based learning that will support the development of the understanding (Larmer et al., 2015; Wiggins & McTighe, 2005).

Backward design processes have become the mainstay for project-based learning because of the clear focus on identifying *understanding* as the goal of the learning process.

Translation of best practices in learning and assessment to effective curriculum design is a major barrier in successful teaching. Creative approaches must be used to embed opportunities for inquiry, innovative problem solving, and critical thinking into a backbone of deep discipline knowledge. (Roth, 2007, p. 95)

Wiggins and McTighe (2005) emphasize the need to identify the understanding—not as a series of small objectives, or busy work activities, but as a deep assimilation of core content knowledge.

In the work of the Center, the *Understanding by Design* framework (Wiggins & McTighe, 2005) is familiar to many teachers (it is often introduced in pre-service teacher classes), but few have had the support to actually work with other teachers and professional developers to design and implement original projects, based on the understandings identified in the common core standards. The process of "co-designing" with Center facilitators and fellow teachers is important because of the support teachers give each other and the support the facilitators give teachers when developing exciting and meaningful projects that position students as creators and knowledge builders.

Importantly, the learning sciences tell us that students learn more effectively when "they can connect what happens in school to their cultural contexts and experiences, when their teachers are responsive to their strengths and needs, and when their environment is 'identity safe' (Steele & Cohn-Vargas, 2013), reinforcing their value and belonging" (Darling-Hammond et al., 2020, p. 102).

Teachers can be seen as core stakeholders in curriculum innovation and in the complex process of curriculum design because, as Fullan (1991) has stated, in the end, "educational change depends on what teachers do and think— it's as simple and complex as that" (p. 117). Because teachers are key, providing them with a means of developing their own design practice is critical. Professional development is the primary means of supporting teachers in this process (Pieters et al., 2019).

Professional Development

An important foundation for the *Innovating Instruction* model is Cochran-Smith and Lytle's (2009) *Inquiry as Stance*, which they define as a grounded theory of action that places practitioners and practitioner knowledge as central in all school improvement efforts designed to "...transform teaching, learning, leading, and schools for democratic purposes and social justice goals" (p. 119). Recognizing the crucial role of practitioner knowledge in this way establishes an inquiry perspective as the core basis of the work.

Fundamental to the notion of inquiry as stance is the idea that educational practice is not simply instrumental in the sense of figuring out how to get things done, but also and more importantly, it is social and political in the sense of deliberating about what to get done, why to get it done, who decides and whose interests are served. (Cochran-Smith & Lytle, 2009, p 121)

Framing the work with teachers as a dialogue also serves to balance the power dynamics between outside "experts" (in this case, university facilitators) and teachers and creates a culture of respect and mutuality that advances communication and collaboration. The goal becomes working together from the practitioner's perspective to address student strengths, interests, and needs.

The professional development sessions should engage teachers as adult learners and professionals in a knowledge-building process. Particular frameworks that have helped shape the *Innovating Instruction* model including Borko's (2004) emphasis on situating the professional development in the life of individual teachers, Ertmer's (1999) work on the first and second barriers for technology integration, and Guskey's (2000) research on teacher change. Guskey explains that there is often a rush to measure student impact rather than focusing on teacher change and their response to the ideas related to the innovation. He contends that professional developers must first understand the response of teachers to the sessions: what did they take away and how are they acting on this new knowledge? Center facilitators maintain the inquiry stance with teachers as a cultural norm for the relationship.

Individual teachers are obviously essential to the shift being described, but teachers work within a particular school organization, and thus it is essential for professional developers to acknowledge the school structure and the organizational theories that could be leveraged to build a more comprehensive foundational theory for school change.

School Change Theories and Leadership

Michael Fullan has written extensively on school change and leadership. His work serves as an important guide for understanding the processes that support immediate and long-term change efforts, including school technology integration efforts (Fullan, 2012). His seminal work, *The New Meaning of Educational Change*, emphasizes the important role teachers play in making change (Fullan, 2015).

While teachers' direct work with students remains the focus of the change effort, teachers are also part of a particular school and community. Leaders of a given intervention must be responsive to the unique needs of each teacher and each school (Borko, 2004). Without situating the work in the lives of each unique group of teachers, there is the risk of using the limited "one size fits all" model, which fails to understand the nuances of their environment. Without an appreciation for the context, it is difficult for professional developers to understand the true needs of the teacher and succeed in helping teachers adopt new materials (e.g., technology), adopt new approaches to instruction, and change their beliefs about teaching practices (Fullan, 2015).

School change theories must take leadership issues into account. The success of a given intervention is heavily dependent on the support teachers receive for engaging with the intervention and the support they receive for following through and implementing changes in their classroom. School leaders thus play a pivotal role in helping to develop a shared vision; even if only a subset of teachers is initially involved, administrative support for the intervention is critical. The Wallace Foundation recently completed a study on the impact of principals and identified four key "drivers" of effective principals: interacting with teachers around instructional practice; creating a positive school climate focused on trust; developing and supporting communities of practice; strategic use of resource allocation (Grissom et al., 2021, p. xv). These four factors can be encouraged and emphasized by those leading the interventions.

In larger interventions, such as *Innovating Instruction*, successful implementation results in a shift in the school culture, as teachers begin evolving their pedagogical practices, the culture becomes more collaborative, and the learning more relevant to the specific interests and needs of the students. To accomplish this shift, ideally, principals establish effective learning communities so that the whole school can become a "learning organization" (Senge, 2006).

All our insights are connected to this one fact—they stem from reflective action. This accounts for the related but counterintuitive findings: behaviors and emotions change before beliefs—we need to act in a new way before we get insights and feelings related to new beliefs. (Fullan, 2015, p. 41)

In a holistic review of what is needed to lead change efforts, Fullan (2007) lists the importance of understanding the change process, along with the importance of building relationships, the need to create and share knowledge, bring coherence to the change process, and champion a moral purpose. Leading with moral purpose—the desire for equity, social justice, and the well-being of *all* students—brings commitment, both internal and external (Fullan, 2007). With commitment, comes motivation and interest in moving towards change.

Equity: Technology Integration and the Opportunity Divide

At the heart of this work is a concern for access, and enriched learning opportunities for all. Technology equity is actually a complex issue that starts with access to the equipment itself. During the pandemic in New York city, the technology needs alone were daunting. In late Fall (nine months after the onset of the pandemic), *The New York Times* (Nierenberg & Pasick, 2020) noted that tens of thousands of New York City students still lacked access to a digital device. Internet access issues were also extremely problematic. Moreover, teachers were in various stages of online fluency: many were uncomfortable using technology as an instructional tool. Warschauer (2011) writes about discrepancies in the use of digital tools, with some teachers using them for traditional teaching practices (often skill-driven), while others use technology for creative student-centered practices. Often, schools with limited resources and limited professional development funding use technology in ways that reinforce skill-driven learning approaches rather than student-centered learning approaches (Warschauer, 2011; Warschauer & Matuchniak, 2010). Thus, the "Opportunity Divide" in learning with technology privileges some students over others.

Figure 1 captures this "Opportunity Divide," used as part of the *Innovating Instruction* approach. It depicts the interdependence of three basic elements. First, there is a need for *access*, pictured in the outer ring. Access to devices and the internet is essential. The second tier, *fluency,* includes the knowledge and use of software, multimodal tools, video-conferencing tools, and learning platforms. Teachers cannot teach comfortably with technology if they are not comfortable using the technology and understand at least some basic software options for using technology creatively. Finally, teachers need support to develop the design skills required to pursue inquiry learning by applying a backward project-based design approach, thus providing a creative structure for online teaching that engages students inclusively, creatively, and rigorously.

The commitment to equity and social justice is not an option for America's schools. Linda Darling-Hammond's 2015 book, *The Flat World and Education,* is subtitled "How America's commitment to equity will determine our future." It is not only a moral imperative—all children have a genuine right to learn—but a reminder that the failure to educate all of America's children puts the country at risk in a globally competitive society.

The Digital Opportunity Divide captures the need to ensure access to equipment and connectivity, and the importance of supporting teachers in developing fluidity in their use of the hardware and software. With access and fluency comes the opportunity to design projects that are inclusive, rigorous, and culturally relevant. True equity comes when technology is used to support the kind of creative and engaging learning found in well-resourced schools.

The real threat of a digital divide in the US is not that some people will have computers and some won't, but that they will be enabled to use them in entirely different ways, with one group able to muster a wide range of semiotic tools and resources to persuade, argue, analyse, critique and interpret, and another group, lacking these semiotics skills, limited to pre-packaged choices. (Warschauer, 2006, p. 2)

Figure 1. The digital opportunity divide (Meier, 2020)

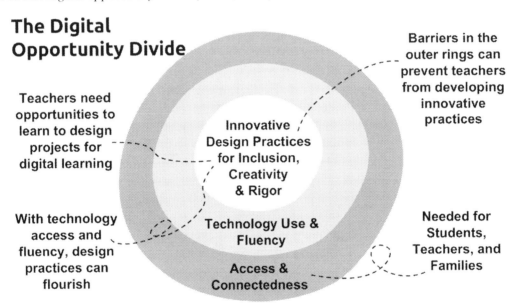

The moral imperative for technology equity requires an ongoing commitment to teacher fluency and the preparation of teachers to use technology effectively. Without a concerted effort to understand and address equity issues, the digital divide will only widen.

These five frameworks—learning theories, design approaches, professional development, school change and leadership, and equity—shape the Center's systems approach for integrating technology and making substantive change in pedagogy. The learning sciences provide the theoretical background for understanding the best conditions for learning, while curriculum design skills provide teachers with a structure for focusing on deeper understandings. Professional development theories provide a rationale and guidance for working with teachers in ways that situate the work in the lives of each teacher and engage them in active, hands-on learning. School change dynamics provide guidance in making decisions about how to work with teachers and building leaders to support the shifts that are needed to support inquiry-based learning. At the center of this dynamic model is a commitment to pursue equity in ways that deeply engage all students through culturally responsive and culturally sustaining teaching.

INNOVATING INSTRUCTION: THE CENTER'S MODEL FOR PROFESSIONAL DEVELOPMENT

The *Innovating Instruction* model is structured around three primary components: design, situate, lead. The professional development is led by skilled facilitators with teaching backgrounds who have been prepared to work closely with adult learners. Facilitators use a "backwards" *design* process to engage teachers in co-developing projects around big understandings and essential questions, working backward to determine the assessments and design the classroom learning environment (Larmer et al., 2015; Wiggins & McTighe, 2005). The facilitators *situate* this work in the particular school, being careful to understand the context of each school and community. Finally, facilitators encourage *leadership* from the principal to support the projects and they look for leadership from the teachers who can emerge as teacher-leaders to support the process going forward. See Figure 2 for an expanded look at the Center's professional development model.

The model itself is content agnostic and can be (and has been) applied to a broad range of disciplines, contexts, and modalities, including the shift to remote learning. Because online learning became a reality for schools in a matter of days, the professional development also had to move online immediately. A successful prototype of the asynchronous professional development had been implemented with an edEx course that was offered twice and selected as one of the ten top science, technology, engineering, and mathematics (STEM) courses offered nationally (Business Insider, 2020).

The professional development is typically organized around key understandings related to project-based design and pedagogy, and developed to be interactive, engaging, and relevant to the particular teachers and school. The total dependence on the technology to deliver the professional development, also provided the facilitators with the ability to model online best practices for the teachers themselves.

Design

Although all the phases in this extended professional development are important, the design phase is the most complex. In this stage, facilitators introduce the pedagogical reasoning teachers need to guide them in creating the inquiry-driven projects that will engage students. Following a backward design development process, facilitators engage teachers in conversations to develop deeper understandings around the content, authentic assessment, and the use of meaningful tools when creating rigorous learning experiences for all students.

Facilitators must be sensitive to the backgrounds and needs of the teachers as they co-design projects with them, encourage collaboration with their peers in the school, introduce new technology tools and software, and eventually help teachers implement the project in their classrooms. Post-implementation, the facilitators reflect as a group on the entire process. Emerging data from a related study (Du, 2021) indicates that it is during the implementation phase that teachers make the greatest strides in understanding the value and deeper meaning of the shift toward inquiry.

During the pandemic, the project design work focused on providing opportunities for students to engage in culturally relevant inquiry online, while maintaining a sense of rigor, and generating opportunities for students to interact with their peers and their teachers online. The facilitators also supported teachers in developing strategies for responding to student needs within their virtual teaching environments.

Figure 2. Instructional innovation, the center's professional development model (Meier, 2018)

DESIGN - Engage teachers as designers of student-centered, authentic learning experiences	
1. Embrace a Design Approach	Model and support a backwards design approach to project planning that creates meaningful learning experiences for students.
2. Enrich Content Knowledge	Provide opportunities for deepening teachers' understanding of content, including cross-curricular connections, learning standards, and student misconceptions.
3. Integrate Assessment Practices	Facilitate the design of authentic assessment and data use to identify and respond to student needs.
4. Leverage Digital Tools	Teach the integration of digital tools as part of the design process to facilitate interactive student learning and to enrich content.
SITUATE - Provide learning experiences for teachers that respect them as professionals and that adapt the learning to their particular school and situation	
1. Contextualize Teacher Learning	Situate the design work in the professional lives of teachers in order to connect deeply to the realities of teachers' classrooms and their students.
2. Model Effective Practice	Provide interactive, hands-on professional development that engages teachers and models project-based learning with available tools and resources.
3. Individualize Support	Co-construct project plans based on student and curricular needs, provide ongoing support for classroom implementation, culturally relevant pedagogy, and facilitate reflection on teaching and learning.
LEAD - Support leaders in guiding and sustaining change initiatives, while positioning teachers as agents of change	
1. Envision Change	Prioritize instructional leadership and develop actionable goals to promote change in self-identified areas of need.
2. Empower Leadership at All Levels	Provide a forum for identifying leaders—administrators, teachers, and community members—who can spearhead efforts that contribute to the common vision.
3. Sustain a Culture for Innovation	Scaffold educators' efforts toward instructional innovation to realize goals beyond the immediate scope of the professional development.
4. Research	Lead research that informs the transformative use of technology in existing and emerging practices in schools, while contributing to evolving scholarship on innovations for teaching and learning.

Situate

Many view the professional development that is typically offered to teachers as superficial and ineffective—a "drive-by" endeavor and often limited to presenting simple techniques, unrelated to the specific needs of teachers. Borko (2004), Cobb et al. (2003), Desimone (2009) among many others explain the need to situate professional development in the lives of teachers—just as teachers are asked to do for their students. The learning must be based on the needs of the school and the community. Facilitators create strong relationships with teachers; the changes they are introducing are substantive and can be challenging. Throughout the process, facilitators address the underlying pedagogical rationale for project design, promote technology literacy, and provide implementation support in the classroom or online. In doing so, facilitators contextualize the learning for teachers, model effective practice, and provide individual support to teachers both before and during implementation.

The following considerations were of critical importance to facilitators in situating the work for the needs of teachers during the pandemic: issues of access, fluency skills of teachers, learning how to operate designated online teaching platforms, structure of the online school day, expectations for students, and institutional expectations for teachers.

Lead

Leadership must be addressed to ensure the sustainability of the work. Principals and teacher leaders can distribute responsibility for ongoing learning (Harris & Spillane, 2008) and can empower teachers to take on leadership responsibilities (Hallinger & Heck, 2010). For instance, often, specific organizational changes are needed to provide time for teacher collaboration, or for team-teaching an interdisciplinary project. Long-term, ongoing learning goals are established as professional developers engage teachers in building their pedagogical skills to embrace new learning approaches and skills that include technology use. The aspirational change being described is nothing short of a cultural change for learning (Fullan, 2015).

Center facilitators support longevity of the ideas and structures by supporting leaders in envisioning the change, empowering leadership at all levels, and building in plans to sustain the work beyond the scope of the professional development.

The facilitators worked closely with leaders during the pandemic to support a vision for online teaching, and to ensure their understanding and fluency with regard to the technology and pedagogy. The facilitators also relied on teacher leaders to contribute to a support system within the school for the shift to remote learning.

RESEARCH ON IMPLEMENTATION OF THE MODEL

The *Innovating Instruction* model approach grew out of the Center's experience in supporting teachers and building leaders with a substantive approach to the integration of technology, undertaken in the context of research on learning and school change. Over the past two decades, Center facilitators have worked with multiple small and large city districts, hundreds of schools, and thousands of teachers to support shifts toward technology infused, project-based inquiry learning. The Center believes in establishing long-term relationships with educators whenever possible to support ongoing design work and shifts in teacher practice over time. Professional development with the Center typically includes a series of workshops, grade-level design work meetings, and classroom coaching.

During the pandemic, this work was done online, mostly synchronously but also asynchronously at times. As reflected in the model, the focus of each component is highly situated to the context of the school and the needs of the faculty and students in the building. Schools often engage with the Center over multiple cycles to reinforce the learning and to develop a sustainable culture for building rigorous, hands-on, culturally relevant approaches to instruction.

Three consecutive grants from the National Science Foundation have enabled the Center to apply the general model—which is content agnostic—to the design and implementation of integrated STEM teaching and learning. Although, STEM is typically simply defined by listing the subjects in the acronym, it is more thoughtfully defined as:

A standards-based, meta-discipline residing at the school level where all teachers, especially science, technology, engineering, and mathematics (STEM) teachers, teach an integrated approach to teaching and learning, where discipline-specific content is not divided, but addressed and treated as one dynamic, fluid study. (Merrill, 2009, p. 6)

The need in this case arises from the proliferation of STEM-focused schools in our nation's cities. Many of these schools have been "rebranded" as STEM schools, but struggle to live up to their new names. In many cases, the onus is on faculty to integrate interdisciplinary learning experiences into their curriculum, without access to proper training or resources. This phenomenon is all too familiar for the participating educators. The Center's professional development work in this case is situated to address educators' beliefs about STEM teaching and learning and provides teachers and leaders with a process for identifying and realizing their STEM missions. Design work is, again, central to the effort with grade-level teams as they develop and implement authentic STEM projects for their students. Leaders are asked to support the effort and initiate the structural changes needed to enable and to sustain the work. The goal of the research was to understand the initial impact of the *Innovating Instruction* model on teachers' pedagogy.

Study Methodology

The second of the three National Science Foundation projects, the *Systemic Transformation of Inquiry Learning Environments* (STILE) study (NSF Project No. 1621387), is the focus of this research discussion. Specifically, the second cohort of STILE teachers were the focus because, for the most part, they were at a midpoint in their professional development experience at the onset of the pandemic. In the pivot to online learning in the third year of the study, and in an effort to situate the work to the immediate needs of the schools, the project focused specifically on supporting inquiry-based work online.

A convergent parallel mixed-methods approach guided the research and analysis (Creswell & Poth, 2016), with a central focus on the impact of the STILE implementation on teachers, especially related to the shift to remote instruction during the pandemic.

A total of 67 teachers, from primarily underserved elementary and middle schools, were initially identified for Cohort 2, 47 of whom persisted through the pandemic to design and implement at least one STEM project alongside Center facilitators. Time spent in professional development varied considerably within and across schools due to the challenges of COVID-19 (see Table 1). Center facilitators offered support to all schools, but not every site was in a position to continue following the shift to remote teaching. Many schools cited new restrictions on their professional development time, largely due to the city's internal efforts to support teachers in reaching their students (they were initially concerned about access). On the other hand, some schools—such as School A—took advantage of STILE as an opportunity to support their teachers in transferring student-centered practices online. It should be noted that professional development hours, or "dosage" hours accrued during the pandemic came primarily from one-on-one or small group virtual coaching sessions focused on designing and implementing student-centered practices online.

Table 1. STILE Cohort 1-2 professional development dosage hours through June 2020

School	Cohort 1				Cohort 2			
	Total No. of Teachers	Avg. Contact Hours	Max. Dosage Hours	Min. Dosage Hours	Total No. of Teachers	Avg. Contact Hours	Max. Dosage Hours	Min. Dosage Hours
A	11	23.4	33.6	7.6	11	41.8	57.0	21.7
B	7	32.1	48.8	16.2	3	22.8	29.1	10.2
C	6	40.8	46.8	29.6	4	29.8	47.3	18.1
D	6	19.7	36.0	1.3	4	7.1	16.2	3.4
E	5	7.2	15.3	2.5	5	7.6	18.4	3.3
F	4	13.9	32.2	NA	6	16.1	30.0	12.0
H	4	18.2	28.5	NA	5	21.9	29.5	15.6
I	5	32.7	48.4	12.0	6	3.3	5.7	1.7
L	6	22.5	32.0	22.5	4	20.7	35.8	4.5
M	6	33.9	47.6	24.8	4	17.3	20.1	13.9
N	7	25.7	38.8	5.0	5	19.4	35.9	9.5
O	4	22.1	24.3	19.3	6	16.4	21.1	8.8
P	7	13.3	17.0	7.0	4	18.0	20.5	17.0

Note. Professional development dosage includes institutes, planning meetings, classroom visitations, and reflection sessions as reported on formal sign-in sheets. Schools G and J dropped out of the program in the first year of the study and are omitted from the table.

Findings

An exploratory factor analysis of the STILE teacher questionnaire analyzed the internal structure of the survey and revealed two key domains: Conceptualizations of STEM (shifting from a disciplinary perspective to an interdisciplinary perspective supported by the exploration of oft messy, real-world problems) and Instruction (shifting from didactic approaches to student-centered approaches focused on individual needs). The observed correlation between the two halves adjusted by the Spearman-Brown prophecy formula suggests a high internal consistency for each domain, at 0.87 for Conceptualizations of STEM and 0.78 for Instruction (Boyle, 1991; Cortina, 1993; Green et al., 1977).

The analysis of questionnaire results from the Cohort 1 treatment condition (when Cohort 2 initially served as a control pre-pandemic), suggested a significant positive effect of the STILE intervention on teachers' shifts in Conceptualizations of STEM at the 95% confidence level ($F(1,68)=4.9781$, p-value=0.029), with a medium estimated Cohen's d effect size of 0.544. However, questionnaire results suggest no significant effect of the STILE intervention on teachers' shifts in Instruction at the 95% confidence level for the Cohort 1 treatment condition ($F(1,68)=1.58$, p-value=0.21), with a small estimated Cohen's d effect size of 0.306 (Cohen, 1988).

The Cohort 2 results found additional changes from the Cohort 1 larger STILE study (see, Meier et al., 2021). Looking at Cohort 2 pre-post intervention measures, teachers show significant positive shifts in *both* Conceptualizations of STEM ($t=3.71$, $df=34$, p-value=0.014) and Instruction ($t=3.90$, $df=34$, p-value=0.002) (see Table 2).

Table 2. Cohort 2 t-test analysis

Domain	N	Descriptive Data				Paired t-test	
		Pre μ^1	Pre SD σ	Post μ^1	Post SD σ	t	p
1: STEM Conceptualization	34	3.71	0.693	4.14	0.79	2.584	0.014*
2: STEM Instruction	34	3.90	0.728	4.34	0.66	3.438	0.002*

*$p < .05$.

The researchers were also interested in the influence of the STILE experience on teachers' preparedness for the shift to online learning spaces in Spring 2020. One question was added to the June 2020 Cohort 2 Teacher Questionnaire to address the ongoing challenges posed by the pandemic. A total of 73 percent (N = 27) of the teachers indicated that STILE experiences prepared them for a remote learning situation, and when asked to explain, many cited the professional development's focus on the use of technology for classroom teaching and curriculum development and planning.

Qualitative findings reinforced the idea that the STILE program influenced teachers' ability to transition to online learning. Eighteen teachers engaged in exit interviews with the project researchers in Summer 2020. When asked about their readiness with regard to remote teaching, most participants pointed to their *Innovating Instruction* experience as a source of preparedness for teaching during the pandemic. According to their comments, two components of the model seemed to transfer to their current situation: the design approach and the integration of digital tools.

Facilitators helped teachers use the backwards planning approach to consider specific learning goals and assessments, before beginning to construct online learning experiences. Moreover, teachers frequently discussed their exposure to creative digital tools during the *Innovating Instruction* experience and described feeling more prepared to make informed choices about how and when to integrate technology into their instruction.

It was the tools, honestly, just taking it day by day and trying to just survive. We were trying to get straight and make sure that my students were okay and the parents were okay and somehow still connect while teaching and learning, Google Meet and Zoom and all these applications that, as a new teacher, I still consider myself a new teacher, I've never really been that person, like "yeah, technology, okay." So now coming into it, it's just like, "Wow, okay." Technology is so needed. And it has to be such. (Cohort 2 Teacher No. 765, 2020)

Especially right now with remote, I have told a million people that I'm so lucky for this, that we have [STILE], because so much of what we were using in remote, I had already tried, when students or set up with students, like Google classrooms and stuff were already set up and Desmos, the kids had actually already seen before. So it was a much smoother transition to online, because we had seen that and then going into blending or into blended with we're not supposed to pass out papers and things like that. (Cohort 2 Teacher No. 924, 2020)

And, you can come to our faculty meeting, you can come to our math meeting. You can come to any of the meetings that we have. And you can experience the thought process that we have fostered or that we have made part of our fabric. And some of it came from [STILE]. Some of it, of course, was some of us, but [STILE] had a major influence on how we approach things. (Cohort 1 Teacher No. 163, 2020)

Center facilitators continued to provide support to Cohort 1 and Cohort 2 participants during a culminating STILE Institute held over Summer 2020. Structured as a three-day series of synchronous and asynchronous learning blocks, the professional development modeled an approach to structured online learning, while challenging participating teachers to rethink ways of working with students via a remote or hybrid setting. While the 44 teachers were motivated to push past the barriers and to reimagine what student-centered, inquiry-based learning looks like in the "new normal," the teachers reflected on how easy it was to fall back on didactic, disciplinary focused approaches to content despite one's beliefs about pedagogy when teaching online.

DISCUSSION

For decades, technology advocates have predicted that the introduction of digital tools would bring about new, more effective ways of teaching, with technology serving as a catalyst for rethinking and reimagining instruction (Cuban, 2001, 2013). Successful implementation of these tools has proven elusive however; many educational critics would say that little substantive pedagogical change has been accomplished with the addition of technology (Cuban, 2001, 2013; Sims, 2017; Warschauer & Matuchniak, 2010). Indeed, it was frustration with the slow pace of change and the lost opportunities to use technology to provide more learning opportunities for students in underserved schools that led to the creation of the Center and its commitment to school change.

In reflecting on this recent research, and ongoing work with hundreds of teachers during the pandemic, it seems that the broad failure of technology to transform educational environments involves at least four key challenges. First, there is no agreement on what constitutes the "shift" expected in teacher practice with the introduction of technology. The goals are vague and too general to provide clear guidance to those interested in pedagogical reform. There are many calls for "21st century learning" that attempt to shift the focus from teacher-centric learning to student-centered learning, but it is far from clear how these general aspirational goals can be used to deepen student learning without a more coherent framework for pedagogical reasoning.

Second, the pedagogical changes often associated with the introduction of technology, i.e., constructivist approaches to teaching (Wenglinsky, 2005) or, more recently, connectivism (Downes, 2004; Siemens, 2005), are also vague and typically provide little specific pedagogical guidance for teachers (Cuban, 2001, 2013; Lowyck, 2014).

Third, professional development for technology is usually focused on the tools and the techniques for classroom use, rather than pedagogical reasoning or on new approaches to teaching and learning that the technology can support. Professional development practices for introducing technology must also evolve. Digital tools provide affordances that have the potential to catalyze new practices, but learning theories should guide these shifts in practice (Meier, 2020).

Finally, educators have not developed an expansive understanding of the scope of the changes required to support new, technology-supported pedagogical practices. If the goal is not simply to introduce technology but to use technology to help shift teacher pedagogical reasoning from traditional classroom practices to "knowledge-building" practices (Scardamalia & Bereiter, 2014), then personal and organizational change issues must be considered. Leadership, for instance, plays an important role in supporting instructional shifts, and enabling the structural changes that schools may need to make (e.g., longer instructional periods) to support these new practices.

Although formal research on the application of *Innovating Instruction* to online learning is not complete, the assistance that was provided in the initial months of the pandemic to a sample of the teachers in the Center's NSF STILE program resulted in teacher-reported shifts in their instructional thinking. The qualitative data also captured teachers' enthusiasm for the support in making the transition to online teaching and learning. In reflecting on this work, it seems that two key elements that directly relate to the *Innovating Instruction* model were at play: improving teacher technology fluency; and providing the design skills for developing student-centered projects based on new pedagogical reasoning represented in inquiry learning. The design work was situated in the immediate needs of teachers during the pandemic, and included leaders and teachers in conversations around the potential for remote teaching.

The model was successfully adapted to the new online environment while still maintaining its strong principles for design, based on findings from the learning sciences about effective teaching and learning. The projects co-designed with teachers ranged from mini learning experiences to larger units and were largely dependent on the needs of the students, teachers, and schools, as well as on the scope of the professional development.

As schools contemplate more online learning—in the months, and perhaps the years ahead—it is possible that remote learning will become an ongoing option for various reasons and for various segments of the school population. A strategic national professional development plan is needed to prepare the nation's teachers for this eventuality. The *Innovating Instruction* model shows promise today as a starting point for helping with these transitions.

DIRECTIONS FOR FUTURE RESEARCH

More research is needed to focus on the critical issue of transitioning from teaching and learning in a face-to-face classroom to teaching and learning online. The pre-COVID evidence gathered from the study of *Innovating Instruction* is promising: the strong foundation teachers receive in developing design practices, pedagogical reasoning, and technology seems to prepare them to make the shifts that are at the heart of the model. It will be important to continue to research the pedagogical practices that support inquiry learning and best practices to prepare teachers to make these pedagogical changes. Lowyck (2014) notes that the very concept of knowledge-building will "change over time, depending on epistemological arguments and evolving learning theories" (p. 9). The authors anticipate that the *Innovating Instruction* model will continue to evolve through ongoing research that captures the important dialogue between emerging learning theories and practice.

Once the relationship between the model and the process of establishing new teaching cultures is more thoroughly understood, student learning will also be studied. Pilot work is already underway to define what student learning should be captured and will be implemented in the research currently funded. The Center's commitment to equity begins with a concern about ensuring that all students, especially those attending underserved schools, have access to an engaging and rigorous schooling experience. Curriculum that is designed around the interests and needs of individual students and reflects students' culture and aspirations, will generate more student agency around learning (Darling-Hammond et al., 2020).

Finally, it is important to understand if the work is scalable. The Center's current funding investigates the usability and feasibility of the model. In anticipation of this question, initial efforts were made over two years ago to develop a blended model that would utilize both online and face-to-face components in a cost-effective and replicable manner. More research is needed to ensure that this combination of online professional development and face-to-face support is sufficient to prepare teachers to do the challenging work needed to shift pedagogical practice while integrating technology in ways that support that shift.

CONCLUSION

The COVID crisis may well prove to be an historic educational change for teachers who were suddenly and totally dependent on technology. However, it is not yet clear what will evolve from this historic moment. The tools, by themselves, do not change existing practices (Blundell et al., 2020; Meier, 2015). It may be that teachers return to their "business as usual" classroom activities as teachers return to the classroom. However, this historic moment, despite its ties to tragedy, has raised new questions and new opportunities for engaging with students at a distance.

Teachers need more than an introduction to the equipment and software; they also need to link the use of technology with the opportunity to learn design practices that can put their students at the center of the learning process. Teachers have been anxious to learn how to use digital tools in ways that lead to student engagement and learning. Learning opportunities for teachers require access to high-quality professional development that supports a transition to new practices that reflect learning science precepts. Teachers also need the design skills to identify and focus on inquiry learning through culturally responsive teaching.

Theories provide the rationale, direction, and insight into next steps for the educational field. Unfortunately, efforts to date to help teachers use technology effectively as a catalyst for shifting instruction have been too fragmented, too limited, and lack the holistic vision needed to realize the potential for using technology wisely. To shape the contours for more holistic system change it will be important to bring together frameworks and theories to support the overall goal of transformative learning.

It is likely that a return to schooling as it existed before COVID is not feasible. Online learning may well become a permanent aspect of schooling, at least for some. For those who return to the classroom, there is much to learn from the crisis. The challenge will be to consider the skills and knowledge the next generation of learners deserve, particularly those in underserved schools who have the right to an engaging, relevant, and productive education. With guidance from the learning sciences, and the development of impactful professional development, educators can use design practices to develop dynamic learning environments for students who want the opportunity to become the life-long learners required for an informed democracy.

ACKNOWLEDGMENT

This material is based, in part, upon work supported by the National Science Foundation under Grant No. 1621387. Any opinions, findings, and conclusions or recommendations expressed in this material are those of the authors and do not necessarily reflect the views of the National Science Foundation.

Select findings regarding effect sizes were first reported in 2021 in an AERA paper.

The authors would like to acknowledge the collective efforts of the facilitators and researchers in the Center who are instrumental to the work reported on in this chapter.

REFERENCES

Adams, C. (2020, April 17). *Teachers need lots of training to do online learning well. Coronavirus closures gave many just days*. The Hechinger Report. https://hechingerreport.org/teachers-need-lots-of-training-to-do-online-learning-well-coronavirus-closures-gave-many-just-days/

Benbunan-Fich, R., Hiltz, S. R., & Harasim, L. (2005). The online interaction learning model: An integrated theoretical framework for learning networks. In S. Hiltz (Ed.), *Learning together online: Research on asynchronous learning networks* (pp. 18–36). Routledge.

Blundell, C., Lee, K., & Nykvist, S. (2020). Moving beyond enhancing pedagogies with digital technologies: Frames of reference, habits of mind and transformative learning. *Journal of Research on Technology in Education*, *52*(2), 178–196. doi:10.1080/15391523.2020.1726235

Borko, H. (2004). Professional development and teacher learning: Mapping the terrain. *Educational Researcher*, *33*(3), 3–15. doi:10.3102/0013189X033008003

Boyle, G. J. (1991). Does item homogeneity indicate internal consistency or item redundancy in psychometric scales? *Personality and Individual Differences*, *12*(3), 291–294. doi:10.1016/0191-8869(91)90115-R

Bransford, J., Brown, A., & Cocking, R. (2000). *How people learn: Brain, mind, experience, and school*. National Academies Press.

Chen, C., & Pugachevsky, J. (2020, October 27). *Ten popular online STEM, coding and gaming courses—all are taught by women*. Business Insider. https://www.businessinsider.com/online-stem-gaming-python-courses-taught-by-women

Cobb, P., McClain, K., de Silva Lamberg, T., & Dean, C. (2003). Situating teachers' instructional practices in the institutional setting of the school and district. *Educational Researcher*, *32*(6), 13–24. doi:10.3102/0013189X032006013

Cochran-Smith, M., & Lytle, S. (2009). *Inquiry as stance: Practitioner research for the next generation*. Teachers College Press.

Cohen, J. (1988). *Statistical power analysis for the behavioral sciences* (2nd ed.). Lawrence Erlbaum Associates.

Cortina, J. M. (1993). What is coefficient alpha: An examination of theory and applications? *The Journal of Applied Psychology*, *78*(1), 98–104. doi:10.1037/0021-9010.78.1.98

Creswell, J. W., & Poth, C. N. (2016). *Qualitative inquiry and research design: Choosing among five approaches*. Sage Publications.

Cuban, L. (2001). *Oversold and underused*. Harvard University Press.

Cuban, L. (2013). *Inside the black box of classroom practice: Change without reform in American education.* Harvard Education Publishing Group.

Darling-Hammond, L. (2015). *The flat world and education: How America's commitment to equity will determine our future.* Teachers College Press.

Darling-Hammond, L., Flook, L., Cook-Harvey, C., Barro, B., & Osher, D. (2020). Implications for educational practice of the science of learning and development. *Applied Developmental Science, 24*(2), 97–140. doi:10.1080/10888691.2018.1537791

Dede, C. (2008). Theoretical perspectives influencing the use of information technology in teaching and learning. In J. Voogt & G. Knezek (Eds.), *International handbook of information technology in primary and secondary education* (Vol. 20, pp. 43–62). Springer. doi:10.1007/978-0-387-73315-9_3

Desimone, L. (2009). Improving impact studies of teachers' professional development: Toward better conceptualizations and measures. *Educational Researcher, 38*(3), 181–199. doi:10.3102/0013189X08331140

Downes, S. (2004). The buntine oration: Learning networks. *International Journal of Instructional Technology & Distance Learning, 1*(11), 3–14. http://www.itdl.org/Journal/Nov_04/Nov_04.pdf

Du, X. (2021). *Technology and special education: Designing effective professional development for equitable and inclusive classrooms* [Unpublished doctoral dissertation]. Teachers College, Columbia University, New York, United States.

Edelson, D., Gordin, D., & Pea, R. (1999). Addressing the challenges of inquiry-based learning through technology and curriculum design. *Journal of the Learning Sciences, 3*(8), 391–450. doi:10.120715327809jls0803&4_3

Ertmer, P. A. (1999). Addressing first- and second-order barriers to change: Strategies for technology integration. *Educational Technology Research and Development, 47*(4), 47–61. doi:10.1007/BF02299597

Fullan, M. (1991). *The new meaning of educational change* (2nd ed.). Teachers College Press.

Fullan, M. (2007). *Leading in a culture of change.* Jossey Bass.

Fullan, M. (2012). *Stratosphere: Integrating technology, pedagogy, and change knowledge.* Pearson.

Fullan, M. (2015). *The new meaning of educational change* (5th ed.). Teachers College Press.

Green, S. B., Lissitz, R. W., & Mulaik, S. A. (1977). Limitations of coefficient alpha as an index of test unidimensionality. *Educational and Psychological Measurement, 37*(4), 827–836. doi:10.1177/001316447703700403

Grissom, J., Egalite, A., & Lindsay, C. (2021). *How principals affect students and schools: A systematic synthesis of two decades of research.* The Wallace Foundation. https://www.wallacefoundation.org/knowledge-center/Documents/How-Principals-Affect-Students-and-Schools.pdf

Grover, S., Catete, V., Barnes, T., Hill, M., Ledeczi, A., & Broll, B. (2020). FIRST principles to design for online, synchronous high school CS teacher training and curriculum co-design. In N. Falkner & O. Seppala (Eds.), *Koli Calling '20: Proceedings of the 20th Koli Calling International Conference on Computing Education Research* (Article 21, pp. 1-5). Association for Computing Machinery. 10.1145/3428029.3428059

Guskey, T. R. (2000). *Evaluating professional development*. Corwin.

Hallinger, P., & Heck, R. H. (2010). Leadership for learning: Does collaborative leadership make a difference in school improvement? *Educational Management Administration & Leadership, 38*(6), 654–658. doi:10.1177/1741143210379060

Harasim, L. (2012). *Learning theory and online technologies*. Routledge. doi:10.4324/9780203846933

Harris, A., & Spillane, J. (2008). Distributed leadership through the looking glass. *Journal of Educational Administration, 46*(2), 31–34. doi:10.1108/jea.2008.07446baa.001

Kamenetz, A. (2020, December 4). *5 things we've learned about virtual school in 2020*. NPR. https://www.npr.org/2020/12/04/938050723/5-things-weve-learned-about-virtual-school-in-2020

Krajcik, J., & Shin, N. (2014). Project-based learning. In R. Sawyer (Ed.), *The Cambridge handbook of the learning sciences* (2nd ed., pp. 275–297). Cambridge University Press. doi:10.1017/CBO9781139519526.018

Ladson-Billings, G. (2014). Culturally relevant pedagogy 2.0: Aka the remix. *Harvard Educational Review, 84*(1), 74–84. doi:10.17763/haer.84.1.p2rj131485484751

Larmer, J., Mergendoller, J., & Boss, S. (2015). *Setting the standard for project based learning*. Association for Supervision and Curriculum Development.

Lowyck, J. (2014). Bridging learning theories and technology-enhanced environments: A critical appraisal of its history. In J. M. Spector, M. D. Merrill, J. Elen, & M. J. Bishop (Eds.), *Handbook of research on communications and educational technology*. Springer. doi:10.1007/978-1-4614-3185-5_1

Meier, E. (2020). Designing and using digital platforms for 21st century learning. *Educational Technology Research and Development, 69*(1), 217–220. doi:10.100711423-020-09880-4 PMID:33456280

Meier, E., Mineo, C., Gabriela Diaz Yanez, K., Du, X., & Ma, Y. (2021). *Educational responsibility for addressing complex problems: STEM research with underserved schools* [Paper presentation]. Annual Meeting of the American Educational Research Association.

Meier. (2015). Beyond a digital status quo: Re-conceptualizing online learning opportunities. *Bank Street Occasional Papers 34*. Retrieved from: https://educate.bankstreet.edu/cgi/viewcontent.cgi?article=1000&context=occasional-paper-series

Meier. (2018). The collaboration imperative. In L. Lin & J. M. Spector (Eds.), *Constructive articulation between the sciences of learning and the instructional design and technology communities* (pp. 131-151). Routledge.

Merrill, C. (2009). The future of TE masters' degrees: STEM [Paper presentation]. Meeting of the International Technology Education Association, Louisville, KY, United States.

National Academies of Sciences, Engineering, and Medicine. (2018). *How people learn II: Learners, context, and cultures.* The National Academies Press.

Nierenberg, A., & Pasick, A. (2020, November 20). Parents erupt in frustration as New York City schools close. *The New York Times.* https://www.nytimes.com/2020/11/20/us/parents-erupt-in-frustration-as-new-york-city-schools-close

Paris, D. (2012). Culturally sustaining pedagogy: A needed change in stance, terminology, and practice. *Educational Researcher, 41*(3), 93–97. doi:10.3102/0013189X12441244

Penuel, W. (2019). Co-design as infrastructuring with attention to power: Building collective capacity for equitable teaching and learning through design-based implementation research. In J. Pieters, J. Voogt, & N. Roblin (Eds.), *Collaborative curriculum design for sustainable innovation and teacher learning.* Springer Open. doi:10.1007/978-3-030-20062-6_21

Pieters, J., Voogt, J., & Roblin, N. (Eds.). (2019). *Collaborative curriculum design for sustainable innovation and teacher learning.* Springer Open. doi:10.1007/978-3-030-20062-6

Roth, D. (2007). Understanding by design: A framework for effecting curricular development and assessment. *CBE Life Sciences Education, 6*(2), 95–97. doi:10.1187/cbe.07-03-0012

Saldaña, J. (2016). *Ethnotheatre: Research from page to stage.* Routledge. doi:10.4324/9781315428932

Sawyer, R. K. (Ed.). (2014). *The Cambridge handbook of the learning sciences.* Cambridge University Press. doi:10.1017/CBO9781139519526

Scardamalia, M., & Bereiter, C. (2014). Knowledge building and knowledge creation: Theory, pedagogy, and technology. In R. Sawyer (Ed.), *The Cambridge handbook of the learning sciences* (2nd ed., pp. 397–417). Cambridge University Press. doi:10.1017/CBO9781139519526.025

Senge, P. M. (2006). *The fifth discipline: The art and practice of the learning organization.* Currency.

Siemens, G. (2005). Connectivism: A learning theory for the digital age. *Instructional Technology and Distance Learning, 2*(1), 3-10. http://itdl.org/Journal/Jan_05/article01.htm

Sims, C. (2017). *Disruptive fixation: School reform and the pitfalls of techno-idealism.* Princeton University Press.

Steele, D. M., & Cohn-Vargas, B. (2013). *Identity safe classrooms, grades K-5: Places to belong and learn.* Corwin.

Vasquez, J. A. (2015). STEM—Beyond the acronym. *Educational Leadership, 72*(4), 10–15.

Warschauer, M. (2006). Literacy and technology: Bridging the divide. In D. Gibbs & K. L. Krause (Eds.), *Cyberlines 2.0: Languages and cultures of the internet* (pp. 163–174). James Nicholas Publishers.

Warschauer, M. (2011). *Learning in the cloud: How (and why) to transform schools with digital media.* Teachers College Press.

Warschauer, M., & Matuchniak, T. (2010). New technology and digital worlds: Analyzing evidence of equity in access, use, and outcomes. In N. Pinkard & V. Gadsden (Eds.), *Review of research in education: What counts as evidence in educational settings? Rethinking equity, diversity, and reform in the 21st century* (Vol. 34, pp. 179–225). Sage. doi:10.3102/0091732X09349791

Wenglinsky, H. (2005). *Using technology wisely: The keys to success in schools*. Teachers College Press.

Wiggins, G., & McTighe, J. (2005). *Understanding by design* (2nd ed.). Association for Supervision and Curriculum Development.

Zimmerman, A., & Gould, J. (2020, April 25). *5 weeks into online learning, NYC is still racing to get thousands of devices to students*. Chalkbeat. https://ny.chalkbeat.org/2020/4/25/21236279/students-lack-devices-nyc-schools-coronavirus

Chapter 6
Using the Technology Integration Planning Cycle to Select Digital Tools for Virtual Instruction

Lindsay Woodward
Drake University, USA

Beth Beschorner
Minnesota State University, Mankato, USA

ABSTRACT

This chapter explores the use of the Technology Integration Planning Cycle (TIPC) for supporting teachers' decision-making as they plan virtual instruction. The TIPC is designed to support teachers in evaluating the possible contributions of digital tools to instruction that facilitates meeting specific learning goals. The use of the TIPC to support pre-service teachers, in-service teachers, and in professional development settings is discussed. Then, examples of a teacher using the TIPC as she plans virtual reading and writing instruction illustrate the potential of the TIPC to support effective virtual instruction. Finally, issues of access, equity, and safety related to use the TIPC are discussed.

INTRODUCTION

Recent changes in global education have not only foregrounded virtual learning for a broader group of teachers and students but have also afforded the opportunity to revisit what is known about learning in digital spaces and the digital tools that are effective in virtual teaching and learning environments. While many elements of effective virtual instruction are similar to effective face to face instruction, such as establishing relationships, clarity of instruction, student engagement, and assessment practices (Fisher et al., 2021), the way in which these elements are enacted can be quite different in virtual environments. Therefore, it is critical that teachers are supported in how to organize all of the elements of

DOI: 10.4018/978-1-7998-7222-1.ch006

virtual learning through high quality instructional planning. While teachers' instructional planning can be supported through a number of different approaches (Kozak & Martin-Chang, 2019; Lowrey et al., 2019; Woodward & Hutchison, 2018), this chapter focuses on the possibilities of using a planning cycle to consider how digital tools can contribute to specific instructional goals.

The Technology Integration Planning Cycle (TIPC; Hutchison & Woodward, 2014) was originally developed to support in-service English Language Arts and Literacy teachers as they sought to integrate digital tools into their in-person instruction. However, follow up studies have indicated that the TIPC can be used to support a wide range of teachers, both pre-service and in-service, and in multiple grade levels and disciplines (e.g. Beschorner & Kruse, 2016; Ciampa, 2017; Hutchison & Colwell, 2016; Hutchison & Woodward, 2018). Thus, there is much potential for how the TIPC can support teachers' pedagogical decision-making as they select digital tools in a virtual learning environment as well. This chapter will describe the TIPC, how it can be used to support pre-service and in-service teachers' pedagogical reasoning, and provide examples of how the TIPC supports instructional planning in virtual learning environments.

BACKGROUND

The TIPC was created to provide a clear decision-making process for teachers who are planning instruction during which students utilize digital tools to meet instructional goals. The TIPC synthesizes best practices in effective instruction and technology integration and provides a process for teachers to prepare them to consider critical elements of using a particular digital tool to meet specific instructional goals. While teachers are often prepared to utilize technology in their instruction and are familiar with a variety of digital tools, a recent study of teacher educators (Carpenter et al., 2020) noted a lack of expectations regarding preparing teachers to evaluate technology for specific instructional purposes. This disconnection between using technology and evaluating the potential of digital tools for instruction continues once teachers are in the field. For practicing teachers, the professional development they receive is often digital tool based and foregrounds a particular type of technology (Colwell et al., 2020; Hillmayr et al., 2020; Panero & Aldon, 2016), rather than how that tool can be used to meet specific curricular goals. Utilizing the TIPC as an approach to integrating technology aims to re-focus technology use on facilitating learning of specific instructional goals.

The TIPC provides a foundation for teachers to consider new and existing digital tools and how they can align with specific, discipline-based instructional objectives. The TIPC provides an opportunity for teachers to focus on their instructional standards, learning objectives, and the overall instructional approach best suited to their learning goals for students, prior to the integration of a digital tool. It also foregrounds the unique contributions that digital tools can make to instruction and provides teachers with a reflective process in which to consider the affordances of a digital tool for student learning, as well as possible constraints that may need to be addressed through instruction.

THE TECHNOLOGY INTEGRATION PLANNING CYCLE

The TIPC emerged from the increased attention to digital and multimodal learning in the Common Core State Standards (CCSSI, 2010) and the struggles that many teachers were experiencing as they sought to integrate technology meaningfully into their instruction (Ertmer et al., 2012). The knowledge utilized throughout the TIPC is grounded in Mishra and Koehler's (2006) Technological Pedagogical Content Knowledge (TPACK) framework. This framework extended Shulman's (1986) pedagogical content knowledge to include technological knowledge. Mishra and Koehler recognized that, like pedagogical knowledge, content knowledge, and pedagogical content knowledge, there were distinct types of knowledge that overlapped as teachers conceptualized instruction that used technology. Thus, they added the overlap of technological knowledge to pedagogical and content knowledge, and identified the overlap of all three as technological pedagogical content knowledge.

Conceptualizing teacher knowledge in virtual learning environments as the intersection among technological, pedagogical, and content knowledge can be a powerful tool in understanding what teachers draw upon when making instructional decisions. However, as a theoretical framework, it may not directly support teachers in enacting these types of knowledge to design meaningful instruction. Thus, Hutchison and Woodward (2014) recognized the need for an instructional planning framework that could support teachers in situating their TPACK within the specific learning they were designing for their students. While this cycle was developed to support teachers in selecting tools for instruction in in-person environments, it may be even more relevant to virtual instruction, as teachers are choosing digital tools over traditional materials for many instructional activities in a virtual environment.

Understanding the Elements of the Technology Integration Planning Cycle

The TIPC (Hutchison & Woodward, 2014), shown in Figure 1, is comprised of seven elements that support teachers as they plan instruction that integrates technology to meet instructional goals.

Figure 1. The Technology Integration Planning Cycle (Source: Hutchison & Woodward, (2014) reprinted with permission

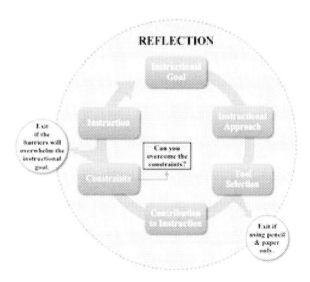

These seven elements represent the considerations that teachers should analyze when selecting a digital tool to use in instruction. Although the cycle has a clear progression, it is situated within a sphere of reflection to allow for teachers to return to the other elements in the cycle as they learn more about their planned instruction and the possibilities for students. This section explains each of the elements of the TIPC.

The first element focuses on identifying clear *instructional goals*. These may come from standards or other curriculum planning documents and serve to guide each subsequent consideration in the cycle. While these goals may be the learning standard itself, teachers have found it most useful to select a specific learning goal that can be met through the instruction planned in this cycle. It is also possible that additional standards or goals may be added later in the cycle, due to discovering additional affordances of the selected digital tool. This element focuses on a teacher's pedagogical content knowledge, as they are both selecting a content objective and considering how to translate that into an achievable learning objective for students.

Once teachers have identified an instructional goal, they should select the best instructional approach. The *instructional approach* reflects the specific pedagogical choices that the teacher believes are most appropriate to teaching the content. These approaches can include a wide range of considerations, such as how much the students have already interacted with the topic, whether they need guided, group, or independent practice, whether the learning should be collaborative, or the depth of knowledge required to achieve the instructional goal. The instructional approach element foregrounds the teacher's pedagogical knowledge and intentionally takes place before the exploration of possible digital tools. The position of the instructional approach decision being made prior to selecting a digital tool supports the idea that it should be sound pedagogy that dictates the instructional approach, rather than the way a particular digital tool is designed. In a virtual learning environment where students are already utilizing a number of digital tools, focusing on the instructional approach prior to selecting the digital tool is exceptionally important to creating equitable learning experiences that are driven by effective teaching.

Then, teachers can consider what *digital tool* might best support the learning of the instructional goal and facilitate the enactment of the instructional approach. In the TIPC, selecting the digital tool is a key decision-making point for teachers, as they may not find a particular digital tool that will meet their needs. In this case, they are advised to consider using traditional materials. In a virtual learning environment, using traditional tools may look like asking students to sketch a diagram using paper and pencil and uploading a photograph, using traditional materials like highlighters and Post It notes for organizational tasks, or drawing a picture. The distinguishing factor of the digital tool in the TIPC is that students are using it to engage with the instructional goal, not necessarily one that functions as a digital intermediary to submit traditionally created work. Meaning that the digital tool adds to students' progress towards meeting the learning goal, not that it simply facilitates the submission of work. For example, the camera or email applications used when emailing a photo of a drawing for an assignment or attaching a Word document of a narrative description would not necessarily be digital tools that contribute to the instructional approach and learning goals, and therefore this cycle may not support a teacher's work in that case. Examples of how digital tools can contribute to student learning are discussed later in this chapter.

Once teachers have identified a possible digital tool to support students' learning, they should identify whether the digital tool contributes to students' learning of digital and nondigital content skills and how it may support students engaging "in the types of multimodal production or consumption" (Hutchison & Woodward, 2014, p.461) that are relevant to the instructional goal. Through analyzing the potential *contributions to instruction* of a particular digital tool, teachers are better able to distinguish their particular goals for the digital tool and any additional contributions one tool may make over another towards meeting the instructional goal. Teachers may also find that there are features of the digital tool that add to the learning goals that students are meeting. For example, a teacher who is using a collaborative annotation digital tool may find that in addition to research-related learning goals, students are also meeting discussion-focused learning goals by using the tool itself and return to the instructional goal element to revise the overall purposes of the instruction. Once teachers have identified the affordances of their selected digital tool, then they should also identify possible constraints. The *constraints* of using a particular digital tool may range from small limitations like needing to set up new class accounts or share access codes to larger ones related to being able to operate the technology or a lack of understanding of how to use the features of the digital tool to produce the desired outcome. After considering the constraints, teachers are at another critical decision point. It may be that the constraints will overwhelm the instruction, meaning that there are too many factors that cannot be overcome in the lesson to make the tool an effective choice for supporting students' learning. In this case, teachers may consider not using a digital tool for this particular instructional approach or goal, or beginning the cycle again with a different type of tool. It is important that the possible contributions to instruction are considered prior to the constraints in order to clearly understand the full potential of the digital tool, as teachers may become overwhelmed by the constraints of a digital tool if they have not identified the possible affordances first (Woodward & Hutchison, 2018). This particularly supportive part of the TIPC situates digital tool selection within the context of instruction that is focused on a learning goal, which can support teachers in identifying the most useful tools for instruction.

Once the decision to move forward, start over with a different digital tool, or use traditional tools has been made, teachers move to the final element of the TIPC, planning *instruction*. At this point in the cycle, the teacher finalizes the details of their instructional planning and specific parts of the lesson that are designed to maximize the contributions and minimize the constraints of the digital tool. This process can include specific classroom management approaches, modeling of how to use the tool, or shorter guided practice with any of the parts of the instructional approach that may be needed. Once the instruction element of the cycle is complete, teachers are asked to revisit each element and *reflect* on their instructional goal to ensure that the final instruction planned still meets this goal.

USING THE TIPC WITH TEACHERS

The use of the TIPC has been studied in a range of contexts and has been used by both pre- and in-service teachers. Revisiting what is known about the use of the TIPC in a more traditional setting is useful for imagining its utility for teaching in digital spaces. Thus, the following sections describe the evidence and support for using the TIPC with pre-service and in-service teachers.

Using the TIPC with Pre-service Teachers

Although the focus of this chapter is on in-service teachers' use of the TIPC, it is important to note that there is an evidence base suggesting that pre-service teachers can also use the TIPC while learning how to plan instruction. The TIPC can be used as a scaffold for pre-service teachers as they are beginning to learn to make instructional decisions (Bergeson & Beschorner, In press), because the TIPC provides clear steps for pre-service teachers to consider as they plan instruction. Pre-service teachers have suggested that using the TIPC heightened their consciousness about all of the decisions that must be made when writing an instructional plan and that it encourages reflection throughout the planning and instruction process (Beschorner & Kruse, 2016). Although pre-service teachers often report feeling unsure of their decisions, evidence indicates that they think critically about the use of digital tools when using the TIPC to plan instruction (Bergeson & Beschorner, 2020).

Benefits of Pre-service Teachers' Use of the TIPC

Utilizing the TIPC with pre-service teachers can draw attention to the consideration of digital tools for instruction that might be overlooked without its use, because pre-service teachers report that using the TIPC helps them to think about each stage of planning instruction, including tool selection (Beschorner & Kruse, 2016). Furthermore, the use of the TIPC can increase pre-service teachers' awareness of many of the digital tools used in educational settings, which is important considering that pre-service teachers typically rely heavily on recommendations from coursework rather than researching digital tools on their own (Hutchison & Colwell, 2016). When pre-service teachers are more conscious of their instructional planning and become more aware of digital tools used in educational settings, it could encourage them to plan instruction that supports students' simultaneous development of traditional and digital literacies.

Considerations for Using the TIPC with Pre-service Teachers

Since pre-service teachers are developing all aspects of their TPACK, significant, intentional support as pre-service teachers begin to use the TIPC is necessary (Bergeson & Beschorner, 2020; Hutchison & Colwell, 2016). For example, teacher educators can model their own thinking while using the TIPC in order to illustrate the types of decisions that are necessary throughout the planning process. Considering that pre-service teachers report that tool selection is the most difficult aspect while planning (Bergeson & Beschorner, 2020), it may be particularly important for teacher educators to model how to determine affordances and constraints of multiple digital tools. It may also be necessary for teacher educators to consider how pre-service teachers can use the TIPC to plan instruction in several courses across content areas throughout their program, because pre-service teachers are often initially unsure of their decisions about the use of digital tools within their instruction (Beschorner & Kruse, 2016; Bergeson & Beschorner, in press).

Using the TIPC with In-Service Teachers

The TIPC holds much promise for supporting K-12 in-service teachers in their virtual instruction as both part of formal graduate coursework as well as in professional development. In their study of the TIPC in a graduate literacy education class, Beschorner and Woodward (2020) found that teachers selected more purposeful digital tools related to literacy instruction through utilizing the TIPC. In another study that explored how the TIPC might be used in professional development, Hutchison & Woodward (2018) found that using the TIPC to undergird a professional development model could support teachers in successfully integrating technology into their instruction to meet specific instructional goals in a variety of grades and content areas. This study found that not only did teachers feel the TIPC provided a valuable approach for selecting meaningful digital tools, but the students in these teachers' classes also scored significantly better on a digital literacy assessment.

Benefits of In-service Teachers' Use of the TIPC

In her recent book, Karchmer-Klein (2020) noted that instructional design must be at the forefront of collaborative and interactive online instruction, which is represented in the TIPC. Yet, approaches to professional development for teachers continue to focus on tool-based instruction, without the time, support, or access to knowledgeable others needed to effectively integrate digital tools into instruction (Hutchison & Woodward, 2018; Kopcha et al., 2020; Thoma et al., 2017). While recent events might have foregrounded connecting virtual instructional practices to familiar face-to face ones, instead more access to more digital tools was given with some support for specific tools teachers can choose to implement, but little guidance was provided as to how to integrate the digital tools for specific instructional purposes (Rauf, 2020).

Although teachers' access to digital tools and resources for purchasing them varies widely, the Internet has facilitated access to a number of free and low-cost digital tools that could be used for a variety of instructional purposes. Yet, teachers can feel overwhelmed with options for interesting new digital tools to use (Schwartz, 2020). Through using the TIPC, teachers are better positioned to evaluate the digital tools to which they already have access and to seek new ones to meet specific instructional needs, rather than only relying on ones that have been used previously or that are most recently promoted. The impact of the TIPC on digital tool selection was especially evident in Woodward and Hutchison's (2018) study of elementary teachers who received weekly professional development support that was grounded in using the TIPC. These teachers had iPads for every student and district curated apps that could be used. After searching the Internet for multiple additional apps that might be used in their classroom, the teachers realized that they needed support in how to identify which apps would be most useful. The TIPC professional development supported these teachers in selecting digital tools that reflected the needs of current students in their classrooms and the instruction they were planning that week, rather than trying to use new digital tools and fitting them into their instruction. For example, one teacher realized that the iPad app Skitch was a better tool for annotating images than iPhoto, because the design was similar to an app they already used previously in class, and she would be able to more easily overcome the constraint of navigating a new tool in her instruction. When teachers are able to begin with specific instructional goals situated in their own context, rather than attempting to find instructional goals to fit a specific digital tool, their instructional planning can result in meaningful learning for students.

There are also benefits to using the TIPC to inform instructional planning over time. Beschorner and Woodward (2019) found that teachers enrolled in a graduate course on literacy utilized the TIPC as they selected digital tools to create a long-term planning matrix that foregrounded the digital tools and digital literacy skills that aligned with their instruction over the course of several months. One teacher recognized that she wanted to utilize a writer's workshop instructional approach and identified a digital tool that would facilitate that work, Google Docs. As she continued to use Google Docs, this teacher reflected and recognized that when she considered the affordances of Google Docs, she could maximize in-the-moment feedback and student-to-student collaboration through incorporating additional features of Google Docs over time. This teacher's experience is just one example of the potential of the TIPC to support both teachers' daily instructional planning, as well as longer term goals and instruction.

Finally, this approach can also support teachers who are advocating for access to more or different digital tools to support their virtual learners through clearly analyzing the unique instructional contributions that possible digital tools can make to student learning. Utilizing the TIPC provides a clear instructional foundation for which to justify purchases of paid digital tools, wider access for students across multiple grades, or school to home connections, that extend beyond just the features of the tools and into clear, standards-supported instructional rationale.

Considerations for Using the TIPC with In-service Teachers

Because in-service teachers have a specific context and students for whom to plan, they may disregard particular digital tools due to perceptions about their students, prior to considering any possible instructional contributions. For example, in their work with first grade teachers, Woodward and Hutchison (2018) found that teachers selected digital tools after considering how they could overcome constraints through instruction, rather than using traditional materials that did not add additional learning opportunities for students. The teachers in that study shared that by taking time to consider both what the constraints were, as well as how to overcome them, that they were better prepared to understand how to use a particular digital tool in their instruction and what it added to student learning.

It is important to remind teachers that many constraints can be overcome with instruction, as long as they are identified in advance of implementation. It can also be helpful to foreground that many of the elements of the TIPC are likely a part of teachers' existing instructional planning. Identifying standards, instructional goals, and instructional approaches are not at all new to teachers in any learning environment, so encouraging teachers to leverage their existing pedagogical content knowledge is key to effectively utilizing the TIPC. Then, teachers can focus on developing their existing technological pedagogical content knowledge to use the TIPC to organize their instructional planning and maximize learning opportunities for their students. Finally, teachers will need to be comfortable with the cyclical nature of the TIPC and recognize that instructional goals, and sometimes instructional approaches, may change as particular digital tools bring more learning opportunities for students.

USING THE TIPC TO PLAN INSTRUCTION

As teachers and pre-service teachers use the TIPC to plan instruction for online environments, they make several decisions. These types of decisions are described in the sections below using an illustrative example of a teacher named Mrs. Peterson, and the elements of the TIPC that she uses are italicized. The ways that Mrs. Peterson might use the TIPC to plan instruction for her third-grade students, who are currently learning at home in a virtual learning environment, are explained. In this example, Mrs. Peterson's students are researching an animal of their choice in order to be able to write an informational digital text. Therefore, Mrs. Peterson needs to plan reading and writing instruction as part of this unit.

Planning for Reading Instruction

Mrs. Peterson plans to teach students to use information gained from illustrations (e.g., maps, photographs) and the words in a text to demonstrate understanding of the text (e.g., where, when, why, and how key events occur), which is Common Core State Standard CCSS.ELA-LITERACY.RI.3.7 (National Governors Association Center for Best Practices, 2010). The following sections explain how Mrs. Peterson uses the TIPC to plan a lesson that models the standard, a lesson that provides students with guided practice, and a lesson that allows students to work toward the standard during independent reading. As she plans the instruction using the TIPC, she relies on what she knows about effective pedagogy in traditional face-to-face settings to make decisions about the approaches she will use. On-going feedback to students is an important aspect of this instructional model, so she frequently reflects on her instruction and returns to different elements of the TIPC as she uses it to guide her instructional planning.

Modeling

The *instructional goal* for this lesson is standard CCSS.ELA-LITERACY.RI.3.7 and is new for Mrs. Peterson's students, so as she considers her *instructional approach*, she knows that she needs to provide modeling and gradually release responsibility (Pearson & Gallagher, 1983) for her students. Therefore, as she begins to select tools for the lesson, she wants to *select a digital tool* that will allow her to record her doing a think-aloud while reading. She decides that if she uses Voice Thread, a media player that allows users to respond to a text using audio, text, or video, she will be able to record herself reading and thinking aloud. Voice Thread will also allow her students to respond as she models using information to demonstrate understanding of the text. She could use a screencasting tool, like Screencastomatic to record a presentation, but she decides on Voice Thread, because she knows that Voice Thread will allow her to pose questions during her recording and students will be able to respond. These features make important *contributions* to the lesson, because Mrs. Peterson wants to monitor students' engagement with her video and assess their understanding during the lesson. She recognizes that VoiceThread will be a new tool to students, which could be a *constraint* of using the tool. She knows students will likely require *instruction* related to using the tool in order to be able to respond to the video that Mrs. Peterson creates. However, she believes that she can overcome this constraint through her classroom instruction.

Since Mrs. Peterson will be conducting her recording her think-aloud on Voice Thread, she knows that she will need to select the text she will use and determine when in the text she will think aloud. After she shares the Voice Thread with her students via the school's learning management system and starts to listen to and read her students' answers, she must *reflect* on the lesson and determine how to develop her next lesson, which will give students the opportunity to practice gaining information from illustrations and the words in a text to demonstrate understanding of the text.

Guided Practice

Mrs. Peterson knows that her students will benefit from practice with using illustration and words in a text to demonstrate understanding, so she plans a lesson where students will work together to "discuss" *African Animals,* an e-book that students can access for free via uniteforliteracy.com. As she considers her *instructional approach*, she would like students to be able to discuss the book during one of their live meetings, but not all students are able to participate due to Internet issues, child care challenges, etc., so, in order to try to be more equitable, Mrs. Peterson decides to plan an asynchronous lesson that students can participate in at their convenience.

After making this determination about her instructional approach, Mrs. Peterson *considers the tools* that she might use for the lesson. Since Mrs. Peterson wants students to be able to work together during this lesson, she determines that she will have students use a Padlet, www.padlet.com, after reading. Mrs. Peterson plans to provide the students the following directions on the school's learning management system:

You will be reading African Animals. As you read, identify at least three facts that you learned about African animals from the photographs or the words in the book. Then, record the facts you learned on (link to class Padlet). You can type your facts, record a video of yourself explaining the facts, or insert an image and include a caption that describes the facts. After you have added your notes, add responses using words or video to your friends' ideas and let them know what you learned about the animal that they wrote or spoke about.

She also plans to include an example of a Padlet entry to serve as a model for her students.

As Mrs. Peterson decides which text to use for the lesson, she determines that a text from the website uniteforliteracy.com would be best because the texts are easily accessible for free. Moreover, if the text is too difficult for any of the students, there is a feature where students can turn on narration and have the text read to them. *African Animals,* and the other texts on uniteforliteracy.com, have high-quality photographs that work exceptionally well for this particular lesson where students can identify details in the photographs to make sense of the text. Additionally, the texts are written in multiple languages, so students who speak multiple languages can read or listen to text with their families.

Additionally, Mrs. Peterson determines that using a Padlet could *contribute to instruction* since it is an effective tool for her students to use to collaborate, and she is able to set up accounts for them and will be able to monitor, and respond to, their work. She feels that the options for writing (e.g. video, images, text, etc.) will provide the differentiation that her students need. She considers having the students just create a Google document, but feels that the response options and organization of padlet.com would help her students meet the learning outcomes in a collaborative way. Additionally, she knows that padlet.com would allow students to see, and respond to, each other's work.

Independent Reading

Mrs. Peterson uses the TIPC to plan another literacy lesson, because she wants her students to apply their ability to use illustrations and words in a text to demonstrate understanding in their own independent reading, which is the *instructional approach* that she selects for the lesson. Next, Mrs. Peterson considers tools that she might use for independent reading. Since each student is doing research about an animal in order to write their own informational text, she decides that she will have students engage in independent reading by researching their animal using www.kids.nationalgeographic.com. She *selects* this website, because she knows that they can easily navigate the website to identity information about the animals that the students have selected. Additionally, the website includes photographs and other types of images (e.g. maps) that students can use to learn about their animals.

She knows that she wants to be able to determine what her students learned about their animals by reading the website, but she also wants students to be able to use the information as they begin to write their information text. Therefore, she *selects another digital tool* and asks students to use Popplet, www.popplet.com, to create a graphic that includes main ideas and supporting details from the text about their animal. She decides to have students use Popplet because there are many *contributions to instruction.* Students can create and design their own graphic organizer using an already familiar concept map approach, which allows them to make connections that are relevant to them as opposed to completing a predefined graphic organizer designed by the teacher. Further, Popplet will allow the students to include written text, screenshots of specific information, hyperlinks, etc. Moreover, Popplet allows users to color code their ideas, which Mrs. Peterson thinks might be helpful to her students, because they can organize their ideas by habitat, type of animal, diet, etc. or in another way that makes sense to the individual students. This way, students can use their notes when they start to write their informational text.

As she considers what possible *constraints* might be, Mrs. Peterson knows that some students might have difficulty sharing their work with her, so she creates a short video that explains the steps to share their Popplet with her. Additionally, in order to overcome this possible constraint through *instruction*, she also decides to be available for a synchronous meeting, because she thinks she can easily help students troubleshoot any difficulty they might have getting started with their Popplet. As students create and submit their work to Mrs. Peterson, she will evaluate their ability to meet the learning outcome and will *reflect* upon the instruction and the potential of additional digital tools that may support her future reading instruction.

Planning for Writing Instruction

Mrs. Peterson's students have been reading about an animal of their choice in order to write an informational text that will be written and shared using Adobe Spark. This unit supports students' ability to meet Common Core State Standard CCSS.ELA-LITERACY.W.3.2, which is to write informative/explanatory texts to examine a topic and convey ideas and information clearly. Specifically, she is working with her students on developing their topic with facts, definitions, and details, which is CCSS.ELA-LITERACY.W.3.2.B.

Similar to her reading instruction, Mrs. Peterson activates her knowledge about effective pedagogy in face-to-face contexts to design her writing instruction. Since she employs the Writer's Workshop model in her face-to-face instruction, which includes a mini-lesson, time for writing, and opportunities to share student writing (Calkins, 1994), she utilizes a similar structure as she plans for her digital instruction. She plans writing mini-lessons that include modeling, gives students opportunities to write that allow her to provide substantive feedback, and creates platforms for students to share their writing. The ways that she uses the TIPC plan this instruction is described in the following sections.

Modeling

Since Mrs. Peterson's *instructional goal* is for her students to add facts, definitions, and details to their writing, she believes that modeling how she adds to her own informative writing will support students to be able to do so in their own writing. As she plans her *instructional approach*, she considers that if she were in a face-to-face setting, her students would be participating in Writer's Workshop where they would receive a short mini-lesson before spending a considerable amount of time writing. During the mini-lesson portion of Writer's Workshop she would model adding details using the shared writing approach, where the teacher holds the pen and the students contribute to the ideas that are written. Although she values eliciting student thinking, she determines that in this case the most important aspect is that the students can hear her thinking as she writes. Therefore, she decides that her instructional approach will involve creating a screencast that records her computer screen and audio while also capturing video in the corner of the screen. As she starts to *consider what tool* she might use, she knows that there are many screencasting tools available, but she decides to use https://screencast-o-matic.com/, because it is free, intuitive, and she can create an MP4 type file that is easily accessed by students on the class's learning management system. She is excited about the *contributions to instruction* of creating the recording, because she knows that the recording will provide a contribution to her instruction, because students will be able to watch it more than once if they need to refer back as they get started on their own independent writing. After she posts the video and students apply what she modeled to her own writing, she is planning to evaluate their ability to develop their topics by reading their writing to inform her future *instruction*. As she reads their writing, she will be able to *reflect* on the effectiveness of the lesson.

Providing Feedback

Next, Mrs. Peterson develops a lesson where she can provide feedback on the students' initial drafts of writing. Although Mrs. Peterson's students are eventually going to create an informative multimodal text using Adobespark, she decides that she wants them to first draft their text using word processing only, because she wants them to focus on skills related to developing facts, definitions, and details first before integrating design skills related to images, audio, etc. She also knows that she wants to be able to provide timely feedback to students as they write. Therefore, when *selecting a tool* for the lesson, she decides to have students draft their initial ideas using Google documents, since the tool would allow her to add comments and make suggestions as students write, which is an important *contribution to her instruction*. Additionally, she is excited that Google documents will allow her to give multiple rounds of feedback as students are writing rather than the slower process of giving written feedback on a piece of paper. She knows that she will be able to provide feedback as her students write rather than waiting for students to submit drafts to her on paper. Her students have created Google documents before, so she thinks they will be able to independently create a document. She knows that typing can be a slow process for some of her students, which might be a *constraint* of using Google documents, but she believes that giving them practice to do so is necessary as part of her *instruction*. As her students share their Google documents with her, she will be leaving feedback for each of them and *reflecting* upon her instructional approach.

Sharing Writing

Typically, in a face-to-face setting, Mrs. Peterson would have her students share their writing using a range of instructional strategies like Author's Chair, partner sharing, etc., so as she is determining her *instructional approach* for sharing writing, she would like to do something similar to those strategies. Since students are not together synchronously to share their writing, and she believes that it is still important for her students to share their writing, she needs to *select a digital tool* that will facilitate this approach. As she thinks about the types of digital tools that might allow her students to share their writing, she decides to use FlipGrid and plans to ask each student to share their favorite part of their informational text. FlipGrid is a free online tool that allows users to create short videos and post them within assigned groups online. After a FlipGrid video has been posted, other users in the small group can respond by recording a video response and/or with emojis. This type of collaborative conversation is one of the affordances of FlipGrid that Mrs. Peterson identifies as being effective for sharing writing. She appreciates that students will be able to listen to one another's videos and provide thoughtful, substantive responses. She knows that her students may need some support for providing effective feedback in this type of environment, which might be a *constraint* of this too, so she plans to make several videos of herself replying to students' writing to model the appropriate discourse for responding to writing in order as part of her *instruction* to overcome this possible constraint. As students post videos and responses, she plans to monitor their conversations and provide video feedback when necessary. While viewing the videos her students create, she will be *reflecting* upon the use of FlipGrid for sharing writing in order to improve her future instruction and is prepared to consider the affordances and constraints of additional digital tools in her writing instruction.

FUTURE RESEARCH DIRECTIONS

While there is much potential for using the TIPC for supporting teachers as they select digital tools in virtual learning environments, there are important areas for additional consideration, which include access, equity, and student safety. Educational leaders must ensure that children have access to the hardware and high-speed Internet that they need (Tierney & Kolluri, 2018) to successfully engage in the rich tasks that can take place during virtual instruction and the bandwidth required to do so. Teachers must consider unique issues that may be present when several members of one family are attempting to use the Internet simultaneously. Using the TIPC in virtual instruction will require teachers to think broadly about the possible affordances and constraints, as well as what they identify as "traditional" versus "digital" tools in contexts and environments that may change daily for students.

Next, there must be recognition that the instructional decisions that are made using the TIPC are not neutral and must be equitable. Teachers must be able recognize whose interests are being served and whose are being marginalized by each of the decisions made within the TIPC. For example, teachers should consider whether or not the texts that they select are historically accurate, provide opportunities for children to see themselves and also learn about others, and allow children to think about equity and justice. Additionally, teachers must identify what scaffolding will be provided and to whom while considering if they are making assumptions about children's capabilities that may be inaccurate. Furthermore, teachers should reflect on how their instruction encourages empathy, critical thinking, creativity, and inquiry and whether or not children are making choices that allow them to take control over their own learning throughout the use of the TIPC.

Finally, further consideration of the technoethics (Krutka et al., 2019) involved when asking students to safely engage in using digital tools is needed when teaching in virtual environments. The potential of using digital tools to support and elevate student learning is high, but with increasingly sophisticated digital tools and possibilities comes additional potential risks for our students. Digital tools that are outside of learning management systems or school-district supported software may expose student data in unanticipated ways. Thus, it is critical to support teachers as they consider what information they ask students to share using digital tools and what agreements to use digital tools entail for both themselves and their students.

CONCLUSION

Teachers can use the TIPC to plan virtual instruction that maintains a focus on learning outcomes and leverages digital tools to add to and enhance students' learning. Specifically, teachers can use the TIPC to plan virtual instruction that maintains effective instructional practices, like modeling and gradual release of responsibility, while also creating opportunities for students to develop digital skills that allow them to represent their understanding in multiple forms. It is possible that using the TIPC can assist teachers in foregrounding rich instruction, rather than relying on digital tools that may reinforce low level skills through drill and practice activities.

REFERENCES

Bergeson, K., & Beschorner, B. (2020). Modeling and scaffolding the Technology Integration Planning Cycle for pre-service teachers: A case study. *International Journal of Education in Mathematics, Science, and Technology, 8*(4), 330–341. doi:10.46328/ijemst.v8i4.1031

Bergeson, K., & Beschorner, B. (2021). Pre-service teachers' use of the Technology Integration Planning Cycle: Lessons learned. *Reading Horizons, 60*(1).

Beschorner, B., & Kruse, J. (2016). Pre-Service Teachers' Use of a Technology Integration Planning Cycle: A Case Study. *International Journal of Education in Mathematics, Science and Technology, 4*(4), 258–271.

Beschorner, B., & Woodward, L. (2019). Engaging teachers in a digital learner-centered approach to support understanding of foundational literacy. In R. Karchmer-Klein & K. Pytash (Eds.), *Effective Practices in Online Teacher Preparation for Literacy Educators* (pp. 284–306). IGI Global.

Beschorner, B., & Woodward, L. (2019). Long-Term Planning for Technology in Literacy Instruction. *The Reading Teacher, 73*(3), 325–337.

Calkins, L. (1994). *The Art of Teaching Writing*. Heinemann.

Carpenter, J. P., Rosenberg, J. M., Dousay, T. A., Romero-Hall, E., Trust, T., Kessler, A., Phillips, M., Morrison, S. A., Fischer, C., & Krutka, D. G. (2020). What should teacher educators known about technology? Perspectives and self-assessments. *Teaching and Teacher Education, 95,* 1–13. doi:10.1016/j.tate.2020.103124

Ciampa, K. (2017). Building Bridges Between Technology and Content Literacy in Special Education: Lessons Learned from Special Educators' Use of Integrated Technology and Perceived Benefits for Students. *Literacy Research and Instruction, 56*(2), 85–113. doi:10.1080/19388071.2017.1280863

Common Core State Standards Initiative. (2010). *Common Core State Standards for English language arts and literacy in history/social studies, science, and technical subjects*. National Governors Association Center for Best Practices and the Council of Chief State School Officers.

Common Core State Standards Initiative. (2010). *Common Core State Standards for English language arts and literacy in history/social studies, science, and technical subjects*. National Governors Association Center for Best Practices and the Council of Chief State School Officers.

Ertmer, P. A., Ottenbreit-Leftwich, A. T., Sadik, O., Sendurur, E., & Sendurur, P. (2012). Teacher Beliefs and Technology Integration Practices: A Critical Relationship. *Computers & Education, 59*(2), 423–435. doi:10.1016/j.compedu.2012.02.001

Fisher, D., Frey, N., & Hattie, J. (2021). *The distance learning playbook: Grades K-12*. Corwin.

Hillmayr, D., Ziernwald, L., Reinhold, F., Hofer, S. I., & Reiss, K. M. (2020). The potential of digital tools to enhance mathematics and science learning in secondary schools: A context-specific meta-analysis. *Computers & Education, 153,* 1–25. doi:10.1016/j.compedu.2020.103897

Hutchison, A., & Colwell, J. (2016). Preservice Teachers' Use of the Technology Integration Planning Cycle to Integrate iPads into Literacy Instruction. *Journal of Research on Technology in Education*, *48*(1), 1–15. doi:10.1080/15391523.2015.1103146

Hutchison, A., & Woodward, L. (2014). A planning cycle for integrating digital technology into literacy instruction. *The Reading Teacher*, *67*(6), 455–464. doi:10.1002/trtr.1225

Hutchison, A., & Woodward, L. (2018). Examining the Technology Integration Planning Cycle Model of Professional Development to Support Teachers' Instructional Practices. *Teachers College Record*, *120*(10), 1–44.

Hutchison, A. C., & Colwell, J. (2014). The Potential of Digital Technologies to Support Literacy Instruction Relevant to the Common Core State Standards. *Journal of Adolescent & Adult Literacy*, *58*(2), 147–156. doi:10.1002/jaal.335

Karchmer-Klein, R. (2020). *Designing interactive and collaborative online learning opportunities for teacher education courses*. Teachers College Press.

Kopcha, T. J., Neumann, K. L., Ottenbreit-Leftwich, A., & Pitman, E. (2020). Process over product: The next evolution of our quest for technology integration. *Educational Technology Research and Development*, *68*(2), 729–749. doi:10.100711423-020-09735-y

Kozak, S., & Martin-Chang, S. (2019). Preservice Teacher Knowledge, Print Exposure, and Planning for Instruction. *Reading Research Quarterly*, *54*(3), 323–338. doi:10.1002/rrq.240

Krutka, D. G., Heath, M. K., & Willet, K. B. S. (2019). Foregrounding Technoethics: Toward Critical Perspectives in Technology and Teacher Education. *Journal of Technology and Teacher Education*, *27*(4), 555–574.

Lowrey, A. K., Classen, A., & Sylvest, A. (2019). Exploring Ways to Support Preservice Teachers' Use of UDL in Planning and Instruction. *Journal of Educational Research and Practice*, *9*(1), 261–281. doi:10.5590/JERAP.2019.09.1.19

Mishra, P., & Koehler, M. (2006). Technological Pedagogical Content Knowledge: A Framework for Teacher Knowledge. *Teachers College Record*, *108*(6), 1017–1054. doi:10.1111/j.1467-9620.2006.00684.x

National Governors Association Center for Best Practices. (2010). Common Core State Standards. National Governors Association Center for Best Practices, Council of Chief State School Officers.

Panero, M., & Aldon, G. (2016). How Teachers Evolve Their Formative Assessment Practices When Digital Tools Are Involved in the Classroom. *Digital Experiences in Mathematics Education*, *2*(1), 70–86. doi:10.100740751-016-0012-x

Pearson, P. D., & Gallagher, M. C. (1983). The instruction of reading comprehension. *Contemporary Educational Psychology*, *8*(3), 317–344. doi:10.1016/0361-476X(83)90019-X

Rauf, D. S. (2020, April 23). How districts are helping teachers get better at tech under coronavirus. *Education Week*. https://www.edweek.org/ew/articles/2020/04/22/how-districts-are-helping-teachers-get-better.html

Schwartz, S. (2020, March 25). Flood of Online Learning Resources Overwhelms Teachers. *Education Week*. https://www.edweek.org/teaching-learning/flood-of-online-learning-resources-overwhelms-teachers/2020/03

Shulman, L. S. (1986). Those Who Understand: Knowledge Growth in Teaching. *Educational Researcher*, *15*(2), 4–14. doi:10.3102/0013189X015002004

Thoma, J., Hutchison, A., Johnson, D., Johnson, K., & Stromer, E. (2017). Planning for Technology Integration in a Professional Learning Community. *The Reading Teacher*, *71*(2), 167–175. doi:10.1002/trtr.1604

Tierney, W., & Kolluri, S. (2018). Mapping the Terrain: Youth and Digital Media. In W. Tierney, Z. B. Corwin, & A. Ochsner (Eds.), *Diversifying Digital Learning* (pp. 1–24). Johns Hopkins University Press.

Woodward, L., & Hutchison, A. (2018). The STAK Model: Exploring Professional Development for Technology Integration Into Instruction. *Journal of Technology and Teacher Education*, *26*(4), 613–644.

ADDITIONAL READING

Beschorner, B., & Hall, A. (2017). Taking a closer look at your informational writing instruction. *The Reading Teacher*, *71*(5), 597–600. doi:10.1002/trtr.1656

Colwell, J. (2019). Selecting Texts for Disciplinary Literacy Instruction. *The Reading Teacher*, *72*(5), 631–637. doi:10.1002/trtr.1762

Karchmer-Klein, R., Mouza, C., Harlow Shinas, V., & Park, S. (2017). Patterns in Teachers' Instructional Design When Integrating Apps in Middle School Content-Area Teaching. *Journal of Digital Learning in Teacher Education*, *33*(3), 91–102. doi:10.1080/21532974.2017.1305305

Kimmons, R., & Hall, C. (2018). How Useful are our Models? Pre-Service and Practicing Teacher Evaluations of Technology Integration Models. *TechTrends*, *62*(1), 29–36. doi:10.100711528-017-0227-8

Leary, H., Dopp, C., Turley, C., Cheney, M., Simmons, Z., Graham, C. R., & Hatch, R. (2020). Professional development for online teaching: A literature review. *Online Learning*, *24*(4), 254–275. doi:10.24059/olj.v24i4.2198

O'Byrne, W. I., & Pytash, K. E. (2015). Hybrid and Blended Learning. *Journal of Adolescent & Adult Literacy*, *59*(2), 137–140. doi:10.1002/jaal.463

Reich, J. (2019). Teaching our way to digital equity. *Educational Leadership*, *76*(5), 30–35.

Siefert, B., Kelly, K., Yearta, L., & Oliveira, T. (2019). Teacher Perceptions and Use of Technology Across Content Areas with Linguistically Diverse Middle School Students. *Journal of Digital Learning in Teacher Education*, *35*(2), 107–121. doi:10.1080/21532974.2019.1568327

KEY TERMS AND DEFINITIONS

Constraints: As used in the TIPC, constraints are those particular instructional obstacles that arise when using a digital tool with students.

Digital Tools: A website, app, program, or other software available on a technology device (e.g. iPad, laptop, smart phone, etc.), including those that are multimodal.

Feedback: A part of the assessment process that involves teachers communicating with students about their progress towards specific instructional goals and is often included as a possible Contribution to Instruction of a digital tool and part of the Instruction element of the TIPC.

Instructional Planning: The approach that teachers utilize when selecting standards-based learning objectives, selecting and/or curating materials, and creating the instruction involved in supporting students' success towards particular learning goals.

Multimodal: Materials that utilize more than a single mode of communication. Examples include written text with visuals, videos, animations, etc.

Reflection: An analysis of a teacher's context in which they are teaching as related to providing instruction for a particular instructional goal.

Technoethics: The social and privacy-related implications of using technology.

Technology Integration: Meaningfully incorporating digital tools to meet instructional goals. This is distinguished from using technology to accomplish tasks, such as a learning management system to submit a paper or sending an email.

Chapter 7
Four Steps to Promote Teacher Creativity When Making the Transition to Virtual Learning Experiences

Matthew Worwood
University of Connecticut, USA

ABSTRACT

This chapter presents four steps for teacher creativity as part of a design-based approach to problem-solving pedagogical challenges using virtual learning environments. Building on existing practices found in creative problem-solving and design thinking methodology, these steps explore change as a journey that begins with an intent to produce an outcome that improves a specific aspect of the learning experience. Glaveanu's five-A framework provides a sociocultural perspective to support the concept of teacher creativity in the classroom, while Kaufman and Beghetto's 4-C model serves as a developmental approach to evaluating outcomes based on the impact they have in the environment. Future opportunities for study, including integrating learning analytics and situating the different stages of creative problem-solving in education, are also discussed.

INTRODUCTION

The global pandemic significantly disrupted K-12 education; students of all ages were thrust into distant learning, while parents were tasked with providing oversight during the workday. Absent procedural norms, teachers were challenged to design solutions to varying problems using new technologies. These solutions were also deployed under entirely new circumstances and have remained in flux when some schools have returned full-time. Others have maintained 100% distant learning, and some have adopted a mix-matched hybrid approach. Furthermore, teachers have had to address increased absences, unprecedented rules around social distancing, and situations where a few students are still learning remotely even while most of the class has returned to school.

DOI: 10.4018/978-1-7998-7222-1.ch007

The events related to the pandemic are extreme, but in many ways, they portray preexisting disruptions already present because of the Digital Age. Teachers are routinely tasked to integrate new technology into their practice to address the pedagogical challenges of virtual learning (Kenney & Zysman, 2016; McLeod & Shareski, 2017; OECD, 2018; OECD, 2019). Those with the characteristics of early adopters may have adjusted well to this reality but those who are part of the late majority may find this aspect of their practice particularly challenging (see Rogers, 2003). Whatever category an individual may reside in, the premise is the same – today's teaching practitioner must develop knowledge and new pedagogical reasoning around new technologies and their relationship to virtual learning experiences; Covid-19 merely accelerated this need to an extreme.

This chapter explores the connection between creative problem-solving methodology and instructional change necessitated when tasked with transitioning to virtual learning environments (VLEs). Specifically, it introduces four steps that promote a design-based approach to teacher creativity when transitioning to a VLE. These four steps take established CPS procedures and situate them inside teaching and learning using new technology.

CHANGE AND TECHNOLOGY

What constitutes a change in education has remained a prominent topic among practitioner-scholars, administrators, and educational researchers (Hancock et al., 2007; Maddux et al., 1997; Montrieux et al., 2017). Alison King's (1993) *Sage on Stage or Guide on the Side* is one example of a change advocated toward existing methods of instruction. Within this popular article, King presents the instructor as a "Sage on the Stage" (p. 30) who facilitates the one-way transfer of information. King promotes change as a transition away from this pedagogical approach and toward a concept coined "Guide on the Side" (p. 30). With greater attention toward strategies like project-based learning, this term became a view to support approaches dedicated to student-centered instruction. Although debates continue for how much guidance is required to make these alternative approaches to learning effective (Kirschner, Sweller, & Clark, 2006; Sweller, Kirschner, & Clark, 2007), technology and teacher beliefs are influential factors when making a transition to something new. (Barak, 2017; Montrieux et al., 2017; Overbay et al., 2010; Zielinski, 2017). However, change toward an instructional approach does not necessarily require a change in the philosophical understanding of teaching and learning.

New technological tools or existing virtual learning platforms can also enhance existing practices supporting subtle changes when transitioning to a VLE. When viewed from this perspective, creativity is less about radical change and more about the discovery of new possibilities inside current constraints. This chapter is dedicated to the latter, focusing on engaging teacher creativity to improve the design of virtual learning experiences in K-12 schooling. A subtle change in a teacher's practice can include modifying an instructional procedure that enhances a single aspect of an existing learning experience instead of a drastic change in teaching philosophy (Guskey, 2002). This change can include modifications in delivering content, feedback, or improving student engagement during a learning task. During the initial stages of the pandemic, these types of modifications took place as teachers began transitioning existing practices to VLEs to support schooling from home. Applications like Loom and Zoom offered an easy way to deliver existing in-class presentations synchronously or asynchronously. These experiences often took place with support from existing learning management systems already available or used in the classroom. Under these conditions, some practitioners would be familiar with the technology, but few would have had experience using the technology to support learning from a distance. Therefore, elements commonly experienced in more traditional face-to-face settings (e.g., in-class presentations, in-class discussions, responding to feedback, etc.) would introduce challenges under the new conditions for teaching and learning.

Highlighting new practices for virtual presentations during the pandemic provides an example to showcase opportunities where subtle changes to an existing presentation format can improve learning outcomes even when teaching via a VLE at a distance. Within these environments, lectures can take the form of a sequence of short video tutorials. Research shows this type of change can improve students' understanding of the material compared to longer-form videos with the same content (Fiorella et al., 2019). Likewise, modifications to the presentation of information on a screen can increase retention, with research emphasizing the benefit of focusing on the design, text, and narration of visuals (Mayer, 2017).

The subtle changes exemplified above highlight the opportunities to improve instruction when teaching using VLEs. However, they also demonstrate that change is a consequence of actions conducted by the teacher. Classroom practitioners possess the power to decide how a technological tool is used (Hall & Hord, 2015) and can also choose to reject it (Blackwell et al., 2016; Ertmer & Ottenbreit-Leftwich, 2010). Therefore, change through technology is not dependent on having access or knowledge of a technological tool, but the capacity to engage in a process that "recreates" and "reorganizes" the delivery of instruction (Mills & Tincher, 2003, p. 383).

CHANGE AND CREATIVITY

Rather than seeing change through technology as something facilitated by an outside force, the concept of teacher creativity looks toward the classroom practitioner as a lifelong learner constantly tasked with responding to disturbances introduced because of technological change. Within the context of this chapter, the disorder is a global pandemic. Still, as outlined in the previous paragraph, the challenges of the pandemic highlighted an already existing situation related to instructional practices and the increasing use of VLEs. When engaged in addressing problems that arise when under these conditions, teachers must think and act creatively to produce solutions.

Within the Concerns-Based Adoption Model, Hall (2010) presents the concept of an innovation bridge to visualize the teacher change process; on one side of the bridge is a teacher's existing practice and on the other side is a change to that practice introduced because of innovation. However, change is not synonymous with improvement. Consequently, teacher creativity offers an opportunity to view this journey as something that should conclude with a new outcome that improves the learning experience. Furthermore, it expands the concept of creativity in education beyond students in the classroom. This view of creativity forms an interesting paradox; teachers are called on to cultivate creativity in students without always having an applied understanding of the concept themselves (Beghetto, 2010; Lin, 2011). The pandemic challenges have demonstrated the importance of teacher creativity in the classroom, therefore seeking ways to promote and facilitate this construct is vital to the future of education and VLE use in K-12 public schooling.

Teacher Creativity

Plucker et al. (2004) define creativity as producing new and valuable outcomes relevant to a specific context. Although novelty is a theme commonly associated with creativity (Plucker & Dow, 2016), many of the stereotypes around this construct often fail to address the importance of an outcome as evaluated within the context to where it exists. This view of teacher creativity assumes a sociocultural perspective for this construct, which has gained momentum in recent years, as demonstrated by a manifesto titled *Advancing Creativity and Research: A Sociocultural Manifesto* (Glaveanu et al., 2019). This document does not challenge previous research that focuses on individualized units of creativity, which include special attention toward the individual, the process, or the outcomes produced (Glaveanu, 2010; Rhodes, 1960), but it does highlight the complexity of creativity and how these varying factors interact inside a specified environment under study.

Sociocultural theories also emphasize an individual's actions as they exist inside an environment. Tools and objects offer action possibilities inside that environment (Gee, 2008; Gibson, 1977), but realizing these possibilities is beholden to how an individual perceives and uses these tools (Blewett & Hugo, 2016; Vygotsky, 1978). Glaveanu's (2013) five-A framework for creativity builds on existing sociocultural theories to emphasize how environmental factors come together to influence creativity (see Glaveanu, 2013). Presenting the intricacies of this framework expands beyond the scope of this chapter. Still, the importance of a teacher's actions in terms of how they perceive and use technological tools helps establish a way to view and promote this construct: teacher creativity considers the actions taken by the teacher in response to a problem and the outcomes they produce because of those actions (see Figure 1).

Figure 1. Situating teacher creativity inside a teacher's professional environment

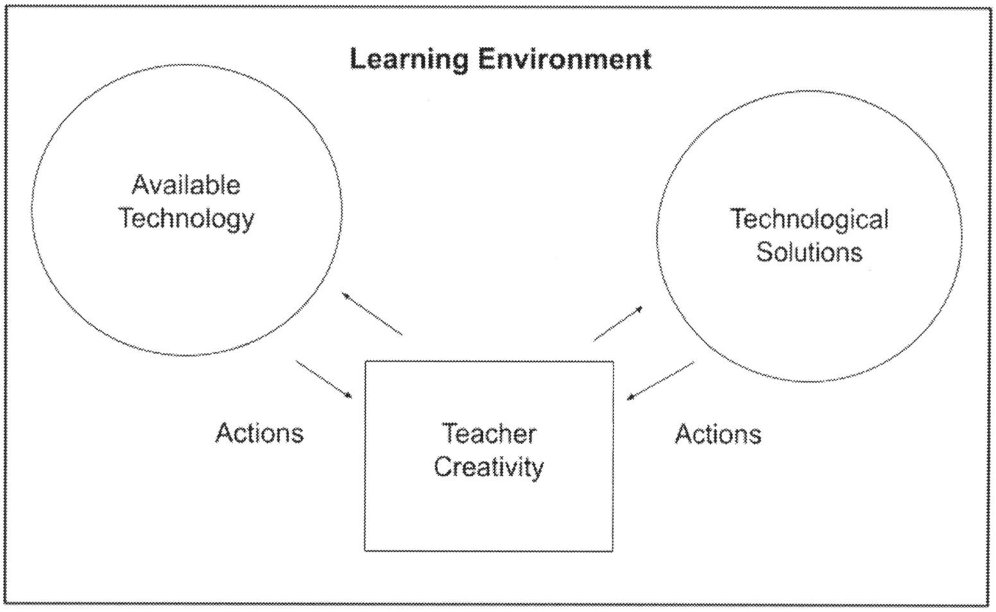

CREATIVE PROBLEM-SOLVING

Creative problem-solving offers an established sequence of evidence-based actions to help facilitate teacher creativity when designing learning experiences for VLEs. Like the concept of the innovation bridge (Hall, 2010), these actions represent a journey with distinct stages (Wallas, 1926) to support change (Puccio et al., 2011). Furthermore, these stages support situations where there is a deliberate intent to produce a new and valuable outcome in response to a problem (Darbellay et al., 2018, Mumford, 2017; Puccio et al., 2011). Therefore, they are appropriate when making a transition to a VLE, as a teacher must assume agency for developing technological solutions to support their learning environment.

Graham Wallas (1926) and Alex Osborn (1963) are two early pioneers of CPS; both were fascinated with creative production and studied stages of the process that were common among creatives. In his book, The Art of Thought (1926), Wallas presented preparation as the first stage of the process, representing exploring problems, followed by a second stage called incubation that considers time taken to process information. Illumination and verification proceed these stages and consider idea selection, development, and implementation. Alex Osborn's (1963) later work on CPS identified similar steps categorized as fact-finding, problem-finding, and idea finding.

Current CPS methods include the creative process model (Mumford et al., 1991) and the thinking skills model (Puccio et al., 2011). There is also increased attention toward design-based approaches to CPS, commonly referred to as design thinking (see IDEO Design Thinking; IBM Enterprise Design Thinking). Detailed examination of differences between CPS and design thinking expands beyond the focus of this chapter; however, design thinking contains a similar profile as CPS but places more emphasis on human-centered design (Worwood & Plucker, 2018). Under these conditions, information gathered about the end-user is placed at the forefront of idea generation, selection, and evaluation (Wolcott et al., 2020; Worwood & Plucker, 2018). From this perspective, design thinking appears more suitable for sociocultural perspectives of creativity because it encourages focus toward environmental factors such as people and context.

Although these recent forms of CPS have expanded upon the initial stages identified by Wallas and Osborn, they still contain the core principles of information gathering, problem definition, idea generation, idea evaluation, and real-world implementation (see Table 1). Training in these core principles is applied to improve creative outcomes among individuals and groups (Hargrove, 2011; Hargrove & Nietfeld, 2014), with research showing it can increase ideas, help clarify problems, and improve creativity overall (Scott et al., 2004a; Scott et al., 2004b; Puccio et al., 2018). With a growing acceptance of these methods, opportunities exist to consider how best to situate core CPS principles inside specific domains (Marcy & Mumford, 2007; Mumford & Mcintosh, 2017).

INTRODUCING FOUR STEPS FOR TEACHER CREATIVITY

The following section introduces four steps for teacher creativity that support an individual's approach to the identification and use of technological tools that improve virtual learning experiences. Although the stages of creative problem-solving and design thinking are considered transferable across domains (Puccio et al., 2011; Worwood & Plucker, 2018), sociocultural theory emphasizes the importance of situating knowledge of procedures inside a specific context when learning to apply them in practice (Gee, 2008). Consequently, the four steps for teacher creativity are targeted toward professional learning

Table 1. Common procedures of CPS and design thinking grouped according to Osborn's CPS process

Method	Fact-Finding	Idea-Finding	Solution-Finding
Art of Thought (Wallas, 1926)	Preparation	Incubation/ Illumination	Verification
Universal Traveler, (Koberg & Bagnall, 1972)	Analyze/Define	Ideate/Select	Select/ Implement
Thinking Skills Model (Puccio et al., 2007)	Clarification: Exploring the Vision/ Formulating Challenges	Transformation: Formulating Ideas	Transformation: Formulating Solutions
IBM Enterprise Design Thinking	Observe/Reflect	Reflect/Make	Make/Reflect
IDEO Design Thinking Creative Thinking Processes (Mumford, 2017)	Empathy/Define Problem Definition/ Information Gathering/ Concept Selection	Ideate/Prototype Conceptual Combination/ Idea Generation/ Idea Evaluation	Prototype/Test Implementation Planning/ Adaptive Execution

when responding to problems using VLEs. This approach supports the need to connect domain-general creativity skills to the realities of a real-world context (Mumford, Martin, Elliott, & McIntosh, 2018).

Within the domain of teaching and learning, classroom practitioners hold existing pedagogical reasoning toward the use of technology in their environment. Some research suggests this reasoning may come with a preference for using technology to support instructional practice and increase student engagement, versus using technology to improve cognitive development in students (Hughes et al., 2020). During the transition to VLEs, both preferences are required as teachers will need to reexamine instructional views when teaching from a distance, while also considering how best to facilitate learning outside a traditional classroom setting. Under these conditions, pedagogical reasoning must consider the way technology is selected and applied when designing learning experiences for an environment dependent on technology use (Niess & Gillow-Wiles, 2013). Therefore, the four steps for teacher creativity are presented as a design-based approach to CPS, with a focus toward the identification and evaluation of technological solutions that improve teaching and learning when using VLEs.

Process Overview

Returning to the concept of the innovation bridge, "change is a process. Not an event" (Hall & Hord, 2015). Like the concept of the innovation bridge, during the early years of creative problem solving, this process was likened to a journey (Koberg & Bagnall, 1972; Wallas, 1926). A prerequisite to successful engagement in this journey is acknowledging a "disturbance" to existing practices (Havelock, 1973, p. 6). This disturbance could arise from an extreme event like the global pandemic. It may also occur because new information changes an individual's current perception of something in their environment.

Although the methods previously outlined suggest a linear progression over the bridge, the journey often presents twists and turns during the design and implementation of new technological solutions. This concept is illustrated in Figure 2, with each designated name representing a step forward on the journey. However, the drastic bends signify the twists and turns that may occur as more information about the situation is acquired. This information interacts with existing pedagogical and technological knowledge, a concept made popular by the TPACK frame, which promotes technology integration by design (see Mishra & Koehler, 2006). Therefore, teacher creativity provides further support to the idea of "adapting, reusing, and repurposing new technology" by harnessing technological, pedagogical, and content knowledge during the design and development of new learning experiences (Koehler et al., 2011, p. 149). Acknowledging existing frameworks for teacher change establishes credible connections to help promote CPS inside the teaching profession. Furthermore, prompting this process as a collection of creative steps introduces new ways to view the design of learning experiences inside VLEs – teachers are designers working to produce new technological solutions applicable to their context.

Figure 2. Four steps to support teacher creativity

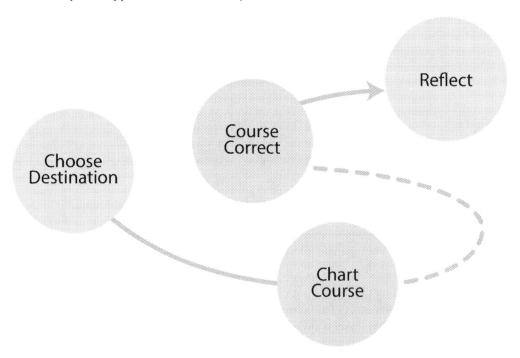

The capacity to think divergently is a popular focus when exploring actions that support creative production (Acar, 2017; Puccio et a., 2018; Runco & Acar, 2012). Divergent thinking considers the production of new and alternative ideas (Torrance & Safter, 1999). However, Cropley (2006) emphasizes the importance of convergent thinking, which considers an individual or group's capacity to identify the most appropriate idea for development and implementation. Like Mishra and Koehler (2006), Cropley (2006) considers knowledge as "a well from which ideas are drawn" (p. 395). Therefore, the journey toward teacher creativity is dependent on an individual's ability to choose their destination, chart their course, and make subsequent course corrections along the way. All while working within the constraints of teaching and learning using a VLE. As teachers participate in these steps they will partake in divergent and convergent thinking exercises to consider alternative ways to view technology, but also make selections that help move the process toward an evidence-based solution.

Most importantly, the final action of this journey challenges the teacher to evaluate their outcome based on its impact within the environment. This last aspect of the journey uses Kauffman and Beghetto's (2009) 4-C framework to categorize outcomes based on the perception by others familiar with the domain. Although change may have occurred at some level, the 4-C framework considers the relationship of this change as viewed by the individual teacher, the students, and colleagues. What follows is an overview of these four steps as they apply to teachers engaged in the transition to a VLE.

Step 1: Choose Destination

The first action, *Choose Destination*, is when an individual begins to address the ambiguity that arises when there is a desired change in circumstances to an existing practice. The first-time transition to VLEs introduces tension between existing pedagogical understandings and how they apply to this new learning environment. As a teacher begins to explore this situation in action, they will interact with new challenges and opportunities related to teaching and learning. During the pandemic, this tension was particularly evident as teachers were tasked with continuing existing practices from a distance with little understanding of a preferred outcome. New technologies were presented as immediate solutions to problems that arose under these new conditions; however, these technologies were introduced with few opportunities for training and support. Soon, new problems emerged because of security concerns, Internet access, screen time, engagement, and a new reliance on parental support. Each of these situations challenged teachers to identify and develop specific technological solutions relevant to their environment. Therefore, the first action of teacher creativity is considering all the problems and opportunities that exist (or may exist) under the new conditions of teaching and learning using VLEs.

As teachers begin this initial stage of the process, they focus on divergent thinking techniques, such as brainstorming or brainwriting. These strategies are common in creative circles and use existing knowledge to generate multiple ideas or suggestions in response to an open-ended prompt. Potential examples to support this initial activity include the following:

- what opportunities exist for teaching and learning inside my VLE;
- what problems exist for teaching and learning inside my VLE;
- what challenges can I expect as I transition my current assignments to my VLE; and
- what equity issues exist inside my VLE.

Although all four questions represent an open-ended prompt to initiate divergent thinking, the latter two focus attention on two themes of potential concern that were made apparent during the pandemic. Therefore, a teacher may assume a broad approach to this activity or choose to focus on a particular area of interest. Furthermore, divergent thinking can take place as a group or individual exercise. Traditionally, brainstorming is an ideation activity where individuals verbally communicate suggestions in a group. A large sheet of paper or something similar is used to record these ideas and make them easily accessible to all participating members. Brainwriting is considered a similar exercise to brainstorming but conducted by the individual and recorded in private. Debates about the influence of judgment and experience during divergent thinking continue within creativity research (Cropley 2006; Tien et al., 2019), but the overall objective for these exercises is to produce as many responses as possible (Osborn, 1963; Puccio et al., 2018). Furthermore, the more knowledge teachers know about the situation, the more suggestions they will likely produce; therefore, there is an advantage in delaying this activity until teachers have had an opportunity to increase their knowledge base of VLEs and related issues.

Once a teacher or group of teachers have produced many items to consider, they are ready to converge on a single theme that will eventually form an intended goal (e.g., grading, feedback, engagement, group work, etc.). There are likely multiple challenges that exist during the transition to VLEs; some challenges may require immediate attention, others may require resources not available to the teacher, and some may have constraints too challenging to overcome. Consequently, the goal of choose destination is not the selection or exploration of technology but the identification and clarification of a single problem firmly situated inside a teacher's environment. When making these selections, a teacher must consider perceived barriers to teacher creativity. These barriers may include the perception of a rigid curriculum, lack of resources, time challenges, and perceived pressures from the administration (Worwood, 2020). Therefore, a significant factor of this first step is not generating lots of ideas but an individual's ability to recognize the constraints and procedures needed to produce a viable solution inside the environment (Davis, 2004; Mumford et al., 2018). Applying this knowledge can help teachers avoid problems they cannot address under the current conditions and select issues that are most likely to impact the learning experience positively. If engaged successfully, this action should increase teacher agency as it challenges individuals to identify unique problems applicable to their practice and level of expertise. After identifying a problem, a teacher can move to the next step in the process.

Step 2: Chart Course

Despite identifying a problem, ambiguity remains until a teacher has selected a tool that can assist the design and development of a solution. Consequently, *Chart Course* encourages a teacher to explore available features and tools available to the VLE. This step continues to reduce ambiguity for the teacher by establishing a destination and guide to begin the creative journey. The activity undertaken for this stage is developing a short problem statement that lists an intended goal, technology, and context for implementation. This activity aligns more toward the creative actions associated with designers as it integrates the production of an artifact that serves the purpose of a client's brief (Gleavean et al., 2013). Likewise, this step requires the inclusion of information to support creativity by documenting the intention of what a teacher plans to change (Ryd, 2004). The phrasing of a problem statement is important, as different approaches can encourage or discourage divergent and convergent thinking (Liu et al., 2018; Silk et al., 2014). Listing the goal establishes the intended change. Including the technology provides the how-to, and stating the context offers focus during exploration and development.

Beginning a problem statement with phrases that encourage divergent thinking is important to the overall production of multiple ideas (Liu et al., 2018). Creativity literature emphasizes this point (Runco & Acar, 2012; Runco et al., 2001; Runco et al., 2014), with research showing how divergent thinking can boost creative output when tasked with producing ideas in response to a problem (Acar, 2017; Runco & Acar, 2012; Puccio et al., 2018). Therefore, a problem statement should avoid phasing that leads to the generation of a single idea and instead encourage the production and consideration of multiple ideas (see Table 2). Problem statements are single sentences that benefit from the information that helps focus thoughts on the problem and context under investigation (Bonnardel & Didier, 2020). Furthermore, problem statements may help teachers evaluate outcomes during the subsequent stages of the creative process and therefore assist teachers in establishing new ways to perceive available tools in the environment (Worwood, 2020).

Table 2. Example of problem statements applicable to VLEs. Problem statements contain an intended goal, technology to help achieve that goal, and a specified context for investigation

Problem-Statement	Technology	Intended Goal	Context
Instruction			
In what ways can I use Flipgrid to establish a closer relationship with students while teaching 9th grade English from a distance?	Flipgrid	Establish close relationships with students	9th Grade English Class
In what ways can the Seasaw app support timely feedback to students?	Seasaw App	Deliver timely feedback	Teaching via Seesaw
How can increased use of Google Translate improve group participation for ELA students during group discussion?	Google Translate	Increase participation for ELA students during class discussions	Activities involving group discussion
How might Google Docs better facilitate break-out activities conducted during class Zoom meetings?	Google Docs (and all available features)	Improve facilitation of group break-out activities conducted via Zoom	Activities involving group discussion
Cognitive Development			
In what ways can podcasting increase deeper thinking when teaching students about scientific methods in my 10th grade Earth Sciences course?	Podcasting Tools	Increase deeper thinking for the scientific method	10th Grade Earth Science Course
In what ways can I use Flipgrid to replicate my preference for using in-class debates to challenge deeper thinking among students in my social studies class?	Flipgrid	Replicate in-class debates	Debates in social studies class

Step 3: Course Correct

The next step in the process is *Course Correct*, which represents the exploration of enacted ideas and technology during instruction. This step is when a teacher begins to implement selected ideas and evaluates success based on the feedback they receive from the environment. During the development and early implementation of ideas, they become outcomes observable to others inside the environment. However, although this step is familiar with existing practices when using something new in the classroom, the teacher must remain committed to the problem statement and seek various channels of feedback to challenge potential bias when making judgments about this outcome. Data is a crucial aspect of any design process, as it provides essential information to refine and improve an idea during implementation (Goodwin, Low Ling, Ng Tee, Yeung, & Cai, 2015). Data obtained from this experience should include opportunities to challenge initial perceptions formed by the teacher. Therefore, self-monitoring is critical during this step; a teacher must learn from failure and resist the temptation to abandon an effort because it is not working as intended. Likewise, they should not accept an idea based on assumptions or observations from one or two students only. Instead, this step is about making informed decisions when making modifications or ratifying a solution.

Although virtual learning experiences may disrupt some methods for obtaining feedback in the classroom, learning management systems provide new ways to receive feedback. For example, quantitative data offered through platforms like Blackboard, Moodle, and Canvas can introduce some teachers to the value of learning analytics (Avella et al., 2016; Zacharoula et al., 2014). Whereas online applications like Flipgrid can help facilitate virtual interactions that produce qualitative data similar to a more traditional learning environment. Likewise, applications like Google Forms make it easy for teachers to create short surveys to obtain regular feedback from students. Thanks to VLEs, this data is becoming increasingly available to teachers and must become part of a system for evaluating ideas and technological solutions.

Some classroom practitioners may already recognize these concepts as iterative design and experimentation with technology; however, Reeves (2008) stresses that this approach must contain a structure with established problems and methods for evaluation. Therefore, when evaluating enacted ideas, a teacher must continue to reflect on the problem statement identified during the previous steps (Figure 3). It is unlikely that focus on the technology alone will meet the goals outlined in the problem statement. Therefore, teachers must continually tweak elements inside the learning experience, including modifications to assignment prompts and changes to the lesson's format. For example, FlipGird provides teachers with the ability to set time durations of student videos and include prompts on the platform. Likewise, when using an application like FlipGrid, a teacher decides the time given to complete the assignment, student grouping, and facilitating peer and teacher feedback. All these factors apply to the problem statement and should receive ongoing review and modifications during this stage. Only when a teacher feels they've produced a meaningful outcome should they transition to the final step of the process.

Figure 3. Course correct challenges teachers to enact ideas and evaluate those ideas based on their relationship to the problem statement. Ideas are then modified to produce a final outcome

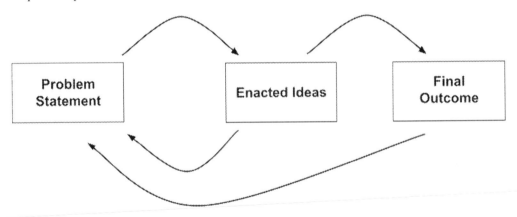

Step 4: Reflect

The final step is when a teacher evaluates the new outcome based on its impact on the environment. Like the previous step, teachers are encouraged to obtain feedback from others who know the context to where the outcome exists. Therefore, this activity supports a preference for collaboration among colleagues when facilitating professional learning opportunities (Learning Forward, 2011; Swan et al., 2014). During this type of discussion, teachers should articulate whether they produced a new outcome within their practice while also determining the extent to which it addressed the intended problem. This reflective activity uses the 4-C framework of creativity, which categories outcomes into mini-, little-c, pro-c, and big-c creativity (see Kaufman & Beghetto, 2009). As the latter represents a level of innovation reserved for elite scientists, inventors, and entrepreneurs, it is excluded from the framework when applied to evaluating teacher creativity during the transition to VLEs (see Table 3).

Table 3. 4-C model of creativity used as a framework to evaluate outcomes of teacher creativity

	Five-A Framework	**Teacher Creativity**
Mini-C	Considers individual accomplishment within a learning process (e.g., learning to play the piano for the first time)	The teacher perceives the outcome as a personal achievement that delivered something new and useful inside the VLE. However, this achievement is difficult to recognize by people other than the individual teacher, including students and fellow colleagues.
Little-C	New and useful accomplishments that others within the social context can identify and appreciate	The teacher perceives the outcome as new and useful when compared to existing practices taking place in VLEs used at the school. The outcome is recognized by other people connected to the environment such as students and fellow colleagues.
Pro-C	Considered as expert level. Builds on substantial knowledgebase to produce outcomes that change existing paradigms	The outcome is perceived as a solution based on evidence. Replication of the idea is taking place among the teaching community and has begun to challenge existing paradigms within the school or wider district.
Big-C	Transformational outcomes that deliver far-reaching change that extends beyond the lifetime of the individual	N/A

Mini-C

Mini-c outcomes are considered those that capture an individual's accomplishment because of a learning event (Kaufman et al., 2013). The newness and usefulness of the result are confined to the individual and do not expand any further (Beghetto & Kaufman, 2007). Kaufman and Beghetto (2009) present mini-c creativity as a helpful way to investigate young children's creativity, who routinely produce creative outcomes as they formulate and explore new ideas about their world. Although these discoveries are likely known and therefore come with little value to others, they remain creative when viewed from the individual's perspective. However, when considering the 4-C model as a developmental framework to teacher creativity, mini-c represents the initial ideas and discoveries a teacher makes when considering problems and solutions applicable to the VLE. These initial discoveries about the environment provide a foundation that can lead to little-c, and eventually pro-c outcomes over time (Kaufman & Beghetto, 2009). Therefore, they are most likely to emerge during the previous stage course correct, when teachers are producing new knowledge about the technology and its potential relationship in the environment.

Little-C

Little-c has a history of representing the everyday acts of creativity that do not constitute significant changes within a domain but remain essential to the immediate environment (Kaufman & Beghetto, 2009). More importantly, little-c is considered a representative of the everyday actions associated with creative teaching in the classroom (Bloom & VanSlyke-Briggs, 2019). The individual's limited knowledge of the situation makes it unlikely this outcome will significantly change the community. Nevertheless, others with direct knowledge of the problem can recognize these individual acts of creativity, promoting some replication among colleagues. Furthermore, little-c outcomes produce valued changes in the environment that improves a learning experience for either the teacher or the students (Bloom & VanSlyke-Briggs, 2019). These outcomes address the problem statement and form initial efforts during the first-time transition to a VLE.

Pro-C

The final category to consider when reflecting on outcomes produced by the teacher is how they impact the community (e.g., school or district). Pro-c outcomes introduce systematic changes inside a profession (Kaufman & Beghetto, 2009). Typically, this would require extensive expertise obtained through years of service, however, when applied to teacher creativity, pro-c outcomes represent those expanding beyond the individual teacher's environment by having a significant impact inside the wider school community (e.g., department, building, district). An idea viewed as a pro-c outcome is an evidence-based solution accepted by colleagues and promoted by members of the administration.

Evaluating Outcomes

Teacher creativity represents a collection of actions that help identify technological solutions to improve an aspect of the learning experience. Using the four steps outlined above, teachers can clarify problems and develop solutions in support of VLEs. Example questions presented in Table 4 demonstrate how the 4-C framework can facilitate a final reflection to categories the level of creativity based on its relationship inside the school community. This activity can take place individually or among colleagues. The latter is considered an essential aspect of professional learning and is therefore considered a preferred approach for this final step (Curwood, 2014; Kuh, 2016; Rohlwing & Spelman, 2014; Swan et al., 2014). Those interacting with a new problem or technological feature inside a VLE will likely begin at mini-c. Still, as their discoveries lead to further implementation and experimentation, they will start to construct new knowledge about their idea, the technology, and its relation to teaching and learning inside the VLE. Although this aspect of the process is relevant throughout the journey toward a creative outcome, teachers must prioritize time to reflect when they feel they've produced a solution that responds to their problem statement.

Table 4. Questions used to guide reflection when evaluating ideas for creativity. Questions are organized using the 4-C framework.

Mini-c	Little-c	Pro-c
What discoveries have I made about my problem? What discoveries have I made about my VLE? What discoveries have I made about the technological tools available to my VLE? What discoveries have I made about the different instructional approaches available inside my VLE? Do I consider my idea a potential solution to my problem?	What do other people in my environment think about my idea? How are students responding to my idea during implementation? What impact does my idea have on individual students in my class? How does my idea compare to other enacted ideas in my school community? Does my solution impact everyone in the same way? How do I know my idea works?	Do I have credible evidence that shows my idea solved the problem? Does my idea address the problem in the same way for everyone? Is my idea being adopted by other people in the school community? Is my idea being promoted as a solution by other people in the school community?

Four Steps to Promote Teacher Creativity When Making the Transition to Virtual Learning Experiences

DISCUSSION

When making the transition to a VLE, classroom practitioners must consider how they view and use technological tools to support learning at a distance. Existing pedagogical practices may not work for all students inside the new environment. Likewise, new challenges will emerge that require attention. This chapter introduced teacher creativity as a sequence of actions to facilitate the design and development of technological solutions to address these problems. Standards for professional learning call for increased teacher agency (Darling-Hammond, Hyler, & Gardner, 2017; Swan et al., 2014). Using the four-step process of choose destination, chart course, course correct, and reflect, teachers can assume increased agency in identifying problems, choosing technology to address those problems, and reflecting on their success from a view of creativity. Presenting these steps as a design-based approach to problem-solving emphasizes the classroom practitioner's role in designing and developing outcomes that improve the learning experience. Furthermore, the sociocultural perspective of creativity highlights the relationship between these outcomes and other people in the environment. Promoting discussion among colleagues and encouraging increased data use challenges the teacher to seek alternative perspectives other than their own as part of a process of design-based implementation research.

FUTURE RESEARCH

The overall concept of teacher creativity supports the vision for a knowledge-creating school (see Hargreaves, 1999) or thinking school (see Atwal, 2017) by viewing problem-solving in the classroom as a method for conducting design-based implementation research (Means & Harris, 2013). With a destination firmly established, a teacher has a vision and purpose of guiding play and experimentation when using new technological tools to support VLEs. This iterative aspect of the process produces new knowledge to help further progression toward little-c and pro-c outcomes (Kaufman & Beghetto, 2009). This type of approach is common among designers routinely challenged to solve complex problems (Michlewski, 2008). Emphasizing the connections between design, change, and professional learning is the overall objective of teacher creativity, as it supports an ongoing cycle for professional learning that challenges current views and approaches held inside a teacher's environment (Clarke & Hollingsworth, 2002).

Future research into teacher creativity should consider ways to strengthen the relationship between existing research on teacher change and the four-step process outlined in this chapter. There is also an opportunity to investigate the level of change produced using this method by exploring the extent and duration of change enacted in practice (Anderson, 2017; Spillane et al., 2002). This research could also consider focused attention on individual steps in the process, such as the production of problem statements designed to reduce ambiguity but also used as a tool to help evaluate outcomes.

Finally, design-based implementation research considers the production of evidence-based solutions developed in the classroom. Therefore, focus on data generated from learning management systems like Blackboard or Google Classrooms can help strengthen the final two stages, of course correct and reflect. This type of research could consider how teachers make modifications and judgments when experimenting with ideas and responding to feedback from the environment. The sociocultural approach to teacher creativity emphasizes how teachers perceive tools and the actions of others. Consequently, investigating the influence of data obtained from learning management systems is another potential area of research to explore when researching teacher creativity when using VLEs.

CONCLUSION

Using VLEs to deliver instruction will continue to challenge teachers after the global pandemic has ended. Although administrators might offer one-off professional development workshops on selected platforms, the individual teacher is tasked with designing solutions to problems that impact their practice when using VLEs. However, this situation isn't too different from what already takes place in the traditional classroom; things often go wrong, and teachers must respond creatively to address the problems that arise (Burnett & Smith, 2019). Teaching in a virtual environment is a new experience, but it's not too far beyond the regular expectations of the classroom; there is a curriculum, and the teacher must design learning experiences to teach that curriculum. The global pandemic has highlighted the creativity of the teaching profession. It has also emphasized the value of VLEs in education. As individual teachers work to address coming challenges post-pandemic, teacher creativity and the use of technology to engage students in the curriculum will continue. The four-step process presented in this chapter can contribute to furthering and improving this effort.

REFERENCES

Acar, S., Burnett, C., & Cabra, J. F. (2017). Ingredients of Creativity: Originality and More. *Creativity Research Journal*, *29*(2), 133–144. doi:10.1080/10400419.2017.1302776

Altwel, K. (2017). *The Thinking School: Developing a dynamic learning community*. John Catt Educational Ltd.

Avella, J. T., Kebritchi, M., Nunn, S. G., & Kanai, T. (2016). Learning analytics methods, benefits, and challenges in higher education: A systematic literature review. *Online Learning*, *20*(2), 13–29. doi:10.24059/olj.v20i2.790

Barak, M. (2017). Science teacher education in the Twenty-First Century: A Pedagogical Framework for Technology-Integrated Social Constructivism. *Research in Science Education*, *47*(2), 283–303. doi:10.100711165-015-9501-y

Beghetto, R., & Kaufman, J. (2007). Toward a Broader Conception of Creativity: A Case for Mini-c Creativity. *Psychology of Aesthetics, Creativity, and the Arts*, *1*(2), 73–79. doi:10.1037/1931-3896.1.2.73

Beghetto, R. A. (2010). Creativity in the classroom. In J. C. Kaufman & R. J. Sternberg (Eds.), *The Cambridge handbook of creativity* (pp. 587–606). Cambridge University Press. doi:10.1017/CBO9780511763205.027

Blackwell, C. K., Lauricella, A. R., & Wartella, E. (2016). The influence of TPACK contextual factors on early childhood educators' tablet computer use. *Computers & Education*, *98*, 57–69. doi:10.1016/j.compedu.2016.02.010

Blewett, C., & Hugo, W. (2016). Actant affordances: a brief history of affordance theory and a Latourian extension for education technology research. *Critical Studies in Teaching and Learning*, *4*, 55-73. doi:10.14426/cristal.v4i1.50

Bloom, E., & VanSlyke-Briggs. (2019). The demise of creativity in tomorrow's teachers. *Journal of Inquiry & Action in Education*, *10*(2), 90–99. Retrieved from https://digitalcommons.buffalostate.edu/

Bonnardel, N., & Didier, J. (2020). Brainstorming variants to favor creative design. *Applied Ergonomics*, *83*, 102987–102987. doi:10.1016/j.apergo.2019.102987 PMID:31710954

Buchanan, R. (1992). Wicked problems in design thinking. *Design Issues*, *8*(2), 5–21. doi:10.2307/1511637

Burnett, C., & Smith, S. (2019). Reaching for the Star: A Model for Integrating Creativity in Education. In C. Mullen (Ed.), *Creativity Under Duress in Education?* Springer International Publishing. doi:10.1007/978-3-319-90272-2_10

Churchman, C. W. (1967). Wicked Problems. *Management Science*, *14*(4), 41–142. http://www.jstor.org/stable/2628678

Clarke, D., & Hollingsworth, H. (2002). Elaborating a model of teacher professional growth. *Teaching and Teacher Education*, *18*(8), 947–967. doi:10.1016/S0742-051X(02)00053-7

Cropley, A. (2006). In praise of convergent thinking. *Creativity Research Journal*, *18*(3), 391–404. doi:10.120715326934crj1803_13

Darbellay, F., Moody, Z., & Lubart, T. (2018). Introduction: Thinking creativity, design, and interdisciplinary in a changing world. In F. Darbellay, Z. Moody, & T. Lubart (Eds.), *Creativity, Design Thinking and Interdisciplinarity* (pp. xi–xxi). Springer., doi:10.1007/978-981-10-7524-7

Darling-Hammond, L., Hyler, M. E., & Gardner, M. (2017). *Effective teacher professional development*. Palo Alto, CA: Learning Policy Institute. Retrieved from https://learningpolicyinstitute.org/product/teacher-prof-dev

Davis, G. A. (2004). *Creativity is forever* (5th ed.). Kendall Hunt.

Ertmer, P. A., & Ottenbreit-Leftwich, A. (2010). Teacher technology change: How knowledge, confidence, beliefs, and culture intersect. *Journal of Research on Technology in Education*, *42*(3), 255–284. doi:10.1080/15391523.2010.10782551

Fiorella, L., Stull, A. T., Kuhlmann, S., & Mayer, R. E. (2019). Fostering generative learning from video lessons: Benefits of instructor-generated drawings and learner-generated explanations. *Journal of Educational Psychology*, *112*(5), 895–906. doi:10.1037/edu0000408

Fishman, B. J., Penuel, W. R., Allen, A. R., Cheng, B. H., & Sabelli, N. (2013). Design-based implementation research: An emerging model for transforming the relationship of research and practice. In B. J. Fishman & W. R. Penuel (Eds.), *National Society for the Study of Education: Design Based Implementation Research* (pp. 136–156). SRI International. Retrieved from https://www.sri.com/sites/default/files/publications/fishman_penuel_allen_cheng_sabelli_2013.pdf

Gee, J. P. (2008). A sociocultural perspective on opportunity to learn. In P. A. Moss, D. C. Pullin, J. P. Gee, E. H. Haertel, & L. J. Young (Eds.), *Assessment, equity, and opportunity to learn* (pp. 76–108). Cambridge University Press. doi:10.1017/CBO9780511802157.006

Gibson, J. J. (1977). The Theory of Affordances. In R. Shaw & J. Bransford (Eds.), *Perceiving, Acting, and Knowing: Toward an Ecological Psychology* (pp. 67–82). Lawrence Erlbaum.

Glaveanu, V. (2010). Paradigms in the study of creativity: Introducing the perspective of cultural psychology. *New Ideas in Psychology, 28*(1), 79–93. doi:10.1016/j.newideapsych.2009.07.007

Glaveanu, V., Lubart, T., Bonnardel, N., Botella, M., de Biaisi, P. M., Desainte-Catherine, M., & Zenasni, F. (2013). Creativity as action: Findings from five creative domains. *Frontiers in Psychology, 4*, 176. doi:10.3389/fpsyg.2013.00176 PMID:23596431

Glaveanu, V. G. (2013). Rewriting the language of creativity: The five A's framework. *Review of General Psychology, 17*(1), 69–81. doi:10.1037/a0029528

Glaveanu, V. P. (2012). Habitual Creativity: Revising Habit, Reconceptualizing Creativity. *Review of General Psychology, 16*(1), 78–92. doi:10.1037/a0026611

Glaveanu, V. P., Hanchett Hanson, M., Baer, J., Barbot, B., Clapp, E. P., Corazza, G. E., . . . Sternberg, R. J. (2019). Advancing Creativity Theory and Research: A Socio-cultural Manifesto. *The Journal of Creative Behavior*. doi:10.1002/jocb.395

Goodwin, A. L., Low Ling, E., Ng Tee, P., Yeung, A. S., & Cai, L. (2015). Enhancing playful teachers' perception of the importance of ICT use in the classroom: The role of risk taking as a mediator. *The Australian Journal of Teacher Education, 40*(4). Advance online publication. https://ro.ecu.edu.au/ajte/. doi:10.14221/ajte.2015v40n4.8

Guskey, T. R. (2002). Professional development and teacher change. *Teachers and Teaching, 8*(3), 381–391. doi:10.1080/135406002100000512

Guskey, T. R. (2014). Measuring the effectiveness of educators' professional development. In L. E. Martin, S. Kragler, D. J. Quatroche, & K. L. Bauserman (Eds.), *Handbook of professional development in education: Successful models and practices, PreK–12* (pp. 447–466). Guilford Press.

Hall, G. E. (2010). Technology's Achilles heel: Achieving high-quality implementation. *Journal of Research on Technology in Education, 42*(3), 231–251. doi:10.1080/15391523.2010.10782550

Hall, G. E., & Hord, S. M. (2015). *Implementing Change: Patterns, Principles, and Potholes*. Pearson Education.

Hancock, R., Knezek, G., & Christensen, R. (2007). Cross-validating measures of technology integration: A first step toward examining potential relationships between technology integration and student achievement. *Journal of Computing in Teacher Education, 24*(1), 15–21. https://www.learntechlib.org/p/105327/

Hargreaves, D. H. (1999). The knowledge-creating school. *British Journal of Educational Studies, 47*(2), 122–144. doi:10.1111/1467-8527.00107

Hargrove, R. A. (2012). Assessing the long-term impact of a metacognitive approach to creative skill development. *International Journal of Technology and Design Education, 23*(3), 489–517. doi:10.100710798-011-9200-6

Hargrove, R. A., & Nietfeld, J. L. (2014). The impact of metacognitive instruction on creative problem solving. *Journal of Experimental Education, 83*(3), 291–318. doi:10.1080/00220973.2013.876604

Hughes, J. E., Cheah, Y. H., Shi, Y., & Hsiao, K. (2020). Preservice and inservice teachers' pedagogical reasoning underlying their most-valued technology-supported instructional activities. *Journal of Computer Assisted Learning, 36*(4), 549–568. doi:10.1111/jcal.12425

IBM Design Thinking. (2019, August 15). *The Framework: Design thinking re-envision for the modern enterprise*. Retrieved from: https://www.ibm.com/design/thinking/page/framework

IDEO Design Thinking. (2019, August 15). *Design Thinking Defined*. Retrieved from: https://design-thinking.ideo.com/

Juelsbo, T., Tanggard, L., & Glaveanu, V. P. (2018). From design thinking to design doing. In F. Darbellay, Z. Moody, & T. Lubart (Eds.), *Creativity, Design Thinking and Interdisciplinarity* (pp. 149–167). Springer. doi:10.1007/978-981-10-7524-7

Kaufman, J. C., & Beghetto, R. A. (2009). Beyond big and little: The four C model of creativity. *Review of General Psychology, 13*(1), 1–12. doi:10.1037/a0013688

Kaufman, J. C., & Beghetto, R. A. (2013). In praise of Clark Kent: Creative metacognition and the importance of teaching kids when (not) to be creative. *Roeper Review: A Journal on Gifted Education, 35*, 155–165. doi:10.1080/02783193.2013.799413

Kenney, M., & Zysman, J. (2016). The rise of the platform economy. *Issues in Science and Technology, 32*(3). https://issues.org/the-rise-of-the-platformeconomy/

King, A. (1993). From sage on the stage to guide on the side. *Journal of College Teacher, 41*(1), 30–35. doi:10.1080/87567555.1993.9926781

Kirschner, P. A., Sweller, J., & Clark, R. E. (2006). Why Minimal Guidance During Instruction Does Not Work: An Analysis of the Failure of Constructivist, Discovery, Problem-Based, Experiential, and Inquiry-Based Teaching. *Educational Psychologist, 41*(2), 75–86. doi:10.120715326985ep4102_1

Koberg, D., & Bagnall, J. (1972). *The Universal Traveler; a soft-systems Guide: To Creativity, Problem-Solving, and the process of Design*. Kaufmann.

Koh, J. H. L., Chai, C. S., Hong, H.-Y., & Tsai, C.-C. (2014). A survey to examine teachers' perceptions of design dispositions, lesson design practices, and their relationships with technological pedagogical content knowledge (TPACK). *Asia-Pacific Journal of Teacher Education, 43*(5), 378–391. doi:10.1080/1359866x.2014.941280

Krish, P., Maros, M., & Siti, H. S. (2012). Sociocultural Factors and Social Presence in an Online Learning Environment. *Journal of Language Studies, 2*(1), 201–213. https://core.ac.uk/download/pdf/11492265.pdf

Learning Forward. (2011). *Standards for professional learning*. Author.

Lin, Ys. (2011). Fostering creativity through education – A conceptual framework of Creative Pedagogy. *Creative Education, 2*, 149–155. doi:10.4236/ce.2011.23021

Liu, L., Li, Y., Xiong, Y., Cao, J., & Yuan, P. (2018). An EEG study of the relationship between design problem statements and cognitive behaviors during conceptual design. *Artificial Intelligence for Engineering Design, Analysis and Manufacturing, 32*(3), 351–362. doi:10.1017/S0890060417000683

Lonergan, D. C., Scott, G. M., & Mumford, M. D. (2004). Evaluative Aspects of Creative Thought: Effects of Appraisal and Revision Standards. *Creativity Research Journal, 16*(2-3), 231–246. doi:10.1 080/10400419.2004.9651455

Maddux, C., Johnson, D., & Willis, J. (1997). *Educational computing: Learning with tomorrow's technologies* (2nd ed.). Allyn & Bacon.

McLeod, S., & Shareski, D. (2017). *Different schools for a different world: School improvement for 21st century skills, global citizenship, and deeper learning.* Solution Tree Press.

Means, B., & Harris, C. J. (2013). Towards an evidence framework for design-based implementation research. In W. R. Penuel, B. Fishman, A. Allen, & B. Cheng (Eds.), *Design-based implementation research. National Society for the Study of Education yearbook* (pp. 350–371). Teachers College Press.

Mills, S. C., & Tincher, R. C. (2003). Be the technology: A developmental model for evaluating technology integration. *Journal of Research on Technology in Education, 35*(3), 382–401. doi:10.1080/15 391523.2003.10782392

Montrieux, H., Raes, A., & Schellens, T. (2017). 'The Best App is the teacher' introducing classroom scripts in technology-enhanced education. *Journal of Computer Assisted Learning, 33*(3), 267–281. doi:10.1111/jcal.12177

Mumford, M. (2017). Creative Thinking Processes: The past and the future. *The Journal of Creative Behavior, 51*, 317–322. doi:10.1002/jocb.197

Mumford, M., Martin, R., Elliott, S., & McIntosh, T. (2018). Creative Thinking in the Real World: Processing in Context. In R. Sternberg & J. Kaufman (Eds.), *The Nature of Human Creativity* (pp. 147–165). Cambridge University Press. doi:10.1017/9781108185936.013

Niess, M. L., & Gillow-Wiles, H. (2017). Expanding teachers' technological pedagogical reasoning with a systems pedagogical approach. *Australasian Journal of Educational Technology, 33*(3). Advance online publication. doi:10.14742/ajet.3473

OECD. (2019). *Trends shaping education 2019.* Paris, France: OECD Publishing. Retrieved from https://www.oecd.org/education/ceri/trends-shaping-education-22187049.htm

Osborn, A. (1963). *Applied imagination: Principles and procedures of creative thinking* (3rd ed.). Charles Scribner's Sons.

Overbay, A., Patterson, A. S., Vasu, E. S., & Grable, L. L. (2010). Constructivism and Technology Use: Findings from the IMPACTing Leadership Project. *Educational Media International, 47*(2), 103–120. doi:10.1080/09523987.2010.492675

Papamitsiou, Z., & Economides, A. A. (2014). Learning Analytics and Educational Data Mining in Practice: A Systematic Literature Review of Empirical Evidence. *Journal of Educational Technology & Society, 17*(4), 49–64. Retrieved February 16, 2021, from http://www.jstor.org/stable/jeductechsoci.17.4.49

Patahuddin, S. M. (2013). Mathematics teacher professional development in and through Internet use: Reflections on an ethnographic study. *Mathematics Education Research, 25*, 503–521. doi:10.100713394-013-0084-5

Plucker, J. A., & Alanazi, R. (2019). Is Creativity Compatible with Educational Accountability? Promise and Pitfalls of Using Assessment to Monitor and Enhance a Complex Construct. In I. Lebuda & V. Glăveanu (Eds.), *The Palgrave Handbook of Social Creativity Research. Palgrave Studies in Creativity and Culture* (pp. 501–514). Palgrave Macmillan. doi:10.1007/978-3-319-95498-1_31

Plucker, J. A., Beghetto, R. A., & Dow, G. T. (2004). Why isn't creativity more important to educational psychologists? Potentials, pitfalls, and future directions in creativity research. *Educational Psychologist, 39*(2), 83–96. doi:10.120715326985ep3902_1

Plucker, J. A., & Dow, G. T. (2010). Attitude change as the precursor to creativity enhancement. In R. A. Beghetto & J. C. Kaufman (Eds.), *Nurturing creativity in the classroom* (pp. 362–379). Cambridge University Press. doi:10.1017/CBO9780511781629.018

Plucker, J. A., & Dow, G. T. (2016). Attitude change as the precursor to creativity enhancement. In R. Beghetto & J. Kaufman (Eds.), *Nurturing Creativity* (pp. 190–211). Cambridge University Press. doi:10.1017/CBO9780511781629

Plucker, J. A., McWilliams, J., & Alanazi, R. A. (2016). Creativity, Culture, and the Digital Revolution: Implications and Considerations for Education. In V. P. Glaveanu (Ed.), *The Palgrave Handbook of Creativity and Cultural Research* (pp. 517–533). Palgrave Macmillan. doi:10.1057/1978-1-137-46344-9

Puccio, G. J., Burnett, C., Acar, S., Yudess, J. A., Holinger, M., & Cabra, J. F. (2018). Creative problem solving in small groups: The effects of creativity training on idea generation, solution creativity, and leadership effectiveness. *The Journal of Creative Behavior*. Advance online publication. doi:10.1002/jocb.381

Puccio, G. J., Mance, M., & Murdock, M. C. (2011). *Creative leadership: Skills that drive change.* SAGE Publications.

Reeves, T. C. (2008). Evaluation of the design and development of IT tools in education. In J. Voogt & G. Knezek (Eds.), *International handbook of information technology in primary and secondary education* (pp. 1037–1051). Springer.

Rhodes, M. (1960). An Analysis of Creativity. *Phi Delta Kappan, 42*(7), 305–310. www.jstor.org/stable/20342603

Rogers, E. M. (2003). *Diffusion of innovations* (5th ed.). Free Press.

Rohlwing, R. L., & Spelman, M. (2014). Characteristics of adult learning: Implications for the design and implementation of professional development programs. In L. E. Martin, S. Kragler, D. J. Quatroche, & K. L. Bauserman (Eds.), *Handbook of professional development in education: Successful models and practices, PreK–12* (pp. 231–245). Guilford Press.

Rowe, P. (1991). *Design Thinking.* MIT Press.

Runco, M. A., & Acar, S. (2012). Divergent Thinking as an Indicator of Creative Potential. *Creativity Research Journal, 24*(1), 66–75. doi:10.1080/10400419.2012.652929

Runco, M. A., Plucker, J. A., & Lim, W. (2001). Development and Psychometric Integrity of a Measure of Ideational Behavior. *Creativity Research Journal, 13*(3), 393–400.

Runco, M. A., Walczyk, J. J., Acar, S., Cowger, E. L., Simundson, M., & Tripp, S. (2014). The incremental validity of a short form of the Ideational Behavior Scale and usefulness of distractor, contraindicative, and lie scales. *The Journal of Creative Behavior, 48,* 185–197. doi:10.1002/jocb.47

Ryd, N. (2004). The design brief as carrier of client information during the construction process. *Design Studies, 25*(3), 231–249. doi:10.1016/j.destud.2003.10.003

Scott, G. M., Leritz, L. E., & Mumford, M. D. (2004a). The effectiveness of creativity training: A meta-analysis. *Creativity Research Journal, 16,* 361–388. doi:10.1080/10400410409534549

Scott, G. M., Leritz, L. E., & Mumford, M. D. (2004b). Types of creativity training: Approaches and their effectiveness. *The Journal of Creative Behavior, 38,* 149–179. doi:10.1002/j.2162-6057.2004.tb01238.x

Silk, E. M., Daly, S. R., Jablokow, K., Yilmaz, S., & Berg, M. N. (2014). The Design Problem Framework: Using Adaption-Innovation Theory to Construct Design Problem Statements. *Industrial Design Conference Presentations, Posters, and Proceedings, 7.* Retrieved from: https://lib.dr.iastate.edu/industrialdesign_conf/7

Swan Dagen, A. S., & Bean, R. M. (2014). High-quality research-based professional development: An essential for enhancing high-quality teaching. In L. E. Martin, S. Kragler, D. J. Quatroche, & K. L. Basuerman (Eds.), *Handbook of professional development in education: Successful models and practices, PreK–12* (pp. 42–63). Guilford Press.

Sweller, J., Kirschner, P. A., & Clark, R. E. (2007). Why minimally guided teaching techniques do not work: A reply to commentaries. *Educational Psychologist, 42*(2), 115–121. doi:10.1080/00461520701263426

Tien, H., Chang, B., & Kuo, Y. (2019). Does experience stimulate or stifle creativity? *European Journal of Innovation Management, 22*(3), 422–445. doi:10.1108/EJIM-02-2018-0042

Torrance, E. P., & Safter, H. T. (1999). *Making the creative leap beyond.* Creative Education Foundation Press.

Vygotsky, L. S. (1978). *Mind in society: The development of higher psychological processes.* Harvard University Press.

Wallas, G. (1926). *The Art of Thought.* Harcourt, Brace and Company.

Wolcott, M. D., McLaughlin, J. E., Hubbard, D. K., Rider, T. R., & Umstead, K. (2020). Twelve tips to stimulate creative problem-solving with design thinking. *Medical Teacher,* •••, 1–8. doi:10.1080/0142159X.2020.1807483

Worwood, M. J. (2020). *From teacher to designer: Promoting teacher creativity when using new technology* (Doctoral dissertation). Retrieved from: http://jhir.library.jhu.edu/handle/1774.2/63559

Worwood, M. J., & Plucker, J. (2018). Domain Generality and Specificity in Creative Design Thinking. In F. Darbellay, Z. Moody, & T. Lubart (Eds.), *Creativity, Design Thinking and Interdisciplinarity* (pp. 83–91). Springer., doi:10.1007/978-981-10-7524-7

Zielinski, D. E. (2017). The Use of Collaboration, Authentic Learning, Linking Material to Personal Knowledge, and Technology in the Constructivist Classroom: Interviews with Community College Faculty Members. *Community College Journal of Research and Practice*, *41*(10), 668–686. doi:10.10 80/10668926.2016.1220338

KEY TERMS AND DEFINITIONS

Creative Problem-Solving: A problem-solving method to support the development of a creative outcome. :

Design Thinking: A human-centered approach to creative problem-solving.:

Environment: A classroom or virtual learning environment that represents the context for teacher creativity. :

Little-C: A category of creative outcomes that are recognized by others but do not produce a change outside an individual's environment. :

Mini-C: A category of creative outcomes that do not extend beyond the individual.:

Outcome: An idea or solution produced because of deliberate actions enacted by the teacher in response to a problem. :

Pro-C: A category of creative outcomes that produce systematic changes throughout a department: building, or school district.

Problem Statement: A short clarifying statement that includes a goal: a technology to help meet that goal, and a specific context.

Teacher Creativity: Actions undertaken by the teacher in response to a problem: and the outcomes produced because of those actions.

Technological Solution: An evidence-based outcome produced using digital technology and proven to address a predetermined problem.:

Section 2
Best Practices And Pedagogical Reasoning In K–12 Grade Levels

Chapter 8
Using Generation Z's Learning Approaches to Create Meaningful Online Learning

Letha Mellman
University of Wyoming, USA

Mia Kim Williams
https://orcid.org/0000-0002-4928-6367
University of Wyoming, USA

David A. Slykhuis
University of Northern Colorado, USA

ABSTRACT

This chapter presents findings from an eDelphi research study through which participant experts of Generation Z established learning approaches for online environments. Experts were members of this generation all being born in 2001 or 2002 who have participated in informal or formal pre-pandemic online learning. Background on Generation Z, description of the eDelphi research method, and implications of the learning approaches provide insight to different pedagogical practices that support successful online teaching and learning aligned with the learning approaches established by Generation Z. This generation bridges the bulk of K12 and undergraduate learners. As educators re-vision classrooms necessitated by the current educational climate, understanding the learning approaches of students provides a critical foundation on which educators can make pedagogical decisions that engage learners in online contexts.

INTRODUCTION

The transformation of K-12 education seemed to happen overnight as the COVID-19 Pandemic swept through the United States in March 2020. Most K-12 educators spent hours reconfiguring lessons to be delivered via virtual conference, struggled with new learning management systems, and questioned

DOI: 10.4018/978-1-7998-7222-1.ch008

how long it would be before they could return to the classroom. At the same time, administrators navigated policy changes, communicated with parents and students, and organized resources like textbooks, educational materials, and Chromebooks for parent pick-up. All the haphazard attempts to keep schools running in the spring made way for summer and an opportunity to revise remote teaching and learning. In preparing new learning experiences, educators often focused on student-centered approaches to best meet the needs of their individual students. Knowing the students as learners improved teaching. Learning and knowing them went beyond the superficial social and administrative data that teachers accessed. How students engaged in learning, including where they sought knowledge and support, how they navigated information and technology tools, and what they privileged in the process, provided insight to students' learning approaches. With this knowledge in hand, educators could identify and employ access points to the curriculum that promoted engagement and student success with virtual learning content. In such a unique situation as the one educators faced in 2020, did educators know enough about their students as learners to successfully re-envision teaching and learning in online contexts?

Individuals born between 1997-2012 make up Generation Z (Dimock, 2019), and they were the bulk of students in K-12 and undergraduate higher education in 2020. Their life experiences went beyond growing up in a digital world. According to The Pew Research Center, Generation Z is identified by several unique characteristics compared to previous generations: more racially and ethnically diverse, on a focused educational trajectory, sharp differences in perspective about social and economic issues from their elders, and value for family and social change (Parker & Igielnik, 2020). Generation Z (Gen Z) also identified YouTube, Instagram, and Snapchat as the top three social media and digital communication tools. Educators have not experienced a generation like Gen Z and knowing them as learners could support the design of curriculum and development of pedagogical practices to best engage in online learning.

Knowing Generation Z as Online Learners

The goal of this research was to understand how Gen Z students learned online in both formal and informal settings. This goal was important because Gen Z individuals made up the majority of students, and it was anticipated, pre-Covid, when this research started, that online learning was a growing part of students' formal educational experiences. Serendipitously, online learning became paramount and intensified the need to understand Gen Z as learners.

This chapter presents findings from an eDelphi research study through which participant experts established learning approaches in online environments. Experts in this study were part of Gen Z and had the additional qualifying characteristic of having participated in pre-pandemic formal or self-directed online learning. Participants were all over the age of 18 in order to participate in the research study, however, they shared characteristics identified as unique to Gen Z collectively. While participants represent a subset of the generation, the findings of this study are relatable to the entire generation who share similar characteristics.

More importantly, this chapter explores different pedagogical practices aligned with Gen Z's established learning approaches promoting successful teaching online. Prior to the spring of 2020, online teaching and learning existed in a variety of contexts, including online schools and courses, and blended learning. The educational climate beginning in March 2020 necessitated online teaching and learning in an even wider variety of configurations. Thus, this chapter seeks to deepen educators' understanding about how students engage in online learning and provide ideas for pedagogical decision making.

BACKGROUND

Generation Z's Approach to Learning

Connectivism builds on the constructivist perspective for today's learners. It is a digital-age learning theory useful in e-learning settings (Siemens, 2005). Connections an individual makes provide diverse opinions and outlooks. When the individual has a background of knowledge, s/he can explore opinions and make decisions about what they believe and why they believe it. Creating connections results in continuous processes of establishing new knowledge (Siemens, 2005).

To learn new information well through connectivism, it needs to be integrated into a learner's thought process. Deep learning has the goal of knowledge transfer and application and creates an ongoing partnership between the learner and the knowledge they acquire. Analyzing, linking, and deconstructing leads the learner to long-term retention and integration of past and new knowledge and problem solving. The ability to connect with information and manipulate it in future problem solving comes from the learner's construction of a deeper meaning (Marton & Säljö, 1976). Deep learning is a successful pedagogical lens for educating Gen Z learners.

Not all approaches to learning are the same. Swedish researchers Marton and Säljö (1976) began exploring *approaches to learning* (ATL) in the late 1900's. Their research looked at "deep" and "surface" learning, these approaches to learning were still widely studied at the time of this research. There was a debate in the literature around the issue of preference vs. effectiveness. It was important to note that in this study, Gen Z's preferred learning approaches may not have translated to best practices for Gen Z. However, there was value in understanding the importance of preferences. For example, in Parmer et al. (2009) research conducted explored the relationship between preference to vegetable consumption, hands on garden exploration and school gardens. They found that having a garden did improve vegetable preference in second graders. There are many variables which may have played into the increased preferences including the participant's knowledge and positive or negative experience growing a garden. The increased knowledge about the vegetables may have been due to prior preferences, increased access to the vegetables, or a host of other variables. Additionally, research showed the importance of being aware of potential problems when preferences were ignored. Taylor and Serna's 2020 article examined college student preferences regarding communication. One finding was "the time and frequency of text messages determine student interaction with the text" (p.139). If the university ignored the student's preferred time and frequency, fewer students may have engaged with the text. If the university sent too many texts or consistently sent texts at an inopportune time, students may have ignored or blocked the texts. This could have detrimentally limited the knowledge the text was attempting to relay. When it came to preferences and effectiveness, educators did well to meld perspectives.

In this study, Gen Z participants identified learning approaches they preferred. The next sections expound on Gen Z's learning approaches and explore ways educators could restructure pedagogical practices to support them.

RESEARCH

Two Delphi panels were implemented simultaneously to compare academic and nonacademic Gen Z online learners. This study began prior to the COVID 19 pandemic and participants had at least some online learning prior to the situation of forced online learning. To be included in the academic sub-group, the Gen Z learners had to have completed at least two online university courses taught by two different educators. Because recruitment of participants took place prior to the pandemic, the online courses were designed as online courses and not emergency remote teaching situations. The members of the non-academic sub-group chose not to enroll in more than one pre-pandemic online university courses, but went online to seek how to learn a skill, purposefully gain knowledge, or pursue informal online learning experiences. Participants needed to reside in the United States and, where applicable, take domestic university courses. Additionally, all participants were born in 2001 or 2002 (at least 18 by the start day of the study). Each participant read and signed an informed consent document to participate in the research project.

The following research questions guided this study:

Q1. How does Generation Z learn in
   a. online academic settings?
   b. nonacademic settings?

During the Delphi process each sub-group received surveys entirely independently of the other about their online learning experiences. The Round 1 survey was developed from the literature review, and results from a pilot study. The survey contained both quantitative (rank order and choose all that apply) and qualitative (open-ended) questions. Subsequent round surveys were based on the responses from the previous rounds' data. The Round 2 surveys contained both quantitative (rank order and choose all that apply) and qualitative (open-ended) questions which culminated in expert consensus. The Round 3 survey gathered qualitative data from participants sharing potentially successful examples for implementation of identified learning approaches. After each survey round the researcher coded and analyzed the results for themes. The data from the prior survey was used to sharpen the questions and narrow the results. This Delphi systematic analysis eventually led to a consensus of opinions in each of the expert groups. The validity of this research was supported by Tomasik (2010), who reports that Delphi research has "good reliability and satisfactory validity" (p. 1) due to the need for individuals to amalgamate individual responses to a group consensus.

Theoretical Framework

In considering how Gen Z students learned online, several learning theories were considered. The constructivist perspective was chosen as a framework because it suggests while learning occurs individually, it is simultaneously a social experience. Learning is heavily influenced by social interactions (Vygotsky, 1962), personal experiences (Dewey, 1938), culture (Hunter & Krantz, 2010), perceptions (Stengers, 2008), language (Lin & Qiyun, 2003), collaboration (Mohr & Mohr, 2017), the individual capacity to teach self (Vygotsky, 1997), and active participation with the individual's world (Tobin, 1993). As an individual reflects upon experiences, knowledge is not transferred but is built and is personally meaningful.

It was important to consider how Gen Z learners in this study know how they learned. Murray-Harvey (1994) noted that *approaches to learning* (ATL) researchers are concerned with learning strategies and characteristics individuals implement when learning. There are six common approaches: deep, surface, achievement-orient (strategic approach), lack of direction, academic self-confidence, and metacognitive awareness of studying (Furnham, 2012). The rationale for ATL may stem from the motivation to learn.

If, for example, a student hoped to get an A by attempting to memorize an entire book the night before a test, she may have been externally motivated by surface learning. If learning was inherent and joy was found in acquiring knowledge, then application of knowledge likely resulted in a deep learning approach. As another example, a student needed bagels for a breakfast party. Prior to needing bagels, this student liked to cook, and while they had never made bagels, they believed, based on previous baking experiences, that successfully make bagels was possible. The student decided to try making bagels. Once the students finished the task, he/she shared the newfound skill (or lack thereof) with friends. Deep learning occurred as they recalled past knowledge and experience and applied it to their need for bagels. They furthered their learning experience when they shared out the results.

Analysis

The study was run in a qualitative-quantitative-qualitative approach, where the quantitative analysis informed the qualitative analysis and together the analysis suggested the need for further exploration. In Round 1 and Round 2, data were coded for frequency and rank order before being analyzed for qualitative open ended participant responses. The additional qualitative responses added depth and clarity to the quantitatively generated lists in each round. Those questions which considered rank and frequency were analyzed using the Henry Garrett Ranking Technique (Garrett & Woodworth, 1969), which is a descriptive statistical test that generates a score for each item according to participant rank. It was chosen to show order of preference along with rank order from the experts. Consensus was measured by the participant response mean.

After each round, the data from the independent expert panels were cleaned. Cleaning the data was achieved by correcting misspellings, excluding and reporting skipped items, item responses that were not considered in line with the question asked, or data provided by inappropriately identified participants (e.g., nickname/pseudonym did not match participant). Furthermore, data were cleaned by organizing documented notes. In each round, themes were identified by the researcher. Participants were not required to participate in each round. Rounds were iterative, thus missing one was not considered an issue in analysis.

Round 3 was designed to be Qualitative to elicit details and recommendations. Thematic analysis was performed through memo writing and codebook creation. Themes within each panel were identified and connected to develop a narrative and define meaning of each learning preference. Thematic analysis was performed following Braun and Clarke's six step method (2006).

IMPLEMENTATION FOR PRESERVICE AND INSERVICE EDUCATORS

One of the reasons for this study was identifying how Gen Z learning approaches could be beneficial for the educators who teach these students. At the time of this study, there was literature exploring learning preference vs. tried-and-true teaching methods. Researchers debated the two methods, as preferred learning did not always reflect best practices nor did the most effective ways of teaching always engage students in preferred ways to learn. Knowing both the most effective teaching method and the learning preferences of students enhanced the educators' pedagogical toolbox. Similarly, learning approaches, used at the time of this study, may not have aligned with the most effective pedagogy, and that did not discredit the value of educators' understanding preferred learning approaches.

The following information presents findings of the study that were common among the academic and nonacademic expert groups organized in themes. Discussion reviews the learning approaches that gained consensus and explores pedagogical practices relevant to the preferred learning.

Gen Z's Call for Restructuring Pedagogical Practices

Teaching online is not the same as teaching face-to-face (Plat et al., 2014). It requires a different scope, different actions, and is fraught with different problems. Gen Z has different expectations about the role of the educator and the learner in online learning contexts. Thus, teaching in an online space likely requires a restructure of pedagogical practice. Educators of all subjects and grades may wonder how they can teach Gen Z when their learning approaches may seem foreign, and the generation gap leaves some baffled. Additionally, educators who would be willing to restructure pedagogical practices to incorporate Gen Z's distinctive call, may be at a loss as to where to begin or how to do so.

Understanding the perspective of Gen Z about teaching and learning is important for inservice and preservice educators. The current educational context has challenged inservice educators to adapt their current pedagogical practices in order to accommodate remote teaching, but in planning to do this in online contexts (synchronous, asynchronous, hyflex, blended, etc.) inservice educators must also understand Gen Z in order to meet their unique needs and learning preference to achieve a student-centered classroom. As members of Gen Z, current preservice educators own the learning preferences which this chapter discusses and have firsthand experience with education which does not embrace their unique perspective of teaching and learning. Preservice educators have the opportunity not only to restructure pedagogical practices, but to lead the re-visioning of education by providing valuable insight, support, and explanation to inservice educators while redesigning student learning experiences. The lived experiences of Gen Z are grounded in existing face to face K-12 practices and learning through self-selected online practices. This unique and evolving situation provides scaffolding for currently unexplored pedagogical practices, particularly in online learning contexts where existing educators may lack experience. Gen Z has established online learning practices, which allow them to learn what they want to learn or hack the required learning of school, but preservice teachers still yield to established practice because like all educators they tend to teach the way they were taught. Inservice teachers and teacher educators can benefit from the insights of preservice educators and collaboratively re-vision educational practice. One of the benefits of growing up in a world with constant communication capabilities is Gen Z has no problem sharing their opinions and ideas, but the older generations will likely have to make space for their new ideas. What follows are recommendations provided by Gen Z participants. These learning preferences can inform pedagogical practices, and if adopted by an individual educator or implemented in school wide professional development, could add to the educational impact on learning in online spaces.

Educator Is the Guide

A norm held by Gen Z, which shifted from the established role of *teacher* in the educational process, was the idea educators are no longer sole proprietors of knowledge. Neither did educators exist simply to curate information and impart knowledge upon students. Rather, educators guided students in the education process (Tomei & Nelson, 2019) and facilitated experiences (Morey & Mouratis, 2016; Seemiller & Grace, 2016; Tomei & Nelson, 2019). Mohr and Mohr (2017) explain Gen Z "often desire relevant, solution-oriented relationships with their mentors and peers but need guidance to respond to contemporary challenges" (p 92). This research supported the desire for guidance as Gen Z participant-experts identified guide as the main role of the educator in learning contexts.

Student-Centered Learning According to Gen Z

In online educational spaces, Gen Z learners had specific expectations of what constituted a guide in their learning experiences, and thus how they understood the role of the educators in learning contexts. Gen Z participants described learning as continual and a multifaceted path embedded with various learning relationships. *Student-Centered,* as explained by Gen Z, went beyond what most educators might consider student-centered. Traditionally, educators successfully moved from the familiar role of teacher as presenter of information to passive students to a classroom figure who functioned as a coach or facilitator while students embraced a more active and collaborative role in their own learning. However, Gen Z expected something more. This study suggested student-centered was a delicate balance of student autonomy and educator guidance. The role of guide was interwoven among many responses throughout the study when participants expressed learning approaches in an online academic space. When outside the academic space the role of guide took on the description of *seeking recommendations* from others. The role of educator as a guide appeared as a significant learning approach for Gen Z and included the following characteristics:

- clear, detailed learning materials
- personalized content and activities
- educator presence in the online space
- way of monitoring progress, or checking with student on a consistent basis

When discussing learning materials, academic panel participants expressed instructor-created materials held the greatest value. Parameters set through course materials kept the learner on track. Within those parameters, the individual had, and wanted, choice of what to engage in through the learning process according to their unique desires or perceived needs.

Table 1. Suggested academic practices that facilitate Gen Z's expectation of educator as guide

Learning Materials	Description
Educator Created Content	module specific; detailed expectation; clear directions
Educator Created Video	minimum of weekly/by module video introduction, demonstration and/or explanation of content and projects; specifically designed for individual classes; personal connection via video encapsulating unique educator attributes
Question/Answer Opportunities	educator to learner; learner to learner; crowdsourcing; global connections
Scaffolded Search Experiences	safe environment; trusted sites and resources; teach how to critically evaluate search results
Unique Curated Resources	specifically chosen materials of others to support learning goals; explanation of purpose

Use of Video

This research noted while YouTube was a preferred approach to learning it was not the primary video preference. Instead, Gen Z participants preferred videos created by the educator, which discussed and described class specific content. They identified this type of educator generated video particularly helpful in online learning. Participants in both panels offered the following criteria for those creating supportive videos:

- "filter relevant information" (nonacademic panel participant)
- "create content which is real and interesting" (nonacademic panel participant)
- "are of high quality" (academic panel participant)
- "are easy to find" (nonacademic panel participant)
- "can teach individuals with varying levels of previous knowledge and offer the educators unique talents" (academic panel participant)
- "short" (academic panel participant)
- "detailed instructional videos" (academic panel participant)
- "pertain to assignments given" (academic panel participant)
- update in "real-time"

Additionally, participants from this study supported Lithner's (2008) finding that Gen Z students observed with the intention of imitation or replication. Gen Z participants gathered and reviewed data (e.g., videos) until they were comfortable combining prior knowledge and experience with new information to generate new knowledge. Specifically, nonacademic panel participants requested multimodal visual examples of finished projects with demonstrative videos (step-by-step successful examples which were engaging, detailed, and easy to understand).

Scaffolding Online Searching

Several participants indicated a need for critical consideration and fact checking of information found online, due to the fact anyone could post anything, which left truth and fiction potentially indecipherable. Interestingly, this concern did not slow participants' affinity for online searches which aligned with research (Kardaras, 2016). One nonacademic panel participant explained searching the internet was a learning preference, "because it is convenient, and I have the internet in my hand or pocket all day long." Gen Z generally reached for their phone about once a minute. Another nonacademic panel participant shared the reason they searched online was because, "there's everything I want to know on the internet." These participants suggested online searches were valuable and convenient.

As with any advancement, technology and access to instant answers provided learners with benefits and downfalls. This study suggested Gen Z had unique concerns with online learning, and an abundance of unregulated search results was one of them. Unlike Sinatra & Lombardi, 2020 cautioned, Gen Z did not properly validate online search findings, this research offered hope; Gen Z was aware of the need for validated search results and wanted to address this need. Participants from both panels called for better "screening" of search results and wanted to ensure "valid" information. One academic panel participant reported when they had a question, "I just look up the answer. I use multiple sources to make sure I'm right, and then I investigate. It's pretty simple." Interestingly, more nonacademic panel participants sought valid results than academic panel participants. One nonacademic panel participant cautioned, "Yes, search engines can basically solve every problem, but there will be some junk information, we have to learn to filter, find quality information." A second nonacademic panel participant explained the validation process, "It's simple, do more screening, do more thinking." These participants echo the warning and simple solution of Sinatra and Lombardi (2020) when searching for answers online, ask yourself, "is this explanation plausible, and how do I know?" (p.1). Technology may have made online searches fast, convenient, and offered a variety of multimodal answers, but it was up to the individual to extract the truth from all potential sources. This concern may have been one of the reasons participants, in this study, reported online classes needed more support from the educator. Academic panel participants seemed to see educators as part of their filter, or at least as the means of learning how to critically sift through search results. In short, online Gen Z learners relied on educators to teach them where and how to find search results which answered questions, and offered pertinent, reliable information.

Reliance on Self

In addition to placing the onus for filter search results on themselves, Gen Z participants in both panels reported strong preferences for approaching learning at an individual level, including "take responsibility for your own learning" (academic panel participant). This research supported Marton and Säljö (1976) finding, autonomous individuals learned on a deeper level, a level which required individuals to critically examine new information and formulate connections to past and current knowledge. The academic panel participants defined reliance on self as the ability to organize and create an individual study plan, one in which they took responsibility for their unique learning path.

While the academic panel manifested a preference for Self-Directed Learning (SDL), they also found having clear guidelines in place and frequent validation imperative to their learning. They requested online projects that had a set framework, detailed expectations, and space where learners experimented, and implemented unique voice and choice. The nonacademic panel added they attempted to learn new skills independently and engaged with projects where learners chose what to do while learning autonomously. They desired SDL (e.g., Knowles, 1975) projects, and choices aligned with constructivist theories (e.g., personal learning process; Goldie, 2016), deep learning (e.g. project-based learning, and student voice and choice) (Fullan & Langworthy, 2014). In both learning methods, the individual was largely responsible for his/her learning (Vygotsky, 1997).

Historically, students have relied on educators to control the learning experience, and the learning space. When it comes to online education, Gen Z students may have had more experience in online learning environments than educators. The findings of this study suggested that while Gen Z students were comfortable in the online learning space, they required a guide who set up their learning path (e.g., educator implemented pedagogical practices, educator facilitated relationships, educator generated videos) and provided sounding boards (e.g., people with whom they asked questions, gathered information and increased clarity) prior to developing new knowledge. It appeared Gen Z learners desired to be in control of themselves, and their educational expedition; however, without a guide they could not achieve this desire.

For Gen Z learners, learning was not stagnant, nor was it one continuous path. It was potentially endless paths, which crisscrossed, entangled, diverted, reconnected, even splintered and regenerated as they progressed. Gen Z participants indicated learning did not end in the classroom, nor did it begin there. With the technological advances of their time, they controlled what questions they asked, and where they found their information at any given time. In short, they learned in any space, at any moment, thanks to the ability to constantly be online, connecting with people, bots, search results...etc. No matter how the path evolved, learning happened through various connections and relationships which connected them with individuals and groups to test beliefs about new knowledge. Participants largely identified the educator as an expert of choice.

The idea of educator as a guide found in this study closely aligned with Vygotsky's social constructivist learning theory (Vygotsky, 1997). Vygotsky stated, "ultimately, the child teaches himself" (1997, p. 47). The educator guides, leads, and offers direction; however, in the end it is the learner who teaches themselves.

If educators wanted to implement only one of the recommended learning approaches provided by Gen Z participants, participant responses indicated guidance had the biggest impact. Guidance was interwoven with the other learning approaches, which made it the most requested and the most complex learning approach. One way Gen Z participants suggested educators guided them was to build strong relationships.

Build Relationships

While Gen Z participants were particularly self-reliant and desired Self-Directed Learning (SDL) opportunities (e.g., Poague, 2018), their independence relied heavily upon a solid relationship with their educator. Both academic and nonacademic panel participants wanted someone who connected with them, engaged in relationship-building, and supported their learning process. Additionally, academic panel participants sought a learning relationship that offered guidance, as needed, and frequent checks on the learning situation. Gen Z literature suggested Gen Z was adept at maintaining daily, on demand relationships (Mohr & Mohr, 2017; Rue, 2018), which may be why one academic panel participant asked educators to check in "daily." Findings suggested the majority of academic participants accepted "checking in" as weekly instructional videos generated by educators, weekly emails, assignment reminders, educators who set up and kept online office hours, and educators who were willing to meet with students or responded to students' emails in a "timely" manner. Open communication, accessible educators, clear boundaries on educator availability, and educators who informed students of changes, appeared to foster desired student/educator relationships. One academic panel participant explained, "just be available. Don't answer in two days. Give a time where you will be on, specifically looking at the class. This gives students a time to ask the educator any questions and get a response." Online Gen Z learners in this study were drawn to educators who "interact with students while teaching" (academic panel participant). Another academic panel participant commented on how simple this interaction could be, "teachers need to talk to the students, have everything ready, and don't overload on reading. As long as the educators are prepared, I believe everything will go great." According to Gen Z participants, materials and connections did not need to be lengthy to be of value.

Participants in this study who had questions during learning activities wanted to connect with their educator(s). In a presentation on Gen Z, Cook (2015) proposed Gen Z's "most pressing need is for immediate response" (slide 8). Participants in this study repeatedly asked for online classes and online learning spaces which were up to date. For instance, academic panel participants called for "real-time updates" and "frequently" updated learning material, and stated, "give us more experience, advance with the times!" Gen Z participants approached learning at the speed of Google, and perhaps unrealistically, expected anyone who wanted to assist them to respond just as quickly. However, their angst for rapid response diminished as trusted relationships with their educator(s) grew.

Learner/Educator Relationships

Relationships between students and educator generated during the learning process were critical to the success of online students, and the research (Graham et al., 2001; Kim & Bonk, 2006; Martin & Bolliger, 2018) aligned with Gen Z's learning approach. Additionally, Gen Z learners in this study, indicated it was crucial the educator included ways for participants to interact and nurture relationships in online courses and suggested projects or discussions foster interaction and student engagement. Benefits of positive relationships in online classes identified by participants included: increased feelings of comfort to ask questions, increased student and educator response rate, improved student desire to navigate and engage in the online learning space, and ultimately heightened the likelihood of retention of information and successful completion of the course. Relationships were additionally important as students needed to ask educators about matters beyond traditional education, such as technology concerns involved in online courses, aligned with research (Bennett & Lockyer, 2004). Good relationships helped create an engaging and safe environment, which was another critical component of successful online classes identified in the research (Graham et al., 2001; Martin & Bolliger, 2018; Nguyen & Hovy, 2019; Rue, 2018; Schwieger & Ladwig, 2018). This study found relationships between educator and student were significant in establishing the role of the educator as guide because the student needed support from someone they trusted to think critically, process information, and move along the learning path outlined in the course.

Individual "Why" of the Learner

When participants responded to survey questions regarding online learning approaches, they often provided a reason they learned a new skill, a personal experience, or what they believed the benefit of learning a new skill would be instead of providing the way they approached learning. For example, a few nonacademic panel participants talked about procuring skills to "survive." One nonacademic panel participant explained they learned new skills, "...to prepare for the future survival." Participants in both panels frequently reported learning was done purposefully because it increased personal knowledge or provided additional skills, which offered work-related promotions or increased quality of life. Poague (2018), of LinkedIn Learning, found 43% of Gen Z were self-directed learners, and felt rushed to gain knowledge as quickly as possible to achieve career goals. As the literature on SDL suggested, establishing career goals relied on learners who acquired knowledge to procure unique achievements (Knowles, 1975). SDL goals were expected, however, participant responses such as learning "some skills that can survive in the future" were not. While participants offered no further explanation, the literature stated that Gen Z preferred to look to the future, vigilantly aware of the end result (Goldie, 2016). At the time of this study, it was estimated that 65% of Gen Z's future jobs did not exist (Fisch & McLeod, 2008). Therefore, it was imperative educators and researchers kept the future need(s) of education as a constant focus (Joordens et al., 2019) to prepare for incoming and upcoming generations of learners.

Create and Apply Meaningful New Knowledge

At the time of this study, eEducational motivation literature suggested students were more likely to succeed in a class (especially an online class which required greater self-motivation) if students found value in the coursework (Wigfield & Eccles, 2000). Value for class content may not be something students came to class with, and educators may have needed to guide students as they found or created value. For example, an instructor may have implemented opportunities for the student to explore the value of the material for them as an individual, and as a whole class thus the student made meaning at both an individual and collective level (Graham et al., 2001). Making meaning is the ability for a student to actively engage in a learning experience while simultaneously internalizing the concept being studied to create unique, individualized value (Bennett & Lockyer, 2004). Making meaning promoted deep learning as it created individual value for students and was invaluable in student retention (Bawa, 2016).

Appropriate Workload and Work Tools

Academic and nonacademic panel participants provided comments highlighting what they referred to as "cognitive overload"; however, what participants described was work overload. Participant descriptions had nothing to do with in-the-moment cognitive processing, but rather, reported being concerned about online courses which had an abundance of busy work, reading, numerous projects, and/or implemented multiple assignments at once. Additionally, participants connected materials and tools engaged with during the learning process as part of their workload. Online learners not only wanted to use personal devices, but also *expected to* use them and other technology when learning. Gen Z also used technology to engage in global connections via video chats and texted to gather information, tested new ideas, and shared meaning they made during the learning process (Beall, 2016; Gale, 2015). Participants expected education to be self-taught, experiential, administered using constantly updated technology, provide opportunities to connect with peers and experts around the globe, offer immediate feedback, and include support from the educator. The way Gen Z participants approached learning, including their distinct self-imposed processes of connecting with others, and their desire to implement technology as educational tools promoted active learning for creation and application of new knowledge.

This research supported past research finding technological speed mattered to Gen Z (Dimock, 2019). Whether they were surfing the web, checking the weather, playing games, or solving equations, Gen Z seemed hardwired for speed. They constantly watched and waited for the next technological advancement, and they lacked tolerance for those who did not keep pace (Schwieger & Ladwig, 2018). This may have frustrated some educators, but Gen Z learners adapted quickly and were willing and capable of teaching themselves and supporting each other as long as they felt supported by their educator. This recognition held implications for which tools promoted learning, and the learners' role in choosing the way to engage in and represent learning.

Making Connections

Equally important to online Gen Z participants were experiences and opportunities that promoted sharing with others. Gen Z grew up with constant access to information on nearly any topic they may have wanted to explore. They expected that their learning aligned with this norm, was personalized, and information was easily and quickly accessible; they sought experiences in which they applied and tested the new knowledge. Online Gen Z learners looked for opportunities to solve problems and constantly posted, Snapchated, and Instagramed experiences. The ability to work with others and share experiences was an integral part of Gen Z (Merriman, 2015; Schwieger & Ladwig, 2018). Working with others, according to Gen Z participants, meant the ability and opportunity to share ideas with several people, gather opinions from inside and outside the course from which they made informed decisions about the topic being learned. Additionally, their ability to establish relationships, through technology, with people around the globe, created a unique learning space for the crowd-sourcing activity of learning. This willingness to engage in learning beyond the classroom broadened their perspective about other cultures (Dabbagh et al., 2016), which provided them with a global connection. These global relationships and the ability to communicate quickly may have helped negate stereotypes and helped students embrace one another through collaborative learning. This research suggested educators who embraced and utilized global connections in education further embraced Gen Z's learning approaches to engage with others and share knowledge. Educator global awareness and engagement also promoted Gen Z's perspective of authentic application of new knowledge.

Additionally, this study found successful online Gen Z educators provided opportunity for learners to ask for clarity, receive validation, gather recommendations, and gather information from participants identified as experts (e.g., classmates, educator, tutors, professionals, discussion forum members deemed more knowledgeable or possessing greater skill in a desired topic area) prior to accepting information as new knowledge. Additionally, Gen Z participants indicated social media groups (e.g., Instagram, Snapchat, Facebook, forums), friends, and network connections were valuable resources of information and recommendations. It appeared these online learners considered the educator to be the head guide, but not the only guide, in their learning process.

Implement Deep Learning Pedagogy

Pedagogical choices in this study were paramount to the educators' ability to successfully implement an online class. Connectivism (Goldie, 2016; Schwieger & Ladwig, 2018; Siemens, 2005) and Constructivist learning theory (Driscoll & Tomiak, 2000) offered relevant pedagogical approaches that were important to 2020 digitally connected students, such as authentic experiences, problem-based learning, passion projects, collaboration, connection to the world around them, interactive learning, offered choices, shared artifacts, as well as student voice and choice. These learning theories aligned well with several of the Gen Z learning approaches.

Deep Learning

Deep learning constituted a shift in pedagogical practices. Fullan and Langworthy (2014) depicted old pedagogies as those which used technology, pedagogical capacity and content knowledge with a goal of "content mastery" (Fullan & Langworthy, 2014, p. 3). New pedagogies sought deep learning outcomes by engaging with current technology which allowed students to "discover and master content knowledge" through a delicate balance of pedagogical capacity and creation of "NEW knowledge in the World" (Fullan & Langworthy, 2014, p. 3). To simplify, old pedagogies were teacher-centered and required content regurgitation, and new pedagogies were often student-centered and focused on the creation and application of knowledge. The deep learning shift was student-focused and created an ongoing partnership for the learner and the knowledge they acquire. Deep learning required a student who was willing to critically explore new information, analyze the new information to understand how the new knowledge enhanced or disassembled past knowledge and personal theories.

If an educator implemented deep learning, the amount of information given to students may have been limited to allow for critical thinking and higher-order cognitive skills. Deep learners need to experiment with the information, think critically about it and develop a more in-depth understanding as they engage with the learning process, if they are to apply the knowledge in their life (Pugh, 2017). Some of the identified learning preferences (e.g. "projects that I can choose what to do and learn the material," and the ability to apply knowledge to enhance the quality of life) aligned with deep learning pedagogy. Deep learning, with the intent for knowledge acquisition and implementation, was identified in this study as a successful pedagogical lens for educating Gen Z learners in online spaces. Poague's, 2018 research explored Gen Z's "shaping a new era of learning" (Poague, 2018 p.1). Results from this study supported the notion an evolution of pedagogical practices may better suit Gen Z's unique learning approaches.

Self-Directed Learning

One learning theory which strongly supported the idea of educator as a guide was self-directed learning (SDL). Optimal SDL learners took responsibility for their own learning (Knowles, 1975). Responsibility would include established individual goals, choice in materials and generation of knowledge according to unique achievements, desires, and experiences (Knowles, 1975). At the time of this study, SDL was a popular adult learning theory, which required learners to take ownership of knowledge acquisition as part of a lifelong endeavor.

SLD provided three perspectives for SDL: personal attribute (e.g. Kasworm, 1988), in which learners became responsible for their moral, emotional, and intellectual development; process (e.g. Harrison, 1978) where the learner chose, constructed, and organized an individual learning process; and context (e.g. Candy, 1991) when self-directed learning was bound by the environment or context. Context, generally thought of as confined to face-to-face learning, did not venture into a virtual learning space; however, twenty-first century researchers, such as Song and Hill (2007), were exploring the expansion of the context perspective in online learning. SDL was anticipated to do well in online settings, in part due to the belief that online learning could be effective for autonomous learners (Song & Bonk, 2016). Furthermore, mobile technology increased the desire and places SDL occurs, which enhanced student-centered learning over teacher-centered learning (Song & Bonk, 2016).

SDL aligned with Gen Z participant learning approaches such as: relying on self, choice of projects, choice in learning materials, and discussing with others. Responsibilities identified in this study were similar to those found in Harrison (1978), which included materials offered choice, personal organization of materials, as well as moral, emotional, and intellectual development. SDL aligned well with autonomous learners (Song & Bonk, 2016), and promotes symbiotic relationships between peers as part of the learning process (Fullan & Langworthy, 2014). This study concurred with literature which presented Gen Z's constant connection to online sources (Kardaras, 2016) and Artificial Intelligence (bot; e.g. Siri, Google, and Alexa) searches (Lovato et al., 2019) as learning preferences. This study added to the literature two learning approaches, complete course materials and ask experts. These two learning preferences detailed Gen Z preference to learn independently but identified their inability to do so without clear and detailed course materials provided by the educator.

LEARNING EXPERIENCES INFLUENCED BY GEN Z

Anyone who has ever gone bowling has likely experienced the crushing defeat of a gutter ball. Even beginning bowlers know throwing the ball down the center of the lane will greatly increase the chances of knocking down the pins. However, having this knowledge does not keep the heavy ball out of the gutter.

Adding bumper pads almost ensures connection with the pins. Educators can think about virtual learning a bit like bowling. The lane is the learning path; the pins are the desired knowledge. Students act as the bowler trying to master the learning, but not always making the strike. Educators, in the perspective of Gen Z, act as the bumper pads to keep learning in the lane, and like the mechanism that resets the pins, educators provide continuous opportunities for a strike. Just as bowlers who utilize bumper pads and the pin setting machine increase the likelihood of rolling a strike, students can comfortably navigate online learning experiences when the educator acts as a guide and provides scaffolding and numerous opportunities for learning.

Communicate in a Personal, Relatable Way

The educator who sets clear expectations for students and clearly identifies what students can expect from the educator are highly preferred. This identification could be accomplished in a syllabus as expectations for a course, or in a specific assignment or learning module. Gen Z suggests educators can share expectations through detailed, written instructions providing the goal, bulleted steps of the process, and expectations for achievement. Within this structure, however, they desire the ability to apply their learning approaches of global communication, technology use, and creation of applicable knowledge – this tenuous balance is a main challenge of fulfilling the role of educator as guide.

To support clarity in communicating learning activity processes and expectations in the online context, Gen Z suggests creating personalized, educator-generated videos. Because constant communication is important to Gen Z, learners ask for educators to generate videos weekly, or at least to accompany each learning module. Table 2 outlines characteristics of video that meet the suggestions of Gen Z.

Table 2. Characteristics of educator-created video for instructional guidance

Length	Short, 10 minutes or less
Content	Explanatory information about the learning activity; key insights; expectations
Style	Casual, Gen Z is interested in knowing the person
Purpose	Personally connect with the learner; clarify or repeat writing directions; establish a replayable soundbite about the learning activity

Keeping in mind that Gen Z's preferred social media (Snapchat, Instagram) is focused on casual video and images, it seems logical that they prefer similar short, personal, and casual video interaction with their educator. Spending time crafting a video specific to each learning activity builds trust while simultaneously creating a connection with students. Videos could be a simple video capturing the educator talking about the learning activity or a little more complex dual-picture video with the talking head and static image of a slide or screencast (i.e., Recorded Zoom http://zoom.com or VidGrid presentation http://www.vidgrid.com). These videos should be professional, but do not have to be a polished production. While Gen Z likes high quality videos, the effort to connect, even in a novice way, is more important.

Instructional videos that introduce new content hold a different expectation for Gen Z. While the communicative videos described above can be casual in nature, the expectation is instructional videos, whether curated or educator-created, are more succinct and polished. Videos can be created using a phone, tablet, computer, and easily recorded on platforms such as Zoom (http://zoom.com), Loom (Apple App Store/Google Play), Flipgrid (http://flipgrid.com), Powtoon (http://powtoon.com), and Adobe Spark (http://spark.adobe.com), but should be polished, clear, and engaging. Gen Z is believed to have the shortest attention span in history (Beall, 2016). Therefore, videos should still be short, approximately 10 minutes or less, and be on focused pertinent content (Wilson & Korn, 2007). If the educator has complex content to share or a lengthy lecture to distribute, breaking it into meaningful smaller pieces is preferred. Current research (Goldie, 2016; Rue, 2018) suggests that this attention span may also be a filter allowing them to quickly sift through information, perhaps not perfectly, or critically, but enough to decipher useful information from irrelevant information in a very short time. Therefore, instructional video should focus on purposeful information pertinent to the learning goal. Educators may consider using video editing software to trim videos and implement multimedia components such as adding text and pictures in order to guide students' viewing process of the instructional video.

Rely on Endless Support from the World

Gen Z expects to use technology, they expect to connect with others regardless of geographic distance, they expect to collaborate and create, and they will use these learning approaches even if the educator does not include them in the formal process. Educators who know the learning approaches of Gen Z can build them into the learning activities as both formal processes and scaffolds for learning. Gen Z seeks learning from educators, each other, crowdsourcing through social media, and searching for information online to ensure validity and clarity of academic concepts. Educators can provide academic, reliable, online, global connections to guide learners to meaningful content. Additionally, global connections and specific audiences provide Gen Z the desired opportunity to share out their learning experiences in safe, purposeful ways. Gen Z participants specifically identified internet searching as a natural part of their learning process, where they found answers to any question by connecting with others to converse, gather advice, deepen understanding, gain clarity, validation, and increase understanding. Educators could design specific assignments providing opportunities for students to search online. Such an activity also includes skill building in critical reading and source verification. Aligning with the educator guidance desired by Gen Z, parameters for searching, expectations of resource type, and possibly examples of age-appropriate, credible sites should be provided by the educator. While Gen Z wants to work independently, they also want guidance, assurance, and modeling from educators in selecting resources.

Gen Z often engages in global connections through asynchronous video chats and texting as opposed to face-to-face interactions and is motivated to share out things they are learning (Beall, 2016; Gale, 2015). The ability to create relationships with people around the globe, through digital technology, creates a unique opportunity for Gen Z to learn more about other cultures and ways of life (Dabbagh et al., 2016). These global relationships and the ability to communicate quickly can help negate stereotypes and help people embrace one another in the learning process.

These examples, along with countless others, provide ideas for educators to embrace the learning approaches of Gen Z and create engaging learning activities. The need for creating and maintaining an online environment in which learners will thrive is up to the individual educator. Online learning is not the same as face-to-face and requires educators who understand and embrace the affordances and drawbacks of the digital world and navigate the variety of cultures and global issues Gen Z learners face on a daily basis. Gen Z participants perceive the educator as their greatest resource in academic settings. Each educator possesses unique attributes, talents, and insights enhancing education and Gen Z is keen to engage with what the individual educator has to offer. Much like the bowling analogy, all the support promotes a refinement of skill so that the bumpers can be removed, and the bowler can be successful. Becoming the educational guide in the online learning context allows students opportunities for learning success that supports their educational preferences.

DIRECTIONS FOR FUTURE EXAMINATION

Participants in both panels repeatedly asked for personalized, explanatory videos, produced by the educator. Further research about asynchronous video communication and relationship building between educator and student could illuminate valuable relationship building and engagement strategies educators could employ to enhance online instruction. Gen Z participants identified the desire for a guide who would facilitate curriculum, check on them to ensure clear understanding of content, and who was concerned with their well-being. Furthermore, Gen Z recommended pedagogical practices promoting technology use and connecting in global contexts. Turning to experts for clarification was critical to their learning approaches, whether that expert be the course instructor or a crowd sourced option. Additional research to explore the nuances and reasoning for the learning approaches could expand educators' knowledge about creating student-centered learning specific for Gen Z. Additionally, participants did not represent the metacognition to detail their process of learning; instead, they explained their unique why for learning. Therefore, a deeper investigation about *how* they learn with the identified approaches and preferences would be valuable to educators. This research established the learning approaches of Generation Z in online contexts through an eDelphi research process, but it yielded only basic understanding about Gen Z as learners. Much can still be learned about how to best meet their needs in the evolving online learning context of education by building further understanding about Gen Z as learners and exploring how to integrate their learning approaches into pedagogical practice. Specifically, this study could be replicated with varying age participants who represent different ranges of the generation. Because the participants in this study were Gen Z young adults with experience in online learning in pre-pandemic contexts, additional research can provide deeper understanding about the learning approaches of the totality of the generation and give insight into needed pedagogical practices for post-pandemic online learning experiences.

CONCLUSION

Two unique panels of experts were chosen to explore a wide variety of Gen Z's learning preferences in both academic and nonacademic online settings. Consensus was reached on many learning approaches with several relating across both panels. Perhaps the most interesting result was the preference for self-directed learning but with a desired guide by an instructor (academic) or reference from others (nonacademic). Pedagogical practices that address the unique characteristics of Gen Z were discussed and related to the prevalent context of online learning.

Implications of this research include:

- A need for educational guidance from online educators, specifically, educators should be available; create class-specific, purposeful content; and communicate through personal videos.

- Online learning happened best when educators balanced student autonomy and educator guidance, so pedagogical practices should rely on clear, purposeful instructional materials that provide project creation choices.
- Relationships were found to be important to online learners' success in the class, thus educators who invest in learning the needs and desires of each student, then created content that supported each student's learning path, can build stronger online relationships and thus promote learner's success.
- Educators should create environments that provide learners with course content and opportunities to seek and test knowledge through social media platforms, experts, and global connections.

This research offered suggestions and examples for how educators could support Gen Z learners in their educational goals and set groundwork for further research regarding Gen Z online learning approaches and best practices. Furthermore, this research pioneers the topic by comparing online academic with online nonacademic preferred learning approaches of Gen Z. And uniquely asked Gen Z to identify their own unique learning process. Understanding the learning approaches of Gen Z deepens educators' understanding and informs future practices. By identifying learning approaches for Gen Z, this study also provides future researchers the ability to test pedagogy specifically designed for online Gen Z learners.

REFERENCES

Bawa, P. (2016). Retention in online courses: Exploring issues and solutions—a literature review. *SAGE Open, 6*(1). Advance online publication. doi:10.1177/2158244015621777

Beall, G. (2016, November). 8 key differences between Gen Z and Millennials. *The Huffington Post.* https://www.huffpost.com

Bennett, S., & Lockyer, L. (2004). Becoming an online teacher: Adapting to a changed environment for teaching and learning in higher education. *Educational Media International, 41*(3), 231–248. doi:10.1080/09523980410001680842

Braun, V., & Clarke, V. (2006). Using thematic analysis in psychology. *Qualitative Research in Psychology, 3*(2), 77–101. doi:10.1191/1478088706qp063oa

Candy, P. C. (1991). *Self-direction for lifelong learning: A comprehensive guide to theory and practice.* Jossey-Bass.

Cook, S. (2015, August). *Engaging Generation Z students* [Workshop presentation]. Greenville College.

Dabbagh, N., Benson, A. D., Denham, A., Joseph, R., Al-Freih, M., Zgheib, G., & Guo, Z. (2016). *Learning technologies and globalization: pedagogical frameworks and applications.* Springer. doi:10.1007/978-3-319-22963-8

Dewey, J. (1938). *Experience and education.* Collier.

Dimock, M. (2019). Defining generations: Where Millennials end and Generation Z begins. *Pew Research Center, 17,* 1-7. http://tony-silva.com/eslefl/miscstudent/downloadpagearticles/defgenerations-pew.pdf

Driscoll, M., & Tomiak, G. R. (2000). Web-based training: Using technology to design adult learning experiences. *Performance Improvement*, *39*(3), 60–61. doi:10.1002/pfi.4140390316

Fisch, K., & McLeod, S. (2008, September). *Shift happens* [YouTube Video]. https://www.youtube.com/watch?v=FdTOFkhaplo

Fullan, M., & Langworthy, M. (2014). *A rich seam: How new pedagogies find deep learning*. Pearson with support of ISTE, MaRS and Nesta. https://www.michaelfullan.ca/wp-content/uploads/2014/01/3897.Rich_Seam_web.pdf

Furnham, A. (2012). Learning styles and approaches to learning. In APA Educational Psychology Handbook: Vol. 2. Individual Differences and Cultural and Continual Factors (pp. 59-81). American Psychological Association. doi:10.1037/13274-003

Gale, S. F. (2015, July). Forget Gen Y: Are you ready for Gen Z? *Chief Learning Officer*. https://www.clomedia.com/2015/07/07/forget-gen-y-are-you-ready-for-gen-z/

Garrett, H., & Woodworth, R. (1969). *Statistics in psychology and education*. Vakils, Feffer & Simons Pvt. Ltd.

Goldie, J. G. S. (2016). Connectivism: A knowledge learning theory for the digital age? *Medical Teacher*, *38*(10), 1064–1069. doi:10.3109/0142159X.2016.1173661 PMID:27128290

Graham, C., Cagiltay, K., Lim, B. R., Craner, J., & Duffy, T. M. (2001). Seven principles of effective teaching: A practical lens for evaluating online courses. *The Technology Source*, *30*(5), 50.

Harrison, R. (1978). How to design and conduct self-directed learning experiences. *Group & Organization Studies*, *3*(2), 149–167. doi:10.1177/105960117800300203

Hunter, J. L., & Krantz, S. (2010). Constructivism in cultural competence education. *The Journal of Nursing Education*, *49*(4), 207–214. doi:10.3928/01484834-20100115-06 PMID:20143755

Joordens, S., Kapoor, A., & Hofman, B. (2019). Let's riff off rifs (relevant, interesting, fun, and social): Best practices for engaging the online mind. In *Handbook of Research on Emerging Practices and Methods for K-12 Online and Blended Learning* (pp. 213–232). IGI Global. doi:10.4018/978-1-5225-8009-6.ch010

Kardaras, N. (2016). Generation Z: Online and at risk. *Scientific American Mind*, *27*(5), 64–69. doi:10.1038cientificamericanmind0916-64

Kasworm, C. E. (1988). *Part-time credit learners as full-time workers: The role of self-directed learning in their lives* [Paper presentation]. Annual conference of the American Association for Adult and Continuing Education, Tulsa, OK.

Kim, K. J., & Bonk, C. J. (2006). The future of online teaching and learning in higher education. *EDUCAUSE Quarterly*, *29*(4), 22–30.

Knowles, M. K. (1975). *Self-directed learning*. Follett.

Lin, F., & Qiyun, Z. (2003). The affinity between constructivist teaching theory and English language teaching reform. *Foreign Languages and Their Teaching*, *4*(7), 89–94.

Lithner, J. (2008). A research framework for creative and imitative reasoning. *Educational Studies in Mathematics*, *67*(3), 255–276. doi:10.100710649-007-9104-2

Lovato, S. B., Piper, A. M., & Wartella, E. A. (2019, June). Hey Google, Do Unicorns Exist? Conversational Agents as a Path to Answers to Children's Questions. In *Proceedings of the 18th ACM International Conference on Interaction Design and Children* (pp. 301-313). 10.1145/3311927.3323150

Martin, F., & Bolliger, D. U. (2018). Engagement matters: Student perceptions on the importance of engagement strategies in the online learning environment. *Online Learning*, *22*(1), 205–222. doi:10.24059/olj.v22i1.1092

Marton, F., & Säljö, R. (1976). On qualitative differences in learning: I—Outcome and process. *The British Journal of Educational Psychology*, *46*(1), 4–11. doi:10.1111/j.2044-8279.1976.tb02980.x

Merriman, M. (2015). *What if the next big disruptor isn't a what but a who. Gen Z is connected, informed and ready for business.* Slideshare, EY. https://www.slideshare.net/wiseknow/what-if-the-next-big-disruptor-isnt-a-what-but-a-who

Mohr, K. A., & Mohr, E. S. (2017). Understanding Generation Z students to promote a contemporary learning environment. *Journal on Empowering Teaching Excellence*, *1*(1), 9.

Morey, S., & Mouratis, J. (2016). *New adobe study shows Gen Z students and teachers see creativity as key to success.* Adobe Press Release.

Murray-Harvey, R. (1994). Learning styles and approaches to learning. *The British Journal of Educational Psychology*, *64*(3), 373–388. doi:10.1111/j.2044-8279.1994.tb01110.x

Nguyen, H., & Hovy, D. (2019, November). Hey Siri. Ok Google. Alexa: A topic modeling of user reviews for smart speakers. *The 5th Workshop on Noisy User-generated Text (W-NUT 2019)*, 76-83. https://www.aclweb.org/anthology/D19-5510/

Parker, K., & Igielnik, R. (2020). On the cusp of adulthood and facing an uncertain future: What we know about Gen Z so far. *Pew Research Center*, (May), 14.

Parmer, S. M., Salisbury-Glennon, J., Shannon, D., & Struempler, B. (2009). School gardens: An experiential learning approach for a nutrition education program to increase fruit and vegetable knowledge, preference, and consumption among second-grade students. *Journal of Nutrition Education and Behavior*, *41*(3), 212–217. doi:10.1016/j.jneb.2008.06.002 PMID:19411056

Poague, E. (2018, December). *Gen z is shaping a new era of learning: Here's what you should know.* Linkedin.com. https://learning.linkedin.com/blog/learning-thought-leadership/gen-z-is-shaping-a-new-era-of-learning--heres-what-you-should-know

Pugh, K. (2017). *Computers, cockroaches, and ecosystems: Understanding learning through metaphor.* Information Age Publishing.

Rue, P. (2018). Make way, millennials, here comes gen z. *About Campus: Enriching the Student Learning Experience*, *23*(3), 5–12. doi:10.1177/1086482218804251

Schwieger, D., & Ladwig, C. (2018). Reaching and retaining the next generation: Adapting to the expectations of Gen Z in the classroom. *Information Systems Education Journal, 16*(3), 45.

Seemiller, C., & Grace, M. (2016). *Generation Z goes to college*. John Wiley & Sons.

Siemens, G. (2005). Connectivism: a learning theory for the digital age. *Instructional Technology and Distance Learning, 2*, 1–8. http://www.itdl.org/Journal/Jan%5f05/article01.htm

Sinatra, G. M., & Lombardi, D. (2020). Evaluating sources of scientific evidence and claims in the post-truth era may require reappraising plausibility judgments. *Educational Psychologist, 55*(3), 120–131. doi:10.1080/00461520.2020.1730181

Song, D., & Bonk, C. J. (2016). Motivational factors in self-directed informal learning from online learning resources. *Cogent Education, 3*(1), 1205838. https://www.cogentoa.com/article/10.1080/2331186X.2016.1205838.pdf

Song, L., & Hill, J. R. (2007). A conceptual model for understanding self-directed learning in online environments. *Journal of Interactive Online Learning, 6*(1), 27–42. http://www.ncolr.org/jiol/issues/pdf/6.1.3.pdf

Stengers, I. (2008). A constructivist reading of process and reality. *Theory, Culture & Society, 25*(4), 91–110. doi:10.1177/0263276408091985

Taylor, Z. W., & Serna, K. L. (2020). Don't Txt Me L8r, Text Me Now: Exploring community college student preferences for receiving a text message from their institution. *Community College Journal of Research and Practice, 44*(2), 133–146. https://naspa.tandfonline.com/doi/full/10.1080/10668926.2018.1560374?scroll=top&needAccess=true

Tobin, K. G. (1993). *The practice of constructivism in science education*. Psychology Press.

Tomasik, T. (2010). Reliability and validity of the Delphi method in guideline development for family physicians. *Quality in Primary Care, 18*(5), 317–326. PMID:21114912

Tomei, L. A., & Nelson, D. (2019). The impact of online teaching on faculty load–revisited: Computing the ideal class size for traditional, online, and hybrid courses. *International Journal of Online Pedagogy and Course Design, 9*(3), 1–12. doi:10.4018/IJOPCD.2019070101

Vygotsky, L. (1962). Thought and language (E. Hanfmann & G. Vakar.). MIT Press. doi:10.1037/11193-000

Vygotsky, L. (1997). *Educational psychology*. St. Lucie Press.

Wigfield, A., & Eccles, J. S. (2000). Expectancy-value theory of achievement motivation. *Contemporary Educational Psychology, 25*(1), 68–81. doi:10.1006/ceps.1999.1015 PMID:10620382

Wilson, K., & Korn, J. H. (2007). Attention during lectures: Beyond ten minutes. *Teaching of Psychology, 34*(2), 85–89. doi:10.1177/009862830703400202

Chapter 9
Intersections of Micro-Level Contextual Factors and Technological Pedagogical Knowledge

Meredith J. C. Swallow
https://orcid.org/0000-0001-6241-9462
University of Maine, Farmington, USA

Mia L. Morrison
University of Maine, Orono, USA

ABSTRACT

Context is an essential component of educator knowledge development and practice. When K-12 learning environments shifted from traditional schools and classrooms to remote learning, teacher knowledge of context was challenged as students were situated in varied and unpredictable settings. In this chapter, researchers examine the ways in which purposeful attention to technological pedagogical knowledge in teacher development and practice can influence the impact of fluctuations in micro level teaching contexts in remote learning environments. To provide direction in enhancing knowledge across contexts, the authors focus on the cross curricular learning skills of critical thinking, communication, collaboration, and creativity. Particular attention is given to learning activities that can span across contexts, grade levels, and subject areas.

INTRODUCTION

It is necessary for educators to have deep knowledge about both the practice of teaching and the application of educational technologies in order to engage in pedagogical strategies that support effective instruction (Koehler & Mishra, 2009). Contextual knowledge is a critical component to education as the influence a teacher has on students depends on the teacher's knowledge and understanding of the

DOI: 10.4018/978-1-7998-7222-1.ch009

specific context (Kelly, 2007; Mishra, 2019). Amidst the many challenges of the COVID-19 global pandemic, educators were confronted with a rapid shift of teaching modalities and environments; this change modified traditional conceptualizations of context including the immediate environment in which students were physically situated (Ferdig et al., 2020). Micro level physical factors (Porras-Hernandez & Salinas-Amescua, 2013) such as the design of the classroom and the availability of resources were disrupted as classrooms relocated to homes, libraries, and parking lots. Additional micro level factors that were impacted include the mutual expectations established between teachers and students as classroom norms, which supported the learning environment.

Rosenberg and Koehler (2015) posit that context is inseparable from teachers and that the development of teacher technological pedagogical knowledge must therefore be developed through a teacher's knowledge of context and within context. When that context is significantly changed - as experienced during the pandemic - questions emerge on the knowledge and actions of teachers. That is, when context is woven together with teacher knowledge as the site of that knowledge (Rosenberg & Koehler, 2015), what happens when that context is disrupted? This chapter addresses the issue through exploration of how the purposeful enhancement of technological pedagogical knowledge development can strengthen the interplay between technology, pedagogy, and context. This exploration focuses on why specific micro level contextual factors support learning and how educators can establish those factors in fluctuating remote learning environments.

BACKGROUND

The Technological Pedagogical Content Knowledge (TPACK) framework (Mishra & Koehler, 2006) is central in educational technology research as a way to characterize the essential knowledge for effective instruction (Chai et al., 2013). The expansion (Figure 1) on Shulman's (1986) pedagogical content knowledge (PCK) framework to include technology introduced four new knowledge domains: technological knowledge (TK), technological pedagogical knowledge (TPK), technological content knowledge (TCK), and technological pedagogical content knowledge (TPACK) (Mishra & Koehler, 2006). The influence of TPACK on scholarship and practice is notable; as of 2020 there have been over 1900 publications focused on or supported by the TPACK framework (Harris & Wildman, 2019). As follows, it is understandable that teacher preparation and professional development continues to be informed by the framework when engaging in learning and knowledge sharing.

Technological Pedagogical Knowledge

This chapter prioritizes the technological pedagogical knowledge (TPK) domain to emphasize the importance of innovations afforded by educational technology to support student learning in remote environments. In the absence of specified content, TPK focuses on the understanding of how to leverage digital tools for appropriate pedagogical practices to support learning outcomes (Mishra & Koehler, 2007). For clarity, Mishra and Koehler (2007) suggested the visualization of a whiteboard; in the physical classroom the location of a whiteboard is often in the front of the room determining the position of the teacher and thus the interactions between the teacher and students. Furthermore, this position often dictates the teacher's pedagogical decisions leaning toward more teacher directed learning tasks. However, when an educator reconsiders the space and use of the whiteboard (e.g. brainstorming), there can be a shift in

Figure 1. TPACK model. Reproduced by permission of the publisher © 2012 by tpack.org.

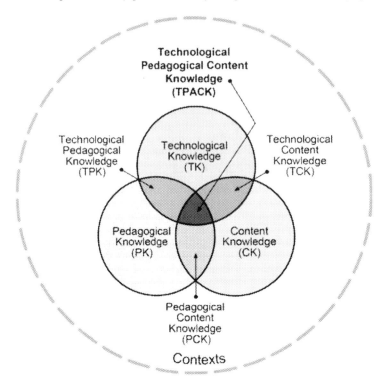

teacher-student interaction as well as pedagogical decisions. TPK, as proposed by Mishra and Koehler, necessitates creative application of tools to support effective teaching and learning.

The research on eliciting the specifics of TPK is not as robust as the focus on the complex integration of TPACK (Koh et al., 2015). However, the importance of TPK is not understated in the limited studies that do pointedly center on the construct. Jaipal and Figg's (2010) cross-case analysis of elementary teacher candidates' teaching practices identified specific characteristics of TPK that lead to successful technology integration. In a follow up survey development, they reemphasized TPK by not differentiating content due to the nature of elementary educators teaching either across the curriculum or through the integration of curriculum (Figg & Jaipal - Jamani, 2011). Heitink et al. (2017) gave additional attention to TPK in their examination of elementary teachers using information and communication technology in practice. They also suggested TPK as an essential construct of the TPACK framework for elementary educators due to the variety of subjects they must teach. Therefore, they placed emphasis on broad pedagogical strategies and argued that teachers' practice is grounded in a reasoning process. Although not explicitly stated as a relationship between the two studies, reasoning is an emphasis that suggests TPK as part of an embedded process of pedagogical decision making based on developing technological knowledge. This aligns to Niess and Gillow-Wiles (2017) approach for a technological pedagogical reasoning process. They considered ways in which integrating technologies as learning tools could engage learners in using critical thinking, creative thinking, communication, and collaboration.

TPK and Context

The aforementioned studies were situated in unique environments; the authors of this study agree that the ability to make informed decisions drawing from one's reasoning skills and TPK requires contextual knowledge, defined as "everything from a teacher's awareness of available technologies, to the teacher's knowledge of the school, district, state, or national policies they operate within" (Mishra, 2019, p. 1). TPACK was developed as embedded in context. However, the perspectives of context have been conceptualized and researched in many different ways (Kelly, 2010; Rosenberg & Koehler, 2015). Kelly (2007) posited that teacher success depends on knowledge and adjustment to each unique context; that is, the changing physical elements of the educational environment. Reviews of relevant literature related to context (see Kelly, 2010; Rosenberg & Koehler, 2015) highlighted the lack of inclusion of context in TPACK studies. Addressing inconsistencies in definitions of context and the omittance of contextual knowledge as an equally important knowledge domain, Mishra's (2019) upgrade (Figure 2) to the well-established TPACK diagram emphasized the outer dotted circle as "XK for ConteXtual Knowledge" (p. 2), highlighting the importance of teachers' knowledge of context.

Figure 2. Revised version of the TPACK image © Punya Mishra, 2018. Reproduced with permission.

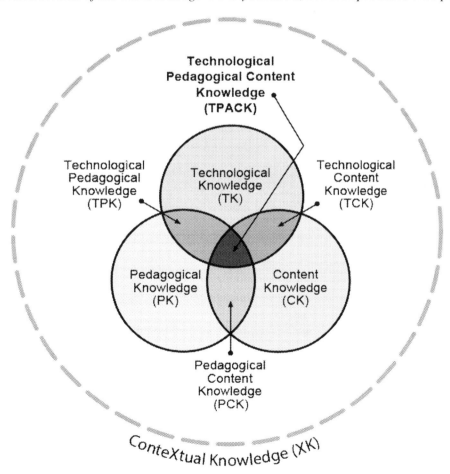

This chapter affirms the importance of XK in teaching and considered research specific to the understanding of context and the intersections of knowledge development. Rosenberg and Koehler (2015) described two perspectives of context which dominate the literature and debate on what constitutes context. "Context as that which surrounds" (p. 442) views context as something that is independent of a teacher's condition. That is, the variables which make up the context are not controlled by the teacher, thus allowing the teacher the ability to develop knowledge *of* the context. In this regard, teacher knowledge can be developed about situational variables, with pedagogies enacted based on such contextual influences. Counter to knowledge *of* context, Rosenberg and Koehler (2015) described the second perspective of "context as woven together with" (p. 422) as context that is inseparable from a teacher. Knowledge in-context considers a teacher's knowledge as it is formed within or by a specific context. The authors of this chapter agree with Rosenberg and Koehler that both views are important and needed for educational research. This chapter focuses specifically on the development of TPK to mitigate the unpredictability of contextual factors due to varied remote learning environments. The authors heighten the focus on both knowledge of context and knowledge in-context as ways for teachers to leverage their understanding of the virtual space in which they are situated and how their development of technological and pedagogical knowledge in that space influences teaching and learning.

Porras-Hernandez and Salinas-Amescua's (2013) conceptual framework for context and the influence of contextual factors on teacher knowledge served as the direction for context in this chapter. The two-dimensional framework follows a bioecological development model (Bronfenbrenner, 1976; Bronfenbrenner & Morris, 2006) consisting of a disaggregation of context along two dimensions: scope and actor. Figure 3 serves as a recreation of their model. Three concentric domains of contextual influences make up the scope of context: (1) the macro level defined as the global and national "social, political, technological, and economic conditions" (Porras-Hernandez & Salinas-Amescua, 2013, p. 228); (2) the meso level - how these elements are established within the local community and individual schools; and (3) the micro level which includes the classroom-level circumstances such as available resources and the physical layout. The actors in this model include teachers and students, and how their own knowledge, attitudes, beliefs, characteristics, and interests interact to shape the learning environment (Porras-Hernandez & Salinas-Amescua, 2013). A more detailed description of Porras-Hernandez and Salinas-Amescua's dimensions follows.

Scope

Porras-Hernandez and Salinas-Amescua's (2013) definition of macro level contextual factors included the national perspective of educational technology and the relevant conditions which may impact technology integration in classrooms. Rosenberg and Koehler (2015) suggested curricular standards as an example of macro level factors that may impact teacher knowledge. Swallow and Olofson (2017) described how specific macro level factors prompted two schools to engage in systemic initiatives focused on curriculum design and technology integration. In this case, they identified relevant demographic trends and state enacted assessment strategies as driving circumstances.

Porras-Hernandez and Salinas-Amescua (2013) defined the meso level as "the social, cultural, political, organizational, and economic conditions established in the local community and the educational institution" (p. 228). Following this definition, they considered the role of power structures, initiatives, and values as factors influencing the success of technology integration. Furthermore, the meso level may include elements that are contiguous to teachers but not within their physical space. For example,

Intersections of Micro-Level Contextual Factors and Technological Pedagogical Knowledge

Figure 3. Authors' recreation of Porras-Hernandez and Salinas-Amescua's (2013) representation of context elements

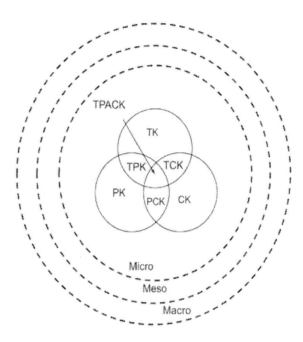

community involvement or support of initiatives may impact teacher actions in the learning space. Swallow and Olofson (2017) found that local support systems (e.g. parent involvement or community partnerships) during a one-to-one technology initiative had direct influence on an educator's motivation to leverage technology to support student learning.

The micro level context is associated with "in-class conditions for learning" (Porras-Hernandez & Salinas-Amescua, 2013, p. 230) and included elements such as resources, activities, and norms. In this regard, the micro level context is that which is most immediate to an educator. In related literature, micro level contextual factors are the most prevalent (Rosenberg & Koehler, 2015) when examining the construct of TPACK. In this regard there might be a question as to whether or not additional research needs to be conducted looking at micro level factors. The authors of this chapter suggest a shift in identifying what the micro level encompasses. With alignment to the Porras-Hernandez and Salinas-Amescua (2013) definition that the micro level context includes "given conditions that influence or determine teachers' practice," the authors aim to contribute explicit attention to micro level factors in a virtual classroom. That is, defining Porras-Hernandez & Salinas-Amescua's "in class" (p. 230) as *a virtual class*.

Actor

Porras-Hernandez and Salinas-Amescua's (2013) framework for context also identifies teachers and students as actors where "each actor brings unique characteristics that influence the interaction and the learning process" (p. 231). The factors related to a teacher's ability to integrate technology into instruction have been studied (Ertmer & Ottenbreit-Leftwich, 2010; Ertmer et al., 2012), contributing to the position that the teacher as an actor, and the subjective variables that contribute to a teacher's knowledge of technology integration, needs to be recognized within knowledge construction (Porras-Hernandez &

Salinas-Amescua, 2013). Thus, the contextual factors related to a teacher need to be considered when integrating technology.

In addition to the understanding of the teacher and their self-contributing factors, the student needs to be recognized as an actor in the conceptualization of context. Porras-Hernandez and Salinas-Amescua (2013) acknowledged students' attitudes and beliefs as contextual factors and identified external conditions (or the external contextual factors for a student) as equally important.

FOCUS OF CHAPTER

As contextual boundaries shift, questions and opportunities emerge in the roles of teachers and students - the actors. Increased attention on the virtual space and the micro-level factors in that space present affordances with the interactions between teachers and students and creates opportunities for redefining the structure of learning. The focus, solutions, and recommendations of this chapter center on the co-construction of learning through the interplay of technological pedagogical knowledge and conteXtual knowledge, and the consideration of learning partnerships among the actors.

Issues

Although not explicitly stated, in reviewing the broad context within studies cited in systematic literature reviews of TPACK (e.g. Chai et al., 2013; Rosenberg & Koehler, 2015; Voogt et al., 2012), context was broadly assumed in the physical space. In a review of more recent studies that consider TPACK in the midst of the pandemic, pedagogical implications consider the shift from physical to online as opposed to centering on the virtual space as the primary context (Ferdig et al., 2020). The authors' intention with this chapter is to draw attention to the virtual space and the micro level factors that can be influenced by increasing technological pedagogical knowledge (TPK). Rosenberg and Koehler (2015) emphasized the interwoven relationships between knowledge and context. Expanding, actors cannot be independent from their context and whether or not knowledge is *of* or *in* context is inseparable from pedagogy. This chapter presents perspectives and solutions situated within the micro level of a virtual context and influenced by the knowledge of context and knowledge in-context (conteXtual knowledge, XK) of the teacher and student as actors.

Learning Skills

To develop TPK to enhance teaching across contexts, researchers and educators must consider why specific micro level contextual factors support learning as well as how to establish those factors in fluctuating and unpredictable remote learning environments. In efforts to provide associable knowledge across contexts, the authors focus on the cross curricular learning and innovation skills of critical thinking, communication, collaboration, and creativity commonly referred to as the 4Cs (Battelle for Kids, 2019). The shift from twentieth to twenty-first century educational thinking prompted stakeholders to challenge the success of a teaching model that emphasized teacher-centered learning through scripted curriculum (Becker & Ravitz, 1999). Educational organizations promoted twenty-first century standards or competencies tied to teaching practices, learning outcomes, and technology integration (Voogt & Roblin, 2010), and the Partnership for 21st Century Skills launched a national conversation on the importance of contemporary and necessary skills for all students (Battelle for Kids, 2019) and emphasized key subjects, learning and innovation skills, information, media, and technology skills, and life and career skills. The 4Cs emerged from the learning and innovation skills as skills "recognized as those that separate students who are prepared for a more and more complex life and work environments in the 21st century, and those who are not" (Battelle for Kids, 2019b, p. 4) with a focus on creativity, critical thinking, communication, and collaboration.

Niess and Gillow-Wiles (2017) questioned the professional knowledge base for educators in the twenty first century and suggested that the teacher orchestration of managing "learning tasks in the content areas in a manner that supports their students in engaging in these critical learning skills [the 4Cs]" (p. 78) is a challenge that reaches beyond an understanding of content. The challenges already faced by educators are further complicated by the radical shift to multiple teaching and learning environments. For example, Roschelle and Teasley (1995) defined collaboration within the scope of "synchronous activity" (p. 73). Additional insights on collaborative work focus the classification of the process and the purpose (Hesse et al., 2015; Kuhn, 2015) without redefining how the participants are situated. There is also the position that collaboration does not benefit all students in learning contexts; some show greater learning gains when working individually (Kuhn, 2015). Thus, if collaboration is an essential skill for learners, the authors of this chapter contend that with the increase to multiple modes of learning spaces there is an opportunity to better understand how the intersections between conteXtual knowledge (XK) and technological pedagogical knowledge (TPK) can transform teaching and learning so that students *can* be better supported. When learning occurs outside a unified singular environment across unpredictably varied locations as in remote learning, each student brings their individual XK to the learning table as they advance their TPK to communicate, collaborate and think critically through creative and diverse, self-chosen modalities. Student actors partake in the construction of knowledge in concert with the teacher actor, building self-awareness and greater autonomy as learners take ownership in the process.

The variability on how educators embrace shifting contexts is far-reaching in the current state of education (Ferdig et al., 2020). Much of this variability has to do with the multiple modalities in which teachers are engaging. For example, common modes of classroom instruction now include online, hybrid, or hyflex when once those same classrooms were exclusively face-to-face. In general, there is an acceptance that most educators will need to embrace some form of virtual instruction. This chapter considers then XK being knowledge of and in-context when the context is situated in a virtual (or remote) environment. In examination of micro level contextual factors, the authors center on learning spaces, available resources, and the interactions among and between teachers and students as the actors (Porras-Hernandez & Salinas-Amescua, 2013) in these new learning environments. Furthermore, they emphasize the 4Cs as the learning skills within this scope.

Learning Spaces

Environments that facilitate a learner-centered model of instruction promote student engagement through tasks that support the development of the 4Cs (Soule & Plucker, 2015). Flexible seating arrangements, for example, can offer physical learner-centered classroom designs. These organizations of classroom physical structures are purposefully designed to support student-focused learning opportunities. To illustrate, students have the ability to move freely around the classroom, work independently or collaborate as needed, and find space that fits their learning needs. In the shift to the virtual classroom, educators are tasked with creating these same considerations. However, they are challenged with mitigating the contextual factors that students are bringing to the virtual classroom. This draws attention to the intersections of students and teachers as actors and the understanding of the context in which each actor brings. Teachers, therefore, are creating knowledge of the context while simultaneously developing knowledge in-context in order to adapt their instruction to support student learning. There is a shift from the physical considerations of the learning space to the virtual. Therefore, the factors that define the learning space broaden to include the variables that contribute to the space. This may, for example, include how specific learning tools create or support new spaces for learning, and expands to consider the pedagogical implications of interacting in these spaces. When examining XK knowledge of and in-context during remote and hybrid learning modalities, both teacher and student actors contribute to XK considerations for effective and productive knowledge construction.

Available Resources

Technological knowledge is knowledge about technologies utilized by educators and requires the ability to adapt and learn with the nature of evolving digital tools and resources (Mishra & Koehler, 2006). The options for available resources in contemporary education are continuously expanding and educators must consider the emerging opportunities to use available tools to enhance learning. This recognition extends beyond the knowledge of hard technologies (Lakhana, 2014) to incorporate the awareness and understanding of the various *applications* of the tools embedded within the hardware and software. The authors consider how then available resources can be defined as both what is accessible to the actors and how it is applicable to support the 4Cs; this underscores the importance of technological pedagogical knowledge as a sophisticated comprehension of resources and their applications will enhance learning. To demonstrate, consider creativity within the 4C framework; teachers need a depth of understanding of available resources to use or may facilitate student exploration of tools as options for expression and creativity. The manner in which students interact with those tools can illuminate how available resources might look differently or be used differently for each individual. This understanding allows for diverse modalities of resources to support knowledge construction and application.

Interactions

When teaching remotely, contextual knowledge is not a consistent, controllable component across the learner population. Rather, each student engages from a personal, unique learning environment. This idea complements the literature viewing students as actors (Porras-Hernandez and Salinas-Amescua, 2013); students bring their unique external conditions to the learning environment since students now are both emotionally *and* physically tied to their individual educational context. In the virtual context, teachers and students are not physically in the traditional classroom space and educators are tasked with weaving a variety of contexts together to create their knowledge of - and in - context. Therefore, it is important to increase TPK in order to leverage the virtual micro contextual factors that support the 4Cs across the multitude of unique contexts. With that in mind, the interactions between the teacher and the student need to leverage the flexibility and unpredictability of the environment as opposed to viewing it as a challenge. The common dichotomy of time in a virtual classroom is delineated as synchronous (occurring at the same time) and asynchronous (not occurring at the same time). Strategies to support communication, for example, need to incorporate both synchronous and asynchronous interactions. With regard to TPK, teachers need to recognize how digital tools can allow for the expansion of time and space to embrace flexible timing. In this way, interactions among actors (teacher-student and student-student) can be enhanced through increased attention to the innovative learning structures afforded through increased TPK. Remote activities and lessons must provide versatility for student actors to determine the pace and schedule of interactions to best suit their unique context. They contribute to both XK and TPK domains as well as experience growth in all 4Cs and autonomy through the learning experience as they take ownership of their education.

Researchers, practitioners, and professional development providers have an opportunity to support educators in enhancing their knowledge development in order to conceptualize their understanding of physical space, resources, and interactions with students for effective online pedagogical strategies. To enhance TPK and micro level contextual knowledge, the proposed solutions present learning experiences that align to dynamic interplay between TPK and virtual XK development, as well as the activation of the 4Cs. In these examples, students are active participants in the construction of knowledge.

SOLUTIONS AND RECOMMENDATIONS

Each learning experience described in this chapter supports technological pedagogical knowledge (TPK) development and includes an investigation of how that experience is further complemented by the micro level contextual factors of space, resources, and interactions. These factors must be re-examined through the lens of remote learning contextual impact and then redesigned to be applicable across virtual learning spaces. The analysis centers on the knowledge development of the actors and the application of the 4Cs.

Note-Taking: Transformation from Face-to-Face to Virtual

The act of taking notes during a lesson can support the 4Cs through the activation of learning by sharing and interacting with peers. In a traditional face-to-face classroom, students might exchange notes, followed by a small group question and answer period to deepen understanding. Students are able to compare and question their interpretation and conclusions. In a virtual space, there are more parameters and workflows to evaluate and from which to select. Teachers are no longer controlling how the space is organized nor what is going on around the student. This change shifts the TPK lens to focus on tools and activities that allow for engagement and completion surrounded by a diverse set of factors. Educators need TPK in order to determine the most suitable and relevant digital tools to support this type of interaction while considering the variable contexts of their learner population. Table 1 illustrates the transformation of note taking from in person to the virtual environment with an accompanying in-practice example. The interplay of enhanced TPK with specific contextual considerations creates new opportunities for students. The focus on technology, pedagogy, and context provides guidance for how educators can use their knowledge to foster engaging learning experiences for students in virtual environments. Two additional transformations of common learning actions (Tables 2 and 3) follow accompanied by in-practice examples.

Table 1. Transformation of Note Taking from Face-to-Face to Virtual Environments

	Face-to-Face Note Taking	**Interplay Between TPK and XK**	**Virtual Note Taking**
Space	Note taking occurs during lesson or class time. Opportunities to extend learning through additional resources occur outside the confines of class and time.	Processes for note taking must incorporate flexibility in access, device or tool, and collaborative platforms. *Focus areas:* mixed media, annotation, sharing, and editing	Untethered by space restrictions or commonality, note taking can occur through self-selected digital or analog methods.
Resources	Tools are single purpose and used to describe, summarize, and capture thinking.	Digital resources and diverse modalities need to be leveraged to support various strategies of knowledge construction and application. *Focus areas:* tools in conjunction with one another, and redesigned use	Resources expand in modality for engagement, access, and diverse environmental consideration. Tools for note taking can span a wider spectrum of modalities and used in conjunction with one another. Sketchnoting, embedded video and audio, typing, and handwriting can interact on platforms with collaborative options.
Interactions	Note taking, communication, and collaboration happens synchronously. Focus and scope remain local, tied to participants inside the classroom.	Strategies for communication need to incorporate synchronous and asynchronous options, with an awareness of broader audiences. *Focus areas:* expansion of time and space, and innovative learning structures	Interactions in the classroom are no longer bound by time or place. Peer to peer collaboration as well as feedback can be ongoing and iterative to provide maximum learning and growth as student selected pacing. There are no boundaries in finding expertise nor engaging in dialogue with anyone.

In-Practice Example: Middle School Science

In person, students take notes on paper as they listen to a lecture or read from a textbook. Most notes are textual and taken on a blank page, whether a physical sheet of paper or digital document. The example of virtual note-taking shows a page out of a digital workbook created by the teacher (Figure 4) using Keynote. The teacher instructs and interacts with her students as they engage with content resources. The students are given the workbook template in which they can follow along during direct instruction. It is also available to guide students as they engage with resources independently and repeatedly as needed, collaborate with others by sharing their workbook with another "owner" in Keynote, and interact with content related apps or websites that are actively linked in the workbook. When students choose to share and work in the same workbook, they strengthen communication and collaboration skills. Students can work both synchronously and asynchronously, independently and collaboratively, to engage with content resources. As well, students are able to connect with teachers or peers to ask questions in a one to one, small group, or whole group setting. Through modeling visual expression and providing optional pathways for showing knowledge, the teacher encourages and activates both critical thinking and creativity as students engage in synthesis of knowledge (Figure 5). Note taking is accomplished through numerous modalities of expression, independent or collaborative environments, and at flexible, self-paced nodes. The examples show a sketchnote made in Pages and textual note taking as they learn and engage with content resources. Other applications for sketchnoting and for the creation of visuals include Explain Everything, Tayasui Sketches, and Procreate.

Figure 4. Example of a student taking notes on a page in a teacher created workbook that accompanies the learning activity

Choose one of the options below and learn more about SPACE! Add what you learned at the bottom by creating sketchnotes!

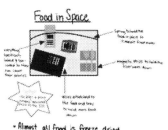
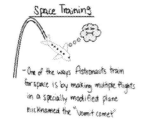

Figure 5. Example of a creative expression (sketchnote) made by a student to express understanding as they engage with resources and synthesize information

The metric system is the universal system used by scientists all over the world. By using the metric system, all scientists can understand each others measurements. Since the metric system in based on units of ten, it also makes it easier to convert from one unit to another.

Measurement	Unit	We usually use:
Length	Meters	cm
Volume	Liters	mL
Mass	Grams	g
Temperature	Celsius (or Kelvin)	C^0
Density	Grams/Liter	g/mL or g/cm^3

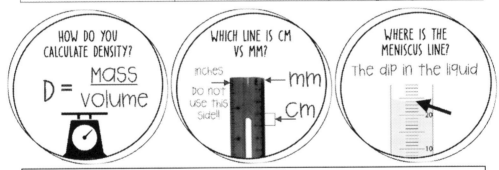

How do you measure the volume of an irregular solid object?
water displacement or how much does the water rise when you add the object?

Add any additional notes you need here. You can also add a blank page after this one or make a copy of the notebook paper on p. 17

Measuring volume of REGULAR solid: length x width x height

Density: how tight the molecules are ~ closer together means more dense.

Presentation: Transformation from Face-to-Face to Virtual

The next example (Table 2) illustrates the enhancement of the 4Cs skill building process during remote learning whereby students share their learning through presentations. In a traditional face-to-face environment, learners must consider the most important aspects of their message (critical thinking) and use creativity in the communication of these points. The transition into virtual spaces opens the door to increased collaboration and creativity, where students can incorporate components of interactivity and even immersive experiences through augmented or virtual reality elements. Presentations can be shared both synchronously together as well as asynchronously for a personalized experience in small groups or solo, to be controlled by viewer(s) in terms of pace, choices, interactivity, and repetition. Not only does the teacher impart an enhanced TPK to scaffold and build opportunities for learners, the students themselves cultivate their own TPK in the creation. All 4Cs are utilized and enhanced during student discovery, innovation and incorporation of their XK to create a personalized expression of their learning.

Table 2. Transformation of Presentations from Face-to-Face to Virtual Environments

	Face-to-Face Presentation	**Interplay Between TPK and XK**	**Virtual Presentation**
Space	Opportunities to share understanding and present knowledge occurs during class time. Sharing is synchronous and unidirectional.	Ability to present findings or share information must incorporate flexibility in access, device or tool, and audience engagement. *Focus areas:* innovative ways to engage audience, creative expression of information and knowledge	Virtual presentations can include both synchronous and asynchronous components. Presentations can be paused or reviewed and can include audience participation.
Resources	Tools are focused on visual aids suited for common space, effective screen view and projection. Users are able to share synchronously and in a one to many modality.	Tools focus on audience experience and engagement rather than creator experience. *Focus areas:* tools for visual impact, audience participation, and experience	Resources expand in modality, creative (multimedia) expression, and audience experience.
Interactions	Presenting and viewing happens synchronously. Focus and scope remain unidirectional, with passive viewing.	Presentations incorporate audience participation to accommodate asynchronous viewing and to sustain engagement and understanding. *Focus areas:* audience engagement, participation, interactivity and multimedia stimulation	Audiences can be engaged with more visuals, participatory elements, and interactive media. Presenter and viewer can interact in both synchronous and asynchronous modalities.

In-Practice Example: Elementary Second Grade

Second grade students present their learning and understanding after a counting and measuring unit using Keynote (Figure 6, Figure 7, Figure 8). The teacher is able to encourage students to engage with their immediate (home) environment as well as found objects. In these activities, students have choice in what they measure, which encourages autonomy, critical thinking, and creativity. They learn technology and media skills as well as build communication and collaboration skills as they share the learning and consider what questions they might pose to others or answer questions from peer presentations. There is a plethora of options for creativity in expression and modes of communication. The presentations are shared digitally so that they can be experienced at the convenience and pace of the individual student situation, need, and learning. This can be done synchronously or asynchronously during presentation, with the artifact left in a shared space that can be accessed at a later time by peers. Each student can watch, review, and respond or collaborate with other students throughout the process as they learn content, create artifacts to share their learning, and both provide and receive responses. These elementary students are bringing their XK and advancing their TPK throughout the learning process. Other applications for creativity and ease of use for elementary include Adobe Spark and Haiku Deck, with collaboration features additionally available on Adobe Spark.

Figure 6. Example of multimedia rich slides from a presentation made by a 2nd grade student that can be shared synchronously and then submitted in a virtual space for reviewing and further exploration

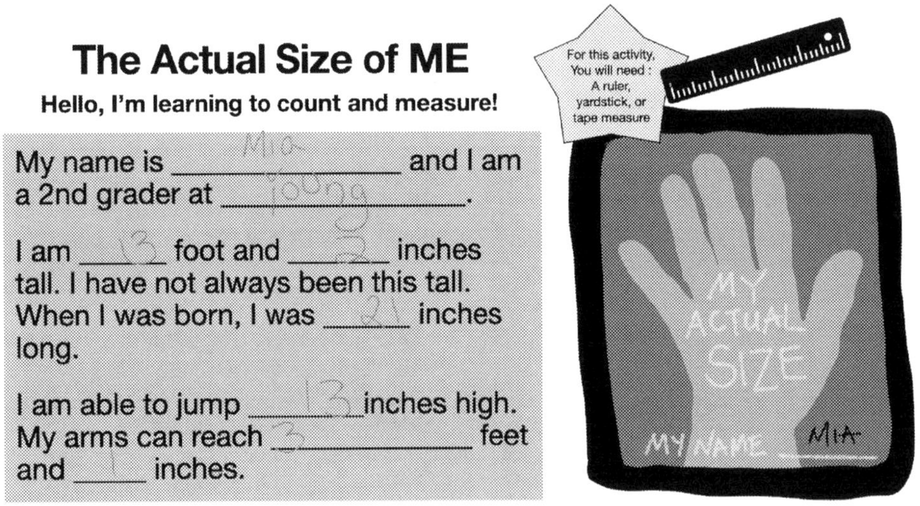

Figure 7. Second example of multimedia rich slides from a presentation that includes embedded audio

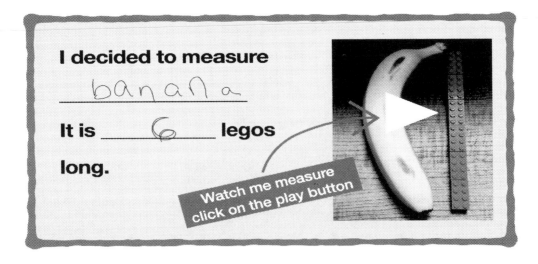

Figure 8. Third example of multimedia rich slides from a presentation that includes embedded audio and opportunities for synchronous or asynchronous student-student interaction

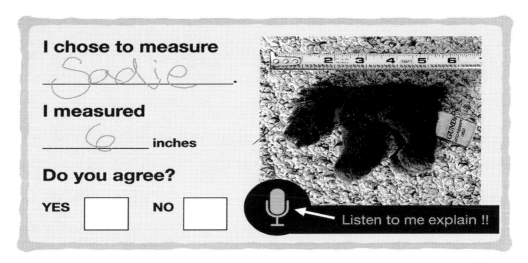

Co-Construction of Knowledge: Transformation of a Literacy Activity from Face-to-Face to Virtual

The last illustration (Table 3) exemplifies the collaborative nature between students and teacher as they each bring knowledge of and in-context (XK) as well as leveraging advanced TPK to co-construct a differentiated, personalized learning experience around literacy. While in traditional face-to-face learning environments, literacy activities tend to be linear in time and space. Additionally, it is common for the teacher to front load information and directions to be followed by student action. Remote learning provides opportunity for active student participation in developing the knowledge construction process as well as actual knowledge construction, synthesis and interactivity. The teacher must leverage TPK and XK (in-context knowledge) to provide workflow and scaffolding that encourages the incorporation of student XK while enhancing development of student TPK. As co-owners of this collaborative knowledge construction process, students are empowered and build critical thinking skills and autonomy. They are able to pace their engagement and comprehension and punctuate synthesis with synchronous and asynchronous interactivity with peers and teachers. When both teacher and student actors are active and participatory in this complex and rich interplay between XK and TPK, learners embrace the 4Cs in personalized, large strides that are customizable to align with their situation, needs, and strengths.

In-Practice Example: High School Literacy

Students reading Macbeth complete activities and collaborate to advance literacy skills and make key connections. As students work to unpack the words of Shakespeare, they are given the opportunity to read independently while interacting with peers. The teacher provides space and resources for students to share ideas, identify key themes or connections as well as discuss, debate, communicate and think critically. The student determines the pace and organization of learning that best suits their XK and needs. Punctuating these common strategies, the teacher has created an interactive activity where students

Table 3. Transformation of Literacy Activity from Face-to-Face to Virtual Environments

	Face-to-Face Literacy	Interplay Between TPK and XK	Virtual Literacy
Space	Building literacy skills (reading, comprehension) is completed during class time. Opportunities to practice are completed outside class time, with feedback provided during the next class or beyond. Commonly, directions are front loaded, reading, answering questions or annotation is completed on paper.	Processes for building literacy skills incorporate increased feedback in both quantity and immediacy. Teachers and students can work together to develop content or activity appropriate environments for interactivity, collaboration, and growth. *Focus areas:* feedback, sharing, and practice	Lessons provide synchronous and asynchronous components. Asynchronous activities can incorporate practice and synthesis (comprehension). Feedback can be both synchronous and asynchronous so that it is timely, frequent, and specific.
Resources	Tools are focused on synchronous listening and responding.	Tools incorporate diverse multimedia options, multiple modes of engagement, creative expression. They should provide opportunities for feedback to be immediate and interactive. *Focus areas:* mix of synchronous and asynchronous activity, ability to pause or review, multiple modes of expression, interactivity, collaboration	Resources must provide students with synchronous and asynchronous activities. Students will engage with resources independently and collaboratively as they practice, share thoughts around comprehension and synthesis. Students then elicit feedback or engage with interactive resources to advance understanding, make connections or create new meaning.
Interactions	Directions, learning and feedback is linear. Feedback and sharing are synchronous, tied to class time and space.	There is increased focus on collaboration and integration of asynchronous components, with frequent and timely interaction. Interactivity with peers and teachers encourages sustained engagement. *Focus areas:* pace and meter of synchronous and asynchronous work, feedback and share cycles	Interactions with peers and teachers occur more frequently in both synchronous and asynchronous modalities. Students can work at their own pace while advancing comprehension and synthesis through critical thinking, discussion, feedback, interactive activities and synthesis.

place visual icons in hexagonal patterns (Figure 9) using Pages book templates and Keynote. When sides touch, the themes or characters must be connected. In this way, students are thinking critically about the reading, synthesizing plot and behaviors, and identifying metaphors and themes. In remote learning environments, students communicate and collaborate through audio and video modalities (Figure 10) to enrich the conversations and support one another as they navigate the ionic pentameter and explore Shakespearean tragedy. The teacher can join and watch the interactions, stepping in as needed to guide their thinking, provide insight, or ask more questions to enrich the conversation. There is a mix of synchronous and asynchronous action that is coupled with peer interactivity to sustain engagement. Further, the design of these activities is scaffolded to encourage independence, ownership, and autonomy. This transformation of literacy exemplifies a shift in leveraging TPK by one actor - the teacher - within an in person context to the potential of collaboration between two actors - teacher and students - in developing TPK in a virtual context to maximize learning and growth. Teachers and students construct differentiated, personalized learning experiences together through a rich interplay of both the student and teacher TPK and XK.

Intersections of Micro-Level Contextual Factors and Technological Pedagogical Knowledge

Figure 9. Example of high school students completing an interactive activity using visual icons to promote comprehension, author's message, and literary connections

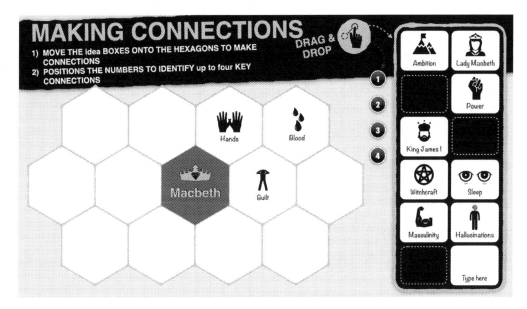

Figure 10. Example of high school students building literacy skills and collaborating with peers through a teacher created workbook as they read Shakespeare's Hamlet

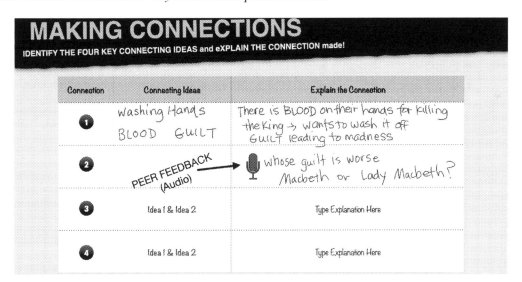

FUTURE RESEARCH DIRECTIONS

The solutions and recommendations illuminate the development of TPK and how the micro level contextual factors for space, resources, and interactions enhance development through the added lens of remote learning contextual impact. From interactive note-taking and expression of knowledge to co-construction of literacy advancement, students take a leadership role in their learning in this new paradigm. There is new interplay between TPK and XK for the teacher and the student. Taking this one step further, the exchange between and role of the teacher and especially the student has shifted. Both have been additionally empowered and offered passport to collaboration and earnest ownership of the learning process.

The authors suggest that directions for future considerations utilizing the ideas put forth in the recommendations include deeper exploration of the interplay between conteXtual knowledge (XK) and technological pedagogical knowledge (TPK) to influence learning. The lens can be expanded to consider the roles of both the teacher and student in the co-construction of essential knowledge and more specifically, the collaboration of these actors in developing skills, autonomy, and creativity as XK and TPK from both actors are leveraged to maximize learning. Further discussion should emphasize diverse knowledge construction as teachers provide a foundation of visible learning punctuated and enhanced by opportunity for learners to participate and embrace their unique contextual perspectives. Instead of managing the known context of a classroom, that is knowledge of context, the above examples show that during hybrid and remote learning, teachers collaborate with learners to incorporate their immediate environment during learning, whereby students interact and guide a teacher's knowledge in-context development. The teacher cannot act alone in personal conteXtual knowledge. Rather, teachers and students are equals and must communicate and collaborate to leverage conteXtual knowledge, which in turn enhances technological pedagogical knowledge of both actors.

As the boundaries of brick and mortar contextual parameters are taken down, learners are afforded increased ownership of conteXtual knowledge construction and power in essential knowledge development. Future studies may look to unpack these shifting frames and explore the vast potential of actor roles as further flattening the hierarchical structures of learning. In the virtual environment, XK is no longer fixed and therefore unpredictable nor controllable by the teacher. The importance of knowledge in-context is heightened simultaneous to the role of the student in developing XK. Teachers leverage their own XK (knowledge of context) and TPK to provide learning activities with embedded opportunities for students to leverage their own XK and TPK, thus sustaining engagement and increasing learner power and ownership. Teacher TPK is important as teachers make learning visible to provide scaffolds, motivation, and direction. Students build upon these visible frames to develop and strengthen their own TPK as they share and embrace their collaborative XK (knowledge in-context) through choice and autonomous thinking. This condition leads to sustained engagement and greater ownership of the learning. Teachers and students are working collaboratively in the construction of a personalized learning experience through the rich interplay TPK and XK from both actors. While the teacher provides a visual map as a foundation, students are empowered to bring in their own XK and TPK for the learning experience to be completed.

As the roles of teachers and students shifts to more collaboration, it becomes increasingly important to provide multiple modes of engagement and expression. Key takeaways for future investigation include best practices and pedagogy around making learning visible through TPK as well as the deep impacts of the newly collaborative interplay of XK and TPK on student expression, ownership, and autonomy. Figure 11 highlights elements to consider as teachers leverage their TPK and XK in the development of learning experiences that empower students. As the teacher introduces an activity or series of activities around content, students are able to leverage their own TPK and XK to continue development of the activity and personalize the experience. Students are no longer simply following directions, with personalization enhanced through choice. Rather, learners are now participants in the activity scope and development to make the activity personally relevant and meaningful. In this way, teachers and students co-construct and collaborate to maximize learning, sustain engagement, stimulate (diverse) knowledge construction, specifically knowledge in-context, and inspire ownership of learning. Future research should embrace not only these new paradigms of TPK and XK interactivity, whether focused on the teacher, students or newly minted collaborative nature of this interactivity, but incorporate the role of technology in empowering each stakeholder.

Figure 11. The elements involved in the collaboration between teachers and students to co-construct differentiated, personalized learning experiences through a rich interplay of TPK and XK of both actors

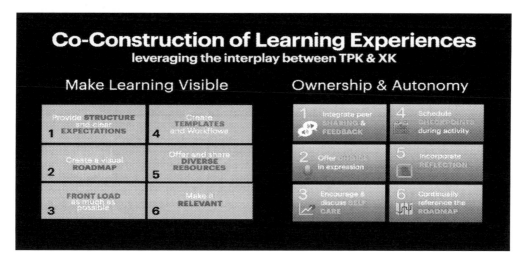

CONCLUSION

The COVID-19 global pandemic forced schools and classrooms to redefine their definitions of a learning space. The traditional and comfortable physical space shifted to flexible and often unpredictable virtual environments bringing together the varied contexts of learners and teachers. While the displacement of instruction created many different challenges (Ferdig et al., 2020), a focus on technological pedagogical knowledge (TPK) and how teachers can leverage their knowledge present an opportunity to rethink the intersections of context, teaching, and learning. Teachers need to recognize and understand the unique contexts of each student in order to develop their own knowledge of and in-context to support pedagogy; in a virtual space conteXtual knowledge (XK) presents even more considerations. Learning spaces fluctuate and the distinctive circumstances of each student contribute to the broader virtual learning environment in unique combinations for each student. The authors of this chapter proposed increased attention on TPK and the intersections of XK in a virtual space with a focus on micro level factors (Porras-Hernandez & Salinas-Amescua, 2013). Examples of how knowledge construction can be enhanced in remote environments were presented with consideration toward space, resources, and interactions between the student and teacher (the actors) (Porras-Hernandez & Salinas-Amescua, 2013). The cross curricular learning skills of critical thinking, communication, collaboration, and creativity served as associable knowledge across varied contexts and content areas. A developing theme throughout the examples provided involves the shift in the role of each actor within the process of knowledge construction. Where once the teacher was the primary focal point of TPK consideration, with their XK defined by *their* knowledge either of or in context, the new opportunities presented by virtual learning allows for a dynamic and complex interplay of the TPK and XK of each student to also emerge as an essential aspect to learning. The focus on space, resources, and interactions illuminated how those micro factors can contribute to the working knowledge of all actors and how the collaboration of the actors can lead to the co-construction of learning experiences. While this chapter situated knowledge in the virtual classroom, the coaction of TPK and XK should not be limited to remote learning. In all environments, teachers need to embolden students' ownership of learning by facilitating opportunities where students are empowered to leverage their unique knowledge to personalize their experiences.

REFERENCES

Battelle for Kids. (2019a). Retrieved from https://www.battelleforkids.org/

Battelle for Kids. (2019b). *A framework for 21st century learning definitions*. Retrieved from http://static.battelleforkids.org/documents/p21/P21_Framework_DefinitionsBFK.pdf

Becker, H. J., & Ravitz, J. (1999). The influence of computer and internet use of teachers' pedagogical practices and perceptions. *Journal of Research on Computing in Education, 31*(4), 356–379. doi:10.1080/08886504.1999.10782260

Bronfenbrenner, U. (1976). The experimental ecology of education. *Educational Researcher, 5*(9), 5–15. doi:10.3102/0013189X005009005

Bronfenbrenner, U., & Morris, P. A. (2006). The bioecological model of human development. In W. Damon & R. M. Lerner (Eds.), Handbook of child psychology (Vol. 1, pp. 793–828). John Wiley & Sons. doi:10.1002/9780470147658.chpsy0114

Chai, C. S., Koh, J. H. L., & Tsai, C.-C. (2013). A review of technological pedagogical content knowledge. *Journal of Educational Technology & Society, 16*(2), 31–51.

Ertmer, P. A., & Ottenbreit-Leftwich, A. T. (2010). Teacher technology change: How knowledge, confidence, beliefs, and culture intersect. *Journal of Research on Technology in Education, 42*(3), 256–284. doi:10.1080/15391523.2010.10782551

Ertmer, P. A., Ottenbreit-Leftwich, A. T., Olgun, S., Sendurur, E., & Sendurur, P. (2012). Teacher beliefs and technology integration practices: A critical relationship. *Computers & Education, 59*(2), 423–435. doi:10.1016/j.compedu.2012.02.001

Ferdig, R. E., Baumgartner, E., Hartshorne, R., Kaplan-Rakowski, R., & Mouza, C. (Eds.). (2020). *Teaching, Technology, and Teacher Education During the COVID-19 Pandemic: Stories from the Field*. Association for the Advancement of Computing in Education (AACE). Retrieved June 15, 2020 from https://www.learntechlib.org/p/216903/

Figg, C., & Jaipal-Jamani, K. (2011). Developing a survey from a taxonomy of characteristics for TK, TCK, and TPK to assess teacher candidates' knowledge of teaching with technology. *Proceedings of Society for Information Technology & Teacher Education International Conference*. Retrieved from: https://www.researchgate.net/publication/277983097

Harris, J., & Wildman, A. (Eds.). (2019). February 28. *TPACK Newsletter*. Retrieved from https://activitytypes.wm.edu/TPACKNewsletters/index.html

Heitink, M., Voogt, J., Fisser, P., Verplanken, L., & van Braak, J. (2017). Eliciting teachers' technological pedagogical knowledge. *Australasian Journal of Educational Technology*, *33*(3), 96–109. doi:10.14742/ajet.3505

Hesse, F., Care, E., Buder, J., Sassenberg, K., & Griffin, P. (2015). A framework for teachable collaborative problem solving skills. In P. Griffin & E. Care (Eds.), *What We Know About Collaboration Assessment and Teaching of 21st Century Skills: Methods and Approach* (pp. 37–56). Springer. doi:10.1007/978-94-017-9395-7_2

Jaipal, K., & Figg, C. (2010). Unpacking the "Total PACKage": Emergent TPACK characteristics from a study of preservice teachers teaching with technology. *Journal of Technology and Teacher Education*, *18*(3), 415–441.

Kelly, M. A. (2007). Culturally sensitive teaching with technology: Implementing TPCK in culturally mixed contexts. In R. Carlsen, K. McFerrin, J. Price, R. Weber, & D. Willis (Eds.), *Proceedings of Society for Information Technology & Teacher Education International Conference 2007* (pp. 2199–2202). Chesapeake, VA: AACE.

Kelly, M. A. (2010). Technological Pedagogical Content Knowledge (TPACK): A Content analysis of 2006–2009 print journal articles. In D. Gibson, & B. Dodge (Eds.), *Proceedings of the Society for Information Technology & Teacher Education International Conference 2010* (pp. 3880–3888). Chesapeake, VA: AACE.

Koehler, M. J., & Mishra, P. (2009). What is technological pedagogical content knowledge? *Contemporary Issues in Technology & Teacher Education*, *9*(1), 60–70.

Koh, J. H. L., Chai, C. S., & Lee, M.-H. (2015). Technological pedagogical content knowledge for pedagogical improvement: Editorial for special issue on TPACK. *The Asia-Pacific Education Researcher*, *24*(3), 459–462. doi:10.100740299-015-0241-6

Kuhn, D. (2015). Thinking together and alone. *Educational Researcher*, *44*(1), 46–53. doi:10.3102/0013189X15569530

Lakhana, A. (2014). What is educational technology? An inquiry into the meaning, use, and reciprocity of technology. *Canadian Journal of Learning and Technology*, *40*(3), 1–41. doi:10.21432/T2H59S

Mishra, P. (2019). Considering contextual knowledge: The TPACK diagram gets an upgrade. *Journal of Digital Learning in Teacher Education*, *35*(2), 76–78. doi:10.1080/21532974.2019.1588611

Mishra, P., & Koehler, M. J. (2006). Technological pedagogical content knowledge: A new framework for teacher knowledge. *Teachers College Record*, *108*(6), 1017–1054. doi:10.1111/j.1467-9620.2006.00684.x

Mishra, P., & Koehler, M. J. (2007). *What is technological pedagogical content knowledge?* Retrieved from: https://citejournal.org/volume-9/issue-1-09/general/what-is-technological-pedagogicalcontent-knowledge/

Niess, M., & Gillow-Wiles, H. (2017). Expanding teachers' technological pedagogical reasoning with a systems pedagogical approach. *Australasian Journal of Educational Technology, 33*(3), 77–95. doi:10.14742/ajet.3473

Porras-Hernandez, L. H., & Salinas-Amescua, B. (2013). Strengthening TPACK: A broader notion of context and the use of teacher's narratives to reveal knowledge construction. *Journal of Educational Computing Research, 48*(2), 223–244. doi:10.2190/EC.48.2.f

Roschelle, J., & Teasley, S. D. (1995). The construction of shared knowledge in collaborative problem solving. In C. E. O'Malley (Ed.), *Computer-supported collaborative learning* (pp. 69–197). SpringerVerlag. doi:10.1007/978-3-642-85098-1_5

Rosenberg, J. M., & Koehler, M. J. (2015). Context and technological pedagogical content knowledge (TPACK): A systematic review. *Journal of Research on Technology in Education, 4*(3), 186–210. doi:10.1080/15391523.2015.1052663

Soule, H., & Plucker, J. (2015). *4Cs research series. Partnership for 21st Century Skills*. Academic Press.

Swallow, M. J. C., & Olofson, M. (2017). Contextual understandings in the TPACK framework. *Journal of Research on Technology in Education, 49*(3), 228–244. doi:10.1080/15391523.2017.1347537

Voogt, J., Fisser, P., Roblin, N. P., Tondeur, J., & van Braak, J. (2012). Technological pedagogical content knowledge - a review of the literature. *Journal of Computer Assisted Learning, 29*(2), 109–121. doi:10.1111/j.1365-2729.2012.00487.x

Voogt, J., & Roblin, N. P. (2010). *21st century skills. Discussienota*. Kennisnet. Retrieved from http://opite.pbworks.com/w/file/fetch/61995295/White%20Paper%2021stCS_Final_ENG_def2.pdf

ADDITIONAL READING

Admiraal, W., van Vugt, F., Kranenburg, F., Koster, B., Smit, B., Weijers, S., & Lockhorst, D. (2017). Preparing pre-service teachers to integrate technology into K–12 instruction: Evaluation of a technology-infused approach. *Technology, Pedagogy and Education, 26*(1), 105-120. https:// doi:10.1080/1475939X.2016.1163283

Archambault, L., & Crippen, K. (2009). Examining TPACK among K-12 online distance educators in the United States. *Contemporary Issues in Technology & Teacher Education, 9*(1). https://citejournal.org/volume-9/issue-1-09/general/examining-tpack-among-k-12-online-distance-educators-in-the-united-states

Baydas, O., Kucuk, S., Yilmaz, R. M., Aydemir, M., & Goktas, Y. (2015). Educational technology research trends from 2002 to 2014. *Scientometrics*. https://link.springer.com/journal/11192

Evans, M., & Boucher, A. R. (2015). Optimizing the power of choice: Supporting student autonomy to foster motivation and engagement in learning. *Mind, Brain and Education, 9*(2), 87-91. https:// doi:10.1111/mbe.12073

Garthwait, A., & Weller, H.G. (2005). A year in the life. *Journal of Research on Technology in Education, 37*(4), 361-377. https:/ doi:10.1080/15391523.2005.10782443

Hartshorne, R., Baumgartner, E., Kaplan-Rakowski, R., Mouza, C., & Ferdig, R. (2020). Special Issue Editorial: Preservice and inservice professional development during the COVID-19 pandemic. *Journal of Technology and Teacher Education, 28*(2), 137–147.

Lambert, J., & Gong, Y. (2010). 21st century paradigms for pre-service teacher technology preparation. *Computers in the Schools, 27*(1), 54-70. https:// doi:10.1080/07380560903536272

López-Pérez, M. V., Pérez-López, M. C., Rodríguez-Ariza, L., & Argente-Linares, E. (2013). The influence of the use of technology on student outcomes in a blended learning context. *Education Tech Research Dev, 61*, 625–638. https://https://-org.wv-o-ursus-proxy02.ursus.maine.edu/10.1007/s11423-013-9303-8

McKenney, S., & Visscher, A. J. (2019). Technology for teacher learning and performance. *Technology, Pedagogy and Education, 28*(2), 129-132. https:// doi:10.1080/1475939X.2019.1600859

McLeod, S., & Graber, J. (2018). *Harnessing technology for deeper learning: A quick guide to educational technology integration and digital learning spaces*. Solution Tree.

Pew Research Center. (2020). Parents attitudes and experiences related to digital technology. https://www.pewresearch.org/internet/2020/07/28/parents-attitudes-and-experiences-related-to-digital-technology/

Scherer, R., Tondeur, J., Siddiq, F., & Baran, E. (2018). The importance of attitudes toward technology for pre-service teachers' technological, pedagogical, and content knowledge: Comparing structural equation modeling approaches. *Computers in Human Behavior, 80*, 67-80. https:// doi:10.1016/j.chb.2017.11.003

Tam, M. (2000). Constructivism, instructional design, and technology: Implications for transforming distance learning. *Journal of Educational Technology & Society, 3*(2), 50–60.

KEY TERMS AND DEFINITIONS

Communication, Collaboration, Creativity, Critical Thinking (4Cs): Cross curricular learning and innovation skills

ConteXtual Knowledge (XK): A teacher's knowledge context; in this chapter the knowledge of and in-context when the context is situated in a virtual (or remote) environment.

Interactions: The relationships between teachers and students and their knowledge construction through knowledge of and in-context.

Learning Space: The places where teaching and learning occur including the digital factors that contribute to the space.

Micro-Level Context: Classroom-level circumstances such as the space and resources.

Resources: Accessible digital tools and their potential applications for teaching and learning.

Technological Pedagogical Knowledge (TPK): A teacher's understanding of how technology can influence instructional decisions to best support student learning.

Chapter 10
Teaching Strategies During a Pandemic:
Learnings and Reflections

Kelly Medellin
Midwestern State University, USA

Dittika Gupta
Midwestern State University, USA

Kym Acuña
Midwestern State University, USA

ABSTRACT

Due to the COVID-19 pandemic, teachers were faced with the insurmountable task of changing teaching methods to virtual online pedagogy, practically overnight, that continued to provide students with quality instruction using best practices. Action research was employed to help seek the answers to the question: During a pandemic with school online and students socially distanced in person simultaneously, how could teachers still provide cooperative learning experiences that give students opportunities to collaborate in class while continuing to use best practices like the 4Cs (communication, collaboration, critical thinking, and creativity)? Through completely online and synchronous (online and face-to-face) instruction, Jamboard, Padlet, Mentimeter, Flipgrid, and Bitmoji Classroom were implemented to support student learning through the 4Cs of 21st century learning. In this chapter, the rationale, implementation, successes, and challenges will be revealed from self-examined action research.

INTRODUCTION

The COVID-19 pandemic has forced educators worldwide to change the layout of their courses and classrooms to online learning. The pedagogy of virtual learning environments is a new landscape for many educators, and there is more to creating these environments than just placing information in an

DOI: 10.4018/978-1-7998-7222-1.ch010

online format for students. The goals and mission for a virtual learning experience include providing culturally relevant instruction with comprehensible input for *ALL* students, facilitating a space for communication and collaboration among peers, and creating opportunities for inquiry based learning and critical Donethinking (González-González & Jiménez-Zarco, 2015; Saadé, et al., 2012). While teachers are prepared in their teacher preparation on how to provide students with a quality education that includes all of the aforementioned goals in a physical classroom setting, meeting the challenge to place all curriculum online and recreate an experience similar to that of a traditional classroom for students is a daunting task.

The aim of this chapter is to provide actual learning activities through which teacher candidates can develop the skills identified through the 4C's of twenty-first century skills: communication, critical thinking, collaboration, and creativity based on best practices and pedagogical reasoning that can be used across grade levels PK-12 and at the university level (Thoughtful Learning, 2016). The 4C's support student learning in all content areas and the technology resources addressed in this paper are tools educators can use to implement critical thinking, creative thinking, communicating, and collaborating (Thoughtful Learning, 2016). Action research has become an important part of educational research in which researchers attempt to address issues in the classroom (Glassman et al., 2013).

BACKGROUND

Implementing the 4C's of twenty-first century skills in a virtual learning environment calls for careful examination of exactly how to engage students in the actions. Action research methodology (Mills, 2020; Stringer & Aragón, 2020) provides a strategy for a continuous refining and revising of the instructional materials and strategies specifically designed to develop these skills among students. Particular technologies are called upon in this process - Jamboard, Mentimeter, Flipgrid, Padlet, and Google Classroom. Each of these resources are considered in detail along with several examples that can be used in a synchronous or asynchronous virtual learning environment. However, as background to this work, a description of the 4C's as well as the action research methodology is provided.

4C'S of Twenty-first Century Skills

Goodwin and Sommervold (2012) call critical thinking, creativity, and communication, the 3C's, to have "universal applicability" in the teaching and learning process. There is no doubt that the concepts of critical thinking, creativity, and communication have woven threads in each and every aspect of the learning process (Thoughtful Learning, 2016). Creativity is not just for an artist or a painter; it is much more than that. Creativity refers to thinking "outside the box" - to think of novel ideas and be able to come up with solutions to problems (Goodwin & Sommervold, 2012). Henriksen et al. (2015) describe creativity as an individual's thoughts, behaviors, and products that can be considered novel, effective and whole.

Another interwoven skill is that of critical thinking. Critical thinking has been identified as one of the most important skills needed for an individual to be successful in life (van der Zanden et al., 2020). To be effective problem solvers, one must be able to analyze and think deeply to make sense of the situation. According to Fischer and Scriven (1997), "critical thinking is skilled and active interpretations and evaluation of observations and communications, information, and argumentation" (p. 21).

Communication is yet another core skill essential for learning in any classroom whether it be between the students, or between the student and teacher. Ortiz-Rodríguez et al. (2005) examined factors affecting the quality of a distance education course from the student's point of view and found that communication was one of the most prominent identified factors for quality education. Traditionally, communication has been done in-person however with the change in education and the change mode of delivery- communication through technology has also become an area to be considered and explored in depth.

A final skill that has emerged as an essential skill in the 21st century has been collaboration. This skill can be considered the fourth C. Saavedra and Opfer (2012) call collaboration as a "condition for optimal learning" (p. 12). Through collaboration, students exchange ideas, justify their thinking, and develop understanding of other ideas to accomplish a meaningful shared goal. Lai (2011) states that collaboration is linked to all other skills and also leads to metacognition and motivation. The scenario of collaboration is also changing. It is more than just meeting face-to-face but rather being able to meet through various platforms, cooperatively work, and analyze to accomplish a task. Hence, it is critical to have tasks, activities, and instructional practices that support achievement of these twenty-first century skills. A curriculum that includes rich tasks that encourage exploration, discovery and creativity with negative constraints of competition has potential for leading to meaningful learning (Russo, 2013; Hinchman & Gupta, 2020).

Given the challenge of the 4C's in an online learning experience, teachers are challenged to identify specific strategies and tasks. But in online experiences, these strategies require examination of various technologies to support students in these engagements. A look at the connection of the 4Cs for teaching with effective use of technologies (Budhai, & Taddei, 2015) during the pandemic was framed through an action research lens.

The researchers sought to use the impetus of pandemic necessitated acceleration of skill building in the use of various technology tools to explore how those tools could promote the inclusion of the 4Cs in a combined face-to-face and virtual classroom or in a synchronous or asynchronous setting. Action research has been defined as "an inquiry conducted by educators in their own settings in order to advance their practice and improve student learning" (Efron & David, 2020, p. 2). The researchers took the opportunity to develop an action research team in order to seek to address an issue that went beyond the single classroom (Spaulding & Falco, 2013). Mertler (2020) identifies six ways in which action research can be used successfully in the educational setting: improvement of educational practice, connecting theory to practice, connection to school improvement, teacher empowerment, professional growth, and social justice advocacy. So, the researchers began exploring the use of five specific apps that could impact instructional practice. The researchers' implementation of the five chosen apps were geared specifically toward those ends.

The researchers used a four-stage procedure for conducting the action research (Mertler, 2006). The four stages include: the planning stage, the acting stage, the developing stage, and the reflecting stage. The planning stage involved determining which technologies might fit the learning goals and available resources then determining how the technologies might be used in the different classrooms. This stage was done by considering the devices available to each student and the comfort level of each instructor in utilizing the technologies in face to face, hybrid, and online settings. For the acting and developing stages, each researcher then individually developed the lessons involving the technologies studied and implemented them in class over various iterations. In the reflection stage, the researchers used student response, student engagement, and written feedback to examine the effectiveness of the use of each technology for use of the 4Cs within their lessons.

Five specific technologies were examined, used in the classroom, and studied as tools for teaching the 4Cs within additional course content. This informal action research collaboration (Sagor, 2000) allowed for three autonomous teachers united by a common vision of student engagement and student success within a greatly changed learning environment to examine various technologies across teaching styles and course subjects.

EXAMINATION OF FIVE TECHNOLOGIES FOR ONLINE LEARNING

The five technologies that were examined included: Jamboard, Mentimeter, Flipgrid, Padlet, and Bitmoji Classroom. The following sections discuss the technology tool, the implementation of, and successes and challenges of the following platforms examined in the action research project. Various aspects and elements of each of the resources/strategies are examined and considered in detail with several examples for use in a synchronous or asynchronous virtual learning environment.

Jamboard

Collaboration is an essential part of every classroom and according to Vygotsky's Sociocultural Theory of Learning (Jaramillo, 1996), collaboration is an essential part of the learning process itself. Students can work together and build on ideas from one another to elevate their learning and open their minds to new ways of thinking. Collaboration, additionally referred to in education as cooperative learning (González-Tejero et al.,2007), also allows space for higher order/ critical thinking skills to be used by students with support from their peers.

In a traditional classroom setting, students work collaboratively on assignments and activities during class in pairs and small groups where they can share an end product like a Venn Diagram or poster. Students can then present or share with other pairs/groups in the class in a manner where their collaboration gives way to knowledge, learning and scholarship amongst the classmates.

The traditional methods of social collaboration in classrooms were threatened due to the COVID-19 pandemic which forced many classrooms to become fully online, hybrid, or socially distanced. Teachers were now faced with the task of teaching via Zoom, teaching in socially distanced classrooms and teaching synchronously to face-to-face and virtual students. Therefore, the question arose, how could teachers still provide cooperative learning experiences that give students opportunities to collaborate in class?

The action research process began by searching for virtual platforms that would allow for collaboration and cooperative learning during COVID-19 pandemic. In looking for ways where students could collaborate in class (whether hybrid, virtually or in a socially distanced classroom), use critical thinking and use creativity, the researchers found that Jamboard provided an easy and free tool to be able to incorporate collaborative brainstorming. Jamboard is a free collaborative tool from Google Suites that permits multiple students' simultaneous use, as with a whiteboard or poster that automatically saves all changes in the document.

Implementation

Jamboard is a free tool provided by Google for the purposes of collaboration. Through the use of Jamboard, the researchers found that students were able to collaborate on a plethora of classroom projects and activities. Instead of using the traditional classroom tools like markers and a poster or whiteboard, students could use Jamboard on their devices to work in collaborative groups while safely social distancing in the classroom or contribute virtually from home. Jamboard serves as a canvas that permits multiple students to simultaneously draw, type, write in free style, add sticky notes, insert a picture, and save the document as a PDF file.

The researchers found that Jamboard allowed students to collaborate safely within a synchronously taught classroom where students were face-to-face (but socially distanced) where all had access to a one-to-one technology. Further, the capability also allowed the students from a Zoom classroom to participate with the students in the face-to-face classroom. Essentially then, both environments merged to feel as if one classroom where they were able to collaborate on ideas with peers throughout the classroom space.

When creating a new Jamboard, the link may be changed to "anyone who has this link can edit" such that students sharing the link can work on projects together on any device from wherever they are physically (six feet apart in a classroom or at home). One can change the background setting and create a template for students to follow or you can let students decide on how their Jamboard looks based on the assignment/task. Students can collaborate by adding ideas via textbox, sticky note, adding an image and drawing/writing.

Figure 1 provides an example where a group of students collaboratively worked to accomplish the task of discussing an educational philosophy using words, quotes, pictures, and other things. The power lies in the fact that they can simultaneously work on it and build off each other's ideas. Additionally, the collaborative whiteboard can be used through breakout rooms with each group having their own page or even during a face-to-face class that requires social distancing or collaboration across the room. When sharing their Jamboard with other classmates, students can share the link to "view only" and then use the laser pen feature to highlight important information they want to reveal. The researchers found that with its multiple uses and functionalities, Jamboard allowed for true peer collaboration in class supporting cooperative learning and quality of classroom instruction to continue at a high level during an unprecedented time.

Successes and Learnings

Overall, the use of the Jamboard tool was a success because it not only helped to answer one of the initial questions: How can teachers still provide cooperative learning experiences that give students opportunities to collaborate in class? However, as it was implemented, students were collaborating and using critical thinking and creativity skills that elevated their learning. When initially using this tool in class, students were able to easily use this product and there was almost a nonexistent learning curve because it was a user-friendly tool. For example, students commented on the overall ease of using the tool and the sticky notes feature. In class, Jamboard was used successfully with small groups presenting activities to class and students could work with others from across socially-distanced classrooms as well as with the synchronously taught virtual students.

Jamboard was also used for whole group collaboration where students could all respond to the same question/section of the chapter and see each other's thoughts and ideas. This action also provided beginnings for class discussions. For some of the activities a template was used and copied so that small groups/pairs collaborated on their own ideas while also using the same formatting. Also, Jamboard allows multiple slides/pages within one application if there is not enough space on the initial page.

Figure 1. Collaborating on an activity through Jamboard

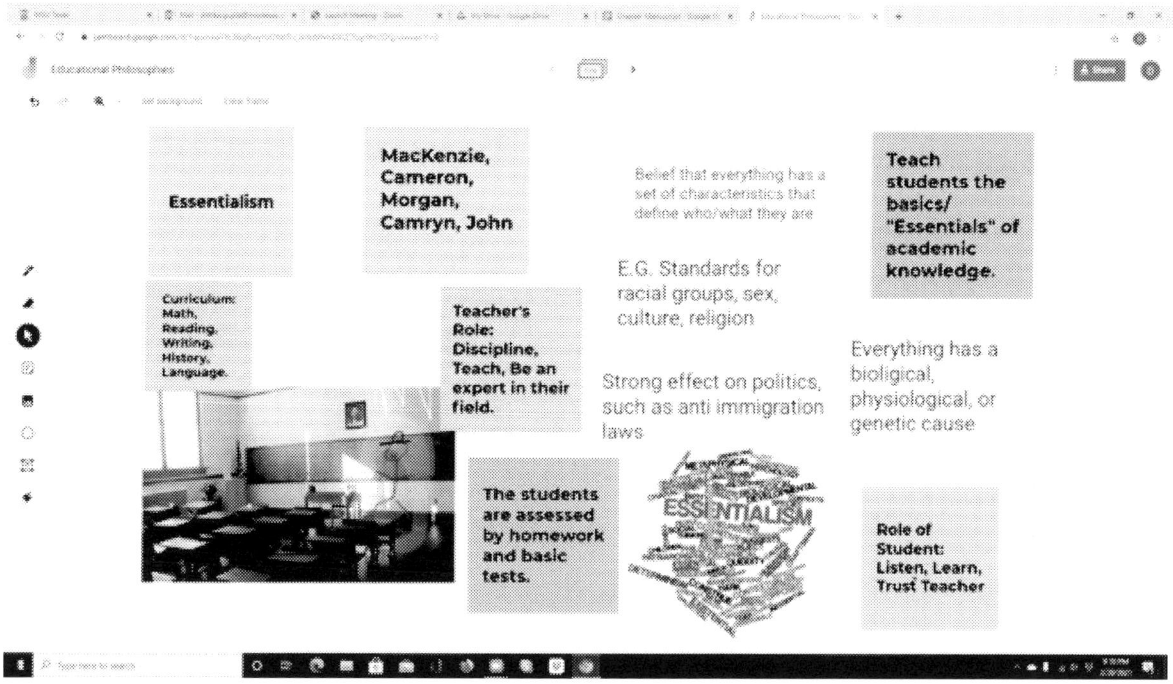

From the action research, the researchers learned not only these tips for using the programming, but that Jamboard is an excellent tool for 21st century collaboration. Virtual learning is within the future of education. Learning to blend virtual learning with the research-based practice of collaborative/cooperative learning was an overall success with Jamboard. However, there were initial challenges.

Concerns and Challenges

As mentioned previously, there was almost a nonexistent learning curve because it is a very user-friendly tool. There were a couple of challenges worth mentioning. First, if there are a large number of students in the class and you are completing a Jamboard as a whole group experience, there may not be enough room for everyone's comments. Some solutions to this issue include planning ahead of time and making a Jamboard with more than one page, or creating a Jamboard with columns where students place different sticky notes or text boxes while the teacher monitors and moves the items around to make room when necessary.

A second issue the researchers found was that if using the Jamboard for a grade, there was not a way to see who added which piece to the Jamboard. This challenge actually could be a benefit when discussing difficult topics and you want anonymity. The solution to this challenge, if needed, is to have students add their initials to their textbox or sticky note following their contribution. These minor challenges were mostly user issues and not concerns with the platform itself. Regardless, Jamboard provides a valuable classroom tool for collaboration.

Padlet

Again, due to the pandemic, the researchers wanted their instruction to still be delivered at a high level even though teaching through Zoom and socially distanced classrooms. Therefore, the action research led researchers to find Padlet. Padlet is a free website that teachers can use to set up spaces for students to create and collaborate via interactive multimedia bulletin boards. This app is easy to use, customizable, and has many uses including, creating timelines, diagrams, and collages.

Two of the best rationales for using this site are that it is free and there is a gallery of ideas that teachers can search, use and/or copy, and recreate for their own classes. When considering how to implement the 4C's, creativity, collaboration, communication, and critical thinking, Padlet generates room for students to have the opportunity to use all the aforementioned areas of twenty-first century learning. Students can access Padlet from home or in a socially distanced classroom using tablets/computers and collaborate and/or communicate on assignments and class activities. For example, students can respond to each other's posts in a twitter style feed using text, pictures, gifs, etc. Padlet also gives way to creativity and critical thinking by allowing students to use different media to express their thoughts on a topic and allows the teacher/professor to use multimedia to spark conversation and critical thinking.

Implementation

The implementation of Padlet efficiently allowed students to collaborate in new ways whether at school or home and learn in a cooperative manner together. Padlet has a free account mode and an upgraded mode that costs a fee for more access to different tools. The researchers found that the free version met the requirements to use the 4C's in classroom instruction during COVID-19.

Once you have an account, one can set up a new Padlet. In setting up a new Padlet, there are many choices including a wall, a grid, a stream, a canvas, and a shelf, all of which students can view and respond to content set up by the instructor. There is a backchannel Padlet, where students can communicate in a chat like environment similar to Twitter. The other two Padlet types are a map and a timeline. On the map you can add content to points on the map and on the timeline you can place content on a horizontal timeline (this could be used by the teacher or students could use this feature to create a timeline).

Examples of using Padlet include, students collaborating to assign a meme or gif to a vocabulary word and definition, communicating back and forth in a twitter-style feed about a classroom topic, or adding content points to a map. For a specific example, consider a Human diversity course where Padlet was used to watch videos of people describing their experiences with microaggressions on a stream Padlet format and students responded using texts and gifs. In Figure 2 students were asked to collaborate in pairs and use critical thinking and creativity to share a given vocabulary word by creating a definition and adding a gif or meme to help explain the concept of their vocabulary word to the class. This activity showed the instructor how students thought but also created an environment where students used their creativity to express themselves. Through this Padlet activity, they were able to look at each other's work, get inspiration from each other's ideas, and comment on what they saw. In essence the activity supported the development of a community of learners. Another example of it was setting Padlets for students to share about their favorite son, wishes, thoughts, and other personal aspects in video, image, or text format to build a community in a virtual environment. As peers and the instructor could comment and/or like the various posts, it fostered personalization.

Teaching Strategies During a Pandemic

Figure 2. An example of Padlet where students express their thoughts in multiple ways

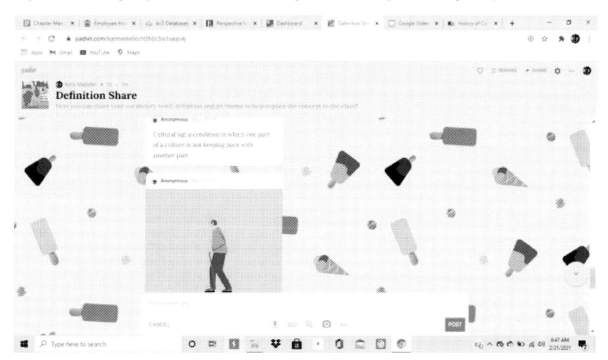

Successes and Learnings

This tool supported several successes in fostering creativity, collaboration, communication, and critical thinking. The first success was that students enjoyed using the platform and were able to engage in academic dialogue in a way that they were able to relate to similar platforms outside of class. Another success in using Padlet was that it allowed students in the classroom to communicate and collaborate with virtual learners on in-class assignments, and they were able to communicate and collaborate in the classroom while staying six feet apart. Lastly, giving students the option to respond using gifs, text, drawing, pictures, film, etc. supported creative responses and fostered building a community.

There were also many learnings from the research and using Padlet in the classroom. One finding was that the creator of the Padlet can require approval by the moderator before the posts become visible to others and there is an option that will filter out profanity. These are good tools that can make this site appropriate for use across many grade levels. Another finding, similar to Jamboard, students are able to remain anonymous or sign in when posting. List allows for monitoring conversations/posts. Lastly, posts show up in real time allowing the activities and discussions to be conducted immediately during class instruction.

Concerns and Challenges

For this project of finding platforms to engage students using the 4C's during pandemic-synchronous online and face-to-face (socially-distanced instruction), Padlet really hit the mark, although there were some concerns and challenges. One challenge that was faced was that incorporation of Padlet takes some planning time for the instructor to play, experiment, get used to, think of how to implement the tool into the curriculum, and ultimately present to students. Once educators take the time to learn all the functions and uses though, Padlet can be a twenty-first century learning tool used in the classroom for years to come. The second challenge was the internet in the classroom. Using Zoom and everyone in all the classrooms using the wifi in the building at times could cause Padlet to run slowly in the classroom. With limited time with students such delays could cause distractions and other issues for engaging the students in the activity experience. Yet another concern was that there are only a limited number of free Padlets for one user. A way to overcome this limitation is by deleting an old Padlet before forming new ones which however also deletes all records. Another way to overcome this challenge is to have students sign-in using the instructor's reference code and every two successful sign-ins gives the instructor one additional Padlet.

Mentimeter

Mentimeter is a tool that can be used to encourage discussions that allow for students' opinions and analysis of data. Initially the researchers had been exposed to Mentimeter in faculty meetings/development to give responses to new information learned from the presenter. This tool is free and similar to some of the features found in other technologies such as Polleverywhere and Nearpod. Mentimeter is user friendly and easy for student interaction, mirroring survey, data display, and brainstorming as done in a traditional classroom with sticky notes. This option provides ways for students to continue to think critically and engage in collaborative learning experiences while being socially-distanced whether virtual or face-to-face. Though similar to surveys, Mentimeters are interactive and powerful ways to navigate displaying data visually, which can be a challenge in virtual learning environments. Students and teachers are able to formulate questions and responses by using multiple question types: multiple choice, word cloud, open ended, scales, ranking of students, and ask a question. Activities completed with Mentimeter allow students to think critically about assignments and collaborate as a class to discuss topics, two critical elements of the 4C's. This tool was aimed as a strategy for teaching during a pandemic, but because of the aforementioned reasonings, it may well continue as the world moves past COVID-19.

Implementation

As mentioned previously, Mentimeter is overtly user friendly and free, both characteristics are important to educators and students. Mentimeter does have an upgrade feature for a fee that can include unlimited questions, the ability to export results to Excel, add user-defined branding and moderate the question-and-answer actions. In the research process, the free version fit the classroom needs of engaging students collaboratively and with critical thinking. After signing up, when creating a new presentation, there are various style slides from which to choose including, question slides and content slides. The question slides were used in this action research project as these allocated the opportunity for critical thinking and collaboration. Depending on the type of question slide chosen, students are able to respond to questions by creating a word cloud, rating statements on a scale or ranking items, placing a pin on an image, open ended, or students can post questions for the instructor to answer. All of this can be done on students' computer/device or on their phone by scanning a QR code. When using Mentimeter, there are options of theme and how the content is displayed, with the ability to add multiple slides to one presentation. Also, a library of examples are available for teachers to search for ideas. Some examples of using Mentimeter in this research was having students post an open-ended question to classmates, creating word clouds for class topics, and ranking sections of the chapter. An example is shown in Figure 3 in which each student ranks educational philosophies through their personal lens. The scale provides a visual representation of the whole class educational philosophy and how it is distributed.

Figure 3. A depiction of the using scale with Mentimeter

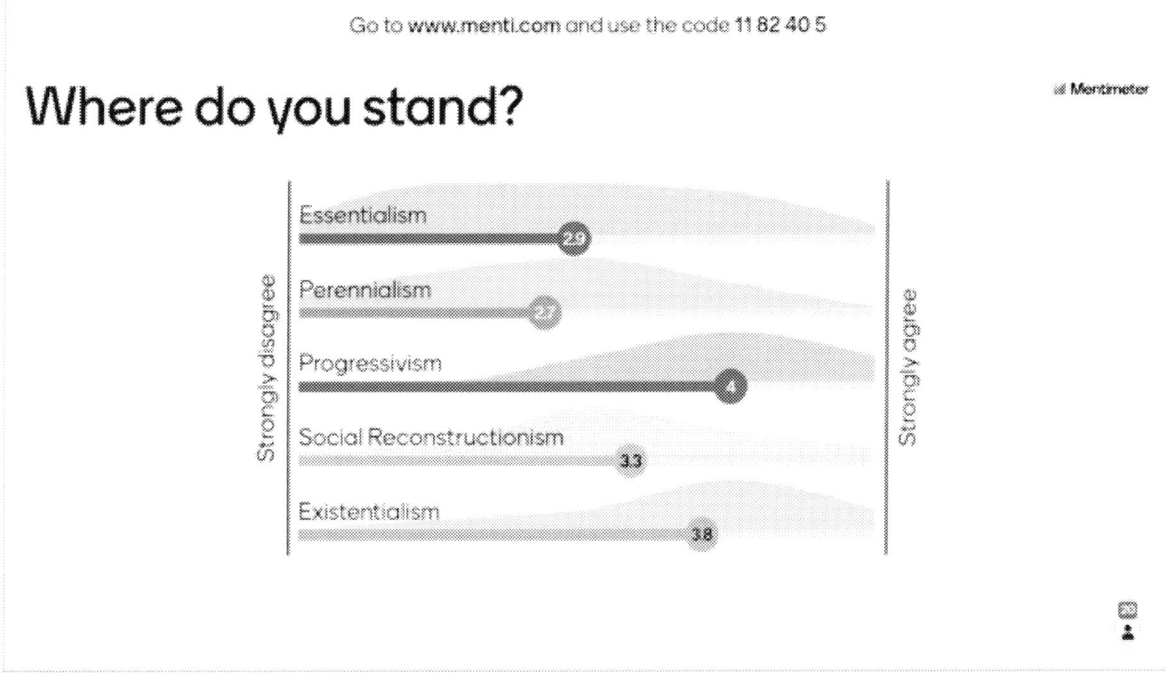

Successes and Learnings

For this action research project, Mentimeter was successful in helping students to think critically and collaborate. The site is user friendly and probably one of the top two easiest sites to set up and manipulate from the selections for this research. Students would collaborate in answering questions through Mentimeter and then their answers would often lead to more in-depth discussions of class topics. For example, students were asked about their thoughts on having a balance of connectedness/disconnectedness and to give their thoughts on whether people should create times and space for solitude and reflection or should people always be connected through their phones, the internet, and social media. They gave their responses in open-ended dialog boxes. This action sparked a great whole group discussion after students organized their ideas.

Posts on mentimeter are anonymous and can allow for students to give open and honest feedback if discussing sensitive topics. For example, in one class activity, students ranked cultural preferences discussed in the course textbook, one being individualism versus collectivism. Then based on the overall class rankings, the discussion focused on the highs and the lows of the rankings and why students leaned towards one ideal or another. Students also created an anonymous class word cloud for words they felt were missing on the list of dimensions of diversity. This activity allowed students to use their critical thinking skills while working collaboratively at home and in class.

Concerns and Challenges

With all of the tools used to enhance the 4C's of creativity, collaboration, communication, and critical thinking, there were great successes and also concerns and challenges. With Mentimeter there were few concerns and challenges, mainly due to the fact that this platform is exceptionally user friendly and teachers do not have to spend much time learning how to use it or implement it in the classroom. The ease of set-up is wonderful for teachers, though it does have limitations. One challenge is that with the free version, only three slides can be made in conjunction with one another. If you want to use more in a presentation, you will have to pay for the upgraded version or make two or more separate presentations. Students were always able to easily access the slides whether in the class or at home using computers, tablets and cell phones. Also, the site never seemed to run slow and once students posted, their responses popped up almost instantaneously. One more possible challenge of Mentimeter was that the posts are anonymous, and this situation could be a positive aspect of the platform or an issue depending on what the activity would be use for in class. But, as mentioned previously, this asset could be good when students want to give their thoughts but want to remain anonymous. Although it will tell you how many responses you have in total and you can wait for all of your students to respond before moving forward or on open-ended questions students can add initials. Yet another challenge is that once a mentimeter presentation is created in the free version, it is only 'active' for a maximum of 14 days. Though this situation can be difficult for teachers that plan their lessons far in advance, an easy way to overcome it is to duplicate the mentimeter, re-active it, and get a new code.

Flipgrid

Flipgrid is currently an extremely popular learning tool used in education from kindergarten through higher education. Flipgrid is a free tool that creates a virtual learning experience to create personalized spaces for dialogue and communication. The researchers chose this strategy for teaching because Flipgrid includes the goal of adding communication to a virtual classroom experience (whether synchronous or asynchronous). In a traditional online learning setting, the students complete discussions through text messaging boards. They write back and forth to one another on varying topics. Flipgrid allows teachers to set up discussion boards for interaction amongst students where students respond to a prompt or question of the teacher and then submit their responses via video and then they can reply to one another via video replies. The video component is a huge factor as it allows for a more personalized communication style. It also mirrors the more informal spoken communication that is typically present in a face-to-face classroom. This tool is also truly built for virtual learning because students do not all have to make videos at the same time as in Zoom or Skype for discussion. This feature worked extremely well for non-traditional students who may need to post videos nights or weekends due to other commitments. This ability serves the K-12 classroom as students learning from home can post and reply at times that work with their family schedule. Students can post their video when they have the most time and then reply to others and share ideas (all while being facilitated and monitored by the instructor). Flipgrid can be used for students to share book reports, communicate about a particular classroom topic, or present findings from an assignment or project.

Implementation

Similar to Mentimeter, Flipgrid is in the top two of the tools/strategies used during this action research project for ease of use. Outside of school, students communicate through social media videos like Snapchat and TikTok, and through the free Flipgrid application students can use video communication in a safe classroom-friendly way. This technology can be set up as private and teachers can supervise and monitor who has access to creating videos, and teachers can set videos to be approved before being visible to other classmates. Flipgrid is a technology that can be used from Kindergarten through grade 12 and is an asset to any face-to-face classroom or virtual classroom. Once an educator account is created, a group can be created for each class. Creating the group involves identification of a class name and personalized class code, personalizing the group cover, and setting the permissions for who can enter the class group by email, public, student usernames, or link to the google classroom. Once the discussion group is created, you can add a topic with a title and prompt, and even set up the maximum recording time, language for captions, your settings for responses, and teacher moderation settings. Then all students have to do is go to the Flipgrid page and click on submit a video response and upload thereby creating their own video. The powerful aspect of this technology tool is that it allows peers and the instructor to provide written or video replies to any created video thereby mirroring a traditional face to face classroom to great extent. Students made several comments about the use of Flipgrid and how much they enjoyed it for class discussions rather than typing class discussions.

Some examples of video discussion used were students presenting a book report, students giving their responses to parts of the class readings, and students presenting findings from a research project. Figure 4 shows an example in which the students had to analyze various education events to discuss five events that they felt had the most impact on education. Since the post and the replies are video, the students get a sense of peer interaction as in a classroom. Additionally, instructor participation helps to extend and enrich the discussion.

Successes and Learnings

There were numerous successes and learnings using Flipgrid. One of the best aspects about Flipgrid is that it has built in American with Disabilities Act (ADA) compliance that will automatically provide closed captioning. Additionally, students can click on a button at the bottom of the video and access a transcript of the video in over 30 languages. The transcript can be read to one as well. One can also move the cursor over words that are unknown or difficult to understand and the tool gives a picture along with the word in the translated language and English. For educators, feedback can be given in several ways: recording a public or a private feedback, texting a public or a private feedback, adding a grading rubric to each video and assigning a grade via the rubric, or adding a sticker to the top of the video like "awesome." One facet learned about Flipgrid was when a class is done with a topic, the topic post can be moved down, thus having the new topic card be at the front of the page. Another learning that is a wonderful aspect for teachers is that one can complete a number of tasks: export data onto an excel spreadsheet about who has posted and when, add a copilot teacher, add it as an app to a phone or device, and can discover Flipgrids other teachers have made. All of these options are available for free! Another worth mentioning aspect of Flipgrid is that one is able to connect with classrooms around the globe and have video pen pals for the students. Thus, this technology has the capability for connecting with all of the 4 C's: communication, collaboration, critical thinking, and creativity.

Figure 4. An example of a Flipgrid discussion board post

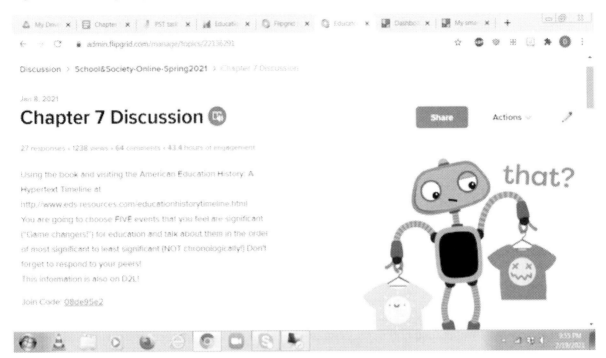

Concerns and Challenges

Few concerns or challenges are evident with this application. Students, as well as educators, find Flipgrid to be user friendly, however recording a video makes a person become more self-conscious than just speaking. This does sometimes lead one to record a video several times to get it to be perfect for viewing by others and the instructor. A way to overcome this challenge is for teachers to not only provide opportunity for practice of recording a video but also to emphasize the goal of flipgrid as developing a discussion rather than a 'perfect' response. Flipgrid provides videos and instructions to show users the various features and tools and how-to information to successfully use the online application site. Flipgrid can be used in Kindergarten through grade 12 for any discipline, and it not only connects to the 4 C's area of communication, but it keeps students engaged and it personalizes education and learning. For younger learners, teachers will have to take time to prepare and coach students on how to use the platform, and for all classroom teachers, they can use the moderation tools to monitor and supervise student activity. Through experiences seen in Kindergarten and first grade classrooms to high school Spanish and at the university level, Flipgrid is a tool that can be used in class, online, or given as homework where schools have technology available to students at home. Yet another challenge the researchers found was that the automated closed captioning was not always correct, but teachers or the students are able to make corrections if necessary.

Bitmoji Classroom

Outside of school students are engaged in aspects of a virtual world that is often beyond compare to what happens in school. When students are attending class in a virtual way, teachers have to strive to find new ways to engage students in creative endeavors that foster critical thinking. Therefore, creating a space where students can feel a part of and engaged in the classroom experience is vital to twenty-first century learning. The researchers found that implementing a Bitmoji classroom employs two of the 4C's - creativity and collaboration. A Bitmoji classroom provides a virtual classroom experience where educators add their Bitmoji to a virtual classroom or slide in order to animate the learning experiences to engage students of any age. A Bitmoji classroom is a virtual classroom created by the teachers using a Bitmoji that resembles themselves engaging students in various ways. In the process, the students see themselves as learners -virtually. The result is that they feel more a part of the classroom. Not only will this tool be useful now with many at home due to COVID 19, virtual learning is only growing and educators must find new pedagogical practices that correlate and connect to the best practices for teaching in this learning environment.

Implementation

There are several ways to implement a Bitmoji classroom into the curriculum for synchronous and asynchronous virtual teaching. For example, one Bitmoji classroom was created for a mathematics course containing a virtual wall of mathematics manipulatives for students to explore and even create lesson plans for the explorations. In another example, students created their own Bitmoji classroom and were required to make a content area center to accompany their lesson plan. Both of these examples engaged students in creativity and critical thinking.

One use for the Bitmoji classroom that aligns with the creativity facet of the 4C's is to have students create their own Bitmoji classrooms for various assignments. This activity would be for upper level middle school students through the university level. Students could create their own Bitmoji classroom for various academic purposes, like giving a presentation on a topic they are learning in class or working with a partner or a group as a Jigsaw cooperative learning assignment and making a Bitmoji classroom Webquest for other students to complete. At the university level, through the action research conducted, preservice teachers created and designed centers for PreK students using Bitmoji classroom. Though this activity was very successful, the main use the researchers found for this platform was teacher-created Bitmoji classrooms.

When creating a Bitmoji classroom, the researchers used Google slides (another free resource) to create Bitmoji classrooms. Teacher-made Bitmoji classroom templates are available for free and/or for purchase. The templates make the process easier for creating the classroom. Several free online videos show the process of creating a classroom step-by-step. Teachers can choose a background that resembles a classroom and set it up using clip art and images from online.

With the completed classroom design, teachers add links to items in the classroom to make an interactive experience for the students. These links can connect to the other strategies/sites as mentioned previously. Figure 5 shows a screenshot of a Bitmoji classroom of one of the researchers. This classroom activity engages students in choosing a podcast to listen to the hyperlinked ipods on the shelf. Then students might use Flipgrid to record their responses to the podcast and reply to one another. Also, from this page students were asked to go to Padlet and listen to a story and post a response in Padlet. Finally, students were able to complete an activity where they listened to three songs and then used Mentimeter to rank the songs and discuss their rankings in Flipgrid. In this example, the researcher used items that were personal to her and the Bitmoji classroom helped students to learn more about the instructor. The picture of kids or images of favorite flowers supported the building of a relationship and collaborative learning.

Figure 5. Screenshot of Bitmoji classroom

Successes and Learnings

The researchers personally found that using the Bitmoji classroom helped to engage students in a way that a typical virtual classroom screen cannot accomplish. Here the teacher was visible, and students engaged with the content in the classroom through the links created by hyperlinking items like books and computers and manipulatives. For example, students were able to click on links on the Bitmoji computer to get into groups and receive directions to work on creating a Google slide to add to the presentation over a topic from the chapter. The hyperlink in Figure 5 sent students to a Jamboard where they collaboratively created a poster. Another example would be hyperlinking a book to e-book or a pdf resource.

Concerns and Challenges

The Bitmoji classroom has many positive attributes in terms of student engagement and fostering creativity and critical thinking, but there were some major concerns. The researchers' main concern for using Bitmoji classroom was that it was the most time consuming of all of the tools presented. Teachers can get lost for hours creating these experiences for students and though the result can be very rewarding, time is one thing most teachers lack.

Another challenge of the Bitmoji classroom is learning how to set up the classroom itself and the activities embedded within it, especially without familiarity with Google Slides, embedding links or formatting pictures/images in slides. An additional concern is about plagiarism and copyright issues of images. Teachers must be cautious of what/whose images are placed in the slide and must be sure to give proper credit. Lastly, there is a concern with issues of ADA compliance and the Bitmoji classroom and ensuring that all students would have equal opportunities to learn using this tool. For example, for students with visual impairments, this platform's words can be very small especially for information about the links or for reading instructions. To address this issue, teachers could turn on the screen reader, magnifier, and braille supports for students using the accessibility tool.

FUTURE DIRECTIONS AND CONSIDERATIONS

The virtual experiences of Jamboard, Padlet, Mentimeter, Flipgrid, and Bitmoji classroom were successful as discussed through student work. Students were able to learn course material in an engaging and relevant way using the 4C's communication, collaboration, critical thinking, and creativity in the virtual classroom. There were also challenges, like having to learn how to use and implement these resources in an effective and meaningful way.

Endless possibilities exist for future examination of transforming teachers' online pedagogical reasoning for K-12 students in virtual learning environments. And, although the pandemic kicked online learning into high gear, once the virus is eradicated or subdued, the researchers do not see the rise in online learning decreasing. With schools considering the establishment of virtual classrooms, it is pivotal that there is a continuation of research for online pedagogy that implements best practices like the 4C's communication, collaboration, critical thinking, and creativity. Moreover, the tools and learnings from this pandemic should not be forgotten. They can be ideas that move education forward and provide an impetus for new teaching methodologies.

Therefore, it is pertinent that researchers press on to new explorations of online pedagogy and virtual learning experiences. Future research with the 4C's and virtual teaching is crucial to the continuation of how to best meet the needs of twenty-first century learners, and keep learning engaging, rigorous, and meaningful. Specifically, for this action research, more inquiry could be conducted through student and teacher interviews of the experiences or taking an in-depth look at culturally relevant pedagogy thorough critical discourse analysis of text and talk being presented in virtual classrooms.

CONCLUSION

With the pandemic, came a necessitation of agile self-learning for educators everywhere. The researchers found ways to adjust their teaching practices, not just to mirror face to face learning in a virtual environment. It is indispensable that teachers return to the foundations of good pedagogy and look to explore how to teach students face-to-face with social distancing and virtually simultaneously without losing the essence of those learning experiences. For this reason, the researchers chose the self-examining practice of action research to scrutinize the use of five technology tools for instruction and how true they could remain to the utilization of the 4Cs of teaching within the dual model of instruction. Jamboard, Padlet, Mentimeter, Flipgrid and Bitmoji classroom were the tools the researchers chose to focus on while navigating through teaching during a pandemic. The researchers found that the use of the technologies served to enhance the engagement of both the face to face and virtual students while serving as tools to utilize the 4Cs in a challenging and new learning environment. All teachers and educators should consider these technologies for the future- to take learning from the pandemic and develop these ideas for meaningful learning.

REFERENCES

Budhai, S. S., & Taddei, L. M. (2015). *Teaching the 4Cs with Technology: How do I use 21st century tools to teach 21st century skills?* ASCD.

Efron, S., & David, R. (2020). *Action Research in Education: A practical guide.* The Guilford Press.

Fisher, A., & Scriven, M. (1997). *Critical Thinking: Its definition and assessment.* Edgepress.

Glassman, M., Erdem, G., & Bartholomew, M. (2013). Action Research and Its History as an Adult Education Movement for Social Change. *Adult Education Quarterly, 63*(3), 272–288. doi:10.1177/0741713612471418

González-González, I., & Jiménez-Zarco, A. I. (2015). Using learning methodologies and resources in the development of critical thinking competency: An exploratory study in a virtual learning environment. *Computers in Human Behavior, 51*, 1359–1366. doi:10.1016/j.chb.2014.11.002

González-Tejero, J. M. S., Parra, R. M. P., & Llamas, M. G. R. (2007). Perspectiva histórica del aprendizaje cooperativo: Un largo y tortuoso camino a través de cuatro siglos. *Revista Española de Pedagogía, 236*, 125–138.

Goodwin, M., & Sommervold, C. L. (2012). *Creativity, critical thinking, and communication: Strategies to increase students' skills.* R&L Education.

Henriksen, D., Mishra, P., & Mehta, R. (2015). Novel, Effective, Whole: Toward a NEW framework for evaluations of creative products. *Journal of Technology and Teacher Education, 23*(3), 455–478. https://www.learntechlib.org/p/151574/

Hinchman, T., & Gupta, D. (2020, April). STEAMED UP: A Mixed Methods Creativity Evaluation. *Proceedings from Association for the Advancement of Computing in Education Conference*, 1121-1127.

Jaramillo, J. A. (1996). Vygotsky's sociocultural theory and contributions to the development of constructivist curricula. *Education, 117*(1), 133–141.

Lai, E. R. (2011). *Collaboration: A literature review.* Pearson Publisher.

Mertler, C. (2006). Action Research: Teachers as researchers in the classroom. *Sage (Atlanta, Ga.).*

Mertler, C. (2020). Action Research: Improving schools and empowering educators. *Sage (Atlanta, Ga.).*

Mills, G. E. (2000). *Action Research: A guide for the teacher researcher.* Prentice-Hall.

Ortiz-Rodríguez, M., Telg, R. W., Irani, T., Roberts, T. G., & Rhoades, E. (2005). College students' perceptions of quality in distance education: The importance of Communication. *Quarterly Review of Distance Education, 6*(2), 97–105.

Russo, L. H. (2013). Play and Creativity at the Center of Curriculum and Assessment: A New York City school's journey to re-think curricular pedagogy. *Online Submission, 61*(1), 131–146. doi:10.13042/brp.2013.65109

Saadé, R. G., Morin, D., & Thomas, J. D. (2012). Critical thinking in E-learning environments. *Computers in Human Behavior, 28*(5), 1608–1617. doi:10.1016/j.chb.2012.03.025

Saavedra, A. R., & Opfer, V. D. (2012). Learning 21st-century skills requires 21st-century teaching. *Phi Delta Kappan, 94*(2), 8–13. doi:10.1177/003172171209400203

Sagor, R. (2000). *Guiding School Improvement with Action Research*. ASCD.

Spaulding, D. T., & Falco, J. (2013). *Action Research for School Leaders*. Pearson.

Stringer, E. T., & Aragón, A. O. (2020). *Action Research*. Sage Publications.

Thoughtful Learning. (2016). *3 Simple steps to the 4 c's*. Retrieved from https://k12.thoughtfullearning.com/blogpost/3-simple-steps-4-cs

Van der Zanden, P., Denessen, E., Cillessen, A., & Meijer, P. (2020). Fostering critical thinking skills in secondary education to prepare students for university: Teacher perceptions and practices. *Research in Post-Compulsory Education, 25*(4), 394–419. doi:10.1080/13596748.2020.1846313

Chapter 11
Crystallizing Moments:
Teacher–Student Interaction and Engagement in Online Primary Grades Education

Charlotte Kristyn Gallagher-Immenschuh
Northcentral University, USA

Maggie Broderick
https://orcid.org/0000-0003-1032-6795
Northcentral University, USA

ABSTRACT

The COVID-19 pandemic has forced K-12 teachers to think differently about their teaching methods. Primary grade teachers must especially consider how to make online learning engaging, motivating, and as hands-on and developmentally appropriate as possible for young learners. This chapter provides insight into purposely created and child-centered crystallizing moments, in which research-based strategies can enhance teacher-student interaction and engagement. Examples from real-world teaching practice are included.

INTRODUCTION

As the central theme of this book stresses, the COVID-19 pandemic has forced K-12 teachers to think differently about their teaching methods. Primary grades teachers, students, and parents have faced an especially rough transition (Rasmitadila et al., 2020) because of a mismatch between typical online education methods and the need for developmentally appropriate and hands-on learning for young learners. Simultaneously, twenty-first century learning and skills, such as communication, collaboration, creativity, and critical thinking, are more critical now than ever before (Guo & Woulfin, 2016). Curriculum, instruction, and assessment (Beebe et al., 2010) are crucial concerns when transitioning to online learning models. Teachers who have suddenly switched to online modalities may lack knowledge regarding

DOI: 10.4018/978-1-7998-7222-1.ch011

best practices for online teaching, especially student engagement. Teachers may also lack the confidence in their ability to effectively communicate, demonstrate, and act creatively with their students through an online platform. A new and mindful approach to helping these teachers move forward is necessary. Educators encounter challenges with redesigning curriculum to be compatible and effective online. One key to enhancing teacher-student interaction and engagement in online primary grades classrooms is the concept of *Crystallizing Moments* (Gardner, 1991; Murphy, 2016), which is the focus of this chapter.

Murphy (2016) emphasizes that Gardner's (1991) concepts of crystallizing moments can happen at any time, upon any moment in a day, without the ability to plan the moment(s). Crystallizing moments are any experience, positive or negative, leaving a lasting impact on the learner, and are deeper than a mere epiphany. The feeling left from the moment of crystallization cannot be undone, erased, or eradicated. Crystallizing moments forge the learner and impact their approach to both learning and learning environments. Remaining cognizant of this concept is vital to remain fully present when with students. Educators always hope students will have an enlightening moment and the memory be positive and exciting. However, no matter how hard teachers try, crystallization may also occur when teachers perform at their worst. Every teacher has feelings of worry and not getting across to students. It is normal and natural to feel this way and is possibly why teachers constantly self-evaluate and strive to continue improving their lessons, delivery, and presentation to their classroom. Teachers are always students themselves, and with this in mind, they too experience crystallizing moments that are unexpected and beneficial to their growth experienced each year.

In March 2020, the entire country faced an exponential shift in classroom delivery. Veteran teachers and novice teachers alike found themselves learning how to create a seamless interaction across a screen. Was there a necessity to only use high-tech systems and online software, or could those moments of personal interaction, classroom sharing with peer collaboration in real-time, and the never-ending curiosity of crystallizing moments? When, where, and how these things occurred would be left to discover.

Whether learning occurs in person, remote, online, or hybrid, experts agree that a positive learning environment is crucial (Fisher et al., 2021). Differentiated Instruction (Tomlinson, 2014) is also key to creating and maintaining engaging learning environments. Differentiated Instruction allows for more student choice by nature and design and is thus more child-led and child-centered than more traditional types of classroom-based instruction. The individualization possibilities within the philosophy of Differentiated Instruction connect with the process involved in creating the *Crystallizing Moments*. These concepts, especially in the primary grades, are discussed later in this chapter. Differentiated Instruction in the primary grades is a powerful tool for reaching and engaging young learners who undergo rapid development. For example, a primary classroom can have students at various levels, such as reading levels and readiness. In the online environment, differentiation is attainable through work modifications without restricting access to the whole lesson or peer interaction (Brodersen et al., 2017). It is also imperative to consider Developmentally Appropriate Practice in Online Education for young learners (Parette et al., 2010). As many parents and teachers realize today (and have especially come to realize during the COVID-19 pandemic), the use of technology for primary grades children is not inherently against the fundamentals of Developmentally Appropriate Practice. It can help to develop necessary twenty-first century learning and skills. However, instructional use of technology should be accomplished mindfully, with the whole and individual child in mind.

The COVID-19 pandemic significantly increased primary grades students studying online and teaching and learning modalities, such as video conferencing (especially using Zoom). Most U.S. children attended school at least partially online for some duration during the pandemic. Most K-12 schools scrambled to provide emergency remote learning in place of traditional on-ground instruction beginning in March of 2020. The emergency transition to online and distance learning during COVID-19 was not the same as ongoing and established programs, chosen as options for parents, students, and teachers. Still, it is more akin to *crisis teaching* or *emergency teaching* (Mutton, 2020). Policymakers and other stakeholders fought to keep schools closed in the fall of 2020 due to growing safety concerns (Will, 2020). Many educators felt that they were not adequately prepared for online and hybrid models, citing a lack of planning and resources. Fisher and Frey (2020) stressed that teachers were especially concerned about their roles during this unique and ever-evolving period. COVID-19 has brought many simmering issues to light and made everything about online and remote education far more mainstream in the discussions for parents, teachers, and others in society. Student participation is not an option; it is a requirement for learning. Therefore, the learning process must shift from teacher-centered to student-centered with maximum engagement opportunities. This chapter describes research supporting the notion of *Crystallizing Moments* and examples from real-world teaching practice. Background information and literature relating to the critical concerns about *Crystallizing Moments* in online primary grades education is presented, followed by a descriptive case study of a first-grade student involved in one-to-one online learning experiences with a teacher-researcher. Primary grades teachers who are increasingly teaching online can consider scaling these *Crystallizing Moments* to their specific online teaching and learning situations.

BACKGROUND

Teachers rely heavily upon in-person observations of students within their brick-and-mortar classrooms for self-reflection and adjustments to lesson plans, student interventions, and designing appropriate activities and lessons. Replicating this type of ongoing ability to observe, self-reflect, and monitor and adjust (Hunter, 1994) can be problematic in the online learning environment. Online learning in the primary grades is not as popular as in other grades/levels. In the 2017-2018 school year, only "3 percent of primary schools offered any courses entirely online" (NCES Fast Facts Tool, n.d., p. 1.) in the U.S. Globally, the statistics are similar (Barbour et al., 2011). For example, in South Korea, "Online education available for primary school students are few, and online supplement and support systems available for the formal school curriculum are even fewer" (Lee et al., 2013, p. 69).

Globally, few schools utilize online modalities for the primary grades, either part-time or full-time for students. The existing evidence clearly shows (Lee et al., 2013) that young students prefer a more human touch. Video conferencing between teacher and student is encouraged. The following example details student feedback on a specific Cyber Home Learning System (CHLS) and a CHLS with a video conferencing element (CHLS-VC):

First, it was found that primary level students preferred CHLS-VC over CHLS and found it recommendable. The teacher's friendliness was considered highly positive with 99.0%. Making synchronous interaction available seems to have increased the humanness in the online environment, which seemed to have caused the students to appreciate the video conferencing feature of the CHLS-VC. (Lee et al., 2013, p. 75)

An additional concern is that most current online learning practices are not developmentally appropriate or geared toward primary grades learners. According to Bowdon (2020):

Crystallizing Moments

When schools suddenly closed down last March, many teachers lacked experience using technology to instruct students and connect with them. In early childhood and early elementary school classes, this challenge was compounded by the fact that many teachers consider e-learning to be developmentally inappropriate for younger students. Teachers' years of experience told them that rather than sitting and learning passively by staring at computers or tablets, young learners need to move their bodies, practice their fine motor skills, interact with peers, use manipulatives, and play. (p. 1)

Now, teachers must recreate their teaching practices to address new gaps developing from the lack of technology, access, understanding of how to use the technology (teacher, student, and parent), and effectively communicating these gaps. Keeping in mind that children drive creative and interactive learning processes, designing and developing a curriculum that represents effective learning is crucial at this juncture and no longer resembles the practices that teachers, students, and parents have become accustomed. *Crystallizing Moments* (Gardner, 1991; Murphy, 2016) can serve to escape a sterile application of lessons, such as using classroom worksheets and not altering them to be more interactive for online learners. Rather than using the worksheet, the teacher may find it more engaging and beneficial to keep young learners using their hands, creativity, and voice while they work and discover. For instance, Figure 1 displays a kindergarten teacher's approach to using technology to meet with the class. The teacher is still using handmade objects and creativity to engage the young learners in the group discussion. The students then have written activities they can display by holding them up for the rest of the class to see. Later, parents upload the documents to SeeSaw (SeeSaw, 2021). Additionally, the 10-year veteran teacher comments, "This has been my view for an entire year now. I teach to a computer and pray the littles on the other side are getting it" (Hand in Hand in Kinderland, 2021).

COVID-19 spurred a monumental shift in the classroom, parent involvement, and the newly defined roles students, teachers, and parents had to adopt. In an instant, learning became inclusive of the entire family, remote, foreign, and disruptive for a traditional classroom's known and learned behaviors. The concept of learning no longer meant being physically present through the learning process with the guidance of a teacher and peers' support for comprehension and deeper connections (Vygotsky, 1978). The question becomes, can a meaningful curriculum be adapted from a learning kit or pre-prescribed curriculum while still piquing the interest and curiosity of the learner? Kohn (2006) contends that denying students a voice does not make problems or issues disappear. Instead, a denial drives the problems to manifest themselves in less productive and often destructive manners.

Kohn (2006) posits a profound need for a student-focused curriculum, where discipline is explored, learned, applied, and thoroughly developed through the curriculum, not as a contingency of the curriculum (Adler, 1955). Geographer Soja (1996) explores thirdspace theory concepts as the space between physical worlds, such as a valley between two mountains or the border between Mexico or Canada and the United States. Within this space exists extreme diversity that negotiating without neglecting the cultures and individuals found within each area. Similarly, students, parents, and educators find themselves dealing with similar territory. As students, families, and teachers migrated into online instruction and learning, there was a more profound sense of thirdspace to consider. On one side of the screen, the teachers are presenting. On the other side, the students are receiving information. Space in-between delivery and reception is of intense interest to the authors. Bridging the gap between school and home is crucial. Learning across a screen meant navigating a new level of thirdspace (Soja, 1996). The question and concern became an element of time and space. As a 20-year veteran teacher recently expressed,

I can't stand programs where I can't directly monitor my kids. So, things like Quizziz, Kahoot, etc., move fast, and I want to see specific data. They [school] have us using Smart Learning Suite, but for some kids, it moves too slow and others too fast. I'm all about connections, but because we aren't together physically, I already lost the power to fully connect. So now, it's called survival. (personal communication with the author, December 9, 2020).

Figure 1. Kindergarten online teaching from the teacher's perspective

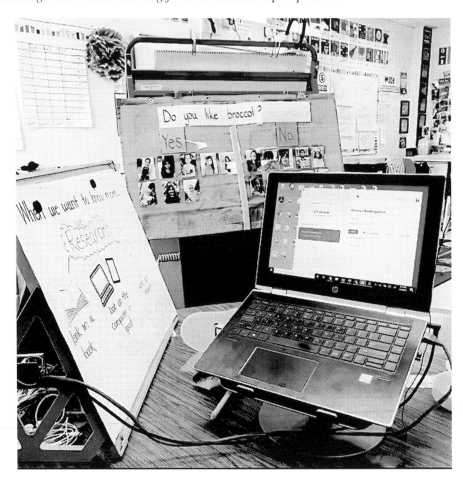

Lu and Hao (2014) examine young children's internet use at home and school. They stress the importance of understanding children's internet use in formal versus informal settings while looking toward a future with more blurred lines and less obvious distinctions about children's internet usage.

The human connection is paramount, whether learning occurs in person or online. Many schools and teachers utilize pre-recorded videos, apps, and similar types of technology for online learning, and these tools can certainly be helpful. However, that human connection is especially crucial for young learners in primary grades classrooms. Creating and finding opportunities for more organic teacher-student engagement via *Crystallizing Moments* is vital. Utilizing more synchronous videoconferencing with face-to-face interaction and hands-on activities can enhance engagement and make the most of online teaching and learning experiences.

Emphasis on Creativity and the 4Cs

It is crucial to make online learning as engaging, motivating, hands-on, and developmentally appropriate as possible. In reaction to non-stop accountability-based and assessment-driven policies over the past two decades, creativity and all 4Cs are regaining prominence. Guo and Woulfin (2016) explain the global trend, especially how "recent years have witnessed a renaissance of global creativity in education...U.S. policymakers and educators have also begun to notice the importance of creativity in maintaining and improving global competitiveness." (p. 154). The Partnership for 21st Century Learning (2019) denotes the *4Cs* of 21st Century Learning, including communication, collaboration, critical thinking, and creativity. Schleicher (2018) connects research, policy, and practice with specific strategies for building twenty-first century schools, while Robinson (2011) stresses that creativity is most missing from today's public schools. Reflecting further on creativity as a crucial aspect of the 4Cs, Guo and Woulfin (2016, p. 157) make a clear distinction between what they term "creative and novel activities." Novel activities may help to attract and engage students but may also be merely superficial and not necessarily involve higher-order thinking skills, such as creativity and problem-solving.

The authors stress teachers' independent roles in being flexible and adaptive toward students' needs, especially in terms of creative expression and problem-solving; "it is vital to raise the capacity of administrators and teachers so their students can receive creative instruction that matches P21" (Guo & Woulfin, 2016, pp. 159). The 4Cs are highly relevant to making online learning more engaging, motivating, and hands-on. A common choice is to utilize more apps and other online learning tools that do not directly involve teacher-student interaction. As will be shown later in this chapter via the case study of an online primary grades learner, the 4Cs are often better integrated via videoconferencing using hands-on items in the learner's hands and shared and explored with the teacher during live sessions.

THE REGGIO EMILIA LENS

Teachers of primary grades students may be familiar with the work of Reggio Emilia. The Reggio Emilia Lens connects directly to focus on creativity and creative thinking described above. It reminds educators that a child's ability to learn, explore, create, and deliver information is lifelong. In contrast, some teaching and learning in typical K-12 schools have become sterile, a laminated lady (Murphy, 2016) of sorts, squashing a student's instinct to look beyond the boundaries of a scripted curriculum. Now more than ever, educators, parents, and students are confronted with learning to find their voice and express their voice in a classroom that may not be face-to-face and further hinder the understood practice of what it means to teach it means to learn. However, if educators focus on the learner's lens and allow them more space to create and manifest ideas (even through interactive, virtual practices), elementary through middle school children can find their way back to being learners and doers of education. To be a doer of education stems from the concepts of being doers of math, which in short means how children understand math and how they perceive themselves as math students (NCTM, 2008; Rock & Shaw, 2000; Steele, 1999).

Jensen (2016) posits mastery of information as "a process and destination…about developing lifelong skills…that makes complex, challenging learning worthwhile" (p.136). Classrooms should be an opportunity for teachers to create a safe space for students to grow and experience a life where all voices are valued and shared (Çubukçu, 2012; Jensen, 2016; Lickona, 1991 Rosenblum & Travis, 2016; Williamson, 2016). Teachers possess an opportunity to create a climate where students develop rapport, are encouraged to take academic risks, explore boundaries, and learn through shared life experiences (Jensen, 2016). Effectively using online platforms' principles and tools, mixed with curated learning modules, encouraged and fostered students' voices, real-time feedback, and genuine engagement can shift a student's experience with online learning.

Meacham and Atwood-Blaine (2018) echo these calls for genuine engagement with their description of the Reggio Emilia-inspired Lego Robotics club's impact. Authentic learning experiences are essential for engaging younger learners, and the school environment plays a prominent role. Similarly, Fernández Santín and Feliu Torruella (2017) connect the Reggio Emilia lens and approach to critical thinking, emphasizing project-based, open-ended, hands-on, creative projects. Children should not merely be recreating works of art but going deeper into creativity and critical thinking. The authors elaborate that the Reggio Emilia approach:

is focused on listening and respecting the children for the potential of witnessing their actions, towards reformulating everyday practices, ideas and projects. The schools associated with the Reggio Emilia philosophy, propose a participatory and democratic educational system, that emphasises research and experimentation. (Fernández Santín & Feliu Torruella, 2017, p. 52)

Open-end art creation is a crucial component of this approach and features directly into the process explained and illustrated later in this chapter. Art can help children think critically about content in other content areas, understand it, and internalize it more deeply. Hands-on, play-based activities can indeed occur in online learning environments with some creative thinking and tools. For instance, sharing via webcam, sharing of media via online tools such as Padlet, the use of hands-on materials that the child utilizes at home (such as KiwiCo Kits, which will be explored later in this chapter), and complete and creative integration between the home and school/learning environments.

Where Do Teachers Begin?

Spring 2020 jettisoned the education system into a virtual world. In this world, teachers, students, and parents found themselves lost in translation. How would the work be productive across a screen? How could a child actively learn and participate in lessons when the teacher, referred to by Vygotsky (1978) as the More Knowledgeable Other (MKO), did not feel in control of the learning situation. Veteran teachers regularly find that prior year's lessons are easily accessible when teaching, frequently going to the arsenal and sticking to the script. There was no longer a script to draw from, no longer an audience that was sterile, predictable, or controllable in one space.

What if the possibility of moving past the tried-and-true lesson plans and twisting the lessons into a newer, technologically applicable model was possible? In a single-student case study, concepts of reimagining the learning experience via Zoom came to fruition. The importance of trying this concept with a first grader in a 100 percent online learning environment will offer teachers and schools to take a step back from survival mode and creatively transition from scripted lessons into a newer chapter of learning. During April through November 2020, a first-grade student and a teacher worked through a new world of education together, as illustrated later in this chapter.

Looking at students from the teacher's perspective and the students through a zone of proximal development (Vygotsky, 1978) has pivoted. Suppose considering geographer Soja's (1996) descriptions of thirdspace as a deep-rooted need to analyze what it means to be in a transitional space. People change depending on their environment. For instance, when children are at a birthday party, they respond to the stimulus and excitement a party brings. Most children have exciting and positive experiences at parties, making transitioning from one person's party to the next a familiar and joyous moment. Equally, when children are about to take a test at school, they would possibly be less enthusiastic than they were at the party—each step of the way requires a transition or pivot. The pivot defines how individuals react to that current space and how they adapt to the new space. If students had a negative experience taking tests in other classes, they might enter with a sense of upset, apprehension, and negativity. On the other hand, if they have had positive experiences, they will more than likely have a smoother transition from one space to the next. Each opportunity can manifest a *Crystallizing Moment* (Gardner, 1991).

The same holds for the current pulse of the education system. The pivot between spaces is generating experiences. The experiences will determine whether the moments are positive or negative. Teachers never know when a crystallizing moment (Gardner, 1991; Murphy, 2016) will impact the students, and in this case, teachers and parents too. They must be aware of how to handle the moments and make them as productive as possible. Capitalizing on moments requires flexibility in mindset and strength to draw from previous experiences. Educators have curricula they follow as a guideline. The guideline, being the key term, serves as a guide, not a tombstone. A successful plan is adjusted as it progresses. Teachers must view their classrooms, especially online classrooms, as areas of enormous change and welcome adjustments. Becoming familiar with the tools available in online platforms, such as Zoom, can make the transition more attainable.

Listening to and Observing Students

Like other educators, the teacher-researchers who are the authors of this chapter found themselves in a situation where they had to take a brick-and-mortar, in-person curriculum and find a way to make the learning process successful when the student was in an alternate space. The teacher-researcher is a former high school teacher with more than 20 years of teaching experience in the public and private sectors. Additionally, the teacher-researcher is an educational coach for students, commonly known as a hakwon in Korea, meaning a "private tutoring system...that provides students with supplementary, after-school education" (Kim, 2016, p. 3). Limitations of the curriculum became profound as there were no online options or resources. Software and online versions of lessons were not in place for this situation. With that in mind, the researcher became encouraged to pivot and look beyond the papers of the lessons. During this analysis, the proverbial light was lit, and the researcher pushed to interact with the students as if they were in the same room, using chalk talk (Ritchhart et al., 2011). Chalk talk is "building understanding in a collaborative way through putting forward ideas, questioning one another, and developing the ideas further" (Ritchhart et al., 2011, p. 78). The researcher listened to what the student needed, wanted, and what enticed a reaction. The researcher capitalized on the active moments online, desiring to make any form of crystallization a positive experience. Acting upon instinct and over 20 years of teaching experience, the researcher pivoted and pivoted and pivoted. During each online meeting, the researcher took notes and reviewed them at the end of the day, searching for repetitive themes from the students and themselves. The researcher often pondered listening to the students and their needs while promoting legitimate peripheral participation (LPP) (Lave & Wenger, 2015). By definition, LPP identifies "learners inevitably participate in communities of practitioners and that the mastery of knowledge and skill requires newcomers to move toward full participation in the sociocultural practices of a community" (Lave & Wenger, 2015, p. 29). Lave and Wenger (2015) do not specifically address 'community' as a classroom and, therefore, the theory extends into a virtual setting. Was the researcher providing the tools, examples, and information that would make the students learning valuable? Each observation led to another trial. Each session aided in the adjustments implemented to make the time with each student more successful.

All curricula have gaps. Through the experience of watching students struggle to make connections, have a relationship with the material, or even lack the confidence to initiate a conversation of what they do not understand, that prompts a change in implementation or supplementation to the current materials. Krashen (2001) discussed an individual's inclination to employ incubation, meaning short breaks and time to think are necessary for transferring information. For instance, in writing, allowing the brain a healthy break to process acquired and active knowledge allows for this additional time. An apparent void exists in research concerning vocabulary acquisition for second language application across curricula. Students often account for the lack of knowledge of applying the words from one subject area to another.

Overemphasis on a standardized score to assess students' language acquisition and connection abilities has become problematic and even harmful to learning outcomes (Herrera & Murry, 2016; Zawacki & Rogers, 2012). Herrera and Murry (2016) discuss destructive issues when teachers *teach a test* [author's emphasis]. The heavy focus on strategies to pass a state or other standardized exam, rather than learning how to make deeper connections with the material, compromises the recognition of content outside of the "test setting" (p. 50). This issue is not limited to native speakers of English. The classrooms' demographic diversity calls for educators to dig deeper and become more willing to pivot from traditional and standard teaching pedagogy.

Furthermore, the cycle diminishes learning opportunities for diverse learners, such as culturally and linguistically diverse (CLD) students. All student populations may experience a "misunderstanding of the role of native language" in a student's academic development (p. 51) when the focus of learning reduces to "objective" education (McLeod, 2012). Reductionist curricula focus too heavily on the value of regenerating information without application, meaning students, CLD and non-CLD alike, are deprived of applying the knowledge into meaningful relationships for future use.

On the other hand, constructivist learning promotes hands-on, progressive education, focusing on individual students' growth in time utilizing previous knowledge and skills to current (grade-level), in-depth, comprehensive values (Herrera & Murry, 2016; Lickona, 1991; Vygotsky, 1978). Learning more about students through an interview process, often referred to as a student bio, before embarking on teaching them is critical to how a teacher develops lessons and supports active learning, shifting from reductionist approaches (Herrera & Murry, 2016). Student bios are appropriate for all learning populations and were instrumental in Oliver's (pseudonym) case study progression and success. Additionally, intentional lesson planning with a constructivist lens and a student bio encapsulates the whole-student learner. For example, the sociocultural process, language development, academic development, and cognitive development of each student allow for a pivot in attitude and intention in teaching online. Previous cultural and educational experiences influence each student's learning process. As the students gain confidence in conversation, language and content development begin to take on a new position in their daily interactions and community involvement. Simultaneously, teachers can effectively and intentionally manipulate the focus of academic development (Herrera & Murry, 2016) through deeper connections across the curriculum (McLeod, 2012), through conversation, and with motivation.

Theory into Praxis

Teachers do the best they can with the knowledge they have. The COVID-19 pandemic brought this issue to the surface. When a pandemic interrupts the course of teaching and learning, there is without a doubt uncertainty in the effectiveness of lesson planning and online delivery. Fenty and Brydon (2017) report a lack of teacher readiness, especially at the elementary level, of how to incorporate "knowledge into content-area instruction" (p. 225). Gained learning experiences support the four dimensions – sociocultural processes, language development, academic development, and cognitive development - to gain richer classroom experiences (Herrera & Murry, 2016). Promoting a similar atmosphere online requires a fresh perspective of how educators deliver content and make student connections. As educators, the authors found themselves in a similar predicament as they relied heavily on reading the room of students and adjusting their delivery according to the audience's needs. The most significant difference in today's virtual climate is that educators and students must learn to communicate without being in the same space.

The fear of letting go in any classroom is a concern of all teachers, especially when online. However, shifting the lessons to be student-centric allows the student to remain in control of their learning. When students have a voice in their education, they are more likely to stay engaged (Tomlinson, 2014). With proper planning, the teacher is really in control. Many teachers fear that knowledge acquisition lacks if students are talking or even silent (Herrera & Murry, 2016).

Projects provide daily assessment opportunities through teacher observation, teacher-student communication, milestone checks, direct classroom instruction, student engagement, and formal presentations or project completions. Project learning offsets the concern of diverse learners who may not test well (Herrera & Murry, 2016; Newkirk-Turner & Johnson, 2018) as they have more opportunities to ingest the content. The fear of not having enough time to prepare and modify eases with completing each project, and each project fosters new ideas and modifications to meet all learners' needs. One way to connect with the students on the other side of the screen is through projects. Project learning holds the advantage of covering multiple state learning objectives daily (TEKS, 2019). This advantage occurs because students work through information at different speeds and then discuss it openly, meaning Student A may be working on the first point. Student B works on the second point, and Student C works on the third point during the same class. This process keeps the project's objectives active, and the conversations that arise during class discussions evolve the knowledge through peer connections and teacher interaction.

Projects are applicable for any grade level and subject content. They can be cross-curricular or as a single-discipline. Single-discipline projects promote the concepts of constructivist ideologies and content-specific comprehension with links to previous and upcoming concepts. For example, suppose an elementary math class is discussing word problems. In that case, a mini-project can be created revolving around math vocabulary to avoid any language barriers, such as a table where one would eat being confused with a table as in a chart for recording information. This type of project then becomes a personal dictionary that feeds into the learner's biographical focus. When the time comes for the students to work individually, all students have self-created personally relevant math dictionaries to aid in solidifying concepts and expanding knowledge. Lickona (1991) encourages students to work in various manners, such as jigsaw, cluster groups, small groups, or whole-class projects. Each style focuses on different organizations. A teacher can quickly reformat a lesson for online learning and distribute pieces to students for small, focused assigned portions followed by presenting in an online discussion. The use of tools, such as screen share and Google Slides, minimizes supplies for successful projects and allows for more substantial use of ZPD online. Students can facilitate working on projects with less hassle as they do not need to leave their homes to meet up with their partners. Guiding students in using online platforms effectively takes practice. Learning is most valuable when the student owns the data.

The Process

The following sections illustrate the ongoing and organic process of continual *Crystallizing Moments* documented in a single case study involving a first-grade student with the pseudonym of Oliver. One of the authors of this chapter, the teacher-researcher, engaged in continual reflection and documentation while engaging with Oliver for several months in an online tutoring capacity. While this case study only provides a glimpse into the online learning experiences of one teacher and student, the overall process and analysis can provide direction for online primary grades teachers in various contexts.

In explaining the approach used during a recent, informal case study, it is essential to disclose that the process developed organically. The action research expanded upon the teacher's dissertation's work (Gallagher-Immenschuh, 2020) and received permission from the student's parent via email to use the work they compeleted together since the beginning of COVID. It is essential to acknowledge that the teacher and student have worked together in an after-school learning center for three years. Their relationship has depth and trust, making the transition from in-person to online smoother. The parent and researcher also have a strong communicative relationship. The researcher acted as both the teacher and the researcher in this case and had a plan going into each session but was open to the possibility that the lesson would need alterations and remained malleable. The parent involvement in the learning process was intense, making the hiccups of technical issues and supplies less likely to disrupt the learning process and classes. Oliver (pseudonym) is in first grade and had no prior experience or exposure to online learning. Oliver previously attended a traditional brick-and-mortar school. Oliver acquired the skills to learn online as each session progressed.

As the teacher, the researcher made a conscious effort to remain unbiased and uncommitted to the original plan. The focus centered on listening to Oliver and watching him determine what modifications were immediately needed to create meaningful learning experiences. The format required the teacher/researcher to wear the instructor's role and the sounding board for Oliver. This dual role required visualizing their work together to think aloud and promote and engage in a sort of chalk talk (Ritchhart et al., 2011). Through the conversations, they could engage in various in-depth learning, including productive mathematical conversations (NCTM, 2013) extending beyond the problems on the page. Mathematical conversations (NCTM, 2013) allow students and teachers to create an enriched understanding of how math communicates in the world and through one another.

Cross-Curricular Learning

Establishing productive and meaningful learning in any classroom requires skill, focused planning, and knowing your students (Herrera & Murry, 2016), especially when the classroom is virtual. Creating legitimate peripheral participation (LPP) with students, meaning the process of understanding and learning takes place through involvement and not in an "individual mind," is the link between successful and effective learning practices and missed learning opportunities (Lave & Wenger, 1991, p.15). Student participation is not an option, rather it is a requirement for learning. Therefore, the learning process must shift from teacher-centered to student-centered with maximum engagement opportunities. Figure 2 displays an example of Oliver's engagement progression during a chalk talk. During a book read from the series *Beep and Bob* (Roth, 2018), Oliver created a parallel universe based on an integrated science lesson about the planets. Using Roth's series (2018) allowed the researcher and Oliver to explore science, language arts, math, art, and social studies. The researcher constructed materials to organize his thoughts and ideas required learning how to make project pieces, such as *Foldables©* (Zike, 2012). Majority of the supplies necessary for this project were readily available to Oliver in his home. The use of standard school supplies generated more inclusivity for students to produce information without resource limitations.

Listening to Oliver as he worked, the project adopted a life of its own, meaning the original layout and lessons were not binding. Screen sharing the interactive National Aeronautics and Space Administration (NASA) website *Space Place* (Erickson, 2021), https://spaceplace.nasa.gov/menu/solar-system/, made using valuable content fast and easy. The Zoom call quickly transformed from a two-way communication into an interactive research discovery. Figure 3 and Figure 4 also display the depth this project encompassed. What was most interesting to the researcher as the MKO (more knowledgeable other) was how involved and critical their role as a peer/project buddy was for his continued growth. Everything Oliver did, the researcher did in real-time. Any hiccups the researcher experienced, Oliver witnessed. Oliver had a slight reservation about offering ways to troubleshoot minor problems and would ask the researcher to display online images that the researcher would locate in real-time as he asked questions or craved more information. The interactive cooperation as project buddies became the new lesson plan and focus; The researcher would listen, and Oliver would lead. The researcher planned, and Oliver would find his path. The researcher would pose questions and lead discussions, and Oliver would channel his creativity. His interest in the solar system grew to a point where he made a solar system to authenticate what they discussed. The solar system inspired him to think of new and exciting details for his stories.

Translating these concepts and methodologies became less about the work and more about the student engagement. Looking at the student and his space became a higher priority. The researcher began conducting mini-interviews to see what was of interest to the student and where his curiosity piqued. The mini-interviews were not formal. They were casual and recorded during session notes (Figure 5). The researcher would pose ideas or questions and allow Oliver to discuss. The student's grade level's scope and sequence were present in the questioning process, meaning questions focused on essential learning components. The researcher wanted to find the avenue to create learning excitingly and dynamically while still covering the necessary materials. Rather than taking an assignment and executing it as initially written, the researcher thought considerably about how Oliver interacted with them online. Again, the researcher took notes and evaluated them, always looking for growth opportunities.

KiwiCo

Upon finding a theme of Oliver's love of math, space, reading, adventure, and how things work, the researcher decided to use KiwiCo (KiwiCo, 2021) to implement science projects and literature, a constant theme. This theme transitioned into math as well. Before Oliver completed the project, the researcher placed herself through the process and looked for connections, links, and opportunities for engagement. The researcher felt that a classroom teacher must accomplish this action in an online project with many moving parts. How could the process be unified and unique? Including a piece of literature with each project enhanced creating an opportunity for a literature-rich, online, engaged project. This flow enabled the researcher and Oliver to deepen content knowledge, remaining involved as learning partners, and understand how to keep a novel as a primary objective to a project. The connections manifested organically through the work and similar outcomes educators would desire in a classroom while watching a group of students working. The KiwiCo (2021) boxes became a means to diversify topics and blend them over multiple disciplines. What the researcher most appreciated about the KiwiCo boxes was the website's free resources for do-it-yourself project ideas and projects, https://www.kiwico.com/diy (KiwiCo, 2021). Understanding the constraints classroom teachers experience with budgets, the researcher found that many curated boxes could transpire without purchasing expensive items. This concept became fundamental in thinking of ways to reproduce and produce lower-budget projects with high-quality content. The projects also expanded the researcher's bravery in pushing the envelope and trying projects with numerous facets. After all, the researcher had to learn to follow how a well-curated kit pulled pieces together. Why not push oneself to do something similar? Enter the dream of the coral reef.

Figure 2. Oliver discussing his creation of a parallel solar system

Figure 3. Oliver recited as researcher typed in real-time the story ideas as he began sketching

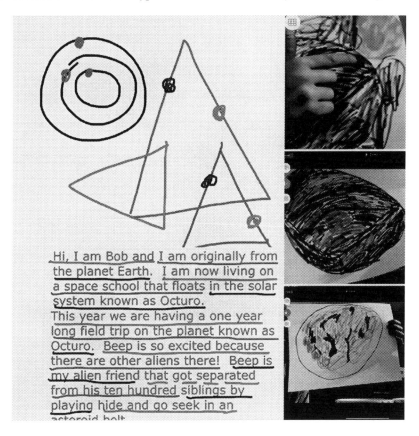

Figure 4. Rounding out Beep and Bob

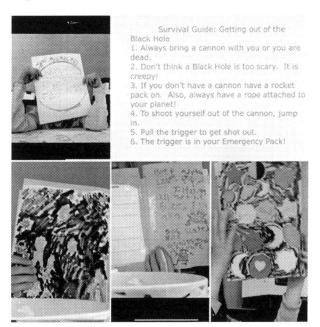

Figure 5. Session and reflection notes

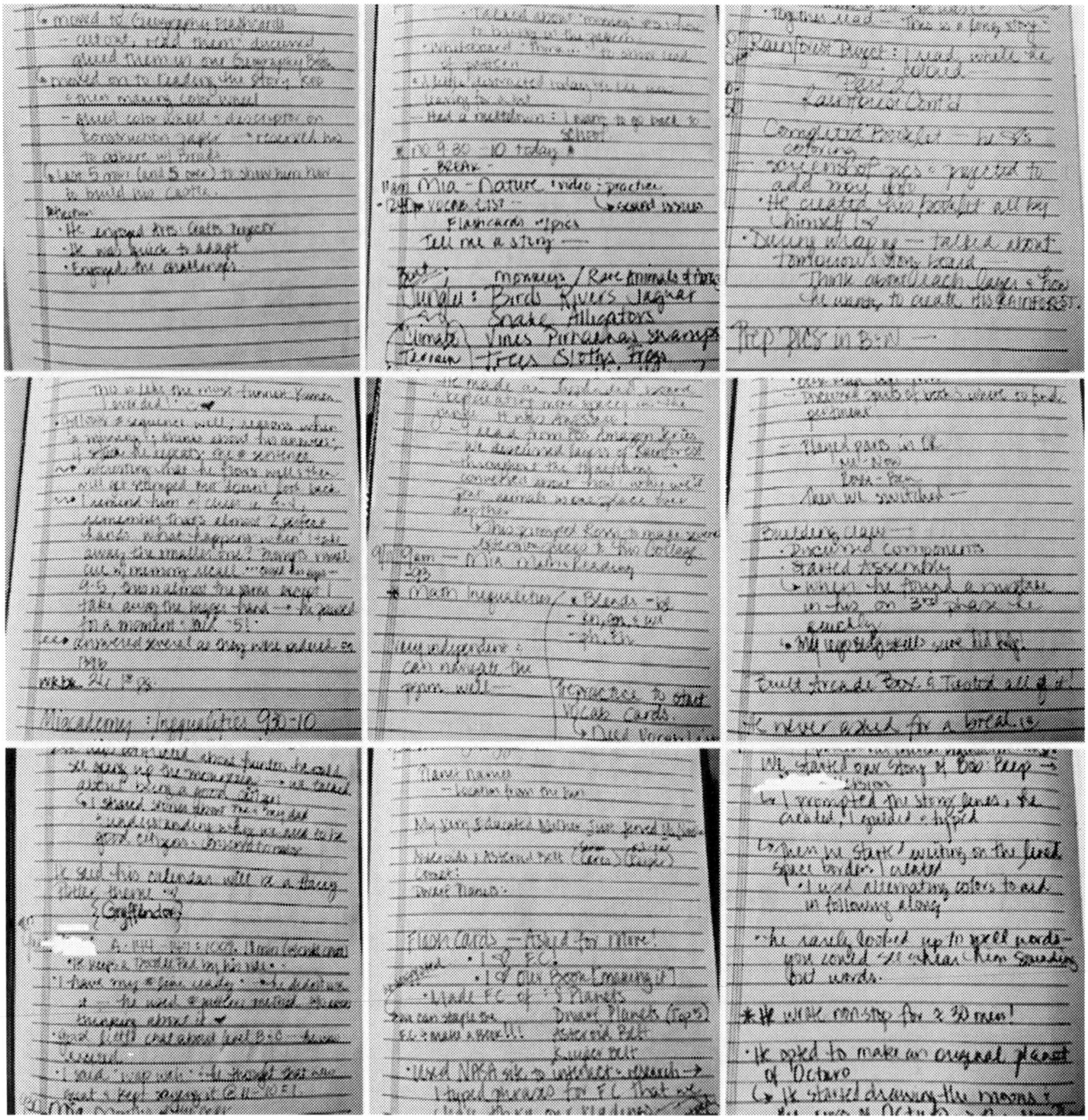

The Coral Reef

Pushing creativity online in a live Zoom session can be daunting. However, the researcher figured that if the project started going awry, it could be modified, just as would be done in a classroom. The decision to embark on a multi-phased project covering coral reefs was the next area of focus. This project was not a pre-existing project, nor was it an online kit. Oliver was interested in coral reefs, and the researcher committed to developing a cross-curricular lesson and focused on soft skills. The focus remained to have an Oliver-centric project, thus expanding Oliver's knowledge base and skillsets. One commitment

Crystallizing Moments

the researcher made to Oliver was that his imagination was the only limitation; in other words, anything goes. The researcher began locating the components necessary.

The researcher began project development with a piece of literature. Sometimes the books were lengthy, even series, and other times they were short. Shorter books provided for multiple literature pieces followed by audiovisuals and, of course, in-depth discussions. The researcher found coordinated videos on *PBS* (2019) to link one of the educational components of understanding the ecosystem and how humans and animals impact coral reefs. This project also stemmed from a rainforest project (Figure 6) recently completed by Oliver and the researcher. The rainforest project emphasized Murphy's (2016) position of allowing students to play and not interrupt their process. The rainforest project gave the researcher a new perspective of watching as the work progressed, grew, and unfolded across a screen. The more Oliver worked, the more the conversation grew regarding the rainforest. The researcher read to Oliver while he produced information (Figure 6). This casual format allowed for learner-driven discussions (Ritchhart et al., 2011; Vygotsky, 1978). The process of reading to him also allowed for his creativity not to be compromised.

Figure 6. The Rainforest Project

Oliver's interest in themes and requests for more knowledge also played a role in the project guidelines for developing a practical virtual project that translated well across a screen. The brainstorm reflection for the coral reef project began as follows:

Okay, follow me through my building/thought process. After our Rainforest and Arcade, I started thinking about the Coral Reef. I re-read a book I have at the house about the Coral Reef and thought this is something that would pique his interest and cover so many educational elements. I am also going to work on him creating a writing component.

This is literally a jumbo curated box about the Coral Reef to include: Lego City Ocean Exploration Submarine with Coral Reef, Lego Creator 3-in-1 Deep Sea Creatures, National Geographic Ultimate

Ocean Play Sand, Lego Classic Creative building kit (which we can use for a multitude of things....he can use it on his own just for fun too!!!), a display box, Creative Kid Flakes (that I will separate and send a certain number of pieces to build coral reefs), the Lego Block Base for the display box, and 2 Leveled National Geographic Books about the Coral Reef and Fish of the Coral Reef. I will loop in the scratch pad art kit (I have plenty at my house that I can add to his box) to build an original backdrop too.

This project will take several days for sure to complete. I think it would be easiest if I order all the components and put it together in an "Oliver Box" so that I make sure he has all the pieces.

The project commenced and finished in a one-session block via Zoom totaling 2.5 hours. Time was of utmost importance as students need time to "reflect, read, and respond without getting bored" (Ritchhart, Church, and Morrison, 2011, p. 81). The literature components of two short stories commenced the flow, followed by viewing a PBS (2019) program before the building and layouts began. Next, the researcher and Oliver reviewed construction materials, and he took the lead on the order of assembly and construction. During assembly, the researcher and Oliver found ample opportunity for chalk talk (Ritchhart et al., 2011). Chalk talk was instrumental for the researcher to draw on multiple assessment moments through conversation and knowledge base explanation versus a traditional paper or objective-based assessment (McLeod, 2012). Soft skills, such as confidence and motivation, were imperative in the long-term success of learning, and there seemed to be a lack of research that honed in on what made the learner feel successful beyond the measure of a test score.

When online, assessments during class are incredibly challenging. However, implementing chalk talk allows for LPP, legitimate peripheral participation, (Lave & Wenger, 1991), as evidenced by Oliver's contributions of soft skills and confidence in asking questions about the lessons. One of the things Oliver began doing was asking for the researcher to project images of coral reefs and fish of coral reefs so he could attempt to construct similar components for his version. The researcher learned to be quick to add any elements he needed to make his learning more fulfilled.

During construction, the LEGO® Creator 3in1 31088 Deep Sea Creatures set (2020) allowed Oliver and the researcher to create different animals using the same pieces. Oliver chose first, and then the researcher's choice was discussed and agreed upon, leaving Oliver with the final say of what he thought would add more excitement to their diverse creations. This level of negotiation was similar to a ZPD, zone of proximal development (Vygotsky, 1978), that would have occurred in a traditional classroom, or even with other peers online to include negotiation, discussion, and collaboration. Oliver's speed in construction exceeded that of the researcher, and he was quick to offer building tips and tricks that he referred to as his "lots of LEGO® building skills" and compassionately encouraged the researcher to "not give up... you'll get it!" This casual conversation transpiring between the two was comparable to ZPD in a classroom orientation. Oliver was completely immersed in learning and would take quick restroom breaks as needed. He never asked to stop, nor did he lose interest. Figure 6 provides a closer look at the project's construction and depicts some of the materials used.

During this project, the researcher scaffolded a prior social studies lesson on maps (see Figure 7) that covered a base 33 Texas Essential Knowledge and Skills (TEKS) (TEA, 2019). Oliver thoroughly enjoyed reusing previous knowledge of his maps to add the estimated location of coral reefs worldwide. While a project across a screen seems like a mess waiting to happen, a comfortable teacher will remain in control. However, the student has the authority of creativity, engagement, interest, and diversity in learning to complete the project. The researcher practices a personal rule of what they refer to as 'guide-

Crystallizing Moments

lines, not tombstones,' meaning everything can and should be free to change (pivot) to find success. By the end of the coral reef project, the researcher learned that no matter how extensive or massive it may feel when detailing the parts, students will exceed and surprise the original expectations. If the student and the teacher have access to the same materials, the margin for error minimizes. Every project organically developed when the student remained at the center of the project. The critical takeaway from any project's development was that the teacher took the time to write and reflect on what worked, did not work, as well as the feelings about the teacher role in the project. This project is reproducible using less expensive items. For instance, students can use their backyards to locate rocks and foliage to paint to represent the coral reef. Students can use their toys, construction paper, plastic cups, straws, canvas and paints, magazine cutouts, or any item a student desires to transform. Students can work individually or in small groups and place their creativity on Google Slides or PowerPoint presentations. The opportunities indeed are limitless and can be cost-effective.

Figure 7. The Coral Reef Project

DISCUSSION

Teachers found themselves in a new world of online teaching and learning during the COVID-19 pandemic. Many schools and teachers have understandably relied more on pre-recorded videos, apps, and similar types of technology for online learning, especially during this unprecedented time. The human connection created and maintained via purposeful engagement and hands-on learning experiences during synchronous videoconferencing sessions is especially crucial for young learners in primary grades classrooms. *Crystallizing Moments* can occur naturally and indeed *humanly* during synchronous videoconferencing with face-to-face interaction and hands-on activities, enhancing engagement and making the most of online teaching and learning experiences. The 4Cs (communication, collaboration, critical thinking, and creativity) are crucial elements of twenty-first century teaching and learning. In the online primary grades classroom via synchronous teacher-student engagement, the 4Cs are best actualized in online primary grades classrooms via synchronous teacher-student engagement. The Reggio Emilia Lens provides insight into approaching engaging, hands-on, *Crystallizing Moments* and can be thoughtfully incorporated into online teaching and learning for young children. The case study of Oliver provided in this chapter offers a glimpse into how the 4Cs and the Reggio Emilia lens can work together within a child-centered teaching and learning environment involving ongoing and purposefully planned teacher-student interactions. Teachers of primary grades learners who are now increasingly teaching online can benefit from using a hands-on approach as was utilized with Oliver. Naturally, teachers have a variety of contexts, needs, goals, budgets, and realities. The general idea of planning synchronous primary grades teaching and learning sessions via videoconferencing, while using hands-on objects, in the actual hands of the child can be creatively applied with considerations of one's own teaching situation and reality. Teachers may consider how to scale up these interactions to include multiple students using their choice of available hands-on materials at home and then interacting with the teacher and other students via videoconferencing.

SUMMARY AND CONCLUSION

This small-scale research project served as an opportunity to observe using alternative methodologies and pedagogy in a time of much change and upheaval in education. While the research was a small-scale approach, the outcomes show promise for current and future classroom adaptations. The flexibility of experimentation with Zoom during the COVID-19 pandemic allowed for diversity in academic presentation. The researcher faced challenges of amplifying a more comprehensive range of academic skills than they had explored. On the other hand, the challenges provided validity to learning and filling in Oliver's gaps in the classroom. The collaboration between the researcher and Oliver promotes the pedagogical concepts of chalk talk (Ritchhart et al., 2011), ZPD and MKO (Vygotsky, 1978), and LPP (Lave & Wenger, 2015).

McLeod (2012) explains the Writing Across the Curriculum (WAC) movement born in the 1970s as a

recent educational movement, one aimed at transforming pedagogy at the college level, at moving away from the lecture model of teaching…to a model of active student engagement with the material and with the genres of the discipline through writing, not just in English classes but in all classes across the university. (p. 54)

Student-centric engagement to learn, understand, and create learning should not wait until teachers face students in person. Equally, challenging educators and students to express themselves in real-time through virtual platforms is possible and productive. As a first-grade student, Oliver rose to the academic and participatory expectations through each project's course. The researcher focused on maintaining the role as an academic coach and facilitator, promoting Oliver's soft and hard skills. Knowledge acquisition in Oliver's academic growth (Figures 1 through 6) is notable. Oliver worried less and less about what to write and how to write it. The researcher maintained the principles of gradual advancement and expectation without limiting his potential through promoting active learning and critical thinking in every exercise and holding the position as a guide and peer support. During this approach, a student possesses the opportunity to revise work after submission after receiving feedback. Learning is scaffolded when students return to their work to fix and polish materials. Even as a first-grader, Oliver successfully made revisions after conversations with the teacher-researcher. Teachers of primary grades learners who are now increasingly teaching online can benefit from using a hands-on approach as described in this chapter. The approach can potentially be scaled up to include multiple students using hands-on materials at home and then interacting with the teacher and other students via videoconferencing.

REFERENCES

Adler, M. (1955). *The great ideas*. Encyclopedia Britannica.

Barbour, M., Brown, R., Waters, L. H., Hoey, R., Hunt, J. L., Kennedy, K., Ounsworth, C., Powell, A., & Trimm, T. (2011). Online and Blended Learning: A Survey of Policy and Practice from K-12 Schools around the World. In *International Association for K-12 Online Learning*. International Association for K-12 Online Learning.

Beebe, R, Vonderwell, S & Boboc, M. (2010). Emerging patterns in transferring assessment practices from F2f to online environments. *Electronic Journal of e-Learning, 8*(1), 1 - 12.

Bowdon, J. (2020, August 25). *Meaningful online education for our youngest learners: Tips to reconcile the need for e-learning with how young children learn best.* https://ies.ed.gov/ncee/edlabs/regions/midwest/blogs/online-education-young-learners.aspx

Brodersen, R. M., & Melluzzo, D. (2017). Summary of Research on Online and Blended Learning Programs That Offer Differentiated Learning Options. REL 2017-228. Regional Educational Laboratory Central.

Çubukçu, Z. (2012). The effect of hidden curriculum on character education process of primary school students. *Educational Sciences: Theory and Practice, 12*(2), 1526–1534.

Fernández Santín, M., & Feliu Torruella, M. (2017). Reggio Emilia: An Essential Tool to Develop Critical Thinking in Early Childhood. *Journal of New Approaches in Educational Research, 6*(1), 50–56. doi:10.7821/naer.2017.1.207

Fisher, D., & Frey, N. (2020). Helping students cope with the pandemic: How educators respond to children's fears now will influence the long-term effects. *Educational Leadership, 78*(2), 76–77.

Fisher, D., Frey, N., & Hattie, J. (2021). *The Distance Learning Playbook, Grades K-12: Teaching for Engagement and Impact in Any Setting*. Corwin.

Gallagher-Immenschuh, C. (2020). *Reading and writing mathematics: A phenomenological qualitative case study of a cross-curricular approach* [Doctoral dissertation, Northcentral University]. ProQuest Dissertations Publishing. https://search.proquest.com/openview/357f41bc90e76955bf337d5313b73435/1?pq-origsite=gscholar&cbl=44156

Gardner, H. (1991). *The unschooled mind: How children think and how schools should teach.* Basic Books.

Guo, J., & Woulfin, S. (2016). Twenty-First Century Creativity: An Investigation of How the Partnership for 21st Century Instructional Framework Reflects the Principles of Creativity. *Roeper Review*, *38*(3), 153–161. doi:10.1080/02783193.2016.1183741

Hand in Hand in Kinderland [@handinhandinkinderland]. (2021, April 17). *This has been my view for an entire year now. I teach to a computer and pray the littles on the other side are getting it* [Photograph]. Instagram. https://www.instagram.com/p/CNyklaKM5KW/?igshid=ip8s6m7hdlt

Hunter, M. (1994). *Mastery Teaching.* Corwin.

KiwiCo. (2021). https://www.kiwico.com/

Kohn, A. (2006). *Beyond discipline: From compliance to community.* Association for Supervision and Curriculum Development.

Lave, J., & Wenger, E. (2015). *Situated learning: Legitimate peripheral participation.* Cambridge University Press.

Lee, J., Yoon, S. Y., & Lee, C. H. (2013). Exploring Online Learning at Primary Schools: Students' Perspectives on Cyber Home Learning System through Video Conferencing (CHLS-VC). *Turkish Online Journal of Educational Technology, 12*(1), 68–76.

LEGO®. (2020). *Creator 3in1 31088 Deep sea creatures set.* Retrieved from https://www.lego.com/en-us/product/deep-sea-creatures-31088

Lickona, T. (1991). *Educating for character: How our schools can teach respect and responsibility.* Bantam Books.

Lu, J., & Hao, Q. (2014). What factors impact on primary school students' online engagement for learning and entertainment at home. *Journal of Computers in Education*, *1*(2–3), 133.

McLeod, S. (2013). The pedagogy of Writing Across the Curriculum. In Writing across the curriculum: A critical sourcebook. Bedford/St. Martin's.

Meacham, S., & Atwood-Blaine, D. (2018). Early Childhood Robotics: A Lego robotics club inspired by Reggio Emilia supports children's authentic learning. *Science and Children*, *56*(3), 57–62.

Murphy, L. (2016). *Lisa Murphy on play: The foundation of children's learning.* Redleaf Press.

Mutton, T. (2020, August). Teacher education and COVID-19: Responses and opportunities for new pedagogical initiatives. *Journal of Education for Teaching.* https://doi.org./10.1080/02607476.2020.1805189

NCES Fast Facts Tool. (n.d.). https://nces.ed.gov/fastfacts/display.asp?id=372#:~:text=In%202017%E2%80%9318%2C%20about%2019,offered%20any%20courses%20entirely%20online

NCTM. (2008). *Getting into the Mathematics conversation: Valuing communication in Mathematics classrooms.* The National Council of Teachers of Mathematics, Inc.

Parette, H. P., Quesenberry, A. C., & Blum, C. (2010). Missing the Boat with Technology Usage in Early Childhood Settings: A 21st Century View of Developmentally Appropriate Practice. *Early Childhood Education Journal, 37*(5), 335–343. https://doi.org/10.1007/s10643-009-0352-x

Partnership for 21st Century Learning. (2019). http://static.battelleforkids.org/documents/p21/P21_Framework_Brief.pdf

Rasmitadila, A. R. R., Rachmadtullah, R., Samsudin, A., Syaodih, E., Nurtanto, M., & Tambunan, A. R. S. (2020). The Perceptions of Primary School Teachers of Online Learning during the COVID-19 Pandemic Period: A Case Study in Indonesia. *Journal of Ethnic & Cultural Studies, 7*(2), 90.

Robinson, K. (2011). *Out of Our Minds: Learning to be Creative.* Capstone Publishing Ltd.

Rock, D., & Shaw, J. M. (2000). *Exploring children's thinking about mathematicians and their work. In Getting into the Mathematics conversation: Valuing communication in Mathematics classrooms.* The National Council of Teachers of Mathematics, Inc.

Rosenblum, K. E., & Travis, T. M. C. (2016). *The meaning of difference: American constructions of race and ethnicity, sex and gender, social class, sexuality, and disability* (7th ed.). McGraw-Hill Education.

Schleicher, A. (2018). *World class: How to build a 21st-Century school system, strong performers and successful reformers in education.* OECD Publishing.

SeeSaw. (2021). https://web.seesaw.me/

Soja, E. W. (1996). *Thirdspace: Journeys to Los Angeles and other real-and-imagined places.* Blackwell Publishing.

Steele, D. F. (1999). *Learning mathematical language in the Zone of Proximal Development. Getting into the Mathematics conversation: Valuing communication in Mathematics classrooms.* The National Council of Teachers of Mathematics, Inc.

Tomlinson, C. A. (2014). *The Differentiated Classroom: Responding to the Needs of All Learners.* ASCD.

Vygotsky, L. S. (1978). *Mind in society: The development of higher psychological processes.* Harvard University Press.

Whalley, R., & Barbour, M. K. (2020). Collaboration and Virtual Learning in New Zealand Rural Primary Schools: A Review of the Literature. *Turkish Online Journal of Distance Education, 21*(2), 102–125.

Will, M. (2020, August 6). New NEA President: 'We are not going to put our students at risk' for COVID-19. *Education Week.* https://www.edweek.org/teaching-learning/new-nea-president-we-are-not-going-to-put-our-students-at-risk-for-covid-19/2020/08

Williamson, T. (2017). Listening to many voices: Enacting social justice literacy curriculum. *Teaching and Teacher Education, 61*, 104–114. https://doi.org. /10.1016/j.tate.2016.10.002

Zike, D. M. (Ed.). (2012). *Envelope graphic organizers: Using repurposed envelopes for projects, study guides, and daily work; Strategies for all subjects, all levels*. Dinah-Might Adventures, LP.

ADDITIONAL READING

Carey, B. (2014). *How we learn: The surprising truth about when, where, and why it happens*. Random House.

Cenoz, J. (2017). Translanguaging in school contexts: International perspectives. *Journal of Language, Identity, and Education*, *16*(4), 193–198. doi:10.1080/15348458.2017.1327816

Fenty, N. S., & Brydon, M. (2017). Integrating literacy and the content curriculum to support diverse learners. *Learning Disabilities (Weston, Mass.)*, *15*(2), 225–238.

Liou, D. D., Martinez, A. N., & Rotheram-Fuller, E. (2015). "Don't give up on me": Critical mentoring pedagogy for the classroom building students' community cultural wealth. *International Journal of Qualitative Studies in Education: QSE*, *29*(1), 104–129. doi:10.1080/09518398.2015.1017849

Schaeffer, M. J., Rozek, C. S., Berkowitz, T., Levine, S. C., & Beilock, S. L. (2018). Disassociating the relation between parents' math anxiety and children's math achievement: Long-Term effects of a math app intervention. *Journal of Experimental Psychology. General*, *47*(12), 1782–1790. doi:10.1037/xge0000490 PMID:30284862

Schalk, L., Saalbach, H., & Stern, E. (2016). Approaches to foster transfer of formal principles: Which route to take? *PLoS One*, *11*(2), e0148787. doi:10.1371/journal.pone.0148787 PMID:26871902

Seo, E. H. (2018). Private tutoring and academic achievement: Self-study as a mediator. *Social Behavior and Personality*, *46*(5), 823–830. doi:10.2224bp.6689

Von Duyke, K., & Matusov, E. (2015). Flowery math: A case for heterodiscoursia in mathematics problems solving in recognition of students' authorial agency. *Pedagogies*, *11*(1), 1–21. doi:10.1080/1554480X.2015.1090904

KEY TERMS AND DEFINITIONS

Creativity: A higher-order thinking skill involving humans/learners utilizing imaginative ideas and original approaches, typically involving synthesis, analysis, problem-solving, and often artistic thinking.

Developmentally Appropriate Practice: The use of instructional materials and strategies that honor the ongoing and specific phases of child development and learning during early childhood.

Differentiated Instruction: The practice of allowing many processes and products to demonstrate mastery of learning outcomes in education, understanding that learners approach tasks differently and learn in unique ways.

Hands-On Learning: A term used to describe students using their hands to create and represent their knowledge and not a software program.

Legitimate Peripheral Participation: Understanding and learning takes place through participation and not within the individual's mind.

Online Learning: Instruction and learning occurring via the internet (either synchronous, asynchronous, or a combination of both).

Primary Grades: Grades K-3 in a United States school system.

Reggio Emilia: A teaching and pedagogy approach usually based on preschool and kindergarten students. The approach is a children-centric and constructivist self-guided curriculum, using self-directed, experiential learning in relationship-driven environments.

Twenty-First Century Learning: Skills recognized as necessary to navigation of and communication within the twenty-first century, such as communication, collaboration, critical thinking, and creativity.

Chapter 12
Using Digital Games in Virtual Classrooms to Make Attitudinal Learning Motivating and Engaging

Shamila Janakiraman
Purdue University, USA

ABSTRACT

The COVID-19 global pandemic has made it difficult for schools to conduct in-person learning, pushing educators to think innovatively to create digital classrooms and engage K-12 learners. This chapter will provide best practices and pedagogical reasoning into the use of digital game-based learning (DGBL) for attitudinal instruction in virtual classrooms of middle and high school students. When it comes to teaching socio-scientific topics, providing cognitive knowledge is not the only goal of education. Young learners need to develop appropriate attitudes and behaviors to ensure the holistic development of their personality. This is where DGBL has been found to be an effective instructional activity. Although the focus of this chapter is on using DGBL in environmental sustainability education, it provides implications that are applicable to other socio-scientific topics as well.

INTRODUCTION

The COVID-19 global pandemic disrupted in-person learning and many schools are still struggling to keep their schools open safely. Educators have the responsibility to help children continue to learn through other paths. Fortunately, the growth in educational technology and the advent of online teaching have made it possible to achieve some of the goals for K-12 education. Online learning has been growing rapidly across the United States and it is not an unfamiliar situation in higher education (Seaman et al., 2018). However, when COVID-19 struck, K-12 teachers found themselves in uncharted territory. Most K-12 educators have never taught online before, and now they had to create digital classrooms. Simply transferring strategies from an in-person class to an online platform has been clearly demonstrated as

DOI: 10.4018/978-1-7998-7222-1.ch012

not working. Teachers have to go the extra mile to engage their students using new and novel strategies (Rockey, 2020). Educators, including school administration and teachers, have to find and implement digital tools that can help their young students learn in an engaging way and complete assigned tasks on time.

Research studies and the application of digital game-based learning (DGBL) in real classrooms have shown that DGBL is an effective instructional strategy to engage and motivate students to learn various subjects (Adams et al., 2012; Gee, 2008; Gros, 2014; Habgood & Ainsworth; 2011; Prensky, 2003; Wen et al., 2018). Considering virtual classrooms, implementing digital games will not only help students learn, but can also reduce the burden on teachers and add some fun moments. Games can reduce Zoom fatigue connected to burnout from overuse of conferencing platforms (Lee, 2020; Schroeder, 2021) and can also be provided as a homework activity or earn credit.

This chapter focuses specifically on teaching socio-scientific topics to K-12 students using DGBL in virtual classrooms. These approaches are different from implementing educational games that are designed to provide cognitive knowledge in subjects like math, science, social studies, languages, and others. First the importance of socio-scientific topics and the need for attitudinal learning is explained using environmental sustainability education (ESE) as an example. Following this example, how DGBL can be an effective pedagogical tool for attitudinal learning, how DGBL can be implemented in virtual classrooms, and how attitudinal learning can be assessed in virtual classrooms are elaborated upon.

TEACHING SOCIO-SCIENTIFIC TOPICS

In addition to teaching subject knowledge, many schools strive to incorporate socio-scientific topics in their curriculum that include real-world problems like environmental, social, and economic sustainability, pollution, use of pesticides, drug abuse, healthy food habits, and so on. There have been considerations about how to include such issues within the school curriculum, and about the pedagogical skills that are required of science teachers to teach such topics (Lewis & Leach, 2007). Socio-scientific topics involve ill-structured problem solving where there are no single correct answers, and the learning cannot be achieved by memorization (Sadler, 2009). These topics have local, national, and global dimensions (Ratcliffe & Grace, 2003). Such issues directly impact people who have competing perspectives and priorities making them controversial in nature, because of their undetermined status and connections to society (Sadler, 2009). Learners are exposed to these issues through media mostly and the way these issues are interpreted by them is impactful (Ratcliffe & Grace, 2003). Hence when teaching such topics, providing cognitive knowledge should not be the only goal; young learners need to develop appropriate attitudes and behaviors, making attitudinal learning very important.

Attitudinal learning comprises cognitive, affective, behavioral, and social learning. Gagne et al. (1992), define an attitude as the psychological evaluation a person has regarding an object, person, or event. Attitude comprises of three components: cognitive component based on information, knowledge, and thoughts; affective component based on emotions or feeling, and behavioral component, the predisposition to act (Kamradt & Kamradt, 1999; Simonson, 1979). In addition, social learning also influences attitude change, where discussions or interactions with others influences attitudes (Watson et al., 2018; Janakiraman et al., 2021b).

The goal of attitudinal instruction is to influence learners' existing attitudes positively or negatively leading to attitudinal learning (Watson et al., 2018). This challenge is possible if learners are made to perform an action that is slightly different from their existing attitude and slightly matching the target attitude (Kamradt & Kamradt, 1999). The following section describes attitudinal learning using environmental sustainability education (ESE) as an example.

Attitudinal Learning in Environmental Sustainability Education

Several studies conducted by the United Nations Educational, Scientific, and Cultural Organization (UNESCO, n.d) and others (Arora, 2018; Brinkmann, 2020) have shown the impact of environmental degradation and climate change on the lives of animals, plants, their habitats and ecosystems. But the truth is that most people refuse to acknowledge that the main causes are human activities (anthropocentric) like burning fossil fuels, rapid construction, and alterations to land use (Karl & Trenberth, 2003; Meya & Eisenack, 2018; UNEP, 2020).

Being an interdisciplinary topic, environmental sustainability is included in the Science and Social Studies curriculum and is also relevant in Environmental Science in many school standards in the U.S. For example, the Human Sustainability section for high schools, and the Ecosystems: Interactions, Energy, and Dynamics section for middle schools cover this topic under the Next Generation Science Standards (NGSS, n.d.) in the U.S. Similarly, educational standards have been stipulated by the departments of education in various states in the U.S. For example, the Indiana Academic Standard 7: Pollution, and the Standard 8: Natural and Anthropogenic Resource Cycles are included in the Indiana Department of Education (DOE, n.d.) standards.

Although, ESE creates awareness regarding harmful human activities, it does not focus on encouraging pro-environmental attitudes and behaviors in real life. While teaching socio-scientific topics like this, teachers have to focus on changing the beliefs and behaviors of their students in order to influence their decisions and actual behaviors in the real world (Tsai, 2018).

As discussed earlier, an attitude is the psychological evaluation a person has regarding an object, person, or event, according to Gagne et al. (1992). It comprises of: (1) the cognitive component based on information, knowledge, and thoughts, (2) the affective component based on emotions or feeling, and (3) the behavioral component, the pre-disposition to act (Kamradt & Kamradt, 1999), and (4) social learning from interaction with others (Watson et al., 2018). The behavioral component refers to the pre-disposition to act, or the behavioral intentions that can predict actual behaviors, according to the theory of planned behavior (Ajzen, 2019).

To promote attitudinal learning, instructional strategies that create awareness (Buchanan et al., 2016; Huckle, 2012) and promote mindfulness (Wang et al., 2019) have to be implemented. Knowledge should be provided as activities and experiences that are situated in scenarios and not as facts and information so that learners develop situated understandings (Gee, 2008). With respect to ESE, studies have shown that attitudinal learning from traditional methods of instruction do not produce long-term behavioral changes because learned environmental attitudes are forgotten and inconvenient to practice (Arbuthnott, 2009; Hungerford & Volk, 1990; Tucker, 1999). However, creating feelings of empathy and encouraging learners to perform environmentally friendly behaviors within the learning environment have been shown to promote attitudinal learning (Janakiraman et al., 2021a; Tan & Biswas, 2008; Yang et al., 2012). Moreover, learners need to develop skills in decision-making, and gain a sense of ownership and empowerment that encourages pro-environmental behaviors (Hungerford & Volk, 1990). To inspire learners to act sustainably, the United Nations Educational, Scientific, and Cultural Organization (UNESCO, n.d.)

recommends "learning in an interactive, learner-centered way that enables exploratory, action oriented and transformative learning," necessitating a transformative pedagogy (Bell, 2016).

Therefore, when teaching socio-scientific topics, it is desirable that the instruction promotes affective, behavioral, and social learning alongside cognitive knowledge. DGBL environments satisfy all the requirements for an effective pedagogical tool to promote attitudinal learning (Janakiramans, 2021; Chen et al., 2019; Troussas et al., 2019). The effectiveness of DGBL in the instruction of various subjects has been discussed extensively. However, studies that discuss the use of DGBL as an effective instructional strategy for attitudinal learning are few (Harker-Schuch et al., 2020; Knol & De Vries, 2011; Ninaus et al., 2019). This chapter addresses this gap to provide insights into the practical application of game activities in attitudinal instruction based on the studies conducted by Janakiraman. These include a literature review on the topic (Janakiraman et al., 2018) and three exploratory mixed methods studies using a game (Janakiraman et al., 2021a; Janakiraman et al., 2021b; Janakiraman et al. 2021c). All these studies used a game designed to teach environmental sustainability education (ESE).

Based on literature and the Janakiraman studies, this chapter provides best practices and pedagogical reasoning for implementing DGBL to promote attitudinal learning among middle school and high school grade students in virtual classrooms. Throughout this chapter ESE is used as an example for a socio-scientific topic and to explain how DGBL was used to teach ESE.

Digital Games for Promoting Attitudinal Learning in ESE

Environmental Sustainability Education (ESE) should be effective in influencing real-world attitudes and behaviors. Since behavioral changes depend on constraints and negative perceptions, it is necessary to implement persuasive pedagogical tools in ESE (Sinatra et al., 2012), such as digital game-based learning (DGBL). Studies have shown that games are stronger alternatives or support activities because they allow learners to test their behaviors and see the consequences of harmful behaviors immediately, thereby facilitating attitudinal learning and retention of learning (Janakiraman, 2020; Yang et al., 2012; Harker-Schuch et al., 2020). DGBL can create feelings of empathy, provide a discovery learning environment, help visualize interrelatedness in the real world, and promote systems thinking (Janakiraman, 2018; Fabricatore & López, 2012). Games encourage players to perform actions that may be inconsistent with their existing attitude and consistent with the target attitude (Kamradt & Kamradt, 1999), and are therefore more effective compared to traditional instructional methods.

Janakiraman's prior studies were based on the premise that creating awareness about environmental sustainability issues alone is not enough. As a first step, a literature review was conducted on this topic (Janakiraman et al., 2018) that showed that digital games not only provide cognitive knowledge but can also engage learners emotionally and allow learners to test new behaviors by examining consequences instantly, something not possible in the real world.

To further explore this a series of studies were conducted. In one study (Janakiraman et al., 2021a) the effectiveness of DGBL in producing attitudinal and behavioral changes was examined by comparing the attitudinal learning between a group of undergraduate students studying in a large university in an educational technology course who played EnerCities, an ESE game, and another group that played a game that was not connected to ESE. The students comprised of freshman, sophomore, and juniors studying different majors and pursuing teaching licenses. Survey data were collected using the Attitudinal Learning Instrument (ALI) administered after one week and after five weeks of game play. Quantitative data analysis using Partial Least Squares Structural Equation Modeling (PLS-SEM) showed that the

ESE game did promote environmentally friendly attitudes and behaviors. Interviews highlighted why and how the game produced the attitudinal changes.

In the second study (Janakiraman et al., 2021b) the effectiveness of games when played collaboratively and when played individually was examined in a high school in India, using the same game, EnerCities. Students studying in three sections of Grade 11 participated in this study. Prior studies involving games in subjects like Math, Science, language literacy, and other subjects showed that knowledge acquisition was more in collaborative learning than individual game play. Such a comparison was not made with respect to attitudinal learning in a socio-scientific topic, and this study bridged that gap. This study employed surveys based on the Theory of Planned Behavior (TPB) and the Attitudinal Learning Instrument (ALI), and found that attitudinal learning from games was similar for collaborative and individual players. A comparison of game players with learners who learned ESE only through traditional instructional methods showed that game players' attitudinal learning was higher. Interviews highlighted the contributions made by the game to the learning experience and how game play strategies differed among collaborative and individual game players.

The third study (Janakiraman et al., 2021c) examined the environmental attitudes of high school students in India about anthropogenic activities that cause environmental degradation related problems. ESE is taught from elementary school in India and the objectives include enabling students to identify environmental problems and the interactive processes of nature, and learn how to care for the environment, conserve energy, prevent pollution, and preserve the environment. In this study differences in environmental attitudes between students who played EnerCities, and students who did not play that game and learned ESE only by traditional methods was examined. Findings using the unidimensional and multidimensional properties of the New Ecological Paradigm (NEP) scale showed significant differences among the two groups. Interviews indicated how EnerCities changed participants' environmental attitudes and their perceptions towards nature and provided insights into the game features that were instrumental in attitudinal learning, establishing the effectiveness of DGBL.

Although these studies were conducted in face-to-face classrooms, implications for implementing games in virtual classrooms can be derived from them. When teaching topics that focus on attitudinal learning, teachers should ensure a holistic and meaningful learning experience. Effective programs provide learners with cognitive knowledge and promote affective, behavioral, and social learning. The following sections consider ESE as an example to explain the following: (1) how teachers can implement DGBL in a virtual environment, (2) how teachers can select a suitable game, (3) the instructional strategies that need to be implemented, and (4) the game features that make the learning experience motivating and engaging. Recommendations are provided for how teachers can assess attitudinal learning using application activities when students demonstrate their learning in the real-world. The examples presented in this chapter may be adapted to the instruction of other socio-scientific topics as well, to make attitudinal learning effective while using DGBL in virtual classrooms.

DIGITAL GAMES FOR VIRTUAL CLASSROOMS

Traditional methods of attitudinal instruction in virtual classrooms encompassing lectures and presentations, quizzes and exams will not be sufficient because students need to learn from experiences (Janakiraman et al., 2021a; Yang et al., 2012; Wu & Huang, 2015). DGBL, on the other hand, offers a near-authentic experience to practice behaviors and learn from one's own actions that are executed in safe simulated environments and are easy to implement in virtual classrooms. When teachers and parents use games purposefully as "objects-to-think-with," they can encourage exploration and experimentation (Holbert & Wilensky, 2019).

Such an impactful platform can be leveraged to promote attitudinal learning regarding socio-scientific topics in virtual classrooms because implementing DGBL as a learning activity reduces time spent on conferencing platforms that cause fatigue (Lee, 2020; Schroeder, 2021). As a virtual experience DGBL offers two modes of interaction: learning for playing and learning from playing (Hong et al., 2013). Either way DGBL can promote attitudinal learning because games provide a platform that is interactive (Meya & Eisenack, 2018), and persuasive (Griset, 2010; Sinatra et al., 2012). Moreover, DGBL can engage learners with the topic and motivate them to complete their assigned work because it offers experiential learning in a highly rewarding, game-based environment (Janakiraman, 2020).

Statistica and Pew Research Center studies have shown the growth in popularity of digital games among young learners across the globe (Gough, 2020; Perrin, 2018). Although, this idea applies to recreational games, Serious Educational Games (SEGs) are also becoming popular. SEGs employ video gaming technology to design engaging learning activities for learners in order to improve their learning experience and learning outcomes (Barclay & Bowers, 2020). Educational games are usually available for free on websites administered by the National Aeronautics and Space Administration (NASA), National Geographic, and other organizations that can be accessed online (see Appendix 1). Hence, educators from traditional and online schools can use digital games as an impactful and persuasive pedagogical tool to teach young learners about desired attitudes and behaviors concerning various socio-scientific topics.

Selecting a Game for Attitudinal Learning in Virtual Classrooms

Selecting a game for attitudinal learning in virtual classrooms requires careful consideration. This action is different from selecting games to teach subjects like math, science, and language/literacy that focus only on cognitive knowledge gain. Attitudinal learning games have to provide cognitive knowledge and also facilitate affective, behavioral, and social learning. Furthermore, in virtual classrooms, since students do not have direct supervision from their teachers, the game has to perform the role of a teacher in guiding players' progress in the game while facilitating the attitudinal learning experience. The following recommendations show how teachers can purposefully select the experiences concerning socio-scientific topics like child abuse, healthy food habits, environmental sustainability, and others by implementing a game that ensures situated understandings (Gee, 2008):

1. Teachers should select games that "have proven their worth for yielding learning outcomes" (van der Meij et al., 2011, p. 656). Games that are designed to provide instruction that will keep players on track and focused on the learning goals are required to enhance cognition and metacognition of players. This is achieved through prompts that are provided by a virtual agent or through pop-up text boxes (Cuccurullo et al., 2013; Knol & De Vries, 2011; Zumbach et al., 2020). Such prompts provide new knowledge and also inform players about correct and wrong decisions by giving immediate feedback.
2. K-12 teachers need to be aware of the availability of digital games for teaching various topics that are suitable for different grades. There are numerous websites with online games for attitudinal learning (see Appendix 1). Although online games are easier to access, instructors can look for offline games too, that can be downloaded and played. There are several empathy games that can

be used to teach about racism, poverty, gender and sexuality, and others, according to Johnson (2019, November).
3. Teachers should select games that align with the learning objectives of the course rather than try to derive objectives from the games (Watson et al., 2011). To help teachers choose the game that best matches their course objectives, different online games that cover various socio-scientific topics are listed in Appendix 1.
4. Games selected for a class should allow learners to think and learn about the interrelationship between events seen within the game. In games, interconnectivity of events is depicted in the form of reactions across the game that depend on the player's actions and choices (Harker-Schuch et al., 2020; Liarakou et al., 2012; Yoon et al., 2017). The reactions may be favorable or disastrous as shown by the increase or decrease in scores and the levels of progress in the game. This experience helps learners understand the real-world ramifications of appropriate and harmful behaviors.
5. Emotional involvement and engagement with game elements promotes affective learning (Janakiraman, 2020; Ninaus et al., 2019). Hence teachers should select games where game mechanics focus on empathy building that will engage players emotionally. This feeling of empathy for game elements may get transferred to real-world situations because players get a first-hand perspective of the consequences of harmful activities (Janakiraman, 2020).
6. Visualizations in games provide situated and meaningful contexts (Gee, 2008; Liarakou et al., 2012; Wu & Huang, 2015; Harker-Schuch et al., 2020), while also providing a discovery learning environment (Tan & Biswas, 2007). Players can learn from visual cues and examine the consequences of actions in real-time in DGBL environments. In real life, however, results of negative actions occur after a long time, and learners may not be able to connect the cause and the result (Arbuthnott, 2009; Tucker, 1999). During a post-game debrief session, teachers can explain that in real-life harmful effects are visible only when they become disastrous.
7. Most games are based on an interesting narrative or story (Dillon, 2005). These stories have to be realistic and relevant to immerse players in the learning experience so that they are connected to the plot and can feel the tension (Janakiraman, 2020).

The advantage of implementing games in virtual classes is that direct supervision by teachers is not required while providing a cost-effective near-authentic virtual learning experience. In addition to providing cognitive knowledge, DGBL environments can emotionally engage players by producing a feeling of empathy (Belman & Flanagan, 2010; Greitemeyer et al., 2010). Moreover, behavioral learning from games could translate into real life daily behaviors because well-practiced behaviors can become habitual, and the processing that initiates and controls their performance becomes automatic guiding future behaviors (Ouellette & Wood, 1998). When behaviors are repeated, behavioral responses are automatically activated because habits are mentally represented as goal-action links. These behavioral intentions may simulate goal-directed automaticity and help form habits (Aarts & Dijksterhui, 2000). Therefore, behaviors in games that are designed to be repetitive and goal-directed may get transferred to real life and be retained. Even learners discussing their game play experience and talking about pro-environmental behaviors with others is considered as a behavioral change (Ballantyne & Packer, 2005) and is also a form of social learning (Watson et al., 2018). Hence game features have the potential for helping achieve the ultimate goal of teachers, that is promote cognitive, affective, behavioral, and social learning among students.

Game Features that Facilitate Attitudinal Learning

Most often, game features usually seen in recreational games are incorporated into educational games designed for subjects like language literacy, social studies, science, and math. When games are designed for attitudinal learning, game features that target attitudes have to be integrated along with regular game features. This section explores how game mechanics or game features can promote attitudinal learning besides making a game motivating, engaging, challenging, and attractive to young people to enhance the learning process.

Plass et al. (2013) recommend game designers to be aware of instructional design principles and learning theories. Also, game designers should incorporate pedagogical support material that can help instructors facilitate their class discussions (Echeverría et al., 2011). Unlike recreational games, motivation to win is not the only goal in attitudinal learning. Winning does not mean reaching the final level as in recreational games, such as reaching the top of a mountain or locating a treasure chest. Similarly, winning is not about answering all the questions correctly while crossing an obstacle course or playing a matching game, like in normal educational games. In attitudinal learning games, winning refers to actual changes in attitudes and behaviors and does not depend on the levels reached, the numeric score, or time spent on the game. Hence, seductive features that may cause cognitive overload (Adams et al., 2012; Mayer, 2005; Sweller, 2010) and distract from the learning are not recommended in attitudinal learning games (Janakiraman, 2020).

Considering ESE, as an example of a socio-scientific topic, the following section explains how the EnerCities game (designed specifically for ESE) provided "rich learning content" and took into consideration the "ease of use" to increase learning effectiveness (Cheng et al., 2013).

Enercities

EnerCities is a 3D game created by Qeam with support from the University of Twente, Netherlands, and other partners to be implemented for ESE in European schools (Knol & DeVries, 2010; Knol & De Vries, 2011). In the game, players are required to perform activities that are not part of their daily lives. They have to build a sustainable city with happy citizens by implementing renewable and non-renewable sources of energy and be economical and eco-friendly at the same time. All of these parameters can be monitored by the player using indicators at the bottom of the screen. See Figure 1 and Figure 2 that are screenshots obtained at two different instances when the game was in progress.

A score board and a Level bar indicate a player's progress in the game. Other indicators include icons on environmentally friendly building upgrades; monitors that reveal the amount of fossil fuels, electric power, and financial resources that are available to a player; a tree icon denoting green cover; options for different types of buildings; and an emoji that indicates the happiness levels of citizens in the virtual city under construction.

The virtual instructor or agent featured on the left-hand side of the game screen provides useful tips about how to use the available resources and balance game play. These tips direct players to consult the resource monitors before performing any action, helping them in decision-making and critical thinking. Real-world scenarios in the game enables systems thinking, and encourages problem solving and discovery learning through active engagement. The visualizations, text prompts at the 'points of action,' and monitors further promote cognitive learning.

Figure 1. Screenshot showing a text prompt about the importance of forests

Game features such as the emojis (citizens' happiness) and the tree icon (green cover) engage players emotionally. Players in studies that implemented the EnerCities game described how the sad emojis and reddening of the tree icon pushed them to stop certain actions, rethink strategies, and take alternate actions even if it resulted in losing some points (Janakiraman, 2020). They realized the effects of harmful human activities instantly. Hence affective learning was promoted by creating empathy towards the human and non-human world, through situating the learning in immersive environments.

Based on the biological basis of learning and memory formation in humans, Friedlander et al. (2011) said that optimal learning occurs when planned redundancies, repetition, multiple modalities, rewards, active engagement, and visualizations are present in instruction. In EnerCities, players are allowed to level up as they added new buildings and increased the population of the virtual city. At each level players perform similar actions gaining more practice with behaviors within the game, that may be effective in producing behavioral learning. Players are hence, testing their behaviors in safe, simulated conditions by active engagement, live action, and practice. At higher levels, EnerCities offers more sophisticated renewable energy options as rewards when players perform correct actions in order to motivate them. These options help upgrade multistory buildings, that further help players increase their city's population. This option in turn allows players to level up and increase their scores that further motivates them to continue playing the game.

In the process, players can learn about alternate energy options, the scale and scope of implementation, locations to install renewable energy generation, population dynamics, and how to construct energy efficient buildings. The game reveals to players that fossil fuels may be necessary to balance the economy and that they should not become extinct. Actions and consequences reveal the inter-connected nature of the environment and seeing the harmful consequences help players to alter behaviors in the game.

Figure 2. Screenshot showing text prompts from the virtual agent and other monitors

This information helps them realize that in real-life it is not possible to alter an action and that once environmental degradation sets in, it will take decades to rectify the effects (Janakiraman, 2020). The behaviors within the game may encourage learners to perform pro-environmental behaviors more readily in their daily lives. The cyclic process, repetitive actions, and reward system engages and motivates learners to play the game and in turn ensures attitudinal learning and are hence necessary features that have to be present in games.

The following could be used as a checklist of game features to evaluate games designed for attitudinal learning when teachers select games for their classes to promote cognitive, affective, and behavioral learning. They also guide instructional designers to design attitudinal learning games.

Attitudinal learning games for socio-scientific topics must:

- provide multiple lessons within the same game incorporated in a storyline that engages players in an enjoyable environment (cognitive learning).
- provide prompts through a virtual agent to improve learning and performance in the game (cognitive learning).
- incorporate several monitors that indicate levels of resources and other parameters (cognitive learning).
- provide dedicated monitors to show improvement/progress .
- make the game look realistic to create an emotional connection to real-life scenarios (affective learning).
- include dedicated icons that reveal the harmful effects of wrong actions to promote empathy (affective learning).

- reveal reactions for every action performed by the player to display consequences in real time that serves as instant feedback (affective learning).
- provide several opportunities to repeat an action but with added variety to engage players and encourage behaviors (behavioral learning).
- offer rewards to motivate players to complete the game with enthusiasm.
- avoid seductive features that cause cognitive overload, e.g., flashing icons, bright colors.
- create game mechanics that do not instruct directly but provides a discovery learning environment.

The process of taking repetitive actions, planned redundancies, multiple modalities, rewards, active engagement, and visualizations (Friedlander et al., 2011) when present in games are effective in promoting attitudinal learning. Games that include the above features when administered in a virtual environment can take on the role of a teacher, provide a discovery learning environment, and enable players to take ownership for their learning when implemented purposefully.

DGBL and Instructional Strategies for the Virtual Classroom

Implementing DGBL in an online attitudinal learning course is different from implementing games in a face-to-face course. When students play a game under direct supervision by a teacher it is possible to monitor their performance as they play the game, direct their attention to the text and virtual agent prompts available within the game, answer questions, provide clarifications, provide tips about strategies they could perform, and see the extent of their progress. However, in a virtual classroom, students are playing the game by themselves and hence teachers have to perform sufficient prework and scaffolding to ensure a holistic attitudinal learning experience for students. The following are recommendations for teachers to implement for facilitating attitudinal learning using DGBL in virtual classrooms.

1. When implementing games, teachers should first take into consideration technology availability. Uninterrupted internet connectivity at home may be a problem with concerns about affordability, cyber safety, and parental permission when online games are considered.
2. Teachers should launch an internet search for games that align with their course objectives and try to procure it in shareable formats. Social media, for example Facebook, is also an active source to learn about new games that have been used successfully by teachers. Appendix 1 provides a list of games and social media links pertaining to various socio-scientific topics.
3. The identified game (that incorporates the features discussed above) can be shared with students on the course learning management system or through email. Teachers may choose to share the game using the chat feature during online web conferences, but this is best done in addition to a more permanently accessible format. Students may not save the link and then be unable to access the game after the online class ends.
4. Playing the game at least once helps teachers in being prepared to implement the game in their classes. Teachers can get familiar with the storyline, game mechanics, levels in the game, and learn a few scoring strategies. This action is similar to preparing for a traditional class. However, implementing a game saves a lot of time for instructors in explaining real life dynamics about the topic, because the game will provide the knowledge required in stages as the player progresses through the game.

5. Game play can be demonstrated by the teacher using pre-recorded videos or a live gameplay session to explain game mechanics. Demonstrations of games are available online or are offered by game designers that can be used as an instructional activity by teachers. This instruction is more effective in a synchronous online class where engaging students on a web conferencing platform is challenging. Although discovery learning is a better instructional strategy, sometimes demonstrating game mechanics benefits players. Their learning experience is facilitated by reducing the time needed to acclimatize with the game environment that may sometimes frustrate learners (Janakiraman, 2020).
6. Before introducing the game, teachers should provide an overview of game goals and explain why students are expected to play the game. A debrief session following game play will enable instructors to answer questions and explain the actions and reactions in the game. This two-step facilitation process provides an opportunity for social learning among students and between students and the teacher and provides an opportunity for the instructor to check that attitudinal learning was successful. This type of facilitation is a powerful instructional strategy because games enhance learning when supported by instructor supervision and guidance (Watson & Fang, 2012).

If students are actively mentored about their behaviors in the real world by adults at home after the online learning experience, then attitudinal learning is even more effective and lifelong. Similar to how teachers provide updates about learning regarding other subjects, they can update parents/adults about the goals of the attitudinal learning topic. This recommendation will provide additional opportunities for demonstration and practice of the new learning in the home environment following the virtual classroom experience. Researchers have found that when players performed real-world, socially, and academically meaningful activities after playing the Quest Atlantis digital game, their social awareness, commitment to communities, and learning was improved (Barab et al., 2005). The above instructional strategies and recommendations for the use of DGBL can be applied to other socio-scientific topics as well where attitudinal learning is the goal (Janakiraman, 2020; Janakiraman et al., 2021).

ASSESSING ATTITUDINAL LEARNING IN VIRTUAL CLASSROOMS

Demonstrating cognitive knowledge about socio-scientific issues on quizzes and exams is not enough since students may still remain insensitive to the issue itself. With respect to environmentally friendly attitudes and behaviors, Harraway et al. (2012) noted that teachers can assess knowledge using these conventional methods but will not be able to assess values, attitudes, and behaviors. Unlike cognitive knowledge gain, attitudinal learning is not a one-time change, rather it should be a lifelong change in attitudes and behaviors in real life.

This recognition highlights the challenges that exist when implementing games for attitudinal learning in virtual classrooms because teachers are unable to observe and assess actual behaviors that indicates retention of learning. For example, in an environmental science face-to-face course, behaviors such as electricity and water consumption, and being mindful in using paper and other resources can help gauge attitudinal learning. This observation is not possible in a virtual learning environment. Furthermore, progress in the game and high scores, as indicated by the scoreboards generated by the game, do not indicate changes in attitudes and behaviors. Learners need to be assessed through activities outside the game environment.

Questionnaires and Interviews

Given these limitations in online learning using games, one feasible method of assessing attitudinal learning in virtual classrooms is through online questionnaires. Research studies have used different instruments to measure attitudes and behaviors concerning socio-scientific topics. Some instruments are based on: (1) the Attitudinal Learning Instrument (ALI; Watson et al., 2018) that measures cognitive, affective, behavioral, and social learning and (2) the Theory of Planned Behavior (TPB; Ajzen, 2019) to measure attitude formation and behavioral intentions that predicts actual behaviors. The ALI and TPB instruments can be adapted for any attitudinal learning topic. Different socio-scientific topics have surveys designed specifically for the topic. For example, to measure environmental attitudes, there is the New Ecological Paradigm scale (NEP; Dunlap et al., 2000). To gain a deeper and more holistic understanding, teachers can also interview students using conferencing platforms to learn about their learning experience to evaluate the attitudinal learning from the game. See Appendix 2 for example instruments and interview questions that can be used to assess attitudinal learning.

Real-World Application

As stated earlier, game scores and progress in the game do not indicate successful attitudinal learning. Learners have to be assessed based on their behaviors in the real-world. Barab et al. (2005), in their study using the Quest Atlantis game, showed that when students performed socially responsible meaningful activities in the real-world, their social awareness, commitment to communities, and learning improved. Quest Atlantis adopted a socially responsive design and included EcoWorld quests that promoted learning about environmental sustainability. In an online class, teachers can assign tasks that can be performed in the real world.

"Performing original work is the ultimate final exam. It fully connects learning to the life of the learner," (Horton, 2012, p. 54). In his book E-learning by Design, Horton (2012) emphasizes the need to provide *absorb, do, and connect* activities to enhance virtual learning experiences. 'Absorb' activities include presenting the content by the teacher in the form of readings, stories, or game play demonstrations. Then students perform the 'do' activities like playing games by themselves for practice and discovery as discussed in previous sections of this chapter. Finally, the 'connect' activities enable learners to connect their learning to the real world while they ponder and question. These activities can be original work such as drawings, job aids, research essays, stories, and other forms of creative expression.

Attitudinal learning can also be demonstrated through the creation of Public Service Announcements (PSAs). This demonstration can be in the form of infographics created using PowerPoint or Picktochart or can be presented as short PSA audio tracks. This activity encourages students to address a real issue to create awareness, in addition to encouraging a behavioral change. These actions not only replace quizzes but can also highlight critical thinking and problem-solving skills.

The tasks and evidence of completion that constitute the original work should match grade levels. A variety of activities can be used to assess attitudes by giving students the freedom to select an activity based on their interest. For example, when using games for environmental sustainability education, middle school students can provide evidence in the form of journal writing that lists the pro-environmental actions they performed or share photos of their actions. High school students can be asked to participate in community projects, design a digital campaign to increase awareness of paper/energy/water consumption, and maintain a journal of energy consumption based on the monthly bills of the household. Students can be encouraged to participate in volunteering work when time permits.

Screenshots, pictures, PSAs, and other digital artifacts serve as application-based evidence of actual behaviors and attitudinal learning gained from the game. They can be shared with the class on online discussion forums on the course learning management system for peer review, or shared with the teacher through email, Google Drive, or Dropbox as evidence of task completion. These activities and modalities of assignment submission facilitate the assessment of attitudinal learning using games in virtual classrooms.

Teachers can judge attitudinal learning from the submitted original work that serves as evidence for the connect/application activity using their expertise and experience. Real world application activities cannot be judged only by the aesthetics of the submission. Teachers can assess submissions based on the demonstration of attitudinal learning as well as some or all of the 21st century skills: creativity, critical thinking, communication, collaboration, and digital literacy (information, media, and technology literacy). While peer reviewing of each other's work provides opportunities for communication and collaboration, creating PSAs and other digital artifacts demonstrate creativity, critical thinking, digital literacy, and media literacy. A customized rubric that addresses the various components of the assignment will help teachers assess student work.

In acknowledgement of impactful work and to motivate learners, teachers can share the best works widely on a neighborhood website, school community, or local newspaper. Some course management systems incorporate a digital badge system which can be leveraged to create and award special badges for students' original work. This replaces grades, encourages lifelong behaviors, and also serves to motivate students to complete activities and perform better even when learning in isolation in virtual classrooms.

Finding one game that addresses all the components of the topic is sometimes difficult. For example, considering ESE, games that are designed to teach mindful daily behaviors like reducing energy usage and climate change are easily available. However, games connected to other aspects of sustainability such as sustainable travel, water consumption, and food waste, that can provide more insights into the importance of pro-environmental attitudes and behaviors, are rare. Teachers can explore various games and select ones that meet their course objectives and implement them throughout the course. Teachers from different schools can crowdsource games utilizing social media to create a repository of games that they can implement for teaching various topics. See Appendix 1 for examples of games on various socio-scientific topics and social media pages devoted to educational games.

CONCLUSION

Educators and instructional designers can achieve instructional objectives by using the motivating properties of games (Adams et al., 2012). It is even more imperative in virtual classrooms where teachers have to engage their students using interactive activities because garnering attention on an online medium and motivating students to listen to lectures is challenging. However, similar to other subjects, playing a game on an attitudinal change topic is not a standalone activity to teach everything about the topic. Digital Game-Based Learning (DGBL) is an effective support tool to traditional forms of attitudinal instruction because it is an engaging, motivating, challenging, and an attractive platform, where players can test their behaviors and see the consequences of harmful behaviors immediately. Attitudinal learning from games has the potential to be retained longer because of the experiences within the game that mimic real life. Games get players immersed in a scenario that they feel responsible for and helps them see the consequences of actions immediately. In visually observing a scenario, making decisions, and performing actions, players are able to see the results in a very short period of time. As seen in the example of student interactions with the EnerCities game above, strategizing game play based on game monitors enhances critical thinking and problem-solving capabilities. This kind of learning experience is possible within a game and difficult to execute in traditional forms of face-to-face and online instruction.

Considering the growing popularity of digital games, it is wise to leverage games to provide knowledge as an experience that is situated in scenarios (Gee, 2008). Games provide multiple opportunities to evaluate the impact of decisions in a safe environment that can persuade young learners to execute correct attitudes and behaviors. In the instruction of socio-scientific topics where attitudinal learning is the goal, digital games can serve as persuasive pedagogical tools. As a digital resource, games can be easily implemented in virtual classrooms. Games can also be implemented virtually during emergency school shutdowns caused by inclement weather or other exigencies to make up for the lost school hours. Teachers can introduce the lesson during online synchronous classes and implement games that address the topic as a practice activity to reinforce the learning.

On the whole, combining introductory online presentations, digital game-based learning activities, online post-game debrief sessions, and real-world application-based tasks enhances the virtual learning experience of students. Games play a major role in making the learning process engaging, motivating, attractive, rewarding, and challenging (Chen et al., 2019; Prensky, 2003; Troussas et al., 2019) in addition to promoting situated understandings (Gee, 2008). Games have been shown to increase emotional engagement, memory consolidation and learning retention (Ninaus et al., 2019) and are easy to use (Cheng et al., 2013). Moreover, this effort reduces zoom fatigue, allows discovery learning, and supports creativity and critical thinking.

ACKNOWLEDGMENT

My sincere thanks to Dr. Sunnie Lee Watson, Dr. William R Watson, Dr. Timothy Newby, and Dr. Daniel P Shepardson, who guided my research projects that contributed to this chapter.

This research received no specific grant from any funding agency in the public, commercial, or not-for-profit sectors.

REFERENCES

Aarts, H., & Dijksterhuis, A. (2000). Habits as knowledge structures: Automaticity in goal-directed behavior. *Journal of Personality and Social Psychology*, *78*(1), 53–63. doi:10.1037/0022-3514.78.1.53 PMID:10653505

Adams, D. M., Mayer, R. E., MacNamara, A., Koenig, A., & Wainess, R. (2012). Narrative games for learning: Testing the discovery and narrative hypotheses. *Journal of Educational Psychology*, *104*(1), 235–249. doi:10.1037/a0025595

Ajzen, I. (2019). *Constructing a theory of planned behavior questionnaire*. Retrieved from https://people.umass.edu/aizen/pdf/tpb.measurement.pdf

Arbuthnott, K. D. (2009). Education for sustainable development beyond attitude change. *International Journal of Sustainability in Higher Education*, *10*(2), 152–163. doi:10.1108/14676370910945954

Arora, N. K. (2018). Environmental Sustainability - necessary for survival. *Environmental Sustainability*, *1*(1), 1–2. doi:10.100742398-018-0013-3

Ballantyne, R., & Packer, J. (2005). Promoting environmentally sustainable attitudes and behavior through free-choice learning experiences: What is the state of the game? *Environmental Education Research*, *11*(3), 281–295. doi:10.1080/13504620500081145

Barab, S., Thomas, M., Dodge, T., Carteaux, R., & Tuzun, H. (2005). Making learning fun: Quest Atlantis, a game without guns. *Educational Technology Research and Development*, *53*(1), 86–107. doi:10.1007/BF02504859

Barclay, P. A., & Bowers, C. (2020). Associations of subjective immersion, immersion subfactors, and learning outcomes in the revised game engagement model. In Learning and Performance Assessment: Concepts, Methodologies, Tools, and Applications (pp. 957-968). Hershey, PA: IGI Global. doi:10.4018/978-1-7998-0420-8.ch044

Bell, D. (2016). Twenty-first century education: Transformative education for sustainability and responsible citizenship. *Journal of Teacher Education for Sustainability*, *18*(1), 48–56. doi:10.1515/jtes-2016-0004

Belman, J., & Flanagan, M. (2010). Designing games to foster empathy. *International Journal of Cognitive Technology*, *15*(1), 11.

Brinkmann, R. (2020). Connections in environmental sustainability: Living in a time of rapid environmental change. In Environmental Sustainability in a Time of Change. Palgrave Studies in Environmental Sustainability (pp. 1-8). Palgrave Macmillan.

Buchanan, J., Schuck, S., & Aubusson, P. (2016). In-school sustainability action: Climate clever energy savers. *Australian Journal of Environmental Education*, *32*(2), 154–173. doi:10.1017/aee.2015.55

Chen, C. H., Law, V., & Huang, K. (2019). The roles of engagement and competition on learner's performance and motivation in game-based science learning. *Educational Technology Research and Development*, *67*(4), 1–22. doi:10.100711423-019-09670-7

Cheng, Y. M., Lou, S. J., Kuo, S. H., & Shih, R. C. (2013). Investigating elementary school students' technology acceptance by applying digital game-based learning to environmental education. *Australasian Journal of Educational Technology*, *29*(1). Advance online publication. doi:10.14742/ajet.65

Cordano, M., Welcomer, S. A., & Scherer, R. F. (2003). An analysis of the predictive validity of the new ecological paradigm scale. *The Journal of Environmental Education*, *34*(3), 22–28. doi:10.1080/00958960309603490

Cuccurullo, S., Francese, R., Passero, I., & Tortora, G. (2013). A 3D serious city building game on waste disposal. *International Journal of Distance Education Technologies*, *11*(4), 112–135. doi:10.4018/ijdet.2013100108

Department of Education. (n.d.). *Indiana Academic Standards for Environmental Science*. https://www.doe.in.gov/sites/default/files/standards/resource-guides-environmental-science-070516.pdf

Dillon, T. (2005). *Adventure games for learning and storytelling*. UK, Futurelab Prototype Context Paper: Adventure Janakiraman. doi:10.1080/00219266.2012.688848

Dunlap, R. E., Van Liere, K. D., Mertig, A. G., & Jones, R. E. (2000). New trends in measuring environmental attitudes: measuring endorsement of the new ecological paradigm: a revised NEP scale. *The Journal of Social Issues*, *56*(3), 425–442. doi:10.1111/0022-4537.00176

Echeverría, A., García-Campo, C., Nussbaum, M., Gil, F., Villalta, M., Améstica, M., & Echeverría, S. (2011). A framework for the design and integration of collaborative classroom games. *Computers & Education*, *57*(1), 1127–1136. doi:10.1016/j.compedu.2010.12.010

Fabricatore, C., & López, X. (2012). Sustainability learning through gaming: An exploratory study. *Electronic Journal of e-Learning*, *10*(2), 209–222.

Fielding, K. S., & Head, B. W. (2012). Determinants of young Australians' environmental actions: *The role of responsibility attributions, locus of control, knowledge, and attitudes*. Environmental Education Research, *18*(2), 171–186. doi:10.1080/13504622.2011.592936

Friedlander, M. J., Andrews, L., Armstrong, E. G., Aschenbrenner, C., Kass, J. S., Ogden, P., Schwartzstein, R., & Viggiano, T. R. (2011). What can medical education learn from the neurobiology of learning? *Academic Medicine*, *86*(4), 415–420. doi:10.1097/ACM.0b013e31820dc197 PMID:21346504

Gagne, R., Briggs, L., & Wagner, W. (1992). *Principles of instructional design*. Wadsworth/Thomson Learning.

Gee, J. (2008). Game-like learning. In P. Moss, D. Pullin, J. Gee, E. Haertel, & L. Young (Eds.), *Assessment, equity, and opportunity to learn (Learning in doing: Social, cognitive, and computational perspectives)* (pp. 200–221). Cambridge University Press., doi:10.1017/CBO9780511802157.010

Gough, C. (October 15, 2020). *Number of video gamers worldwide 2015-2023*. https://www.statista.com/statistics/748044/number-video-gamers-world/

Greitemeyer, T., Osswald, S., & Brauer, M. (2010). Playing prosocial video games increases empathy and decreases schadenfreude. *Emotion (Washington, D.C.)*, *10*(6), 796–802. doi:10.1037/a0020194 PMID:21171755

Griset, O. L. (2010). Meet us outside! *Science Teacher (Normal, Ill.)*, *77*(2), 40–46.

Gros, B. (2014). Digital games in education: The design of games-based learning environments. *Journal of Research on Technology in Education*, *40*(1), 23–38. doi:10.1080/15391523.2007.10782494

Habgood, M. J., & Ainsworth, S. E. (2011). Motivating children to learn effectively: Exploring the value of intrinsic integration in educational games. *Journal of the Learning Sciences*, *20*(2), 169–206. doi:10.1080/10508406.2010.508029

Harker-Schuch, I. E., Mills, F. P., Lade, S. J., & Colvin, R. M. (2020). CO2peration–Structuring a 3D interactive digital game to improve climate literacy in the 12-13-year-old age group. *Computers & Education*, *144*, 103705. doi:10.1016/j.compedu.2019.103705

Harraway, J., Broughton, F., Deaker, L., Jowett, T., & Shephard, K. (2012). Exploring the use of the revised New Ecological Paradigm scale (NEP) to monitor the development of students' ecological worldviews. *The Journal of Environmental Education*, *43*(3), 177–191. doi:10.1080/00958964.2011.634450

Holbert, N., & Wilensky, U. (2019). Designing educational video games to be objects-to-think-with. *Journal of the Learning Sciences*, *28*(1), 32–72. doi:10.1080/10508406.2018.1487302

Hong, J. C., Hwang, M. Y., Chen, Y. J., Lin, P. H., Huang, Y. T., Cheng, H. Y., & Lee, C. C. (2013). Using the saliency-based model to design a digital archaeological game to motivate players' intention to visit the digital archives of Taiwan's natural science museum. *Computers & Education*, *66*, 74–82. doi:10.1016/j.compedu.2013.02.007

Horton, W. (2012). *E-learning by Design* (2nd ed.). Pfeiffer.

Huckle, J. (2012). Towards greater realism in learning for sustainability. In A. Wals & P. Corcoran (Eds.), *Learning for sustainability in times of accelerating change* (pp. 35–48). Wageningen Academic Publishers. doi:10.3920/978-90-8686-757-8_01

Hungerford, H. R., & Volk, T. L. (1990). Changing learner behavior through environmental education. *The Journal of Environmental Education*, *21*(3), 8–21. doi:10.1080/00958964.1990.10753743

Janakiraman, S. (2020). *Exploring the effectiveness of digital games in producing pro-environmental attitudes and behaviors* (Doctoral dissertation). Purdue University Graduate School.

Janakiraman, S., Watson, S. L., & Watson, W. R. (2018). Using game-Based learning to facilitate attitude change for environmental sustainability. *Journal of Education for Sustainable Development*, *12*(2), 176–185. doi:10.1177/0973408218783286

Janakiraman, S., Watson, S. L., & Watson, W. R. (2021b). Exploring the effectiveness of digital games in producing pro-environmental behaviors when played collaboratively and individually: A mixed methods study in India. *TechTrends*, *65*(3), 331–347. doi:10.100711528-020-00571-8 PMID:33521794

Janakiraman, S., Watson, S. L., Watson, W. R., & Newby, T. (2021a). Effectiveness of digital games in producing environmentally friendly attitudes and behaviors: A mixed methods study. *Computers & Education*, *160*, 104043. doi:10.1016/j.compedu.2020.104043

Janakiraman, S., Watson, S. L., Watson, W. R., & Shepardson, D. P. (2021c). Exploring the influence of digital games on environmental attitudes and behaviours based on the new ecological paradigm scale: A mixed-methods study in India. *Journal of Education for Sustainable Development*, *15*(1), 1–28. doi:10.1177/0973408221997844

Johnson, A. (2019, November 11). Using empathy games in the social sciences. *Educause Review*. https://er.educause.edu/articles/2019/11/using-empathy-games-in-the-social-sciences

Kamradt, T. F., & Kamradt, E. J. (1999). Structured design for attitudinal instruction. In C. M. Reigeluth (Ed.), *Instructional design theories and models: A new paradigm of instructional theory* (Vol. 2, pp. 563–590). Lawrence Erlbaum Associates.

Karl, T. R., & Trenberth, K. E. (2003). Modern global climate change. *Science*, *302*(5651), 1719–1723. doi:10.1126cience.1090228 PMID:14657489

Knol, E., & De Vries, P. W. (2010). EnerCities: educational game about energy. *Proceedings CESB10 Central Europe towards Sustainable Building*. Retrieved from http://www.qeam.com/docs/Knol_Vries_de_EnerCities-educational-game-about-energy-CESB10.PDF

Knol, E., & De Vries, P. W. (2011). EnerCities, a serious game to stimulate sustainability and energy conservation: Preliminary results. *eLearning Papers, 25*, 1-10. https://papers.ssrn.com/sol3/papers.cfm?abstract_id=1866206

Lee, J. (2020, November 17). A neuropsychological exploration of zoom fatigue. *Psychiatric Times*. https://www.psychiatrictimes.com/view/psychological-exploration-zoom-fatigue

Lewis, J., & Leach, J. (2006). Discussion of socio-scientific issues: The role of science knowledge. *International Journal of Science Education, 28*(11), 1267–1287. doi:10.1080/09500690500439348

Liarakou, G., Sakka, E., Gavrilakis, C., & Tsolakidis, C. (2012). Evaluation of serious games, as a tool for education for sustainable development. *European Journal of Open, Distance and E-learning, 15*(2).

Mayer, R. E. (2005). Cognitive theory of multimedia learning. The Cambridge handbook of multimedia learning, 41, 31-48.

Meya, J. N., & Eisenack, K. (2018). Effectiveness of gaming for communicating and teaching climate change. *Climatic Change, 149*(3-4), 319–333. doi:10.100710584-018-2254-7

Next Generation Science Standards. (n.d.). *HS. Human Sustainability*. https://www.nextgenscience.org/topic-arrangement/hshuman-sustainability

Next Generation Science Standards. (n.d.). *MS-LS2-1 Ecosystems: Interactions, Energy, and Dynamics*. https://www.nextgenscience.org/pe/ms-ls2-1-ecosystems-interactions-energy-and-dynamics

Nickerson, R. S. (2003). *Psychology and Environmental Change*. Lawrence Erlbaum Associates.

Ninaus, M., Greipl, S., Kiili, K., Lindstedt, A., Huber, S., Klein, E., Karnath, H.-O., & Moeller, K. (2019). Increased emotional engagement in game-based learning–A machine learning approach on facial emotion detection data. *Computers & Education, 142*, 103641. doi:10.1016/j.compedu.2019.103641

Ouellette, J. A., & Wood, W. (1998). Habit and intention in everyday life: The multiple processes by which past behavior predicts future behavior. *Psychological Bulletin, 124*(1), 54–74. doi:10.1037/0033-2909.124.1.54

Perrin, A. (2018). *5 facts about Americans and video games*. https://www.pewresearch.org/fact-tank/2018/09/17/5-facts-about-americans-and-video-games/

Plass, J. L., O'keefe, P. A., Homer, B. D., Case, J., Hayward, E. O., Stein, M., & Perlin, K. (2013). The impact of individual, competitive, and collaborative mathematics game play on learning, performance, and motivation. *Journal of Educational Psychology, 105*(4), 1050–1066. doi:10.1037/a0032688

Prensky, M. (2003). Digital game-based learning. *Computers in Entertainment, 1*(1), 21–21. doi:10.1145/950566.950596

Ratcliffe, M., & Grace, M. (2003). *Science education for citizenship: Teaching socio-scientific issues*. McGraw-Hill Education.

Sadler, T. D. (2009). Situated learning in science education: Socio-scientific issues as contexts for practice. *Studies in Science Education*, *45*(1), 1–42. doi:10.1080/03057260802681839

Schroeder, R. (2021, January 20). Zoom fatigue: What we have learned. *Inside Higher Ed.* https://www.insidehighered.com/digital-learning/blogs/online-trending-now/zoom-fatigue-what-we-have-learned

Seaman, J. E., Allen, I. E., & Seaman, J. (2018). *Grade Increase: Tracking Distance Education in the United States*. Babson Survey Research Group.

Sinatra, G. M., Kardash, C. M., Taasoobshirazi, G., & Lombardi, D. (2012). Promoting attitude change and expressed willingness to take action toward climate change in college students. *Instructional Science*, *40*(1), 1–17. doi:10.100711251-011-9166-5

Sweller, J. (2010). Element interactivity and intrinsic, extraneous, and germane cognitive load. *Educational Psychology Review*, *22*(2), 123–138. doi:10.100710648-010-9128-5

Tan, J., & Biswas, G. (2007). Simulation-based game learning environments: Building and sustaining a fish tank. *IEEE Xplore Digital Library*, 73-80. . doi:10.1109/DIGITEL.2007.44

Troussas, C., Krouska, A., & Sgouropoulou, C. (2019). Collaboration and fuzzy-modeled personalization for mobile game-based learning in higher education. *Computers & Education*, 1–18. doi:10.1016/j.compedu.2019.103698

Tsai, C. Y. (2018). The effect of online argumentation of socio-scientific issues on students' scientific competencies and sustainability attitudes. *Computers & Education*, *116*, 14–27. doi:10.1016/j.compedu.2017.08.009

Tucker, P. (1999). A survey of attitudes and barriers to kerbside recycling. *Environmental and Waste Management*, *2*(1), 55–63.

UNEP. (2020). *COVID-19: Four sustainable development goals that help future-proof global recovery*. https://www.unenvironment.org/news-and-stories/story/covid-19-four-sustainable-development-goals-help-future-proof-global

UNESCO. (n.d.). *Education for Sustainable Development*. https://en.unesco.org/themes/education-sustainable-development/what-is-esd

van der Meij, H., Albers, E., & Leemkuil, H. (2011). Learning from games: Does collaboration help? *British Journal of Educational Technology*, *42*(4), 655–664. doi:10.1111/j.1467-8535.2010.01067.x

Wang, J., Geng, L., Schultz, P. W., & Zhou, K. (2019). Mindfulness increases the belief in climate change: The mediating role of connectedness with nature. *Environment and Behavior*, *51*(1), 3–23. doi:10.1177/0013916517738036

Watson, S. L., Watson, W. R., & Tay, L. (2018). The development and validation of the Attitudinal Learning Inventory (ALI): A measure of attitudinal learning and instruction. *Educational Technology Research and Development*, *66*(6), 1601–1617. doi:10.100711423-018-9625-7

Watson, W. R., & Fang, J. (2012). PBL as a framework for implementing video games in the classroom. *International Journal of Game-Based Learning*, *2*(1), 77–89. doi:10.4018/ijgbl.2012010105

Watson, W. R., Mong, C. J., & Harris, C. A. (2011). A case study of the in-class use of a video game for teaching high school history. *Computers & Education*, *56*(2), 466–474. doi:10.1016/j.compedu.2010.09.007

Wen, C. T., Chang, C. J., Chang, M. H., Chiang, S. H. F., Liu, C. C., Hwang, F. K., & Tsai, C. C. (2018). The learning analytics of model-based learning facilitated by a problem-solving simulation game. *Instructional Science*, *46*(6), 847–867. doi:10.100711251-018-9461-5

Wu, K., & Huang, P. (2015). Treatment of an anonymous recipient: Solid-waste management simulation game. *Journal of Educational Computing Research*, *52*(4), 568–600. doi:10.1177/0735633115585928

Yang, J. C., Chien, K. H., & Liu, T. C. (2012). A digital game-based learning system for energy education: An energy COnservation PET. *Turkish Online Journal of Educational Technology*, *11*(2), 27-37.

Yoon, S. A., Anderson, E., Koehler-Yom, J., Evans, C., Park, M., Sheldon, J., Schoenfeld, I., Wendel, D., Scheintaub, H., & Klopfer, E. (2017). Teaching about complex systems is no simple matter: Building effective professional development for computer-supported complex systems instruction. *Instructional Science*, *45*(1), 99–12. doi:10.100711251-016-9388-7

Zumbach, J., Rammerstorfer, L., & Deibl, I. (2020). Cognitive and metacognitive support in learning with a serious game about demographic change. *Computers in Human Behavior*, *103*, 120–129. doi:10.1016/j.chb.2019.09.026

KEY TERMS AND DEFINITIONS

Creativity: Creativity involves making something new and valuable and it includes both intangible things like an idea, music or scientific theory, or it can be tangible things like a painting, poem, or story. It also includes ideas presented in innovative ways that can solve practical problems.

DGBL: Digital game-based learning refers to the implementation of a computer-based game into a learning environment where the game serves as the medium of instruction.

PLS-SEM: Partial least squares-structural equation modelling enables researchers to analyze relationships simultaneously in complex models that comprise of multiple constructs, indicator variables and structural paths. The analysis does not make any distributional assumptions on the data.

APPENDIX 1

Additional Resources: Attitudinal Learning Games

1. Explore earth and space. NASA. https://spaceplace.nasa.gov/menu/play/
2. Empathy games in the Social Sciences.
    a. http://playspent.org/html/
    b. https://store.steampowered.com/app/227080/Papo__Yo/
3. Games4Sustainability. Teaching, Learning and Practicing Sustainability Through Serious Games. https://games4sustainability.org/gamepedia/
4. Links to 10 empathy games. Help students understand empathy with these interactive games. https://www.commonsense.org/education/articles/13-top-games-that-teach-empathy
5. National Geographic. https://kids.nationalgeographic.com/games/action-and-adventure/recycle-roundup-new/
6. National Oceanic & Atmospheric Administration. https://sanctuaries.noaa.gov/education/sam/welcome.html
7. The Cloud Institute for Sustainability Education. Play the fish game. https://cloudinstitute.org/fish-game
8. The Oregon Trail mobile game. https://apps.apple.com/us/app/the-oregon-trail-american-settler/id460062770
9. World Rescue. http://worldrescuegame.com/
10. Three sustainability related educational games. https://medium.com/the-wild-thoughts-blog/top-3-video-games-about-sustainability-f0d53a195c0
11. ECO. Build a civilization in a simulated ecosystem. https://play.eco/#tree
12. Aven Colony. https://store.steampowered.com/app/484900/Aven_Colony/
13. Raft. https://store.steampowered.com/app/648800/Raft/
14. Social media pages devoted to educational games:
    a. https://www.facebook.com/groups/learningwithgames/announcements
    b. https://www.facebook.com/WebAdventuresRice
    c. https://www.facebook.com/ScienceGameCenter
    d. https://www.facebook.com/sciencegamesforkids
    e. https://www.facebook.com/NASA.STI.Program
    f. https://www.facebook.com/cloudinstitute

APPENDIX 2

A: Questionnaire for ESE Based on the Attitudinal Learning Instrument (ALI)

All items are to be answered on a 5-point scale (1 – 'strongly disagree' to 5 – 'strongly agree')

1. I learned new information about the environment.
2. I am more knowledgeable about environmental sustainability.

3. I picked up new ideas about environmental sustainability.
4. I feel excitement about the topic of environmental sustainability.
5. I feel eager to learn more about environmental sustainability.
6. I feel passionate about the environment.
7. My behaviors related to the environment have changed.
8. I did something new related to environmental sustainability.
9. I made changes to my behavior related to environmental sustainability.
10. I do things differently now with respect to environmental sustainability.
11. I talk to others about environmental sustainability.
12. I educate others about environmental sustainability.
13. I am confident discussing about environmental sustainability with others.
14. I connect with other people regarding environmental sustainability.
15. I intend to switch off my PC when not in use.
16. I intend to reduce my water usage.
17. I expect to recycle waste as much as possible.
18. I intend to switch off the lights when not required.

B: Questionnaire for ESE Based on the Theory of Planned Behavior (TPB)

All items are to be answered on a 5-point scale (1 – 'strongly disagree' to 5 – 'strongly agree')

1. Turning my laptop off whenever I leave my desk is worthwhile.
2. It is necessary to use less water.
3. Recycling waste as much as possible is worthwhile.
4. Switching off the lights when I leave an unoccupied room is good.
5. People I live with (like parents and other family members) expect me to use less water.
6. My friends recycle waste as much as possible.
7. I switch off the lights when I leave an unoccupied room.
8. I am confident that I can use less water.
9. Switching off the lights when leaving a room is within my control.
10. Whether I recycle waste is entirely up to me.
11. I intend to switch off my PC when not in use.
12. In the past week I have reduced my water usage.
13. I expect to recycle waste as much as possible.
14. I intend to switch off the lights when not required.

C: Example Questions for Evaluation

1. Tell me about your experience while playing the game - Free response.
2. Did you know about this topic before playing the game? - Give examples.
3. Talk about your learning experience - Free response!
4. What are your perceptions now? - Give examples
5. What did you do after playing the game? - Give examples

Chapter 13
Building Community in Online Learning Environments:
Strategies for High School Teachers

Jason Anthony Singh
University of Toronto, Canada

ABSTRACT

This self-study assesses the impact on classroom communities using distance learning activities. Five activities used in the author's high school science classes during the COVID-19 pandemic are analyzed based on a bilateral framework interweaving transactional distance (student-teacher interactions) and social interaction (student-student interaction). A reflective narration of activity development leads to a discussion of the effects of activity design on student-teacher and student-student interactions. The intersection between these interactions serves as a foundation for analyzing their impact on the classroom community. A predominant theme is the psychological separation students face when learning remotely and how activity design can intensify or diminish this perceived detachment. This chapter provides an exemplar for other educators to consider how transactional distance and social interaction play a role in the development of their own classroom communities.

INTRODUCTION

Teachers have been called upon to pivot in these unprecedented times amid the COVID-19 pandemic, which disrupted the learning of nearly 1.5 billion students worldwide in March 2020 and continues to prevent schools from providing uninterrupted in-person learning (United Nations Educational, Scientific and Cultural Organization, 2020). With the uncertainty and mixed messaging that spread around the world, many teachers were thrust into distance learning without sufficient professional development. In addition to the stressors of personal health, family health and safety, social distancing, and mask wearing, teachers faced the additional challenge of bringing students together in an unfamiliar environment and engaging them in learning (Darling-Hammond, 2020). While many teachers have been able to create

DOI: 10.4018/978-1-7998-7222-1.ch013

these environments for their students, this chapter helps teachers begin or continue to move beyond the "physical" creation of an online learning environment to the creation of a classroom community.

In this chapter, the author describes a range of activities successfully facilitated at a private high school in Toronto, Canada. The author uses these activities to explore key strategies for educational practitioners to build a sense of community within a distance learning model, regardless of the geographical location of their students. Readers will recognize distance learning as a psychological separation between the learner and instructor, rather than solely a spatial separation (Moore, 2018). This separation, termed transactional distance, is "a space of potential misunderstanding between the inputs of instructor and those of the learner" (Moore, 1997, p. 22). The acknowledgement of transactional distance allows educators to utilize differentiated instruction to promote the well-being and academic success of their students by creating a positive classroom community. Moreover, readers will learn that an increase in social interaction does not necessarily lead to a decrease in transactional distance. This chapter is guided by the following key questions:

1. How do the levels of transactional distance between learners and their teacher and social interaction between learners and their peers vary between distance learning activities?
2. How do varying levels of transactional distance and social interaction assist teachers in building a sense of community within a distance learning model?

The present analysis benefits high school teachers, middle school teachers, teacher researchers, and educational designers and developers who are creating and facilitating distance learning environments across a range of subjects. Moreover, teachers using any learning management system (LMS) can implement these activities, as they are sufficiently broad in scope to be transferable to a wide range of contexts. Finally, readers may also consider their own pedagogy through the lens of transactional distance, allowing them to construct activities that better support student well-being and academic performance in distance learning environments.

This chapter begins with a review of the literature on building classroom community and the distance learning model. Next, the author conceptualizes transactional distance as a framework to analyze a narrative of five activities personally used in a distance learning environment created due to the COVID-19 pandemic. Subsequently, an analysis integrating current research considers the five activities based on how students engage with each other, how students engage with the teacher, and the intersection between social interaction and transactional distance towards the development of the classroom community. After reflecting on the concerns and limitations of this chapter, the closing remarks suggest directions for future examination of the use of transactional distance and social interaction in the design of distance learning activities to solidify this chapter's position in the literature.

BACKGROUND

When accounting for both student autonomy (Weiss & Belland, 2018) and e-learning context (Benson & Samarawickrema, 2009), online learning activities can build community in ways that mirror in-person learning. Earlier work by Rovai (2001) identifies four tenants that underlie the manifestation of classroom community:

1. A feeling of belonging
2. A feeling that members matter to one another and to the group
3. The presence of duties and obligations to each other and to the school
4. The presence of shared expectations that members' educational needs will be met through commitment to shared goals (Rovai, 2001, p. 34)

Rovai (2001) urged education practitioners to "move away from imparting feelings of isolation and move toward generating greater feelings of community and personal attention" (p. 33). While earlier distance learning models have focused on the logistics of delivering content online (Martin et al., 2013), which continue to evolve alongside new technologies including LMS and content management systems (CMS) (Mesfin et al., 2018), fingerprints of the four tenets can be seen on several distance learning models aimed at moving teachers beyond the mere delivery of content. The Mediating Teacher Model guides the teacher to "encourage the students to feel confident… mediate for meaning and strengthen the motivation to learn" (Ben-Chayim & Offir, 2019, p. 8). The Learning Experience Theory labels the teacher as a mediator, focusing on intentionality, reciprocity, meaning, transcendence, feelings of competence and regulation of behaviour in students (Ben-Chayim et al., 2020). Thus, in both models, the teacher is thought to act as a mediator who bridges the gap between students and content, rather than solely delivering that content.

In addition to establishing the teacher as a mediator, several studies (Huang et al., 2016) ground the distance learning model in Moore's Theory of Transactional Distance, which considers distance learning as a pedagogical concept in addition to a geographic separation of teachers and learners. Moore (1997) identifies transactional distance as a continuous and relative variable, rather than a discrete and absolute term. Thus, rather than using a defined scale, as is common with distance measurements, transactional distance considers pedagogical strategies in relation to each other, within specific educational contexts. Correspondingly, one strategy of grouping transactional distances for comparisons is by considering learner-instructor, learner-content, and learner-learner interactions, which are all deemed to be essential in distance education (Chen, 2001). Both learner-instructor and learner-learner interactions are elements of instructional dialogue, identified by Moore (1997) as "purposeful, constructive, and valued by each party" (p. 23). Thus, instructional dialogue is critical to enhance the classroom community.

However, researchers have argued that distance learning, especially asynchronous distance learning, lacks adequate opportunity for student-teacher and student-student dialogue, leading to a lack of in-depth understanding of the learned material (Ben-Chayim et al., 2020). Moreover, from the student perspective, the Quality of Experience (QoE) Prediction Model establishes extrinsic (external) and intrinsic (self-determined) motivators to be key factors in driving learning behaviours (Malinovski et al., 2014). Taken together, these models emphasize the need to develop pedagogy that prioritizes interactions which satisfy student needs while lowering the transactional distance between students and teachers through enhanced opportunities for interaction.

A recent study of 381 secondary-school students in South Korea found that classroom social climate was a significant predictor of learners' basic psychological needs, which include autonomy, competence, and relatedness (Joe et al., 2017). Unfortunately, few studies analyze specific learning activities that address these needs. An earlier study at the post-secondary level of 201 undergraduate and graduate students across three universities in the United States argues that "how a course is delivered is not as critical to learner satisfaction as how it is structured and how opportunities for interaction are build into it" (Stein et al., 2005, p. 114). The researchers found that learner-instructor and learner-learner interactions that were initiated by students, rather than the instructor, significantly contributed to student satisfaction with perceived knowledge gained (Stein et al., 2005). In a more recent Delphi study of 23 instructional designers from across the United States, Wheatley (2016) argued that instructional design strategies should support interaction with the teacher, other learners, and the course content to reduce transactional distance. However, these suggestions were not accompanied with specific activities that could be implemented.

At the K–12 level, a study involving 12 teachers in a cyber-charter school in Pennsylvania discovered that an interactive whiteboard, along with collaboration tools including a chat box, digital polling, and breakout sessions, were the most common learning activities and assessment tools employed in distance education (O'Brien & Fuller, 2018). In another study, Clyde (2016) considered how course designers approach learner/content interactions in virtual high school classrooms. Clyde (2016) found that their use of synchronous and asynchronous learning activities focused around providing ample opportunity for varying forms of dialogue, enabling learner autonomy, and providing course structure to facilitate learning. Although none of the 10 participants were aware of transactional distance, the author found that these foci were based on Moore's theory of Transactional Distance.

Consequently, this chapter satiates the need for analyses of specific activities based on their transactional distance within a distance learning environment and the resultant influence on the classroom community. Moore's Theory of Transactional Distance is used as a basis for this analysis, with further considerations for the interaction between students.

FRAMEWORK AND METHODOLOGY

The activities presented in this chapter are categorized by the degrees of transactional distance and social interaction. Following Moore's (1997) conception of transactional distance as a relative variable, the author uses Park's (2011) framework of categorizing educational activities based on high and low transactional distance and individualized versus social activity. Accordingly, each activity is analyzed based on both the psychological distance separating teachers from their students and the level of social interaction between students and their peers.

Both types of interactions are representative of the cognitive separation between the self and other. Cognitive separation can be "temporal, spatial, hypothetical, or social, so that any target that exists beyond the ego is experienced as existing at some psychological distance from the self" (Kalkstein et al., 2016, p. 2). An example can be seen in mentally constructing, or *construing*, the idea of being healthy. A low-distance construal may consider specific behaviours, such as choosing to eat oatmeal for breakfast instead of a donut, while a high-distance construal may focus on the conception of being healthy as a personal trait, or considering the reasons why being healthy is important. Thus, a low-level construal is concrete, local, and contextualized, whereas a high-level construal is abstract, global, and decontextualized (Kalkstein et al., 2016). Thus, an analysis of the transactional distance and social interaction provides insight into students' construing during each activity.

Earlier work in the use of technology in the classroom offers admonition "not to focus on what the technology can do, but rather on the effect of that technology on 'learner actions, activities, intentions and goals as they engage in learning'" (Beckman, 2010, p. 162). In congruence with this advice, the author uses a self-study methodology to offer insight into the design and implementation of five distance learning activities. A self-study methodology is used to intentionally and systematically inquire into one's own practice for the purpose of improvement by examining personal values and professional work (Hamilton et al., 2008).

Multiple resources are sourced to develop the narrative, including a teaching journal documenting conversations and observations with students, student video responses, student discussion posts, an optional end-of-course survey, and personal reflections. Since these sources were designed for use as formative assessments, they were not tested for validity or reliability as research tools. Accordingly, the use of multiple sources allows for the triangulation of data, enhancing the validity of the qualitative methodology employed in this chapter (McMillan & Wergin, 2010).

Congruent with self-study, the following narrative of five distance learning activities provide the first level of interaction between the author and his students, while his personal reflections offer a second level of interaction beyond the surface story, termed reflexivity (Hamilton et al., 2008). By bracketing his position, the reader is provided with additional information to consider as they compare the use of each activity in their own setting (McMillan & Wergin, 2010). Consequently, this chapter provides readers with an understanding of the context and reasoning behind the author's decisions and actions, allowing the determination of the transferability of the findings to personal practices.

FIVE ACTIVITIES TO BUILD CLASSROOM COMMUNITY

The author and 34 high school students engaged in the following five activities from March through December of 2020 during the COVID-19 pandemic. The activities were used across a range of Grade 11 and Grade 12 Science courses, including Biology, Chemistry, and Physics. Each activity was implemented within a distance learning model with students from Canada, South Korea, and China. The author facilitated 3-4 classes during each quadmester using an LMS. The high school, located in an urban setting in Toronto, Canada, is attended predominantly by international students seeking admission into post-secondary institutions in Canada, the United States, and the United Kingdom. International students live in homestay near the school with an appointed guardian, while local students live in the city with their parents and guardians.

The school runs on a quadmester system from September to June, with an additional summer semester over July and August. The third quadmester, which runs from February to mid-April, was interrupted in March of 2020 by the COVID-19 pandemic. Two days prior to the start of the March Break, the Ontario government announced the termination of in-person classes in all schools across the province. The order called for an immediate shift to distance learning for two weeks following the March Break, which was later extended to May 31st, and finally to the end of the school year (Ontario Newsroom, 2020). In response to the initial announcement, the school's international students rushed to book flights home to be with their families before further travel restrictions were imposed, while teachers prepared materials and activities on the LMS to facilitate their classes following the March Break. As no training was provided, teachers spent most of this time uploading documents, recording videos, and transitioning assessments into digital versions.

Once classes resumed, after a subjectively short week, both students and teachers began to navigate the complexities of distance learning. Of significant hinderance to learning were logistical issues such as device availability and broadband connectivity; pedagogical issues such as providing adequate pathways through learning for students engaging with the course material at different paces and providing sufficient variety in daily learning activities; and social issues such as opportunities for students to collaborate with the teacher, collaborate amongst their peers, and for teachers to engage in and model professional collaboration amongst staff. In response to these identified challenges, the author endeavoured to create and implement activities that would allow students to employ both low- and high-level construals by utilizing low- and high-transactional distance alongside both individualized and social activities.

The activities presented in this chapter were used to create a sense of community by allowing students to engage with course concepts and each other beyond the traditional written discussion posts often observed in distance learning models. To adequately compare the levels of transactional distance and social interaction, the author includes written discussion posts as a baseline to allow readers to analyze the differences in categorization. The remaining activities utilize different forms of digital storytelling, a technique that allows students to communicate personal narratives in the classroom using voice, sound, and images (Walters and Gillern, 2018).

Within the author's context, a combination of synchronous and asynchronous activities was used, largely due to the time zone differences between students engaging in the course from different areas of the world. The following sub-sections describe the creation and implementation of five activities: written discussion posts and replies; video discussion posts and replies; thought experiments (coupled with think-pair-share); podcasts; and group stories.

Written Discussion Posts and Replies

Written discussion posts and replies are traditionally used in online environments to facilitate interactions between students and teachers as well as amongst students. Generally, the teacher poses a series of questions and sets a deadline by which students are required to post their replies. A further deadline is set for students to reply to 2–3 of their peers. The teacher may also post personal replies to stimulate interaction or consolidate learning. Thus, written discussion posts and replies are used as an asynchronous learning activity. Ideally, the teacher uses written discussion posts in the hopes that conversations flourish as students become deeply engaged in the topics being discussed.

However, in implementing this strategy, very few instances of discussion beyond the requirements were observed across all the author's classes. By only completing what was required, students were losing the opportunity to engage in authentic conversations both about the course material and about themselves. Without these gateways, it became apparent that the classroom community did not translate well to asynchronous virtual learning, as the first group of students were initially together in-person in March of 2020.

In the end-of-course survey for the first term, several students described the challenges of this transition: "I think sometimes it would be good to communicate with each other in real-time using zoom"; "I think students would benefit if you [the teacher] could set a specific time period for q&a [question-and-answer] sessions on platforms like google hangouts." It was evident that the students were proficient in the technology and wanted to see it utilized to its full potential.

Another student described the experience pessimistically, stating "It is hard to get feedback and give some questions but these things are unavoidable." Thus, while students were able to maintain existing relationships developed before the transition to distance learning, the physical and social separation led to the deterioration of these associations.

Compounding the issue of disconnectedness was the looming fourth term where the students would not have had prior opportunity to meet in-person, especially considering that many students were joining the school for the first time. As one student put it, the "most difficult thing was meeting people, I want to

Building Community in Online Learning Environments

socialize with teacher and classmates." Consequently, the author, with feedback from his fellow teachers and his support network comprised of educators and researchers in other institutions, endeavoured to implement additional pedagogical strategies to address these feelings of disconnectedness experienced by students. The resultant activities are presented chronologically as they were implemented across the author's courses through term four in April 2020, the summer term in July and August 2020, and terms one and two of the 2020–2021 school year beginning in September 2020.

Video Discussion Posts and Replies

Video discussion posts and replies are a modification of written posts that provide the ability to augment the content using both auditory and visual stimuli. In considering differentiated instruction, using video seemed like a logical transition to amplify the capture of student voice. Generally, these posts are used in a similar manner as written posts, with students answering questions and replying to each other in an asynchronous fashion. The author used these posts to elicit opinions on science topics in current news, including technologies or treatments being researched and developed. Examples include the emergence of Space Tourism as an industry in Physics, and the development of the COVID-19 vaccine in Biology.

At the outset, most students prepared written responses and read them like a script. To elicit more natural responses to mimic the in-person environment, the author used these as teachable moments to give suggestions on what makes a good presentation. Through consistent modeling and reminders to engage with the audience by making eye contact and considering both body language and the use of nonverbal gestures, subsequent posts saw students relying less on their written notes. Arguably, this action demonstrated an increase in confidence over time as students became more comfortable and practiced with recording themselves, which was observed in each subsequent quadmester. Notably, students who took a second or third course involving video posts demonstrated an immediate ability to create videos in which they connected with the audience. New students were able to use these as exemplars to quickly develop their own techniques in delivering video messages, including those that enhanced their engagement with the audience as discussed previously.

Through class discussions, students noted that while video posts could be recorded on their cell phones or laptops, they generally required more preparation as they needed to consider both the content of the post and the presentation of their ideas. This recognition may have contributed to the author's observation that most of the replies to the initial video posts remained in written form, even though video replies were given as an option. Indeed, even the author's replies were in written form due to the time investment required in rehearsing and producing video responses. Thus, while videos did allow students to see each other by adding a layer of interaction, the issue of building relationships remained. The next activity attempted to address this situation by giving students a common issue to work on collaboratively.

Thought Experiments (Coupled with Think-Pair-Share)

Thought experiments are used both synchronously and asynchronously to promote the critical analysis of a concept or address misconceptions in prior knowledge. The teacher poses a question or a series of questions that allow students to create connections between course concepts and a topic of interest. From prior experience, open-ended questions were generally more effective at generating a variety of responses. For example, a thought experiment with a Chemistry class in the electrochemistry unit asked students, "Why is gold so expensive in comparison to other metals?" Students were provided with a list of the price of gold over the last several years, alongside the prices of silver and aluminum. After a few minutes of student discussion, responses, which were shared with the entire class, included the aesthetic appeal, malleability to shape into jewelry, and, importantly, the longevity of gold due to its inability to be oxidized by oxygen in the air. Thus, the thought experiment not only led students towards the realization of how different substances undergo oxidation-reduction reactions – a key learning objective in electrochemistry – but also allowed students to consider the economic value of different materials and their physical properties, broadening their understanding of how these elements are intertwined. Thus, the question allowed students to consider their prior knowledge and, importantly, take other students' ideas into consideration.

When used asynchronously, required readings or videos can accompany the question to ensure students are informed and thereby equipped to approach the question from multiple perspectives. Since asynchronous learning potentially allows students to work at their own pace, the complexity and depth of the question can be enhanced. When used synchronously, the thought experiment was modified using the think-pair-share strategy. Students were presented with a question that ought to be answered without requiring additional resources. These questions were often opinion questions, or problems to solve that consolidated prior learning, such as the price of gold question. Students were given a set amount of time to consider the question independently, then additional time to pair with each other to discuss their thoughts. In a virtual environment, this was performed by using breakout rooms in a video conference platform, or the chat feature on the LMS. Finally, students reunited, and partners shared their thoughts with the class, allowing the teacher to elaborate on or question student responses to enrich the discussion.

The use of the think-pair-share strategy was based on previous observations of the confidence-building elicited in students by being able to vocalize their ideas and receive feedback prior to sharing with the class. The idea originated when the author reflected on the asynchronous strategies used in recently taken Massive Open Online Courses (MOOCs), including the consumption of static course material and the use of written discussion posts and quizzes to engage with that material. Unfortunately, the pre-recorded videos in MOOCs do not provide the opportunity to challenge students to address current misunderstandings that were not identified when the content was originally created. Accordingly, thought experiments and the accompanying think-pair-share activity provided a strategy for the teacher to respond to student misconceptions without the need for extensive preparation. Through conversations and observations, the teacher can identify prior misconceptions that were creating difficulties in learning and pose questions or problems that required students to address these misconceptions. Thus, thought experiments allowed for a dynamic classroom that considered specific challenges that students experienced, as well as provided flexibility to address the changing needs of students that accompanies each iteration of the course.

Podcasts

Podcasts are pre-recorded audio clips created by one or more students that are focused on a specific topic or set of concepts and ideas. While podcasts are asynchronous to the class, they allow for synchronous work between a pair or group of students. Podcasts allow students to vocalize their opinions and ideas while receiving immediate feedback from their peers. In a distance learning environment, podcasts can imitate the interactions in group work, allowing students to enhance their interpersonal skills.

Moreover, while previous activities focused on providing opportunities for enhanced student interaction, podcasts were primarily introduced to provide students with agency over the choices they could make in the classroom. Students chose group members and a topic to analyze and evaluate based on success criteria that ensured they connected their ideas to learning goals in the course. For example, students in Physics were asked to choose a technology based on the principles of light, such as lasers or Li-Fi, explain how it operates based on course concepts, and evaluate it based on its positive and negative effects on individuals, societies, and the environment. This opportunity provided students with a choice of topic, which contrasts with previous activities in which only the mode of presentation was differentiated.

Podcasts were also given as an option for the final project in all courses, which required students to choose a topic that could be connected to a minimum of two of the five units in the course. In reflection of her Chemistry 12 course, a student identified her favorite assignment as the final project:

I liked connecting the material we learned in class with topics that I am interested in. I also liked being able to introduce those topics the way I wanted to format it (and worrying less about meeting specific grading criteria and covering topics that I'm supposed to be covering).

Thus, following the gradual release of responsibility (Webb et al., 2019), podcasts, among other options, afford students the opportunity to choose a topic of personal interest while demonstrating their knowledge and understanding of course concepts.

Group Stories

Group stories are synchronous activities that can be used for any fictional or non-fictional topic (Singh, 2020). The teacher begins the story by introducing characters, a setting, and a conflict. At a critical point, often before the next noun or verb, the teacher stops and selects a student to continue to the story. Once students have added to the story, they are similarly stopped before a noun or verb, and the story continues to be passed along until every student has contributed. While initially created for elementary school students, this activity was thought to be a creative way to discuss the legal and ethical issues surrounding many technologies and treatments in Science education.

Group stories became possible when the school decided to incorporate bi-weekly synchronous sessions into the distance learning model in September 2020. These sessions were held in the late evening in Toronto, on different days of the week for different courses, allowing students from South Korea and China to join on the following morning. While the school's intention was to use these as question-and-answer sessions, the author used this opportunity to further enhance the classroom community. The group story accomplished this action by providing students the opportunity to share their opinions while accepting the opinions of others.

An example of a group story is the use of CRISPR-Cas9, a tool used in biotechnology to edit individual genes towards the treatment of chronic conditions such as Alzheimer's disease or cancer. In one story, Andrea ended up in the hospital two months after trying the treatment for her terminal cancer, which had re-emerged. As she was still on probation at her new job, she did not have health care coverage, and "could not cover the ridiculous hospital bills." Her brother, who had convinced her to get the treatment, felt an enormous amount of guilt, putting strain on their relationship. In the story, students introduced issues of accountability for unintended side effects of the treatment, its pricing, and the personal choice surrounding experimental treatments. There were several segments of the story where the author took an additional turn to offer some new information, as students were unaware of the costs and length of cancer treatment. In the post-story class discussion, students voiced their support and disapproval for CRISPR-Cas9 gene therapy. Ultimately, the consensus was that it should be a personal choice, with acknowledgement of the difficulties created in conditions leading to impaired reasoning or judgment, such as with Alzheimer's disease (National Institute on Aging, 2017).

Though not attempted by the author, group stories can also be performed asynchronously using a series of written, verbal or video responses. However, the pressure and urgency of real-time storytelling, in addition to the comradery experienced during the activity, leads to more genuine stories. This argument stems from the observations during the initial written discussion posts in which students completed no more than what was required of them. Similarly, the use of asynchronous group stories may lead students to research for the perfect answer, rather than allow the story to blossom organically. Consequently, an important consideration for the teacher is choosing topics the students are well-versed in, while also providing additional information in preparation for and during the activity as required.

DISCUSSION AND ANALYSIS

The activities presented vary in levels of both transactional distance and social interaction (Table 1). Activities with high-level transactional distance presented minimal opportunities for students to engage with the teacher through the learning process, while teacher observations of the student learning process, conversations with students, and consolidation of students' ideas were prevalent in activities with low-level transactional distance. The levels of social interaction were similarly dichotomous, with activities completed individually providing scarce opportunity for students to engage with their peers, while those identified as social created multiple opportunities for students to negotiate and communicate their ideas with each other.

Table 1. Transactional distance and social interaction levels based on Park (2011)

	Level of Transactional Distance	**Level of Social Interaction**
Written Discussion Posts and Replies	• High • Students search for information and gain knowledge without the intervention of the teacher	• Individual • Posts and replies are completed independently • Limited opportunities for social experiences
Video Discussion Posts and Replies	• High • Students search for information and gain knowledge without the intervention of the teacher	• Individual • Posts and replies are completed independently • Limited opportunities for social experiences
Thought Experiments (coupled with Think-Pair-Share)	• Low • Specific learning outcomes are not defined at the beginning of the activity • The teacher observes and contributes to student conversations (synchronous) • The teacher compiles student input to consolidate student learning	• Individual (thought experiment) • Ideas are considered independently • Social (think-pair-share) • Ideas are negotiated through collaboration with peers, but communicated individually
Podcasts	• High • The teacher has minimal involvement	• Social • Ideas are negotiated through collaboration with peers and communicated together
Group Stories	• Low • Specific learning outcomes are not defined at the beginning of the activity • The teacher compiles student input to consolidate student learning	• Social • Ideas are communicated collaboratively

Notably, the level of transactional distance did not necessarily correspond with the level of social interaction, creating a variety of learning scenarios. These variations in the levels of transactional distance and social interaction are examined in two areas of analysis: how students engage with each other and how students engage with the teacher. Next, the intersection between both types of engagements serves as a foundation to analyze their impact on the classroom community.

How Students Engage with Each Other

Chronologically, the author introduced activities that attempted to shift the level of social interaction from individual to social, promoting interpersonal experiences among students. While written discussion posts and replies remained individual activities, corresponding to a lack of social interaction, the author believed that video discussions would allow students to enhance their interactivity by moving beyond certain limitations of written posts. Just as the reader of this chapter would have difficulty describing the author's personality based solely on the writing, written posts prevent students from using social communication cues such as tone, body language, and facial expressions to confer meaning. Thus, the introduction of video posts allowed students the opportunity to employ social communication cues through their recordings.

The thought experiment, coupled with the think-pair-share pedagogical strategy, was introduced to provide students with the opportunity to enhance peer-to-peer interaction. Unlike discussion posts, which remained on the LMS to be viewed throughout a course, this low-stakes strategy allowed students to contemplate their thoughts (the "think") and negotiate their ideas (the "pair") before communicating their conclusions to the class (the "share"). This strategy is in line with calls in the literature to shift the learning process in the digital world from overrating specific material, such as PowerPoint files, to problem-based learning. By doing so, students are afforded the opportunity to "select the essential and meaningful [sources of information], which can be organized into visual and verbal mental models with appropriate association links" (Velichova et al., 2020, p. 1634). Thought experiments accomplish this idea by providing students with an open-ended question accompanied by a wide array of information, ranging from text and diagrams to videos and sound clips. Coupled with the pedagogical strategy of a think-pair-share, this activity allows students to transition their level of social interaction beyond the individual, engaging with the ideas of their peers to determine the level of congruence with their own mental models.

The final two activities, podcasts and group stories, were both introduced to enhance the level of social interaction, albeit in different ways. Podcasts allowed students to fully engage with a partner or a small group while remaining isolated from the rest of the class. This ability to interact with their peers in a sustained manner allowed students to build motivation when engaging in achievement-related contexts such as a podcast assessment. The pursuit of motivation, termed a social achievement goal, was achieved by "developing and sustaining high-quality friendships and improving social competence" (Makara & Madjar, 2015, p. 474). Thus, the informal interactions required to negotiate and develop a podcast provided the peer-to-peer interactions necessary to pursue this social achievement goal alongside academic goals. Moreover, since the creation of a podcast took place in a low-stakes environment, students were able to build confidence in their academic goals alongside these social achievement goals. Indeed, social achievement goals have been identified as predictors in adaptive interactions with peers and seeking out academic help at school (Makara & Madjar, 2015).

Conversely, group stories are a high-stakes social event, as students share a response in front of the class with no preparation time. While the group story is a social activity, it is most effective if adequate consolidation occurs after the narrative, allowing students to openly discuss their thoughts and ideas. In doing so, students can organize their mental models, as discussed previously, while exploring new avenues of idea-building, and perhaps building their relationships in the process.

Overall, student-student interaction was increased with each successive activity. However, another consideration is the level of transactional distance between the student and the teacher, discussed in the following section.

How Students Engage with the Teacher

Unlike social distance, the transactional distance between students and the teacher did not follow a linear progression. Both written and video discussion posts and replies maintained a high transactional distance, as students principally engaged with the material independently from the teacher. Additionally, students' use of asynchronous feedback from the teacher sustained the high transactional distance.

The introduction of the thought experiment, coupled with the think-pair-share strategy, employed connective instruction by lowering the student-teacher transactional distance. This situation led to positive relationship-building, in which the teacher supported both student learning and their individuality, the latter termed *humanizing* the relationship (Garcia-Moya et al., 2020). In a qualitative study of 42 students from England and Spain, humanizing the student-teacher relationship favored connectedness, as students responded positively to teachers straying from the neutral, de-personalized interactions they related with negative student-teacher relationships (Garcia-Moya et al., 2020).

While the final two activities increased social interaction, they differed in their levels of transactional distance. Podcasts, like discussion and video posts, have a high transactional distance, as students predominantly negotiate and produce the final product in the absence of the teacher. Conversely, group stories lower transactional distance, as the teacher can interact directly with students in a consolidating group discussion, or, as described in the example used, interject with additional information to support students' learning. The presence of enhanced teacher support increases the levels of personal mastery and learning-oriented goals, thus supporting student learning (Rolland, 2012).

The Intersection Between Social Interaction and Transactional Distance

The previous analyses demonstrate that an increase in social interaction does not necessarily correlate to a decrease in transactional distance. Consequently, the intersection between social interaction and transactional distance is an important consideration when designing distance learning activities that will impact the classroom community and ultimately student well-being. In comparison to face-to-face learning, online learning places a higher cognitive load and attention-splitting problems on students as there are fewer instances of natural communication. A study by Blau et al. (2017) argues that while the cognitive aspect of learning can be enhanced in online learning, both the social and emotional aspects of learning suffer. Socially, students lose the naturalness associated with face-to-face interactions, as online learning is highly structured and does not provide opportunity for distraction nor the ability to convey social communication cues. Emotionally, students perceive online learning as more difficult and boring, largely due to the repetitiveness of tasks and the limitations in opportunities to engage with each other.

These limitations were observed in both written and video discussion posts in which a lack of social interaction and a high transactional distance engendered a lack of classroom community, evidenced by students' frustrations with receiving teacher support and feeling disconnected from their peers. Thus, the classroom community, which considers connective instruction, allows students to relate to the content, the teacher, and the instruction of the class (Cooper, 2004), in addition to teacher-student relationships, which have been shown to strongly associate with student engagement (Roorda et al., 2011). Calderon and Sood (2018) identify three parameters to evaluate the use of asynchronous online discussions: contextual learning, interpersonal communication, and meta-learning. While the discussion posts succeeded in contextual learning (content mastery) and often included evidence of meta-learning (reflecting on one's own learning), video posts did not provide any opportunities to engage in peer-to-peer interaction beyond what written posts enabled. Indeed, due to the investment of time and energy required for video responses, all students, and even the author, defaulted to written posts when replying to each other. Thus, the investment required to produce videos undermined the intention of enhancing interactivity, ultimately leading to its failure for this purpose.

Consequently, the remaining activities were introduced to eliminate the repetitiveness and perceived tediousness of online learning using differentiated instruction (DI). DI can adjust a common task, introduce specific resources to students that need them, or individualize practice to support a diverse group of learners (Bondie, 2019). Both the thought experiments and group stories adjusted a common task (discussion posts) by transitioning student responses from individual to social and providing instructor support. The combination of a higher level of social interaction with a lower transactional distance increased both student-teacher and student-student interactions.

As discussed previously, both types of interactions contribute to the positive social climate in a learning environment. Thus, through opportunities to engage with both the teacher and their peers, students were able to develop academic competence through contextual learning, while simultaneously enhancing their relatedness to each other through peer-to-peer interaction. As Joe et al. (2017) argue:

Positive student-teacher relationships support the idea that students' perceptions that their teacher cares about their learning and is invested in their well-being and success, on the one hand, and their feelings of support, caring, and encouragement from peers, on the other, will promote the necessary need satisfaction. (p. 139)

Consequently, teachers need to consider both student-teacher and student-student relations to increase social interaction and decrease transactional distance, ultimately leading to a positive influence on the classroom community.

CONCERNS AND LIMITATIONS

In addition to the challenges identified within the analysis, several other key concerns remain to be recognised when considering the transactional distance and social interaction in distance learning classroom activities. These include students' self-regulation, autonomy, motivation, and context, all of which play a role in the classroom community as well as students' academic success and social well-being.

Self-regulation, which is the ability to set, monitor, and reflect on academic goals, is crucial in distance learning environments, as instructors are limited in their opportunities to monitor and support students in ways that parallel in-class learning. Especially when engaged in asynchronous distance learning, students are faced with competition for their attention from the ever-expanding social media multiverse, which include Instagram, Snapchat, TikTok, YouTube, Twitter, Discord, Twitch, and Tumblr, among many others. In fact, according to a study by the Pew Research Center (Lenhart, 2015), 92% of adolescence in the United States use social media daily, with 24% of these teens reporting being online almost constantly. While strategies like scaffolding have been suggested to aid in students' development of self-regulation (Bol & Garner, 2011), it remains unclear how an enhanced level of social interaction and a decreased level of transactional distance influence the development of self-regulation skills.

As discussed previously, the activities presented in this chapter addressed students' basic psychological needs, including academic competence and relatedness. However, to satisfy a student's basic psychological needs, autonomy needs to be enabled within the classroom environment. One strategy used by the author was providing students with choices in their topics as well as modes of presentation on their final projects and podcasts, thereby empowering them to achieve their personal learning goals. The presence of choice also enhanced student motivation, as evidenced by a student's identification of the final project as her favorite, because she was not focused on "meeting specific grading criteria and covering topics that I'm supposed to be covering." Thus, while some activities incorporated higher-level thinking, thereby eliciting increased engagement (Raković et al., 2020), this chapter did not attempt to empirically measure the impact of these activities on the classroom community, as investigated in previous studies (Huang et al., 2016).

A limitation of this chapter is how the use of activities that consider the levels of social interaction and transactional distance are influenced by student traits and context. For example, previous studies at the post-secondary level found that extroverts prefer communicating their ideas through revealing forms of communication, including audio and video, while introverts prefer text-based interaction (Blau & Barak, 2012). Another avenue of exploration found a positive alignment between students' academic achievements and both transactional distance theory and Bloom's taxonomy theory (Abuhassna et al., 2020). Additionally, many other aspects of context may influence how students are (dis)engaging with distance learning, including the learning infrastructure, access issues, teacher support, and technology proficiency (Benson & Samarawickrema, 2009), indicating the multifaceted worth of applying contextual analyses to future research on this topic.

Further, the COVID-19 pandemic has shifted the world to online learning unexpectedly, forcing unwilling learners to engage in distance education. A recent study of 2824 secondary and post-secondary students found that "most of the respondents (53,4%) do not agree with the statement that the online learning should be preferred more than traditional [in-person] education" (Velichova et al., 2020, p. 1636). Taken together, it is important to acknowledge that although this chapter has demonstrated how activities can be designed and implemented with consideration for both student-student and student-teacher interactions, it should be regarded as a steppingstone into a much larger area of research of pedagogical strategies and student realities that need to be considered when building classroom community in online learning environments.

CONCLUDING REMARKS AND FUTURE DIRECTIONS

The emergence of the COVID-19 pandemic has shifted the world to online learning, generating a renewed interest in distance learning. Even though the transition to online learning has been abrupt and uncomfortable, it has also presented a unique opportunity for students and educators to engage in the distance learning model. While this chapter provides insight into the design and implementation of distance learning activities through a consideration of transactional distance and social interaction, it only sends out a ripple into a much larger ocean of research. Several areas remain to be studied to analyze the relationships between transactional distance, social interaction, and different components of the distance learning model.

First, a significant gap in the literature that remains to be filled is the use of specific distance learning activities in their ability to lower transactional distance within and across varying contexts. Admittedly, the author did not design the activities presented in this chapter with transactional distance in mind. Instead, it was realized through reflective research, then later analyzed through the self-study methodology. Therefore, further studies providing resources for teachers or methods of reflective practice in the use of transactional distance and social interaction for activity design are required to augment the current literature.

Second, the relationship between transactional distance, social interaction, and student autonomy and motivation is notably absent in the literature. The framework of transactional distance considers it as "a function of dialogue, structure and learner autonomy" (Huang et al., 2016, p. 743). Indeed, in considering distance learning, Joe et al., (2017), argue the "primary issue facing teachers may be related more to helping learners transition from the more controlled types of regulation to identified or integrated (i.e., autonomous) regulation than about fostering intrinsic motivation per se" (p. 140). Thus, the effects of transactional distance and social interaction on both autonomous regulation and student confidence should be a focus of future research.

Third, the relationship between transactional distance, social interaction, and student outcomes needs to be explored, building on existing literature identifying school climate as predictive of student academic, behavioral, and psychosocial outcomes (Wang & Degol, 2016). Previous meta-analyses and large-scale studies have demonstrated a correlation between student achievement, as measured by grade attainment, and both teacher support (Rolland, 2012) and feelings of connectedness and belongingness to the school (Pate et al., 2017). A cogent continuation of this line of research would measure the impact of social interaction and transactional distance on student outcomes both independently and concurrently to gain further insight into their impact.

Fourth, the relationship between transactional distance, social interaction, and student satisfaction ought to be studied. Positive perceptions of school climate have been correlated to improved mental health (Suldo et al., 2012), while student perceptions of available emotional and service support have been shown to predict future orientation, or the attitude and premonition toward the future a student holds (Johnson et al., 2016). Thus, these relationships should be considered in varying contexts to determine the effectiveness of incorporating transactional distance and social interaction into pedagogical models.

With continued experiences in these unprecedented times, it is evident that distance learning will play a crucial role in education around the world for the foreseeable future. As educators endeavour to develop classroom communities in online environments, it is important to acknowledge that increasing social interaction does not necessarily decrease transactional distance. Instead, educators should consider the interaction between both to best develop learning communities at a distance. By dipping a toe into the uses of transactional distance and social interaction in the creation of distance learning activities, the author eagerly awaits the resultant ripples that disturb and intrigue other educators and researchers to dabble in the use of such activities to positively support the classroom community.

ACKNOWLEDGMENT

The author is eternally grateful to Tanjin Ashraf, his role model, colleague, and friend. Her unwavering support since meeting at the Ontario Institute for Studies in Education at the University of Toronto (OISE/UT) and her meticulous copyediting made this chapter possible. This research received no specific grant from any funding agency in the public, commercial, or not-for-profit sectors.

REFERENCES

Abuhassna, H., Al-Rahmi, W. M., Yahya, N., Zakaria, M. A. Z. M., Kosnin, A. B. M., & Darwish, M. (2020). Development of a new model on utilizing online platforms to improve students' academic achievements and satisfaction. *International Journal of Educational Technology in Higher Education*, *17*(1), 38–60. doi:10.118641239-020-00216-z

Beckman, E. A. (2010). Learners on the move: Mobile modalities in development studies. *Distance Education*, *31*(2), 159–173. doi:10.1080/01587919.2010.498081

Ben-Chayim, A., & Offir, B. (2019). Model of the mediating teaching in distance learning environments: Classes that combine asynchronous distance learning via videotaped lectures. *Journal of Educators Online*, *16*(1), 1–11. doi:10.9743/jeo.2019.16.1.1

Ben-Chayim, A., Reychav, I., McHaney, R., & Offir, B. (2020). Mediating teacher for distance teaching and learning model: An exploration. *Education and Information Technologies*, *25*(1), 105–140. doi:10.100710639-019-09938-8

Benson, R., & Samarawickrema, G. (2009). Addressing the context of e-learning: Using transactional distance theory to inform design. *Distance Education*, *30*(1), 5–21. doi:10.1080/01587910902845972

Blau, I., & Barak, A. (2012). How Do Personality, Synchronous Media, and Discussion Topic Affect Participation? *Journal of Educational Technology & Society*, *15*(2), 12–24. https://www.jstor.org/stable/jeductechsoci.15.2.12

Blau, I., Weiser, O., & Eshet-Alkalai, Y. (2017). How do medium naturalness and personality traits shape academic achievement and perceived learning? An experimental study of face-to-face and synchronous e-learning. *Research in Learning Technology*, *25*(0), 1945. doi:10.25304/rlt.v25.1974

Bol, L., & Garner, J. K. (2011). Challenges in supporting self-regulation in distance education environments. *Journal of Computing in Higher Education*, *23*(2-3), 104–123. doi:10.100712528-011-9046-7

Bondie, R. (2019). Demystifying Differentiated Instruction. *Science & Children*, *57*(2), 14-19. https://doi/org/ doi:10.2505/4c19_057_02_14

Calderon, O., & Sood, C. (2018). Evaluating learning outcomes of an asynchronous online discussion assignment: A post-priori content analysis. *Interactive Learning Environments*, *28*(1), 1, 3–17. doi:10.1080/10494820.2018.1510421

Chen, Y. (2001). Dimensions of transactional distance in the world wide web learning environment: A factor analysis. *British Journal of Educational Technology*, *32*(4), 459–470. doi:10.1111/1467-8535.00213

Clyde, R. G. (2016). *How instructional designers bridge learner-content transactional distances in virtual high school courses* (Publication No. 10151287) [Doctoral dissertation, Capella University]. ProQuest Dissertations Publishing.

Cooper, K. S. (2014). Eliciting engagement in the high school classroom: A mixed methods examination of teaching practices. *American Educational Research Journal, 51*(2), 363–402. doi:10.3102/0002831213507973

Darling-Hammond, L., & Hyler, M. E. (2020). Preparing educators for the time of COVID … and beyond. *European Journal of Teacher Education, 43*(4), 457–465. doi:10.1080/02619768.2020.1816961

Garcia-Moya, I., Brooks, F., & Moreno, C. (2020). Humanizing and conducive to learning: An adolescent students' perspective on the central attributes of positive relationships with teachers. *European Journal of Psychology of Education, 35*(1), 1–20. doi:10.100710212-019-00413-z

Hamilton, M. L., Smith, L., & Worthington, K. (2008). Fitting the methodology with the research: An exploration of narrative, self-study, and auto-ethnography. *Studying Teacher Education, 4*(1), 17–28. doi:10.1080/17425960801976321

Huang, X., Chandra, A., DePaolo, C. A., & Simmons, L. L. (2016). Understanding transactional distance in web-based learning environments: An empirical study. *British Journal of Educational Technology, 47*(4), 734–747. doi:10.1111/bjet.12263

Joe, H., Hiver, P., & Al-Hoorie, A. H. (2017). Classroom social climate, self-determined motivation, willingness to communicate, and achievement: A study of structural relationships in instructed second language settings. *Learning and Individual Differences, 53*, 133–144. doi:10.1016/j.lindif.2016.11.005

Johnson, S. L., Pas, E., & Bradshaw, C. P. (2016). Understanding the association between school climate and future orientation. *Journal of Youth and Adolescence, 45*(8), 1575–1586. doi:10.100710964-015-0321-1 PMID:26104381

Kalkstein, D. A., Kleiman, T., Wakslak, C. J., Liberman, N., & Trope, Y. (2016). Social learning across psychological distance. *Journal of Personality and Social Psychology, 110*(1), 1–19. doi:10.1037/pspa0000042 PMID:26727663

Lenhart, A. (2015, April 9). *Teens, social media & technology: overview 2015*. Pew Research Center. https://www.pewresearch.org/internet/2015/04/09/teens-social-media-technology-2015/

Makara, K. A., & Madjar, N. (2015). The role of goal structures and peer climate in trajectories of social achievement goals during high school. *Developmental Psychology, 51*(4), 473–488. doi:10.1037/a0038801 PMID:25730313

Malinovski, T., Vasileva, M., Vasileva-Stojanovska, T., & Trajkovik, V. (2014). Considering high school students' experience in asynchronous and synchronous learning environments: QoE prediction model. *International Review of Research in Open and Distance Learning, 15*(4), 91–112. doi:10.19173/irrodl.v15i4.1808

Martin, F., Parker, M., & Allred, B. (2013). A case study on the adoption and use of synchronous virtual classrooms. *The Electronic Journal of e-Learning, 11*(2), 124-138. https://files.eric.ed.gov/fulltext/EJ1012878.pdf

McMillan, J. H., & Wergin, J. F. (2010). Qualitative Designs. In *Understanding and evaluating educational research* (4th ed., pp. 89–93). Pearson/Merrill.

Mesfin, G., Ghinea, G., Gronli, T., & Hwang, W. (2018). Enhanced agility of E-learning adoption in high schools. *Journal of Educational Technology & Society, 21*(4), 157–170. https://www.jstor.org/stable/10.2307/26511546

Moore, M. G. (1997). Theory of transactional distance. In D. Keegan (Ed.), *Theoretical Principles of Distance Education* (pp. 22–38). Routledge.

Moore, M. G. (2018). The theory of transactional distance. In M. G. Moore & W. C. Diehl (Eds.), *Handbook of Distance Education* (4th ed.). Routledge. doi:10.4324/9781315296135-4

National Institute on Aging. (2017). *What is Alzheimer's disease?* https://www.nia.nih.gov/health/what-alzheimers-disease

O'Brien, A., & Fuller, R. (2018). Synchronous teaching techniques from the perspective and observation of virtual high school teachers: An investigate study. *International Journal of Information and Communication Technology Education, 14*(3), 55–67. doi:10.4018/IJICTE.2018070105

Ontario Newsroom. (2020, May 19). *Health and safety top priority as schools stay closed*. https://news.ontario.ca/en/release/56971/health-and-safety-top-priority-as-schools-remain-closed

Park, Y. (2011). A pedagogical framework for mobile learning: Categorizing educational applications of mobile technologies into four types. *International Review of Research in Open and Distance Learning, 12*(2), 78–102. doi:10.19173/irrodl.v12i2.791

Pate, C. M., Maras, M. A., Whitney, S. D., & Bradshaw, C. P. (2017). Exploring psychosocial mechanisms and interactions: Links between adolescent emotional distress, school connectedness, and educational achievement. *School Mental Health, 9*(1), 28–43. doi:10.100712310-016-9202-3 PMID:28947921

Raković, M., Marzouk, Z., Liaqat, A., Winne, P. H., & Nesbit, J. C. Fine grained analysis of students' online discussion posts. *Computers & Education, 157*, Article 103982. doi:10.1016/j.compedu.2020.103982

Rolland, R. G. (2012). Synthesizing the evidence on classroom goal structures in middle and secondary schools: A meta-analysis and narrative review. *Review of Educational Research, 82*(4), 396–435. doi:10.3102/0034654312464909

Roorda, D. L., Koomen, H. M. Y., Spilt, J. L., & Oort, F. J. (2011). The influence of affective teacher-student relationships on students' social engagement and achievement: A meta-analytic approach. *Review of Educational Research, 81*(4), 493–529. doi:10.3102/0034654311421793

Rovai, A. P. (2001). Building classroom community at a distance: A case study. *Educational Technology Research and Development, 49*(4), 33–48. https://www.jstor.org/stable/30221135. doi:10.1007/BF02504946

Singh, J. A. (2020). *Teambuilding activities handbook: the physical distancing edition.* https://www.amazon.com/Teambuilding-Activities-Handbook-Physical-Distancing-ebook/dp/B08JP91XBD/

Stein, D. S., Wanstreet, C. E., Calvin, J., Overtoom, C., & Wheaton, J. E. (2005). Bridging the transactional distance gap in online learning environments. *American Journal of Distance Education, 19*(2), 105–118. doi:10.120715389286ajde1902_4

Suldo, S. M., McMahan, M. M., Chappel, A. M., & Loker, T. (2012). Relationships between perceived school climate and adolescent mental health across genders. *School Mental Health, 4*(2), 69–80. doi:10.100712310-012-9073-1

United Nations Educational, Scientific and Cultural Organization. (2020, Dec. 12). *From COVID-19 learning disruption to recovery: a snapshot of UNESCO's work in education in 2020.* https://en.unesco.org/news/covid-19-learning-disruption-recovery-snapshot-unescos-work-education-2020

Velichova, L., Orbanova, D., & Kubekova, A. (2020). The COVID-19 pandemic: Unique opportunity to develop online learning. *Journal of the Association for Information Communication Technologies. Education in Science, 9*(4), 1633–1639. doi:10.18421/TEM94-40

Walters, L. M., & Gillern, S. V. (2018). We learn in the form of stories: How digital storytelling supports critical digital literacy for pre-service teachers. *International Journal of Digital Literacy and Competence, 9*(3), 12–26. doi:10.4018/IJDLDC.2018070102

Wang, M., & Degol, J. L. (2016). School climate: A review of the construct, measurement, and impact on student outcomes. *Educational Psychology Review, 28*(2), 315–352. https://www.jstor.org/stable/24761235. doi:10.100710648-015-9319-1

Webb, S., Massey, D., Goggans, M., & Flajole, K. (2019). Thirty-five years of the gradual release of responsibility: Scaffolding toward complex and responsive teaching. *The Reading Teacher, 73*(1), 75–83. doi:10.1002/trtr.1799

Weiss, D. M., & Belland, B. R. (2018). PBL group autonomy in a high school environmental science class. *Tech Know Learn, 23*(1), 83–107. doi:10.100710758-016-9297-5

Wheatley, D. M. (2016). *Virtual high schools and instructional design strategies to reduce transactional distance and increase student engagement: a Delphi study* (Publication No. 10168359) [Doctoral dissertation, Capella University]. ProQuest Dissertations Publishing.

Chapter 14
TACTivities:
A Way to Promote Hands-On, Minds-On Learning in a Virtual Learning Environment

Angie Hodge-Zickerman
Northern Arizona University, USA

Eric Stade
University of Colorado, Boulder, USA

Cindy S. York
Northern Illinois University, USA

ABSTRACT

The need to keep students engaged is particularly acute in virtual environments. In this chapter, the authors describe TACTivities (learning activities with tactile components), designed to help encourage student participation, collaboration, and communication. Originally developed for in-person instruction, TACTivities are readily adaptable to online learning environments. TACTivities are intended to foster a sense of play, creative problem-solving, and exploration among the students who undertake to complete these tasks, and also among the teachers who design them. Unlike other tactile learning ventures, which may involve various kinds of physical props, TACTivities entail only moveable pieces of paper, or electronic equivalents. This feature means that TACTivities are quite portable, and they are easily implemented, shared, and modified (particularly in remote settings). Further, TACTivities allow for inclusion of discipline-specific content, language, and formalism, while still cultivating physical engagement in problem-solving and critical thinking in any subject area.

INTRODUCTION

K-12 teachers must make decisions in their classroom on a daily basis to help their students learn. Pedagogical reasoning (Niess & Gillow-Wiles, 2017) and technological pedagogical reasoning (Smart et al., 2016) help teachers make such decisions in their classrooms. One way to make such decisions is that

DOI: 10.4018/978-1-7998-7222-1.ch014

TACTivities

K-12 teachers often use hands-on activities and manipulatives to cultivate creativity and playfulness in the classroom, and to engage their students in the learning process. Indeed, engagement (Claxton, 2007), creativity (Beghetto et al., 2015; Bourdeau & Wood, 2019; Cooper & Heaverlo, 2013; Nadjafikhah et al, 2012), and playfulness—especially creative play (James & Nerantzi, 2019; Michelman, 1971; Russ, 1998; Singha et al., 2020), have all been identified as key factors influencing student learning.

When K-12 students have something to do with their hands, they are likely to naturally play with that object and figure out how it works – whatever it may be. Remember Fidget Spinners? They were advertised as a way to provide students something to do with their hands that was quiet and not distracting (more specifically they were advertised for students on the autism spectrum, with attention deficit hyperactivity disorder (ADHD), stress, or anxiety) (see Schecter et al., 2017 for more information). So why not have those random objects in the students' hands to serve a purpose and a so-called solution to a problem the students did not even know existed, or multiple solutions to really get their brain juices flowing? Such approaches have been implemented in face-to-face environments; now the challenge is to find ways to apply similar approaches to help engage students in the online context. Teachers who are teaching in an emergency remote environment are faced with the challenge of how to motivate and engage their students without being able to provide them with concrete items that help students be actively involved in the learning process.

Many teachers around the world have turned to emergency remote teaching on virtual or online platforms due to the COVID-19 pandemic. It has been reported that the online platform is proving to be frustrating and/or boring for K12 students and teachers alike (Dhawan, 2020; Lake, 2020), mostly because the existing curricula were not intended to be taught in an online manner (Hodges et al., 2020). Remote emergency online teaching is not the same as planned online classroom teaching (Hodges et al., 2020), activities are different and student attention span is different. Some children (and adults) can spend hours playing video games in front of a computer but are not able to spend more than an hour or two in front of a remote online classroom. It is pretty obvious why – because the classroom is boring and they are just listening and maybe doing a little talking, whereas video gaming is active, fun, and action-packed time. So how can the monotony of the remote classroom environment be changed, and pedagogical reasoning be used to make teaching decisions in a digital age (Starkey, 2010)? The authors of this chapter believe they have found one solution to increase student and teacher engagement and help make online learning more fun. The suggested learning activities have already been implemented effectively in face-to-face classes, and as the third author has said many times to the first author, "tell me something you do face-to-face and I'll help you figure out how you can do it online" (personal communication, 2017). In fact, all three of the authors are now, of necessity, experienced at figuring out how to do something online that they typically do in a face-to-face classroom, as are many other teachers who have had to teach online because of COVID-19.

That said, many K12 teachers do not have the experience or know-how to figure out how to do some of the hands-on activities they typically do in a face-to-face classroom, in an online classroom. Activities might not look exactly the same, but the authors believe that with a bit of creativity, this type of learning can still be accessible in online classrooms. That said, with emergency remote teaching, sometimes the best a teacher can do is try to replicate online what they do face-to-face; the authors believe this is acceptable in the age of COVID-19. However, true online teaching should examine school reform over merely replicating a face-to-face classroom; see Cuban (2013) for more information on school reform.

In this chapter, the reader is provided with one way in which K12 teachers can still provide their students with these hands-on experiences in the online classroom using tactile learning activities that the authors call TACTivities (Hodge et al., 2015). In order to accomplish this task, active learning is first defined and discussed for better understanding regarding engaging learners. Then, TACTivity is defined and how it works is described. Finally, how to implement TACTivities in an online environment is discussed, as well as providing the reader with TACTivity examples they can immediately put to use. This chapter uses the terms online environment and virtual environment interchangeably.

WHAT IS ACTIVE LEARNING?

Like art, active learning can be difficult to define precisely, though one tends to recognize it when one sees it. In one of the early comprehensive investigations of the subject, Bonwell and Eison (1991) proposed that "active learning be defined as anything that 'involves students in doing things and thinking about the things they are doing'" (p. 2). Those authors supplemented that working definition with some "general characteristics" of active learning approaches: for example, "students are involved in more than just listening", "students are involved in higher-order thinking", and "greater emphasis is placed on students' exploration of their own attitudes and values" (Bonwell & Eison, 1991, p. 2).

At the heart of the active learning paradigm is the theory of *constructivism*, which has its origins in the work of Piaget (Piaget & Inhelder, 1969). Constructivism posits that students (and learners in the more general sense) are architects of their own understandings of the world, rather than mere vessels into which knowledge is to be transferred. Various other teaching and learning philosophies and theories support, complement, and overlap with the active learning approach: student-centered learning, inquiry-based learning (IBL), inquiry-based mathematics education (Laursen & Rasmussen, 2019), collaborative learning, metacognition (e.g., Bonwell & Eison's (1991) vision of "students…thinking about what they're doing" (p. 2)), discovery learning, and others are among the ideas that often surface in the context of active learning discussions. The common thread in all of these ideas is an acknowledgement of—indeed, a respect for—students as a primary agent in their own learning. For more information on instructional learning theories, see https://www.instructionaldesign.org/theories.

Because of its emphasis on exploration and on doing things, active learning helps foster creative thinking and creative problem solving. As noted by Mayer (1989), "Creative learning occurs when students use active learning strategies for mentally representing new material in ways that lead to problem solving transfer" (p. 203).

The effectiveness of active learning has been documented extensively; see, for example, Laursen et al. (2014), Freeman et al. (2014), and Deslauriers et al. (2019). Much of this assessment has been performed in the context of STEM (science, technology, engineering, and mathematics) disciplines. However, there is also compelling evidence in favor of active learning in other fields (McCarthy & Anderson, 2000; Mello & Less, 2013).

The recent shift to remote learning, born of necessity, heightens the need for increased student engagement. Online learning can exacerbate feelings of isolation and alienation and can negatively impact a student's sense of community and feelings of agency (Farrell & Brunton, 2020; McInnerney & Roberts, 2004). To help address some of these issues, the authors of the present work have developed an electronic framework for what they call *TACTivities*: instruments, originally designed for the physical classroom, that foster participation, collaboration, and active—indeed, tactive (to coin a term)—learning (Hodge et al, 2015; Hodge-Zickerman et al., 2020). The innate aspect of TACTivities, promoting engagement and collaboration among students, can address the lack of social aspects in online learning, when used appropriately (Khan et al., 2017).

WHAT IS A TACTIVITY?

The term TACTivity is a portmanteau of the words tactile and activity (Hodge et al., 2015). Thus, a TACTivity is a tactile activity. The authors emphasize that with TACTivities, it is the students, and not (just) the teacher, who are engaged in the tactile experience (Hodge-Zickerman et al., 2020).

It should be noted though, the authors' meaning of tactile only entails moving pieces of paper, or the virtual equivalent (Hodge et al., 2015). This idea can differ from other approaches that involve physical manipulatives (e.g., pipe cleaners, yarn, Spirographs, building blocks, and so on). The authors believe their TACTivities add a different dimension to tactile learning. For example, an advantage of TACTivities over props is that the former look more like formal mathematics (or whatever discipline the TACTivity encompasses) rather than just a fun activity (Hodge-Zickerman et al., 2021). If teachers really want to teach relevant subject matter to their students, at some point teachers have to get the students to appreciate the appropriate language, notation, and formalism of that subject. TACTivities do this, but in a way that can perhaps be more engaging than only using pencil and paper, or word processing software, to do this work. Additionally, TACTivities are easier to adapt to and implement in a virtual environment than are activities requiring physical props (Hodge-Zickerman et al., 2021).

TACTivities are also collaborative in nature and allow for inherent engagement with the subject matter (e.g., mathematics) by the nature of the design (Hodge et al., 2015). In a face-to-face classroom, TACTivities were designed to be completed collaboratively in groups of two to four students ideally on flat tables (Hodge et al., 2015). However, in an online learning environment TACTivities have the flexibility to either be used as an individual learning activity or as a group activity (Hodge-Zickerman et al., 2021), which the authors discuss in greater detail later in this chapter. When presented with a bag of movable pieces, students are expected to align or combine the pieces in such a way that a mathematical outcome is determined (in other words, how do these pieces fit together or align mathematically). The students are engaging with mathematics concepts via the nature of the particular TACTivity and while working, they are talking aloud to each other about the TACTivity (Hodge et al., 2015). Each TACTivity is designed to be given to students with little to no written instructions, and the teacher saying very little other than helpful hints or posing directed questions to the students about their thinking process. In fact, sometimes figuring out the rules to the sorting TACTivities is part of the learning process (and what generates a lot of the rich discussion among students). Another feature that makes TACTivities so appealing is that many of them are self-checking (Hodge-Zickerman et al., 2021). For example, the students will know when they are done with the dominoes TACTivities because they will have completed an enclosed shape with the cards (and all ends match up in a meaningful way – like the game of dominoes).

Although the bulk of the authors' examples and experiences are from the field of mathematics, TACTivities are activities designed to be utilized in any level classroom, from preK-12 to higher education and beyond. TACTivities merge art and science in a manner that requires both students (as TACTivity end users) and teachers (as TACTivity designers) to think creatively, and playfully, while learning and/or teaching content skills.

Virtual TACTivities

The framework used to inform the development of the virtual learning experience provided through doing TACTivities stems from an active learning perspective (Ernst et al., 2017) as previously described. The authors' goals for virtual TACTivities are the same as their goals for TACTivities in a face-to-face classroom. The constructivist goal of active learning approaches is to encourage students to engage vigorously in the building of their own knowledge and understanding, with teachers playing the crucial role of guiding students in their journeys of discovery, rather than merely delivering content. The authors also have a goal to foster creativity and communication through collaborative learning using TACTivities (Hodge et al., 2019; Hodge-Zickerman et al., 2020). To show the readers how one can achieve these goals, the authors will describe what this looks like in the classroom.

In a face-to-face classroom, the collaborative nature of the TACTivities provides the teacher with the knowledge of what the students are thinking as they must *think aloud* to work with other students (i.e., say aloud what they are thinking so others will know what is going on in their head). From this, the teacher can facilitate the situation, providing hints and tips, but not solutions, if and when students get stuck. Or, the teacher can use the time to guide students by asking them questions that will further their thinking about the mathematics (Hodge-Zickerman et al., 2020). In both cases, the students are actively engaged in the learning process. How does a teacher facilitate such active learning in a virtual setting by using TACTivities?

In order to understand what a virtual TACTivity (Hodge-Zickerman et al., 2021) is (or options for what a virtual TACTivity can be), how a teacher can facilitate active learning in a remote environment, and what student engagement looks like in a virtual environment, three examples of virtual TACTivities are presented. In these examples, options are provided for different types of virtual TACTivities, as well as ways in which some of the activities can be printed and administered by parents/guardians (keeping the tactile nature of the original TACTivity design while discussing how to integrate these into a remote learning setting). The authors would like to point out that TACTivities are different than Techtivities (Olson & Johnson, 2021) in that TACTivities are more about having students sort moving pieces to learn or review subject matter (Hodge et al., 2015) whereas Techtivities are designed to have the students interacting with technology to learn mathematical concepts.

Examples of Virtual TACTivities

Three examples describe the virtual TACTivities: a tactile variation on the classic *four fours* order-of-operations activity, a card sort TACTivity that can be completed either virtually or with printouts and the sharing done virtually, and a domino matching TACTivity that is completed by moving virtual cards. Two of these TACTivities have a mathematical theme, and the other is geographical in nature. However, they are all aimed at general audiences, and are intended to be accessible to teachers of any grade level who teach any subject. The solution strategies that these TACTivities entail are not subject-specific; the game play is adaptable to any discipline.

Three different styles of TACTivities are provided that can be completed by anyone to offer opportunities for any teacher to benefit from this chapter. These three examples illustrate the online instructional strategies that are employed when both designing and implementing TACTivities. Actual experiences using these TACTivities in the virtual classroom is discussed as well as other successes and challenges while guiding the reader through these example TACTivities. The utility of Google Slides and Desmos

Activity Builder as a means of creating TACTivities are demonstrated and can be shared freely (without requiring additional apps be purchased), and performed remotely, in synchronous or asynchronous modality, using breakout rooms. The TACTivities should be tried as if the teacher were a student to get the experience of being a student completing the TACTivities. The TACTivities do take some thinking time, so try not to be in a race or under a time constraint when exploring each of the example TACTivities.

Four Fours

In the iconic *Four Fours* activity (Anderson, 1987), students' understandings of order-of-operations rules and strategies are tested through construction of various whole numbers, using only the four basic operations (addition, subtraction, multiplication, and division), parentheses, and four instances of the number four. The paper-and-pencil version of this activity is well-known in elementary education circles. The authors of the present work have developed a tactile version of this activity and have found their TACTivity to be popular with students—and teachers—at all grade levels, even outside of mathematics teaching-and-learning communities. This TACTivity has proven to work well as a hands-on introduction to TACTivities in general.

A virtual version of this TACTivity may be created using Google Slides. It begins with one or more placemats, or slides, onto which the students build their mathematical sentences. Figure 1 is an example.

Figure 1. A Four Fours master slide

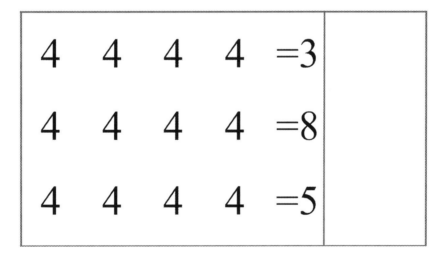

Note the empty space on the right part of the slide; this space is used for the operation signs (addition, subtraction, multiplication, and division) and parentheses that are needed to construct the appropriate equations. Also note the spacing between the fours, which allows placement of these signs and parentheses.

First, though, some comments are in order about developing the master slides themselves. The one in Figure 1 was created using only the text box and line tools within Google Slides itself; no external apps were needed. However, an extra step or two was implemented to assure that the master slide was not editable, so that neither the text nor the linework could be modified, or accidentally moved, deleted, etc. This was achieved using the following steps:

Step 1: After the side was created, it was saved to the computer desktop as a JPEG file, using the Download tool under the File menu within Google Slides.
Step 2: A new slide was opened up within the existing presentation.
Step 3: Using the Background menu in the Google Slides menu bar, the saved JPEG was selected from the desktop as the background for the new slide.
Step 4: Operation symbols and parentheses were added to the sidebar on the right.

Unfortunately, certain mathematics symbols, like the division symbol ($\div$), do not seem to be native to Google Slides. As a work-around, a PDF file with the desired symbols was created (using the LaTeX mathematical typesetting package, although the equation editor in Microsoft Word will work as well). Screenshots of each symbol were then taken from the PDF file, and those screenshots were then pasted as image files onto the slide. Note that if this process is to be followed, it might be necessary to first magnify the PDF image before taking the screenshot, so that it will appear at sufficiently high resolution when pasted onto the slide. Obtaining a suitable resolution seems to be something of an art, may be machine-dependent, and will likely require some experimentation. See Figure 2.

Figure 2. Master slide with symbols added

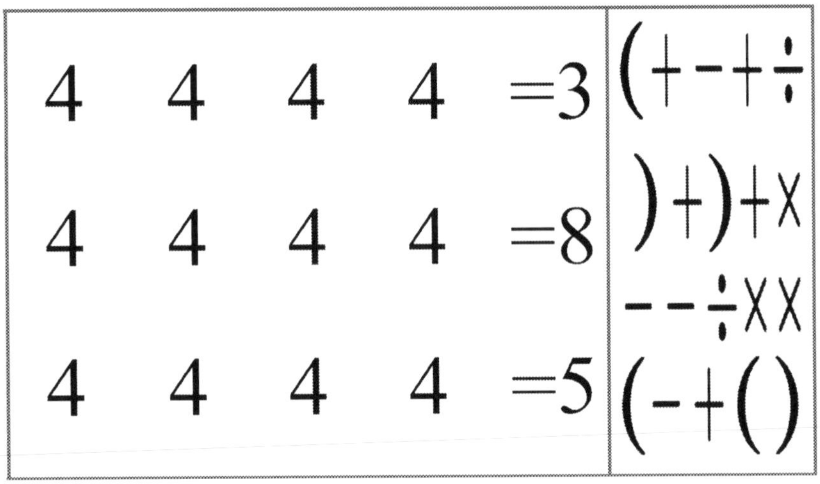

$$\begin{array}{cccccl}
4 & 4 & 4 & 4 & =3 & (+-+\div \\
4 & 4 & 4 & 4 & =8 &)+)+\times \\
& & & & & --\div\times\times \\
4 & 4 & 4 & 4 & =5 & (-+()
\end{array}$$

(Alternatively, a division symbol might be constructed "from scratch" within Google Slides, using the Circle and Line tools.) The symbols were added one-at-a-time, so that they can now be moved into the appropriate places among the numerals, to construct correct equations, for the TACTivity itself. A partial solution is presented in Figure 3.

In the example shown in Figure 3, more symbols were provided than was strictly necessary for correct equations. This provision allows for some variety in solutions to the exercises. On the other hand, some students may at first believe that there are too few symbols—in particular, that there are not a sufficient number of parentheses. In such situations, students should be encouraged to reflect further on the problem, and determine whether some parentheses might be redundant, or might be removed, because of appropriate precedence rules.

Figure 3. Partial solution to the Four Fours TACTivity

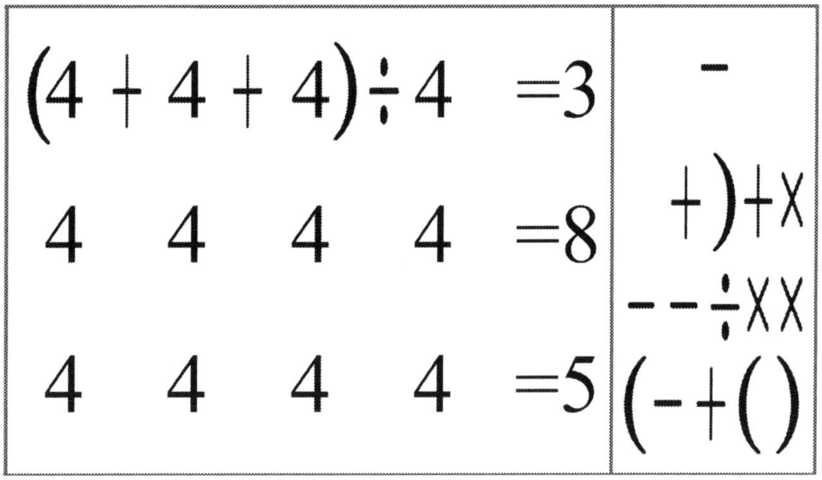

$$(4+4+4) \div 4 = 3$$
$$4 \quad 4 \quad 4 \quad 4 = 8$$
$$4 \quad 4 \quad 4 \quad 4 = 5$$

Available symbols: $-$, $+$, $)$, $+$, $\times$, $-$, $-$, $\div$, $\times$, $\times$, $($, $-$, $+$, $($, $)$

A set of three Four-Fours slides, one as above and the other two involving the other six single-digit whole numbers, with symbols that can be moved around, is available at https://tinyurl.com/6qbxj6th. Teachers are encouraged to adapt and modify these slides as desired. A view-only version is provided, but teachers can make their own copy of the slide and manipulate the copy. It is easy to duplicate an entire presentation, using the Make a copy command under the Google Slides File menu. To do so, questions like the following might be addressed: What other integers can be constructed from four fours? What if one also allows exponentiation? What about juxtaposition—for example, 44+4÷4=12? In this case, one might prefer a master slide that is editable, so that a pair of 4's may be moved closer together.

To use a Google Slides TACTivity in a virtual classroom, a teacher should first make sure to give the students edit access to the presentation, using the Share button in the upper right corner of Google Slides. Also, if Zoom breakout rooms are to be employed to divide the class into small groups, it is advisable to have a separate Google Slides copy of the given presentation made up for each room. Then each breakout room can be supplied with a link to a presentation that is unique to that room, so that each group can operate independently of the others.

Also, the authors strongly recommend that this TACTivity be presented to the students without explicit instructions on how to complete it. Figuring out the rules of the game can be part of the challenge, and often leads to fruitful brainstorming and collaboration among the participants.

Math Joke Card Sort

Card sort TACTivities are always a student favorite (Hodge-Zickerman et al., 2021). Every student can contribute something to sorting a pile of cards, and by working together a group of students can have a rich discussion while learning the subject matter. In person, students would see a baggie of laminated cards (or paper cards if it is the teacher's first time trying out the TACTivity) on their tables when they walked into the room. Then they would dump out the contents of the baggie and figure out what they were supposed to do with the cards on their tables. Sometimes the cards are sorted with only one match and other times they are sorted in piles of three. In any case, the card sort game is complete when all cards have a match (or two), depending on how teachers choose to design their card sort TACTivity.

Virtual card sort TACTivities are very similar, in that Desmos has a free program called Desmos Activity Builder where teachers can create their own cards. These cards can include pictures, words, graphs, or a combination thereof. There are even options that allow teachers to use larger print for visual accommodations in the card sort – a virtual bonus! The teacher can create an answer key to the card sort. Although, if the teacher is doing a paired card sort, the cards are often self-checking. The student is done when all pairs match in a way that makes sense leaving no cards unused and ensuring the final cards left also make a match.

In order to create a virtual card sort TACTivity using Desmos Activity Builder, a teacher should take the following steps:

Step 1: Go to the website: https://teacher.desmos.com
Step 2: Create a free account, so activities can be saved and easily accessed.
Step 3: Click Custom on the left-hand side of the screen.
Step 4: Click New Activity near the top of the screen.
Step 5: Give your new TACTivity a title.
Step 6: Select if you would like your TACTivity to be private or publicly available.
Step 7: Add a description of your TACTivity.
Step 8: Click Create new activity.
Step 9: Scroll down to the bottom of the card options on the left-hand side and select Card Sort.
Step 10: Click on the type of card you would like to create (math or text, image, or graph). You can create different types of cards in the same activity.
Step 11: Add as many cards as you would like.
Step 12: Click Answer Key when you are ready to create a key for your TACTivity.
Step 13: Click Preview to give your TACTivity a beta test.
Step 14: Click Publish to complete your TACTivity.
Step 15: Select Student Preview to make sure it is ready to go.
Step 16: Select Assign to get a link to share with your class.
Step 17: Practice with a friend before sending the link to your class.

Note there are help features if you want to learn more such as *teacher tips* and *learn more*. There are also YouTube videos to help you learn new features of Desmos Activity Builder as the program develops.

Teachers may also use any of the already created mathematics card sort activities, which are currently available at no cost to both teachers and students. Most activities can either be modified to fit the teacher's learning goals or used as they were created by the author of the activity. Again, although most of the activities found on Desmos Activity Builder are mathematical in nature, teachers of all subject areas are encouraged to explore these activities. Most activities found here can be an inspiration to ideas in other subject areas.

The readers of this chapter can actually try it! The authors encourage the reader to explore a *Math Joke Virtual Card Sort* TACTivity using the Student Preview mode: . See Figure 4. Using the Student Preview Mode will not change the original TACTivity, but the teacher can see what is being done in real time when these activities are given to a class.

Figure 5 illustrates the beginnings of a solution to the Math Joke Virtual Card Sort TACTivity.

TACTivities

Figure 4. Math Joke Virtual Card Sort TACTivity

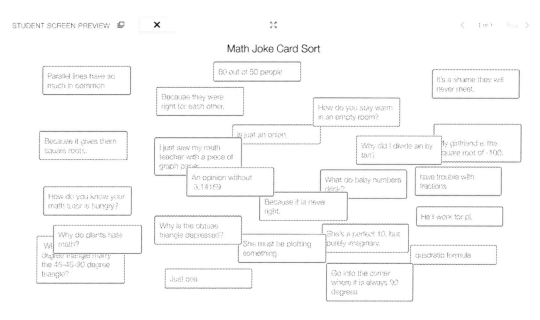

Figure 5. Partial Solution to the Math Joke TACTivity

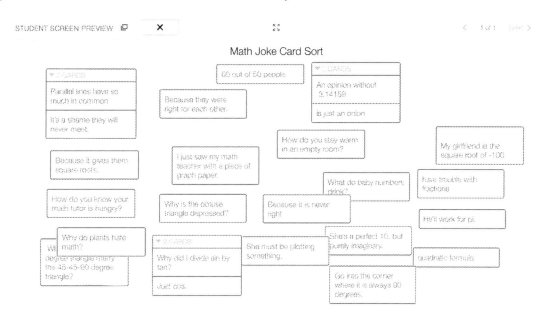

As previously mentioned, a teacher can import this Math Joke Card Sort TACTivity into their own Desmos account (using the Copy and edit command underneath the three vertical dots in the top right-hand corner of the above page) and can then customize this TACTivity to their own goals.

While the card-sort TACTivity entails the pairing of cards, various other sorting paradigms are possible. In the context of mathematics, for example, the authors have created a TACTivity where cards are to be grouped into sets of three; in each set, one card gives a formula for a function, another card a graph of that function, and a third card a unique property of that function. In the example provided, a different color was used for each of the three categories of cards. One could also create a large batch of cards, each of which names a country; students might be asked to group these cards by continent. Another option is for students to be supplied the cards without direction; it might prove interesting to see how they decide to sort them. Or perhaps a group of cards containing individual words could be sorted according to which parts of speech they represent.

Other sorting paradigms might require cards be arranged in a particular order. In a mathematics course, for example, the goal might be forming an increasing sequence of numbers. Depending on the level of that course, the numbers to choose from might include only whole numbers; only integers (positive, negative, or zero); only rational numbers; rational and irrational numbers; and so on. Such a card set could in fact serve multiple purposes—one might also sort them according to type (i.e., whole number, integer, rational, irrational, etc.). Card sets that can be sorted in more than one way are especially effective, not only because they can provide material for multiple lessons, but also because they can be used to reinforce multiple representations of related concepts.

Yet another variation on the sorting notion is the *fridge magnets* idea. Here, one might create a large batch of cards that can be strung together to form complete sentences. The authors have had success doing so with mathematical sentences as well! A card set of this type can be used to teach parts of speech, syntax, poetry (for example, students might be asked to write haikus using the cards), and so on.

Domino State Matching

The authors have used variants on the domino theme as the basis for a number of TACTivities. In the physical manifestation of this concept, the dominoes are actually rectangular pieces of paper, where either the upper or lower half of each piece contains a question of some sort, and the other half an answer. More specifically, the question on one half (upper or lower) of a domino will match the answer on the other half (lower or upper) of a different domino.

A virtual implementation of this idea may be achieved through Google Slides (for example). In Figure 6, each domino is a union of two squares chosen with the Shape tool under the Google Slides Insert menu. The questions and answers are then added to each domino via the Google Slides Text box menu.

As an example, the authors have developed a *Fun Facts: States* domino TACTivity. Only twenty states are represented in this example. Even with this limited subset, the slide is quite dense.

This TACTivity may be also presented without preamble or specific directions. Students should be afforded the satisfaction of determining the desired procedure on their own.

In particular, players should eventually notice that, if a domino is selected, a short line segment ending in a dot will appear at the top of the domino, and the domino may then be rotated by clicking and dragging on this dot. Thus, a domino can be juxtaposed at right angles to another; dominoes can be placed in an upside-down orientation, and so on. See the beginnings of a solution in Figure 7.

A self-check has been built into the above TACTivity, in that a correct solution will loop back to the start. That is, the state specified on the last domino placed will correspond to the Fun Fact cited on the first one. This, too, is a feature that students may be left to discover on their own. Some virtual engineering skills are required to fit such a loop on the slide, with all dominoes properly matched. Instead

TACTivities

Figure 6. Fun Facts: States—a virtual domino TACTivity

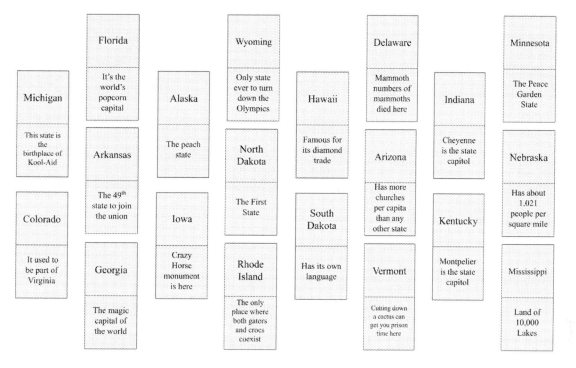

Figure 7. An incomplete solution (commencing at the bottom right) to Fun Facts: States

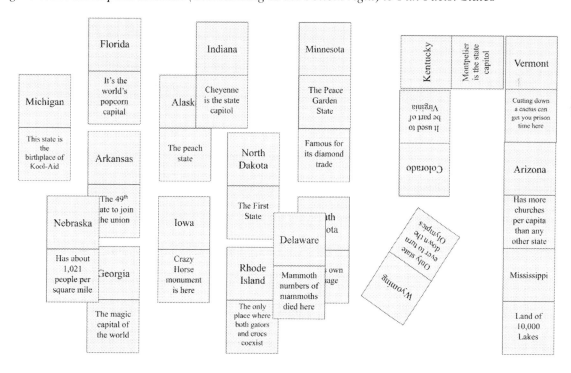

of requiring that the TACTivity be completed in this way, the teacher might leave it to the students to recognize that such a solution is possible, and to fashion such a solution if they wish.

It may not be possible to include a self-check in every TACTivity that one might imagine, but the authors do try to incorporate such a feature when possible. Dominoes are a great example of when the self-checking feature of a TACTivity is evident and easily done.

In the development of the above domino TACTivity, some technical issues were encountered. For one thing, the dominoes that were originally used were constructed from a single rectangle with a line added across the middle. However, the resulting dominoes ended up not fitting together very well. It works best if each half of the domino is an actual square, so that the dominoes line up correctly when placed at right angles to each other.

There was also an issue regarding movement of the dominoes. The Arrange menu in Google Slides contains a Group tool, which will, presumably, lock together elements added separately to the slide. However, functionality of this tool seems inconsistent. That is, attempting to drag a domino seemed sometimes to move only the half that was selected. Further, clicking on or near the text within a domino would sometimes lead to selection of the text itself, rather than the domino as an object, at which point any attempt to drag the domino would fail. Such an issue will not doom the TACTivity. Students are generally adept at recognizing these kinds of pitfalls and working around them. Further, glitches and imperfections constitute important teachable moments, and are therefore hallmarks of the skillful teacher. Still, if these technical irregularities are a concern, one might want to create the dominoes in a separate drawing or word processing program, and import them, via screenshots, as indivisible images into Google Slides. As noted in the context of the Four Fours TACTivity, one might need to experiment with scale when using screenshots, to assure sufficient resolution in the imported images.

The above Fun Facts: States TACTivity is freely available for modification, adaptation, and play, here (remember it is view only, so make a copy first): https://tinyurl.com/qu4vz1ig.

Another helpful hint when creating a domino TACTivity is to draft the virtual card sort on paper or in a Word document in way such that you have an answer key. To do this, start in the upper-left hand corner of the paper and have the upper-left hand entry match with the lower-right hand entry. If all other entries match with the card below until the bottom entry matches with the top entry in the next column, a ready-made key will be created.

Opportunities for virtual domino TACTivities are not limited to fun state facts—or limited at all. For example, the authors have used dominoes in mathematical contexts, where half of each domino is a math problem and the other half a solution. Doubtless there are myriad applications in other disciplines as well. And if inspiration is lacking, students are an excellent resource. Tasking them with designing their own domino TACTivities will engage them in next-level active learning.

TACTivities as a Creative Outlet

The literature abounds with evidence that creativity is integral to learning and to problem-solving, even in disciplines that are not always associated with creativity, such as mathematics and science (e.g., Bourdeau & Wood, 2019; Cooper & Heaverlo, 2013; Nadjafikhah et al., 2012; Scheerer, 1963). The authors are strong proponents of encouraging creativity in all teaching and learning environments and experiences as part of pedagogical reasoning.

Further, the authors share the point of view (see, for example, Laudel, 2001; Paulus & Nijstad, 2003) that creativity is fostered by collaboration. Certainly, TACTivities can be completed—or designed—individually. But the richness of dialogue and of shared inspiration that occurs when TACTivities are created or solved in small groups is valuable and rewarding to all involved (Hodge-Zickerman et al., 2020).

TACTivities can cultivate a spirit of creative problem-solving, as well as collaboration and communication skills, in students (and hopefully address any feelings of tedium). Encouraging student communication may be of particular importance to teachers who are unsure how to get their students talking in a classroom that is not face-to-face. This communication could be in the form of virtual breakout rooms where smaller groups of student-to-student collaboration on the TACTivity takes place versus whole classroom discussion.

TACTivities not only serve as a way to make both the face-to-face and the online environments more engaging for students, but they can also serve as a creative outlet for teachers when engaging in pedagogical reasoning in a digital age (Starkey, 2010). This creative outlet can perhaps provide some relief from the monotony the virtual environment sometimes seems to bring about for teachers. TACTivities provide an opportunity for teachers to think of ideas that match up on cards in ways that are creative. They can all challenge themselves to design the pairing or sorting of cards to require students to use what they have learned (or are learning) and think deeply about what the cards have in common. TACTivities can put the tactile back into the classroom – even remotely. They can give students something to discuss that is fun and more than merely comparing their answers on a worksheet. The authors have shared a few variations of TACTivities, but they challenge all readers of this chapter to develop other variations of TACTivities (both virtual TACTivities and ones that can be completed in a face-to-face classroom). The virtual TACTivities, however, provide new opportunities for teachers to use free apps, sites, and card sorts to make their virtual classrooms come to life. Our inspirations for creating TACTivities often came from childhood games – games with simple rules that spark curiosity and provide a fun way to learn. The remote/virtual world provides many opportunities for teachers to transform existing lesson plans, tasks, and assignments into TACTivities that foster the kind of active, discovery-based learning that is, in the view of the authors, so important.

THE FUTURE OF TACTIVITIES

The future of TACTivities is multifaceted. The authors plan on conducting research comparing and contrasting the success of the paper TACTivities versus virtual card sort TACTivities. Some questions to examine: Are the students engaged at the same level in the face-to-face classroom and in the virtual classroom when using TACTivities? How can the less engaging TACTivities be improved? Does the engagement level depend on the technology used to support the online TACTivity? What will happen to engagement and learning if a computer-based TACTivity is used in a face-to-face classroom? In what ways can computer-based TACTivities enhance the face-to-face classroom after the COVID-19 pandemic? What are the best practices for collaboration in the virtual implementation of TACTivities?

In addition, the authors plan to consider possible avenues for assessing the effectiveness of TACTivities in promoting various kinds of learning goals. Some of these learning goals for students include communication, creativity, problem solving skills, enjoyment in the subject matter, and daily learning objectives related to the TACTivity that is being completed. Explorations for successes and challenges could be conducted across different grade bands and different subject areas.

Funding will be sought to create a website of TACTivities that are open-educational resources for all teachers and students to use around the world. It is the hope that all users of TACTivities will submit their TACTivities to that website with perhaps a Creative Commons license. Funding will also be sought to host both virtual and in-person workshops to train teachers on the creation and implementation of TACTivities in a variety of classroom settings.

CONCLUSION

Small children excitedly learn through play (Singer et al., 2006). Sadly, the authors have noticed anecdotally that students and adults often lose the sense of play in learning somewhere along their educational journeys. The authors have found that TACTivities can help bring back that sense of play, in their students as well as in themselves. Perhaps the latter is particularly important, since teachers still have not really finished school/learning. The authors hope they have communicated the real learning and the real playing that TACTivities provide in all types of learning environments.

TACTivities use the tactile, but simple, play paradigms of childhood games and turn them into activities that promote learning and/or review of a subject. As illustrated in this chapter, this subject matter can be anything from procedural skills (e.g., order of operations in arithmetic as illustrated in the Four Fours TACTivity) to sense making of words (e.g., creating pairs that match in a meaningful way such as the Math Jokes TACTivity) to factual knowledge (e.g., sorting dominoes in a way that all ends that meet make a true statement match). Since this chapter is written to be inclusive to a wide audience, it was not shown how the TACTivities could also be used to enhance both procedural and conceptual knowledge of subject matter such as mathematics. An example of how this is done is when students have to match graphs to functions to other cards in ways in which the matching may not be obvious without a deep understanding of the content. It is envisioned that when teachers who are subject matter experts start to share new ideas for TACTivities that the use of TACTivities and how they can help students learn will grow in many ways.

TACTivities not only make learning more playful, but they can also foster creativity in both teachers and students (Hodge-Zickerman et al., 2020). Teachers can be creative in how they modify existing TACTivities and in how they design new formats for TACTivities that best fit their learning objectives, students' interests, grade-band, and subject matter. Students will naturally be creative in solving the TACTivities, especially when little to no directions are provided as to how they should complete the TACTivities.

In a world where our classrooms have been transformed and many classrooms have become virtual environments, playfulness and creativity can make a two-dimensional windowed classroom come to life. By taking a more holistic approach and sparking the interests of the students, TACTivities can make even a virtual learning environment more engaging and fun. In turn, students are more engaged in active learning and the creation of their own knowledge.

REFERENCES

Anderson, O. D. (1987). Four fours are one, two, three..... *International Journal of Mathematical Education in Science and Technology*, *18*(6), 863–866. doi:10.1080/0020739870180609

Beghetto, R. A., Kaufman, J. C., & Baer, J. (2015). *Teaching for creativity in the common core classroom*. Teacher's College Press.

Bonwell, C. C., & Eison, J. A. (1991). Active learning: Creating excitement in the classroom. ASHE-ERIC Higher Education Report No. 1. The George Washington University, School of Education and Human Development.

Bourdeau, D. T., & Wood, B. L. (2019). What is humanistic STEM and why do we need it? *Journal of Humanistic Mathematics, 9*(1), 205-216. https://scholarship.claremont edu/jhm/vol9/ iss1/11

Claxton, G. (2007). Expanding young people's capacity to learn. *British Journal of Educational Studies, 55*(2), 115–134. doi:10.1111/j.1467-8527.2007.00369.x

Cooper, R., & Heaverlo, C. (2013). Problem solving and creativity and design: What influence do they have on girls' interest in STEM subject areas? *American Journal of Engineering Education, 4*(1), 27–38. doi:10.19030/ajee.v4i1.7856

Cuban, L. (2013). *Inside the black box of classroom practice. Change without reform in American Education*. Harvard Education Press.

Deslauriers, L., McCarty, L. S., Miller, K., Callaghan, K., & Kestin, G. (2019). Measuring actual learning versus feeling of learning in response to being actively engaged in the classroom. *Proceedings of the National Academy of Sciences of the United States of America, 116*(39), 19251–19257. doi:10.1073/pnas.1821936116 PMID:31484770

Dhawan, S. (2020). Online learning: A panacea in the time of COVID-19 crisis. *Journal of Educational Technology Systems, 49*(1), 5–22. doi:10.1177/0047239520934018

Ernst, D. C., Hodge, A., & Yoshinobu, S. (2017). What is inquiry-based learning? *Notices of the American Mathematical Society, 64*(6), 570–574. doi:10.1090/noti1536

Farrell, O., & Brunton, J. (2020). A balancing act: A window into online student engagement experiences. *International Journal of Educational Technology in Higher Education, 17*(1), 25. doi:10.118641239-020-00199-x

Freeman, S., Eddy, S. L., McDonough, M., Smith, M. K., Okoroafor, N., Jordt, H., & Wenderoth, M. P. (2014). Active learning increases student performance in science, engineering, and mathematics. *Proceedings of the National Academy of Sciences of the United States of America, 111*(23), 8410–8415. doi:10.1073/pnas.1319030111 PMID:24821756

Hodge, A., Rech, J., Liu, F., Bunning, K., Stade, E., Tubbs, R., & Webb, D. (2015, January). *Teaching inquiry through calculus TACTivities*. Presentation at the *Joint Mathematics Meetings*, San Antonio, TX.

Hodge, A., Wanek, K., & Rech, J. (2019). TACTivities: A tactile way to learn interdisciplinary communication skills. *Problems, Resources, and Issues in Mathematics Undergraduate Studies, 30*(2), 160–171.

Hodge-Zickerman, A., Stade, E., York, C. S., & Rech, J. (2020). TACTivities: Fostering creativity through tactile learning activities. *Journal of Humanistic Mathematics, 10*(2), 377–390. doi:10.5642/jhummath.202002.17

Hodge-Zickerman, A., York, C. S., & Stade, E. (2021). Using technology and TACTivities to engage learners in mathematics classrooms [*Online Workshop*]. Society for Information Technology and Teacher Education.

Hodges, C., Moore, S., Lockee, B., Trust, T., & Bond, A. (2020). The difference between emergency remote teaching and online learning. *Educause Review*. https://er.educause.edu/articles/2020/3/the-difference-between-emergency-remote-teaching-and-online-learning

James, A., & Nerantzi, C. (Eds.). (2019). *The power of play in higher education: Creativity in tertiary learning*. Palgrave Macmillan. doi:10.1007/978-3-319-95780-7

Khan, A., Egbue, O., Palkie, B., & Madden, J. (2017). Active learning: engaging students to maximize learning in an online course. *The Electronic Journal of e-Learning, 15*(2), 107-115.

Lake, R. (2020, July 7). *Students count: Highlights from COVID-19 student surveys*. Center on Reinventing Public Education. https://www.crpe.org/thelens/students-count-highlights-covid-19-student-surveys

Laudel, G. (2001). Collaboration, creativity, and rewards: Why and how scientists collaborate. *International Journal of Technology Management, 22*(7-8), 762–781. doi:10.1504/IJTM.2001.002990

Laursen, S. L., Hassi, M.-L., Kogan, M., & Weston, T. J. (2014). Benefits for women and men of inquiry-based learning in college mathematics: A multi-institution study. *Journal for Research in Mathematics Education, 45*(4), 406–418. doi:10.5951/jresematheduc.45.4.0406

Laursen, S. L., & Rasmussen, C. (2019). I on the prize: Inquiry approaches in undergraduate mathematics. *International Journal of Research in Undergraduate Mathematics Education, 5*(1), 129–146. doi:10.100740753-019-00085-6

Mayer, R. E. (1989). Cognitive views of creativity: Creative teaching for creative learning. *Contemporary Educational Psychology, 14*(3), 203–221. doi:10.1016/0361-476X(89)90010-6

McCarthy, J. P., & Anderson, L. (2000). Active learning techniques versus traditional teaching styles. *Innovación Educativa (México, D.F.), 24*(4), 279–294. doi:10.1023/B:IHIE.0000047415.48495.05

McInnerney, J. M., & Roberts, T. S. (2004). Online learning: Social interaction and the creation of a sense of community. *Journal of Educational Technology & Society, 7*(3), 73–81.

Mello, D., & Less, C. A. (2013). Effectiveness of active learning in the arts and sciences. *Humanities Department Faculty Publications & Research*. Paper 45. https://scholarsarchive.jwu.edu/humanities_fac/45

Michelman, S. (1971). The importance of creative play. *The American Journal of Occupational Therapy, 25*(6), 285–290. PMID:5111632

Nadjafikhah, M., Yaftian, N., & Bakhshalizadeh, S. (2012). Mathematical creativity: Some definitions and characteristics. *Procedia: Social and Behavioral Sciences, 31*, 285–291. doi:10.1016/j.sbspro.2011.12.056

Niess, M. L., & Gillow-Wiles, H. (2017). Expanding teachers' technological pedagogical reasoning with a systems pedagogical approach. *Australasian Journal of Educational Technology, 33*(3), 76–95. doi:10.14742/ajet.3473

Olson, G. A., & Johnson, H. L. (2021). Promote students' function reasoning with Techtivities. *Problems, Resources, and Issues in Mathematics Undergraduate Studies*, 1-13.

Paulus, P. B., & Nijstad, B. A. (Eds.). (2003). *Group creativity: Innovation through collaboration.* Oxford University Press. doi:10.1093/acprof:oso/9780195147308.001.0001

Piaget, J., & Inhelder, B. (1969). *The psychology of the child* (2nd ed.). Basic Books.

Russ, S. W. (1998). Play, creativity, and adaptive functioning: Implications for play interventions. *Journal of Clinical Child Psychology*, 27(4), 469–480. doi:10.120715374424jccp2704_11 PMID:9866084

Schecter, R. A., Shah, J., Fruitman, K., & Milanaik, R. L. (2017). Fidget spinners: Purported benefits, adverse effects and accepted alternatives. *Current Opinion in Pediatrics*, 29(5), 616–618. doi:10.1097/MOP.0000000000000523 PMID:28692449

Scheerer, M. (1963). Problem solving. *Scientific American*, 208(4), 118–128. doi:10.1038cientificamerican0463-118 PMID:13986996

Singer, D. G., Golinkoff, R. M., & Hirsh-Pasek, K. (Eds.). (2006). *Play = learning: How play motivates and enhances children's cognitive and social-emotional growth.* Oxford University Press. doi:10.1093/acprof:oso/9780195304381.001.0001

Singha, S., Warr, M., Mishra, P., & Henriksen, D. (2020). Playing with creativity across the lifespan: A conversation with Dr. Sandra Russ. *TechTrends*, 64(4), 550–554. doi:10.100711528-020-00514-3 PMID:32838402

Smart, V., Finger, G., & Sim, C. (2016). Envisioning technological pedagogical reasoning. In M. C. Herring, M. J. Koehler, & P. Mishra (Eds.), *Handbook of technological pedagogical content knowledge (TPACK) for educators* (2nd ed., pp. 53–62). Routledge.

Starkey, L. (2010). Teachers' pedagogical reasoning and action in the digital age. *Teachers and Teaching*, 16(2), 233–244. doi:10.1080/13540600903478433

KEY TERMS AND DEFINITIONS

Active Learning: Teaching and learning approaches, philosophies, paradigms, and strategies that leverage and cultivate students' own agency in their acquisition of knowledge and construction of understanding.

Asynchronous: Not happening at the same time. Asynchronous work is work that may be completed at the students' own pace (though typically subject to due dates). In the context of remote learning (see definition below), asynchronous activities may include watching a pre-recorded lecture; completing online homework.

Manipulative: An object—physical or virtual—that can be moved around, or otherwise engaged with in a tactile manner, a part of a learning exercise or activity.

Online Environment: The use of a computer-based internet learning environment in which a class between teacher and students is taking place. This is used interchangeably with virtual environment in this chapter.

Remote Learning: Education that takes place with participants in separate physical spaces. This usually refers to situations where teachers and learners are communicating, sharing, and engaging over the internet.

Student Engagement: Mental presence, attentiveness, and enthusiasm of the learner.

Synchronous: Happening at the same time. Synchronous remote learning activities might include attending a lecture presented live over the internet; engaging in live online discussions with other students; working together with other students to complete guided learning activities.

TACTivity: A portmanteau of the words *tactile* and *activity*. A TACTivity is a tactile learning activity. For the authors, this means not physical props, but pieces of paper—or electronic equivalents—that may be repositioned, linked, matched, sorted, and so on to answer questions and solve problems embodied within the activity itself.

Virtual: The simulation of something done in an online, computer-based manner instead of face-to-face (or in person). It is made to appear to exist via the use of software.

Virtual Environment: The use of a computer-based internet learning environment in which a class between teacher and students is taking place. This term is used interchangeably with online environment in this chapter.

Chapter 15
The 4Cs of Academic Language and Literacy:
Facilitating Structured Discussions in Remote Classrooms

Salika A. Lawrence
The College of New Jersey, USA

Tiffany Labissiere
Literacy Network, USA

Monique C. Stone
Literacy Network, USA

ABSTRACT

This chapter describes how teachers have used structured discussions and digital tools to transition from traditional classrooms to remote, online instruction during the COVID-19 pandemic. With emphasis on culturally and linguistically diverse students, the chapter includes examples of how teachers reinforce literacy while supporting 21st century skills such as collaboration, communication, critical thinking, and creativity. Tools and strategies are presented along with examples teachers can use to facilitate student learning across content areas in virtual classrooms.

INTRODUCTION

The P21 Framework for twenty-first century learning indicates that students are expected to demonstrate creativity and innovation, critical thinking and problem-solving, communication, and collaboration (Partnership for 21st Century Skills, 2009; Thoughtful Learning, 2021). These practices suggest that students should demonstrate learning, literacy, and life skills (Thoughtful Learning, 2021) needed to navigate the information-rich environment we live in today. Twenty-first century skills enable students to use

DOI: 10.4018/978-1-7998-7222-1.ch015

their background content knowledge and skills to engage in real-world experiences that prepare them to work in a global, technologically driven economy (Partnership for 21st Century Skills, 2009). However, many students from underrepresented groups including economically-disadvantaged and some second language learners (Johnson, 2009), face challenges when working with content area texts because these texts use unfamiliar "language patterns that differ from the more everyday ways of using language" (Fang & Schleppegrell, 2010, p. 588). Transitioning to remote learning can magnify linguistic differences that pose academic barriers particularly for culturally and linguistically diverse students.

With the shift to remote learning caused by worldwide lockdowns prompted by the COVID-19 pandemic, teachers have had to rethink how they teach and engage students virtually. Prior to the pandemic, some challenges teachers may have faced when using student-centered classroom discussions include, ensuring there was shared space for all students to engage (quiet vs. students who don't talk back), keeping the discussion focused, making sure students are prepared for the discussion, finding time within the traditional middle and high school 45 minute classroom period for discussion and negotiating the importance of talk given the demands of high stakes assessment outcomes such as performance on interim and final standardized tests. In addition, for some teachers no matter how effective their classroom management, the admonitions to students, or classroom structures and procedures they put in place, students were going to find ways to communicate with each other about topics outside the curriculum. Whether it is passing notes in class via paper, texting each other under the desk, or instant messaging (IM) each other on their technology device, students, particularly adolescents are social and want to communicate with peers. Many teachers perceived these behaviors as off-task discussions between students and some educators consider it to be disruptive. In many instances, students have been reprimanded for off-task behaviors and discussions.

Despite the in-class challenges with student-centered talk, for about two decades much of the K-12 students' virtual discussions outside-of-school have occurred via social media, texting, email, chat rooms and discussion boards. These spaces allow students to stay connected across space and time, sometimes with people they never see or meet in-person. Many of these outside-of-school digital practices have traditionally differed from experiences in school. One reason is that technology use in face-to-face classrooms may have been limited because some teachers struggle to seamlessly integrate technology and many teachers stop teaching content to teach technology (Kjellsdotter, 2020). In contrast, seamless technology integration is evident when teachers and students use technology in a myriad of ways to communicate, problem-solve, create, and build content knowledge in authentic ways to enhance teaching and learning (Florida Center for Instructional Technology, 2021). Transitioning from a face-to-face class to a virtual/remote class means bridging the gap between students' outside-of-school literacy practices and their in-school expectations by using multimodal tools, many of which were previously used socially.

The COVID-19 pandemic prompted significant shifts in classroom practice, and opportunities for engaging, student-centered discussions was paramount. Now that most classrooms around the world are currently remote, teachers are seeking ways to better engage students in meaningful discussions. In a remote, virtual classroom, teachers need to be strategic when planning and making instructional choices. Teachers have had to be intentional about providing opportunities for students to talk and share with peers. For instance, when planning and designing learning experiences, teachers must consider the multimodal tools, the structures and formats for using those tools, and the purposes for class discussions as a pedagogical approach. These kinds of intentional teaching (Epstein, 2009) decisions include explicit instruction and engaging experiences in academic literacy which according to Johnson (2009) places focus on

The 4Cs of Academic Language and Literacy

- distinguishing between academic listening, reading, writing, and speaking;
- developing language and vocabulary, not necessarily memorizing words by helping students understand how to use words in a particular vernacular to convey ideas; and
- facilitating ways for students to investigate and engage with complex ideas so they can closely examine abstract processes by analyzing, evaluating, and synthesizing information from different sources.

This chapter examines how teachers are using classroom discussions to facilitate opportunities for students to demonstrate creativity, critical thinking, communication, and collaboration – the 4Cs - in remote classrooms during the pandemic. The following questions guided our investigation of current remote teaching practices.

1. What stayed the same and what shifts are evident in practice as teachers transitioned from traditional to remote classrooms?
2. What kinds of multimodal tools are teachers using to support students' academic language and literacy development in virtual spaces?

The chapter begins with some background about the importance of student-centered talk in academic spaces and the ways in which teachers can facilitate opportunities for students to hone critical thinking, communication, creativity, and collaboration in traditional and virtual classrooms. Then, a brief discussion about the instructional needs of culturally and linguistically diverse learners, including students learning English as a new language, raises awareness of effective practices and what should transition to remote teaching. Next, the chapter provides some examples of strategies, activities, and resources teachers have used to facilitate discussions as they shifted from traditional, face-to-face classrooms to virtual classrooms. The chapter concludes with recommendations for future research on using discussion protocols in traditional and virtual classrooms.

STUDENT-CENTERED DISCUSSIONS IN ACADEMIC CONTEXTS

In our current media-driven context, students need to the able to think critically and evaluate information and sources including media sources (Media Literacy Now, 2020). Today, twenty-first century skills, specifically critical thinking, creativity, communication, and collaboration - the 4Cs - are essential lifeskills (Thoughtful Learning, 2021). To meet Common Core Standards (National Governors Association Center for Best Practices & Council of Chief State School Officers, 2010), these skills are at the root of successful citizenship and provide the foundation for academic practices needed today. For example, students can build on this foundation to problem-pose and problem-solve local and global social issues through close examination of texts, sources, and other material in academic contexts. The ability to effectively communicate and work collaboratively will foster the creative thinking that comes from dialogue and discussions. Furthermore, fostering learning and innovation skills helps students to develop a critical lens so they shift from passive consumers to take action as producers of knowledge by creating their own digital content. Using digital tools and online resources and allowing space for students to share, evaluate, and ask questions can help foster twenty-first century skills such as critical and creative thinking while communicating and collaborating with others. Below, is an overview of the expectations for discussion in twenty-first century classrooms, followed by perspectives on supporting diverse learners.

Classroom Discussions in Twenty-first Century Classrooms

Kids love to talk and share stories and experiences with peers, asking questions about real-life issues, particularly for older kids, learning from peers can help when problem-solving, and they talk when interacting with multimedia texts such as video games, websites, and videologs. Despite these expectations and social benefits, talk is often overlooked in classrooms. From an academic perspective, listening, speaking, reading and writing are interconnected. Social interaction helps to foster the multiple literacy skills students bring to the classroom. During discussions, students expand their academic language including use of processes and vocabularies to critique texts and generate their own counter-narratives (Behrman, 2006).

Various student-centered activities can help to foster student voice and provide opportunity for them to share their perspectives. For example, social action projects facilitate opportunities for students to hone their speaking and academic literacy skills. VanDerHeida and Juzwik (2018) describe how students wrote argument letters to the principal for outside time during their lunch break. The students had conversations with classmates, teachers, and the principal as well as other community folks both in and beyond the school community to argue their position. The conversations helped students use a real-world issue to engage in purposeful talk to prepare for argument writing (VanDerHeida & Juzwik, 2018, p. 68). The classroom discussions helped to support student agency and voice. Critical conversations about controversial topics provided a scaffold and bridge for students to complete academic writing tasks such as argument essays. Nippold and Ward-Lonergan (2010) found that argument writing helped improve students' analytical skills. Writing essays about real topics, namely arguing against the use of animals in the circus helped students understand issues from multiple perspectives and enhance students' reasoning in their essays (Nippold & Ward-Lonergand, 2010). Talking about social issues in the community and then taking action through writing, helped students to develop critical thinking and analysis skills, which helped enhance their argument essays.

In addition to discussing real life issues, the teacher's text-selection is also important. Teacher decision-making when selecting texts can help facilitate meaningful classroom discussions. The teacher's role in facilitating group discussions can help students learn how to interact in academic spaces. Park et al. (2015) found that students' discussion practices mirror the teacher's practices, particularly when the teacher is actively involved and engaged in online discussions or passive students' practices are influenced by the teacher's behaviors. Students learning to navigate academic spaces, regardless of their academic level look towards the teacher for guidance on academic expectations. Park et al. (2015) found that students often mimic the teacher's role when engaging in class discussions - using similar discourses to the teacher during online discussions, such as asking questions, prompting, practicing, defending their own or another's position, and reflecting on their learning. These results suggest that repositioning students in the class can help to empower them and increase their agency during class discussions.

Similar to the social action writing projects mentioned above, Kersten (2017) found that authentic writing opportunities such as creating a nonfiction book allowed students to use multiple literacy skills and hone their scientific inquiry and knowledge as they worked collaboratively as scientists. The second-grade students in Kersten's (2017) study read numerous nonfiction texts, synthesized information from the texts and shared their knowledge with peers throughout the research process. The students demonstrated increased engagement as "they worked in pairs and small groups on the research, design, and content decisions around their books" (Kersten, 2017, p. 39). Using a project-based approach to the Science unit, provided space for students to feel proud of their work, take ownership, and reposition themselves as authors and experts who can communicate their knowledge orally and in writing. These kinds of authentic experiences help move students' discussions beyond surface-level interaction to critical analysis of the implications of the text within a broader social context. For example, when working with primary sources students can juxtapose informational texts with authentic literature as a springboard into critical conversations about social issues by summarizing and synthesizing information from the text to develop new meaning (Marschall & Davis, 2012). Through close reading, students can position themselves in relation to the text by asking questions, critiquing and analyzing the text (Afflerbach, Cho, Kim, Crassas, & Doyle, 2013).

These literacy practices demonstrated in relation to academic tasks can characterize students' ability to use twenty-first century skills such as problem-solving; communicating through different mediums, with various audiences; thinking critically; and working collaboratively (International Society for Technology in Education, 2016; Partnership for 21st Century Learning, 2015). Rigorous academic tasks can facilitate opportunities for students to build self-efficacy as independent learners, enhance their metacognition, and other dispositions so they can demonstrate twenty-first century skills while solving real-world issues. Mastering these practices requires that students learn specific language features or registers for interacting in academic contexts: this is especially true for second language learners. Typically, the expectation for formal language found in classrooms, which is evident in curriculum materials as well as ways of communicating, is also conveyed in specific disciplines and professions (Johnson, 2009).

Supporting Diverse Learners

Classrooms today are diverse, with a wide range of students who bring multi-dimensional language skills (Souto-Manning, 2016). Critical Race Theory helps educators face the reality of racial inequality in schools so they can use more equitable practices so classrooms are more inclusive and the curriculum is representative of the students. This perspective is not limited to traditional academic rhetoric and instead may use storytelling to, as Delgado (1995) explains to "Analyze myths presuppositions, and received wisdoms that make up the common culture about race that invariably render blacks and other minorities as one-down" (p. xiv).

During face-to-face instruction, teachers have used digital tools such as iPads to differentiate for diverse learners particularly students learning English as a second language (Engin & Donanci, 2015; Hong, Lawrence, Mongillo, & Donnantuono, 2015; Lawrence, Hong, Donnantuono, & Mongillo, 2015). With the transition to remote teaching, teachers working with culturally and linguistically diverse (CLD) face several challenges. One obstacle teachers may face with serving linguistically diverse students in the virtual classroom is being able to provide the correct resources so that students can work independently. Without appropriate tools that meet the development and linguistic needs of students, teachers have limited resources to scaffold and support students while learning independently. Teachers have shared anecdotally that many students are not able to navigate the various platforms and access knowledge because of the forms in which they are presented online. With limited access to content material needed to build background knowledge, students are not able to have rich discussions and engage in critical thinking and creative problem solving expected in twenty-first century classrooms.

Compounding the problem for CLD students is that many teachers are not using traditional strategies during remote teaching, which have helped CLD students in the past such as shared reading, chunking text, opportunities to discuss and share before writing, etc. Teachers need to understand how the tools can help support CLD students, but they have encountered some barriers. Peer feedback helps students develop usage, pronunciation, and fluency skills that support a stronger foundation of language development. Also, hearing the words in conversation and then using the words in writing helps students develop more knowledge on how English words change in grammatical functions.

Although there is no conclusive knowledge on an exclusive pathway to language acquisition, most children talk before they read and write. This verbal interaction creates a foundation for later reading and writing. Some students who studied English in their native or primary language may have been exposed to the grammar translation method of learning a language, while this offers them terrific grammar knowledge (often exceeding that of native speakers) it does not give students the chance to use the language in conversation. On the other hand, students may have been immersed in speaking English in work or social settings but have little or no experience with written forms and convention. Conversation allows students to use their more advanced aural skills to support the development of writing. Some conceptualize students' language development around the ideas of Basic Interpersonal Communication Skills (BICS) and Cognitive Academic Language Proficiency (CALPS) (Cummins, 2000), but this conceptualization delineates academic from social communication, when in fact the two overlap and need not be mutually exclusive from one another. The delineation of BICS, the social language and CALPS, the academic language, should be expanded to consider the language skills CLD students bring with them as assets, rather than placing the higher value on the idea of a standardized version (i.e., White) of English. The goal for teachers is how to draw upon the strengths of CLD students to foster their literacy development in academic spaces. Teachers can provide the support students need so that they can effectively communicate with each other, and instead of emphasizing correct or standard English, have students work towards being understood and clearly communicating their ideas. In both academic writing and speaking the ultimate goal is communication - sharing ideas and being understood.

STRATEGIES FOR TRADITIONAL AND REMOTE CLASSROOMS

When making the transition from traditional face-to-face instruction to virtual instruction teachers need to consider the diverse learners, students' cognitive demands and workloads across classes and subjects, as well as the students' technology skills and needs. More specifically, when planning for remote instruction teachers need to consider background knowledge and experience of the content and technology, accessibility, time, and the technology divide which can include limited wi-fi, tools, shared devices. To support student success in a remote classroom teacher should

- Use color-coding & visuals
- Give different kinds of examples
- Give clear expectations
- Assign Small tasks
- Use tasks that scaffold over time
- Choose 1 or 2 tools and stick with it/them for consistency
- Establish means for student accountability

The 4Cs of Academic Language and Literacy

To facilitate student interaction, one instructional approach necessary for student-centered classrooms in traditional and remote contexts is discussions. Discussions can increase student engagement and provide scaffolding for learners through peer-to-peer interaction. To facilitate this idea in virtual classrooms, teachers need to plan strategically by frontloading resources that will promote critical thinking, collaboration, communication, and creativity in the content areas. Two solutions that help facilitate classroom discussions in online classrooms are protocols for discussing texts, and digital tools.

Numerous online social media posts over the past year have shown that teachers are seeking ways to engage students in online discussions. Several online sources (e.g., blogs, Twitter, Facebook, online educational publications) have identified resources to help teachers foster discussion in online classrooms (Table 1).

Table 1. Using digital resources for the 4Cs

Communication	Book Brain provides ideas for virtual classroom discussions https://picturebookbrain.com/virtual-classroom-discussions/?utm_medium=social&utm_source=pinterest&utm_campaign=tailwind_tribes&utm_content=tribes&utm_term=1030109066_47632086_288619
Creativity	How to use Getty Unshuttered to spark creativity and ELA connections https://writeonwithmissg.com/2020/04/29/how-to-use-getty-unshuttered-to-spark-creativity-ela-connections/
Collaboration	Wakelet allows students to collaborate on projects https://www.erintegration.com/2020/04/08/remote-learning-made-easier-with-wakelet/
Critical Thinking	Parlay has a collection of content-specific and controversial topics that promote critical thinking https://universe.parlayideas.com/roundtables/browse

Teachers know that class discussion is important, but even with the best methods, it can be a struggle to implement discussions that are meaningful and include all students that is also equitable. One tool, Parlay, uses discussion prompts on various topics to prompt discussions in class or online. Parlay uses icebreakers, content-specific prompts, and current events to spark discussions and promote reflection on a wide variety of topics. In one Parlay collection, students are asked to closely explore journalism and media by looking at the parallels between Orwell's 1984 and Fake News (https://universe.parlayideas.com/roundtables/browse). As students prepare for and engage in the discussions, they interact with a wide variety of texts including primary sources. Their discussions require analysis as they consider contemporary issues including religion, science, politics, economics, media to name a few (https://universe.parlayideas.com/roundtables/browse).

Many teachers are also seeking ways to adapt these experiences for culturally and linguistically diverse (CLD) students. While working with middle school teachers during virtual coaching meetings and professional development workshops, a literacy coach shared and modeled various digital tools that can be used to support student engagement, literacy development, and the oral language development of CLD students. After discussing ways to integrate the technology into their classroom, teachers self-selected tools introduced to them by the literacy coach to try during remote teaching. Then they provided feedback to the literacy coach about the benefits of using the digital tools. Table 2 shows a few of the most popular tools used by the teachers along with their reactions. Overall, the teachers believed these digital tools can support students to navigate text independently.

Table 2. Teachers' reactions to using digital tools in remote classrooms

Virtual Tool	Description / Purpose & Use	Reactions and Feedback from Teachers
Virtual Notebook https://onlinenotebook.net	A place where students go consistently to access their notes. Microsoft offers Classnotebook, a tool that allow for teachers and student to have access to student knowledge and understanding	Teachers like that students can have an individual notebook and that they can distribute pages in the notebook to support reading and writing.
Immersive Reader https://www.microsoft.com/en-us/education/products/learning-tools	Reading accessibility tool that allows for changing the format of the text, have the text read aloud, change the color of the background, font style and translate an original document into their home language.	Teachers like this tool because it has a variety of functions and allows students to manipulate the text so that they can gain access to the content.
Flipgrid https://flipgrid.com	A video recording tool used for capturing student responses. Students can rehearse their ideas in this forum to prepare for class discussion	Great tool for practicing oral language and listening to ideas of their classroom. Get tool before a whole class discussion
Padlet https://padlet.com	A virtual bulletin board website that allows students to share ideas in a variety of formats. Includes audio, pictures and text.	Great tool. Allows students to choose how they will share their ideas. Easy to use. Small cost for premium features
Virtual Anchor Charts https://www.storyboardthat.com/create/anchor-charts	Interactive Anchor chart that includes hyperlinks so that students have access tools for reading, writing and discussion	Easy to make in google doc. Great supports for students

Most of the teachers reported that they tried the Microsoft tool called the Immersive Reader, which is an accessibility tool for diverse learners and students with varied reading levels across genres. It allows the teacher or student to change the format of a written text, provide tools to make the text more accessible, and control the amount of text in front of a student at any given time. Linguistically diverse students also benefit from using the Immersive Reader because it also has tools like a picture dictionary. The tool can also identify parts of speech and offers translation functions. The middle school teachers who used these tools reported by incorporating these supports into remote teaching, students were able to gain access to text in ways that make learning fun and supportive. In addition, it helped to prepare students for conversations by providing a wide array of scaffolding within the tool.

Several social media posts document how teachers are adapting practices from face-to-face instruction for virtual classrooms to support CLD students via digital tools. For example, one teacher stated in a Twitter post

I finally discovered how students can translate Google Meet into another language! Chat and closed captioning are automatically translated! Some ELLs finally participated in the class discussion. Love technology. (https://twitter.com/hashtag/CanZoomDoThis?src=hash)

In the past, many teachers have used Student Interest Surveys to get to know students. These surveys include questions such as

- What kinds of books do you like to read?
- What was the last book you read?
- What movies do you like to watch?
- Do you consider yourself a good reader or writer?

Teachers typically use this information to make instructional decisions and create a classroom community where students see their interests reflected in the curriculum. With the transition to remote learning, teachers have reported using FlipGrid to achieve similar goals. Many teachers report using it to facilitate social interaction in the class. Teachers have used it for student-to-student interaction, to allow students to share interests and ideas with peers, and to get to know students at the beginning of the school year. One fifth grade teacher shared on Twitter,

The first way I plan on using @flipgrid in the new year is in a welcome letter to my students. I am most excited to use this because it will give me a peek inside my students' home lives and I can learn what is important to them (before even meeting them!). #eloned #flipgridfever (https://twitter.com/TheNewFriz)

When posting an introductory meeting for the students, the teacher shared a FlipGrid called "Meet the Teacher!" she created along with instructions for students to create their own. The teacher shared a short video about herself and asked students and their family to record a short video of their own. Using the tool in this way, helps the teacher get to know where students are coming from on the individual/family level. One teacher's Twitter post stated,

@Flipgrid scaffolding features - sending the students to the prompt with sentence stems and walking through adding text to the screen to remember elements of culture to talk about. #ELLs can! Can't wait for responses! #RPEMSJourney (https://twitter.com/search?q=%40Flipgrid%20scaffolding%20features%20-%20sending%20the%20students%20to%20the%20prompt%20with%20sentence%20stems%20)

Another teacher asked students to post a picture of their solution of a math problem. The teacher referred to the Padlet as the "digital math word wall" (personal communication 10/22/20 https://twitter.com/MrsViennaOR) which included examples of how in-person and remote students solved various math problems to illustrate key concepts such as addition, subtraction, difference, open number line, equation.

Several teachers report using Padlet for content. After reading an article on the rise of e-cigarettes and vaping, a teacher and basketball coach used Padlet for students to discuss and share their responses to a reading about the health impact of vaping. The teacher posed a question, "Vaping – is it an issue?" and they were asked to post a comment about the impact of vaping (https://twitter.com/CoachZiobrowski).

Planning is an important part of remote instruction. During a virtual professional development workshop on writing, the presenters modeled how to use Padlet for online discussions (Figure 1). During the virtual workshop, teachers experienced simulated tasks that replicated and modeled activities for use in their own classrooms. Teachers in the workshop posted their comments, responded to each other, and responded to structured prompts.

Other online apps can be used to promote visual literacy through creativity by using pictures, emojis, memes, and videos. For example, a high school English language arts teacher posted on her blog that she used Getty Unshuttered for students to foster students' curiosity and creative skills through various activities. Getty Unshuttered is a free photo-sharing app that encourages teens to express themselves through photography. Created by the Getty Museum, the app is a community where teens can come together to learn, create, share, and support others. For example, students can do a photo scavenger hunt by using their smart phone to share what they notice in their environment (https://writeonwithmissg.com/2020/04/29/how-to-use-getty-unshuttered-to-spark-creativity-ela-connections/). Similarly for real-life symbolism,

Figure 1. Example of Padlet used for online discussions

students take pictures of objects and write a caption to explain what the object represents (https://writeonwithmissg.com/2020/04/29/how-to-use-getty-unshuttered-to-spark-creativity-ela-connections/).

To foster critical thinking and analysis in English Language Arts, teachers can help students expand their argumentative skills by quoting sources and explaining their reasons for using the sources. For example, in her podcast, Potash (2017) recommends a search and explore activity where students locate a number of songs that can be used for a soundtrack for a reading, students can quote experts from the song and explain the connection to reading (http://www.nowsparkcreativity.com/2017/12/episode-023-discussion-warm-ups.html).

Using discussion protocols can help foster students' creativity, communication, critical thinking, and collaboration skills. One discussion protocol that educators can use in the virtual classroom is the Waterfall Chat. For this activity, the teacher provides a stimulus—music, art, quotes, comic strips or questions— and the students reply in the chat with comments and reactions to the prompt presented. This time allows teachers to give students appropriate thinking time and writing time as they do not press enter until time is up. After the allotted time, the teacher calls "waterfall" and all the students press enter at the same time. Students can answer with one word, a sentence or with a short paragraph. The purpose of this protocol is to allow students to share their authentic and creative thinking at the same time as all the other students. This strategy provides the teacher with a formative assessment of thinking and creates a game-like atmosphere in the remote classroom. The use of a timer can engage students to think quickly and provides parameters for this thinking and brainstorming activity.

Another protocol that can be used to discuss text is a Building Block Question Protocol. In this protocol, teachers provide a stimulus question and students ask questions about the initial question posed about a common text. This protocol allows students to deconstruct questions, notice key words in questions and prepare for discussions and writing about the texts they are reading. It can also give students choice and

The 4Cs of Academic Language and Literacy

the opportunity to explore the stimulus question from many different points of view. Students can think critically about topics across subject areas and develop creative theories that add to class discussions in creative ways. Using this protocol, the teacher can encourage the use of divergent thinking and allow students to brainstorm innovative ideas when problem-solving with peers or when writing. One example of a Building Block Question for the text Fences by August Wilson is:

Stimulus question: Who is Troy Maxson?
Follow up questions (from students):
- How did Troy Maxson learn to be a father?
- What character trait best describes Troy Maxson?
- What life experiences shaped Troy Maxson?
- What choice has Troy Maxson made to change his life?
- Did Troy Maxson have a choice in life or were the cards already dealt for him?

Another questioning protocol, the One Question Interview allows students to create questions and interview peers in the class. Using digital tools like Padlet (padlet.com) teachers can modify the protocols to create opportunities for students to practice asking questions in virtual spaces. The worksheet in Figure 2, provides students with directions for conducting a virtual One Question Interview. The worksheet is easily adapted for use on Padlet where students will have space to note ideas as they complete their virtual interview. Padlet allows students to type responses or record their voice and film to simulate face-to-face interaction.

Many discussion protocols for text-based discussions frequently used in traditional, face-to-face classrooms can be adapted for online classes. These include,

- Small group instruction (e.g., guided reading)
- Teacher-student conferences
- Collaborative projects (e.g., research)
- Cooperative learning (e.g., literature circles, jigsaw)
- Discussion Boards
- Accountable talk
- Inquiry groups
- Workstations/ learning centers

In particular, small group discussions about texts using accountable talk prompts, group activities at workstations, and literature circles can help scaffold students' comprehension. Similarly, workstation and learning center task sheets can be linked to Padlet with hyperlinks to outside sources for students to build background knowledge about content. Collaborative experiences help to capitalize on students' affinity for oral discussion and experiences interacting with digital texts.

In the traditional classroom, some teachers have used a Gallery Walk or Carousel—students walk around the room to respond to texts posted on big chart paper to share their interpretations with peers. Similarly, interactive notebooks for reader response allow students to reflect on what they are reading and share their ideas with peers. Adapting these kinds of discussion protocols for virtual classrooms requires some pedagogical shifts for using technology as a mechanism for engagement. As shown on Table 3 students can use various tool for synchronous and asynchronous group meetings.

Figure 2. Digital workshop for One Question Interview

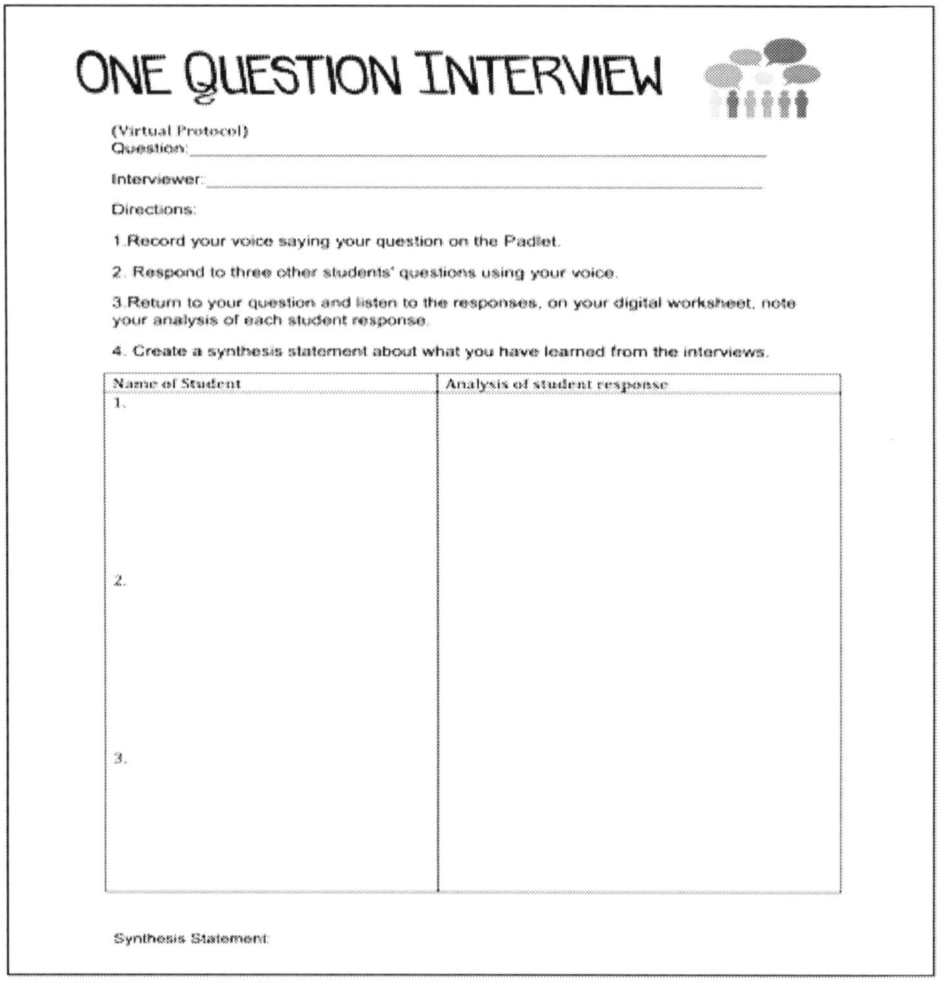

ONE QUESTION INTERVIEW

(Virtual Protocol)
Question: _____
Interviewer: _____
Directions:
1. Record your voice saying your question on the Padlet.
2. Respond to three other students' questions using your voice.
3. Return to your question and listen to the responses, on your digital worksheet, note your analysis of each student response.
4. Create a synthesis statement about what you have learned from the interviews.

Name of Student	Analysis of student response
1.	
2.	
3.	

Synthesis Statement:

Table 3. Text-based discussions in traditional and remote classrooms

Traditional Classroom	Remote Classroom	Remote Tools
Turn and talk	Using the chat feature with diverse learners	● Pre-recorded video or presentation (e.g., Screencastify, PowerPoint) Flipgrid ● Synchronous (e.g., Webex, Skype, Zoom, Google Meet) ● Asynchronous (e.g., Google Doc, Jamboard, Padlet)
Small groups	Breakout rooms (or google meets), discussion boards, games, text messaging, Flipgrid, responding with voice recording on Padlet, digital workstations, literature circles	
Whole group discussions	Protocols- Ex: Confirm-Extend Challenge	

Literature circles and book clubs have been used in traditional classrooms for decades to facilitate student-centered discussions about texts in K-12 classrooms (Daniels, 2002). Typically, students meet several times over a few weeks to discuss a text they are all reading. All groups in the class can read the same book but meet in groups to discuss it or each group can read a different text on a common theme connecting the books being read in the class. Students usually complete role sheets to facilitate their close reading of the text by focusing on specific aspects: word wizard (vocabulary), discussion director (asking questions), travel tracer (setting), illustrator (noting details). Assessments often include a written response to the text to share their interpretation of the text and a culminating group project that focuses on the themes of the text.

Literature circles and book clubs can be used synchronously (live real-time, video chat or meeting to interact with the class) and asynchronously (offline activities and tasks completed over time with a deadline/due date) in her remote classroom. Using sentence stems and role sheets, Padlet can easily be adapted for literature circles and book club meetings. Google can also be used to facilitate these small group discussions. First, the teacher should form literature circles or book clubs based on students' self-selected texts. Then, set up a separate Google Meet link for each group to facilitate the small group discussions. This preparation allows the teacher to rotate amongst the groups via the different Meet links. Next, the teacher should create a Google Doc for each group to build in student-accountability and create a space for notes during live group meetings.

During live, synchronous group meetings assign students questions (Table 4) to facilitate their text-based discussions. These structured questions can afford students opportunities to examine texts from nontraditional perspectives, namely using psychoanalytic criticism to examine characters or feminist criticism to examine the role of women in text, or Critical Race Theory to examine social issues in contemporary society and prompt civic engagement.

Using the structured discussion questions fosters critical thinking and analysis of the text by focusing on critical social issues that allow for close examination of the text and its broader implications (Figure 3). During their meeting, the groups can capture notes of their discussions on Google Docs and comment on each other's notes. Having access to the Google Doc provides the teacher with access to students' notes to offer feedback and pose additional questions to scaffold the discussion.

Table 4. Example of literary analysis questions. Source: Purdue Online Writing Lab https://owl.purdue.edu/owl/subject_specific_writing/writing_in_literature/literary_theory_and_schools_of_criticism/index.html

Psychoanalytic	Feminist	Critical Race Theory
1. How do the characters in the text mirror the archetypal figures? 2. How does the text mirror the archetypal narrative patterns? 3. How does the protagonist reflect the hero of myth? 4. Does the "hero" embark on a journey in either a physical or spiritual sense? 5. What trials or ordeals does the protagonist face? What is the reward for overcoming them?	1. How is the relationship between men and women portrayed? 2. What are the power relationships between men and women (or characters assuming male/female roles)? 3. How are male and female roles defined? 4. What constitutes masculinity and femininity? 5. How do characters embody these traits? 6. Do characters take on traits from opposite genders? How so? How does this change others' reactions to them? 7. What does the work reveal about the operations (economically, politically, socially, or psychologically) of patriarchy? 8. What does the work imply about the possibilities of sisterhood as a mode of resisting patriarchy? 9. What does the work say about women's creativity?	1. What is the significance of race in contemporary American society? 2. Where, in what ways, and to what ends does race appear in dominant American culture and shape the ways we interact with one another? 3. What types of texts and other cultural artifacts reflect dominant culture's perceptions of race? 4. How can scholars convey that racism is a concern that affects all members of society? 5. How does racism continue to function as a persistent force in American society? 6. How can we combat racism to ensure that all members of American society experience equal representation and access to fundamental rights? 7. How can we accurately reflect the experiences of victims of racism?

Figure 3. Excerpt from one group's Google Doc used for note-taking during literature circle along with feedback from the teacher

1. The reading is about why black males are the ones who are getting in trouble the most.
2. Ferguson examines examines beliefs, social relationship, and everyday practices that give rise to these patterns where children being punished in "Jailhouses" are predominantly black and male.
   a. Reaction - It is a very overwhelming to think that in society and the numbers are not what everyone thinks
3. Concepts
   a. Kids that come from troubled homes are given up on easily and labeled "at-risk" of failing, "unsalvageable" and "bound for jail".
   b. Two cultural images that stigmatize black males: as criminals and as endangered species
   c. The role of race and gender identities in the punishment of African American boys
4. Theme stuffs
   a. Escape from classroom to punishing room (social hub)
   b. Teachers giving up on minority students and seeing them as a waste of resources to help (self fulfilling prophecy)
   c. Testing: failure is something that cannot be helped
   d. Schoolboys and Troublemakers
   e.
      i. Outside forces as an influence on the role
      ii. No return from troublemaker role
   f. Hidden curriculum and cultural capital
   g. Someone who is "troubled" in the school context can be a model in other concepts
5. " My observations in the compensatory education classroom confirmed the argument of radical schooling theorists that low-income and minority kids will be schooled to take their place in the bottom rungs of the class structure. " (page 59)
   a. Showing that if they believe that there is not a reason to work with the kids they won't. Only work with the students that know that have a chance to succeed in society.

2:56 PM Mar 26
This is a brilliant point. I encourage you to keep discussing, unpacking this idea. Why do you think that is the case? Why is it important for some people to be perceived and labeled a certain way? What purpose does it serve? I guess the bigger question is why don't more people question the inaccuracies? Why do people accept these falsehoods? It only perpetuates inequity...
Good start to your discussion!
Show less

Reply

2:58 PM Mar 26
What do you think it does to a person when they are characterized and perceived this way? Think about it.

3:01 PM Mar 26
One of the things I thought about when reading this book was that some students (remember when we read and discussed different "types" of students) prefer to be suspended or asked to leave class. For some students they get more validation and acceptance from being in the "punishing room" or being out of school. In many urban schools they recognize this and seek to make suspension an absolutely last resort knowing that students prefer that and will often times do things that get them removed from class. What does that say about the classroom, teachers, curriculum? For some students they do not feel the connection to what is happening in some classes. As we have discussed, this is not all the time. It goes to show you that part of being Culturally Responsive is understanding how to help student connect with the curriculum and creating a classroom environment where they want to (prefer to stay) in class.

During their live group meetings, students can also work creatively to synthesize the themes and ideas from the text to prepare a final presentation for the class. Students can collaborate to summarize their notes into a PowerPoint presentation to lead the class in discussion about some of the key ideas and implications of the text. When planning literature circles using Google Apps, the teacher should place emphasis on

- Groups working collaboratively on the culminating project (e.g., presentation to the class)
- Identifying a time for live meetings and be consistent - same time for each live meeting
- Allowing for multiple forms of participation and interaction including asynchronous opportunities (audio recording, notes and contributions on Google Doc)
- Using pre-recorded videos for instruction and building background knowledge (e.g., students watch video lesson/PowerPoint offline)

The final grade for this experience is calculated based on the amount of time students worked asynchronously, synchronously, their final group presentation, plus quizzes and tests. Identifying multiple and varied student outcomes for the class allows for student success rather than being punitive because student may not be able to attend all the synchronous/live sessions. Balancing synchronous and asynchronous expectations includes considerations for time commitments from other courses, as well as technical and wi-fi issues that might arise.

Using games and simulations in face-to-face and virtual classrooms can also help students interact orally while using digital tools. For example, when playing Speed Dating, culturally and linguistically diverse (CLD) students, particularly those learning English as a new language can write down three to five things they know about a specific topic and then share it with partners and changing partners multiple times, so they rehearse what they say. Think of it as practicing and perfecting an "elevator speech." This game allows students to repeat the same thing multiple times and receive feedback from both native and non-native English speakers. The game-like nature of the simulation benefits students because students can immediately apply the feedback they receive. The simulation makes it possible to drill and repeat the language patterns contextually in an authentic situation. To build fluency in a new language a long process including practice and feedback is necessary. Games that require students to repeat the same thing multiple times, like the speed dating example, accelerates and condenses this process so that learners can build confidence and build positive experiences around language learning. One way to use this game in a literature context to support learners of English as a new language would be to have students pick a character in the text and describe personality or physical traits of a selected character. A benefit is that it helps learners understand differences and similarities between characters and clarify confusion about who is who in a story. Supporting learners with a plot and character level understanding through games builds a foundation for more complex discussions on theme and analysis. When studying poetry this game can be used by having students first talking about what is literally happening in the poem and when the poem lends itself to this approach, particularly when reading more difficult texts.

Vocabulary development is critical for all students to meet academic standards and demonstrate English language proficiency (Gardner & Davies, 2014). Vocabulary is also an important part of language acquisition for students learning English. To better support students' oral language and vocabulary development in virtual classrooms teachers need assistance in leveraging and accessing technology that allows for both interactive and prepared speech. For example, prepared speech is an activity that allows students to practice particular vocabulary without the worry of impressing their peers, or the fear of embarrassment that comes from inevitable mistakes that are part of learning a new language or vocabulary. However, to truly learn and remember vocabulary, students need to interact in real time through simulations and other experiences to practice and experiment with language. Students will be able to receive feedback from their peers to see if their choice of vocabulary conveyed their intended meaning.

FUTURE RESEARCH DIRECTIONS

Future research should continue to examine transitioning to virtual classrooms and how it bridged outside-of-school and inside-of-school practices, particularly with technology. Many teachers and students use technology and digital tools for social purposes outside of school. Future research should look at student and teacher efficacy using digital tools for academic purposes. The Technology Integration Matrix (Florida Center for Instructional Technology, 2021) can be used to explore the level of technology use in these contexts.

Additionally, future research that focuses on the ways in which diverse learners perform in virtual classrooms is warranted. More in-depth investigations can focus on the performance of specific student populations such as special education students, students learning English as a new language, and African American or Black students across subject areas. Research should include more diversity in student and teacher populations. These studies can examine the specific tools used to support students' multiple literacy skills across content areas in remote classes. Studies should also examine inequalities in the infrastructure supporting technology including, bandwidth, maintenance of hardware, and technical support available to teachers.

Research can also use an experimental design to examine which digital tools facilitate more high-quality discussions. These studies can also look at the level of interaction between and among students; and test the effectiveness of these digital tools on quality and impact of students' discussions. For some digital tools, such as Flipgrid, the communication is one-way, perhaps used for reflection, or limited to teacher-student interaction for feedback and scaffolding. In these instances, the student's posts or ideas they share might be communicated with minimal feedback and/or interaction with peers. While other tools such as Padlet and discussion boards allow for more interaction.

CONCLUSION

This chapter explored how teachers can use structured discussions to support the academic development of students in remote classrooms. Although there is some discussion about how to differentiate for diverse learners, particularly culturally and linguistically diverse students in the remote classroom, the chapter highlights ways teachers can use digital tools across subject areas to foster critical thinking, collaboration, communication, and creativity. Looking around our information-rich and technology-driven context today, there are a wide range of digital tools and resources available to facilitate discussions that align with the 4Cs. Whether teaching remotely or face-to-face in classrooms, digital tools can be used to facilitate student-centered discussion and increase student engagement. Teachers should consider a few steps particularly when teaching virtually. First, teachers should begin by self-assessing their own comfort level and efficacy using technology. By thinking about their own skills using digital tools and biases towards technology, teachers can consider the ways in which they use technology and how it can impact their instruction. For instance, when teachers reflect on whether and how they use technology to communicate and socialize, learn, and create digital content will reveal whether their technology skills and practices can be updated through professional development. During self-assessment a teacher can determine whether they are currently more likely to share a word document as an email attachment vs. a shared Google Doc for collaboration. The latter is more feasible for use in virtual classes to facilitate collaboration, communication, and creativity as students work together. Teachers can use The Technology

Integration Matrix (Florida Center for Instructional Technology, 2021) to guide their self-assessment and subsequent professional development. Next, teachers should consider the ways in which they currently interact with students in face-to-face classrooms, which might include teacher/student conferences, whole class lectures, or teacher-generated questions. These practices seamlessly move between face-to-face and remote contexts. However, when teaching virtually teachers need to think more strategically about how to reposition themselves to facilitate more student-centered discussions, student-generated questions, and opportunities for students to demonstrate what they know in creative ways. Using digital tools can be effective for creating multiple and varied opportunities for student discussions. Technology resources, namely virtual notebook and Padlet are invitations for students to engage with peers and share ideas. In addition, using the prompts suggested by Parlay can help to scaffold students who may not know what topics to discuss; these prompts can be good entry points for discussion. Allowing students to use tools such as blogging, vidlogs to communicate with peers, and work collaboratively to create content that demonstrates their learning can empower students to have more ownership of their learning. Having varied options to communicate with peers allows for differentiation. Some students would rather discuss ideas orally via Flipgrid while other students would rather use discussion board posts to type their comments. Providing students with options allows for multiple entry points into the discussion based on students' comfort level and personality because extroverts communicate differently than introverts (Banaji & Greenwald, 2013). Third, which aligns with repositioning the teacher in the classroom, teachers should empower students to problem-solve and share what they know as leaders in the class. The teacher does not need to know everything. Students bring a wide range of skill sets, particularly in the use of digital tools, and teachers should create culturally responsive classrooms by validating and empowering students (Gay, 2018) so they can lead and teach each other.

As teachers transitioned from face-to-face, traditional classrooms to remote teaching during the COVID-19 pandemic, some instructional practices in face-to-face classrooms have been seamlessly adapted for use in virtual spaces. Teachers have also been able to use a wide range of digital tools, previously used for social interactions, to foster students' academic literacy. Digital tools and protocols have allowed students to collaborate in real-time and offline to explore and discuss real-world topics. Teachers have also been able to use digital tools to scaffold students' foundational language and literacy skills in developmentally appropriate ways while also creating opportunities for students to discuss various texts, explore contemporary issues, and develop critical thinking skills by asking questions and conducting research around self-selected topics.

REFERENCES

Afflerbach, P., Cho, B., Kim, J., Crassas, M., & Doyle, B. (2013). Reading: What else matters besides strategies and skills. *The Reading Teacher*, 66(6), 440–448. doi:10.1002/TRTR.1146

Banaji, M. R., & Greenwald, A. G. (2013). *Blindspot: Hidden biases of good people*. Delacorte Press.

Behrman, E. H. (2006). Teaching about language, power, and text: A review of classroom practices that support critical literacy. *Journal of Adolescent & Adult Literacy*, 49(6), 490–498. doi:10.1598/JAAL.49.6.4

Cummins, J. (2000). *Language, power and pedagogy: Bilingual children in the crossfire*. Multilingual Matters. doi:10.21832/9781853596773

Daniels, H. (2002). *Literature circles: Voice and choice in book clubs & reading groups* (2nd ed.). Stenhouse Publishers.

Delgado, R. (Ed.). (1995). *Critical race theory: The cutting edge*. Temple University Press.

Epstein, A. S. (2009). Think before you (inter)act: What it means to be an intentional teacher. *Exchange*, 46–49. http://citeseerx.ist.psu.edu/viewdoc/download?doi=10.1.1.476.9053&rep=rep1&type=pdf

Fang, Z., & Schleppegrell, M. J. (2010). Disciplinary literacies across content areas: Supporting secondary reading through functional language analysis. *Journal of Adolescent & Adult Literacy, 53*(7), 587–597. doi:10.1598/JAAL.53.7.6

Florida Center for Instructional Technology. (2021). *The technology integration matrix*. Retrieved from https://fcit.usf.edu/matrix/matrix/

Gardner, D., & Davies, M. (2014). A new academic vocabulary list. *Applied Linguistics, 35*(3), 305–327. doi:10.1093/applin/amt015

Gay, G. (2018). *Culturally responsive teaching: Theory, research, and practice* (3rd ed.). Teachers College Press.

Hong, C. E., Lawrence, S. A., Mongillo, G., & Donnantuono, M. (2015). Using iPads to support K-12 struggling readers: A case study of iPad implementation in a university-based reading clinic. In H. An, S. Alon, & D. Fuentes (Eds.), *Tablets in K-12 Education: Integrated Experiences and Implications* (pp. 296–309). IGI Global. doi:10.4018/978-1-4666-6300-8.ch017

International Society for Technology in Education. (2016). *ISTE Standards for students*. Retrieved from https://www.iste.org/standards/for-students

Johnson, E. R. (2009). *Academic language! Academic literacy!: A guide for K-12 educators*. Corwin.

Kersten, S. (2017). Becoming nonfiction authors: Engaging in Science inquiry. *The Reading Teacher, 71*(1), 33–41. doi:10.1002/trtr.1577

Lawrence, S. A., Hong, E., Donnantuono, M., & Mongillo, G. (2015). Using literacy iPad apps for reading motivation. In T. V. Rasinski, R. E. Ferdig, & K. E. Pytash (Eds.), *Using Technology to Enhance Reading: Innovative Approaches to Literacy Instruction* (pp. 187–202). Solution Tree.

Marschall, S., & Davis, C. (2012). A conceptual framework for teaching critical reading to adult college students. *Adult Learning, 23*(2), 63–68. doi:10.1177/1045159512444265

Media Literacy Now. (2020). *What is media literacy?* Retrieved from https://medialiteracynow.org/what-is-media-literacy/

National Governors Association Center for Best Practices & Council of Chief State School Officers. (2010). *Common Core State Standards for English language arts and literacy in history/social studies, science, and technical subjects*. Authors.

Nippold, M. A., & Ward-Lonergan, J. M. (2010). Argumentative writing in pre-adolescents: The role of verbal reasoning. *Child Language Teaching and Therapy, 26*(3), 238–248. doi:10.1177/0265659009349979

Park, J. H., Schallert, D. L., Sanders, A. J. Z., Williams, K. M., Seo, E., Yu, L., Volger, J. S., Song, K., Williamson, Z. H., & Knox, M. C. (2015). Does it matter if the teacher is there?: A teacher's contribution to emerging patterns of interactions in online classroom discussions. *Computers & Education*, *82*, 315–328. doi:10.1016/j.compedu.2014.11.019

Partnership for 21st Century Skills. (2009). *P21 Framework Definitions*. Retrieved from https://files.eric.ed.gov/fulltext/ED519462.pdf

Potash, B. (2017). *Episode 23: Discussion Warm Ups*. http://www.nowsparkcreativity.com/2017/12/episode-023-discussion-warm-ups.html

Souto-Manning, M. (2016). Honoring and building on the rich literacy practices of young bilingual and multilingual learners. *The Reading Teacher*, *70*(3), 263–271. doi:10.1002/trtr.1518

Thoughtful Learning. (2021). *What are 21st century skills*. Retrieved from https://k12.thoughtfullearning.com/FAQ/what-are-21st-century-skills

VanDerHeide, J., & Juzwik, M. M. (2018). Argument as conversation: Students responding through writing to significant conversations across time and place. *Journal of Adolescent & Adult Literacy*, *62*(1), 67–77. doi:10.1002/jaal.754

Write on with Miss G. (2020). *How to use Getty Unshuttered to spark creativity and ELA connections*. Retrieved from https://writeonwithmissg.com/2020/04/29/how-to-use-getty-unshuttered-to-spark-creativity-ela-connections/

ADDITIONAL READING

Anderson, M. (2020). Your words matter: Three language shifts teachers can make to get classroom discussions flowing. *Educational Leadership*, *77*(7), 22–26.

Carpenter, S. L., Kim, J., Nilsen, K., Irish, T., Bianchini, J. A., & Berkowitz, A. R. (2020). Secondary science teachers' use of discourse moves to work with student ideas in classroom discussions. *International Journal of Science Education*, *42*(15), 2513–2533. doi:10.1080/09500693.2020.1820620

Duff, P. (2002). Pop culture and ESL students: Intertextuality, identity, and participation in classroom discussions. *Journal of Adolescent & Adult Literacy*, *45*(6), 482–487.

Engin, M., & Donanci, S. (2015). Dialogic teaching and iPads in the EAP classroom. *Computers & Education*, *88*, 268–279. doi:10.1016/j.compedu.2015.06.005

Florida Center for Instructional Technology. (2021). The technology integration matrix. Retrieved from https://fcit.usf.edu/matrix/matrix/

Groenke, S. L. (2008). Missed opportunities in cyberspace: Preparing preservice teachers to facilitate critical talk about literature through computer-mediated communication. *Journal of Adolescent & Adult Literacy*, *52*(3), 224–233. doi:10.1598/JAAL.52.3.5

Hong, C. E., Lawrence, S. A., Mongillo, G., & Donnantuono, M. (2015). Using iPads to support K-12 struggling readers: A case study of iPad implementation in a university-based reading clinic. In H. An, S. Alon, & D. Fuentes (Eds.), *Tablets in K-12 Education: Integrated Experiences and Implications* (pp. 296–309). IGI Global. doi:10.4018/978-1-4666-6300-8.ch017

Lawrence, S. A., Hong, E., Donnantuono, M., & Mongillo, G. (2015). Using literacy iPad apps for reading motivation. In T. V. Rasinski, R. E. Ferdig, & K. E. Pytash (Eds.), *Using Technology to Enhance Reading: Innovative Approaches to Literacy Instruction* (pp. 187–202). Solution Tree.

Lee, A. V. Y. (2021). Determining quality and distribution of ideas in online classroom talk using learning analytics and machine learning. *Educational Technology & Society, 24*(1), 236.249.

Media Literacy Now. (2020). What is media literacy? Retrieved from https://medialiteracynow.org/what-is-media-literacy/

Riddle, J. (2010). Podcasting in the classroom: A sound success. *Multimedia & Internet @ Schools, 17*(1), 23-26.

Walatka, T. (2012). Hub-and-spoke student blogging and advantages for classroom discussion. *Teaching Theology and Religion, 15*(4), 372–383. doi:10.1111/j.1467-9647.2012.00830.x

Zheng, B., & Warschauer, M. (2015). Participation, interaction, and academic achievement in an online discussion environment. *Computers & Education, 84*, 78–89. doi:10.1016/j.compedu.2015.01.008

KEY TERMS AND DEFINITIONS

Academic Literacy: Literacy practices demonstrated or performed in relation to school-based activities and expectations across subject areas.

Asynchronous: Offline activities and tasks that do not require live, real-time meeting but are completed over time with a deadline/due date.

Culturally and Linguistically Diverse Students: Students from ethnically, linguistically, and culturally different backgrounds including Black, Indigenous, People of color, students learning English as a Second Language also referred to as English Language Learners.

Prepared Speech: Students use technology tools to create text of what they want to communicate and then practice saying it orally.

Student-Centered: Student-initiated learning and ideas generated based on students' interests and experiences rather than teacher-directed learning.

Synchronous: Live real-time, video chat or meeting to interact with the class.

Compilation of References

Aarts, H., & Dijksterhuis, A. (2000). Habits as knowledge structures: Automaticity in goal-directed behavior. *Journal of Personality and Social Psychology*, *78*(1), 53–63. doi:10.1037/0022-3514.78.1.53 PMID:10653505

Abramovich, S., & Schunn, C. (2012). Studying teacher selection of resources in an ultra-large scale interactive system: Does metadata guide the way? *Computers & Education*, *58*(1), 551–559. doi:10.1016/j.compedu.2011.09.001

Abuhassna, H., Al-Rahmi, W. M., Yahya, N., Zakaria, M. A. Z. M., Kosnin, A. B. M., & Darwish, M. (2020). Development of a new model on utilizing online platforms to improve students' academic achievements and satisfaction. *International Journal of Educational Technology in Higher Education*, *17*(1), 38–60. doi:10.118641239-020-00216-z

Acar, O., Tarakci, M., & van Knippenberg, D. (2019). Why constraints are good for innovation. *Harvard Business Review*. https://hbr.org/2019/11/why-constraints-are-good-for-innovation

Acar, S., Burnett, C., & Cabra, J. F. (2017). Ingredients of Creativity: Originality and More. *Creativity Research Journal*, *29*(2), 133–144. doi:10.1080/10400419.2017.1302776

Adams, C. (2020, April 17). *Teachers need lots of training to do online learning well. Coronavirus closures gave many just days*. The Hechinger Report. https://hechingerreport.org/teachers-need-lots-of-training-to-do-online-learning-well-coronavirus-closures-gave-many-just-days/

Adams, D. M., Mayer, R. E., MacNamara, A., Koenig, A., & Wainess, R. (2012). Narrative games for learning: Testing the discovery and narrative hypotheses. *Journal of Educational Psychology*, *104*(1), 235–249. doi:10.1037/a0025595

Adams, N. E. (2015). Bloom's taxonomy of cognitive learning objectives. *Journal of the Medical Library Association: JMLA*, *103*(3), 152–154. doi:10.3163/1536-5050.103.3.010 PMID:26213509

Addessi, A. R., Anelli, F., Benghi, D., & Friberg, A. (2017). Child–Computer interaction at the beginner stage of music learning: Effects of reflexive interaction on children's musical improvisation. *Frontiers in Psychology*, *8*. Advance online publication. doi:10.3389/fpsyg.2017.00065 PMID:28184205

Adelman, H. S. (1992). LD: The next 25 years. *Journal of Learning Disabilities*, *25*(1), 17–22. doi:10.1177/002221949202500103 PMID:1740634

Adesoji, F. A., & Idika, M. I. (2015). Effects of 7E Learning Cycle Model and Case-Based Learning Strategy on Secondary School Students' Learning Outcomes in Chemistry. *Journal of the International Society for Teacher Education*, *19*(1), 7–17.

Adler, M. (1955). *The great ideas*. Encyclopedia Britannica.

Afflerbach, P., Cho, B., Kim, J., Crassas, M., & Doyle, B. (2013). Reading: What else matters besides strategies and skills. *The Reading Teacher*, *66*(6), 440–448. doi:10.1002/TRTR.1146

Compilation of References

Afterschool Alliance. (2015). *Full STEM ahead: Afterschool programs step up as key partners in STEM education*. http://www.afterschoolalliance.org/aa3pm/STEM.pdf

Agee, S. (2019). Equal access+equal opportunity=success for all learners. *Knowledge Quest*, *48*(2), 24–29. https://files.eric.ed.gov/fulltext/EJ1233107.pdf

Ainscow, M., Booth, T., & Dyson, A. (2006). *Improving schools, developing inclusion?* Routledge., doi:10.4324/9780203967157

Ainsworth, S. E., & Fleming, P. F. (2006). Teachers as instructional designers: Does involving a classroom teacher in the design of computer-based learning environments improve their effectiveness? *Computers in Human Behavior*, *22*, 131–148. doi:10.1016/j.chb.2005.01.010

Ajzen, I. (2019). *Constructing a theory of planned behavior questionnaire*. Retrieved from https://people.umass.edu/aizen/pdf/tpb.measurement.pdf

Akyol, Z., & Garrison, D. R. (2011). Assessing metacognition in an online community of inquiry. *The Internet and Higher Education*, *14*(3), 183–190. doi:10.1016/j.iheduc.2011.01.005

Al Mamun, M. A., Lawrie, G., & Wright, T. (2020). Instructional design of scaffolded online learning modules for self-directed and inquiry-based learning environments. *Computers & Education*, *144*, 103695–103712. doi:10.1016/j.compedu.2019.103695

Alanazi, M. H. (2019). A study of the pre-service trainee teachers problems in designing lesson plans. *Arab World English Journal*, *10*(1), 166–182. doi:10.24093/awej/vol10no1.15

Albert, J., Jocius, R., Barnes, T., Joshi, D., Catete, V., Robinson, R., O'Byrne, I., & Andrews, A. (2020). Research-based design recommendations for transitioning a computational thinking summer professional development to a virtual format. In *Teaching, technology, and teacher education during the COVID-19 pandemic: Stories from the field* (pp. 59-64). Association for the Advancement of Computing in Education (AACE). Available: https://www.learntechlib.org/p/216903/

Al-dheleai, Y., Tasir, Z., Al-Rahmi, W., Al-Sharafi, M., & Mydin, A. (2020). Modeling of Students Online Social Presence on Social Networking Sites and Academic Performance. *International Journal of Emerging Technologies in Learning*, *15*(12), 56–71. doi:10.3991/ijet.v15i12.12599

Alexander, P. A. (2020). About readers' struggles with comprehension in the digital age: Moving beyond the phonics versus whole language debate. *Reading Research Quarterly*, *55*(S1). Advance online publication. doi:10.1002/rrq.331

Allen, I. E., & Seaman, J. (2013). *Changing Course: Ten Years of Tracking Online Education in the United States*. Sloan Consortium. https://search.ebscohost.com/login.aspx?direct=true&AuthType=ip,shib&db=eric&AN=ED541571&site=ehost-live&scope=site&authtype=ip,shib&custid=s3555202

Al-Samarraie, H., & Saeed, N. (2018). A systematic review of cloud computing tools for collaborative learning: Opportunities and challenges to the blended-learning environment. *Computers & Education*, *124*, 77–91. doi:10.1016/j.compedu.2018.05.016

Altwel, K. (2017). *The Thinking School: Developing a dynamic learning community*. John Catt Educational Ltd.

Ambrose, M. (2019, March 14). *Panel warns US faces STEM workforce supply challenges*. American Institute of Physics. https://www.aip.org/fyi/2019/panel-warns-us-faces-stem-workforce-supply-challenges

Anant, S. S. (1966). Need to belong. *Canada's Mental Health*, *14*(2), 21–27.

An, D., & Carr, M. (2017). Learning styles theory fails to explain learning and achievement: Recommendations for alternative approaches. *Personality and Individual Differences*, *116*, 410–416. doi:10.1016/j.paid.2017.04.050

Anderson, T. (2011). Towards a theory of online learning. In T. Anderson (Ed.), The theory and practice of online learning (2nd ed., pp. 45-74). AU Press.

Anderson, O. D. (1987). Four fours are one, two, three..... *International Journal of Mathematical Education in Science and Technology*, *18*(6), 863–866. doi:10.1080/0020739870180609

Anderson, R. K., Boaler, J., & Dieckmann, J. A. (2018). Achieving elusive teacher change through challenging myths about learning: A blended approach. *Education Sciences*, *8*(3), 98. doi:10.3390/educsci8030098

Angeli, C., & Valanides, N. (2008). *TPCK in pre-service teacher education: Preparing primary education student to teach with technology*. Paper presented at the annual meeting of the American Education Research Association, New York, NY.

Angeli, C., & Valanides, N. (2005). Preservice teachers as ICT designers: An instructional design model based on an expanded view of pedagogical content knowledge. *Journal of Computer Assisted Learning*, *21*(4), 292–302. doi:10.1111/j.1365-2729.2005.00135.x

Angus, S. D., & Watson, J. (2009). Does regular online testing enhance student learning in the numerical sciences? Robust evidence from a large data set. *British Journal of Educational Technology*, *40*(2), 255–272. doi:10.1111/j.1467-8535.2008.00916.x

Annamma, S. A., Connor, D., & Ferri, B. (2013). Dis/ability critical race studies (DisCrit): Theorizing at the intersections of race and dis/ability. *Race, Ethnicity and Education*, *16*(1), 1–31. doi:10.1080/13613324.2012.730511

Annamma, S., & Morrison, D. (2018). DisCrit Classroom Ecology: Using praxis to dismantle dysfunctional education ecologies. *Teaching and Teacher Education*, *73*, 70–80. doi:10.1016/j.tate.2018.03.008

Arbaugh, F., Ball, D. L., Grossman, P., Heller, D. E., & Monk, D. (2015). Deans' Corner: Views on the state of teacher education in 2015. *Journal of Teacher Education*, *66*(5), 435–445. doi:10.1177/0022487115602314

Arbuthnott, K. D. (2009). Education for sustainable development beyond attitude change. *International Journal of Sustainability in Higher Education*, *10*(2), 152–163. doi:10.1108/14676370910945954

Archambault, L. (2011). The practitioner's perspective on teacher education: Preparing for the K-12 online classroom. *Journal of Technology and Teacher Education*, *19*(1), 73–91.

Armstrong, A. (2020). Emergent technological practices of middle school students with mathematics learning disabilities. *General Report*. https://doi.org/ doi:10.5206/eei.v30i1.10912

Arora, N. K. (2018). Environmental Sustainability - necessary for survival. *Environmental Sustainability*, *1*(1), 1–2. doi:10.100742398-018-0013-3

Asbury, K., & Kim, L. (2020). "Lazy, lazy teachers": Teachers' perceptions of how their profession is valued by society, policymakers, and the media during COVID-19. doi:10.31234/osf.io/65k8qosf.io/65k8q

Asbury, K., Fox, L., Deniz, E., Code, A., & Toseeb, U. (2020). How is COVID-19 affecting the mental health of children with special educational needs and disabilities and their families? *Journal of Autism and Developmental Disorders*, 1–9. doi:10.100710803-020-04577-2 PMID:32737668

Asbury, K., Fox, L., Deniz, E., Code, A., & Toseeb, U. (2020). How is COVID-19 Affecting the Mental Health of Children with Special Educational Needs and Disabilities and Their Families? *Journal of Autism and Developmental Disorders*, 1–9. doi:10.31234/osf.ioevyd PMID:32737668

Compilation of References

Ashton, J. (2014). Barriers to implementing STEM in K–12 virtual programs. *Distance Learning, 11*(1), 51–57.

Assessing Women and Men in Engineering. (2010). *Lower elementary school pre-participation survey*. http://aweonline.org/pre_college.html#elementary

Assunção Flores, M., & Swennen, A. (2020). The COVID-19 pandemic and its effects on teacher education. *European Journal of Teacher Education, 43*(4), 453–456. doi:10.1080/02619768.2020.1824253

Astin, A. W. (1984). Student involvement: A developmental theory for higher education. *Student Involvement: A Developmental Theory for Higher Education, 25*(4), 297–308.

Atabey, D. (2018). A Study into the Effective Communication and Social Skills of Preschool Children Derya. Alanya Alaaddin Keykubat University, 19, 185–199. doi:10.17679/inuefd.323598

Atherton, M. C. (2014). Academic Preparedness of First-Generation College Students: Different Perspectives. *Journal of College Student Development, 55*(8), 824–829. doi:10.1353/csd.2014.0081

Atmatzidou, S., & Demetriadis, S. (2016). Advancing students' computational thinking skills through educational robotics: A study on age and gender relevant differences. *Robotics and Autonomous Systems, 75*, 661–670. doi:10.1016/j.robot.2015.10.008

August, D. (n.d.). *A Review of the Latest Research Educating ELLs*. Academic Press.

August, D. (2018). Educating English language learners: A review of the latest research. *American Educator, 42*(3), 4–9.

Avella, J. T., Kebritchi, M., Nunn, S. G., & Kanai, T. (2016). Learning analytics methods, benefits, and challenges in higher education: A systematic literature review. *Online Learning, 20*(2), 13–29. doi:10.24059/olj.v20i2.790

Baffoe, J. (2020). Subini Ancy Annamma: The pedagogy of pathologization: Dis/abled girls of color in the school-prison nexus. *Journal of Youth and Adolescence, 49*(2), 565–568. doi:10.100710964-019-01169-x

Bagchi-Sen, S. (2001). Product innovation and competitive advantage in an area of industrial decline: The Niagara region of Canada. *Technovation, 21*(1), 45–54. doi:10.1016/S0166-4972(00)00016-X

Bai, H., & Ertmer, P. A. (2008). Teacher educators' beliefs and technology uses as predictors of preservice teachers' beliefs and technology attitudes. *Journal of Technology and Teacher Education, 16*(1), 93–112.

Baker, C. K., Bitto, L. E., Wills, T., Galanti, T. M., & Eatmon, C. C. (2019). Developing teacher leaders through self-study: a mathematics education field experience. In T. E. Hodges & A. Baum (Eds.), *Handbook of research on field-based teacher education* (pp. 635–658). IGI Global. doi:10.4018/978-1-5225-6249-8.ch027

Baker, C. K., & Hjalmarson, M. (2019). Designing purposeful student interactions to advance synchronous learning experiences. *International Journal of Web-Based Learning and Teaching Technologies, 14*(1), 1–16. doi:10.4018/IJWLTT.2019010101

Balingit, M. (2020, August 16). 'A national crisis': As coronavirus forces many schools online this fall, millions of disconnected students are being left behind. *Washington Post*.

Ballam, N., & Cosgriff, M. (2018). Enabling ability and growing talent: The contribution of self, place, and belonging. *Australasian Journal of Gifted Education, 27*(1), 21–30. doi:10.21505/ajge.2018.0003

Ballantyne, J., Barrett, M., Temmerman, N., Harrison, S., & Meissner, E. (2009). Music teachers oz online: A new approach to school-university collaboration in teacher education. *International Journal of Education & the Arts, 10*(6). http://www.ijea.org/v10n6/

Ballantyne, R., & Packer, J. (2005). Promoting environmentally sustainable attitudes and behavior through free-choice learning experiences: What is the state of the game? *Environmental Education Research*, *11*(3), 281–295. doi:10.1080/13504620500081145

Bal-Taştan, S., Davoudi, S. M. M., Masalimova, A. R., Bersanov, A. S., Kurbanov, R. A., Boiarchuk, A. V., & Pavlushin, A. A. (2018). The Impacts of Teacher's Efficacy and Motivation on Student's Academic Achievement in Science Education among Secondary and High School Students. *Eurasia Journal of Mathematics, Science and Technology Education*, *14*(6), 2353–2366. doi:10.29333/ejmste/89579

Banaji, M. R., & Greenwald, A. G. (2013). *Blindspot: Hidden biases of good people*. Delacorte Press.

Bao, X., Qu, H., Zhang, R., & Hogan, T. P. (2020). *Literacy loss in kindergarten children during COVID-19 school closures*. Academic Press.

Barab, S., Thomas, M., Dodge, T., Carteaux, R., & Tuzun, H. (2005). Making learning fun: Quest Atlantis, a game without guns. *Educational Technology Research and Development*, *53*(1), 86–107. doi:10.1007/BF02504859

Barak, M. (2017). Science teacher education in the Twenty-First Century: A Pedagogical Framework for Technology-Integrated Social Constructivism. *Research in Science Education*, *47*(2), 283–303. doi:10.100711165-015-9501-y

Baran, E., Correia, A. P., & Thompson, A. (2011). Transforming online teaching practice: Critical analysis of the literature on the roles and competencies of online teachers. *Distance Education*, *32*(3), 421–439. doi:10.1080/01587919.2011.610293

Baratè, A., Haus, G., & Ludovico, L. A. (2020). Learning, teaching, and making music together in the COVID-19 era through IEEE 1599. *2020 International Conference on Software, Telecommunications and Computer Networks (SoftCOM)*, 1–5. 10.23919/SoftCOM50211.2020.9238238

Barbour, M., Brown, R., Waters, L. H., Hoey, R., Hunt, J. L., Kennedy, K., Ounsworth, C., Powell, A., & Trimm, T. (2011). Online and Blended Learning: A Survey of Policy and Practice from K-12 Schools around the World. In *International Association for K-12 Online Learning*. International Association for K-12 Online Learning.

Barclay, P. A., & Bowers, C. (2020). Associations of subjective immersion, immersion subfactors, and learning outcomes in the revised game engagement model. In Learning and Performance Assessment: Concepts, Methodologies, Tools, and Applications (pp. 957-968). Hershey, PA: IGI Global. doi:10.4018/978-1-7998-0420-8.ch044

Barlow, A., Edwards, C., Robichaux-Davis, R., & Sears, R. (2020). Enhancing and transforming virtual instruction. *Mathematics Teacher: Learning and Teaching Pk-12*, *113*(12), 972-982.

Barnard-Brak, L., Stevens, T., & Ritter, W. (2017). Reading and mathematics equally important to science achievement: Results from nationally-representative data. *Learning and Individual Differences*, *58*, 1–9. doi:10.1016/j.lindif.2017.07.001

Bartlett, M. (2018). Using Flipgrid to increase students' connectedness in an online class. *eLearn*, *2018*(12). https://dl.acm.org/doi/abs/10.1145/3302261.3236703

Barton, A. C., Tan, E., & Greenberg, D. (2016). The makerspace movement: Sites of possibilities for equitable opportunities to engage underrepresented youth in STEM. *Teachers College Record*, *119*(6), 11–44.

Bates, T. (2020, November 12). *How Canadian schools (k-12) prepared for the fall in 2020*. Retrieved from https://www.tonybates.ca/2020/11/12/how-canadian-schools-k-12-prepared-for-the-fall-in-2020/

Battelle for Kids. (2019a). Retrieved from https://www.battelleforkids.org/

Battelle for Kids. (2019b). *A framework for 21st century learning definitions*. Retrieved from http://static.battelleforkids.org/documents/p21/P21_Framework_DefinitionsBFK.pdf

Compilation of References

Battista, M. T. (2006). Understanding the development of students' thinking about length. *Teaching Children Mathematics*, *13*(3), 140–146. doi:10.5951/TCM.13.3.0140

Bauml, M., Patton, M. M., & Rhea, D. (2020). A Qualitative Study of Teachers' Perceptions of Increased Recess Time on Teaching, Learning, and Behavior. *Journal of Research in Childhood Education*, *34*(4), 506–520. doi:10.1080/02568543.2020.1718808

Bawa, P. (2016). Retention in online courses: Exploring issues and solutions—a literature review. *SAGE Open*, *6*(1). Advance online publication. doi:10.1177/2158244015621777

Beall, G. (2016, November). 8 key differences between Gen Z and Millennials. *The Huffington Post*. https://www.huffpost.com

Bear, D. R., Invernizzi, M., Templeton, S., & Johnston, F. (2020). *Words their way: Word study for phonics, vocabulary, and spelling instruction* (7th ed.). Pearson.

Becker, H. J., & Ravitz, J. (1999). The influence of computer and internet use of teachers' pedagogical practices and perceptions. *Journal of Research on Computing in Education*, *31*(4), 356–379. doi:10.1080/08886504.1999.10782260

Beckman, E. A. (2010). Learners on the move: Mobile modalities in development studies. *Distance Education*, *31*(2), 159–173. doi:10.1080/01587919.2010.498081

Beckmann, E., & Minnaert, A. (2018). Non-cognitive characteristics of gifted students with learning disabilities: An in-depth systematic review. *Frontiers in Psychology*, *9*, 504. doi:10.3389/fpsyg.2018.00504 PMID:29731728

Beebe, R, Vonderwell, S & Boboc, M. (2010). Emerging patterns in transferring assessment practices from F2f to online environments. *Electronic Journal of e-Learning, 8*(1), 1 - 12.

Beer, C., Clark, K., & Jones, D. (2010) Indicators of engagement. In C.H. Steel, M.J. Keppell, P. Gerbic, & Housego, M. (Eds.), *Proceedings of the Curriculum, Technology & Transformation for an Unknown Future Conference* (*ASCILITE 2010*) (pp. 75–86). The University of Queensland.

Beghetto, R. A. (2010). Creativity in the classroom. In J. C. Kaufman & R. J. Sternberg (Eds.), *The Cambridge handbook of creativity* (pp. 587–606). Cambridge University Press. doi:10.1017/CBO9780511763205.027

Beghetto, R. A., Kaufman, J. C., & Baer, J. (2015). *Teaching for creativity in the common core classroom*. Teacher's College Press.

Beghetto, R., & Kaufman, J. (2007). Toward a Broader Conception of Creativity: A Case for Mini-c Creativity. *Psychology of Aesthetics, Creativity, and the Arts*, *1*(2), 73–79. doi:10.1037/1931-3896.1.2.73

Behrman, E. H. (2006). Teaching about language, power, and text: A review of classroom practices that support critical literacy. *Journal of Adolescent & Adult Literacy*, *49*(6), 490–498. doi:10.1598/JAAL.49.6.4

Bell, D. (2016). Twenty-first century education: Transformative education for sustainability and responsible citizenship. *Journal of Teacher Education for Sustainability*, *18*(1), 48–56. doi:10.1515/jtes-2016-0004

Belman, J., & Flanagan, M. (2010). Designing games to foster empathy. *International Journal of Cognitive Technology*, *15*(1), 11.

Benbunan-Fich, R., Hiltz, S. R., & Harasim, L. (2005). The online interaction learning model: An integrated theoretical framework for learning networks. In S. Hiltz (Ed.), *Learning together online: Research on asynchronous learning networks* (pp. 18–36). Routledge.

Ben-Chayim, A., & Offir, B. (2019). Model of the mediating teaching in distance learning environments: Classes that combine asynchronous distance learning via videotaped lectures. *Journal of Educators Online*, *16*(1), 1–11. doi:10.9743/jeo.2019.16.1.1

Ben-Chayim, A., Reychav, I., McHaney, R., & Offir, B. (2020). Mediating teacher for distance teaching and learning model: An exploration. *Education and Information Technologies*, *25*(1), 105–140. doi:10.100710639-019-09938-8

BengtsonD. (2021). *LBR Problem 2.1*. https://teacher.desmos.com/activitybuilder/custom/6040ee84f10a370d55f38d29

Bennett, D., & Chong, E. K. M. (2018). Singaporean pre-service music teachers' identities, motivations and career intentions. *International Journal of Music Education*, *36*(1), 108–123. doi:10.1177/0255761417703780

Bennett, S., & Lockyer, L. (2004). Becoming an online teacher: Adapting to a changed environment for teaching and learning in higher education. *Educational Media International*, *41*(3), 231–248. doi:10.1080/09523980410001680842

Bennison, A., & Merrilyn, G. (2010). Learning to teach mathematics with technology: A survey of professional development needs, experience and impacts. *Mathematics Education Research Journal*, *22*(1), 31–56. doi:10.1007/BF03217558

Benson, R., & Samarawickrema, G. (2009). Addressing the context of e-learning: Using transactional distance theory to inform design. *Distance Education*, *30*(1), 5–21. doi:10.1080/01587910902845972

Bergeson, K., & Beschorner, B. (2020). Modeling and scaffolding the Technology Integration Planning Cycle for pre-service teachers: A case study. *International Journal of Education in Mathematics, Science, and Technology*, *8*(4), 330–341. doi:10.46328/ijemst.v8i4.1031

Bergeson, K., & Beschorner, B. (2021). Pre-service teachers' use of the Technology Integration Planning Cycle: Lessons learned. *Reading Horizons*, *60*(1).

Berquist, E. (2017). *UDL: Moving from exploration to integration*. CAST Publishing.

Bers, M. U., Flannery, L., Kazakoff, E. R., & Sullivan, A. (2014). Computational thinking and tinkering: Exploration of an early childhood robotics curriculum. *Computers & Education*, *72*, 145–157. doi:10.1016/j.compedu.2013.10.020

Beschorner, B., & Kruse, J. (2016). Pre-Service Teachers' Use of a Technology Integration Planning Cycle: A Case Study. *International Journal of Education in Mathematics, Science and Technology*, *4*(4), 258–271.

Beschorner, B., & Woodward, L. (2019). Engaging teachers in a digital learner-centered approach to support understanding of foundational literacy. In R. Karchmer-Klein & K. Pytash (Eds.), *Effective Practices in Online Teacher Preparation for Literacy Educators* (pp. 284–306). IGI Global.

Beschorner, B., & Woodward, L. (2019). Long-Term Planning for Technology in Literacy Instruction. *The Reading Teacher*, *73*(3), 325–337.

Biggs, J. (1996). Enhancing Teaching through Constructive Alignment. *Higher Education*, *32*(3), 347–364. doi:10.1007/BF00138871

Bingham, C., & Sidorkin, A. (Eds.). (2004). *No education without relation*. Peter Lang.

Bjorklund, D. F., & Green, B. L. (1992). The adaptive nature of cognitive immaturity. *The American Psychologist*, *47*(1), 46–54. doi:10.1037/0003-066X.47.1.46

Bjork, R. A. (1994). Memory and metamemory considerations in the training of human beings. In J. Metcalfe & A. P. Shimamura (Eds.), *Metacognition: Knowing about knowing* (Vol. 185, pp. 185–206). MIT Press.

Compilation of References

Black, P., & Wiliam, D. (1998). Assessment and classroom learning. *Assessment in Education: Principles, Policy & Practice*, *5*(1), 7–74. doi:10.1080/0969595980050102

Black, P., & Wiliam, D. (2009). Developing the theory of formative assessment. *Educational Assessment, Evaluation and Accountability*, *21*(1), 5–31. doi:10.100711092-008-9068-5

Black, P., & Wiliam, D. (2018). Classroom assessment and pedagogy. *Assessment in Education: Principles, Policy & Practice*, *25*(6), 551–575. doi:10.1080/0969594X.2018.1441807

Black, R. D., Weinberg, L. A., & Brodwin, M. G. (2015). Universal design for learning and instruction: Perspectives of students with disabilities in higher education. *Exceptionality Education International*, *25*(2). Advance online publication. doi:10.5206/eei.v25i2.7723

Blackwell, C. K., Lauricella, A. R., & Wartella, E. (2016). The influence of TPACK contextual factors on early childhood educators' tablet computer use. *Computers & Education*, *98*, 57–69. doi:10.1016/j.compedu.2016.02.010

Blackwell, L. S., Trzesniewski, K. H., & Dweck, C. S. (2007). Implicit theories of intelligence predict achievement across an adolescent transition: A longitudinal study and an intervention. *Child Development*, *78*(1), 246–263. doi:10.1111/j.1467-8624.2007.00995.x PMID:17328703

Blair, C. (2016). The development of executive functions and self-regulation: A bidirectional psychological model. In K. D. Vohs & R. F. Baumeister (Eds.), *Handbook of self-regulation* (3rd ed., pp. 417–440). The Guilford Press.

Blank, R. (2013). Science instructional time is declining in elementary schools: What are the implications for student achievement and closing the gap? *Science Education*, *97*(6), 830–847. doi:10.1002ce.21078

Blau, I., & Barak, A. (2012). How Do Personality, Synchronous Media, and Discussion Topic Affect Participation? *Journal of Educational Technology & Society*, *15*(2), 12–24. https://www.jstor.org/stable/jeductechsoci.15.2.12

Blau, I., Weiser, O., & Eshet-Alkalai, Y. (2017). How do medium naturalness and personality traits shape academic achievement and perceived learning? An experimental study of face-to-face and synchronous e-learning. *Research in Learning Technology*, *25*(0), 1945. doi:10.25304/rlt.v25.1974

Blewett, C., & Hugo, W. (2016). Actant affordances: a brief history of affordance theory and a Latourian extension for education technology research. *Critical Studies in Teaching and Learning*, *4*, 55-73. doi:10.14426/cristal.v4i1.50

Bloom, E., & VanSlyke-Briggs. (2019). The demise of creativity in tomorrow's teachers. *Journal of Inquiry & Action in Education*, *10*(2), 90–99. Retrieved from https://digitalcommons.buffalostate.edu/

Blundell, C., Lee, K., & Nykvist, S. (2020). Moving beyond enhancing pedagogies with digital technologies: Frames of reference, habits of mind and transformative learning. *Journal of Research on Technology in Education*, *52*(2), 178–196. doi:10.1080/15391523.2020.1726235

Bocconi, S., Chioccariello, A., Dettori, G., Ferrari, A., & Engelhardt, K. (2016). *Computational thinking in compulsory education*. Technical report, European Union Scientific and Technical Research Reports, 2016. EUR 28295 EN.

Boden, K. (2011). Perceived Academic Preparedness of First-Generation Latino College Students. *Journal of Hispanic Higher Education*, *10*(2), 96–106. doi:10.1177/1538192711402211

Boehrer, J., & Linsky, M. (1990). Teaching with cases: Learning to question. *New Directions for Teaching and Learning*, *1990*(42), 41–57. doi:10.1002/tl.37219904206

BoGL. (2020). *A Board Game Language*. Academic Press.

Bol, L., & Garner, J. K. (2011). Challenges in supporting self-regulation in distance education environments. *Journal of Computing in Higher Education*, *23*(2-3), 104–123. doi:10.100712528-011-9046-7

Bol, L., & Strage, A. (1996). The contradiction between teachers' instructional goals and their assessment practices in high school biology courses. *Science Education*, *80*(2), 145–163. doi:10.1002/(SICI)1098-237X(199604)80:2<145::AID-SCE2>3.0.CO;2-G

Bolliger, D. U., & Martin, F. (2018). Instructor and student perceptions of online student engagement strategies. *Distance Education*, *39*(4), 568–583. doi:10.1080/01587919.2018.1520041

Bondie, R. (2019). Demystifying Differentiated Instruction. *Science & Children*, *57*(2), 14-19. https://doi/org/doi:10.2505/4c19_057_02_14

Bonnardel, N., & Didier, J. (2020). Brainstorming variants to favor creative design. *Applied Ergonomics*, *83*, 102987–102987. doi:10.1016/j.apergo.2019.102987 PMID:31710954

Bonwell, C. C., & Eison, J. A. (1991). Active learning: Creating excitement in the classroom. ASHE-ERIC Higher Education Report No. 1. The George Washington University, School of Education and Human Development.

Boonpleng, W., Park, C., Gallo, A., Corte, C., McCreary, L., & Bergren, M. (2013). Ecological Influences of Early Childhood Obesity: A Multilevel Analysis. *Western Journal of Nursing Research*, *35*(6), 742–759. doi:10.1177/0193945913480275 PMID:23493675

Booth, T. (2020, January 29). *Bilingual Augmentative and Alternative Communication (AAC) Users*. Retrieved August 03, 2020, from https://hespinterpretation.com/2019/10/07/bilingual-augmentative-and-alternative-communication-aac-users/comment-page-1/

Borko, H. (2004). Professional development and teacher learning: Mapping the terrain. *Educational Researcher*, *33*(3), 3–15. doi:10.3102/0013189X033008003

Boud, D. (2000). Sustainable assessment: Rethinking assessment for the learning society. *Studies in Continuing Education*, *22*(2), 151–167. doi:10.1080/713695728

Bourdeau, D. T., & Wood, B. L. (2019). What is humanistic STEM and why do we need it? *Journal of Humanistic Mathematics*, *9*(1), 205- 216. https://scholarship.claremont edu/jhm/vol9/ iss1/11

Bowdon, J. (2020, August 25). *Meaningful online education for our youngest learners: Tips to reconcile the need for e-learning with how young children learn best*. https://ies.ed.gov/ncee/edlabs/regions/midwest/blogs/online-education-young-learners.aspx

Boyle, G. J. (1991). Does item homogeneity indicate internal consistency or item redundancy in psychometric scales? *Personality and Individual Differences*, *12*(3), 291–294. doi:10.1016/0191-8869(91)90115-R

Bradbury, L. (2014). Linking science and language arts: A review of the literature which compares integrated versus non-integrated approaches. *Journal of Science Teacher Education*, *25*(4), 465–488. doi:10.100710972-013-9368-6

Branch, R. M. (2009). *Instructional design: The ADDIE approach*. Springer., doi:10.1007/978-0-387-09506-6

Branscombe, N. A., Castle, K., Surbeck, E., & Burcham, J. G. (2013). *Early Childhood Curriculum: A Constructivist Perspective* (2nd ed.). Routledge., doi:10.4324/9780203808849

Bransford, J., Brown, A., & Cocking, R. (2000). *How people learn: Brain, mind, experience, and school*. National Academies Press.

Braun, V., & Clarke, V. (2006). Using thematic analysis in psychology. *Qualitative Research in Psychology*, *3*(2), 77–101. doi:10.1191/1478088706qp063oa

Brevik, L. M., Olsen, R. V., & Hellekjær, G. O. (2016). The complexity of second language reading: Investigating the L1-L2 relationship. *Reading in a Foreign Language*, *28*(2), 161–182.

Brinkmann, R. (2020). Connections in environmental sustainability: Living in a time of rapid environmental change. In Environmental Sustainability in a Time of Change. Palgrave Studies in Environmental Sustainability (pp. 1-8). Palgrave Macmillan.

Britt, J., & Howe, M. (2014). Developing a vision for the common core classroom: What does elementary social studies look like? *Social Studies*, *105*(3), 158–163. doi:10.1080/00377996.2013.866930

Broadbent, J., Panadero, E., & Boud, D. (2018). Implementing summative assessment with a formative flavour: A case study in a large class. *Assessment & Evaluation in Higher Education*, *43*(2), 307–322. doi:10.1080/02602938.2017.1343455

Brodersen, R. M., & Melluzzo, D. (2017). Summary of Research on Online and Blended Learning Programs That Offer Differentiated Learning Options. REL 2017-228. Regional Educational Laboratory Central.

Bronfenbrenner, U. (1976). The experimental ecology of education. *Educational Researcher*, *5*(9), 5–15. doi:10.3102/0013189X005009005

Bronfenbrenner, U., & Morris, P. A. (2006). The bioecological model of human development. In W. Damon & R. M. Lerner (Eds.), Handbook of child psychology (Vol. 1, pp. 793–828). John Wiley & Sons. doi:10.1002/9780470147658.chpsy0114

Brookhart, S. M. (2010). *Assessing higher order thinking skills in your classroom*. ASCD.

Brooks, S. K., Webster, R. K., Smith, L. E., Woodland, L., Wessely, S., Greenberg, N., & Rubin, G. J. (2020). The psychological impact of quarantine and how to reduce it: Rapid review of the evidence. *Lancet*, *395*(10227), 912–920. doi:10.1016/S0140-6736(20)30460-8 PMID:32112714

Brown, J. S., Collins, A., & Duguid, P. (1989). Situated Cognition and the Culture of Learning. *Educational Researcher*, *18*(1), 32–42. doi:10.3102/0013189X018001032

Buchanan, J., Schuck, S., & Aubusson, P. (2016). In-school sustainability action: Climate clever energy savers. *Australian Journal of Environmental Education*, *32*(2), 154–173. doi:10.1017/aee.2015.55

Buchanan, R. (1992). Wicked problems in design thinking. *Design Issues*, *8*(2), 5–21. doi:10.2307/1511637

Budhai, S. S., & Taddei, L. M. (2015). *Teaching the 4Cs with Technology: How do I use 21st century tools to teach 21st century skills?* ASCD.

Burgess, S., & Sievertsen, H. H. (2020). *Schools, skills, and learning: The impact of COVID-19 on education*. https://voxeu.org/article/impact-covid-19-education

Burnett, C., & Smith, S. (2019). Reaching for the Star: A Model for Integrating Creativity in Education. In C. Mullen (Ed.), *Creativity Under Duress in Education?* Springer International Publishing. doi:10.1007/978-3-319-90272-2_10

Cabell, S. Q., & Hwang, H. (2020). Building content knowledge to boost comprehension in the primary grades. *Reading Research Quarterly*, *55*(51). Advance online publication. doi:10.1002/rrq.338

Cabell, S. Q., Tortorelli, L. S., & Gerde, H. K. (2013). How do I write…? Scaffolding preschoolers' early writing. *The Reading Teacher*, *66*(8), 650–659. doi:10.1002/trtr.1173

Calderon, O., & Sood, C. (2018). Evaluating learning outcomes of an asynchronous online discussion assignment: A post-priori content analysis. *Interactive Learning Environments*, *28*(1), 1, 3–17. doi:10.1080/10494820.2018.1510421

Calefato, F., Iaffaldano, G., & Lanubile, F. (2018). *Collaboration success factors in an online music community*. In Proceedings of 2018 ACM conference on Supporting Groupwork. Association for Computing Machinery. doi:10.1145/3148330.3148346

Calkins, L. (1994). *The Art of Teaching Writing*. Heinemann.

Campaign for Grade-Level Reading. (2016). *3rd grade reading success matters*. http://gradelevelreading.net

Candy, P. C. (1991). *Self-direction for lifelong learning: A comprehensive guide to theory and practice*. Jossey-Bass.

Carder, L., Willingham, P., & Bibb, D. (2001). Case-based, problem-based learning: Information literacy for the real world. *Research Strategies*, *18*(3), 181–190. doi:10.1016/S0734-3310(02)00087-3

Carey, L. B. (2020). *Executive function and online learning: Linking research to classroom*. https://www.kennedykrieger.org/stories/linking-research-classrooms-blog/executive-function-and-online-learning

Carey, L. B., Sadera, W. A., Cai, Q., & Filipiak. (2020). Creating a community of practice for educators forced to transition to remote teaching. *Teaching, Technology, and Teacher Education during the COVID-19 Pandemic: Stories from the Field*, 251-255. https://www.learntechlib.org/p/216903/

Carey, L. B., Schmidt, J., Dommestrup, A. K., Pritchard, A. E., van Stone, M., Grasmick, N., ... Jacobson, L. A. (2020). Beyond learning about the brain: A situated approach to training teachers in mind, brain, and education. *Mind, Brain and Education: the Official Journal of the International Mind, Brain, and Education Society*, *14*(3), 200–208. doi:10.1111/mbe.12238

Carpenter, J., Cassaday, A., & Monti, S. (2018, March). Exploring how and why educators use Pinterest. In *Society for Information Technology & Teacher Education International Conference* (pp. 2222-2229). Association for the Advancement of Computing in Education (AACE).

Carpenter, J., Morrison, S., Craft, M., & Lee, M. (2019). Exploring how and why educators use Instagram. In K. Graziano (Ed.), *Proceedings of Society for Information Technology & Teacher Education (SITE) International Conference 2019* (pp. 2686–2691). Las Vegas, NV: Association for the Advancement of Computing in Education (AACE).

Carpenter, J. P. (2016). Teachers at the wheel. *Educational Leadership*, 3–35.

Carpenter, J. P., Rosenberg, J. M., Dousay, T. A., Romero-Hall, E., Trust, T., Kessler, A., Phillips, M., Morrison, S. A., Fischer, C., & Krutka, D. G. (2020). What should teacher educators known about technology? Perspectives and self-assessments. *Teaching and Teacher Education*, *95*, 1–13. doi:10.1016/j.tate.2020.103124

Carter, C. (2017, April 13). *Diversity in STEM—Important for society, good for business*. Huffington Post. https://www.huffpost.com/entry/diversity-in-stem-important-for-society-good-for_b_58efe99fe4b04cae050dc5ea

Cartwright, T. (2014). Confronting barriers to teaching elementary science: After-school science teaching experiences for preservice teachers. *Teacher Education and Practice*, *27*(2/3), 464–487.

Cashmore, P. (2010, December 30). How Facebook eclipsed Google in 2010. *CNN*. https://www.cnn.com/2010/TECH/social.media/12/30/facebook.beats.google.cashmore/index.html

Castelo, M. (2020). *Here's What to Know About Moving Classroom Management Online*. Retrieved from https://edtechmagazine.com/k12/article/2020/07/heres-what-know-about-moving-classroom-management-online-perfcon

Cayari, C. (2020). Popular practices for online musicking and performance: Developing creative dispositions for music education and the Internet. *Journal of Popular Music Education, 4*(2), 131–134. doi:10.1386/jpme_00021_2

Center for Applied Special Technology (CAST). (2011). *Universal Design for Learning guidelines version 2.0*. http://www.udlcenter.org/aboutudl/udlguidelines

Center for Applied Special Technology (CAST). (2018). *Universal design for learning guidelines version 2.2*. https://udlguidelines.cast.org

Center for Applied Special Technology (CAST). (2020). *CAST announces a community-driven process to update UDL guidelines*. https://www.cast.org/news/2020/community-driven-process-update-udl-guidelines

Center on Online Learning and Students with Disabilities (COLSWD). (2016). *Equity matters: Digital & online learning for students with disabilities*. Lawrence, KS: Author. http://www.centerononlinelearning.res.ku.edu/equity-matters-2016-digital-and-online-learning-for-students-with-disabilities/

Cervetti, G. N., Pearson, P. D., Palinsar, A. S., Afflerbach, P., Kendeou, P., Biancaros, G., Higgs, J., Fitzgerald, M. S., & Berman, A. I. (2020). How the reading for understanding initiative's research complicates the simple view of reading invoked in the science of reading. *Reading Research Quarterly, 55*(51). Advance online publication. doi:10.1002/rrq.343

Cervetti, G., Barber, J., Dorph, R., Pearson, D., & Goldschmidt, P. (2012). The impact of an integrated approach to science and literacy in elementary school classrooms. *Journal of Research in Science Teaching, 49*(5), 631–658. doi:10.1002/tea.21015

Çetin, I., & Erdoğan, A. (2018). Development, validity and reliability of study of technological pedagogical content knowledge (TPACK) efficiency scale for mathematics teacher candidates. *International Journal of Contemporary Educational Research, 5*(1), 50–62.

Chai, C. S., Koh, J. H. L., & Tsai, C.-C. (2013). A review of technological pedagogical content knowledge. *Journal of Educational Technology & Society, 16*(2), 31–51.

Chamberlain, L., Lacina, J., Bintz, W. P., Jimerson, J. B., Payne, K., & Zingale, R. (2020). Literacy in lockdown: Learning and teaching during COVID-19 school closures. *The Reading Teacher, 74*(3), 243–253. doi:10.1002/trtr.1961 PMID:33362300

Chapin, S. H., O'Connor, C., O'Connor, M. C., & Anderson, N. C. (2009). *Classroom discussions: Using math talk to help students learn, Grades K-6*. Math Solutions.

Charsky, D., & Ressler, W. (2011). "Games are made for fun": Lessons on the effects of concept maps in the classroom use of computer games. *Computers & Education, 56*(3), 604–615. doi:10.1016/j.compedu.2010.10.001

Chen, C., & Pugachevsky, J. (2020, October 27). *Ten popular online STEM, coding and gaming courses—all are taught by women*. Business Insider. https://www.businessinsider.com/online-stem-gaming-python-courses-taught-by-women

Chen, B., Bastedo, K., & Howard, W. (2018). Exploring Design Elements for Online STEM Courses: Active Learning, Engagement & Assessment Design. *Online Learning, 22*(2), 59–75. doi:10.24059/olj.v22i2.1369

Chen, C. H., Law, V., & Huang, K. (2019). The roles of engagement and competition on learner's performance and motivation in game-based science learning. *Educational Technology Research and Development, 67*(4), 1–22. doi:10.100711423-019-09670-7

Cheng, Y. M., Lou, S. J., Kuo, S. H., & Shih, R. C. (2013). Investigating elementary school students' technology acceptance by applying digital game-based learning to environmental education. *Australasian Journal of Educational Technology, 29*(1). Advance online publication. doi:10.14742/ajet.65

Chen, Y. (2001). Dimensions of transactional distance in the world wide web learning environment: A factor analysis. *British Journal of Educational Technology, 32*(4), 459–470. doi:10.1111/1467-8535.00213

Children's Defense Fund. (2020). *The state of America's children.* https://www.childrensdefense.org/policy/resources/soac-2020-child-poverty-tables/

Chiu, M. M., Chow, B. W. Y., McBride, C., & Mol, S. T. (2016). Students' Sense of Belonging at School in 41 Countries: Cross-Cultural Variability. *Journal of Cross-Cultural Psychology, 47*(2), 175–196. doi:10.1177/0022022115617031

Christodoulou, D. (2020). Teachers vs tech? The case for an ed tech revolution. Oxford University Press.

Churchman, C. W. (1967). Wicked Problems. *Management Science, 14*(4), 41–142. http://www.jstor.org/stable/2628678

Ciampa, K. (2016). Implementing a digital reading and writing workshop model for content literacy instruction in an urban elementary (K-8) school. *The Reading Teacher, 70*(3), 295–306. doi:10.1002/trtr.1514

Ciampa, K. (2017). Building Bridges Between Technology and Content Literacy in Special Education: Lessons Learned from Special Educators' Use of Integrated Technology and Perceived Benefits for Students. *Literacy Research and Instruction, 56*(2), 85–113. doi:10.1080/19388071.2017.1280863

Ciccone, M. (2019). Teaching adolescents to communicate (better) online. *The Journal of Media Literacy Education, 11*(2), 167–170. doi:10.23860/JMLE-2019-11-2-9

Cicconi, M. (2014). Vygotsky meets technology: A reinvention of collaboration in the early childhood mathematics classroom. *Early Childhood Journal, 42*(1), 57–65. doi:10.100710643-013-0582-9

Clapp, E. P., Ross, J., Ryan, J. O., & Tishman, S. (2017). *Maker-centered learning: Empowering young people to shape their worlds.* Jossey-Bass.

Clarke, D., & Hollingsworth, H. (2002). Elaborating a model of teacher professional growth. *Teaching and Teacher Education, 18*(8), 947–967. doi:10.1016/S0742-051X(02)00053-7

Clark, R. E., Feldon, D. F., van Merriënboer, J., Yates, K. A., & Early, S. (2008). Cognitive Task Analysis. In M. Spector, M. D. Merrill, J. van Merrienboer, & M. P. Driscoll (Eds.), *Handbook of research on educational communications and technology* (3rd ed., pp. 1801–1856). Routledge.

Clark, S., & Lott, K. (2017). Integrating science inquiry and literacy instruction for young children. *The Reading Teacher, 70*(6), 701–710. doi:10.1002/trtr.1572

Claro, S., Paunesku, D., & Dweck, C. S. (2016). Growth mindset tempers the effects of poverty on academic achievement. *Proceedings of the National Academy of Sciences of the United States of America, 113*(31), 8664–8668. doi:10.1073/pnas.1608207113 PMID:27432947

Claxton, G. (2007). Expanding young people's capacity to learn. *British Journal of Educational Studies, 55*(2), 115–134. doi:10.1111/j.1467-8527.2007.00369.x

Clay, M. M. (2001). *Change over time in children's literacy development.* Heinemann.

Clowes, G. (2011). *The essential 5: A starting point for Kagan cooperative learning.* Kagan Online Magazine.

Clyde, R. G. (2016). *How instructional designers bridge learner-content transactional distances in virtual high school courses* (Publication No. 10151287) [Doctoral dissertation, Capella University]. ProQuest Dissertations Publishing.

Cobb, P., McClain, K., de Silva Lamberg, T., & Dean, C. (2003). Situating teachers' instructional practices in the institutional setting of the school and district. *Educational Researcher, 32*(6), 13–24. doi:10.3102/0013189X032006013

Coburn, C. E., Penuel, W. R., & Geil, K. E. (2013). *Practice Partnerships: A Strategy for Leveraging Research for Educational Improvement in School Districts*. William T. Grant Foundation.

Cochran-Smith, M., & Lytle, S. (2009). *Inquiry as stance: Practitioner research for the next generation*. Teachers College Press.

Cohen, J. (1988). *Statistical power analysis for the behavioral sciences* (2nd ed.). Lawrence Erlbaum Associates.

Colao, A., Piscitelli, P., Pulimeno, M., Colazzo, S., Miani, A., & Giannini, S. (2020). Rethinking the role of the school after COVID-19. *The Lancet Public Health*, 5(7), e370. PMID:32464100

Collier-Meek, M. A., Johnson, A. H., Sanetti, L. H., & Minami, T. (2019). Identifying critical components of classroom management implementation. *School Psychology Review*, 48(4), 348–361. doi:10.17105/SPR-2018-0026.V48-4

Collins, K. H. (2018). Confronting color-blind STEM talent development: Toward a contextual model for Black student STEM identity. *Journal of Advanced Academics*, 29(2), 143–168. doi:10.1177/1932202X18757958

Common Core State Standards Initiative. (2010). *Common Core State Standards for English language arts and literacy in history/social studies, science, and technical subjects*. National Governors Association Center for Best Practices and the Council of Chief State School Officers.

Conde, M. Á., Fernández, C., Alves, J., Ramos, M. J., Celis-Tena, S., Gonçalves, J., ... Peñalvo, F. J. G. (2019, October). RoboSTEAM: A challenge based learning approach for integrating STEAM and developing computational thinking. In *Proceedings of the Seventh International Conference on Technological Ecosystems for Enhancing Multiculturality* (pp. 24-30). ACM. 10.1145/3362789.3362893

Conn, C. A., Bohan, K. J., Pieper, S. L., & Musumeci, M. (2020). Validity inquiry process: Practical guidance for examining performance assessments and building a validity argument. *Studies in Educational Evaluation*, 65, 100843. doi:10.1016/j.stueduc.2020.100843

Cook, S. (2015, August). *Engaging Generation Z students* [Workshop presentation]. Greenville College.

Cooper, R., & Murphy, E. (2016). *Hacking Project Based Learning*. Times 10 Publications.

Cooper, K. S. (2014). Eliciting engagement in the high school classroom: A mixed methods examination of teaching practices. *American Educational Research Journal*, 51(2), 363–402. doi:10.3102/0002831213507973

Cooper, R., & Heaverlo, C. (2013). Problem solving and creativity and design: What influence do they have on girls' interest in STEM subject areas? *American Journal of Engineering Education*, 4(1), 27–38. doi:10.19030/ajee.v4i1.7856

Cooper, R., Warren, L., Hogan-Chapman, A., & Mills, L. (2020). Pre-service teachers and their self-efficacy toward online teaching. *Southeastern Regional Association of Teacher Educators*, 29(2), 5–7.

Cope, B., & Kalantzis, M. (2013). Multiliteracies: New literacies, new learning. In M. R. Hawkins (Ed.), *Framing language and literacies: Socially situated views and perspectives* (pp. 54–66). Routledge.

Copp, S. B., Cabell, S. Q., & Tortorelli, L. S. (2016). See, say, write: A writing routine for the preschool classroom. *The Reading Teacher*, 69(4), 447–451. doi:10.1002/trtr.1419

Corbin, J., & Strauss, A. (2014). *Basics of qualitative research: Techniques and procedures for developing grounded theory*. https://books.google.com/books?hl=en&lr=&id=MaKWBQAAQBAJ&oi=fnd&pg=PP1&dq=Constructing+Grounded+Theory+(Introducing+Qualitative+Methods+series)&ots=QrDftQ67U2&sig=u_iUtIvlfgpuhRsnJC7-pNRmIEY

Cordano, M., Welcomer, S. A., & Scherer, R. F. (2003). An analysis of the predictive validity of the new ecological paradigm scale. *The Journal of Environmental Education*, 34(3), 22–28. doi:10.1080/00958960309603490

Cortiella, C., & Horowitz, S. H. (2014). The state of learning disabilities: Facts, trends, and emerging issues. *National Center for Learning Disabilities, 25*, 2-45. https://www.ncld.org/wp-content/uploads/2014/11/2014-State-of-LD.pdf

Cortina, J. M. (1993). What is coefficient alpha: An examination of theory and applications? *The Journal of Applied Psychology, 78*(1), 98–104. doi:10.1037/0021-9010.78.1.98

Coy, K., Marino, M. T., & Serianni, B. (2014). Using universal design for learning in synchronous online instruction. *Journal of Special Education Technology, 29*(1), 63–74. doi:10.1177/016264341402900105

Crabtree, L., Richardson, S., & Lewis, C. (2019). The gifted gap, STEM education, and economic immobility. *Journal of Advanced Academics, 30*(2), 203–231. doi:10.1177/1932202X19829749

Cremata, R., & Powell, B. (2015). Online music collaboration project: Digitally mediated, deterritorialized music education. *International Journal of Music Education, 35*(2), 302–315. doi:10.1177/0255761415620225

Creswell, J. W., & Poth, C. N. (2016). *Qualitative inquiry and research design: Choosing among five approaches*. Sage Publications.

Crompton, H. (2017). *ISTE Standards for educators: A guide for teachers and other professionals*. International Society for Technology in Education.

Cropley, A. (2006). In praise of convergent thinking. *Creativity Research Journal, 18*(3), 391–404. doi:10.120715326934crj1803_13

Croxton, R. A., & Chow, A. S. (2015). Using ADDIE and systems thinking as the framework for developing a MOOC: A case study. *Quarterly Review of Distance Education, 16*(4), 83–96.

Csikszentmihalyi, M. (2013). *Creativity: The psychology of discovery and invention*. Harper Perennial Modern Classics.

Cuban, L. (2001). *Oversold and underused*. Harvard University Press.

Cuban, L. (2013). *Inside the black box of classroom practice. Change without reform in American Education*. Harvard Education Press.

Cuban, L. (2013). *Inside the black box of classroom practice: Change without reform in American education*. Harvard Education Publishing Group.

Çubukçu, Z. (2012). The effect of hidden curriculum on character education process of primary school students. *Educational Sciences: Theory and Practice, 12*(2), 1526–1534.

Cuccurullo, S., Francese, R., Passero, I., & Tortora, G. (2013). A 3D serious city building game on waste disposal. *International Journal of Distance Education Technologies, 11*(4), 112–135. doi:10.4018/ijdet.2013100108

Cummins, J. (2000). *Language, power and pedagogy: Bilingual children in the crossfire*. Multilingual Matters. doi:10.21832/9781853596773

Cureton, A., & Hill, T. (2018). Disability in Practice: Attitudes, Policies, and Relationships. In *Disability in Practice*. Oxford University Press. doi:10.1093/oso/9780198812876.001.0001

Cutri, M. R., Mena, J., & Feinauer Whiting, E. (2020). Faculty readiness for online crisis teaching: Transitioning to online teaching during the COVID-19 pandemic. *European Journal of Teacher Education, 43*(4), 523–541. doi:10.1080/02619768.2020.1815702

Compilation of References

Czeisler, M. É., Lane, R. I., Petrosky, E., Wiley, J. F., Christensen, A., Njai, R., & Czeisler, C. A. (2020). Mental health, substance use, and suicidal ideation during the COVID-19 pandemic—United States, June 24–30, 2020. *Morbidity and Mortality Weekly Report*, *69*(32), 1049–1060. doi:10.15585/mmwr.mm6932a1 PMID:32790653

Dabbagh, N., Benson, A. D., Denham, A., Joseph, R., Al-Freih, M., Zgheib, G., & Guo, Z. (2016). *Learning technologies and globalization: pedagogical frameworks and applications*. Springer. doi:10.1007/978-3-319-22963-8

Daniels, H. (2002). *Literature circles: Voice and choice in book clubs & reading groups* (2nd ed.). Stenhouse Publishers.

Darbellay, F., Moody, Z., & Lubart, T. (2018). Introduction: Thinking creativity, design, and interdisciplinary in a changing world. In F. Darbellay, Z. Moody, & T. Lubart (Eds.), *Creativity, Design Thinking and Interdisciplinarity* (pp. xi–xxi). Springer., doi:10.1007/978-981-10-7524-7

Darling-Hammond, L., Hyler, M. E., & Gardner, M. (2017). *Effective teacher professional development*. Palo Alto, CA: Learning Policy Institute. Retrieved from https://learningpolicyinstitute.org/product/teacher-prof-dev

Darling-Hammond, L. (2015). *The flat world and education: How America's commitment to equity will determine our future*. Teachers College Press.

Darling-Hammond, L., Flook, L., Cook-Harvey, C., Barro, B., & Osher, D. (2020). Implications for educational practice of the science of learning and development. *Applied Developmental Science*, *24*(2), 97–140. doi:10.1080/10888691.2018.1537791

Darling-Hammond, L., & Hyler, M. E. (2020). Preparing educators for the time of COVID … and beyond. *European Journal of Teacher Education*, *43*(4), 457–465. doi:10.1080/02619768.2020.1816961

Darling-Hammond, L., Hyler, M. E., & Gardner, M. (2017). *Effective teacher professional development*. Learning Policy Institute.

Davis, G. A. (2004). *Creativity is forever* (5th ed.). Kendall Hunt.

Dawley, L. K., Rice, E. D. G. & Hinck. (2010). *The Status of Professional Development and Unique Needs of K-12 Online Teachers November, 2010*. Academic Press.

DEC Recommended Practices. (2015). DEC Recommended Practices. *Young Exceptional Children*, *18*(3), 54–54. doi:10.1177/1096250615605690

Dede, C. (2008). Theoretical perspectives influencing the use of information technology in teaching and learning. In J. Voogt & G. Knezek (Eds.), *International handbook of information technology in primary and secondary education* (Vol. 20, pp. 43–62). Springer. doi:10.1007/978-0-387-73315-9_3

DeJarnette, N. K. (2012). America's children: Providing early exposure to STEM (Science, Technology, Engineering and Mathematics) initiatives. *Education*, *133*(1), 77–84.

Dekeyser, S., & Watson, R. (2006). *Extending Google Docs to collaborate on research papers*. Technical Report. The University of Southern Queensland, Australia. Accessed May 8, 2021, from http://www.sci.usq.edu.au/staff/dekeyser/googledocs.pdf

Delgado, R. (Ed.). (1995). *Critical race theory: The cutting edge*. Temple University Press.

Delmas, P. M., & Moore, P. R. (2019). Student perceptions of video-based discussions in online and blended learning. In *Proceedings of the E-Learn 2019 Annual Conference* (pp. 1280–1286). Association for the Advancement of Computing in Education.

Denckla, M. B. (2018). *Understanding learning and related disabilities: Inconvenient brains.* Routledge. doi:10.4324/9780429425981

Department of Education (ED), O. for C. R. (OCR) & Office of Special Education and Rehabilitative Services, (ED). (2020b). *Supplemental Fact Sheet: Addressing the Risk of COVID-19 in Preschool, Elementary and Secondary Schools While Serving Children with Disabilities* (Office for Civil Rights, US Department of Education). Office for Civil Rights, US Department of Education.

Department of Education. (n.d.). *Indiana Academic Standards for Environmental Science.* https://www.doe.in.gov/sites/default/files/standards/resource-guides-environmental-science-070516.pdf

Desimone, L. (2009). Improving impact studies of teachers' professional development: Toward better conceptualizations and measures. *Educational Researcher, 38*(3), 181–199. doi:10.3102/0013189X08331140

Deslauriers, L., McCarty, L. S., Miller, K., Callaghan, K., & Kestin, G. (2019). Measuring actual learning versus feeling of learning in response to being actively engaged in the classroom. *Proceedings of the National Academy of Sciences of the United States of America, 116*(39), 19251–19257. doi:10.1073/pnas.1821936116 PMID:31484770

Desmos Activities. (n.d.). https://teacher.desmos.com/

Desmos Bank. (n.d.). https://sites.google.com/site/desmosbank/

Desmos Graphing Calculator. (n.d.). https://www.desmos.com/calculator

Desmos. (2015). *The Desmos Activity Builder Community - Des-Blog.* https://blog.desmos.com/articles/the-desmos-activity-builder-community/

Desmos. (n.d.). *Desmos | About Us.* Accessed February 19, 2021. https://www.desmos.com/about

Dewey, J. (1938). *Experience and education.* Collier.

DeWitt, P. (2012). *Rigor, relevance, & relationships: An interview with Bill Daggett.* EducationWeek. https://blogs.edweek.org/edweek/finding_common_ground/2012/01/rigor_relevance_relationships_an_interview_with_bill_daggett.html

Dhawan, S. (2020). Online learning: A panacea in the time of COVID-19 crisis. *Journal of Educational Technology Systems, 49*(1), 5–22. doi:10.1177/0047239520934018

Di Pietro, G. (2018). The academic impact of natural disasters: Evidence from L'Aquila earthquake. *Education Economics, 26*(1), 62–77. doi:10.1080/09645292.2017.1394984

Diamond, A. (2013). Executive functions. *Annual Review of Psychology, 64*(1), 135–168. doi:10.1146/annurev-psych-113011-143750 PMID:23020641

Dickman, G. (2018). Ladder of reading infographic. *Examiner, 7*(3). https://dyslexiaida.org

Digital, R., Rowan, W., Works, D. & Elder, B. (2020). *Decolonizing inclusive education: A collection of practical inclusive CDS-and DisCrit-informed teaching practices implemented in the global South* (Vol. 7). Academic Press.

Dikkers, A., Whiteside, A., & Lewis, S. (2013). Virtual high school teacher and student reactions to the social presence model. *Journal of Interactive Online Learning, 12*(3).

Dillon, T. (2005). *Adventure games for learning and storytelling.* UK, Futurelab Prototype Context Paper: Adventure Janakiraman. doi:10.1080/00219266.2012.688848

Dimock, M. (2019). Defining generations: Where Millennials end and Generation Z begins. *Pew Research Center, 17,* 1-7. http://tony-silva.com/eslefl/miscstudent/downloadpagearticles/defgenerations-pew.pdf

Dixson, D. D., & Worrell, F. C. (2016). Formative and summative assessment in the classroom. *Theory into Practice*, *55*(2), 153–159. doi:10.1080/00405841.2016.1148989

Dominguez, O., & Carugno, P. (2020). Learning Disability. StatPearls Publishing.

Dorfman, J. (2017). Considering music technology and literacy. In A. Ruthmann & R. Mantie (Eds.), *The Oxford handbook of technology and music education*. Oxford University Press.

Dorroll, C., & Dorroll, P. (2020). Finding connection virtually through shared deep stories. *Teaching Theology and Religion*, *23*(4), 287–289. doi:10.1111/teth.12561

Dougherty, D. (2012). The maker movement. *Innovations: Technology, Governance, Globalization*, *7*(3), 11–14. doi:10.1162/INOV_a_00135

Douglas, K., Rynearson, A., Yoon, S., & Diefas-Dax, H. (2016). Two elementary schools' developing potential for sustainability of engineering education. *International Journal of Technology and Design Education*, *26*(3), 309–334. doi:10.100710798-015-9313-4

Downes, S. (2004). The buntine oration: Learning networks. *International Journal of Instructional Technology & Distance Learning*, *1*(11), 3–14. http://www.itdl.org/Journal/Nov_04/Nov_04.pdf

Doyle, M. A. (2013). Marie M. Clay's theoretical perspective: A literacy processing theory. In D. E. Alvermann, N. J. Unrau, & R. B. Ruddell (Eds.), Theoretical models and processes of reading (6th ed.). International Reading [Literacy] Association.

Draus, P., Curran, M., & Trempus, M. (2014). The influence of instructor-generated video content on the satisfaction with and engagement in asynchronous online classes. *Journal of Online Learning and Teaching*, *10*(2), 240–254.

Driscoll, M., & Tomiak, G. R. (2000). Web-based training: Using technology to design adult learning experiences. *Performance Improvement*, *39*(3), 60–61. doi:10.1002/pfi.4140390316

Drolet, M., & Arcand, I. (2013). Positive development, sense of belonging, and support of peers among early adolescents: Perspectives of different actors. *International Education Studies*, *6*(4), 29–38. doi:10.5539/ies.v6n4p29

Du, X. (2021). *Technology and special education: Designing effective professional development for equitable and inclusive classrooms* [Unpublished doctoral dissertation]. Teachers College, Columbia University, New York, United States.

Dunlap, R. E., Van Liere, K. D., Mertig, A. G., & Jones, R. E. (2000). New trends in measuring environmental attitudes: measuring endorsement of the new ecological paradigm: a revised NEP scale. *The Journal of Social Issues*, *56*(3), 425–442. doi:10.1111/0022-4537.00176

Durak, H., & Saritepeci, M. (2017). Investigating the effect of technology use in education on classroom management within the scope of the FATİH project. *Çukurova Üniversitesi Eğitim Fakültesi Dergisi*, *46*(2), 441-457. doi:10.14812/cufej.303511

Dweck, C. (2006). *Mindset: The new psychology of success*. Ballantine Books.

Dweck, C. (2016). What having a "growth mindset" actually means. *Harvard Business Review*, *13*, 213–226.

Dweck, C. S. (2010). Even geniuses work hard. *Educational Leadership*, *68*(1), 16–20.

Dweck, C. S., & Yeager, D. S. (2019). Mindsets: A view from two eras. *Perspectives on Psychological Science*, *14*(3), 481–496. doi:10.1177/1745691618804166 PMID:30707853

Dwyer, H., Hill, C., Carpenter, S., Harlow, D., & Franklin, D. (2014). Identifying elementary students' pre-instructional ability to develop algorithms and step-by-step instructions. In *Proceedings of the 45th ACM Technical Symposium on Computer Science Education* (pp. 511-516). ACM. 10.1145/2538862.2538905

Dye, K. (2016). Student and instructor behaviors in online music lessons: An exploratory study. *International Journal of Music Education*, *34*(2), 161–170. doi:10.1177/0255761415584290

Dyscalculia. (2021). *Best tools*. https://www.dyscalculia.org/math-tools

Echeverría, A., García-Campo, C., Nussbaum, M., Gil, F., Villalta, M., Améstica, M., & Echeverría, S. (2011). A framework for the design and integration of collaborative classroom games. *Computers & Education*, *57*(1), 1127–1136. doi:10.1016/j.compedu.2010.12.010

Economic Modelling Specialists International. (2017). *Economic Modelling Specialists International (EMSI) state reports*. https://www.economicmodelling.com.au/state-reports

Edelson, D., Gordin, D., & Pea, R. (1999). Addressing the challenges of inquiry-based learning through technology and curriculum design. *Journal of the Learning Sciences*, *3*(8), 391–450. doi:10.120715327809jls0803&4_3

Edwards, C. M., & Robichaux-Davis, R. R. (2020). Digital first: Not just an add-on. *Mathematics Teacher: Learning and Teaching PK-12, 113*(6), 442–443.

Edwards, L. (2020, Aug. 11). *What is Flipgrid and How Does it Work for Teachers and Students? Tech & Learning: Tools & Ideas to Transform Education*. https://www.techlearning.com/how-to/what-is-flipgrid-and-how-does-it-work-for-teachers-and-students

Edwards, C. (2018). By way of introduction: Productive struggle. *Mathematics Teaching in the Middle School*, *23*(4), 183. doi:10.5951/mathteacmiddscho.23.4.0183

Edyburn, D. L. (2013). Critical issues in advancing the special education technology evidence base. *Exceptional Children*, *80*(1), 7–24. doi:10.1177/001440291308000107

Efron, S., & David, R. (2020). *Action Research in Education: A practical guide*. The Guilford Press.

Elaine, Amanda, Burcham, Gunnels, Castle, & Surbeck. (2013). *The Aims of Constructivist Curriculum*. Routledge.

Elbaum, B., & Vaughn, S. (2003). For which students with learning disabilities are self-concept interventions effective? *Journal of Learning Disabilities*, *36*(2), 101–108. doi:10.1177/002221940303600203 PMID:15493426

Elbow, P. (2004). Writing first! *Educational Leadership*, 8–13.

Elder, B. C., & Migliarini, V. (2020). Decolonizing inclusive education: A collection of practical inclusive CDS and DisCrit-informed teaching practices implemented in the global South. *Disability and the Global South*, *7*(1), 1852–1872.

Engel, R. (1997). Instrument for locating students with suspected learning disabilities: A quantitative approach. *International Journal of Rehabilitation Research. Internationale Zeitschrift fur Rehabilitationsforschung. Revue Internationale de Recherches de Readaptation*, *20*, 169–181. doi:10.1097/00004356-199706000-00006 PMID:9226500

Engeström, Y. (1999). Activity theory and individual and social transformation. In Y. Engeström, P. Rajja-Leena, & R. Miettinen (Eds.), *Perspectives on activity theory* (pp. 19–37). Cambridge University Press. doi:10.1017/CBO9780511812774.003

Engeström, Y. (2001). Expansive learning at work: Toward an activity theoretical reconceptualization. *Journal of Education and Work*, *14*(1), 133–156. doi:10.1080/13639080020028747

Compilation of References

Epstein, A. S. (2009). Think before you (inter)act: What it means to be an intentional teacher. *Exchange*, 46–49. http://citeseerx.ist.psu.edu/viewdoc/download?doi=10.1.1.476.9053&rep=rep1&type=pdf

Erduran, A., & Ince, B. (2018). Identifying mathematics teachers' difficulties in technology integration in terms of Technological Pedagogical Content Knowledge (TPCK). *International Journal of Research in Education and Science*, *4*(2), 555–576. doi:10.21890/ijres.428955

Erickson, F. (2006). Definition and analysis of data from videotape: Some research procedures and their rationales. In J. L. Green, G. Camilli, & P. B. Elmore (Eds.), *Handbook of complementary methods in educational research* (pp. 177–191). American Educational Research Association.

Ernst, D. C., Hodge, A., & Yoshinobu, S. (2017). What is inquiry-based learning? *Notices of the American Mathematical Society*, *64*(6), 570–574. doi:10.1090/noti1536

Ertmer, P. A. (1999). Addressing first- and second-order barriers to change: Strategies for technology integration. *Educational Technology Research and Development*, *47*(4), 47–61. doi:10.1007/BF02299597

Ertmer, P. A., & Ottenbreit-Leftwich, A. (2010). Teacher technology change: How knowledge, confidence, beliefs, and culture intersect. *Journal of Research on Technology in Education*, *42*(3), 255–284. doi:10.1080/15391523.2010.10782551

Ertmer, P. A., Ottenbreit-Leftwich, A. T., Sadik, O., Sendurur, E., & Sendurur, P. (2012). Teacher Beliefs and Technology Integration Practices: A Critical Relationship. *Computers & Education*, *59*(2), 423–435. doi:10.1016/j.compedu.2012.02.001

Evans, A. D., & Lockee, B. B. (2008). At a distance: An instructional design framework for distance education. *Distance Learning*, *5*(3), 11–16.

Evans, D. (2002). *Lost in the Desert!* Pennsylvania State University, Department of Natural Sciences.

Evans, T. (2021). Negotiating the hazards of the "just-in-time" online writing course. In J. Borgman & C. McArdle (Eds.), *PARS in practice: More resources and strategies for online writing instructors* (pp. 167–180). WAC Clearinghouse. doi:10.37514/PRA-B.2021.1145.2.10

Eveland, T. J. (2020). Supporting first-generation college students: Analyzing academic and social support's effects on academic performance. *Journal of Further and Higher Education*, *44*(8), 1039–1051. doi:10.1080/0309877X.2019.1646891

Fabricatore, C., & López, X. (2012). Sustainability learning through gaming: An exploratory study. *Electronic Journal of e-Learning*, *10*(2), 209–222.

Facione, P. A., & Facione, N. C. (2013). Critical thinking for life: Valuing, measuring, and training critical thinking in all its forms. *Inquiry*, *28*(1), 5–25.

Fact Sheet: Impact of COVID-19 on Assessments and Accountability under the Elementary and Secondary Education Act. (2020). Academic Press.

Falloon, G. (2020). From digital literacy to digital competence: The teacher digital competency (TDC) framework. *Educational Technology Research and Development*, *68*(5), 1–24. doi:10.100711423-020-09767-4

Fang, Z., & Schleppegrell, M. J. (2010). Disciplinary literacies across content areas: Supporting secondary reading through functional language analysis. *Journal of Adolescent & Adult Literacy*, *53*(7), 587–597. doi:10.1598/JAAL.53.7.6

Farrell, O., & Brunton, J. (2020). A balancing act: A window into online student engagement experiences. *International Journal of Educational Technology in Higher Education*, *17*(1), 25. doi:10.118641239-020-00199-x

Fenton, D., & Essler-Petty, S. (2019). Self-efficacy and STEM: An integrated pedagogical approach for pre-service elementary teachers. *International Journal for Cross-Disciplinary Subjects in Education, 10*(4), 4160–4168. doi:10.20533/ijcdse.2042.6364.2019.0508

Ferdig, R. E., Baumgartner, E., Hartshorne, R., Kaplan-Rakowski, R., & Mouza, C. (Eds.). (2020). *Teaching, Technology, and Teacher Education During the COVID-19 Pandemic: Stories from the Field*. Association for the Advancement of Computing in Education (AACE). Retrieved June 15, 2020 from https://www.learntechlib.org/p/216903/

Ferdig, R. E., Baumgartner, E., Hartshorne, R., Kaplan-Rakowski, R., & Mouza, C. (Eds.). (2020). *Teaching, technology, and teacher education during the COVID-19 pandemic: Stories from the field*. Association for the Advancement of Computing in Education.

Fernández Santín, M., & Feliu Torruella, M. (2017). Reggio Emilia: An Essential Tool to Develop Critical Thinking in Early Childhood. *Journal of New Approaches in Educational Research, 6*(1), 50–56. doi:10.7821/naer.2017.1.207

Fichten, C., Olenik-Shemesh, D., Asuncion, J., Jorgensen, M., & Colwell, C. (2020). Higher education, information and communication technologies and students with disabilities: An overview of the current situation. *Improving accessible digital practices in higher education*, 21-44. https://doi.org/ doi:10.1007/978-3-030-37125-8_2

Fielding, K. S., & Head, B. W. (2012). Determinants of young Australians' environmental actions: *The role of responsibility attributions, locus of control, knowledge, and attitudes. Environmental Education Research, 18*(2), 171–186. doi:10.1080/13504622.2011.592936

Figg, C., & Jaipal-Jamani, K. (2011). Developing a survey from a taxonomy of characteristics for TK, TCK, and TPK to assess teacher candidates' knowledge of teaching with technology. *Proceedings of Society for Information Technology & Teacher Education International Conference*. Retrieved from: https://www.researchgate.net/publication/277983097

Fiorella, L., Stull, A. T., Kuhlmann, S., & Mayer, R. E. (2019). Fostering generative learning from video lessons: Benefits of instructor-generated drawings and learner-generated explanations. *Journal of Educational Psychology, 112*(5), 895–906. doi:10.1037/edu0000408

Fırat, T., & Ergül, C. (2020). The effect of TWA strategy instruction on students with learning disabilities developing cognitive and metacognitive strategies. *Kastamonu Education Journal, 28*(3), 1390–1406.

Fisch, K., & McLeod, S. (2008, September). *Shift happens* [YouTube Video]. https://www.youtube.com/watch?v=FdTOFkhaplo

Fischer, K. W., Bullock, D., Rotenberg, E. J., & Raya, P. (1993). The dynamics of competence: How context contributes directly to skill. *Development in Context: Acting and Thinking in Specific Environments, 1*, 93–117.

Fischer, K. W., Daniel, D. B., Immordino-Yang, M. H., Stern, E., Battro, A., & Koizumi, H. (2007). Why mind, brain, and education? Why now? *Mind, Brain and Education: the Official Journal of the International Mind, Brain, and Education Society, 1*(1), 1–2. doi:10.1111/j.1751-228X.2007.00006.x

Fisher, A., & Scriven, M. (1997). *Critical Thinking: Its definition and assessment*. Edgepress.

Fisher, D., & Frey, N. (2020). Helping students cope with the pandemic: How educators respond to children's fears now will influence the long-term effects. *Educational Leadership, 78*(2), 76–77.

Fisher, D., Frey, N., & Akhavan, N. (2019). *This is balanced literacy, grades K-6*. Corwin.

Fisher, D., Frey, N., & Hattie, J. (2021). *The distance learning playbook, grades K-12: Teaching for engagement and impact in any setting*. Corwin Press.

Compilation of References

Fisher, D., Frey, N., & Hattie, J. (2021). *The Distance Learning Playbook, Grades K-12: Teaching for Engagement and Impact in Any Setting*. Corwin.

Fisher, D., Frey, N., & Hattie, J. (2021). *The distance learning playbook: Grades K-12*. Corwin.

Fishman, B. J., Penuel, W. R., Allen, A. R., Cheng, B. H., & Sabelli, N. (2013). Design-based implementation research: An emerging model for transforming the relationship of research and practice. In B. J. Fishman & W. R. Penuel (Eds.), *National Society for the Study of Education: Design Based Implementation Research* (pp. 136–156). SRI International. Retrieved from https://www.sri.com/sites/default/files/publications/fishman_penuel_allen_cheng_sabelli_2013.pdf

Flick, M., & Kuchey, D. (2015). Contest corner: Increasing classroom discourse and computational fluency through number talks. *Ohio Journal of School Mathematics, 71*, 38-41. https://kb.osu.edu/bitstream/handle/1811/78915/1/OJSM_71_Spring2015_38.pdf

Florida Center for Instructional Technology. (2021). *The technology integration matrix*. Retrieved from https://fcit.usf.edu/matrix/matrix/

Flynn, A. E., & Klein, J. D. (2001). The influence of discussion groups in a case-based learning environment. *Educational Technology Research and Development, 49*(3), 71–86. doi:10.1007/BF02504916

Foorman, B., Beyler, N., Borradaile, K., Coyne, M., Denton, C. A., Dimino, J., Furgeson, J., Hayes, L., Henke, J., Justice, L., Keating, B., Lewis, W., Sattar, S., Streke, A., Wagner, R., & Wissel, S. (2016). *Foundational skills to support reading for understanding in kindergarten through 3rd grade* (NCEE 2016-4008). Washington, DC: National Center for Education Evaluation and Regional Assistance (NCEE), Institute of Education Sciences, U.S. Department of Education. Retrieved from the NCEE website: http://whatworks.ed.gov

Fortuna, L., Tolou-Shams, M., Robles-Ramamurthy, B., & Porsche, M. (2020). Inequity and the disproportionate impact of COVID-19 on communities of color in the United States: The need for a trauma-informed social justice response. *Psychological Trauma: Theory, Research, Practice, and Policy, 12*(5), 443–445. doi:10.1037/tra0000889 PMID:32478545

Fourie, I., & Meyer, A. (2015). What to make of makerspaces. *Library Hi Tech, 33*(4), 519–525. doi:10.1108/LHT-09-2015-0092

Fox, B. J. (2014). *Phonics and word study for the teacher of reading: Programmed for self-instruction* (11th ed.). Pearson.

Fransson, G., & Grannäs, J. (2013). Dilemmatic spaces in educational contexts - towards a conceptual framework for dilemmas in teachers work. *Teachers and Teaching, 19*(1), 4–17. doi:10.1080/13540602.2013.744195

Fransson, G., Holmberg, J., & Westelius, C. (2020). The challenges of using Head Mounted Virtual Reality in K-12 schools from a teacher perspective. *Education and Information Technologies, 25*(4), 3383–3404. doi:10.100710639-020-10119-1

Freeman, S., Eddy, S. L., McDonough, M., Smith, M. K., Okoroafor, N., Jordt, H., & Wenderoth, M. P. (2014). Active learning increases student performance in science, engineering, and mathematics. *Proceedings of the National Academy of Sciences of the United States of America, 111*(23), 8410–8415. doi:10.1073/pnas.1319030111 PMID:24821756

Freischlag, K., Ji, K., Kamyszek, R. W., Leraas, H. J., Olivere, L. A., Gefter, L., Mann, B., Migaly, J., & Tracy, E. T. (2019). Health Career Academy: Addition of a Surgical Case-Based Learning Curriculum Captures the Interest of High School Students. *Journal of Surgical Education, 76*(2), 401–407. doi:10.1016/j.jsurg.2018.07.016 PMID:30111518

Friday Institute for Educational Innovation. (2012). *Teacher efficacy and attitudes toward STEM (T-STEM) survey: Elementary teachers*. Author. http://stelar.edc.org/sites/stelar.edc.org/files/T-STEM%20Survey.pdf

Friedlander, M. J., Andrews, L., Armstrong, E. G., Aschenbrenner, C., Kass, J. S., Ogden, P., Schwartzstein, R., & Viggiano, T. R. (2011). What can medical education learn from the neurobiology of learning? *Academic Medicine*, *86*(4), 415–420. doi:10.1097/ACM.0b013e31820dc197 PMID:21346504

Friend, M., & Bursuck, W. D. (2012). *Including students with special needs: A practical guide for classroom teachers* (6th ed.). Pearson.

Fullan, M., & Langworthy, M. (2014). *A rich seam: How new pedagogies find deep learning*. Pearson with support of ISTE, MaRS and Nesta. https://www.michaelfullan.ca/wp-content/uploads/2014/01/3897.Rich_Seam_web.pdf

Fullan, M. (1991). *The new meaning of educational change* (2nd ed.). Teachers College Press.

Fullan, M. (2007). *Leading in a culture of change*. Jossey Bass.

Fullan, M. (2012). *Stratosphere: Integrating technology, pedagogy, and change knowledge*. Pearson.

Funk, C., & Parker, K. (2018). *Women and men in STEM often at odds over workplace equity*. PEW Research Center Analysis. https://www.pewresearch.org/social-trends/2018/01/09/women-and-men-in-stem-often-at-odds-over-workplace-equity/

Funk, J. (2018). *How to code a rollercoaster*. Viking Books.

Funk, J. (2019). *How to code a sandcastle*. Viking Books.

Furnham, A. (2012). Learning styles and approaches to learning. In APA Educational Psychology Handbook: Vol. 2. Individual Differences and Cultural and Continual Factors (pp. 59-81). American Psychological Association. doi:10.1037/13274-003

Gablasova, D. (2014). Issues in the assessment of bilingually educated students: Expressing subject knowledge through L1 and L2. *Language Learning Journal*, *42*(2), 151–164. doi:10.1080/09571736.2014.891396

Gadanidis, G., & Geiger, V. (2010). A social perspective on technology-enhanced mathematical learning: From collaboration to performance. *ZDM*, *1*(42), 91–104. doi:10.100711858-009-0213-5

Gagne, R., Briggs, L., & Wagner, W. (1992). *Principles of instructional design*. Wadsworth/Thomson Learning.

Gaible, E., & Burns, M. (2005). *Using Technology to Train Teachers: Appropriate Uses of ICT for Teacher Professional Development in Developing Countries*. Washington, DC: infoDev / World Bank. http://www.infodev.org/en/Publication.13.html

Galanti, T. M., Baker, C. K., Morrow-Leong, K., & Kraft, T. (2020). Enriching TPACK in mathematics education: Using digital interactive notebooks in synchronous online learning environments. *Interactive Technology and Smart Education*, *ahead-of-print*(ahead-of-print). Advance online publication. doi:10.1108/ITSE-08-2020-0175

Gale, S. F. (2015, July). Forget Gen Y: Are you ready for Gen Z? *Chief Learning Officer*. https://www.clomedia.com/2015/07/07/forget-gen-y-are-you-ready-for-gen-z/

Gallagher, K. & Kittle, P. (n.d.). *180 Days*. Heinemann.

Gallagher, S. (2012, June 28). *Hands-on with the Google Drive for iOS app: mostly read only*. ARS Technica. https://arstechnica.com/information-technology/2012/06/hands-on-with-the-google-drive-for-ios-app-mostly-read-only/

Gallagher-Immenschuh, C. (2020). *Reading and writing mathematics: A phenomenological qualitative case study of a cross-curricular approach* [Doctoral dissertation, Northcentral University]. ProQuest Dissertations Publishing. https://search.proquest.com/openview/357f41bc90e76955bf337d5313b73435/1?pq-origsite=gscholar&cbl=44156

Compilation of References

Gallardo, V., Finnegan, P., Ingram, A., & Martin, S. (2020). *Supporting multilingual/English learners during school closures* [Guidebook]. Washington Office of Superintendent of Public Instruction.

Galway, T. M., & Metsala, J. L. (2011). Social cognition and its relation to psychosocial adjustment in children with nonverbal learning disabilities. *Journal of Learning Disabilities*, *44*(1), 33–49. doi:10.1177/0022219410371680 PMID:20574062

Garcia-Moya, I., Brooks, F., & Moreno, C. (2020). Humanizing and conducive to learning: An adolescent students' perspective on the central attributes of positive relationships with teachers. *European Journal of Psychology of Education*, *35*(1), 1–20. doi:10.100710212-019-00413-z

Gardner, D., & Davies, M. (2014). A new academic vocabulary list. *Applied Linguistics*, *35*(3), 305–327. doi:10.1093/applin/amt015

Gardner, H. (1991). *The unschooled mind: How children think and how schools should teach*. Basic Books.

Gargiulo, R. M., & Bouck, E. C. (2018). *Special education in contemporary society: An introduction to exceptionality* (6th ed.). Sage.

Garrett, H., & Woodworth, R. (1969). *Statistics in psychology and education*. Vakils, Feffer & Simons Pvt. Ltd.

Garrison, D. (2017). *E-learning in the 21st century: A Community of Inquiry framework for research and practice* (3rd ed.). Routledge.

Garrison, D. R. (2011). *E-learning in the 21st century: A framework for research and practice* (2nd ed.). Routledge. doi:10.4324/9780203838761

Garrison, D. R., & Akyol, Z. (2012). Toward the development of a metacognition construct for communities of inquiry. *The Internet and Higher Education*, *17*, 14–89.

Garrison, D. R., & Akyol, Z. (2013). The community of inquiry theoretical framework. In M. G. Moore (Ed.), *Handbook of distance education* (3rd ed., pp. 104–120). Routledge. doi:10.4324/9780203803738.ch7

Garrison, D. R., Anderson, T., & Archer, W. (1999). Critical inquiry in a text-based environment: Computer conferencing in higher education. *The Internet and Higher Education*, *2*(2–3), 87–105. doi:10.1016/S1096-7516(00)00016-6

Garrison, D. R., Anderson, T., & Archer, W. (1999). Critical thinking and computer conferencing: A model and tool to assess cognitive presence. *American Journal of Distance Education*, *15*(1), 7–23. doi:10.1080/08923640109527071

Garrison, D. R., Anderson, T., & Archer, W. (2010). The first decade of the community of inquiry framework: A retrospective. *The Internet and Higher Education*, *13*(1-2), 5–9. doi:10.1016/j.iheduc.2009.10.003

Garrison, D. R., & Cleveland-Innes, M. (2005). Facilitating cognitive presence in online learning: Interaction is not enough. *American Journal of Distance Education*, *19*(3), 133–148. doi:10.120715389286ajde1903_2

Garrison, D. R., Cleveland-Innes, M., & Fung, T. (2004). Student role adjustment in online communities of inquiry: Model and instrument validation. *Journal of Asynchronous Learning Networks*, *8*(2), 61–74. doi:10.24059/olj.v8i2.1828

Garrison, D. R., Cleveland-Innes, M., & Fung, T. S. (2010). Exploring causal relationships among teaching, cognitive and social presence: Student perceptions of the community of inquiry framework. *The internet and higher education*, *13*(1-2), 31–36. doi:10.1016/j.iheduc.2009.10.002

Gartland, D., & Strosnider, R. (2018). Learning Disabilities: Implications for Policy Regarding Research and Practice: A Report by the National Joint Committee on Learning Disabilities. *Learning Disability Quarterly*, *41*(4), 195–199. doi:10.1177/0731948718789994

Gay, G. (2018). *Culturally responsive teaching: Theory, research, and practice* (3rd ed.). Teachers College Press.

Gee, J. (2008). Game-like learning. In P. Moss, D. Pullin, J. Gee, E. Haertel, & L. Young (Eds.), *Assessment, equity, and opportunity to learn (Learning in doing: Social, cognitive, and computational perspectives)* (pp. 200–221). Cambridge University Press., doi:10.1017/CBO9780511802157.010

Gee, J. P. (2001). Education identity as an analytic lens for research. *Review of Research in Education, 25*, 99–125.

Gee, J. P. (2008). A sociocultural perspective on opportunity to learn. In P. A. Moss, D. C. Pullin, J. P. Gee, E. H. Haertel, & L. J. Young (Eds.), *Assessment, equity, and opportunity to learn* (pp. 76–108). Cambridge University Press. doi:10.1017/CBO9780511802157.006

GeoGebra. (n.d.). https://www.geogebra.org/

Gersten, R., Fuchs, L. S., Williams, J. P., & Baker, S. (2001). Teaching reading comprehension strategies to students with learning disabilities: A review of research. *Review of Educational Research, 21*, 279–320. doi:10.3102/00346543071002279

Gerstenschlager, N. E., & Strayer, J. F. (2019). Number talks for statistics and probability: Short, mathematical discussions can elicit students' reasoning and focus on foundational ideas. *Mathematics Teaching in the Middle School, 24*(6), 362–367. doi:10.5951/mathteacmiddscho.24.6.0362

Gibson, J. J. (1977). The Theory of Affordances. In R. Shaw & J. Bransford (Eds.), *Perceiving, Acting, and Knowing: Toward an Ecological Psychology* (pp. 67–82). Lawrence Erlbaum.

Giesbers, B., Rienties, B., Tempelaar, D., & Gijselaers, W. (2014). A dynamic analysis of the interplay between asynchronous and synchronous communication in online learning: The impact of motivation. *Journal of Computer Assisted Learning, 30*(1), 30–50. doi:10.1111/jcal.12020

Gikandi, J. W., Morrow, D., & Davis, N. E. (2011). Online formative assessment in higher education: A review of the literature. *Computers & Education, 57*(4), 2333–2351. doi:10.1016/j.compedu.2011.06.004

Gilbertson, A. (2015, April 17). Schools dealing with aftermath of LAUSD's iPad fiasco. *Southern California Public Radio.* https://www.scpr.org/news/2015/04/17/51093/schools-dealing-with-aftermath-of-lausd-s-ipad-fia/

Gilles, C., Wang, Y., Smith, J., & Johnson, D. (2013). I'm no longer just teaching history: Professional development for teaching common core state standards for literacy in social studies by identifying the reading strategies they regularly use within their disciplines; content area teachers are better able to teach students how to derive meaning from texts. *Middle School Journal, 44*(3), 34–43. doi:10.1080/00940771.2013.11461853

Gioia, G. A., Isquith, P. K., Guy, S. C., & Kenworthy, L. (2015). *BRIEF: Behavior rating inventory of executive function.* Psychological Assessment Resources.

Glassman, M., Erdem, G., & Bartholomew, M. (2013). Action Research and Its History as an Adult Education Movement for Social Change. *Adult Education Quarterly, 63*(3), 272–288. doi:10.1177/0741713612471418

Glaveanu, V. P., Hanchett Hanson, M., Baer, J., Barbot, B., Clapp, E. P., Corazza, G. E., . . . Sternberg, R. J. (2019). Advancing Creativity Theory and Research: A Socio-cultural Manifesto. *The Journal of Creative Behavior.* doi:10.1002/jocb.395

Glaveanu, V. (2010). Paradigms in the study of creativity: Introducing the perspective of cultural psychology. *New Ideas in Psychology, 28*(1), 79–93. doi:10.1016/j.newideapsych.2009.07.007

Glaveanu, V. G. (2013). Rewriting the language of creativity: The five A's framework. *Review of General Psychology, 17*(1), 69–81. doi:10.1037/a0029528

Glaveanu, V. P. (2012). Habitual Creativity: Revising Habit, Reconceptualizing Creativity. *Review of General Psychology*, *16*(1), 78–92. doi:10.1037/a0026611

Glaveanu, V., Lubart, T., Bonnardel, N., Botella, M., de Biaisi, P. M., Desainte-Catherine, M., & Zenasni, F. (2013). Creativity as action: Findings from five creative domains. *Frontiers in Psychology*, *4*, 176. doi:10.3389/fpsyg.2013.00176 PMID:23596431

Goffney, I., & Gutiérrez, R. (Eds.). (2018). Rehumanizing mathematics for Black, Indigenous, and Latinx students. In *Annual perspectives in mathematics education*. Reston, VA: National Council of Teachers of Mathematics.

Goldenberg, C., Hicks, J., & Lit, I. (2013). Dual language learners: Effective instruction in early childhood. *American Educator*, *37*(2), 26–29.

Goldie, J. G. S. (2016). Connectivism: A knowledge learning theory for the digital age? *Medical Teacher*, *38*(10), 1064–1069. doi:10.3109/0142159X.2016.1173661 PMID:27128290

Goldstein, D. (2020). Research shows students falling months behind during virus disruptions. *The New York Times*, 5. https://www.nytimes.com/2020/06/05/us/coronavirus-education-lost-learning.html?smid=tw-share

Goldstein, D., Popescu, A., & Hannah-Jones, N. (2020, April 6). As School Moves Online, Many Students Stay Logged Out. *The New York Times*.

González-González, I., & Jiménez-Zarco, A. I. (2015). Using learning methodologies and resources in the development of critical thinking competency: An exploratory study in a virtual learning environment. *Computers in Human Behavior*, *51*, 1359–1366. doi:10.1016/j.chb.2014.11.002

González, N., & Moll, L. C. (2001). Cruzando el Puente: Building bridges to funds of knowledge. *Educational Policy*, *16*(4), 623–641. doi:10.1177/0895904802016004009

Gonzalez-Sanmamed, M., Sangra, A., & Munoz-Carril, P. C. (2017). We can, we know how. But do we want to? Teaching attitudes towards ICT based on the level of technology integration in schools. *Technology, Pedagogy and Education*, *26*(5), 633–647. doi:10.1080/1475939X.2017.1313775

González-Tejero, J. M. S., Parra, R. M. P., & Llamas, M. G. R. (2007). Perspectiva histórica del aprendizaje cooperativo: Un largo y tortuoso camino a través de cuatro siglos. *Revista Española de Pedagogía*, *236*, 125–138.

Good, C., Aronson, J., & Inzlicht, M. (2003). Improving adolescents' standardized test performance: An intervention to reduce the effects of stereotype threat. *Journal of Applied Developmental Psychology*, *24*(6), 645–662. doi:10.1016/j.appdev.2003.09.002

Goodenow, C. (1993). Classroom Belonging among Early Adolescent Students: Relationships to Motivation and Achievement. *The Journal of Early Adolescence*, *13*(1), 21–43. doi:10.1177/0272431693013001002

Goodman, G., Arbona, C., & Dominguez de Rameriz, R. (2008). High-Stakes, Minimum-Competency Exams: How Competent Are They for Evaluating Teacher Competence? *Journal of Teacher Education*, *59*(1), 24–39. doi:10.1177/0022487107309972

Goodwin, A. L., Low Ling, E., Ng Tee, P., Yeung, A. S., & Cai, L. (2015). Enhancing playful teachers' perception of the importance of ICT use in the classroom: The role of risk taking as a mediator. *The Australian Journal of Teacher Education*, *40*(4). Advance online publication. https://ro.ecu.edu.au/ajte/. doi:10.14221/ajte.2015v40n4.8

Goodwin, M., & Sommervold, C. L. (2012). *Creativity, critical thinking, and communication: Strategies to increase students' skills*. R&L Education.

Goodyear, P. (2005). Educational Design and Networked Learning: Patterns, Pattern Languages and Design Practice. *Australasian Journal of Educational Technology*, *21*(1), 82–101. doi:10.14742/ajet.1344

Goodyear, P. (2015). Teaching as design. *HERDSA Review of Higher Education*, *2*(2), 27–50.

Gordon, D. G. (2001). Classroom management problems and solutions: A few basic guidelines for classroom management can improve student behavior and reduce stress on the music educator. *Music Educators Journal*, *88*(2), 17–23. doi:10.2307/3399737

Gorlewski, J., Meyer, T., Young, M., & Lieberstein-Solera, F. (2012). Research for the classroom: Lost in translation: Assessing writing of English language learners. *English Journal*, *101*(5), 93–96.

Gough, C. (October 15, 2020). *Number of video gamers worldwide 2015-2023*. https://www.statista.com/statistics/748044/number-video-gamers-world/

Graf, N., Fry, R., & Funk, C. (2018). *7 facts about the STEM workforce*. Pew Research Center. https://medium.com/@pewresearch/7-facts-about-the-stem-workforce-fe2a9fb87cad

Graham, C., Cagiltay, K., Lim, B. R., Craner, J., & Duffy, T. M. (2001). Seven principles of effective teaching: A practical lens for evaluating online courses. *The Technology Source*, *30*(5), 50.

Graham, S. (2020). The sciences of reading and writing must become more fully integrated. *Reading Research Quarterly*, *55*(51). Advance online publication. doi:10.1002/rrq.332

Graham, S., Collins, A. A., & Rigby-Wills, H. (2017). Writing characteristics of students with learning disabilities and typically achieving peers: A meta-analysis. *Exceptional Children*, *83*(2), 199–218. doi:10.1177/0014402916664070

Granberg, C. (2016). Discovering and addressing errors during mathematics problem-solving—A productive struggle? *The Journal of Mathematical Behavior*, *42*, 33–48. doi:10.1016/j.jmathb.2016.02.002

Graziano, K. J., & Feher, L. (2016). A dual placement approach to online student teaching. *Contemporary Issues in Technology & Teacher Education*, *16*(4), 495–513.

Green, M. (2018). *A case study on the use of best practices within the MRI program in a Midwest school district* [Master's Thesis]. Lindenwood University.

Greenberg, D., Calabrese Barton, A., Turner, C., Hardy, K., Roper, A., Williams, C., Herrenkohl, L. R., Davis, E. A., & Tasker, T. (2020). Community infrastructuring as necessary ingenuity in the COVID-19 pandemic. *Educational Researcher*, *49*(7), 518–523. doi:10.3102/0013189X20957614

Green, S. B., Lissitz, R. W., & Mulaik, S. A. (1977). Limitations of coefficient alpha as an index of test unidimensionality. *Educational and Psychological Measurement*, *37*(4), 827–836. doi:10.1177/001316447703700403

Gregg, K. (2011). A document analysis of the National Association for the Education of Young Children's Developmentally Appropriate Practice Position Statement: What does it tell us about supporting children with disabilities? *Contemporary Issues in Early Childhood*, *12*(2), 175–186. doi:10.2304/ciec.2011.12.2.175

Greitemeyer, T., Osswald, S., & Brauer, M. (2010). Playing prosocial video games increases empathy and decreases schadenfreude. *Emotion (Washington, D.C.)*, *10*(6), 796–802. doi:10.1037/a0020194 PMID:21171755

Gresham, G. (2018). Mathematics teacher efficacy and mathematics anxiety in preservice teachers. *Proceedings for the 45th Annual Meeting of the Research Council on Mathematics Learning*, 17.

Griffin, N., & Wohlstetter, P. (2001). Building a plane while flying it: Early lessons from developing charter schools. *Teachers College Record*, *103*(2), 336–365. doi:10.1111/0161-4681.00118

Compilation of References

Griffith, M., Melnick, H., Darling-Hammond, L., & Cardichon, J. (2020). *Restarting and reinventing school: Learning in the time of COVID and beyond.* Learning Policy Institute.

Griffiths, M. & Graham, C. (2019). *Using asynchronous video in online classes: Results from a pilot study.* Brigham Young University.

Grigorenko, E. L., Compton, D. L., Fuchs, L. S., Wagner, R. K., Willcutt, E. G., & Fletcher, J. M. (2020). Understanding, educating, and supporting children with specific learning disabilities: 50 Years of science and practice. *The American Psychologist, 75*(1), 37. doi:10.1037/amp0000452 PMID:31081650

Griset, O. L. (2010). Meet us outside! *Science Teacher (Normal, Ill.), 77*(2), 40–46.

Grissom, J., Egalite, A., & Lindsay, C. (2021). *How principals affect students and schools: A systematic synthesis of two decades of research.* The Wallace Foundation. https://www.wallacefoundation.org/knowledge-center/Documents/How-Principals-Affect-Students-and-Schools.pdf

Gros, B. (2014). Digital games in education: The design of games-based learning environments. *Journal of Research on Technology in Education, 40*(1), 23–38. doi:10.1080/15391523.2007.10782494

Grossman, P. L. (1989). A study in contrast: Sources of pedagogical content knowledge for secondary English. *Journal of Teacher Education, 40*(5), 24–31. doi:10.1177/002248718904000504

Grossman, P. L. (1991). Overcoming the apprenticeship of observation in teacher education coursework. *Teaching and Teacher Education, 7*(4), 245–257. doi:10.1016/0742-051X(91)90004-9

Grover, S., Catete, V., Barnes, T., Hill, M., Ledeczi, A., & Broll, B. (2020). FIRST principles to design for online, synchronous high school CS teacher training and curriculum co-design. In N. Falkner & O. Seppala (Eds.), *Koli Calling '20: Proceedings of the 20th Koli Calling International Conference on Computing Education Research* (Article 21, pp. 1-5). Association for Computing Machinery. 10.1145/3428029.3428059

Grover, S. (2017). Assessing algorithmic and computational thinking in K-12: Lessons from a middle school classroom. In *Emerging research, practice, and policy on computational thinking* (pp. 269–288). Springer. doi:10.1007/978-3-319-52691-1_17

Grubaugh, S. (1989). Non-verbal language techniques for better classroom management and discipline. *High School Journal, 73*(1), 34–40.

Guo, J., & Woulfin, S. (2016). Twenty-First Century Creativity: An Investigation of How the Partnership for 21st Century Instructional Framework Reflects the Principles of Creativity. *Roeper Review, 38*(3), 153–161. doi:10.1080/02783193.2016.1183741

Guskey, T. R. (2000). *Evaluating professional development.* Corwin Press.

Guskey, T. R. (2002). Professional development and teacher change. *Teachers and Teaching, 8*(3), 381–391. doi:10.1080/135406002100000512

Guskey, T. R. (2014). Measuring the effectiveness of educators' professional development. In L. E. Martin, S. Kragler, D. J. Quatroche, & K. L. Bauserman (Eds.), *Handbook of professional development in education: Successful models and practices, PreK–12* (pp. 447–466). Guilford Press.

Guskey, T. R., & Yoon, K. S. (2009). What works in professional development? *Phi Delta Kappan, 90*(7), 495–500. doi:10.1177/003172170909000709

Habgood, M. J., & Ainsworth, S. E. (2011). Motivating children to learn effectively: Exploring the value of intrinsic integration in educational games. *Journal of the Learning Sciences*, *20*(2), 169–206. doi:10.1080/10508406.2010.508029

Hagerty, B. M. K., Lynch-Sauer, J., Patusky, K. L., Bouwsema, M., & Collier, P. (1992). Sense of belonging: A vital mental health concept. *Archives of Psychiatric Nursing*, *6*(3), 172–177. doi:10.1016/0883-9417(92)90028-H PMID:1622293

Hagerty, B. M., Williams, R. A., & Oe, H. (2002). Childhood antecedents of adult sense of belonging. *Journal of Clinical Psychology*, *58*(7), 793–801. doi:10.1002/jclp.2007 PMID:12205719

Hakkarainen, K. (2009). A knowledge-practice perspective on technology-mediated learning. *Computer-Supported Collaborative Learning*, *4*(2), 213–231. doi:10.100711412-009-9064-x

Hall, A. H., Simpson, A., Guo, Y., & Wang, S. (2015). Examining the effects of preschool writing instruction on emergent literacy skills: A systematic review of the literature. *Literacy Research and Instruction*, *54*(2), 115–134. doi:10.1080/19388071.2014.991883

Hall, G. E. (2010). Technology's Achilles heel: Achieving high-quality implementation. *Journal of Research on Technology in Education*, *42*(3), 231–251. doi:10.1080/15391523.2010.10782550

Hall, G. E., & Hord, S. M. (1987). *Change in schools: Facilitating the process*. State University of New York Press.

Hall, G. E., & Hord, S. M. (2015). *Implementing Change: Patterns, Principles, and Potholes*. Pearson Education.

Hallinger, P., & Heck, R. H. (2010). Leadership for learning: Does collaborative leadership make a difference in school improvement? *Educational Management Administration & Leadership*, *38*(6), 654–658. doi:10.1177/1741143210379060

Halverson, E. R., & Sheridan, K. (2014). The maker movement in education. *Harvard Educational Review*, *84*(4), 495–504. doi:10.17763/haer.84.4.34j1g68140382063

Hamilton, L. S., Grant, D., Kaufman, J. H., Diliberti, M., Schwartz, H. L., Hunter, G. P., Claude, M. S., & Young, C. J. (2020). *COVID-19 and the State of K-12 Schools: Results and Technical Documentation from the Spring 2020 American Educator Panels COVID-19 Surveys*. RAND Corporation. doi:10.7249/RRA168-1

Hamilton, M. L., Smith, L., & Worthington, K. (2008). Fitting the methodology with the research: An exploration of narrative, self-study, and auto-ethnography. *Studying Teacher Education*, *4*(1), 17–28. doi:10.1080/17425960801976321

Hammack, R., & Ivey, T. (2019). Elementary teachers' perceptions of K–5 engineering education and perceived barriers to implementation. *Journal of Engineering Education*, *108*(4), 503–522. doi:10.1002/jee.20289

Hancock, D., & Algozzine, B. (2011). *Designing case study research: A practical guide for beginning researchers* (2nd ed.). Teachers College Press.

Hancock, R., Knezek, G., & Christensen, R. (2007). Cross-validating measures of technology integration: A first step toward examining potential relationships between technology integration and student achievement. *Journal of Computing in Teacher Education*, *24*(1), 15–21. https://www.learntechlib.org/p/105327/

Hand in Hand in Kinderland [@handinhandinkinderland]. (2021, April 17). *This has been my view for an entire year now. I teach to a computer and pray the littles on the other side are getting it* [Photograph]. Instagram. https://www.instagram.com/p/CNyklaKM5KW/?igshid=ip8s6m7hdlt

Hansel, L. (n.d.). Embracing anti-bias education. *YC Young Children*, *5*(4–5).

Harasim, L. (2012). *Learning theory and online technologies*. Routledge. doi:10.4324/9780203846933

Compilation of References

Hargreaves, D. H. (1999). The knowledge-creating school. *British Journal of Educational Studies, 47*(2), 122–144. doi:10.1111/1467-8527.00107

Hargrove, R. A. (2012). Assessing the long-term impact of a metacognitive approach to creative skill development. *International Journal of Technology and Design Education, 23*(3), 489–517. doi:10.100710798-011-9200-6

Hargrove, R. A., & Nietfeld, J. L. (2014). The impact of metacognitive instruction on creative problem solving. *Journal of Experimental Education, 83*(3), 291–318. doi:10.1080/00220973.2013.876604

Harker-Schuch, I. E., Mills, F. P., Lade, S. J., & Colvin, R. M. (2020). CO2peration–Structuring a 3D interactive digital game to improve climate literacy in the 12-13-year-old age group. *Computers & Education, 144*, 103705. doi:10.1016/j.compedu.2019.103705

Harraway, J., Broughton, F., Deaker, L., Jowett, T., & Shephard, K. (2012). Exploring the use of the revised New Ecological Paradigm scale (NEP) to monitor the development of students' ecological worldviews. *The Journal of Environmental Education, 43*(3), 177–191. doi:10.1080/00958964.2011.634450

Harrington, R. A., Driskell, S. O., Johnston, C. J., Browning, C. A., & Niess, M. L. (2016). Technological Pedagogical Content Knowledge: Preparation and support of mathematics teachers. In Handbook of Research on Transforming Mathematics Teacher Education in the Digital Age (pp. 1-22). IGI Global.

Harris, J. (2016, January 17). *Did Michael Jackson have vitiligo?* Vitiligo Clinic & Research Center. https://www.umassmed.edu/vitiligo/blog/blog-posts1/2016/01/did-michael-jackson-have-vitiligo/

Harris, J., & Wildman, A. (Eds.). (2019). February 28. *TPACK Newsletter*. Retrieved from https://activitytypes.wm.edu/TPACKNewsletters/index.html

Harris, A., & Spillane, J. (2008). Distributed leadership through the looking glass. *Journal of Educational Administration, 46*(2), 31–34. doi:10.1108/jea.2008.07446baa.001

Harrison, M. (2018). Space as a tool for analysis: Examining digital learning spaces. *Open Praxis, 10*(1), 17. doi:10.5944/openpraxis.10.1.782

Harrison, R. (1978). How to design and conduct self-directed learning experiences. *Group & Organization Studies, 3*(2), 149–167. doi:10.1177/105960117800300203

Hart, M., & Rush, R. (2007). E-learning and the development of 'voice' in business studies education. *International Journal of Educational Management, 21*(1), 68–77. doi:10.1108/09513540710716830

Harvey, B., & Mönig, J. (2010). Bringing "no ceiling" to scratch: Can one language serve kids and computer scientists. *Proc. Constructionism*, 1-10.

Hashey, A. I., & Stahl, S. (2014). Making online learning accessible for students with disabilities. *Teaching Exceptional Children, 46*(5), 70–78.

Hattie, J. A. (2008). *Visible Learning: A Synthesis of Over 800 Meta-Analyses Relating to Achievement*. Routledge. doi:10.4324/9780203887332

Hattie, J. A. (2012). *Visible learning for teachers: Maximizing impact on learning*. Routledge. doi:10.4324/9780203181522

Hattie, J., & Timperley, H. (2007). The power of feedback. *Review of Educational Research, 77*(1), 81–112. doi:10.3102/003465430298487

Hauge, C. (2020). Agency with virtual learning: Prioritizing children's social emotional health in the pandemic. *Childhood Education, 96*(6), 54–59. doi:10.1080/00094056.2020.1846391

Heafner, T. L., & Fitchett, P. G. (2012). National trends in elementary instruction: Exploring the role of social studies curricula. *Social Studies*, *103*(2), 67–72. doi:10.1080/00377996.2011.592165

Healy, M., & Richardson, M. (2017). Images and identity: Children constructing a sense of belonging to Europe. *European Educational Research Journal*, *16*(4), 440–454. doi:10.1177/1474904116674015

Heft, M. T., & Swaminathan, S. (2002). Effect of computers on the social behaviour of preschoolers. *Journal of Research in Childhood Education*, *16*(2), 162–174. doi:10.1080/02568540209594982

Hegedus, S., Laborde, C., Brady, C., Dalton, S., Hans-Siller, S., Tabach, M., Trgalova, J., & Moreno-Armella, L. (2017). *Uses of technology in upper secondary mathematics education. ICME-13 Topical surveys.* Springer International Publishing., doi:10.1007/978-3-319-42611-2

Heikkila, M., Iiskala, T., & Mikkila-Erdmann, M. (2020). Voices of student teachers' professional agency at the intersection of theory and practice. *Learning, Culture and Social Interaction*, *25*, 100405. Advance online publication. doi:10.1016/j.lcsi.2020.100405

Heinisch, B. P. (2018). *DigitalCommons@University of Nebraska-Lincoln Rural Students' Sense of Belonging at a Large Public University.* https://digitalcommons.unl.edu/cehsedaddiss/291

Heitink, M., Voogt, J., Fisser, P., Verplanken, L., & van Braak, J. (2017). Eliciting teachers' technological pedagogical knowledge. *Australasian Journal of Educational Technology*, *33*(3), 96–109. doi:10.14742/ajet.3505

Hembree, R. (1990). The nature, effects, and relief of mathematics anxiety. *Journal for Research in Mathematics Education*, *21*(1), 33–46. doi:10.2307/749455

Henriksen, D., Mishra, P., & Fisser, P. (2016). Infusing creativity and technology in 21st century education: A systemic view for change. *Journal of Educational Technology & Society*, *19*(3), 27–37. https://punyamishra.com/wp-content/uploads/2016/08/henriksen-Mishra-Fisser-Creativity-ETS2016.pdf

Henriksen, D., Mishra, P., & Mehta, R. (2015). Novel, Effective, Whole: Toward a NEW framework for evaluations of creative products. *Journal of Technology and Teacher Education*, *23*(3), 455–478. https://www.learntechlib.org/p/151574/

Hernández-Bravo, J. R., Cardona-Moltó, M. C., & Hernández-Bravo, J. A. (2016). The effects of an individualised ICT-based music education programme on primary school students' musical competence and grades. *Music Education Research*, *18*(2), 176–194. doi:10.1080/14613808.2015.1049255

Herreid, C. F. (1994). Case studies in science-A novel method of science education. *Journal of College Science Teaching*, *23*, 221–221.

Herreid, C. F. (2004). Can case studies be used to teach critical thinking? *Journal of College Science Teaching*, *33*(6), 12–14.

Herrington, J., Reeves, T. C., & Oliver, R. (2014). Authentic learning environments. In J. M. Spector, M. D. Merrill, J. Elen, & M. J. Bishop (Eds.), *Handbook of research on educational communications and technology* (4th ed., pp. 401–412). Springer. doi:10.1007/978-1-4614-3185-5_32

Hesse, F., Care, E., Buder, J., Sassenberg, K., & Griffin, P. (2015). A framework for teachable collaborative problem solving skills. In P. Griffin & E. Care (Eds.), *What We Know About Collaboration Assessment and Teaching of 21st Century Skills: Methods and Approach* (pp. 37–56). Springer. doi:10.1007/978-94-017-9395-7_2

Hiebert, J. S., & Grouws, D. A. (2007). The effects of classroom mathematics teaching on students' learning. In F. K. Lester (Ed.), *Second handbook of research on mathematics teaching and learning* (pp. 371–404). Information Age Publishing.

Compilation of References

Hill, F. (2020). The pandemic is a crisis for students with special needs. *The Atlantic.* https://www.theatlantic.com/education/archive/2020/04/special-education-goes-remote-covid-19-pandemic/610231/

Hill, J., Song, L., & West, R. (2009). Social Learning Theory and Web-Based Learning Environments: A Review of Research and Discussion of Implications. *American Journal of Distance Education, 23*(2), 88–103. doi:10.1080/08923640902857713

Hillmayr, D., Ziernwald, L., Reinhold, F., Hofer, S. I., & Reiss, K. M. (2020). The potential of digital tools to enhance mathematics and science learning in secondary schools: A context-specific meta-analysis. *Computers & Education, 153,* 1–25. doi:10.1016/j.compedu.2020.103897

Hinchman, T., & Gupta, D. (2020, April). STEAMED UP: A Mixed Methods Creativity Evaluation. *Proceedings from Association for the Advancement of Computing in Education Conference*, 1121-1127.

Hipkins, R. (2010). Reshaping the secondary school curriculum: Building the plane while flying it. *Findings from NZCER National Survey of Secondary Schools 2009.*

Hodge, A., Rech, J., Liu, F., Bunning, K., Stade, E., Tubbs, R., & Webb, D. (2015, January). *Teaching inquiry through calculus TACTivities*. Presentation at the *Joint Mathematics Meetings*, San Antonio, TX.

Hodge, A., Wanek, K., & Rech, J. (2019). TACTivities: A tactile way to learn interdisciplinary communication skills. *Problems, Resources, and Issues in Mathematics Undergraduate Studies, 30*(2), 160–171.

Hodges, C., Moore, S., Lockee, B., Trust, T., & Bond, A. (2020). The difference between emergency remote teaching and online learning. *Educause Review*. https://er.educause.edu/articles/2020/3/the-difference-between-emergency-remote-teaching-and-online-learning

Hodges, C., Moore, S., Lockee, B., Trust, T., & Bond, A. (2020). The difference between emergency remote teaching and online learning. *EDUCAUSE Review*. https://er.educause.edu/articles/2020/3/the-difference-between-emergency-remote-teachingand-online-learning

Hodges, C., Moore, S., Lockee, B., Trust, T., & Bond, A. (2020). The Difference Between Emergency Remote Teaching and Online Learning. *Educause Review*. https://er.educause.edu/articles/2020/3/the-difference-between-emergency-remote-teaching-and-online-learning

Hodges, C., Moore, S., Lockee, B., Trust, T., & Bond, A. (2020, March 27). The difference between emergency remote teaching and online learning. *Edu-CAUSE Review*. https://er.educause.edu/articles/2020/3/the-difference-between-Emergency-remote-teaching-and-online-learning

Hodges, T. S., Kerch, C., & Fowler, M. (2020). Teacher education in the time of COVID-19: Creating digital networks as university-school-family partnerships. *Middle Grades Review, 6*(2).

Hodges, T. S. (2021). Teaching all students to write during a pandemic: Best practices for writing instruction. In L. Kyei-Blankson, J. Blankson, & E. Ntuli (Eds.), *Handbook of Research on Inequities in Online Education During Global Crises*. IGI Global. doi:10.4018/978-1-7998-6533-9.ch015

Hodge-Zickerman, A., Stade, E., York, C. S., & Rech, J. (2020). TACTivities: Fostering creativity through tactile learning activities. *Journal of Humanistic Mathematics, 10*(2), 377–390. doi:10.5642/jhummath.202002.17

Hodge-Zickerman, A., York, C. S., & Stade, E. (2021). Using technology and TACTivities to engage learners in mathematics classrooms [*Online Workshop*]. Society for Information Technology and Teacher Education.

Holbert, N., & Wilensky, U. (2019). Designing educational video games to be objects-to-think-with. *Journal of the Learning Sciences, 28*(1), 32–72. doi:10.1080/10508406.2018.1487302

Holmberg, J. (2019). *Designing for added pedagogical value: A design-based study of teachers' educational design with ICT* [Doctoral dissertation]. Department of Computer and Systems Sciences. Stockholm University.

Holmberg, J., Fransson, G. & Fors, U. (2018). Teachers' pedagogical reasoning and reframing of practice in digital contexts. *The International Journal of Information and Learning Technology, 35*(2), 130-142. doi:10.1108/IJILT-09-2017-0084

Holmes, E. A., O'Connor, R. C., Perry, V. H., Tracey, I., Wessely, S., Arseneault, L., Ballard, C., Christensen, H., Cohen Silver, R., Everall, I., Ford, T., John, A., Kabir, T., King, K., Madan, I., Michie, S., Przybylski, A. K., Shafran, R., Sweeney, A., ... Bullmore, E. (2020). Multidisciplinary research priorities for the COVID-19 pandemic: A call for action for mental health science. *The Lancet Psychiatry, 7*(6), 547–560. doi:10.1016/S2215-0366(20)30168-1 PMID:32304649

Holum, A., & Gahala, J. (2001). Critical issue: Using technology to enhance literacy instruction. *Northern Central Regional Educational Laboratory (NCREL)*. Retrieved from https://eric.ed.gov/?id=ED480229

Hong, C. E., Lawrence, S. A., Mongillo, G., & Donnantuono, M. (2015). Using iPads to support K-12 struggling readers: A case study of iPad implementation in a university-based reading clinic. In H. An, S. Alon, & D. Fuentes (Eds.), *Tablets in K-12 Education: Integrated Experiences and Implications* (pp. 296–309). IGI Global. doi:10.4018/978-1-4666-6300-8.ch017

Hong, J. C., Hwang, M. Y., Chen, Y. J., Lin, P. H., Huang, Y. T., Cheng, H. Y., & Lee, C. C. (2013). Using the saliency-based model to design a digital archaeological game to motivate players' intention to visit the digital archives of Taiwan's natural science museum. *Computers & Education, 66*, 74–82. doi:10.1016/j.compedu.2013.02.007

Horn, I. S. (2010). Teaching replays, teaching rehearsals, and re-visions of practice: Learning from colleagues in a mathematics teacher community. *Teachers College Record, 112*(1), 225–259.

Horowitz, S. H., Rawe, J., & Whittaker, M. C. (2017). *The state of learning disabilities: Understanding the 1 in 5*. National Center for Learning Disabilities.

Horton, W. (2012). *E-learning by Design* (2nd ed.). Pfeiffer.

Hoyles, C., & Jean-Baptiste, L. (2005). 17th ICMI study digital technologies and mathematics teaching and learning: Rethinking the domain-short announcement. *Educational Studies in Mathematics, 60*(2), 267–268. doi:10.100710649-005-4491-8

Hsu, L. (2011). The perceptual learning styles of hospitality students in a virtual learning environment: The case of Taiwan. *Journal of Hospitality, Leisure, Sport and Tourism Education, 10*(1), 114–127. doi:10.3794/johlste.101.325

Hsu, Y. C., Baldwin, S., & Ching, Y. H. (2017). Learning through making and maker education. *TechTrends, 61*(6), 589–594. doi:10.100711528-017-0172-6

Huang, D., & Manouchehri, A. (2019). Online mathematics teacher education in the U.S.: A status report. *Contemporary Issues in Technology & Teacher Education, 19*(2), 171–194. https://www.learntechlib.org/primary/p/182476/

Huang, X., Chandra, A., DePaolo, C. A., & Simmons, L. L. (2016). Understanding transactional distance in web-based learning environments: An empirical study. *British Journal of Educational Technology, 47*(4), 734–747. doi:10.1111/bjet.12263

Huckins, J. F., daSilva, A. W., Wang, W., Hedlund, E., Rogers, C., Nepal, S. K., Wu, J., Obuchi, M., Murphy, E. I., Meyer, M. L., Wagner, D. D., Holtzheimer, P. E., & Campbell, A. T. (2020). Mental Health and Behavior of College Students During the Early Phases of the COVID-19 Pandemic: Longitudinal Smartphone and Ecological Momentary Assessment Study. *Journal of Medical Internet Research, 22*(6), e20185. doi:10.2196/20185 PMID:32519963

Compilation of References

Huckle, J. (2012). Towards greater realism in learning for sustainability. In A. Wals & P. Corcoran (Eds.), *Learning for sustainability in times of accelerating change* (pp. 35–48). Wageningen Academic Publishers. doi:10.3920/978-90-8686-757-8_01

Hughes, G. (2011). Towards a personal best: A case for introducing ipsative assessment in higher education. *Studies in Higher Education*, *36*(3), 353–367. doi:10.1080/03075079.2010.486859

Hughes, G. (2014). *Ipsative assessment: Motivation through marking progress*. Springer. doi:10.1057/9781137267221

Hughes, G., Wood, E., & Kitagawa, K. (2014). Use of self-referential (ipsative) feedback to motivate and guide distance learners. *Open Learning*, *29*(1), 31–44. doi:10.1080/02680513.2014.921612

Hughes, J. E., Cheah, Y. H., Shi, Y., & Hsiao, K. (2020). Preservice and inservice teachers' pedagogical reasoning underlying their most-valued technology-supported instructional activities. *Journal of Computer Assisted Learning*, *36*(4), 549–568. doi:10.1111/jcal.12425

Humphreys, C., & Parker, R. (2015). *Making number talks matter: Developing mathematical practices and deepening understanding grades 4-10*. Stenhouse Publishing.

Hungerford, H. R., & Volk, T. L. (1990). Changing learner behavior through environmental education. *The Journal of Environmental Education*, *21*(3), 8–21. doi:10.1080/00958964.1990.10753743

Hunt, J., & Stein, M. K. (2020). Constructing Goals for Student Learning through Conversation. *Mathematics Teacher: Learning and Teaching PK-12*, *113*(11), 904–909.

Hunter, J. L., & Krantz, S. (2010). Constructivism in cultural competence education. *The Journal of Nursing Education*, *49*(4), 207–214. doi:10.3928/01484834-20100115-06 PMID:20143755

Hunter, M. (1994). *Mastery Teaching*. Corwin.

Hutchison, A. C., & Colwell, J. (2014). The Potential of Digital Technologies to Support Literacy Instruction Relevant to the Common Core State Standards. *Journal of Adolescent & Adult Literacy*, *58*(2), 147–156. doi:10.1002/jaal.335

Hutchison, A., & Colwell, J. (2016). Preservice Teachers' Use of the Technology Integration Planning Cycle to Integrate iPads into Literacy Instruction. *Journal of Research on Technology in Education*, *48*(1), 1–15. doi:10.1080/15391523.2015.1103146

Hutchison, A., & Woodward, L. (2014). A planning cycle for integrating digital technology into literacy instruction. *The Reading Teacher*, *67*(6), 455–464. doi:10.1002/trtr.1225

Hutchison, A., & Woodward, L. (2018). Examining the Technology Integration Planning Cycle Model of Professional Development to Support Teachers' Instructional Practices. *Teachers College Record*, *120*(10), 1–44.

Hyun, E., & Davis, G. (2005). Kindergarten conversations in a computer-based technology classroom. *Communication Education*, *54*(2), 118–135. doi:10.1080/03634520500213397

IBM Design Thinking. (2019, August 15). *The Framework: Design thinking re-envision for the modern enterprise*. Retrieved from: https://www.ibm.com/design/thinking/page/framework

IDEO Design Thinking. (2019, August 15). *Design Thinking Defined*. Retrieved from: https://designthinking.ideo.com/

Impact of COVID-19 on assessments and accountability under the Elementary and Secondary Education Act . (2020). Department of Education.

Individuals with Disabilities Education Act, 20 U.S.C. § 1400 (2004).

Individuals With Disabilities Education Improvement Act. (2004). Public Law 105-17 (20 U. S. C. § 1400 et seq.).

Inside Mathematics. (n.d.). *Number talks.* https://www.insidemathematics.org/classroom-videos/number-talks

International Society for Technology in Education. (2000). *National educational technology standards for students: connecting curriculum and technology.* International Society for Technology in Education.

International Society for Technology in Education. (2016). *ISTE Standards for students.* Retrieved from https://www.iste.org/standards/for-students

International Society for Technology in Education. (2021). *Online learning: Creating transformational learning experiences online.* https://www.iste.org/learn/online-learning

Islam, M. S., & Grönlund, Å. (2016). An international literature review of 1: 1 computing in schools. *Journal of Educational Change*, *17*(2), 191–222. doi:10.100710833-016-9271-y

Israel, M., Pearson, J. N., Tapia, T., Wherfel, Q. M., & Reese, G. (2015). Supporting all learners in school-wide computational thinking: A cross-case qualitative analysis. *Computers & Education*, *82*, 263–279. doi:10.1016/j.compedu.2014.11.022

Iuculano, T., Rosenberg-Lee, M., Richardson, J., Tenison, C., Fuchs, L., Supekar, K., & Menon, V. (2015). Cognitive tutoring induces widespread neuroplasticity and remediates brain function in children with mathematical learning disabilities. *Nature Communications*, *6*(1), 1–10. doi:10.1038/ncomms9453 PMID:26419418

Ives, J., & Castillo-Montoya, M. (2020). First-generation college students as academic learners: A systematic review. *Review of Educational Research*, *90*(2), 139–178. doi:10.3102/0034654319899707

Jack, B., & Clarke, A. M. (1998). The purpose and use of questionnaires in research. *Professional Nurse (London, England)*, *14*(3), 176–179. PMID:10095687

Jacobson, L. A., & Mahone, E. M. (2012). Educational implications of executive dysfunction. *Executive Function and Dysfunction*, 232-246. doi:10.1017/CBO9780511977954.021

Jaffe, D. (1997). Asynchronous learning: Technology and pedagogical strategy in a distant learning course. *Teaching Sociology*, *25*(4), 262–277. doi:10.2307/1319295

Jain, S., Lall, M., & Singh, A. (2021). Teachers' voices on the impact of COVID-19 on school education. Are ed-tech companies really the panacea? *Contemporary Education Dialogue*, *18*(1), 58–89. doi:10.1177/0973184920976433

Jaipal, K., & Figg, C. (2010). Unpacking the "Total PACKage": Emergent TPACK characteristics from a study of preservice teachers teaching with technology. *Journal of Technology and Teacher Education*, *18*(3), 415–441.

James, A., & Nerantzi, C. (Eds.). (2019). *The power of play in higher education: Creativity in tertiary learning.* Palgrave Macmillan. doi:10.1007/978-3-319-95780-7

Janakiraman, S. (2020). *Exploring the effectiveness of digital games in producing pro-environmental attitudes and behaviors* (Doctoral dissertation). Purdue University Graduate School.

Janakiraman, S., Watson, S. L., & Watson, W. R. (2018). Using game-Based learning to facilitate attitude change for environmental sustainability. *Journal of Education for Sustainable Development*, *12*(2), 176–185. doi:10.1177/0973408218783286

Janakiraman, S., Watson, S. L., & Watson, W. R. (2021b). Exploring the effectiveness of digital games in producing pro-environmental behaviors when played collaboratively and individually: A mixed methods study in India. *TechTrends*, *65*(3), 331–347. doi:10.100711528-020-00571-8 PMID:33521794

Compilation of References

Janakiraman, S., Watson, S. L., Watson, W. R., & Newby, T. (2021a). Effectiveness of digital games in producing environmentally friendly attitudes and behaviors: A mixed methods study. *Computers & Education, 160*, 104043. doi:10.1016/j.compedu.2020.104043

Janakiraman, S., Watson, S. L., Watson, W. R., & Shepardson, D. P. (2021c). Exploring the influence of digital games on environmental attitudes and behaviours based on the new ecological paradigm scale: A mixed-methods study in India. *Journal of Education for Sustainable Development, 15*(1), 1–28. doi:10.1177/0973408221997844

Jaramillo, J. A. (1996). Vygotsky's sociocultural theory and contributions to the development of constructivist curricula. *Education, 117*(1), 133–141.

Joan, D. R. R. (2018). Virtual Classroom: A gift for disabled children. *I-Manager's Journal on School Educational Technology, 14*(2), 7. http://doi. doi:10.26634/jsch.14.2.15100

Jocius, R. (2017). Good student/bad student: Situated identities in the figured worlds of school and creative multimodal production. *Literacy Research: Theory, Method, and Practice, 66*(1), 198–217. doi:10.1177/2381336917718177

Jocius, R. (2018). Becoming entangled: The emergence of collaborative multimodal practices. *Computers and Composition, 46*, 14–30. doi:10.1016/j.compcom.2017.12.008

Jocius, R., Albert, J., Andrews, A., & Blanton, M. (2020). A study in contradictions: Exploring standards-based making in elementary classrooms. *The Journal of Educational Research, 113*(5), 396–403. doi:10.1080/00220671.2020.1838409

Joe, H., Hiver, P., & Al-Hoorie, A. H. (2017). Classroom social climate, self-determined motivation, willingness to communicate, and achievement: A study of structural relationships in instructed second language settings. *Learning and Individual Differences, 53*, 133–144. doi:10.1016/j.lindif.2016.11.005

John Hopkins University. (2021, February). CoronaVirus Resource Center. *CoronaVirus*. https://coronavirus.jhu.edu/

Johnson, A. (2019, November 11). Using empathy games in the social sciences. *Educause Review*. https://er.educause.edu/articles/2019/11/using-empathy-games-in-the-social-sciences

Johnson, E. R. (2009). *Academic language! Academic literacy!: A guide for K-12 educators*. Corwin.

Johnson, J., Uline, C. L., & Perez, L. G. (2020). *Teaching practices from America's best urban schools: A guide for school and classroom leaders* (2nd ed.). Routledge.

Johnson, N., Veletsianos, G., & Seaman, J. (2020). US Faculty and Administrators' Experiences and Approaches in the Early Weeks of the COVID-19 Pandemic. *Online Learning, 24*(2), 6–21. doi:10.24059/olj.v24i2.2285

Johnson, S. L., Pas, E., & Bradshaw, C. P. (2016). Understanding the association between school climate and future orientation. *Journal of Youth and Adolescence, 45*(8), 1575–1586. doi:10.100710964-015-0321-1 PMID:26104381

Johnson, T., & Dabney, K. (2018). Voices from the field: Constraints encountered by early career elementary science teachers. *School Science and Mathematics, 118*(6), 244–256. doi:10.1111sm.12290

Johnston, E. M. (2020). *Invited to the feast? Problems of hospitality, coloniality and identity in the music classroom* (PhD Dissertation). York University, YorkSpace Institutional Repository. http://hdl.handle.net/10315/37898

Jones, C. D. (2015). Effects of writing instruction on kindergarten students' writing achievement: An experimental study. *The Journal of Educational Research, 108*(1), 35–44. doi:10.1080/00220671.2013.836466

Jones, W. M., Cohen, J. D., Schad, M., Caratachea, M., & Smith, S. (2020). Maker-centered teacher professional development: Examining K-12 teachers' learning experiences in a commercial makerspace. *TechTrends, 64*(1), 37–49. doi:10.100711528-019-00425-y

Jones, W. M., & Dexter, S. (2014). How teachers learn: The roles of formal, informal, and independent learning. *Educational Technology Research and Development*, *62*(3), 367–384. doi:10.100711423-014-9337-6

Joordens, S., Kapoor, A., & Hofman, B. (2019). Let's riff off rifs (relevant, interesting, fun, and social): Best practices for engaging the online mind. In *Handbook of Research on Emerging Practices and Methods for K-12 Online and Blended Learning* (pp. 213–232). IGI Global. doi:10.4018/978-1-5225-8009-6.ch010

Joshi, M., Treiman, R., Carreker, S., & Moats, L. C. (2008). How words cast their spell: Spelling is an integral part of learning the language, not a matter of memorization. *American Educator*, 6–16, 42–43.

Jost, N. S., Jossen, S. L., Rothen, N., & Martarelli, C. S. (2021). The advantage of distributed practice in a blended learning setting. *Education and Information Technologies*, *26*(3), 3097–3113. doi:10.100710639-020-10424-9 PMID:33424416

Joswick, C., Meador, A., Fletcher, N., Conner, K., & McMillian, B. (2020). Responding to current field experience challenges with the virtualization of number talks. *Association of Mathematics Teacher Educators Connections*, *30*(2), 1–5.

Journell, W., & Schouweller, D. (2019). Moving K-12 coursework online: Considerations and strategies. In T. L. Heafner, R. Hartshorne, & R. Thripp (Eds.), *Handbook of research on emerging practices and methods for K-12 online and blended learning* (pp. 477–499). IGI Global. doi:10.4018/978-1-5225-8009-6.ch023

Jung, J., Ding, A.-C. E., Lu, Y.-H., Ottenbreit-Leftwich, A., & Glazewski, K. (2020). Is digital inequality a part of preservice teachers' reasoning about technology integration decisions? *The American Behavioral Scientist*, *64*(7), 994–1011. doi:10.1177/0002764220919141

Kaden, U. (2020). COVID-19 School Closure-Related Changes to the Professional Life of a K–12 Teacher. *Education Sciences*, *10*(6), 165–181. doi:10.3390/educsci10060165

Kahn, P., Everington, L., Kelm, K., Reid, I., & Watkins, F. (2017). Understanding student engagement in online learning environments: The role of reflexivity. *Educational Technology Research and Development*, *65*(1), 203–218. doi:10.100711423-016-9484-z

Kahoot! (2020). *A game-based learning platform*. Retrieved from: https://kahoot.it/

Kalkstein, D. A., Kleiman, T., Wakslak, C. J., Liberman, N., & Trope, Y. (2016). Social learning across psychological distance. *Journal of Personality and Social Psychology*, *110*(1), 1–19. doi:10.1037/pspa0000042 PMID:26727663

Kalyanpur, M., & Kirmani, M. H. (2005). Diversity and technology: Classroom implications of the digital divide. *Journal of Special Education Technology*, *20*(4), 9–18. doi:10.1177/016264340502000402

Kamenetz, A. (2020, December 4). *5 things we've learned about virtual school in 2020*. NPR. https://www.npr.org/2020/12/04/938050723/5-things-weve-learned-about-virtual-school-in-2020

Kamins, M. L., & Dweck, C. S. (1999). Person versus process praise and criticism: Implications for contingent self-worth and coping. *Developmental Psychology*, *35*(3), 835–847. doi:10.1037/0012-1649.35.3.835 PMID:10380873

Kamradt, T. F., & Kamradt, E. J. (1999). Structured design for attitudinal instruction. In C. M. Reigeluth (Ed.), *Instructional design theories and models: A new paradigm of instructional theory* (Vol. 2, pp. 563–590). Lawrence Erlbaum Associates.

Kao, G. Y.-M., Lin, S. S. J., & Sun, C.-T. (2008). Beyond Sharing: Engaging Students in Cooperative and Competitive Active Learning. *Journal of Educational Technology & Society*, *11*(3), 82–96.

Kaplon-Schilis, A., & Lyublinskaya, I. (2021, April 8-12). *Analysis of differences in the levels of TPACK: Unpacking performance indicators in the TPACK Levels Rubric* [Paper presentation]. AERA 2021: Accepting Educational Responsibilities.

Compilation of References

Karacop, A., & Diken, E. H. (2017). The effects of jigsaw technique based on cooperative learning on prospective science teachers' science process skill. *Journal of Education and Practice, 8*(6), 86–97.

Karanja, K. (2018). *Gabi's if/then garden*. Picture Window Books.

Karchmer-Klein, R. (2020). *Designing interactive and collaborative online learning opportunities for teacher education courses*. Teachers College Press.

Karchmer-Klein, R., & Shinas, V. H. (2013). Guiding principles for supporting new literacies in your classroom. *The Reading Teacher, 65*(5), 288–294. doi:10.1002/TRTR.01044

Kardaras, N. (2016). Generation Z: Online and at risk. *Scientific American Mind, 27*(5), 64–69. doi:10.1038cientificamericanmind0916-64

Karimi, H., Torphy, K. T., Derr, T., Frank, K. A., & Tang, J. (2020, August). Characterizing Teacher Connections in Online Social Media: A Case Study on Pinterest. In *Proceedings of the Seventh ACM Conference on Learning@ Scale* (pp. 249-252). 10.1145/3386527.3405941

Karl, T. R., & Trenberth, K. E. (2003). Modern global climate change. *Science, 302*(5651), 1719–1723. doi:10.1126cience.1090228 PMID:14657489

Kasworm, C. E. (1988). *Part-time credit learners as full-time workers: The role of self-directed learning in their lives* [Paper presentation]. Annual conference of the American Association for Adult and Continuing Education, Tulsa, OK.

Kaufman, J. C., & Beghetto, R. A. (2013). In praise of Clark Kent: Creative metacognition and the importance of teaching kids when (not) to be creative. *Roeper Review*: *A Journal on Gifted Education, 35*, 155–165. doi:10.1080/02783193.2013.799413

Kaufman, J. C., & Beghetto, R. A. (2009). Beyond big and little: The four C model of creativity. *Review of General Psychology, 13*(1), 1–12. doi:10.1037/a0013688

Kavale, K. A., & Forness, S. R. (2000). What definitions of learning disability say and don't say: A critical analysis. *Journal of Learning Disabilities, 33*, 239–256. http://ldx.sagepub.com/ PMID:15505963

Kay, R., & Schellenberg, D. (2017, June). Integrating a BYOD program in high school English: Advantage or distraction? In EdMedia+ Innovate Learning (pp. 12-16). Association for the Advancement of Computing in Education (AACE).

Kecskemeti, M. (2013). Competent students and caring teachers: Is a good pedagogy always the best pedagogy? *Teachers & Curriculum, 13*, 94–95. doi:10.15663/tandc.v13i0.18

Kelly, M. A. (2007). Culturally sensitive teaching with technology: Implementing TPCK in culturally mixed contexts. In R. Carlsen, K. McFerrin, J. Price, R. Weber, & D. Willis (Eds.), *Proceedings of Society for Information Technology & Teacher Education International Conference 2007* (pp. 2199–2202). Chesapeake, VA: AACE.

Kelly, M. A. (2010). Technological Pedagogical Content Knowledge (TPACK): A Content analysis of 2006–2009 print journal articles. In D. Gibson, & B. Dodge (Eds.), *Proceedings of the Society for Information Technology & Teacher Education International Conference 2010* (pp. 3880–3888). Chesapeake, VA: AACE.

Kempka-Wagner, D. (2018). Building Augmentative Communication Skills in Homes Where English and Spanish Are Spoken: Perspectives of an Evaluator/Interventionist. *Perspectives of the ASHA Special Interest Groups, 3*(12), 172–185. doi:10.1044/persp3.sig12.172

Kennedy, K., & Ferdig, R. E. (Eds.). (2018). *Handbook of Research of K12 Online and Blended Learning* (2nd ed.). Carnegie Mellon University: ETC Press.

Kennedy, M. J., Thomas, C. N., Meyer, J. P., Alves, K. D., & Lloyd, J. W. (2014). Using evidence-based multimedia to improve vocabulary performance of adolescents with LD: A UDL approach. *Learning Disability Quarterly*, *37*(2), 71–86. doi:10.1177/0731948713507262

Kenney, M., & Zysman, J. (2016). The rise of the platform economy. *Issues in Science and Technology*, *32*(3). https://issues.org/the-rise-of-the-platformeconomy/

Kersten, S. (2017). Becoming nonfiction authors: Engaging in Science inquiry. *The Reading Teacher*, *71*(1), 33–41. doi:10.1002/trtr.1577

Key Curriculum Press. (2001). *The geometer's sketchpad: Dynamic geometry software for exploring mathematics*. Key Curriculum Press.

Khan, A., Egbue, O., Palkie, B., & Madden, J. (2017). Active learning: engaging students to maximize learning in an online course. *The Electronic Journal of e-Learning, 15*(2), 107-115.

Khasawneh, M., Alkhawaldeh, M., & Al-Khasawneh, F. (2020). The levels of metacognitive thinking among students with learning disabilities. *International Journal of English Linguistics*, *10*(5). Advance online publication. doi:10.5539/ijel.v10n5p343

Khazanchi, P., & Khazanchi, R. (2019). Hands-On Activities to Keep Students With Disabilities Engaged in K-12 Classrooms. In Handmade Teaching Materials for Students With Disabilities (pp. 185-211). IGI Global.

Khazanchi, R., & Khazanchi, P. (2020). Effective Pedagogical Practices in Inclusive Classrooms for Students with Disabilities. In *Special Education Design and Development Tools for School Rehabilitation Professionals* (pp. 38–60). IGI Global. doi:10.4018/978-1-7998-1431-3.ch003

Khazanchi, R., Khazanchi, P., Mehta, V., & Tuli, N. (2021). Incorporating Social–Emotional Learning to Build Positive Behaviors. *Kappa Delta Pi Record*, *57*(1), 11–17.

Kilis, S., & Yıldırım, Z. (2018). Investigation of community of inquiry framework in regard to self-regulation, metacognition and motivation. *Computers & Education*, *126*, 53–64. doi:10.1016/j.compedu.2018.06.032

Kim, A. Y., Sinatra, G. M., & Seyranian, V. (2018). Developing a STEM identity among young women: A social identity perspective. *Review of Educational Research*, *88*(4), 589–625. doi:10.3102/0034654318779957

Kim, K. J., & Bonk, C. J. (2006). The future of online teaching and learning in higher education. *EDUCAUSE Quarterly*, *29*(4), 22–30.

King, A. (1993). From sage on the stage to guide on the side. *Journal of College Teacher*, *41*(1), 30–35. doi:10.1080/87567555.1993.9926781

King, K. A. (2012). Writing workshop in preschool: Acknowledging children as writers. *The Reading Teacher*, *65*(6), 392–401. doi:10.1002/TRTR.01059

Kinsel, E., Cleveland-Innes, M., & Garrison, D. R. (2005). *Student Role Adjustment in Online Environments: From the Mouths of Online Babes*. uwex.edu

Kirby, M. S., Spencer, T. D., & Chen, Y.-J. I. (2021). Oral narrative instruction improves kindergarten writing. *Reading & Writing Quarterly*, 1–18. Advance online publication. doi:10.1080/10573569.2021.1879696

Kirschner, P. A., Sweller, J., & Clark, R. E. (2006). Why Minimal Guidance During Instruction Does Not Work: An Analysis of the Failure of Constructivist, Discovery, Problem-Based, Experiential, and Inquiry-Based Teaching. *Educational Psychologist*, *41*(2), 75–86. doi:10.120715326985ep4102_1

Compilation of References

KiwiCo. (2021). https://www.kiwico.com/

Knight, M., & Cunningham, C. (2004, June). *Draw an Engineer Test (DAET): Development of a tool to investigate students' ideas about engineers and engineering.* Paper presented at 2004 ASEE Annual Conference, Salt Lake City, UT. https://peer.asee.org/12831 doi:10.18260/1-2--12831

Knol, E., & De Vries, P. W. (2010). EnerCities: educational game about energy. *Proceedings CESB10 Central Europe towards Sustainable Building.* Retrieved from http://www.qeam.com/docs/Knol_Vries_de_EnerCities-educational-game-about-energy-CESB10.PDF

Knol, E., & De Vries, P. W. (2011). EnerCities, a serious game to stimulate sustainability and energy conservation: Preliminary results. *eLearning Papers, 25,* 1-10. https://papers.ssrn.com/sol3/papers.cfm?abstract_id=1866206

Knowles, M. K. (1975). *Self-directed learning.* Follett.

Koberg, D., & Bagnall, J. (1972). *The Universal Traveler; a soft-systems Guide: To Creativity, Problem-Solving, and the process of Design.* Kaufmann.

Koehler, M. J., & Mishra, P. (2005). What happens when teachers design educational technology? The development of technological pedagogical content knowledge. *Journal of Educational Computing Research, 32*(2), 131–152. doi:10.2190/0EW7-01WB-BKHL-QDYV

Koehler, M. J., & Mishra, P. (2009). What is technological pedagogical content knowledge? *Contemporary Issues in Technology & Teacher Education, 9*(1), 60–70.

Koehler, M. J., Mishra, P., & Cain, W. (2013). What is technological pedagogical content (TPACK)? *Journal of Education, 193*(3), 13–19. doi:10.1177/002205741319300303

Koenig, R. (2020). *Pandemic May (Finally) Push Online Education Into Teacher Prep Programs.* Retrieved from https://www.edsurge.com/news/2020-05-28-pandemic-may-finally-push-online-education-into-teacher-prep-programs

Koh, J. H. L., Chai, C. S., Hong, H.-Y., & Tsai, C.-C. (2014). A survey to examine teachers' perceptions of design dispositions, lesson design practices, and their relationships with technological pedagogical content knowledge (TPACK). *Asia-Pacific Journal of Teacher Education, 43*(5), 378–391. doi:10.1080/1359866x.2014.941280

Koh, J. H. L., Chai, C. S., & Lee, M.-H. (2015). Technological pedagogical content knowledge for pedagogical improvement: Editorial for special issue on TPACK. *The Asia-Pacific Education Researcher, 24*(3), 459–462. doi:10.100740299-015-0241-6

Kohn, A. (2006). *Beyond discipline: From compliance to community.* Association for Supervision and Curriculum Development.

KoksalI. (2020). *The Rise of Online Learning.* Retrieved from https://www.forbes.com/sites/ilkerkoksal/2020/05/02/the-rise-of-online-learning/?sh=671deaa472f3

Kolb, L. (2017). *Learning first, technology second: The educator's guide to designing authentic lessons.* International Society for Technology Education.

König, J., Jäger-Biela, D. J., & Glutsch, N. (2020). Adapting to online teaching during COVID-19 school closure: Teacher education and teacher competence effects among early career teachers in Germany. *European Journal of Teacher Education, 43*(4), 608–622. doi:10.1080/02619768.2020.1809650

Kopcha, T. J., Neumann, K. L., Ottenbreit-Leftwich, A., & Pitman, E. (2020). Process over product: The next evolution of our quest for technology integration. *Educational Technology Research and Development, 68*(2), 729–749. doi:10.100711423-020-09735-y

Korkut, S., Dornberger, R., Diwanji, P., Simon, P., & Maerki, M. (2015). Success factors of online learning videos. *International Journal of Interactive Technologies, 10*(1), 116–182. doi:10.3991/ijim.v9i4.4460

Kosanovich, M., Lee, L., & Foorman, B. (2020). *A Kindergarten Teacher's Guide to Supporting Family Involvement in Foundational Reading Skills* (REL 2020-016). Washington, DC: U.S. Department of Education, Institute of Education Sciences, National Center for Education Evaluation and Regional Assistance, Regional Educational Laboratory Southeast. Retrieved from https://ies.ed.gov/ncee/edlabs

Koshy, V. (2005). *Action research for improving practice: A practical guide*. Sage Publications.

Kozak, S., & Martin-Chang, S. (2019). Preservice Teacher Knowledge, Print Exposure, and Planning for Instruction. *Reading Research Quarterly, 54*(3), 323–338. doi:10.1002/rrq.240

Krajcik, J., & Shin, N. (2014). Project-based learning. In R. Sawyer (Ed.), *The Cambridge handbook of the learning sciences* (2nd ed., pp. 275–297). Cambridge University Press. doi:10.1017/CBO9781139519526.018

Krishnan, J., Yim, S., Wolters, A., & Cusimano, A. (2019). Supporting online synchronous collaborative writing in the secondary classroom. *Journal of Adolescent & Adult Literacy, 63*(2), 138–140. doi:10.1002/jaal.969

Krish, P., Maros, M., & Siti, H. S. (2012). Sociocultural Factors and Social Presence in an Online Learning Environment. *Journal of Language Studies, 2*(1), 201–213. https://core.ac.uk/download/pdf/11492265.pdf

Krutka, D. G., Heath, M. K., & Willet, K. B. S. (2019). Foregrounding Technoethics: Toward Critical Perspectives in Technology and Teacher Education. *Journal of Technology and Teacher Education, 27*(4), 555–574.

Kuhfeld, M., & Tarasawa, B. (2020). *The COVID-19 slide: What summer learning loss can tell us about the potential impact of school closures on student academic achievement*. NWEA.

Kuhn, D. (2015). Thinking together and alone. *Educational Researcher, 44*(1), 46–53. doi:10.3102/0013189X15569530

Kulkarni, S., & Parmar, J. (2017). Culturally and linguistically diverse student and family perspectives of AAC. *Augmentative and Alternative Communication, 33*(3), 170–180. https://doi.org/10.1080/07434618.2017.1346706

Kumari, E., Chakraborty, S., & Ray, B. (2015). Traumatic globe luxation: A case report. *Indian Journal of Ophthalmology, 63*(8), 682–684. doi:10.4103/0301-4738.169795 PMID:26576530

Kunz, K. (2020). *Literacy changemakers: Bringing the joy of reading and writing into focus for teachers and students*. Guilford Press.

Kurti, R. S., Kurti, D. L., & Fleming, L. (2014). The philosophy of educational makerspaces part 1 of making an educational makerspace. *Teacher Librarian, 41*(5), 8–11.

Kushlev, K., Dunn, E., & Proulx, J. D. E. (2017). Digitally Connected, Socially Disconnected: The Effects of Relying on Technology Rather Than Other People. *Computers in Human Behavior, 76*, 68–74. doi:10.1016/j.chb.2017.07.001

Ladson-Billings, G. (2014). Culturally relevant pedagogy 2.0: Aka the remix. *Harvard Educational Review, 84*(1), 74–84. doi:10.17763/haer.84.1.p2rj131485484751

Lai, E. R. (2011). *Collaboration: A literature review*. Pearson Publisher.

Compilation of References

Lake, R. (2020, July 7). *Students count: Highlights from COVID-19 student surveys.* Center on Reinventing Public Education. https://www.crpe.org/thelens/students-count-highlights-covid-19-student-surveys

Lakhana, A. (2014). What is educational technology? An inquiry into the meaning, use, and reciprocity of technology. *Canadian Journal of Learning and Technology, 40*(3), 1–41. doi:10.21432/T2H59S

Lankshear, C., & Knobel, M. (2008). New literacies as a remix. In *New literacies: Everyday practices and classroom learning* (2nd ed., pp. 105–136). Open University Press.

Lantz-Andersson, A., Peterson, L., Hillman, T., Lundin, M., & Rensfeldt, A. B. (2017). Sharing repertoires in a teacher professional Facebook group. *Learning, Culture and Social Interaction, 100*(15), 44–55. doi:10.1016/j.lcsi.2017.07.001

Lappan, G., Phillips, E. D., Fey, J. T., & Friel, S. N. (2014). Connected Mathematics 3. Let's Be Rational. Boston, MA: Pearson Prentice Hall.

Lappan, G., Phillips, E. D., Fey, J. T., & Friel, S. N. (2014). *Connected Mathematics 3. Stretching and Shrinking.* Pearson Prentice Hall. Mathematica. https://www.wolfram.com/mathematica/

Larmer, J., Mergendoller, J., & Boss, S. (2015). *Setting the standard for project based learning.* Association for Supervision and Curriculum Development.

Latour, B. (1999). *Pandora's hope: essays on the reality of science studies.* Harvard University Press.

Laudel, G. (2001). Collaboration, creativity, and rewards: Why and how scientists collaborate. *International Journal of Technology Management, 22*(7-8), 762–781. doi:10.1504/IJTM.2001.002990

Laurillard, D. (2002). *Rethinking University teaching: A conversational framework for the effective use of learning technologies* (2nd ed.). RoutledgeFalmer. doi:10.4324/9780203160329

Laurillard, D. (2012). *Teaching as a design science: Building pedagogical patterns for learning and technology.* Routledge.

Laursen, S. L., Hassi, M.-L., Kogan, M., & Weston, T. J. (2014). Benefits for women and men of inquiry-based learning in college mathematics: A multi-institution study. *Journal for Research in Mathematics Education, 45*(4), 406–418. doi:10.5951/jresematheduc.45.4.0406

Laursen, S. L., & Rasmussen, C. (2019). I on the prize: Inquiry approaches in undergraduate mathematics. *International Journal of Research in Undergraduate Mathematics Education, 5*(1), 129–146. doi:10.100740753-019-00085-6

Lave, J., & Wenger, E. (1991). *Situated Learning: Legitimate Peripheral Participation.* Cambridge University Press. doi:10.1017/CBO9780511815355

Lave, J., & Wenger, E. (2015). *Situated learning: Legitimate peripheral participation.* Cambridge University Press.

Lawrence, S. A., Hong, E., Donnantuono, M., & Mongillo, G. (2015). Using literacy iPad apps for reading motivation. In T. V. Rasinski, R. E. Ferdig, & K. E. Pytash (Eds.), *Using Technology to Enhance Reading: Innovative Approaches to Literacy Instruction* (pp. 187–202). Solution Tree.

Learning Forward. (2011). *Standards for professional learning.* Author.

Learning Forward. (2021). *Standards for professional learning.* https://learningforward.org/standards-for-professional-learning/

Lee, J. (2020, November 17). A neuropsychological exploration of zoom fatigue. *Psychiatric Times.* https://www.psychiatrictimes.com/view/psychological-exploration-zoom-fatigue

Lee, J., Yoon, S. Y., & Lee, C. H. (2013). Exploring Online Learning at Primary Schools: Students' Perspectives on Cyber Home Learning System through Video Conferencing (CHLS-VC). *Turkish Online Journal of Educational Technology, 12*(1), 68–76.

LEGO®. (2020). *Creator 3in1 31088 Deep sea creatures set.* Retrieved from https://www.lego.com/en-us/product/deep-sea-creatures-31088

Lei, J., & Zhao, Y. (2008). One-to-one computing: What does it bring to schools? *Journal of Educational Computing Research, 39*(2), 97–122. doi:10.2190/EC.39.2.a

Lenhart, A. (2015, April 9). *Teens, social media & technology: overview 2015.* Pew Research Center. https://www.pewresearch.org/internet/2015/04/09/teens-social-media-technology-2015/

Leu, D. J., Forzani, E., Rhoads, C., Maykel, C., Kennedy, C., & Timbrell, N. (2014). The new literacies of online research and comprehension: Rethinking the reading achievement gap. *Reading Research Quarterly, 50*(1), 37–59. doi:10.1002/rrq.85

Lewis, J., & Leach, J. (2006). Discussion of socio-scientific issues: The role of science knowledge. *International Journal of Science Education, 28*(11), 1267–1287. doi:10.1080/09500690500439348

Liarakou, G., Sakka, E., Gavrilakis, C., & Tsolakidis, C. (2012). Evaluation of serious games, as a tool for education for sustainable development. *European Journal of Open, Distance and E-learning, 15*(2).

Lickona, T. (1991). *Educating for character: How our schools can teach respect and responsibility.* Bantam Books.

Liljendahl, P. (2020). *Building thinking classrooms in mathematics.* Corwin Mathematics.

Lim, W., Son, J. W., & Kim, D. J. (2018). Understanding pre-service teacher skills in construct lesson plans. *International Journal of Science and Mathematics Education, 16*(3), 519–538. doi:10.100710763-016-9783-1

Lin, F., & Qiyun, Z. (2003). The affinity between constructivist teaching theory and English language teaching reform. *Foreign Languages and Their Teaching, 4*(7), 89–94.

Lin, Ys. (2011). Fostering creativity through education – A conceptual framework of Creative Pedagogy. *Creative Education, 2*, 149–155. doi:10.4236/ce.2011.23021

Lithner, J. (2008). A research framework for creative and imitative reasoning. *Educational Studies in Mathematics, 67*(3), 255–276. doi:10.100710649-007-9104-2

Litts, B. K. (2015). *Making learning: Makerspaces as learning environments* [Doctoral dissertation]. The University of Wisconsin-Madison.

Liu, L., Li, Y., Xiong, Y., Cao, J., & Yuan, P. (2018). An EEG study of the relationship between design problem statements and cognitive behaviors during conceptual design. *Artificial Intelligence for Engineering Design, Analysis and Manufacturing, 32*(3), 351–362. doi:10.1017/S0890060417000683

Lonergan, D. C., Scott, G. M., & Mumford, M. D. (2004). Evaluative Aspects of Creative Thought: Effects of Appraisal and Revision Standards. *Creativity Research Journal, 16*(2-3), 231–246. doi:10.1080/10400419.2004.9651455

Looi, C. K., & Wu, L. (2015). *Reflection and preflection prompts and scaffolding.* SAGE.

Louie, N. L. (2017). The culture of exclusion in mathematics education and its persistence in equity-oriented teaching. *Journal for Research in Mathematics Education, 48*(5), 488–519. doi:10.5951/jresematheduc.48.5.0488

Compilation of References

Lovato, S. B., Piper, A. M., & Wartella, E. A. (2019, June). Hey Google, Do Unicorns Exist? Conversational Agents as a Path to Answers to Children's Questions. In *Proceedings of the 18th ACM International Conference on Interaction Design and Children* (pp. 301-313). 10.1145/3311927.3323150

Lowenthal, P., West, R., Archambault, L., & Borup, J. (2020, August). Engaging students through asynchronous video-based discussions in online courses. *EDUCAUSE Review*. https://er.educause.edu/articles/2020/8/engaging-students-through-asynchronous-videobased-discussions-in-online-courses

Lowenthal, P. R., & Moore, R. L. (2020). Exploring student perceptions of Flipgrid in online courses. *Online Learning*, *24*(4), 28–41. doi:10.24059/olj.v24i4.2335

Lowenthal, P. R., & Snelson, C. (2017). In search of a better understanding of social presence: An investigation into how researchers define social presence. *Distance Education*, *38*(2), 141–159. doi:10.1080/01587919.2017.1324727

Lowrey, A. K., Classen, A., & Sylvest, A. (2019). Exploring Ways to Support Preservice Teachers' Use of UDL in Planning and Instruction. *Journal of Educational Research and Practice*, *9*(1), 261–281. doi:10.5590/JERAP.2019.09.1.19

Lowyck, J. (2014). Bridging learning theories and technology-enhanced environments: A critical appraisal of its history. In J. M. Spector, M. D. Merrill, J. Elen, & M. J. Bishop (Eds.), *Handbook of research on communications and educational technology*. Springer. doi:10.1007/978-1-4614-3185-5_1

Lu, J., & Hao, Q. (2014). What factors impact on primary school students' online engagement for learning and entertainment at home. *Journal of Computers in Education*, *1*(2–3), 133.

Lyle, K. E. (2009). *Teacher Perceptions of their Technology Education Curricula* (Order No. 3385448). Available from ProQuest Dissertations & Theses Global: The Humanities and Social Sciences Collection. (305158541). Retrieved from https://tamusa.idm.oclc.org/login?url=https://www.proquest.com/dissertations-theses/teachers-perceptions-their-technology-education/docview/305158541/se-2?accountid=130967

Lyublinskaya, I., & Du, X. (2021). Analysis of preservice teachers' TPACK learning trajectories in an online summer academic program. In E. Langran & L. Archambault (Eds.), *Proceedings of Society for Information Technology & Teacher Education International Conference* (pp. 1316-1326). Association for the Advancement of Computing in Education (AACE). Retrieved April 7, 2021 from https://www.learntechlib.org/primary/p/219323/

Macià, M., & García, I. (2016). Informal online communities and networks as a source of teacher professional development: A review. *Teaching and Teacher Education*, *55*, 291–307. doi:10.1016/j.tate.2016.01.021

MacIntyre, P. D., Gregersen, T., & Mercer, S. (2020). Language teachers' coping strategies during the Covid-19 conversion to online teaching: Correlations with stress, wellbeing and negative emotions. *System*, *94*, 102352. doi:10.1016/j.system.2020.102352

Maddux, C., Johnson, D., & Willis, J. (1997). *Educational computing: Learning with tomorrow's technologies* (2nd ed.). Allyn & Bacon.

Magen-Nagar, N., & Shonfeld, M. (2018). Attitudes, openness to multiculturalism, and integration of online collaborative learning. *Journal of Educational Technology & Society*, *21*(3), 1–11.

Maguire, E. A., Woollett, K., & Spiers, H. J. (2006). London taxi drivers and bus drivers: A structural MRI and neuropsychological analysis. *Hippocampus*, *16*(12), 1091–1101. doi:10.1002/hipo.20233 PMID:17024677

Mahar, A. L., Cobigo, V., & Stuart, H. (2013). Conceptualizing belonging. *Disability and Rehabilitation*, *35*(12), 1026–1032. doi:10.3109/09638288.2012.717584 PMID:23020179

Makara, K. A., & Madjar, N. (2015). The role of goal structures and peer climate in trajectories of social achievement goals during high school. *Developmental Psychology*, *51*(4), 473–488. doi:10.1037/a0038801 PMID:25730313

Male, T. (2016). Digital technologies: Implications for educational organisations and settings in the twenty-first century. *EducationalFutures*, *7*(3), 5–25.

Malhotra, T. (2014). Integration of technology in kindergarten literacy learning [Unpublished masters major research project]. York University, North York, Toronto, Canada.

Malinovski, T., Vasileva, M., Vasileva-Stojanovska, T., & Trajkovik, V. (2014). Considering high school students' experience in asynchronous and synchronous learning environments: QoE prediction model. *International Review of Research in Open and Distance Learning*, *15*(4), 91–112. doi:10.19173/irrodl.v15i4.1808

Malloy, P. J. (2019). *Secondary teachers' and students' perceptions of the bring your own device (BYOB) technology policy and practices* [Dissertation]. Houston Baptist University. http://hdl.handle.net/20.500.12262/213

Map: Coronavirus and School Closures. (2020, March 6). *Education Week*. Retrieved from https://www.edweek.org/ew/section/multimedia/map-coronavirus-and-school-closures.html

Mardi, F. (2019). How to create meaningful learning experiences in an online environment: Components from coding student reflections. *Research on Education and Media*, *11*(1), 50–62. doi:10.2478/rem-2019-0008

Margerum-Leys, J., & Marx, R. W. (2002). Teacher knowledge of educational technology: A study of student teacher/mentor teacher pairs. *Journal of Educational Computing Research*, *26*(4), 427–462.

Marschall, S., & Davis, C. (2012). A conceptual framework for teaching critical reading to adult college students. *Adult Learning*, *23*(2), 63–68. doi:10.1177/1045159512444265

Marsh. (2007). New literacies and old pedagogies: Recontextualizing rules and practices. *International Journal of Inclusive Education*, *11*(3), 267-281.

Marshall, H. W. (2020). Fostering teaching presence through the synchronous online flipped learning approach. *TESL-EJ, Teaching English as a second or foreign language*, *24*(2), 7–9.

Martin, F., Parker, M., & Allred, B. (2013). A case study on the adoption and use of synchronous virtual classrooms. *The Electronic Journal of e-Learning*, *11*(2), 124-138. https://files.eric.ed.gov/fulltext/EJ1012878.pdf

Martinez, S. L., & Stager, G. (2013). *Invent to learn*. Constructing Modern Knowledge Press.

Martin, F., & Bolliger, D. U. (2018). Engagement matters: Student perceptions on the importance of engagement strategies in the online learning environment. *Online Learning*, *22*(1), 205–222. doi:10.24059/olj.v22i1.1092

Martin-Hansen, L. (2018). Examining ways to meaningfully support students in STEM. *International Journal of STEM Education*, *5*(1), 1–6. doi:10.118640594-018-0150-3 PMID:30631742

Martin, J. (2019). Building relationships and increasing engagement in the virtual classroom: Practical tools for the online instructor. *Journal of Educators Online*, *16*(1). Advance online publication. doi:10.9743/jeo.2019.16.1.9

Marton, F., & Säljö, R. (1976). On qualitative differences in learning: I—Outcome and process. *The British Journal of Educational Psychology*, *46*(1), 4–11. doi:10.1111/j.2044-8279.1976.tb02980.x

Marzano, R. J., Marzano, J. S., & Pickering, D. (2003). *Classroom management that works: Research-based strategies for every teacher*. ASCD.

Compilation of References

Marzano, R. J., Pickering, D., & Pollock, J. E. (2001). *Classroom instruction that works: Research-based strategies for increasing student achievement.* Association for Supervision and Curriculum Development.

Maslow, A. H. (1962). *Toward a psychology of being.* Van Nostrand. doi:10.1037/10793-000

Masonbrink, A. R., & Hurley, E. (2020). Advocating for children during the COVID-19 school closures. *Pediatrics, 146*(3), e20201440. Advance online publication. doi:10.1542/peds.2020-1440 PMID:32554517

Matney, G., Lustgarten, A., & Nicholson, T. (2020). Black holes of research on instructional practice: The case of number talks. *Investigations in Mathematics Learning, 12*(4), 246–260. doi:10.1080/19477503.2020.1804273

Mayer, R. E. (2005). Cognitive theory of multimedia learning. The Cambridge handbook of multimedia learning, 41, 31-48.

Mayer, R. E. (1989). Cognitive views of creativity: Creative teaching for creative learning. *Contemporary Educational Psychology, 14*(3), 203–221. doi:10.1016/0361-476X(89)90010-6

Mayer, R. E. (2019). How multimedia can improve learning and instruction. In J. Dunlosky & K. A. Rawson (Eds.), *The Cambridge handbook of cognition and education* (pp. 460–479). Cambridge University Press. doi:10.1017/9781108235631.019

McCarthy, J. P., & Anderson, L. (2000). Active learning techniques versus traditional teaching styles. *Innovación Educativa (México, D.F.), 24*(4), 279–294. doi:10.1023/B:IHIE.0000047415.48495.05

McCulloch, A. W., Leatham, K. R., Lovett, J. N., Bailey, N. G., & Reed, S. D. (2021). How we are preparing secondary mathematics teachers to teach with technology: Findings from a nationwide survey. *Journal for Research in Mathematics Education, 52*(1), 94–107. doi:10.5951/jresematheduc-2020-0205

McDonald, M. (2003). Building a plane while flying it: Adventures in the integration of social justice in teacher education. *Annual meeting of the American Educational Research Association.*

McDougall, J., Readman, M., & Wilkinson, P. (2018). The uses of (digital) literacy. *Learning, Media and Technology, 43*(3), 263–279. doi:10.1080/17439884.2018.1462206

McInnerney, J. M., & Roberts, T. S. (2004). Online learning: Social interaction and the creation of a sense of community. *Journal of Educational Technology & Society, 7*(3), 73–81.

McKenna, M. C., & Kear, D. J. (1990). Measuring attitude toward reading: A new tool for teachers. *The Reading Teacher, 43*(9), 626–639. doi:10.1598/RT.43.8.3

McLaughlin, T., & Yan, Z. (2017). Diverse delivery methods and strong psychological benefits: A review of online formative assessment. *Journal of Computer Assisted Learning, 33*(6), 562–574. doi:10.1111/jcal.12200

McLeod, S. (2013). The pedagogy of Writing Across the Curriculum. In Writing across the curriculum: A critical sourcebook. Bedford/St. Martin's.

McLeod, S., & Shareski, D. (2017). *Different schools for a different world: School improvement for 21st century skills, global citizenship, and deeper learning.* Solution Tree Press.

McMillan, J. H., & Wergin, J. F. (2010). Qualitative Designs. In *Understanding and evaluating educational research* (4th ed., pp. 89–93). Pearson/Merrill.

McTighe, J., & Ferrara, S. (1998). *Assessing learning in the classroom.* National Education Association.

McTighe, J., & Wiggins, G. P. (2005). *Understanding by Design.* Association for Supervision and Curriculum Development.

Meacham, S., & Atwood-Blaine, D. (2018). Early Childhood Robotics: A Lego robotics club inspired by Reggio Emilia supports children's authentic learning. *Science and Children, 56*(3), 57–62.

Means, B., & Harris, C. J. (2013). Towards an evidence framework for design-based implementation research. In W. R. Penuel, B. Fishman, A. Allen, & B. Cheng (Eds.), *Design-based implementation research. National Society for the Study of Education yearbook* (pp. 350–371). Teachers College Press.

Media Literacy Now. (2020). *What is media literacy?* Retrieved from https://medialiteracynow.org/what-is-media-literacy/

Meece, J. L., Blumenfeld, P. C., & Hoyle, R. H. (1988). Students' goal orientations and cognitive engagement in classroom activities. *Journal of Educational Psychology*, *80*(4), 514–523. doi:10.1037/0022-0663.80.4.514

Mehta, K. J., Miletich, I., & Detyna, M. (2021). Content-specific differences in Padlet perception for collaborative learning amongst undergraduate students. *Research in Learning Technology*, 29.

Meier. (2015). Beyond a digital status quo: Re-conceptualizing online learning opportunities. *Bank Street Occasional Papers 34*. Retrieved from: https://educate.bankstreet.edu/cgi/viewcontent.cgi?article=1000&context=occasional-paper-series

Meier. (2018). The collaboration imperative. In L. Lin & J. M. Spector (Eds.), *Constructive articulation between the sciences of learning and the instructional design and technology communities* (pp. 131-151). Routledge.

Meier, E. (2020). Designing and using digital platforms for 21st century learning. *Educational Technology Research and Development*, *69*(1), 217–220. doi:10.100711423-020-09880-4 PMID:33456280

Meier, E., Mineo, C., Gabriela Diaz Yanez, K., Du, X., & Ma, Y. (2021). *Educational responsibility for addressing complex problems: STEM research with underserved schools* [Paper presentation]. Annual Meeting of the American Educational Research Association.

Mello, D., & Less, C. A. (2013). Effectiveness of active learning in the arts and sciences. *Humanities Department Faculty Publications & Research*. Paper 45. https://scholarsarchive.jwu.edu/humanities_fac/45

Melzer, D. K., & Grant, R. M. (2016). Investigating Differences in Personality Traits and Academic Needs Among Prepared and Underprepared First-Year College Students. *Journal of College Student Development*, *57*(1), 99–103. doi:10.1353/csd.2016.0004

Meo, S. A., Abukhalaf, D. A. A., Alomar, A. A., Sattar, K., & Klonoff, D. C. (2020). COVID-19 pandemic: Impact of quarantine on Medical Students' mental wellbeing and learning behaviors. *Pakistan Journal of Medical Sciences*, *36*(S4), S43–S48. doi:10.12669/pjms.36.COVID19-S4.2809 PMID:32582313

Merrill, C. (2009). The future of TE masters' degrees: STEM [Paper presentation]. Meeting of the International Technology Education Association, Louisville, KY, United States.

Merriman, M. (2015). *What if the next big disruptor isn't a what but a who. Gen Z is connected, informed and ready for business*. Slideshare, EY. https://www.slideshare.net/wiseknow/what-if-the-next-big-disruptor-isnt-a-what-but-a-who

Mertler, C. (2006). Action Research: Teachers as researchers in the classroom. *Sage (Atlanta, Ga.)*.

Mertler, C. (2020). Action Research: Improving schools and empowering educators. *Sage (Atlanta, Ga.)*.

Mesfin, G., Ghinea, G., Gronli, T., & Hwang, W. (2018). Enhanced agility of E-learning adoption in high schools. *Journal of Educational Technology & Society*, *21*(4), 157–170. https://www.jstor.org/stable/10.2307/26511546

Metcalf, S. J., Reilly, J. M., Kamarainen, A. M., King, J., Grotzer, T. A., & Dede, C. (2018). Supports for deeper learning of inquiry-based ecosystem science in virtual environments: Comparing virtual and physical concept mapping. *Computers in Human Behavior*, *87*, 459–469. doi:10.1016/j.chb.2018.03.018

Meya, J. N., & Eisenack, K. (2018). Effectiveness of gaming for communicating and teaching climate change. *Climatic Change*, *149*(3-4), 319–333. doi:10.100710584-018-2254-7

Compilation of References

Meyer, T., Young, M., & Lieberstein-Solera, F. (2012). *Research for the Classroom: Lost in Translation--Assessing Writing of English Language Learners*. *101*(5), 93–96. https://search.ebscohost.com/login.aspx?direct=true&AuthType=ip,shib&db=eric&AN=EJ998954&site=ehost-live&scope=site&authtype=ip,shib&custid=s3555202 http://www.ncte.org/journals/ej/issues/v101-5

Meyer, A., & Rose, D. H. (2005). The future is in the margins: The role of technology and disability in educational reform. In D. H. Rose, A. Meyer, & C. Hitchcock (Eds.), *The universally designed classroom: Accessible curriculum and digital technologies* (pp. 13–35). Harvard Education Press.

Meyer, A., Rose, D. H., & Gordon, D. T. (2014). *Universal design for learning: Theory and practice*. CAST Professional Publishing.

Meyers, J. D., Chappell, A., Elder, M., Geist, A., & Schwidder, L. (2003). Re-Integrating the research record. *Computing in Science & Engineering*, *5*(3), 44–50.

Michelman, S. (1971). The importance of creative play. *The American Journal of Occupational Therapy*, *25*(6), 285–290. PMID:5111632

Middleton, K. V. (2020). The longer-term impact of COVID-19 on K–12 student learning and assessment. *Educational Measurement: Issues and Practice*, *39*(3), 41–44. doi:10.1111/emip.12368

Mills, G. E. (2000). *Action Research: A guide for the teacher researcher*. Prentice-Hall.

Mills, S. C., & Tincher, R. C. (2003). Be the technology: A developmental model for evaluating technology integration. *Journal of Research on Technology in Education*, *35*(3), 382–401. doi:10.1080/15391523.2003.10782392

Milou, E. (1999). The graphing calculator: A survey of classroom usage. *School Science and Mathematics*, *3*(99), 133–140. doi:10.1111/j.1949-8594.1999.tb17461.x

Minhas, R. S. (2020). How Covid-19 is widening disparity in children's developmental potential. *Toronto Star*. https://www.thestar.com/opinion/contributors/2020/10/27/how-covid-19-is-widening-disparity-in-childrens-developmental-potential.html

Miriti, M. (2020). The elephant in the room: Race and STEM diversity. *Bioscience*, *70*(3), 237–242. doi:10.1093/biosci/biz167

Mishra, P., & Koehler, M. J. (2007). *What is technological pedagogical content knowledge?* Retrieved from: https://citejournal.org/volume-9/issue-1-09/general/what-is-technological-pedagogicalcontent-knowledge/

Mishra, P. (2019). Considering contextual knowledge: The TPACK diagram gets an upgrade. *Journal of Digital Learning in Teacher Education*, *35*(2), 76–78. doi:10.1080/21532974.2019.1588611

Mishra, P., & Koehler, M. (2006). Technological Pedagogical Content Knowledge: A Framework for Teacher Knowledge. *Teachers College Record*, *108*(6), 1017–1054. doi:10.1111/j.1467-9620.2006.00684.x

Mishra, P., & Koehler, M. J. (2006). Technological pedagogical content knowledge: A framework for integrating technology in teacher knowledge. *Teachers College Record*, *108*(6), 1017–1054.

Moallem, M. (2015). The impact of synchronous and asynchronous communication tools on learner self-regulation, social presence, immediacy, intimacy and satisfaction in collaborative online learning. *The Online Journal of Distance Education and e-Learning*, *3*(3), 55.

Mohr, K. A., & Mohr, E. S. (2017). Understanding Generation Z students to promote a contemporary learning environment. *Journal on Empowering Teaching Excellence*, *1*(1), 9.

Montrieux, H., Raes, A., & Schellens, T. (2017). 'The Best App is the teacher' introducing classroom scripts in technology-enhanced education. *Journal of Computer Assisted Learning, 33*(3), 267–281. doi:10.1111/jcal.12177

Moore, E. J. (2018). Voices From the Field: Implementing and Scaling-Up Universal Design for Learning in Teacher Preparation Programs. *Journal of Special Education Technology, 33*(1), 40–53.

Moore, M. G. (1997). Theory of transactional distance. In D. Keegan (Ed.), *Theoretical Principles of Distance Education* (pp. 22–38). Routledge.

Moore, M. G. (2018). The theory of transactional distance. In M. G. Moore & W. C. Diehl (Eds.), *Handbook of Distance Education* (4th ed.). Routledge. doi:10.4324/9781315296135-4

Moore, R. L. (2016). Interacting at a distance: Creating engagement in online learning environments. In L. Kyei-Blankson, J. Blankson, E. Ntuli, & C. Agyeman (Eds.), *Handbook of research on strategic management of interaction, presence, and participation in online courses* (pp. 401–425). IGI Global. doi:10.4018/978-1-4666-9582-5.ch016

Moorhouse, B. L. (2019). Seesaw. *RELC Journal, 50*(3), 493-496. https://doi.org/ doi:10.1177/0033688218781976

Morey, S., & Mouratis, J. (2016). *New adobe study shows Gen Z students and teachers see creativity as key to success.* Adobe Press Release.

Morrison, G. M., & Cosden, M. A. (1997). Risk, resilience, and adjustment of individuals with learning disabilities. *Learning Disability Quarterly, 20*(1), 43–60. doi:10.2307/1511092

Mourlam, D. J., DeCino, D. A., Newland, L. A., & Strouse, G. A. (2020). "It's fun!": Using students' voices to understand the impact of school digital technology integration on their well-being. *Computers & Education, 159*, 104003. doi:10.1016/j.compedu.2020.104003

Mouza, C., Yang, H., Pan, Y.-C., Ozden, S. Y., & Pollock, L. (2017). Resetting educational technology coursework for pre-service teachers: A computational thinking approach to the development of technological pedagogical content knowledge (TPACK). *Australasian Journal of Educational Technology, 33*(3), 61–76. doi:10.14742/ajet.3521

Mueller, C. M., & Dweck, C. S. (1998). Praise for intelligence can undermine children's motivation and performance. *Journal of Personality and Social Psychology, 75*(1), 33–52. doi:10.1037/0022-3514.75.1.33 PMID:9686450

Mumford, J. M., Fiala, L., & Daulton, M. (2017). An agile K-12 approach: Teacher PD for new learning ecosystems. In *Handbook of research on teacher education and professional development* (pp. 367–384). IGI Global. doi:10.4018/978-1-5225-1067-3.ch020

Mumford, M. (2017). Creative Thinking Processes: The past and the future. *The Journal of Creative Behavior, 51*, 317–322. doi:10.1002/jocb.197

Mumford, M., Martin, R., Elliott, S., & McIntosh, T. (2018). Creative Thinking in the Real World: Processing in Context. In R. Sternberg & J. Kaufman (Eds.), *The Nature of Human Creativity* (pp. 147–165). Cambridge University Press. doi:10.1017/9781108185936.013

Murphy, L. (2016). *Lisa Murphy on play: The foundation of children's learning.* Redleaf Press.

Murray-Harvey, R. (1994). Learning styles and approaches to learning. *The British Journal of Educational Psychology, 64*(3), 373–388. doi:10.1111/j.2044-8279.1994.tb01110.x

Museum of Science, Boston. (n.d.). *PreK to 8th grade STEM curricula.* EiE. Retrieved December, 2020 from https://eiestore.com/

Compilation of References

Mutton, T. (2020, August). Teacher education and COVID-19: Responses and opportunities for new pedagogical initiatives. *Journal of Education for Teaching*. https://doi.org. /10.1080/02607476.2020.1805189

Nadelson, L., Sias, C., & Seifert, A. (2016, June). *Challenges for integrating engineering into K–12 curriculum: Indicators of K–12 teachers' propensity to adopt innovation*. Paper presented at 2016 ASEE Annual Conference and Exposition, New Orleans, LA. https://peer.asee.org/26471

Nadjafikhah, M., Yaftian, N., & Bakhshalizadeh, S. (2012). Mathematical creativity: Some definitions and characteristics. *Procedia: Social and Behavioral Sciences, 31*, 285–291. doi:10.1016/j.sbspro.2011.12.056

National Academies of Sciences, Engineering, and Medicine. (2018). *How people learn II: Learners, context, and cultures*. The National Academies Press.

National Academies of Sciences, Engineering, and Medicine. (2018). *How people learn II: Learners, contexts, and cultures*. National Academies Press.

National Academy of Engineering. (2008). *Changing the conversation: Messages for improving public understanding of engineering*. The National Academies Press., doi:10.17226/12187

National Association for the Education of Y. C. (2009). Developmentally Appropriate Practice in Early Childhood Programs Serving Children from Birth through *Age 8*. Author.

National Center for Case Study Teaching in Science. (n.d.). *Publications*. https://sciencecases.lib.buffalo.edu/teaching/publications/

National Center for Education Statistics. (2020). *Children and Youth with Disabilities*. https://nces.ed.gov/programs/coe/indicator_cgg.asp

National Center for Learning Disabilities. (2020). *Exploring intersectionality: Understanding student identity to promote equitable social, emotional, cognitive, and academic development during and beyond the covid -19 pandemic*. https://www.ncld.org/wp-content/uploads/2020/11/2020-SEL_Exploring-Intersectionality-Guide_FINAL.pdf

National Center for Learning Disabilities. (2021). *What is MTSS?* https://www.pbisrewards.com/blog/what-is-mtss/

National Commission on Social, Emotional, and Academic Development. (2019). From a nation at risk to a nation at hope. *The Aspen Institute*. https://www.aspeninstitute.org/programs/national-commission-on-social-emotional-and-academic-development

National Council for Teachers of Mathematics. (2011, October). *Strategic use of technology in teaching and learning mathematics*. https://www.nctm.org/Standards-and-Positions/Position-Statements/Strategic-Use-of-Technology-in-Teaching-and-Learning-Mathematics/

National Council for Teachers of Mathematics. (2018). *A fresh look at formative assessments in mathematics education*. Author.

National Council of Teachers of Mathematics and National Council of Supervisors of Mathematics. (2020). *Moving forward: Mathematics learning in the era of COVID-19*. https://www.nctm.org/uploadedFiles/Research_and_Advocacy/NCTM_NCSM_Moving_Forward.pdf

National Council of Teachers of Mathematics. (2000). *Principles and standards for school mathematics*. National Council of Teachers of Mathematics.

National Council of Teachers of Mathematics. (2014). *Principles to actions: Ensuring mathematical success for all*. National Council of Teachers of Mathematics.

National Education Association. (2012). *Preparing 21st century students for a global society: An educator's guide to the "Four Cs."* Author.

National Governors Association Center for Best Practices, Council of Chief State School Officers. (2010). *Common core state standards for mathematics.* http://corestandards.org/

National Governors Association Center for Best Practices. (2010). Common Core State Standards. National Governors Association Center for Best Practices, Council of Chief State School Officers.

National Institute on Aging. (2017). *What is Alzheimer's disease?* https://www.nia.nih.gov/health/what-alzheimers-disease

National Joint Committee on Learning Disabilities. (2008). Adolescent literacy and older students with learning disabilities: A report from the National Joint Committee on Learning Disabilities. *Learning Disability Quarterly*, 211–218. doi:10.2307/25474653

National Research Council (NRC). (2012). *A framework for K-12 science education: Practices, crosscutting concepts, and core ideas.* The National Academy Press.

National Research Council. (2001). *Classroom assessment and the National Science Education Standards.* National Academies Press. https://www.nap.edu/catalog/9847

National Science Board. (2015). *Revisiting the STEM workforce: A companion to science and engineering indicators 2014.* National Science Foundation (NSB-2015-10). https://nsf.gov/pubs/2015/nsb201510/nsb201510.pdf

National Telecommunications and Information Administration. (2018). *New Data Show Substantial Gains and Evolution in Internet Use.* Author.

NCES Fast Facts Tool. (n.d.). https://nces.ed.gov/fastfacts/display.asp?id=372#:~:text=In%202017%E2%80%9318%2C%20about%2019,offered%20any%20courses%20entirely%20online

NCTM. (2008). *Getting into the Mathematics conversation: Valuing communication in Mathematics classrooms.* The National Council of Teachers of Mathematics, Inc.

New American Economy. (2017). *Sizing up the gap in our supply of STEM workers.* https://research.newamericaneconomy.org/report/sizing-up-the-gap-in-our-supply-of-stem-workers/

Next Generation Science Standards. (n.d.). *HS. Human Sustainability.* https://www.nextgenscience.org/topic-arrangement/hshuman-sustainability

Next Generation Science Standards. (n.d.). *MS-LS2-1 Ecosystems: Interactions, Energy, and Dynamics.* https://www.nextgenscience.org/pe/ms-ls2-1-ecosystems-interactions-energy-and-dynamics

NGSS Lead States. (2013). *Next Generation Science Standards: For States, By States.* The National Academies Press.

Nguyen, H., & Hovy, D. (2019, November). Hey Siri. Ok Google. Alexa: A topic modeling of user reviews for smart speakers. *The 5th Workshop on Noisy User-generated Text (W-NUT 2019)*, 76-83. https://www.aclweb.org/anthology/D19-5510/

Niche. (n.d.). *Students at Ferguson-Florissant R-II School District.* https://www.niche.com/k12/d/ferguson-florissant-r-ii-school-district-mo/students/

Nichols, B. E. (2020). Equity in music education: Access to learning during the pandemic and beyond. *Music Educators Journal*, *107*(1), 68–70. doi:10.1177/0027432120945151

Nickerson, R. S. (2003). *Psychology and Environmental Change.* Lawrence Erlbaum Associates.

Compilation of References

Nicol, D. (2007). E-assessment by design: Using multiple-choice tests to good effect. *Journal of Further and Higher Education, 31*(1), 53–64. doi:10.1080/03098770601167922

Nicol, D., Thomson, A., & Breslin, C. (2014). Rethinking feedback practices in higher education: A peer review perspective. *Assessment & Evaluation in Higher Education, 39*(1), 102–122. doi:10.1080/02602938.2013.795518

Nierenberg, A., & Pasick, A. (2020, November 20). Parents erupt in frustration as New York City schools close. *The New York Times.* https://www.nytimes.com/2020/11/20/us/parents-erupt-in-frustration-as-new-york-city-schools-close

Niess, M. L., Suharwoto, G., Lee, K., & Sadri, P. (2006). *Guiding inservice mathematics teachers in developing TPCK* [Paper presentation]. American Education Research Association Annual Conference, San Francisco, CA, United States.

Niess, M. L. (2005). Preparing teachers to teach science and mathematics with technology: Developing a technology pedagogical content knowledge. *Teaching and Teacher Education, 21*(5), 509–523. doi:10.1016/j.tate.2005.03.006

Niess, M. L. (2011). Investigating TPACK: Knowledge growth in teaching with technology. *Journal of Educational Computing Research, 44*(2), 299–317. doi:10.2190/EC.44.3.c

Niess, M. L. (2013). Central component descriptors for levels of technological pedagogical content knowledge. Special issue on Technological Pedagogical Content Knowledge. *Journal of Educational Computing Research, 48*(2), 173–198.

Niess, M. L. (Ed.). (2019). *Blended online learning and instructional design for TPACK: Emerging research and opportunities.* IGI Global. doi:10.4018/978-1-5225-8879-5

Niess, M. L., & Gillow-Wiles, H. (2017). Expanding teachers' technological pedagogical reasoning with a systems pedagogical approach. *Australasian Journal of Educational Technology, 33*(3). Advance online publication. doi:10.14742/ajet.3473

Niess, M. L., Sadri, P., & Lee, K. (2008). Variables and dynamic spreadsheets connect with real world problems. *Mathematics Teaching in the Middle School, 13*(7), 423–431.

Niess, M. L., van Zee, E. H., & Gillow-Wiles, H. (2010). Knowledge growth in teaching mathematics/science with spreadsheets: Moving PCK to TPACK through online professional development. *Journal of Digital Learning in Teacher Education, 27*(2), 42–52. doi:10.1080/21532974.2010.10784657

Nigg, J. T. (2017). Annual research review: On the relations among self-regulation, self-control, executive functioning, effortful control, cognitive control, impulsivity, risk-taking, and inhibition for developmental psychopathology. *Journal of Child Psychology and Psychiatry, and Allied Disciplines, 58*(4), 361–383. doi:10.1111/jcpp.12675 PMID:28035675

Ninaus, M., Greipl, S., Kiili, K., Lindstedt, A., Huber, S., Klein, E., Karnath, H.-O., & Moeller, K. (2019). Increased emotional engagement in game-based learning–A machine learning approach on facial emotion detection data. *Computers & Education, 142*, 103641. doi:10.1016/j.compedu.2019.103641

Nippold, M. A., & Ward-Lonergan, J. M. (2010). Argumentative writing in pre-adolescents: The role of verbal reasoning. *Child Language Teaching and Therapy, 26*(3), 238–248. doi:10.1177/0265659009349979

Niu, L. (2017). Family socioeconomic status and choice of STEM major in college: An analysis of a national sample. *College Student Journal, 51*(2), 298–312.

Norman, D. A. (2013). *The design of everyday things.* Basic Books.

Northrop, L., & Killeen, E. (2013). A framework for using iPads to build early literacy skills. *The Reading Teacher, 66*(7), 531–537. doi:10.1002/TRTR.1155

O'Brien, A., & Fuller, R. (2018). Synchronous teaching techniques from the perspective and observation of virtual high school teachers: An investigate study. *International Journal of Information and Communication Technology Education*, *14*(3), 55–67. doi:10.4018/IJICTE.2018070105

O'Keefe, P. (2013). a Sense of Belonging: Improving Student Retention. *College Student Journal*, *47*(4), 605–613. http://proxygsu-col1.galileo.usg.edu/login?url=http://search.ebscohost.com/login.aspx?direct=true&db=slh&AN=93813989&site=eds-live&scope=site

O'Rourke, E., Haimovitz, K., Ballweber, C., Dweck, C., & Popović, Z. (2014). Brain points: A growth mindset incentive structure boosts persistence in an educational game. *Proceedings of the SIGCHI Conference on Human Factors in Computing Systems*, 3339–3348. 10.1145/2556288.2557157

Obama, B. (2013). *Educate to innovate*. The White House. https://www.whitehouse.gov/issues/education/k-12/educate-innovate

Odowd, E. (2010). The development of linguistic complexity: A functional continuum. *Language Teaching*, *45*(3), 329–346. doi:10.10170261444810000510

OECD. (2019). *Trends shaping education 2019*. Paris, France: OECD Publishing. Retrieved from https://www.oecd.org/education/ceri/trends-shaping-education-22187049.htm

Ogborn, D., Beverley, J., Del Angel, L. N., Tsabary, E., & McLean, A. (2017). Estuary: Browser-based collaborative projectional live coding of musical patterns. In Proceedings of *International Conference on Live Coding, 2017*. ICLC. https://iclc.toplap.org/2017/cameraReady/ICLC_2017_paper_78.pdf

Oh, C. S., Bailenson, J. N., & Welch, G. F. (2018). A systematic review of social presence: Definition, antecedents, and implications. *Frontiers in Robotics and AI*, *5*(OCT), 1–35. doi:10.3389/frobt.2018.00114 PMID:33500993

Ok, M. W., Kim, M. K., Kang, E. Y., & Bryant, B. R. (2016). How to find good Apps: An evaluation rubric for instructional apps for teaching students with learning disabilities. *Intervention in School and Clinic*, *51*(4), 244–252. doi:10.1177/1053451215589179

Olson, G. A., & Johnson, H. L. (2021). Promote students' function reasoning with Techtivities. *Problems, Resources, and Issues in Mathematics Undergraduate Studies*, 1-13.

Olson, C. (2010). Making the tech connection. *Teaching Music*, *17*(5), 30–35.

Olwell, R., & Raphael, N. (2006). The problems of elementary social studies: Are curricular and assessment sprawl to blame? *Social Studies*, *97*(5), 222–224. doi:10.3200/TSSS.97.5.222-224

ons=5fc7ee08eb61e84538790058.

Ontario Newsroom. (2020, May 19). *Health and safety top priority as schools stay closed*. https://news.ontario.ca/en/release/56971/health-and-safety-top-priority-as-schools-remain-closed

Ortiz-Rodríguez, M., Telg, R. W., Irani, T., Roberts, T. G., & Rhoades, E. (2005). College students' perceptions of quality in distance education: The importance of Communication. *Quarterly Review of Distance Education*, *6*(2), 97–105.

Osborn, A. (1963). *Applied imagination: Principles and procedures of creative thinking* (3rd ed.). Charles Scribner's Sons.

Osterman, K. F. (2000). Students' need for belonging in the school community. *Review of Educational Research*, *70*(3), 323–367. doi:10.3102/00346543070003323

Otake, S., Treiman, R., & Yin, L. (2017). Differentiation of writing and drawing by U.S. two- to five-year-olds. *Cognitive Development*, *43*, 119–128. doi:10.1016/j.cogdev.2017.03.004 PMID:29056820

Compilation of References

Ouellette, J. A., & Wood, W. (1998). Habit and intention in everyday life: The multiple processes by which past behavior predicts future behavior. *Psychological Bulletin*, *124*(1), 54–74. doi:10.1037/0033-2909.124.1.54

Oumet, A. (2011). *Culturally relevant literature: How to identify and use culturally relevant literature* (Publication No. 15) [Master's thesis, St. John Fisher College]. Fisher Digital Publications. https://fisherpub.sjfc.edu/cgi/viewcontent.cgi?article=1014&context=education_ETD_masters

Overbay, A., Patterson, A. S., Vasu, E. S., & Grable, L. L. (2010). Constructivism and Technology Use: Findings from the IMPACTing Leadership Project. *Educational Media International*, *47*(2), 103–120. doi:10.1080/09523987.2010.492675

Owston, R., Wideman, H., Thumlert, K., & Malhotra, T. (2016). *Transforming learning everywhere: A study of second year of implementation*. Retrieved from http://www.ontariodirectors.ca/CODE_TLE/TLE%20Complete%20Report%20Final%20FINAL-AODA.PDF

Oxford, R. L. (1990). Language learning strategies: What every teacher should Know. Newbury House, Harper Collins.

Ozdemir, E. (2021). Views of science teachers about online STEM practices during the COVID-19 period. *International Journal of Curriculum and Instruction*, *13*(1), 854–869.

Oztok, M., Zingaro, D., Brett, C., & Hewitt, J. (2013). Exploring asynchronous and synchronous tool use in online courses. *Computers & Education*, *60*(1), 87–94. doi:10.1016/j.compedu.2012.08.007

Ozverir, I., Osam, U. V., & Herrington, J. (2017). Investigating the Effects of Authentic Activities on Foreign Language Learning: A Design-based Research Approach. *Journal of Educational Technology & Society*, *20*(4), 261–274.

Padlet Blog. (2018). *Introducing formats*. https://padlet.com/blog/formats

Paganelli, A., Cribbs, J. D., 'Silvie' Huang, X., Pereira, N., Huss, J., Chandler, W., & Paganelli, A. (2017). The makerspace experience and teacher professional development. *Professional Development in Education*, *43*(2), 232–235. doi:10.1080/19415257.2016.1166448

Palincsar, A. S., Brown, A. L., & Campione, J. C. (1993). First-grade dialogues for knowledge acquisition and use. In E. A. Forman, N. Minick, & C. Addison Stone (Eds.), *Contexts for learning: Sociocultural dynamics in children's development* (pp. 43–57). Oxford University Press.

Panero, M., & Aldon, G. (2016). How Teachers Evolve Their Formative Assessment Practices When Digital Tools Are Involved in the Classroom. *Digital Experiences in Mathematics Education*, *2*(1), 70–86. doi:10.100740751-016-0012-x

Papamitsiou, Z., & Economides, A. A. (2014). Learning Analytics and Educational Data Mining in Practice: A Systematic Literature Review of Empirical Evidence. *Journal of Educational Technology & Society*, *17*(4), 49–64. Retrieved February 16, 2021, from http://www.jstor.org/stable/jeductechsoci.17.4.49

Papanikolaou, K., Makri, K., & Roussos, P. (2017). Learning design as a vehicle for developing TPACK in blended teacher training on technology enhanced learning. *International Journal of Educational Technology in Higher Education*, *14*(1), 1–14. doi:10.118641239-017-0072-z

Parette, H. P., Quesenberry, A. C., & Blum, C. (2010). Missing the Boat with Technology Usage in Early Childhood Settings: A 21st Century View of Developmentally Appropriate Practice. *Early Childhood Education Journal*, *37*(5), 335–343. https://doi.org/10.1007/s10643-009-0352-x

Paris, D. (2012). Culturally sustaining pedagogy: A needed change in stance, terminology, and practice. *Educational Researcher*, *41*(3), 93–97. doi:10.3102/0013189X12441244

Parker, K., & Igielnik, R. (2020). On the cusp of adulthood and facing an uncertain future: What we know about Gen Z so far. *Pew Research Center*, (May), 14.

Park, J. H., Schallert, D. L., Sanders, A. J. Z., Williams, K. M., Seo, E., Yu, L., Volger, J. S., Song, K., Williamson, Z. H., & Knox, M. C. (2015). Does it matter if the teacher is there?: A teacher's contribution to emerging patterns of interactions in online classroom discussions. *Computers & Education*, *82*, 315–328. doi:10.1016/j.compedu.2014.11.019

Park, Y. (2011). A pedagogical framework for mobile learning: Categorizing educational applications of mobile technologies into four types. *International Review of Research in Open and Distance Learning*, *12*(2), 78–102. doi:10.19173/irrodl.v12i2.791

Parmer, S. M., Salisbury-Glennon, J., Shannon, D., & Struempler, B. (2009). School gardens: An experiential learning approach for a nutrition education program to increase fruit and vegetable knowledge, preference, and consumption among second-grade students. *Journal of Nutrition Education and Behavior*, *41*(3), 212–217. doi:10.1016/j.jneb.2008.06.002 PMID:19411056

Parrish, S. (2010). *Number talks: Helping children build mental math and computation strategies, grades K-5*. Math Solutions.

Parrish, S. (2011). Number talks build numerical reasoning. *Teaching Children Mathematics*, *18*(3), 198–206. doi:10.5951/teacchilmath.18.3.0198

Parrish, S., & Dominick, A. (2016). *Number talks: Fractions, decimals, and percentages*. Math Solutions.

Partin, T. C. M., Robertson, R. E., Maggin, D. M., Oliver, R. M., & Wehby, J. H. (2010). Using teacher praise and opportunities to respond to promote appropriate student behavior. *Preventing School Failure*, *54*(3), 172–178. doi:10.1080/10459880903493179

Partnership for 21st Century Learning. (2019). http://static.battelleforkids.org/documents/p21/P21_Framework_Brief.pdf

Partnership for 21st Century Skills. (2009). *P21 Framework Definitions*. Retrieved from https://files.eric.ed.gov/fulltext/ED519462.pdf

Partti, H. (2017). Building a broad view of technology in music teacher education. In A. Ruthmann & R. Mantie (Eds.), *The Oxford handbook of technology and music education*. Oxford University Press.

Patahuddin, S. M. (2013). Mathematics teacher professional development in and through Internet use: Reflections on an ethnographic study. *Mathematics Education Research*, *25*, 503–521. doi:10.100713394-013-0084-5

Pate, C. M., Maras, M. A., Whitney, S. D., & Bradshaw, C. P. (2017). Exploring psychosocial mechanisms and interactions: Links between adolescent emotional distress, school connectedness, and educational achievement. *School Mental Health*, *9*(1), 28–43. doi:10.100712310-016-9202-3 PMID:28947921

Patel, K. (2020). Mental health implications of COVID-19 on children with disabilities. *Asian Journal of Psychiatry*, *54*, 102273. doi:10.1016/j.ajp.2020.102273 PMID:32653852

Paulus, P. B., & Nijstad, B. A. (Eds.). (2003). *Group creativity: Innovation through collaboration*. Oxford University Press. doi:10.1093/acprof:oso/9780195147308.001.0001

Peacock, J. G., & Grande, J. P. (2016). An online app platform enhances collaborative medical student group learning and classroom management. *Medical Teacher*, *38*(2), 174–180. doi:10.3109/0142159X.2015.1020290 PMID:25782601

Peacock, S., & Cowan, J. (2016). From Presences to Linked Influences Within Communities of Inquiry. *International Review of Research in Open and Distributed Learning*, *17*(5), 267–286. doi:10.19173/irrodl.v17i5.2602

Compilation of References

Peacock, S., & Cowan, J. (2019). Promoting sense of belonging in online learning communities of inquiry in accredited courses. *Online Learning Journal*, *23*(2), 67–81. doi:10.24059/olj.v23i2.1488

Peacock, S., Cowan, J., Irvine, L., & Williams, J. (2020). An Exploration Into the Importance of a Sense of Belonging for Online Learners. *International Review of Research in Open and Distributed Learning*, *21*(2), 18–35. doi:10.19173/irrodl.v20i5.4539

Pea, R. D. (1985). Beyond amplification: Using the computer to reorganize mental functioning. *Educational Psychologist*, *20*(4), 167–182. doi:10.120715326985ep2004_2

Pearson, P. D., & Gallagher, M. C. (1983). The instruction of reading comprehension. *Contemporary Educational Psychology*, *8*(3), 317–344. doi:10.1016/0361-476X(83)90019-X

Pearson, P., Moje, E., & Greenleaf, C. (2010). Literacy and science: Each in the service of the other. *Science*, *328*(5977), 459–463. doi:10.1126cience.1182595 PMID:20413491

Pellegrini, A. D., & Bjorklund, D. F. (1997). The role of recess in children's cognitive performance. *Educational Psychologist*, *32*(1), 35–40. doi:10.120715326985ep3201_3

Pellegrini, A. D., & Bohn, C. M. (2005). The Role of Recess in Children's Cognitive Performance and School Adjustment. *Educational Researcher*, *34*(1), 13–19. doi:10.3102/0013189X034001013

Penuel, W. (2019). Co-design as infrastructuring with attention to power: Building collective capacity for equitable teaching and learning through design-based implementation research. In J. Pieters, J. Voogt, & N. Roblin (Eds.), *Collaborative curriculum design for sustainable innovation and teacher learning*. Springer Open. doi:10.1007/978-3-030-20062-6_21

Peppler, K., & Bender, S. (2013). Maker movement spreads innovation one project at a time. *Phi Delta Kappan*, *95*(3), 22–27. doi:10.1177/003172171309500306

Perera-Diltz, D. M., & Moe, J. L. (2014). Formative and Summative Assessment in Online Education. *Counseling & Human Services Faculty Publications*, 37. https://digitalcommons.odu.edu/chs_pubs/37

Perin, D., & Holschuh, J. P. (2019). Teaching academically underprepared postsecondary students. *Review of Research in Education*, *43*(1), 363–393. doi:10.3102/0091732X18821114

Perkmen, S., & Cevik, B. (2010). Relationship between pre-service music teachers' personality and motivation for computer-assisted instruction. *Music Education Research*, *12*(4), 415–425. doi:10.1080/14613808.2010.519768

Perper, R. (2020, April 12). New York City public school teachers describe being unprepared and overwhelmed as the coronavirus forces schools to shut down. *Business Insider*. Retrieved from https://www.businessinsider.com/new-york-city-teachers-overwhelmed-unprepared-for-school-shutdowns-2020-4

Perrenet, J. C., Bouhuijs, P. A., & Smits, J. G. (2000). The suitability of problem-based learning for engineering education: Theory and practice. *Teaching in Higher Education*, *5*(3), 345–358. doi:10.1080/713699144

Perrin, A. (2018). *5 facts about Americans and video games*. https://www.pewresearch.org/fact-tank/2018/09/17/5-facts-about-americans-and-video-games/

Persaud, R. (2007). Why teaching creativity requires more than just producing more 'creativity.'. *Thinking Skills and Creativity*, *2*(1), 68–69. doi:10.1016/j.tsc.2006.11.001

Peters, L. L., Robledo, R. F., Bult, C. J., Churchill, G. A., Paigen, B. J., & Svenson, K. L. (2007). The mouse as a model for human biology: A resource guide for complex trait analysis. *Nature Reviews. Genetics*, *8*(1), 58–69. https://doi.org/10.1038/nrg2025

Peterson, C. (2003). Bringing ADDIE to life: Instructional design at its best. *Journal of Educational Multimedia and Hypermedia, 12*(3), 227–241.

Peterson, L., Scharber, C., Thuesen, A., & Baskin, K. (2020). A rapid response to COVID-19: One district's pivot from technology integration to distance learning. *Information and Learning Science, 121*(5/6), 461–469. doi:10.1108/ILS-04-2020-0131

Petscher, Y., Cabell, S. Q., Catts, H. W., Compton, D. L., Foorman, B. R., Hart, S. A., Lonigan, C. J., Phillips, B. M., Schatschneider, C., Steachy, L. M., Terry, N. P., & Wagner, R. K. (2020). How the science of reading informs 21st-century education. *Reading Research Quarterly, 55*(51). Advance online publication. doi:10.1002/rrq.352 PMID:34007089

Philippakos, Z. A. T., & Voggt, A. (2021). The effects of distant professional development model on second grade teachers' instruction and students' quality of procedural papers. *Reading and Writing*. Advance online publication. doi:10.100711145-021-10120-1 PMID:33519085

Piaget, J., & Inhelder, B. (1969). *The psychology of the child* (2nd ed.). Basic Books.

Picciano, A. G. (2017). Theories and frameworks for online education: Seeking an integrated model. *Online Learning, 21*(3), 166–190. doi:10.24059/olj.v21i3.1225

Pickl, G. (2011). Communication intervention in children with severe disabilities and multilingual backgrounds: Perceptions of pedagogues and parents. *Augmentative and Alternative Communication, 27*, 229–244. doi:10.3109/07434618.2011.630021

Pierson, M. E. (2001). Technology integration practices as function of pedagogical expertise. *Journal of Research on Computing in Education, 33*(4), 413–429.

Pieters, J., Voogt, J., & Roblin, N. (Eds.). (2019). *Collaborative curriculum design for sustainable innovation and teacher learning*. Springer Open. doi:10.1007/978-3-030-20062-6

Pinsk, R., Curran, M. J., Poirier, R., & Coulson, G. (2014). Student perceptions of the use of studentgenerated video in online discussions as a mechanism to establish social presence for nontraditional students: A case study. *Issues in Information Systems, 15*(I), 267–276.

Pittard, E. A. (2017). Gettin' a little crafty: Teachers Pay Teachers©, Pinterest© and neo-liberalism in new materialist feminist research. *Gender and Education, 29*(1), 28–47. doi:10.1080/09540253.2016.1197380

Plass, J. L., O'keefe, P. A., Homer, B. D., Case, J., Hayward, E. O., Stein, M., & Perlin, K. (2013). The impact of individual, competitive, and collaborative mathematics game play on learning, performance, and motivation. *Journal of Educational Psychology, 105*(4), 1050–1066. doi:10.1037/a0032688

Plucker, J. A., & Alanazi, R. (2019). Is Creativity Compatible with Educational Accountability? Promise and Pitfalls of Using Assessment to Monitor and Enhance a Complex Construct. In I. Lebuda & V. Glăveanu (Eds.), *The Palgrave Handbook of Social Creativity Research. Palgrave Studies in Creativity and Culture* (pp. 501–514). Palgrave Macmillan. doi:10.1007/978-3-319-95498-1_31

Plucker, J. A., Beghetto, R. A., & Dow, G. T. (2004). Why isn't creativity more important to educational psychologists? Potentials, pitfalls, and future directions in creativity research. *Educational Psychologist, 39*(2), 83–96. doi:10.120715326985ep3902_1

Plucker, J. A., & Dow, G. T. (2010). Attitude change as the precursor to creativity enhancement. In R. A. Beghetto & J. C. Kaufman (Eds.), *Nurturing creativity in the classroom* (pp. 362–379). Cambridge University Press. doi:10.1017/CBO9780511781629.018

Compilation of References

Plucker, J. A., & Dow, G. T. (2016). Attitude change as the precursor to creativity enhancement. In R. Beghetto & J. Kaufman (Eds.), *Nurturing Creativity* (pp. 190–211). Cambridge University Press. doi:10.1017/CBO9780511781629

Plucker, J. A., McWilliams, J., & Alanazi, R. A. (2016). Creativity, Culture, and the Digital Revolution: Implications and Considerations for Education. In V. P. Glaveanu (Ed.), *The Palgrave Handbook of Creativity and Cultural Research* (pp. 517–533). Palgrave Macmillan. doi:10.1057/1978-1-137-46344-9

Poague, E. (2018, December). *Gen z is shaping a new era of learning: Here's what you should know*. Linkedin.com. https://learning.linkedin.com/blog/learning-thought-leadership/gen-z-is-shaping-a-new-era-of-learning--heres-what-you-should-know

Porras-Hernandez, L. H., & Salinas-Amescua, B. (2013). Strengthening TPACK: A broader notion of context and the use of teacher's narratives to reveal knowledge construction. *Journal of Educational Computing Research*, *48*(2), 223–244. doi:10.2190/EC.48.2.f

Posey, A. (2019). *Engage the brain: How to design for learning that taps into the power of emotions*. Association for Supervision & Curriculum Development.

Poston, B. (2009). An Exercise in Personal Exploration: Maslow's Hierarchy of Needs. *The Surgical Technologist*, *41*(8), 347–353. http://www.ast.org/pdf/308.pdf

Post, Y., Boyer, W., & Brett, L. (2006). A historical examination of self-regulation: Helping children now and in the future. *Early Childhood Education Journal*, *34*(1), 5–14. doi:10.100710643-006-0107-x

Potash, B. (2017). *Episode 23: Discussion Warm Ups*. http://www.nowsparkcreativity.com/2017/12/episode-023-discussion-warm-ups.html

Poyo, S. (2018). Transforming teacher preparation: Assessing digital learners' needs for instruction in dual learning environments. In E. Langran & J. Borup (Eds.), *Proceedings of Society for Information Technology & Teacher Education International Conference* (pp. 1682-1689). AACE.

Prensky, M. (2003). Digital game-based learning. *Computers in Entertainment*, *1*(1), 21–21. doi:10.1145/950566.950596

Pricing. (n.d.). Retrieved July 14, 2020, from https://www.goosechase.com/edu/pricing/

Prilop, C., Bobo, L., & Spurlock, A. (2020). Effects of digital video-based feedback environments or pre-service teachers' feedback competence. *Computers in Human Behavior*, *102*, 126–128. doi:10.1016/j.chb.2019.08.011

Project Lead the Way. (2020, December). *2.1.1 Genetic Case Studies*. mypltw.org.

Project Lead the Way. (2021, January). *1.1.2 Investigating an Outbreak*. mypltw.org

Protacio, M. S. (2012). Reading motivation: A focus on English learners. *The Reading Teacher*, *66*(1), 69–77. doi:10.1002/TRTR.01092

Puccio, G. J., Burnett, C., Acar, S., Yudess, J. A., Holinger, M., & Cabra, J. F. (2018). Creative problem solving in small groups: The effects of creativity training on idea generation, solution creativity, and leadership effectiveness. *The Journal of Creative Behavior*. Advance online publication. doi:10.1002/jocb.381

Puccio, G. J., Mance, M., & Murdock, M. C. (2011). *Creative leadership: Skills that drive change*. SAGE Publications.

Puentedura, R. (2014). *Building transformation: An introduction to the SAMR model*. http://www.hippasus.com/rrpweblog/archives/2014/06/29/LearningTechnologySAMRModel.pdf

Puentedura, R. R. (2010). *SAMR and TPCK: Intro to advanced practice*. Hippasus. Retrieved from: http://hippasus.com/resources/sweden2010/SAMR_TPCK_IntroToAdvancedPractice.pdf

Puentedura, R. R. (2013, May 29). *SAMR: Moving from enhancement to transformation* [Web log post]. http://www.hippasus.com/rrpweblog/archives/000095.html

Puentedura, R. R. (2013, May 29). *SAMR: Moving from enhancement to transformation* [Web log post]. Retrieved from http://www.hippasus.com/rrpweblog/archives/2013/05/29/SAMREnhancementToTransformation.pdf

Pugh, K. (2017). *Computers, cockroaches, and ecosystems: Understanding learning through metaphor*. Information Age Publishing.

Pulham, E., & Graham, C. R. (2018). Comparing K-12 online and blended teaching competencies: A literature review. *Distance Education*, *39*(3), 411–432. doi:10.1080/01587919.2018.1476840

Pyc, M. A., & Rawson, K. A. (2009). Testing the retrieval effort hypothesis: Does greater difficulty correctly recalling information lead to higher levels of memory? *Journal of Memory and Language*, *60*(4), 437–447. doi:10.1016/j.jml.2009.01.004

Quezada, R. L., Talbot, C., & Quezada-Parker, K. B. (2020). From bricks and mortar to remote teaching: A teacher education program's response to COVID-19. *Journal of Education for Teaching*, 1–12. doi:10.1080/02607476.2020.1801330

Quinn, M. F., Gerde, H. K., & Bingham, G. E. (2016). Help me where I am: Scaffolding writing in preschool classrooms. *The Reading Teacher*, *70*(3), 353–357. doi:10.1002/trtr.1512

Raković, M., Marzouk, Z., Liaqat, A., Winne, P. H., & Nesbit, J. C. Fine grained analysis of students' online discussion posts. *Computers & Education*, *157*, Article 103982. doi:10.1016/j.compedu.2020.103982

Ramirez-Chase, M. (2018, March 6). *Earlywood Educational Services / Homepage*. Retrieved August 03, 2020, from https://www.earlywood.org/site/default.aspx?PageType=3

Ramstetter, C., & Murray, R. (2017). Time to Play: Recognizing the Benefits of Recess. *American Educator*, *41*(1), 17.

Rapanta, C., Botturi, L., Goodyear, P., Guardia, L., & Koole, M. (2020). Online university teaching during and after the Covid-19 crisis: Refocusing teacher presence and learning activity. *Postdigital Science Education*, *2*(3), 923–945. doi:10.100742438-020-00155-y

Rasinski, T. V., & Smith, M. C. (2018). *The megabook of fluency*. Scholastic.

Rasinski, T., Rupley, W. H., & Nichols, W. D. (2008). Two essential ingredients: Phonics and fluency getting to know each other. *The Reading Teacher*, *62*(3), 257–260. doi:10.1598/RT.62.3.7

Rasmitadila, A. R. R., Rachmadtullah, R., Samsudin, A., Syaodih, E., Nurtanto, M., & Tambunan, A. R. S. (2020). The Perceptions of Primary School Teachers of Online Learning during the COVID-19 Pandemic Period: A Case Study in Indonesia. *Journal of Ethnic & Cultural Studies*, *7*(2), 90.

Rasmussen, K. (2004). Places for children - Children's places. *Childhood*, *11*(2), 155–173. doi:10.1177/0907568204043053

Ratcliffe, M., & Grace, M. (2003). *Science education for citizenship: Teaching socio-scientific issues*. McGraw-Hill Education.

Rauf, D. S. (2020, April 23). How districts are helping teachers get better at tech under coronavirus. *Education Week*. https://www.edweek.org/ew/articles/2020/04/22/how-districts-are-helping-teachers-get-better.html

Compilation of References

Rea, P. J., McLuaghlin, V. L., & Walter-Thomas, C. (2002). Outcomes for students with learning disabilities in inclusive and pullout programs. *Exceptional Children, 68*(2), 203–222. doi:10.1177/001440290206800204

Rebora, A. (2016). *Teachers Still Struggling to Use Tech to Transform Instruction, Survey Finds*. Retrieved from https://www.edweek.org/technology/teachers-still-struggling-to-use-tech-to-transform-instruction-survey-finds/2016/06

Reddy, L. A., Fabiano, G. A., Dudek, C. M., & Hsu, L. (2013). Instructional and behavior management practices implemented by elementary general education teachers. *Journal of School Psychology, 51*(6), 683–700. doi:10.1016/j.jsp.2013.10.001 PMID:24295143

Reetz, N. T. (2020, September 15). *Expert: COVID makes STEM education gaps more dire*. Futurity. https://www.futurity.org/stem-education-equity-covid-19-2438882-2/

Reeves, T. C. (2008). Evaluation of the design and development of IT tools in education. In J. Voogt & G. Knezek (Eds.), *International handbook of information technology in primary and secondary education* (pp. 1037–1051). Springer.

Reutzel, D., & Cooter, R. Jr. (2018). *Teaching children to read: The Teacher makes the difference* (8th ed.). Pearson.

Reyes, M. R., Brackett, M. A., Rivers, S. E., White, M., & Salovey, P. (2012). Classroom emotional climate, student engagement, and academic achievement. *Journal of Educational Psychology, 104*(3), 700-712. https://doi:10.1037/a0027268

Rhodes, M. (1960). An Analysis of Creativity. *Phi Delta Kappan, 42*(7), 305–310. www.jstor.org/stable/20342603

Rice & Ortiz. (2020). Perceptions of accessibility in online course materials: A survey of teachers from six virtual schools. *Journal of Online Learning Research, 6*(3), 245–254. https://www.learntechlib.org/primary/p/217628/paper_217628.pdf

Rice, K., & Dawley, L. (2007). *Going virtual! The status of professional development for K–12 online teachers*. Retrieved from https://edtech.boisestate.edu/goingvirtual/goingvirtual.htm

Rice, M., & Dykman, B. (2018). The emerging research base for online learning and students with disabilities. Handbook of research on K-12 online and blended learning, 189-206.

Richards, J., & Bohlke, D. (2011). *Creating Effective Language Lessons*. Cambridge University Press.

Rizk, J., & Davies, S. (2021). Can digital technology bridge the classroom engagement gap? Findings from a qualitative study of K-8 classrooms in 10 Ontario school boards. *Social Sciences, 10*(1), 12. doi:10.3390ocsci10010012

Roberts, K. (2015, November 2-4). *Theories of change: Concerns-based adoption model*. 2015 USAID Global Education Summit, Washington, DC. https://2012-2017.usaid.gov/sites/default/files/documents/1865/Roberts.pdf

Roberts, B. (1991). Music teacher education as identity construction. *International Journal of Music Education, 18*(1), 30–39. doi:10.1177/025576149101800104

Roberts, T., Jackson, C., Mohr-Schroeder, M. J., Bush, S. B., Maiorca, C., Cavalcanti, M., Schroeder, D. C., Delaney, A., Putnam, L., & Cremeans, C. (2018). Students' perceptions of STEM learning after participating in a summer informal learning experience. *International Journal of STEM Education, 5*(35), 1–14. doi:10.118640594-018-0133-4 PMID:30631725

Robinson, K. (2011). *Out of Our Minds: Learning to be Creative*. Capstone Publishing Ltd.

Rock, D., & Shaw, J. M. (2000). *Exploring children's thinking about mathematicians and their work. In Getting into the Mathematics conversation: Valuing communication in Mathematics classrooms*. The National Council of Teachers of Mathematics, Inc.

Rodenbaugh, D. W. (2015). Maximize a team-based learning gallery walk experience: Herding cats is easier than you think. *Advances in Physiology Education, 39*(4), 411–413. doi:10.1152/advan.00012.2015 PMID:26628668

Rogers, E. M. (2003). *Diffusion of innovations* (4th ed.). Free Press.

Rogoff, B. (1990). *Apprenticeship in thinking: Cognitive development in social context*. Oxford university press.

Rohlwing, R. L., & Spelman, M. (2014). Characteristics of adult learning: Implications for the design and implementation of professional development programs. In L. E. Martin, S. Kragler, D. J. Quatroche, & K. L. Bauserman (Eds.), *Handbook of professional development in education: Successful models and practices, PreK–12* (pp. 231–245). Guilford Press.

Roitsch, J., Gumpert, M., Springle, A., & Raymer, A. M. (2021). 2020;). Writing instruction for students with learning disabilities: Quality appraisal of systematic reviews and meta-analyses. *Reading & Writing Quarterly*, *37*(1), 32–44. doi:10.1080/10573569.2019.1708221

Rolland, R. G. (2012). Synthesizing the evidence on classroom goal structures in middle and secondary schools: A meta-analysis and narrative review. *Review of Educational Research*, *82*(4), 396–435. doi:10.3102/0034654312464909

Romero-Hall, E., & Vicentini, C. R. (2017). Multimodal interactive tools for online discussions and assessment. In P. Vu, S. Fredrickson, & C. Moore (Eds.), *Handbook of research on blended learning pedagogies and professional development in higher education* (pp. 85–105). IGI Global. doi:10.4018/978-1-5225-1851-8.ch005

Roorda, D. L., Koomen, H. M. Y., Spilt, J. L., & Oort, F. J. (2011). The influence of affective teacher-student relationships on students' social engagement and achievement: A meta-analytic approach. *Review of Educational Research*, *81*(4), 493–529. doi:10.3102/0034654311421793

Roschelle, J., & Teasley, S. D. (1995). The construction of shared knowledge in collaborative problem solving. In C. E. O'Malley (Ed.), *Computer-supported collaborative learning* (pp. 69–197). SpringerVerlag. doi:10.1007/978-3-642-85098-1_5

Rose, D. H., & Meyer, A. (2002). *Teaching every student in the digital age: Universal design for learning*. Association for Supervision & Curriculum Development.

Rosenberg, J. M., & Koehler, M. J. (2015). Context and technological pedagogical content knowledge (TPACK): A systematic review. *Journal of Research on Technology in Education*, *4*(3), 186–210. doi:10.1080/15391523.2015.1052663

Rosenberg, J. M., Reid, J. W., Dyer, E. B. J., Koehler, M., Fischer, C., & McKenna, T. J. (2020). Idle chatter or compelling conversation? The potential of the social media-based #NGSSchat network for supporting science education reform efforts. *Journal of Research in Science Teaching*, *57*(9), 1322–1355. doi:10.1002/tea.21660

Rosenblum, K. E., & Travis, T. M. C. (2016). *The meaning of difference: American constructions of race and ethnicity, sex and gender, social class, sexuality, and disability* (7th ed.). McGraw-Hill Education.

Roth, D. (2007). Understanding by design: A framework for effecting curricular development and assessment. *CBE Life Sciences Education*, *6*(2), 95–97. doi:10.1187/cbe.07-03-0012

Rovai, A. P. (2001). Building classroom community at a distance: A case study. *Educational Technology Research and Development*, *49*(4), 33–48. https://www.jstor.org/stable/30221135. doi:10.1007/BF02504946

Rovai, A. P. (2007). Facilitating online discussions effectively. *The Internet and Higher Education*, *10*(1), 77–88. doi:10.1016/j.iheduc.2006.10.001

Rowe, P. (1991). *Design Thinking*. MIT Press.

Rozek, C. S., Ramirez, G., Fine, R. D., & Beilock, S. L. (2019). Reducing socioeconomic disparities in the STEM pipeline through student emotion regulation. *Proceedings of the National Academy of Sciences of the United States of America*, *116*(5), 1553–1558. doi:10.1073/pnas.1808589116 PMID:30642965

Compilation of References

Rue, P. (2018). Make way, millennials, here comes gen z. *About Campus: Enriching the Student Learning Experience*, *23*(3), 5–12. doi:10.1177/1086482218804251

Runco, M. A., & Acar, S. (2012). Divergent Thinking as an Indicator of Creative Potential. *Creativity Research Journal*, *24*(1), 66–75. doi:10.1080/10400419.2012.652929

Runco, M. A., Plucker, J. A., & Lim, W. (2001). Development and Psychometric Integrity of a Measure of Ideational Behavior. *Creativity Research Journal*, *13*(3), 393–400.

Runco, M. A., Walczyk, J. J., Acar, S., Cowger, E. L., Simundson, M., & Tripp, S. (2014). The incremental validity of a short form of the Ideational Behavior Scale and usefulness of distractor, contraindicative, and lie scales. *The Journal of Creative Behavior*, *48*, 185–197. doi:10.1002/jocb.47

Russell, S. J., Economopoulos, K., & Wittenberg, L. (2008). *Investigations in Number, Data, and Space* (2nd ed.). Pearson.

Russell, V., & Murphy-Judy, K. (2020). *Teaching language online: A guide for designing, developing, and delivering online, blended, and flipped language courses*. Routledge. doi:10.4324/9780429426483

Russo, L. H. (2013). Play and Creativity at the Center of Curriculum and Assessment: A New York City school's journey to re-think curricular pedagogy. *Online Submission*, *61*(1), 131–146. doi:10.13042/brp.2013.65109

Russ, S. W. (1998). Play, creativity, and adaptive functioning: Implications for play interventions. *Journal of Clinical Child Psychology*, *27*(4), 469–480. doi:10.120715374424jccp2704_11 PMID:9866084

Ryd, N. (2004). The design brief as carrier of client information during the construction process. *Design Studies*, *25*(3), 231–249. doi:10.1016/j.destud.2003.10.003

Saadé, R. G., Morin, D., & Thomas, J. D. (2012). Critical thinking in E-learning environments. *Computers in Human Behavior*, *28*(5), 1608–1617. doi:10.1016/j.chb.2012.03.025

Saavedra, A. R., & Opfer, V. D. (2012). Learning 21st-century skills requires 21st-century teaching. *Phi Delta Kappan*, *94*(2), 8–13. doi:10.1177/003172171209400203

Sableski, M. C., Pinnell, M. F., Driskell, S. O., Smith, T. B., & Franco, S. (2021). STEM stories: Connecting STEM and literacy in an afterschool program. In L. A. Henry & N. A. Stahl (Eds.), *Literacy Across the Community: Research, Praxis, and Trends* (pp. 311–326). Routledge.

Sacks, A. (2018). *Special education: A reference book for policy and curriculum development*. Grey House.

Sadler, T. D. (2009). Situated learning in science education: Socio-scientific issues as contexts for practice. *Studies in Science Education*, *45*(1), 1–42. doi:10.1080/03057260802681839

Sagor, R. (2000). *Guiding School Improvement with Action Research*. ASCD.

Saldaña, J. (2016). *Ethnotheatre: Research from page to stage*. Routledge. doi:10.4324/9781315428932

Salomon, G., & Perkins, D. (2005). Do technologies make us smarter? Intellectual amplification with, of, and through technology. In R. J. Sternberg & D. D. Preiss (Eds.), *Intelligence and technology: The impact of tools on the nature and development of human abilities* (pp. 71–86). Erlbaum.

Sanders, M., & George, A. (2017). Viewing the changing world of educational technology from a different perspective: Present realities, past lessons, and future possibilities. *Education and Information Technologies*, *22*(6), 2915–2933. doi:10.100710639-017-9604-3

Santelli, B., Stewart, K., & Mandernach, J. (2020). Supporting high quality teaching in online programs. *Journal of Education Online*, *17*(1), 11–13.

Savage, J. (2007). Reconstructing music education through ICT. *Research in Education*, *78*(1), 65–77. doi:10.7227/RIE.78.6

Sawyer, R. K. (Ed.). (2014). *The Cambridge handbook of the learning sciences*. Cambridge University Press. doi:10.1017/CBO9781139519526

Scardamalia, M., & Bereiter, C. (2014). Knowledge building and knowledge creation: Theory, pedagogy, and technology. In R. Sawyer (Ed.), *The Cambridge handbook of the learning sciences* (2nd ed., pp. 397–417). Cambridge University Press. doi:10.1017/CBO9781139519526.025

Schaffhauser, D. (2020a, June 2). Educators feeling stressed, anxious, overwhelmed and capable. *THE Journal*. https://thejournal.com/articles/2020/06/02/survey-teachers-feeling-stressed-anxious-overwhelmed-and-capable.aspx

Schaffhauser, D. (2020b, June 11). Free STEM & STEAM resources during the COVID 19 Outbreak. *THE Journal*. https://thejournal.com/articles/2020/04/28/updated-free-stem-and-steam-resources-for-schools-during-the-covid-19-outbreak.aspx

Schecter, R. A., Shah, J., Fruitman, K., & Milanaik, R. L. (2017). Fidget spinners: Purported benefits, adverse effects and accepted alternatives. *Current Opinion in Pediatrics*, *29*(5), 616–618. doi:10.1097/MOP.0000000000000523 PMID:28692449

Scheerer, M. (1963). Problem solving. *Scientific American*, *208*(4), 118–128. doi:10.1038cientificamerican0463-118 PMID:13986996

Scherer, R., Tondeur, J., Siddiq, F., & Baran, E. (2018). The importance of attitudes toward technology for pre-service teachers' technological, pedagogical, and content knowledge: Comparing structural equation modeling approaches. *Computers in Human Behavior*, *80*, 67–80. doi:10.1016/j.chb.2017.11.003

Schifter, D., Bastable, V., Russell, S. J., & Woleck, K. R. (2017). *Geometry: Measuring space in one, two, and three dimensions: Casebook*. National Council of Teachers of Mathematics.

Schleicher, A. (2018). *World class: How to build a 21st-Century school system, strong performers and successful reformers in education*. OECD Publishing.

Schoenfeld, A. H. (2015). Summative and formative assessments in mathematics supporting the goals of the common core standards. *Theory into Practice*, *54*(3), 183–194. doi:10.1080/00405841.2015.1044346

Schön, S., Ebner, M., & Kumar, S. (2014). The Maker Movement: Implications of new digital gadgets, fabrication tools and spaces for creative learning and teaching. *eLearning Papers*, *39*, 14-25.

Schott, M. C. (2017). Technology reading programs and their impact on listening comprehension. *Technology*. https://core.ac.uk/download/pdf/233575767.pdf

Schroeder, R. (2021, January 20). Zoom fatigue: What we have learned. *Inside Higher Ed*. https://www.insidehighered.com/digital-learning/blogs/online-trending-now/zoom-fatigue-what-we-have-learned

Schroeder, N. L., Nesbit, J. C., Anguiano, C. J., & Adesope, O. O. (2018). Studying and constructing concept maps: A meta-analysis. *Educational Psychology Review*, *30*(2), 431–455. doi:10.100710648-017-9403-9

Schroeder, S., Curcio, R., & Lundgren, L. (2019). Expanding the Learning Network: How Teachers Use Pinterest. *Journal of Research on Technology in Education*, *51*(2), 166–186. doi:10.1080/15391523.2019.1573354

Compilation of References

Schwartz, S. (2020, March 25). Flood of Online Learning Resources Overwhelms Teachers. *Education Week*. https://www.edweek.org/teaching-learning/flood-of-online-learning-resources-overwhelms-teachers/2020/03

Schwartz, C. S., Morge, S. P., Rachlin, S. L., & Hargrove, T. Y. (2017). A blended online model for instruction: The North Carolina story. In M. B. McGatha & N. R. Rigelman (Eds.), *Elementary mathematics specialists: Developing, refining, and examining programs that support mathematics teaching and learning* (pp. 69–76). Information Age Publishing.

Schwartz, D. L., Tsang, J. M., & Blair, K. P. (2016). *The ABCs of how we learn: 26 scientifically proven approaches, how they work, and when to use them*. WW Norton & Company.

Schwieger, D., & Ladwig, C. (2018). Reaching and retaining the next generation: Adapting to the expectations of Gen Z in the classroom. *Information Systems Education Journal*, *16*(3), 45.

Schwirzke, K., Vashaw, L., & Watson, J. (2018). A history of K-12 online and blended instruction in the United States. In K. Kennedy & R. E. Ferdig (Eds.), *Handbook of research on K-12 online and blended learning* (2nd ed., pp. 7–20). ETC Press.

Scott, G. M., Leritz, L. E., & Mumford, M. D. (2004a). The effectiveness of creativity training: A meta-analysis. *Creativity Research Journal*, *16*, 361–388. doi:10.1080/10400410409534549

Scott, G. M., Leritz, L. E., & Mumford, M. D. (2004b). Types of creativity training: Approaches and their effectiveness. *The Journal of Creative Behavior*, *38*, 149–179. doi:10.1002/j.2162-6057.2004.tb01238.x

Scott, I. (2020). Education during COVID-19: Pivots and consequences. *The Clinical Teacher*, *17*(4), 443–444. https://doi.org/10.1111/tct.13225

Scott, S. J. (2012). Rethinking the roles of assessment in music education. *Music Educators Journal*, *98*(3), 31–35. doi:10.1177/0027432111434742

Screencastify. (2020). https://www.screencastify.com/

Seaman, J. E., Allen, I. E., & Seaman, J. (2018). *Grade Increase: Tracking Distance Education in the United States*. Babson Survey Research Group.

Sedgwick, M. G., & Yonge, O. (2008). "We're it", "we're a team", "we're family" means a sense of belonging. *Rural and Remote Health*, *8*(3), 1021. PMID:18771338

Seemiller, C., & Grace, M. (2016). *Generation Z goes to college*. John Wiley & Sons.

SeeSaw. (2021). https://web.seesaw.me/

Senge, P. M. (2006). *The fifth discipline: The art and practice of the learning organization*. Currency.

Shahabadkar, P., Joshi, A., & Nandurkar, K. (2019, February). Developing IT enabled mechanism for SWOC analysis: A case study. In *Proc. of the 2nd International Conference on Manufacturing Excellence (ICMAX-2019)* (pp. 158-164). Academic Press.

Shaheen, N. L., & Lohnes, W. S. (2019). Bringing disability into the discussion: Examining technology accessibility as an equity concern in the field of instructional technology. *Journal of Research on Technology in Education*, *51*(2), 187–201.

Shamir, A., & Dushnitzky, G. (2019). Metacognitive Intervention with e-Books to Promote Vocabulary and Story Comprehension Among Children at Risk for Learning Disabilities. In *Reading in the Digital Age: Young Children's Experiences with E-books* (pp. 237–257). Springer. doi:10.1007/978-3-030-20077-0_13

Shapiro, D. (2020, December). *Teaching STEM during a pandemic*. National Science Teaching Association. https://www.nsta.org/resources/teaching-stem-during-pandemic

Shaywitz, S. (2003). *Overcoming dyslexia: A new and complete science-based program for reading problems at any level*. Random House.

Shelton, C., Aguilera, E., & Gleason, B. (2020). Resisting dehumanizing assessments: enacting critical humanizing pedagogies in online teacher education. In R. E. Ferdig, E. Baumgartner, R. Hartshorne, R. Kaplan-Rakowski, & C. Mouza (Eds.), *Teaching, technology, and teacher education during the COVID-19 Pandemic: Stories from the field*. Association for the Advancement of Computing in Education.

Shelton, K., & Saltsman, G. (2011). Applying the ADDIE model to online instruction. In M. Khosrow-Pour (Ed.), *Instructional design: Concepts, methodologies, tools and applications* (pp. 566–582). IGI Global. doi:10.4018/978-1-60960-503-2.ch305

Sheridan, K., Halverson, E. R., Litts, B., Brahms, L., Jacobs-Priebe, L., & Owens, T. (2014). Learning in the making: A comparative case study of three makerspaces. *Harvard Educational Review*, 84(4), 505–531. doi:10.17763/haer.84.4.brr34733723j648u

Shernoff, D. J., Sinha, S., Bressler, D. M., & Ginsburg, L. (2017). Assessing teacher education and professional development needs for the implementation of integrated approaches to STEM education. *International Journal of STEM Education*, 4(1), 13. doi:10.118640594-017-0068-1 PMID:30631669

Sherry, T. L. (2013). "She puts clues in our head:" Interactive and independent writing instruction in a first grade classroom. *Mid-Western Educational Researcher*, 25(3), 22–42.

Shifflet, R., & Weilbacher, G. (2015). Teacher Beliefs and Their Influence on Technology Use: A Case Study. *Contemporary Issues in Technology & Teacher Education*, 15(3). https://citejournal.org/volume-15/issue-3-15/social-studies/teacher-beliefs-and-their-influence-on-technology-use-a-case-study

Shulman, L. S. (1986). Those who understand: A conception of teacher knowledge. *American Educator*, 10(1), 9–15, 43–44.

Shulman, L. S. (1986). Those Who Understand: Knowledge Growth in Teaching. *Educational Researcher*, 15(2), 4–14. doi:10.3102/0013189X015002004

Shulman, L. S. (1986). Those wo understand: Knowledge growth in teaching. *Educational Researcher*, 5, 4–14.

Shulman, L. S. (1987). Knowledge and teaching: Foundations of the new reform. *Harvard Educational Review*, 57(1), 1–22. doi:10.17763/haer.57.1.j463w79r56455411

Shumow, L., Schmidt, J. A., & Kackar-Cam, H. (2013). Exploring teacher effects in outcomes of a growth mindset intervention in seventh grade science. *Middle Grades Research Journal*, 10(2), 17–32.

Siemens, G. (2005). Connectivism: A learning theory for the digital age. *Instructional Technology and Distance Learning*, 2(1), 3-10. http://itdl.org/Journal/Jan_05/article01.htm

Siemens, G. (2005). Connectivism: a learning theory for the digital age. *Instructional Technology and Distance Learning*, 2, 1–8. http://www.itdl.org/Journal/Jan%5f05/article01.htm

Siemens, G. (2004). Connectivism: A theory for the digital age. *International Journal of Instructional Technology and Distance Learning*, 2(1), 3–10. http://www.itdl.org/Journal/Jan_05/article01.htm

Compilation of References

Silk, E. M., Daly, S. R., Jablokow, K., Yilmaz, S., & Berg, M. N. (2014). The Design Problem Framework: Using Adaption-Innovation Theory to Construct Design Problem Statements. *Industrial Design Conference Presentations, Posters, and Proceedings, 7*. Retrieved from: https://lib.dr.iastate.edu/industrialdesign_conf/7

Simonsen, B., Freeman, J., Goodman, S., Mitchell, B., Swain-Bradway, J., Flannery, B., Sugai, G., George, H., & Putman, B. (2015). *Supporting and responding to student behavior: Evidence-based classroom strategies for teachers.* OSEP Technical Assistance Brief. Retrieved from https://osepideasthatwork.org/sites/default/files/ClassroomPBIS_508.pdf

Sims, C. (2017). *Disruptive fixation: School reform and the pitfalls of techno-idealism.* Princeton University Press.

Sinatra, G. M., Kardash, C. M., Taasoobshirazi, G., & Lombardi, D. (2012). Promoting attitude change and expressed willingness to take action toward climate change in college students. *Instructional Science, 40*(1), 1–17. doi:10.100711251-011-9166-5

Sinatra, G. M., & Lombardi, D. (2020). Evaluating sources of scientific evidence and claims in the post-truth era may require reappraising plausibility judgments. *Educational Psychologist, 55*(3), 120–131. doi:10.1080/00461520.2020.1730181

Singal, N., & Muthukrishna, N. (2014). Introduction: Education, childhood and disability in countries of the South: Repositioning the debates. *Childhood, 21*(3), 293–307.

Singer, N. (2020). *How Google took over the classroom.* Retrieved from https://www.nytimes.com/2017/05/13/technology/google-education-chromebooks-schools.html

Singer, D. G., Golinkoff, R. M., & Hirsh-Pasek, K. (Eds.). (2006). *Play = learning: How play motivates and enhances children's cognitive and social-emotional growth.* Oxford University Press. doi:10.1093/acprof:oso/9780195304381.001.0001

Singh, J. A. (2020). *Teambuilding activities handbook: the physical distancing edition.* https://www.amazon.com/Teambuilding-Activities-Handbook-Physical-Distancing-ebook/dp/B08JP91XBD/

Singha, S., Warr, M., Mishra, P., & Henriksen, D. (2020). Playing with creativity across the lifespan: A conversation with Dr. Sandra Russ. *TechTrends, 64*(4), 550–554. doi:10.100711528-020-00514-3 PMID:32838402

Skylar, A. A., Fitzpatrick, M. & Brown, M. R. (2008). *Assistive Technology Associate Editor's Column Assistive Technology Access and Use: Considerations for Culturally and Linguistically Diverse Students and Their Families* (Vol. 23). Academic Press.

Smart, V., Finger, G., & Sim, C. (2016). Envisioning technological pedagogical reasoning. In M. C. Herring, M. J. Koehler, & P. Mishra (Eds.), *Handbook of technological pedagogical content knowledge (TPACK) for educators* (2nd ed., pp. 53–62). Routledge.

Smith, S. J., & Basham, J. D. (2014). Designing online learning opportunities for students with disabilities. *Teaching Exceptional Children, 46*(5), 127–137. doi:10.1177/0040059914530102

Soja, E. W. (1996). *Thirdspace: Journeys to Los Angeles and other real-and-imagined places.* Blackwell Publishing.

Sokal, L. J., Trudel, L. G. E., & Babb, J. C. (2020). Supporting Teachers in Times of Change: The Job Demands-Resources Model and Teacher Burnout During the COVID-19 Pandemic. *International Journal of Contemporary Education, 3*(2), 67–74. doi:10.11114/ijce.v3i2.4931

Song, D., & Bonk, C. J. (2016). Motivational factors in self-directed informal learning from online learning resources. *Cogent Education, 3*(1), 1205838. https://www.cogentoa.com/article/10.1080/2331186X.2016.1205838.pdf

Song, L., & Hill, J. R. (2007). A conceptual model for understanding self-directed learning in online environments. *Journal of Interactive Online Learning, 6*(1), 27–42. http://www.ncolr.org/jiol/issues/pdf/6.1.3.pdf

Soule, H., & Plucker, J. (2015). *4Cs research series. Partnership for 21st Century Skills*. Academic Press.

Southern Regional Education Board (SREB). (2009). *Guidelines of professional development for online teachers*. Retrieved from https://www.sreb.org/sites/main/files/file-attachments/09t01_guide_profdev_online_teach.pdf

Souto-Manning, M. (2016). Honoring and building on the rich literacy practices of young bilingual and multilingual learners. *The Reading Teacher, 70*(3), 263–271. doi:10.1002/trtr.1518

Spaulding, D. T., & Falco, J. (2013). *Action Research for School Leaders*. Pearson.

Sprague, D. (2004). Technology and Teacher Education: Are We Talking to Ourselves? *Contemporary Issues in Technology & Teacher Education, 3*(4). https://citejournal.org/issue-4-03/volume-3/editorial/technology-and-teacher-education-are-we-talking-to-ourselves

Stadel, A. (n.d.). *Battery - percents, decimals & fractions • Activity Builder by Desmos*. Accessed December 7, 2020. https://teacher.desmos.com/activitybuilder/custom/5a21b4c53909e70d138d2bc5?collecti

Stahnke, R., & Blömeke, S. (2021). Novice and expert teachers' situation-specific skills regarding classroom management: What do they perceive, interpret and suggest? *Teaching and Teacher Education, 98*, 103243. doi:10.1016/j.tate.2020.103243

St-Amand, J., Girard, S., & Smith, J. (2017). Sense of Belonging at School: Defining Attributes, Determinants, and Sustaining Strategies. *IAFOR Journal of Education, 5*(2), 105–119. doi:10.22492/ije.5.2.05

Starkey, L. (2010). Teachers' pedagogical reasoning and action in the digital age. *Teachers and Teaching, 16*(2), 233–244. doi:10.1080/13540600903478433

Starkey, L. (2011). Evaluating learning in the 21st century: A digital age learning matrix. *Technology, Pedagogy and Education, 20*(1), 19–39. doi:10.1080/1475939X.2011.554021

Staudt Willet, K. B., Koehler, M. J., & Greenhalgh, S. P. (2017). A tweet by any other frame: Comparing three theoretical frameworks for studying educator interactions on Twitter. *Research highlights in technology and teacher education*, 63-70.

Staudt Willet, K., & Carpenter, J. P. (2020). Teachers on Reddit? Exploring contributions and interactions in four teaching-related subreddits. *Journal of Research on Technology in Education, 52*(2), 216–233. doi:10.1080/15391523.2020.1722978

Steele, D. F. (1999). *Learning mathematical language in the Zone of Proximal Development. Getting into the Mathematics conversation: Valuing communication in Mathematics classrooms*. The National Council of Teachers of Mathematics, Inc.

Steele, D. M., & Cohn-Vargas, B. (2013). *Identity safe classrooms, grades K-5: Places to belong and learn*. Corwin.

Stein, D. S., Wanstreet, C. E., Calvin, J., Overtoom, C., & Wheaton, J. E. (2005). Bridging the transactional distance gap in online learning environments. *American Journal of Distance Education, 19*(2), 105–118. doi:10.120715389286ajde1902_4

Stein, M. K., & Smith, M. S. (1998). Mathematical tasks as framework for reflection: From research to practice. *Mathematics Teaching in the Middle School, 3*(4), 268–275. doi:10.5951/MTMS.3.4.0268

Stengers, I. (2008). A constructivist reading of process and reality. *Theory, Culture & Society, 25*(4), 91–110. doi:10.1177/0263276408091985

Stenman, S., & Pettersson, F. (2020). Remote teaching for equal and inclusive education in rural areas? An analysis of teachers' perspectives on remote teaching. *The International Journal of Information and Learning Technology, 37*(3), 87–98. doi:10.1108/IJILT-10-2019-0096

Stetter, M. E. (2018). The use of technology to assist school-aged students with high incidence special needs in reading. *Education in Science*, *8*(2), 61. doi:10.3390/educsci8020061

Stokes, P. D. (2010). Using constraints to develop creativity in the classroom. In R. A. Beghetto & J. C. Kaufman (Eds.), *Nurturing creativity in the classroom* (pp. 88–112). Cambridge University Press. doi:10.1017/CBO9780511781629.006

Stringer, E. T., & Aragón, A. O. (2020). *Action Research*. Sage Publications.

Strutz, M. L., Orr, M. K., & Ohland, M. W. (2012). Low socioeconomic status individuals: An invisible minority in engineering. In C. Baillie, A. Pawley, & D. Riley (Eds.), *Engineering and social justice: In the university and beyond* (pp. 143–156). Purdue University Press. doi:10.2307/j.ctt6wq5pf.11

Suarez, A., Specht, M., Prinsen, F., Kalz, M., & Ternier, S. (2018). A review of the types of mobile activities in mobile inquiry-based learning. *Computers & Education*, *118*, 38–55. doi:10.1016/j.compedu.2017.11.004

Suh, J., Graham, S., Ferranone, T., Kopeinig, G., & Bertholet, B. (2011). Developing persistent and flexible problem solvers with a growth mindset. In D. J. Brahier (Ed.), *Motivation and disposition: Pathways to learning mathematics* (pp. 169–184). National Council of Teachers of Mathematics.

Suldo, S. M., McMahan, M. M., Chappel, A. M., & Loker, T. (2012). Relationships between perceived school climate and adolescent mental health across genders. *School Mental Health*, *4*(2), 69–80. doi:10.100712310-012-9073-1

Sulistia, S., Lidinillah, D. A. M., Nugraha, A., & Karlimah, A. (2019). Promoting engineering for fourth-grade students through STEM learning. *Journal of Physics: Conference Series*, *1318*(1), 6. doi:10.1088/1742-6596/1318/1/012054

Sullivan, S., & Glanz, J. (2013). *Supervision that improves teaching and learning: Strategies and techniques*. Corwin Press.

Summerville, J. B. (2002). Taking ID online: Developing an online instructional design course. *TechTrends*, *46*(4), 29–32. doi:10.1007/BF02763261

Sung, E., & Mayer, R. E. (2012). Five facets of social presence in online distance education. *Computers in Human Behavior*, *28*(5), 1738–1747. doi:10.1016/j.chb.2012.04.014

Sun, K. L., Baldinger, E. E., & Humphreys, C. (2018). Number talks: Gateway to sense making. *Mathematics Teacher*, *112*(1), 48–54.

Svenson, K. L., Churchill, G. A., Peters, L. L., Bult, C. J., Paigen, B. J., & Robledo, R. F. (2007). *The mouse as a model for human biology: a resource guide for complex trait analysis*. doi:10.1038/nrg2025

Swain, M., Kinnear, P., & Steinman, L. (2010). *Sociocultural theory in second language education: An introduction through narratives*. Multilingual Matters.

Swallow, M. J. C., & Olofson, M. (2017). Contextual understandings in the TPACK framework. *Journal of Research on Technology in Education*, *49*(3), 228–244. doi:10.1080/15391523.2017.1347537

Swan Dagen, A. S., & Bean, R. M. (2014). High-quality research-based professional development: An essential for enhancing high-quality teaching. In L. E. Martin, S. Kragler, D. J. Quatroche, & K. L. Basuerman (Eds.), *Handbook of professional development in education: Successful models and practices, PreK–12* (pp. 42–63). Guilford Press.

Swan, K. (2005). A constructivist model for thinking about learning online. *Elements of Quality Online Education: Engaging Communities*, *6*, 13–30.

Swan, K., & Shih, L. F. (2005). On the nature and development of social presence in online course discussions. *Journal of Asynchronous Learning Networks*, *9*(3), 115–136.

Swanson, H. L. (1991). Operational definitions and learning disabilities: An overview. *Learning Disability Quarterly*, *14*(4), 242–254. doi:10.2307/1510661

Swanson, H. L. (1993). Working memory in learning disability subgroups. *Journal of Experimental Child Psychology*, *56*(1), 87–114. doi:10.1006/jecp.1993.1027 PMID:8366327

Swanson, H. L., Christie, L., & Rubadeau, R. J. (1993). The relationship between metacognition and analogical reasoning in mentally retarded, learning disabled, average, and gifted children. *Learning Disabilities Research & Practice*, *8*, 70–81.

Swanson, L., Harris, K. R., & Graham, S. (2013). *Handbook of Learning Disabilities* (2nd ed.).

Sweller, J. (2010). Element interactivity and intrinsic, extraneous, and germane cognitive load. *Educational Psychology Review*, *22*(2), 123–138. doi:10.100710648-010-9128-5

Sweller, J., Kirschner, P. A., & Clark, R. E. (2007). Why minimally guided teaching techniques do not work: A reply to commentaries. *Educational Psychologist*, *42*(2), 115–121. doi:10.1080/00461520701263426

Swennen, A., & White, E. (Eds.). (2021). Being a Teacher Educator Research-Informed Methods for Improving Practice. Routledge.

Tabletopia. (2021). *Online arena for playing board games*. Retrieved from: https://tabletopia.com

Tallvid, M. (2016). Understanding teachers' reluctance to the pedagogical use of ICT in the 1:1 classroom. *Education and Information Technologies*, *21*(3), 503–519. doi:10.100710639-014-9335-7

Tallvid, M., Lundin, J., Svensson, L., & Lindström, B. (2015). Exploring the relationship between sanctioned and unsanctioned laptop use in a 1:1 classroom. *Journal of Educational Technology & Society*, *18*(1), 237–249. https://www.jstor.org/stable/jeductechsoci.18.1.237

Tan, J., & Biswas, G. (2007). Simulation-based game learning environments: Building and sustaining a fish tank. *IEEE Xplore Digital Library*, 73-80. . doi:10.1109/DIGITEL.2007.44

Tassell, J., Gerstenschlager, N. E., Syzmanski, T., & Denning, S. (2020). A study of factors impacting elementary mathematics preservice teachers: Improving mindfulness, anxiety, self-efficacy, and mindset. *School Science and Mathematics*, *120*(6), 333–344. doi:10.1111sm.12425

Taylor & Francis Group. (2020, February 26). *'Low' socioeconomic status is the biggest barrier to STEM participation*. ScienceDaily. https://www.sciencedaily.com/releases/2020/02/200226171121.htm

Taylor, Z. W., & Serna, K. L. (2020). Don't Txt Me L8r, Text Me Now: Exploring community college student preferences for receiving a text message from their institution. *Community College Journal of Research and Practice*, *44*(2), 133–146. https://naspa.tandfonline.com/doi/full/10.1080/10668926.2018.1560374?scroll=top&needAccess=true

Teaching Tolerance Anti-Bias Framework. (n.d.). Retrieved July 14, 2020, from https://www.tolerance.org/sites/default/files/general/TT%20anti%20bias%20framework%20pamphlet_final.pdf

Tekkumru-Kisa, M., Stein, M. K., & Schunn, C. (2015). A framework for analyzing cognitive demand and content-practices integration: Task analysis guide in science. *Journal of Research in Science Teaching*, *52*(5), 659–685.

Terenzini, P. T., Springer, L., Yaeger, P. M., Pascarella, E. T., & Nora, A. (1996). First-generation college students: Characteristics, experiences, and cognitive development. *Research in Higher Education*, *37*(1), 1–22. doi:10.1007/BF01680039

Terry, R., Taylor, J., & Davies, M. (2019). Successful teaching in virtual classrooms. In *Learning and Teaching in Higher Education*. Edward Elgar Publishing.

Compilation of References

The Learning Space. (n.d.). *Number talk processes and resources*. https://www.learning-space.org/cms/lib/WA02221164/Centricity/Domain/41/Number%20Talk%20Process%20and%20Resources.pdf

The Math Learning Center. (2015). *Bridges in Mathematics* (2nd ed.). Author.

The Math Learning Center. (2020a). *COVID-19 Survey, March 2020* [Unpublished data]. Author.

The Math Learning Center. (2020b). *Remote Learning Survey, June 2020* [Unpublished data]. Author.

The Math Learning Center. (2020c). *District Focus Groups July–August 2020* [Unpublished data]. Author.

The Math Learning Center. (2020d). *Next Steps in 2020 Survey, November 2020* [Unpublished data]. Author.

The Math Learning Center. (2020e). *Teacher Interviews, October 2020–February 2021* [Unpublished data]. Author.

Thoma, J., Hutchison, A., Johnson, D., Johnson, K., & Stromer, E. (2017). Planning for Technology Integration in a Professional Learning Community. *The Reading Teacher*, *71*(2), 167–175. doi:10.1002/trtr.1604

Thomas, S., & Golden, J. (2021). *Better wumps hats*. https://www.geogebra.org/m/uq2bkjd9

Thomas, A., & Trainin, G. (2019). Creating laboratories of practice for developing preservice elementary teachers' TPACK: A programmatic approach. In *Handbook of Research on TPACK in the Digital Age* (pp. 155–172). IGI Global. doi:10.4018/978-1-5225-7001-1.ch008

Thompson, S. D., & Raisor, J. M. (2013, May). *Meeting the sensory needs of young children*. Retrieved February 18, 2017, from https://www.naeyc.org/yc/files/yc/file/201305/Meeting_Sensory_Needs_Thompson_0513.pdf

Thoughtful Learning Organization. (2016). Retrieved from https://k12.thoughtfullearning.com/FAQ/what-are-learning-skills

Thoughtful Learning. (2015, August 17). *What are learning skills? K-12 Thoughtful Learning*. Retrieved from https://k12.thoughtfullearning.com/FAQ/what-are-learning-skills

Thoughtful Learning. (2016). *3 Simple steps to the 4 c's*. Retrieved from https://k12.thoughtfullearning.com/blogpost/3-simple-steps-4-cs

Thoughtful Learning. (2021). *What are 21st century skills*. Retrieved from https://k12.thoughtfullearning.com/FAQ/what-are-21st-century-skills

Thumlert, K., Owston, R., & Malhotra, T. (2018). Transforming school culture through inquiry-driven learning and iPads. *Journal of Professional Capital and Community*, *3*(2), 79–96. doi:10.1108/JPCC-09-2017-0020

Tien, H., Chang, B., & Kuo, Y. (2019). Does experience stimulate or stifle creativity? *European Journal of Innovation Management*, *22*(3), 422–445. doi:10.1108/EJIM-02-2018-0042

Tierney, R. J. (2013). Literacy education 2.0: Looking through the rear vision mirror as we move ahead. In *Changing literacies for changing times* (pp. 283–303). Routledge.

Tierney, W., & Kolluri, S. (2018). Mapping the Terrain: Youth and Digital Media. In W. Tierney, Z. B. Corwin, & A. Ochsner (Eds.), *Diversifying Digital Learning* (pp. 1–24). Johns Hopkins University Press.

Timmers, C. F., Walraven, A., & Veldkamp, B. P. (2015). The effect of regulation feedback in a computer-based formative assessment on information problem solving. *Computers & Education*, *87*, 1–9. doi:10.1016/j.compedu.2015.03.012

Tobin, K. G. (1993). *The practice of constructivism in science education*. Psychology Press.

Tomasik, T. (2010). Reliability and validity of the Delphi method in guideline development for family physicians. *Quality in Primary Care*, *18*(5), 317–326. PMID:21114912

Tomei, L. A., & Nelson, D. (2019). The impact of online teaching on faculty load–revisited: Computing the ideal class size for traditional, online, and hybrid courses. *International Journal of Online Pedagogy and Course Design*, *9*(3), 1–12. doi:10.4018/IJOPCD.2019070101

Tomlinson, C. A. (2014). *The Differentiated Classroom: Responding to the Needs of All Learners*. ASCD.

Tompkins, G. E. (2019). *Teaching writing: Balancing process and product* (7th ed.). Pearson.

Torrance, E. P., & Safter, H. T. (1999). *Making the creative leap beyond*. Creative Education Foundation Press.

Townsend, C., Slavit, D., & McDuffie, A. R. (2018). Supporting all learners in productive struggle. *Mathematics Teaching in the Middle School*, *23*(4), 216–224. doi:10.5951/mathteacmiddscho.23.4.0216

Trainin, G., & Swanson, H. L. (2005). Cognition, metacognition, and achievement of college students with learning disabilities. *Learning Disability Quarterly*, *28*, 261–272. doi:10.2307/4126965

Triple E. Framework. (n.d.). https://www.tripleeframework.com/

Troussas, C., Krouska, A., & Sgouropoulou, C. (2019). Collaboration and fuzzy-modeled personalization for mobile game-based learning in higher education. *Computers & Education*, 1–18. doi:10.1016/j.compedu.2019.103698

Trust, T., & Whalen, J. (2020). Should teachers be trained in emergency remote teaching? Lessons learned from the COVID-19 pandemic. *Journal of Technology and Teacher Education*, *28*(2), 189–199.

Trust, T., & Whalen, J. (2020). Should Teachers be Trained in Emergency Remote Teaching? Lessons Learned from the COVID-19 Pandemic. *Journal of Technology and Teacher Education*, *28*(2), 189–199.

Tsai, C. Y. (2018). The effect of online argumentation of socio-scientific issues on students' scientific competencies and sustainability attitudes. *Computers & Education*, *116*, 14–27. doi:10.1016/j.compedu.2017.08.009

Tuapawa, K. (2016). Challenges faced by key stakeholders using educational online technologies in blended tertiary environments. *International Journal of Web-Based Learning and Teaching Technologies*, *2*(11), 116. doi:10.4018/IJWLTT.2016040101

Tucker, P. (1999). A survey of attitudes and barriers to kerbside recycling. *Environmental and Waste Management*, *2*(1), 55–63.

Turkan, S. (2016). In-service teachers' reasoning about scenarios of teaching mathematics to English language learners. *The Mathematics Enthusiast*, *13*(1), 130–148.

U.S. Department of Commerce. (2012). *The competitiveness and innovative capacity of the United States*. https://www.commerce.gov/sites/default/files/migrated/reports/thecompetitivenessandinnovativecapacityoftheunitedstates.pdf

U.S. Department of Education, National Center for Education Statistics (NCES). (2019). *Schools and Staffing Survey. Public and Private Teachers: 2011-12*. Retrieved from https://nces.ed.gov/datalab/QuickStats/Workspace/Index?dataSetId=64

U.S. Department of Education, Office of Planning, Evaluation, and Policy Department. (2010). *Evaluation of Evidence-Based Practices in Online Learning: A Meta-Analysis and Review of Online Learning Studies*. Retrieved from https://www2.ed.gov/rschstat/eval/tech/evidence-based-practices/finalreport.pdf

U.S. President's Council of Advisors on Science and Technology. (2010). *Prepare and inspire: K–12 education in STEM for America's future*. doi:10.1126cience.1198062

Compilation of References

UNEP. (2020). *COVID-19: Four sustainable development goals that help future-proof global recovery.* https://www.unenvironment.org/news-and-stories/story/covid-19-four-sustainable-development-goals-help-future-proof-global

UNESCO. (n.d.). *Education for Sustainable Development.* https://en.unesco.org/themes/education-sustainable-development/what-is-esd

UNICEF. (2020). *Leaving no child behind during the pandemic: Children with disabilities and COVID-19.* https://data.unicef.org/topic/child-disability/covid-19/

United Nations Educational, Scientific and Cultural Organization. (2020, Dec. 12). *From COVID-19 learning disruption to recovery: a snapshot of UNESCO's work in education in 2020.* https://en.unesco.org/news/covid-19-learning-disruption-recovery-snapshot-unescos-work-education-2020

United States Department of Education (USDE). (2020). *Supplemental fact sheet: Addressing the risk of COVID-19 in preschool, elementary and secondary schools while serving children with disabilities.* https://www2.ed.gov/about/offices/list/ocr/frontpage/faq/rr/policyguidance/Supple%20Fact%20Sheet%203.21.20%20FINAL.pdf

United States Department of Education, Office for Civil Rights. (2020). *Addressing the risk of COVID-19 in preschool, elementary and secondary schools while serving children with disabilities.* Author.

United States Department of Education, Office of Elementary and Secondary Education. (2020a). *Addressing the risk of COVID-19 while serving migratory children.* Author.

United States Department of Education, Office of Elementary and Secondary Education. (2020b) *Providing services to English learners during the COVID-19 outbreak.* Author.

University of Missouri. (2020). *Show Me Renewal: Plan for Students.* https://renewal.missouri.edu/

University of Washington. (2014). *Teacher education by design (TEDD).* https://tedd.org/

Uslu, F., & Gizir, S. (2017). School belonging of adolescents: The role of teacher–student relationships, peer relationships and family involvement. *Kuram ve Uygulamada Egitim Bilimleri, 17*(1), 63–82. doi:10.12738/estp.2017.1.0104

Valencia, R. R. (1997). Conceptualizing the notion of deficit thinking. In R. R. Valencia (Ed.), *The evolution of deficit thinking: Educational thought and practice* (pp. 113–131). Routledge Falmer.

Valenzuela, F. R., Fisher, J., Whale, S., & Adapa, S. (2013). Developing and evaluating social presence in the online learning environment. *International Proceedings of Economics Development and Research, 60,* 95.

van der Meij, H., Albers, E., & Leemkuil, H. (2011). Learning from games: Does collaboration help? *British Journal of Educational Technology, 42*(4), 655–664. doi:10.1111/j.1467-8535.2010.01067.x

Van der Sande, L., Henick, X., Marloes, M. H. G., Boor-Klip, H. J., & Mainhard, T. (2018). Learning disabilities and low social status: The role of peer academic reputation and peer reputation of teacher liking. *Journal of Learning Disabilities, 51*(3), 211–222. doi:10.1177/0022219417708172 PMID:28470105

Van der Zanden, P., Denessen, E., Cillessen, A., & Meijer, P. (2020). Fostering critical thinking skills in secondary education to prepare students for university: Teacher perceptions and practices. *Research in Post-Compulsory Education, 25*(4), 394–419. doi:10.1080/13596748.2020.1846313

Van Horne, C., Frayret, J., & Poulin, D. (2006). Creating value with innovation: From centre of expertise to forest products industry. *Forest Policy and Economics, 8*(7), 751–761. doi:10.1016/j.forpol.2005.06.003

van Leeuwen, A., & Janssen, J. (2019). A systematic review of teacher guidance during collaborative learning in primary and secondary education. *Educational Research Review, 27,* 71–89. doi:10.1016/j.edurev.2019.02.001

Vander Ark, T. (2011). Desmos Introduced at TechCrunch Disruptive Conference. *Getting Smart*. https://www.gettingsmart.com/2011/05/desmos-introduced-at-techcrunch-disruptive-conference/

VanDerHeide, J., & Juzwik, M. M. (2018). Argument as conversation: Students responding through writing to significant conversations across time and place. *Journal of Adolescent & Adult Literacy, 62*(1), 67–77. doi:10.1002/jaal.754

Vasquez, J. A. (2015). STEM—Beyond the acronym. *Educational Leadership, 72*(4), 10–15.

Veblen, K., Kruse, N., Messenger, S., & Letain, M. (2018). Children's clapping games on the virtual playground. *International Journal of Music Education, 36*(4), 547–559. doi:10.1177/0255761418772865

Vekiri, I. (2002). What is the value of graphical displays in learning? *Educational Psychology Review, 14*(3), 261–312.

Velichova, L., Orbanova, D., & Kubekova, A. (2020). The COVID-19 pandemic: Unique opportunity to develop online learning. *Journal of the Association for Information Communication Technologies. Education in Science, 9*(4), 1633–1639. doi:10.18421/TEM94-40

Villarroel, V., Bloxham, D., Bruna, D., Bruna, C., & Herrera-Seda, C. (2018). Authentic Assessment: Creating a Blueprint for Course Design. *Assessment & Evaluation in Higher Education, 43*(5), 840–854. doi:10.1080/02602938.2017.1412396

Vincent-Ruz, P., & Schunn, C. D. (2018). The nature of science identity and its role as the driver of student choices. *International Journal of STEM Education, 5*(1), 1–12. doi:10.118640594-018-0140-5 PMID:30631738

Vines, N., Jordan, J., & Broemmel, A. D. (2020). Reenvisioning spelling instruction: Developmental word study nonnegotiable. *The Reading Teacher, 73*(6), 711–722. doi:10.1002/trtr.1882

Virginia Department of Education (VDOE). (2020). *School Reopening Frequently Asked Questions – Updated August 10, 2020*. Retrieved August 12, 2020, from https://www.doe.virginia.gov/support/health_medical/office/covid-19-faq-reopening.shtml

Vonderwell, S., Liang, X., & Alderman, K. (2007). Asynchronous discussions and assessment in online learning. *Journal of Research on Technology in Education, 39*(3), 309–328. doi:10.1080/15391523.2007.10782485

Voogt, J., Fisser, P., Roblin, N. P., Tondeur, J., & van Braak, J. (2012). Technological pedagogical content knowledge - a review of the literature. *Journal of Computer Assisted Learning, 29*(2), 109–121. doi:10.1111/j.1365-2729.2012.00487.x

Voogt, J., & Roblin, N. P. (2010). *21st century skills. Discussienota*. Kennisnet. Retrieved from http://opite.pbworks.com/w/file/fetch/61995295/White%20Paper%2021stCS_Final_ENG_def2.pdf

Vue, G., Hall, T. E., Robinson, K., Ganley, P., Elizalde, E., & Graham, S. (2015). Informing understanding of young students' writing challenges and opportunities. *Learning Disability Quarterly, 39*(2), 83–94. doi:10.1177/0731948715604571

Vygotsky, L. (1962). Thought and language (E. Hanfmann & G. Vakar.). MIT Press. doi:10.1037/11193-000

Vygotsky, L. (1930/1978). *Tool and symbol in child development. Mind in Society: The development of higher psychological processes*. Harvard University Press.

Vygotsky, L. (1978). Interaction between learning and development. *Readings on the Development of Children, 23*(3), 34–41.

Vygotsky, L. (1997). *Educational psychology*. St. Lucie Press.

Vygotsky, L. S. (1978). *Mind in society: The development of higher psychological processes*. Harvard University Press.

Vygotsky, L. S. (1986). *Thought and Language* (A. Kozulin, Trans.). MIT Press.

Compilation of References

Vygotsky, L. S. (1994). The problem of the environment. In R. Van-der-Veer & J. Valsiner (Eds.), *The Vygotsky reader* (pp. 338–354). Blackwell Publishers.

Wade, E., Boon, R. T., & Spencer, V. G. (2010). Use of kidspiration software to enhance the reading comprehension of story grammar components for elementary-age students with specific learning disabilities. *Learning Disabilities (Weston, Mass.)*, *8*, 31–41.

Wai, J., Lubinski, D., Benbow, C. P., & Steiger, J. H. (2010). Accomplishment in science, technology, engineering, and mathematics (STEM) and its relation to STEM educational dose: A 25-year longitudinal study. *Journal of Educational Psychology*, *102*(4), 860–871. doi:10.1037/a0019454

Walker, L., & Avant, K. C. (2011). *Strategies for theory construction* (5th ed.). Prentice Hall.

Wallas, G. (1926). *The Art of Thought*. Harcourt, Brace and Company.

Walters, L. M., & Gillern, S. V. (2018). We learn in the form of stories: How digital storytelling supports critical digital literacy for pre-service teachers. *International Journal of Digital Literacy and Competence*, *9*(3), 12–26. doi:10.4018/IJDLDC.2018070102

Wang, H., Hall, N. C., & Rahimi, S. (2015). Self-efficacy and causal attributions in teachers: Effects on burnout, job satisfaction, illness, and quitting intentions. *Teaching and Teacher Education*, *47*, 120–130. doi:10.1016/j.tate.2014.12.005

Wang, J., Geng, L., Schultz, P. W., & Zhou, K. (2019). Mindfulness increases the belief in climate change: The mediating role of connectedness with nature. *Environment and Behavior*, *51*(1), 3–23. doi:10.1177/0013916517738036

Wang, M., & Degol, J. L. (2016). School climate: A review of the construct, measurement, and impact on student outcomes. *Educational Psychology Review*, *28*(2), 315–352. https://www.jstor.org/stable/24761235. doi:10.100710648-015-9319-1

Wang, S., & Hsu, H. (2009). Using the ADDIE model to design Second Life activities for online learners. *TechTrends*, *53*(6), 76–81. doi:10.100711528-009-0347-x

Wang, T. H. (2008). Web-based quiz-game-like formative assessment: Development and evaluation. *Computers & Education*, *51*(3), 1247–1263. doi:10.1016/j.compedu.2007.11.011

Wang, V. C. X., & Torrisi-Steele, G. (2015). Online teaching, change, and critical theory. *New Horizons in Adult Education and Human Resource Development*, *27*(3), 18–26. doi:10.1002/nha3.20108

Ward, L., Siegel, M. J., & Davenport, Z. (2012). *First-generation college students: Understanding and improving the experience from recruitment to commencement*. John Wiley & Sons.

Warschauer, M. (2006). Literacy and technology: Bridging the divide. In D. Gibbs & K. L. Krause (Eds.), *Cyberlines 2.0: Languages and cultures of the internet* (pp. 163–174). James Nicholas Publishers.

Warschauer, M. (2011). *Learning in the cloud: How (and why) to transform schools with digital media*. Teachers College Press.

Warschauer, M., & Matuchniak, T. (2010). New technology and digital worlds: Analyzing evidence of equity in access, use, and outcomes. In N. Pinkard & V. Gadsden (Eds.), *Review of research in education: What counts as evidence in educational settings? Rethinking equity, diversity, and reform in the 21st century* (Vol. 34, pp. 179–225). Sage. doi:10.3102/0091732X09349791

Warshauer, H. K. (2015). Strategies to support productive struggle. *Mathematics Teaching in the Middle School*, *20*(7), 390–393. doi:10.5951/mathteacmiddscho.20.7.0390

Watson, S. L., Watson, W. R., & Tay, L. (2018). The development and validation of the Attitudinal Learning Inventory (ALI): A measure of attitudinal learning and instruction. *Educational Technology Research and Development*, *66*(6), 1601–1617. doi:10.100711423-018-9625-7

Watson, W. R., & Fang, J. (2012). PBL as a framework for implementing video games in the classroom. *International Journal of Game-Based Learning*, *2*(1), 77–89. doi:10.4018/ijgbl.2012010105

Watson, W. R., Mong, C. J., & Harris, C. A. (2011). A case study of the in-class use of a video game for teaching high school history. *Computers & Education*, *56*(2), 466–474. doi:10.1016/j.compedu.2010.09.007

Watts-Taffe, S., Gwinn, C., Johnson, J., & Horn, M. (2003). Preparing preservice teachers to integrate technology with the elementary literacy program. *The Reading Teacher*, *57*(2), 130–138. http://www.jstor.org/stable/20205332

Waxenfelter, A., Watson, C., & Harry, J. (2013). *Bilingual AAC Apps*. https://www.pdx.edu/multicultural-topics-communication-sciences-disorders/bilingual-aac-apps

Webb, S., Massey, D., Goggans, M., & Flajole, K. (2019). Thirty-five years of the gradual release of responsibility: Scaffolding toward complex and responsive teaching. *The Reading Teacher*, *73*(1), 75–83. doi:10.1002/trtr.1799

Weiss, D. M., & Belland, B. R. (2018). PBL group autonomy in a high school environmental science class. *Tech Know Learn*, *23*(1), 83–107. doi:10.100710758-016-9297-5

Wei, Y., Spear-Swerling, L., & Mercurio, M. (2021). Motivating students with learning disabilities to read. *Intervention in School and Clinic*, *56*(3), 155–162. doi:10.1177/1053451220928956

Wen, C. T., Chang, C. J., Chang, M. H., Chiang, S. H. F., Liu, C. C., Hwang, F. K., & Tsai, C. C. (2018). The learning analytics of model-based learning facilitated by a problem-solving simulation game. *Instructional Science*, *46*(6), 847–867. doi:10.100711251-018-9461-5

Wenger, E. (1999). *Communities of practice: Learning, meaning, and identity*. Cambridge University Press.

Wenglinsky, H. (2005). *Using technology wisely: The keys to success in schools*. Teachers College Press.

Weng, P.-L. (2015). Developing an app evaluation rubric for practitioners in special education. *Journal of Special Education Technology*, *30*(1), 43–58.

Wertsch, J. V. (1998). *Mind As Action*. Oxford University Press.

Whalley, R., & Barbour, M. K. (2020). Collaboration and Virtual Learning in New Zealand Rural Primary Schools: A Review of the Literature. *Turkish Online Journal of Distance Education*, *21*(2), 102–125.

Wheatley, D. M. (2016). *Virtual high schools and instructional design strategies to reduce transactional distance and increase student engagement: a Delphi study* (Publication No. 10168359) [Doctoral dissertation, Capella University]. ProQuest Dissertations Publishing.

Whiteside, A. L. (2015). Introducing the social presence model to explore online and blended learning experiences. *Online Learning*, *19*(2), n2. doi:10.24059/olj.v19i2.453

WIDA Screener. (n.d.). Retrieved from https://wida.wisc.edu/assess/screener

Widjaja, W., Groves, S., & Ersozlu, Z. (2021). Designing and delivering an online lesson study unit in mathematics to pre-service primary teachers: opportunities and challenges. *International Journal for Lesson & Learning Studies*.

Wiedemann, C. (2019, February 6). *Why diversity is crucial to success in STEM*. CERIC. https://ceric.ca/2019/02/why-diversity-is-crucial-to-success-in-stem/

Compilation of References

Wigfield, A., & Eccles, J. S. (2000). Expectancy-value theory of achievement motivation. *Contemporary Educational Psychology*, *25*(1), 68–81. doi:10.1006/ceps.1999.1015 PMID:10620382

Wiggins, G. (2006, April 3). *Healthier testing made easy: the idea of authentic assessment*. Edutopia Magazine. https://www.edutopia.org/authentic-assessment-grant-wiggins

Wiggins, G. (1989). A true test: Toward more authentic and equitable assessment. *Phi Delta Kappan*, *70*(9), 703–713. https://www.jstor.org/stable/20404004

Wiggins, G. P. (1993). *Assessing student performance: Exploring the purpose and limits of testing*. Jossey-Bass.

Wiggins, G., & McTighe, J. (2005). *Understanding by design* (2nd ed.). Association for Supervision and Curriculum Development.

Wilfley, D. (1989). *Interpersonal analyses of bulimia: Normal-weight and obese* [Unpublished doctoral dissertation]. University of Missouri, Columbia, MO, United States.

Wiliam, D. (2007). *Keeping learning on track: classroom assessment and the regulation of learning*. Information Age Publishing.

Wiliam, D., & Black, P. (1996). Meanings and consequences: A basis for distinguishing formative and summative functions of assessment. *British Educational Research Journal*, *22*(5), 537–548. doi:10.1080/0141192960220502

Wilkens, C., Eckdahl, K., Morone, M., Cook, V., Giblin, T., & Coon, J. (2014). Communication, community, and disconnection: Pre-Service teachers in virtual school field experiences. *Journal of Educational Technology Systems*, *43*(2), 143–157. https://doi.org/10.2190/ET.43.2.c

Will, M. (2020, August 6). New NEA President: 'We are not going to put our students at risk' for COVID-19. *Education Week*. https://www.edweek.org/teaching-learning/new-nea-president-we-are-not-going-to-put-our-students-at-risk-for-covid-19/2020/08

Williams, B. (2005). Case based learning—a review of the literature: Is there scope for this educational paradigm in prehospital education? *Emergency Medicine Journal*, *22*(8), 577–581. doi:10.1136/emj.2004.022707 PMID:16046764

Williams, D. A. (2017). Music technology pedagogy and curricula. In A. Ruthmann & R. Mantie (Eds.), *The Oxford handbook of technology and music education*. Oxford University Press.

Williamson, T. (2017). Listening to many voices: Enacting social justice literacy curriculum. *Teaching and Teacher Education*, *61*, 104–114. https://doi.org. /10.1016/j.tate.2016.10.002

Wills, T. (2021). *Teaching math at a distance: A practical guide to rich remote instruction*. Corwin Press.

Wilson, K., & Korn, J. H. (2007). Attention during lectures: Beyond ten minutes. *Teaching of Psychology*, *34*(2), 85–89. doi:10.1177/009862830703400202

Wing, J. (2006). Computational thinking. *Communications of the ACM*, *49*(3), 33–35. doi:10.1145/1118178.1118215

Winstead, L. (2011). The impact of NCLB and accountability on social studies: Teacher experiences and perceptions about teaching social studies. *Social Studies*, *102*(5), 221–227. doi:10.1080/00377996.2011.571567

Wohlwend, K. E., Peppler, K. A., Keune, A., & Thompson, N. (2017). Making sense and nonsense: Comparing mediated discourse and agential realist approaches to materiality in a preschool makerspace. *Journal of Early Childhood Literacy*, *17*(3), 444–462. doi:10.1177/1468798417712066

Wolcott, M. D., McLaughlin, J. E., Hubbard, D. K., Rider, T. R., & Umstead, K. (2020). Twelve tips to stimulate creative problem-solving with design thinking. *Medical Teacher*, •••, 1–8. doi:10.1080/0142159X.2020.1807483

Wong, H. K., & Wong, R. T. (2009). *The first days of school: how to be an effective teacher*. Harry K. Wong Publications. Print

Woods, M. (2021, January 13). Sea shanty TikTok is the new best thing on the internet. *Huffington Post*. Retrieved from https://www.huffingtonpost.ca/entry/sea-shanty-tiktok-trend-song_ca_5fff6bb5c5b63642b7019816

Woodward, L., & Hutchison, A. (2018). The STAK Model: Exploring Professional Development for Technology Integration Into Instruction. *Journal of Technology and Teacher Education*, 26(4), 613–644.

Woollett, K., & Maguire, E. A. (2011). Acquiring "the Knowledge" of London's layout drives structural brain changes. *Current Biology*, 21(24), 2109–2114. doi:10.1016/j.cub.2011.11.018 PMID:22169537

World-Class Instructional Design and Assessment (WIDA). (2021). *Distance teaching and learning: Supporting all multilingual learners during COVID-19*. https://wida.wisc.edu/teach/distance-teaching-learning

Worwood, M. J. (2020). *From teacher to designer: Promoting teacher creativity when using new technology* (Doctoral dissertation). Retrieved from: http://jhir.library.jhu.edu/handle/1774.2/63559

Write on with Miss G. (2020). *How to use Getty Unshuttered to spark creativity and ELA connections*. Retrieved from https://writeonwithmissg.com/2020/04/29/how-to-use-getty-unshuttered-to-spark-creativity-ela-connections/

Wu, K., & Huang, P. (2015). Treatment of an anonymous recipient: Solid-waste management simulation game. *Journal of Educational Computing Research*, 52(4), 568–600. doi:10.1177/0735633115585928

Wurzer, G. (n.d.). Scientific Writing with Google Docs (Digital Architecture and Regional Planning). Technical University of Vienna.

Yamagata-Lynch, L. C. (2014). Blending online asynchronous and synchronous learning. *International Review of Research in Open and Distance Learning*, 15(2), 189–212. doi:10.19173/irrodl.v15i2.1778

Yang, J. C., Chien, K. H., & Liu, T. C. (2012). A digital game-based learning system for energy education: An energy COnservation PET. *Turkish Online Journal of Educational Technology*, 11(2), 27-37.

Yang, D. (2017). Instructional strategies and course design for teaching statistics online: Perspectives from online students. *International Journal of STEM Education*, 4(1), 1–15. doi:10.118640594-017-0096-x PMID:30631690

Yarmosky, A. (n.d.). *Governor Northam Orders Statewide Closure of Certain Non-Essential Businesses, K-12 Schools*. Retrieved August 12, 2020, from https://www.governor.virginia.gov/newsroom/all-releases/2020/march/headline-855292-en.html

Yeager, D. S., Hanselman, P., Walton, G. M., Murray, J. S., Crosnoe, R., Muller, C., Tipton, E., Schneider, B., Hulleman, C. S., Hinojosa, C. P., Paunesku, D., Romero, C., Flint, K., Roberts, A., Trott, J., Iachan, R., Buontempo, J., Yang, S. M., Carvalho, C. M., ... Dweck, C. S. (2019). A national experiment reveals where a growth mindset improves achievement. *Nature*, 573(7774), 364–369. doi:10.103841586-019-1466-y PMID:31391586

Yilmaz, K. (2008). Constructivism: Its theoretical underpinnings, variations, and implications for classroom instruction. *Educational Horizons*, 86(3), 161–172.

Yin, R. (2014). *Case study research: Design and methods* (5th ed.). Sage.

Compilation of References

Yoon, S. A., Anderson, E., Koehler-Yom, J., Evans, C., Park, M., Sheldon, J., Schoenfeld, I., Wendel, D., Scheintaub, H., & Klopfer, E. (2017). Teaching about complex systems is no simple matter: Building effective professional development for computer-supported complex systems instruction. *Instructional Science*, *45*(1), 99–12. doi:10.100711251-016-9388-7

Young, J. M. (2016). Unpacking TPACK in mathematics education research: A systematic review of meta-analyses. *International Journal of Educational Methodology*, *2*(1), 19–29. doi:10.12973/ijem.2.1.19

Yu, P., & Golden, J. (2019). Developing TPACK in elementary mathematics education : a framework to design activities with pre-service teachers. In M. Niess, H. Gillow-Wiles, & C. Angeli (Eds.), *Handbook of research on TPACK in the digital age*. IGI Global. doi:10.4018/978-1-5225-7001-1.ch003

Yurkofsky, M. M., Blum-Smith, S., & Brennan, K. (2019). Expanding outcomes: Exploring varied conceptions of teacher learning in an online professional development experience. *Teaching and Teacher Education*, *82*, 1–13. doi:10.1016/j.tate.2019.03.002

Zeki, C. P. (2009). The importance of non-verbal communication in classroom management. *Procedia: Social and Behavioral Sciences*, *1*(1), 1443–1449. doi:10.1016/j.sbspro.2009.01.254

Zhao, Y. (2003). *What teachers should know about technology? Perspectives and practices*. Information Age Publishing.

Zhi, Q., & Su, M. (2015, October). *Enhance collaborative learning by visualizing process of knowledge building with Padlet. In 2015 international conference of educational innovation through technology (eitt)*. IEEE.

Zhong, R. (2020, March 17). The Coronavirus exposes education's digital divide. *The New York Times*. Retrieved from https://www.nytimes.com/2020/03/17/technology/china-schools-coronavirus.html

Zhou, W., Simpson, E., & Domizi, D. P. (2012). Google Docs in an out-of-class collaborative writing activity. *International Journal on Teaching and Learning in Higher Education*, *24*(3), 359–375.

Zielinski, D. E. (2017). The Use of Collaboration, Authentic Learning, Linking Material to Personal Knowledge, and Technology in the Constructivist Classroom: Interviews with Community College Faculty Members. *Community College Journal of Research and Practice*, *41*(10), 668–686. doi:10.1080/10668926.2016.1220338

Zike, D. M. (Ed.). (2012). Envelope graphic organizers: Using repurposed envelopes for projects, study guides, and daily work; Strategies for all subjects, all levels. Dinah-Might Adventures, LP.

Zimmerman, A., & Gould, J. (2020, April 25). *5 weeks into online learning, NYC is still racing to get thousands of devices to students*. Chalkbeat. https://ny.chalkbeat.org/2020/4/25/21236279/students-lack-devices-nyc-schools-coronavirus

Zoom. (n.d.). https://zoom.us/

Zughoul, O., Momani, F., Almasri, O. H., Zaidan, A. A., Zaidan, B. B., Alsalem, M. A., Albahri, O. S., Albhar, A. S., & Hashim, M. (2018). Comprehensive insights into the criteria of student performance in various educational domains. *IEEE Access : Practical Innovations, Open Solutions*, *6*, 73245–73264. doi:10.1109/ACCESS.2018.2881282

Zumbach, J., Rammerstorfer, L., & Deibl, I. (2020). Cognitive and metacognitive support in learning with a serious game about demographic change. *Computers in Human Behavior*, *103*, 120–129. doi:10.1016/j.chb.2019.09.026

Zumbrunn, S., & Bruning, R. (2013). Improving the writing and knowledge of emergent writers: The effects of self-regulated strategy development. *Reading and Writing*, *26*(1), 91–110. doi:10.100711145-012-9384-5

Zupancic, N. (2012). The importance of lesson planning. *Making a Difference: The Official Blog of Teach and Learn with Georgia*. Retrieved from https://teachandlearnwithgeorgia.wordpress.com/2012/07/26/the-importance-of-lesson-planning/#:~:text=Lesson%20planning%20lets%20you%20track,your%20own%20mistakes%20and%20missteps

About the Contributors

Margaret (Maggie) L. Niess, Ph.D., is a Professor Emeritus of Mathematics Education at Oregon State University. Her research has focused primarily on the knowledge teachers rely on for integrating technologies in teaching mathematics and science, otherwise called Technological Pedagogical Content Knowledge or TPACK. Her current research focuses on teachers' knowledge development for teaching in multiple contexts including online virtual environments. She has authored multiple peer-reviewed journals and chapters including multiple teacher preparation books. She directed the design, implementation, and evaluation of an online Master of Science degree program for in-service K-12 mathematics and science teachers with an interdisciplinary science, mathematics, and technology emphasis. She has chaired multiple committees for the Association of Mathematics Teacher Educators, American Educational Research Association, and the Society for Information Technology and Teacher Education.

Henry Gillow-Wiles has both a Ph.D. in Mathematics Education and a M.S. in Mathematics from Oregon State University. His research centers on investigating the impact of online community of inquiry structures on teaching and learning. His most recent project focused on helping college level faculty redesign their courses to more fully engage first-year and first-generation students using a High Impact Practices structure to create signature assignments. With a student-centered pedagogical perspective, these vulnerable students were better able to transition to the tasks for college students. As part of sharing his research, he has edited several research compendiums and co-authored multiple peer-reviewed journals and chapters. In addition to delivering numerous conference presentations, he has served as the chair for the SITE math education SIG and the Internet officer in the American Education Research Association as for the SIG-TACTL (Technology as a Change Agent in Teaching and Learning).

* * *

Kym Acuña has an Ed.D. in Educational Leadership, Administration, and Policy from Pepperdine University. She has over 20 years of experience in teaching and as a school administrator. She is an Associate Professor at Midwestern State University. Currently she is the chair of Graduate and Adult Education and teaches in the Masters and EdD program in Educational Leadership. Her research interests include personal leadership, service learning, and developing school leaders for equitable schools.

Jennifer Albert received her Ph.D. in Science Education from North Carolina State University and has an M.A. in Curriculum and Instruction from Austin Peay State University. She also specializes in STEM educational evaluation and research with an emphasis on K-16 computer science education,

About the Contributors

science education, educational assessment, and STEM classroom implementation. She has worked on several grants specializing in broadening participation of underrepresented minorities, particularly in rural schools. She taught high school science and now teaches both undergrad and graduate courses in STEM Education (Instructional Technology, Research Methods, etc.) at The Citadel. She is currently Director of the STEM Center of Excellence and an Assistant Professor in the Zucker Family School of Education at The Citadel.

Ashley Andrews is the Assistant Director of the STEM Center of Excellence. Ashley completed her undergraduate and Master's work at James Madison University. She then began her teaching career at an International Baccalaureate school with Arlington Public Schools, where she taught middle school social studies and reading. Ashley also has experience with Adult Education and Instructional Design and her interests include STEM and curriculum development.

Courtney K. Baker is an assistant professor in Mathematics Education Leadership at George Mason University, in Fairfax, Virginia. An educator and advocate for public education for over 15 years, Baker's research agenda is centered in mathematics education and teacher development. Specifically, her work includes advancing the role of mathematics specialists, and developing effective mathematics teacher leaders that both influence learning and increase interest in mathematics. She is co-developer of the Decision-Making Protocol for Mathematics Coaching: a four-phase protocol that provides guidance to individuals as they support the skillful implementation Principles to Actions' Mathematics Teaching Practices (NCTM, 2014).

Phyllis Balcerzak, Ph.D., is an Associate Teaching Professor in the College of Education at the University of Missouri-St. Louis where she works with teams to explore, design, and build innovative programming for K-20 students and educators. Balcerzak received her Ph.D. from Kent State University in Ecology (1990). She joined the UMSL-COE in 2015 after retiring from her career at Washington University where she was a clinical associate professor of teacher preparation (1996-2006) and director of professional development in science education (2006-2014). Through the course of her career, Balcerzak has designed and implemented several national and state STEM initiatives for K-12 teachers, among these the Center for Inquiry in Science Teaching and Learning (CISTL), a collaboration between higher education and informal science institutions; Life Sciences for a Global Community, a national MS in biology degree program for secondary teachers; and, Tools of Inquiry, a graduate degree program for educators interested in the design of professional development for K-12 educators. Prior to her work in higher education, Balcerzak was a teacher of science and social studies for students in grades 4-12, where she focused her attention on the processes and strategies for teaching a student-centered curriculum. This foundational experience as a practitioner has informed her subsequent goals to place research in the service to practice and to generate research from the study of practice.

Amy Barrios is an Associate Professor of Curriculum and Instruction at Texas A&M University-San Antonio. Her research interests include adolescent literacy, teacher preparation, online instruction, and culturally relevant pedagogies.

Douglas Bengtson is a 6-12 certified mathematics teacher with nine years of teaching experience. Douglas earned his Bachelor's Degree in 2012 from the University of Illinois in Urbana Champaign with a major in mathematics and a minor in secondary education.

Beth Beschorner is an Associate Professor in the Elementary and Literacy Education Department at Minnesota State University, Mankato where she teaches coursework related to literacy and scholarly writing. Her research interests include integrating technology into literacy instruction, pre-service teacher education, and anti-racist education. She has published articles in journals such as The Reading Teacher, Reading Horizons, and Journal of Research in Childhood Education.

Melanie Blanton is the outreach coordinator for the STEM Center of Excellence and an adjunct instructor at The Citadel. A former classroom teacher and teacher mentor, she has served as a project manager on several grants to support teachers in integrating making and computational thinking into their classrooms.

Maggie Broderick, PhD, currently teaches and serves as a Dissertation Chair at Northcentral University in the position of Associate Professor - Curriculum and Assessment. Dr. Broderick has taught online for 10 years at various universities and previously taught on-ground in both higher education and K-12 education in the Pittsburgh, PA area.

Emma Bullock, Ph.D., is an Assistant Professor of Mathematics Education at Sam Houston State University. She researches teachers' use of digital math apps and other visual representations including the use of guided notes and studies the intersection between student mathematics achievement and school leadership, modelling schools as complex adaptive systems (CAS).

Lisa Beth Carey is a teacher educator and researcher using the lens of Mind, Brain, and Education science to enhance learning opportunities and outcomes for students with neurodevelopmental disabilities. In her role as the Assistant Director of the Center for Innovation and Leadership in Special Education at Kennedy Krieger Institute, Dr. Carey collaborates with medical providers and neurocognitive researchers to bridge the divide between pediatric medicine and K-12 schooling. Dr. Carey has a special interest in inclusive educational practices, Universal Design for Learning, instructional and assistive technologies, and student neurodevelopmental skills. She is dedicated to enhancing both pre-service and in-service professional development opportunities for educators as well as pediatric medical providers serving children and adolescents with neurodevelopmental disabilities. To that end, Dr. Carey collaborates with the Johns Hopkins University School of Education as an Assistant Research Scientist as well as University of Maryland as special graduate faculty.

Mona M. Choucair, Ph.D., is a Senior Lecturer with a dual appointment in the School of Education and the College of Arts & Sciences in the English Department. Dr. Choucair teaches American Literature survey courses as well as an Advanced Grammar course in the English department and teaches Young Adult Literature and Secondary Methods courses in the School of Education. She also supervises secondary teaching interns. She has been a Councilor for the Council for College Teachers of English, is an active member of South Central Modern Language Association, and continues her annual role as an invited grader and question leader for The College Board, specifically in the Advanced Placement English language exams.

About the Contributors

Beth Cory, Ph.D., is an Associate Professor of Mathematics Education at Sam Houston State University. Her research interests include the teaching and learning of calculus concepts, concept inventory development for Calculus I, and developing students' understanding of geometry with a current focus on the use of guided notes to improve student mathematics achievement.

Shannon Driskell is a Professor of Mathematics Education in the Department of Mathematics at the University of Dayton in Dayton, Ohio. She teaches undergraduate mathematics content courses for preservice teachers. Her research focuses on the use of technology to support teaching and learning mathematics, mathematical content knowledge for teaching, and mathematical mindsets.

Xiaoxue Du earned Ed.D and Ed.M. in Instructional Technology and Media, from Teachers College, Columbia University. Previously, she earned an M.A. in Education Technology Specialist from Teachers College, Columbia University, which led to an initial teaching certificate from New York State. Her research focuses on professional development, assistive technology, and special education.

Jamie Ewing is a National Board Certified Teacher teaching as the Science/STEM Specialist at PS277x, the Bronx, in the New York City Public School system. He works with 2nd, 3rd, 4th, and 5th graders in exploring all things STEAM! Jamie is featured in the www.Code.org video alongside Bill Gates, Mark Zuckerberg, and other industry leaders. STEM + Design Think + PBL + 21st Century Skills = 21st century education! Mentor, Innovator, Coach & Believer Students Come First. He also believes that he does not go into the classroom to inspire his students rather he believes that he is inspired to be a better educator daily by his students. A 13 year veteran educator, he has been recognized nationally/international for the way he inspires learning. Jamie is the 2015 Henry Ford Innovative Teacher of the Year, 2014 MOHAI Teacher of the Year, and the 2013 National Academy of Arts and Science in Education Innovative Teacher of the Year. A 2010-2019 Microsoft Innovative Educator. Represented the USA at the 2013/2014 Microsoft PIL Global Forum in Prague, CR and Barcelona, Spain Jamie has a degree in Fashion Design from Virginia Commonwealth University and pursued that for 15 years before making the GREAT move over into teaching. He received his masters in education from Antioch University.

Nicole Fletcher is an Assistant Professor of Educational Studies and Teacher Preparation at Fairfield University in Fairfield, CT. She taught in classrooms for ten years, including preschool, kindergarten, and first grade, in both general education and special education classrooms in New York City. She has also worked as a K-5 mathematics coordinator and has facilitated professional development for elementary mathematics teachers and teacher trainers both in the US and abroad. Her research interests include symmetry teaching and learning as well as early mathematics assessment, and she enjoys exploring the fascinating world of children's mathematical thinking and working to make mathematics teaching and learning equitable and accessible for all students.

Göran Fransson was a Professor in Curriculum Studies and an Associate Professor of Education at the Faculty of Education and Business Studies, University of Gävle, Sweden. His research centres on digital technologies in educational contexts, teacher commitment, teachers' professional development and induction and mentoring in different professions, with a primary focus on teachers. He has been published in different journals, books, and anthologies.

Terrie Galanti is an Assistant Professor of Secondary Mathematics and STEM Integration/Computational Thinking at the University of North Florida. She was the first woman in history to graduate at the top of her class from the United States Air Force Academy and earned a master's degree in electrical engineering from Stanford University. She synthesizes her thirty years of experience as an engineer, parent, and K-12 mathematics educator in her research on conceptual readiness for STEM fields of study. She studies online synchronous learning in mathematics education and connects mathematical reasoning and sense-making to computational thinking in K-12 curriculum and classrooms.

Charlotte K. Gallagher-Immenschuh, Ph.D., is an alumna of Northcentral University with a degree in Curriculum and Instruction - English as a Second Language. She graduated with honors as a member of Kappa Delta Pi. She is interested in researching the qualitative value of student-driven curricula through project learning, teacher-student mentorship, and bilingual learners. She has presented at national and local conferences. She currently teaches and serves as the owner and Director of an after-school, K-12 educational center for mathematics, reading, and writing. She also serves as an online homeschool teacher for students across the United States. She began her teaching career in 2001 as a high school mathematics teacher and went on to develop and conduct professional development and coaching for teachers. Dr. Gallagher-Immenschuh has 20 years of experience as a teacher, both in-person and online, in San Antonio, TX.

Dittika Gupta has a Ph.D. in Curriculum and Teaching with a focus in mathematics education from Baylor University. She has over 10 years of experience in teaching and is an Associate Professor at Midwestern State University. Currently she works with pre-service teachers in mathematics methods courses and in field experiences. Her research interests include noticing children's mathematical thinking, lesson study, and preparation of teacher candidates.

Julie Herron, Ph.D., is an Associate Professor of Elementary Mathematics and the Associate Dean of the College of Education at Augusta University. Her research interests are in early childhood mathematics assessments and pre-service teachers' perceptions about teaching and learning mathematics.

Angie Hodge-Zickerman is an Associate Professor in the Department of Mathematics and Statistics at Northern Arizona University. She earned her PhD in mathematics education in 2007 from Purdue University. Her research interests include active learning in the mathematics classroom, technology and its role in active learning, and equity issues in the STEM disciplines.

Tracey S. Hodges is an assistant professor of Literacy Education and the Associate Director of the Belser-Parton Literacy Center at the University of Alabama. She earned her Ph.D. in 2015 from Texas A&M University, majoring in Curriculum and Instruction with a literacy emphasis and Advanced Research Methods certificate. She is a former middle school English teacher, which influenced her interest in developing high quality literacy teachers. Her current research interests include developing methods, strategies, and interventions for improving writing instruction in grades K-8 and integrating children's literature in content area and literacy instruction. She integrates high-quality literature with science, social studies, mathematics, and other content areas to improve reading and writing outcomes. She is also interested in studying how children develop empathy through reading multicultural literature and engaging in thoughtful discussions.

About the Contributors

Jörgen Holmberg is Assistant Professor of Curriculum Studies at the Faculty of Education and Business Studies, University of Gävle, Sweden. He has experience in teacher education, digital technologies and design-based research. He is deeply involved in explorative research, for example at the University of Gävle's Digital Learning Lab (DLL). This includes a close cooperation with schoolteachers with a focus on the pedagogical use of digital technologies and the potential added pedagogical value of this use for teaching and learning.

Shamila Janakiraman is a visiting faculty of Learning Design and Technology in the department of Curriculum and Instruction at Purdue University. Her research interests are in emerging technologies like game-based learning and augmented reality, attitude change instruction in socio-scientific topics, online teaching and learning, MOOCs, and adult education. Her dissertation research focused on the use of game-based learning to change attitudes in environmental sustainability education.

Robin Jocius has interdisciplinary research that focuses on teacher learning and children and adolescents' interactions with digital media. A former classroom teacher and reading interventionist, she has collaborated on several grants to support teachers in integrating making and computational thinking into their classrooms. Her research interests include digital literacies, computational thinking, making, teacher learning, and culturally responsive instruction.

Eleanor M. Johnston recently completed her Ph.D. in Education: Language, Culture and Teaching at York University. Her work explores the ways in which curriculum, pedagogy and the resulting objects we choose for study, interact with dominant discourses, belonging and identity. She has collaborated with performers in creating lecture-concerts exploring Canadian musical responses to the Holocaust, and Jewish diasporic works in America, exoticism and colonialism in vocal music, as well as other artistic and social themes. In conferences, she has presented work on democratizing music curricula and pedagogy for AERA, and the work of praxis and poesis using opera in curriculum for AAACS. In addition to her scholarly work, she has worked in the public school board as an elementary and music teacher and as the education coordinator for the Buffalo Philharmonic where she collaborated on teacher workshops, public education, student concerts (including the logistics of unloading and seating students from a hundred school buses within 30 minutes) and related teaching materials.

Deepti Joshi is an Associate Professor of Computer Science at The Citadel, the Military College of South Carolina. Her research interests include spatio-temporal data analytics, integrating wide variety of data for story building purposes, using data-driven approaches to model complex phenomena, and natural language processing. She is currently working in the domains related to anticipating social unrest, understanding natural disaster response, and identifying user writing attributes to develop their Email DNA. She received the Faculty Excellence Award for Research in 2018 from The Citadel. Dr. Joshi's work on social unrest anticipation is funded by the Department of Defense. She also works extensively in the K-12 space to help the teachers learn how to integrate computing the core-disciplines. This is work is funded through the NSF STEM+C, NSF RPP, and other state grants. She earned her Ph.D. in 2011 from the University of Nebraska-Lincoln (UNL) in Computer Science with a focus on polygonal spatial clustering. She still continues to maintain close ties with UNL and works on collaborative research projects.

Candace Joswick is an Assistant Professor of Mathematics Education in Curriculum and Instruction in the College of Education at the University of Texas at Arlington. Her research interests, projects, and publications are in the areas of learning progressions and trajectories, language and classroom discourse, and technology. She has 5 years of experience as a secondary mathematics teacher, 8 years of experience instructing in higher education, and has given myriad professional developments to inservice and preservice teachers.

Lisa Kasmer is a professor of mathematics education at Grand Valley State University.

Pankaj Khazanchi is a doctoral candidate at Liberty University. Mr. Khazanchi received his Educational Specialist Degree in Curriculum and Instruction from Lincoln Memorial University, TN. He has a Master's in Psychology and Childcare and Education. Mr. Khazanchi has over 28 years of experience teaching students with disabilities and has served in several leadership positions. He presently holds a position at Cobb County School District as an Autism Specialist Teacher. He has presented in well-known international and national conferences both in India and United States. His expertise includes integrating technology to support students with disabilities, gamification, artificial intelligence, inclusive education, behavior modification, cognitive load theories, learning disability, and autism. He served as a Co-Chair of New Possibilities with Information Technology, for a period of three years, at Society for Teacher Education and Information Technology. He is Microsoft Innovative Educator and Seesaw Certified Educator.

Rashmi Khazanchi presently serves as a science/ inclusion teacher at Mitchell County High School in Camilla, Georgia. She is a doctoral candidate at the Open University of the Netherlands. Her research focuses on Artificial Intelligence in Education. Ms. Khazanchi has an Educational Specialists Degree in Curriculum and Instruction from Lincoln Memorial University, TN, and a Post Graduate Diploma in Health Psychology and Behavior Modification, and a Master's Degree in Organic Chemistry. She has two decades of teaching experience in K-12 classrooms. Her interest area includes artificial intelligence in education, inclusive education, gamification of learning, Augmented Reality, and Virtual Reality. She has been associated with professional educational organizations, such as SITE, AIED, and AERA, and is actively involved with different SIGs as a reviewer and presenter. She has presented and authored various papers, book chapters, and articles related to teaching science and integrating technology in K-12 classrooms at various national and international conferences. Presently she is serving as a co-chair for Research and Evaluation SIG at Society for Teacher Education and Information Technology.

Karen Kohler is currently an Assistant Professor of Curriculum and Instruction at Texas A&M University-San Antonio. Her research interests include family engagement, teacher preparation, Open Education Resources (OER) and educational collaboration between teachers.

Jennifer Lee Kouo is an Assistant Professor in the Department of Special Education at Towson University. Dr. Kouo is passionate about both instructional and assistive technology, as well as Universal Design for Learning (UDL), and utilizing inclusive practices to support all learners. Dr. Kouo is currently engaged in multiple research projects that involve multidisciplinary collaborations in the field of engineering, medicine, and education, as well as research on teacher preparation and the conducting of evidence-based interventions in school environments. Dr. Kouo received a B.A. in Integrated Elementary

About the Contributors

and Special Education from Towson University, a M.S. in Education of Students with Autism and Other Pervasive Developmental Disorders, and Advanced Methods for Differentiated Instruction, Inclusive Education for Mild to Moderate Disabilities from Johns Hopkins University, and a Ph.D. in Special Education with an emphasis in severe disabilities and Autism Spectrum Disorders from University of Maryland, College Park.

Tammy Kraft is a doctoral student at George Mason University in Fairfax, Virginia, studying mathematics education leadership and teacher education. As a career-switcher from business to mathematics education, she recognizes the value and importance of mathematics in the real world. During her teaching career, her top priority was helping all students see the practicality and relevance of mathematics to their daily lives. As she transitions from middle school mathematics teacher to teacher educator, that same priority continues. Her research interest addresses the persistent achievement gap in middle school mathematics through online teacher professional development.

Tiffany Labissiere is a citywide literacy coach and educational leader in NYC. She has both a Masters in secondary education and educational leadership. Over the past 19 years in education, she has dedicated her work to teaching middle and high school students in urban settings. Tiffany has also presented at national conferences and has published several research articles and book chapters. Tiffany's interest in student engagement and inquiry guide her coaching and research work.

Salika Lawrence is professor and Campbell Endowed Chair of Urban Education at The College of New Jersey where she teaches teacher education courses in literacy and urban education. She is a former middle school and high school teacher, and literacy coach. Dr. Lawrence is also the founder of Literacy Network. Her research interests include critical literacy, teacher education and professional development, sociology of education, social contexts of education, and adolescent literacy.

Victor R. Lee is an Associate Professor in the Graduate School of Education at Stanford University. Through his research, he tries to understand the new opportunities for people of all ages to learn STEM content and practices with the support of emerging digital technologies. Current research examines K-12 teaching and learning about data - and data science in particular, computational thinking in elementary school, and maker education in out of school settings. Longer standing lines of work involve studying self-tracking and learning from "Quantified Self" practices and research on science teaching and learning.

Kimberly Morrow-Leong is a mathematics education specialist, teacher, and adjunct instructor at George Mason University. She is an author of the Mathematize It! series of books for K-8 teachers and is a 2009 recipient of the Presidential Award for Excellence in Mathematics and Science Teaching. After teaching and coaching K-8 mathematics, working as an educator researcher and as a coordinator at NCTM, she is happy to return to the classroom as a teacher-researcher to explore real online learning. Dr. Morrow-Leong's research program promotes evidence-based assessment and explores the nature of teachers' engagement with artifacts of student thinking.

Irina Lyublinskaya received her Ph.D. in Theoretical and Mathematical Physics from Leningrad State University in 1991. Currently she is a full professor of mathematics and education at the Teachers College, Columbia University in New York City. She has over 30 years of teaching and research experience. She is a recipient of various awards for teaching excellence, including Radioshack/Tandy Prize for Teaching Excellence in Mathematics, Science, and Computer Science, NSTA Distinguished Science Teaching Award and citation, Education's Unsung Heroes Award for innovation in the classroom, and NSTA Vernier Technology Award. In 2011, she was inducted to NYS Mathematics Educators Hall of Fame. In 2019 she was elected as a full member of the Russian Academy of Natural Sciences. She is a recipient of several outstanding paper awards from AACE and SITE, an author of 16 books, co-author of 11 chapters in books, and has published substantially in internationally recognized academic journals.

Taru Malhotra is a Ph.D. candidate in the Faculty of Education at York University. She completed her Master's degree in Education and her Graduate Diploma in Early Childhood Education from York University. Before that, she completed her Bachelor's in Science from Delhi University. Taru's interests and research center around literacy and technology, instructor-created videos, blended and online learning, educators' beliefs, adoption of technologies, attitudes, pedagogies, and practices across disciplines in K-20. Her dissertation focuses on instructors' beliefs, attitudes, and practices in STEM and non-STEM blended courses. Her Master's research project focused on technology integration within kindergarten literacy learning. Taru has helped evaluate a few K-20 research projects. One such project examined the effectiveness of one-on-one iPad implementation in a Canadian school board. Another project explored instructors' and students' perceptions around teaching and learning in online and blended courses in a Canadian University's Arts and Design department.

Fatemeh Mardi is an engineer and PMP. Her passion for teacher education led her to a Master's in TESOL and teaching certificates in math and elementary education. She earned her Ph.D. in Teaching and Learning from University of Missouri, St. Louis with a focus on instructional technology. At UMSL, she is a post-doctoral fellow writing STEM grants. She teaches educational technology, math education, and curriculum & instruction. Her research is focused on enhancing student online learning experiences and providing support for teachers. She has experience in teacher education in Iran as well. Her transdisciplinary academic background and cultural competence positions her to facilitate professional learning in a variety of content areas. She is interested in finding ways to integrate skills needed to be a 'literate citizen' in this century (technology, writing, global awareness, growth mindset, and computational thinking) into course content.

Audrey Meador is an Assistant Professor of Mathematics Education at West Texas A&M University in Canyon, Texas. Prior to joining WTAMU, she taught 9-12 grade mathematics in various school districts in the Texas Panhandle. Her current research interests include assessment, diverse populations, and virtual learning in mathematics education, as well as K-20 science, technology, engineering, and mathematics teaching and learning.

Kelly Medellin has a Ph.D. in Curriculum and Instruction with a focus in Early Childhood Studies from the University of North Texas. She has over 10 years of experience in teaching and is an Assistant Professor at Midwestern State University. Currently she works with pre-service teachers in bilingual education and early childhood studies courses, and is a university supervisor for clinical teachers. Her research interests include diversity within children's picturebooks and multicultural/multilingual education..

About the Contributors

Ellen B. Meier is Professor of Computing and Educational Practice at Teachers College, Columbia University, where she also directs the Center for Technology and School Change, and the Educational Technology Certification program. Her research interests include the catalytic role of technology for pedagogical change, with an emphasis on school reform issues in urban schools nationally and internationally.

Letha Mellman, Ph.D., is a passionate visionary who is outgoing and determined. Her current research includes creativity, education, online education, deep learning, and providing learners with learning experiences to enrich a lifetime of learning. She currently works as an Adjunct Professor of Learning, Design, and Technology at the University of Wyoming.

Caron Mineo is the Senior Associate Director of Research at the Center for Technology and School Change at Teachers College, Columbia University. Caron oversees several of the Center's long-term grant projects, serves as a liaison between the Center and the schools, and participates in the development of the Center's research-based model. Caron's personal research focuses on issues of leadership surrounding innovation in schools.

Mia Morrison is an instructional technology specialist and a lecturer in instructional technology with the collaborative graduate instructional technology program, a partnership between the University of Maine, the University of Maine Farmington and the University of Southern Maine. She teaches and coaches across diverse technology environments, presents locally, regionally and nationally, and served on the Apple Distinguished Educator international advisory board to advance the utilization of educational technology around the world. In teaching PK12 students, undergraduates and graduates, her courses emphasize incorporation of technology tools, pedagogy, and practice to promote curiosity, customize the learning experience, and inspire student ownership and growth.

Andrea Parrish is the Director of Development and Learning Systems and an Assistant Research Scientist at the IDEALS Institute. Dr. Parrish's areas of expertise include foundations of special education and inclusion; technology integration; assistive technologies; Universal Design for Learning; and serving students with a range of disabilities, particularly Autism Spectrum Disorder. Her research focuses on the translation of evidence-based practices for practitioners, effective technology integration, online learning, and innovative teaching practices to support diverse populations of learners. At the IDEALS Institute, Parrish leads applied research projects related to educational technology, special education and systems change.

Margaret Pinnell is an Associate Dean for Faculty and Staff Development at the University of Dayton in Dayton, Ohio. She is also a Professor in the Department of Mechanical and Aerospace Engineering and The Bernhard Schmidt Chair in Engineering Leadership. She has been involved in K-12 STEM research and engagement since 2007.

Simran Randhawa is a consultant in Disability Studies with over 25 years of experience currently consulting at Assessment Mentoring & Impact Evaluation (AMIE). She received her doctorate from Punjab University, Chandigarh, and specializes in Intellectual Disabilities & Learning Disabilities. Formerly Assistant Professor in Disability Studies for the B. Ed (Learning Disabilities) degree Programme at the same university, she has been conducting professional development programs for regular and special education teachers across schools for Identification and assessment of Learning disabilities, curriculum adaptations for diversity in the classroom, Multisensory Language teaching, Behavioral management, and life skills.

Amy Ray is an Assistant Professor of Mathematics Education in the School of Teaching and Learning at Sam Houston State University. Her research focuses on mathematics teaching and assessment developments aimed at broadening what it means to know and do mathematics as well as demonstrate mathematics understanding. Dr. Ray is currently exploring pre-service elementary teachers' perceptions of mathematics and the use of student work in methods courses.

Nicole Rigelman, Ed.D., is a professor of mathematics education at Portland State University and the Chief Academic Officer for The Math Learning Center (MLC). Her work focuses on teaching through problem solving, promoting meaningful mathematical discourse, and engaging with meaningful assessments. She has worked on a variety of projects focused on developing mathematics teacher leaders.

Mary-Kate Sableski is an Associate Professor in the Department of Teacher Education in the School of Education and Health Sciences at the University of Dayton in Dayton, Ohio. She teaches undergraduate and graduate courses in children's literature, literacy methods, and literacy intervention and assessment. Her research focuses on diversity in children's literature and instructional support for struggling readers.

Emily Saxton, Ph.D., is the Director of Research for The Math Learning Center (MLC), where she contributes to the design of MLC's research agenda, leads research and evaluation projects, and facilitates internal reflection on data. She is a mixed methods researcher and program evaluator. She specializes in STEM education and Social and Emotional Learning. She has worked on a variety of projects focused on improving teacher professional development and testing the efficacy of programs for PK-12 students.

Jason Singh is Head Science Teacher and Vice-Principal at a private high school in Toronto, Ontario, Canada. He has taught the Ontario curriculum for seven years to predominantly international English language learners. In his Master of Education studies at the Ontario Institute for Studies in Education, University of Toronto (OISE/UT), conferred in 2021, he focused on Educational Leadership and Policy and the creation and equitable learning environments. Jason's previous experiences include Principal at a K-8 school on a remote Indigenous reserve in northern Ontario, an Invigilator with Accessibility Services at the University of Toronto, and a Site Coordinator at beyond 3:30, an after-school program for disadvantaged middle school youth in the Toronto District School Board. His research focuses on educational leadership, equity in education, and supporting teachers and students through change and transition.

David A. Slykhuis, Ph.D, is an Assistant Dean and Professor at the University of Northern Colorado. He is the Chair of the National Technology Leadership Summit, co-Chair of the American Association of Colleges of Teacher Education (AACTE) standing committee on Innovation and Technology, and a member of the Steering Committee of the EdTech Genome Project sponsored by the EdTech Evidence Exchange. David is a past President of the Society for Information Technology and Teacher Education (SITE). He is one of the four researchers who developed the Teacher Educator Technology Competencies.

About the Contributors

Jess Smith serves as a graduate writing coordinator at Baylor University, where she earned her Ph.D. in Curriculum and Teaching. While earning her terminal degree, she taught preservice secondary and middle grades teachers. Before joining Baylor School of Education, Dr. Smith worked in 5-12 Title I schools, teaching ELAR and social studies as well as serving as an interventionist and instructional coach. She earned a M.Ed. from Tarleton State University and a B.A. with secondary teaching certificate from the University of North Texas. Dr. Smith, a teacher at heart, researches in the field of preservice teacher development, teacher and student autonomy, writing development, and mentoring.

Emily Southerton is a doctoral candidate in the Learning Sciences and Technology Design and Curriculum and Teacher Education programs at Stanford's Graduate School of Education. She studies the design of learning environments and technologies which promote literacy, agency, and equity. Before coming to Stanford, Emily taught middle school Humanities and Computer Science and created the Poet Warriors Project, a digital publishing platform that amplifies the work of youth poets from low-income schools across the country.

Eric Stade is Professor of Mathematics at University of Colorado Boulder. He is interested in pure mathematics, applied mathematics, and mathematics education. In his spare time, he enjoys rock climbing, rock drumming, and learning Japanese.

Monique Stone earned her PhD in Language Literacy and Socio-Cultural Studies from the University of New Mexico. She has worked in k-12 schools in multiple states as well as community colleges and community-based organizations. Her teaching roles have been in reading, writing, language arts and English as a second language. Her research interests are in culturally responsive teaching, reader response theory, and supporting teachers in developing meaningful and respectful relationships with students.

Meredith Swallow is an Associate Professor of Elementary Education at the University of Maine Farmington. She holds a PhD in Educational Leadership and Policy Studies with a research focus on instructional technology. Dr. Swallow taught for many years as a mathematics teacher focused on engaged and active learning by supporting the connection of knowledge with application and creativity. Her current teaching and research centers on supporting pre-service teachers and in-service graduate-level educators in developing, and engaging with, innovative teaching practices that support active, learner-driven environments, and effective technology integration.

Chris Swanson is the founding executive director of the Johns Hopkins IDEALS Institute in the School of Education where he is also an associate research scientist. Swanson leads a team committed to the discovery and implementation of best practices that promote healthy development and learning across the life-span through integration of the sectors of education, two-generational health, and social services. His particular areas of expertise center on systems' transformation and coordinated, high-quality service delivery models. Swanson previously served as the Principal for the National Connections Academy School, a flagship virtual public and private hybrid program. Prior to that, Swanson was a central office autism and cognitive delay specialist with Baltimore County Public Schools after being a classroom special educator and inclusion resource teacher.

About the Contributors

Sandra Talbert has been an educator for over 30 years and is a strong proven leader in the field. Her service in education has ranged from elementary schools to the college level, including roles as teacher, assistant principal, principal, superintendent, professor, and state-wide trainer. Prior to joining Baylor School of Education, Dr. Talbert most recently served as Superintendent of Schools for a Texas 4A public school district. Dr. Talbert received her bachelor's degree from Stephen F. Austin State University, her master's from Sam Houston State University, and her doctorate from Tarleton State University. She has taught education courses at Tarleton State University and Mississippi State University. Dr. Talbert is known as an instructional leader who has a deep understanding of curriculum and a commitment to sharing that information through intentional and practical staff development, workshops, and keynote addresses. Dr. Talbert also has expertise on the topics of leadership and organizational change. She has a unique ability to engage those she teaches and is known for creating and maintaining a positive, rich learning environment and culture in the organizations in which she serves.

Rachel Terlop is a globally recognized educator who was born in Worthington, OH, and started her educational career in Green Bay, WI. She received her Bachelor of Science in Early Childhood Education from Baldwin Wallace University in 2013, and her Master of Education from Trinity Washington University in 2017. In 2017, Rachel also pursued her yoga teacher certification through Breathe for Change. In 2019, Rachel was awarded the Henry Ford Innovation Nation Teacher of the Year award, and traveled to Uganda to train as an academic coach in the Bwindi school district with Limited Resource Teacher Training (LRTT). The program involved researching, modeling, sharing, and reflecting on 'best practices' with government officials, administrators, and educators. Following these training sessions, there was a large amount of discussion on how American culture and Ugandan culture complimented each other. When she returned home she published her 1st children's book, Maggie the Moomaid, which won a Mom's Choice Award in June 2020. After her training in Uganda, Rachel joined the PhD program at George Mason University and began to reflect on current teaching practices that are meant to support culturally, linguistically, and cognitively diverse students. Finding the research lacking in how to support students communicating non-verbally, Rachel began collaborating on a research text that combines metaphysics, image based communication, and educational pedagogy. Rachel is currently finishing her Bachelors of Divination at the University of Minnesota and is completing editing a book called Cases on Supreme Court Rulings and Inclusivity for Culturally, Linguistically, and Cognitively Diverse Students due out late 2021. She resides in Alexandria, VA with her husband and is the interim editor for the American Educational Research Association Graduate Student Council Newsletter.

Sarah Thomas is in her fifth year of teaching and currently teaches 7th grade math.

Patrick Vennebush, when not solving problems, telling jokes, or playing Ultimate Frisbee, is the Chief Learning Officer for The Math Learning Center, a nonprofit organization that inspires and enables individuals to discover and develop their mathematical confidence and ability. He previously served as the Director of Mathematics at Discovery Education and as the Online Projects Manager at the National Council of Teachers of Mathematics. He regularly speaks at regional, state, and national conferences, and he is the author of multiple articles and three books: Math Jokes 4 Mathy Folks, More Jokes 4 Mathy Folks, and One Hundred Problems Involving the Number 100.

About the Contributors

Elizabeth Walsh-Rock is a high school science teacher in the Ferguson-Florissant School District at the STEAM Academy at McCluer South Berkeley where she teaches Biology, Anatomy and Physiology, and Project Lead the Way Biomedical Science courses. Walsh-Rock received her B.S. in Biology and Secondary Education from Valparaiso University (2017) where she was a cohort member of the Mathematics and Science Education Enrollment and Development (MSEED) Program funded by the National Science Foundation. She has taught middle school and high science and coached national qualifying middle school Science Olympiad students in Missouri and Indiana. She has been involved in curriculum writing at the high school and middle school levels in FFSD, developing environmental stewardship curriculum through an Environmental Protection Agency program, and works with other science educators to create anti-racist classrooms.

Lorrie Webb is currently a Professor at Texas A&M University-San Antonio. She is also the Chair of the Department of Curriculum & Instruction under the College of Education & Human Development. Her research interests include teacher preparation and technology integration.

Mia Kim Williams, Ph.D., is known for her work in innovative and critical pedagogy and is currently Assistant Professor and program coordinator in Learning, Design, and Technology at the University of Wyoming. She works with practicing and preservice teachers as well as doctoral students interested in promoting change in a variety of educational contexts. Her current research projects include using game design as a critical pedagogy and designing transformative learning spaces to promote active learning.

Lindsay Woodward is an Associate Professor in the School of Education at Drake University. Her background as a high school English teacher informs much of her teaching in disciplinary literacy and scholarship in professional development for teachers. Lindsay's research agenda focuses on technology in literacy, broadly. She explores best practices for supporting teachers as they integrate technology into their content area instruction, as well as how secondary students make sense of the diverse texts they encounter when searching online. Currently, Lindsay's research lies in understanding how personal beliefs about knowledge can influence secondary students' reading online and how teachers can support sophisticated personal epistemologies.

Matthew Worwood is Associate Director of UConn Digital Media Design and Director of Digital Media CT, a statewide collaborative dedicated to furthering Digital Media education in Connecticut. Matthew's research focuses on design-based approaches that support the creative development and implementation of educational technology in K-12 education. Much of this work takes place within the Class of 2032 Project, which uses design thinking to explore education change in response to new technology. Matthew served as an advisor to the NMC Horizon Report between 2013-2018, and until recently, was an executive board member of Everwonder Children's Museum. He is currently a contributor to Creativity and Education, founded the fueling creativity podcast, and has a parenting blog called DadsforCreativity.com.

Cindy S. York is an Associate Professor in the Instructional Technology Program of the Educational Technology, Research & Assessment Department at Northern Illinois University. Her research interests include online learning, instructional design, and technology integration.

Paul Yu is a professor of mathematics education with interests in teaching with technology, integrated STEM education, and culturally sustaining pedagogy.

Index

21st century learning 101, 106, 190, 194, 212, 217, 233, 301, 402
4Cs 176-179, 183, 185, 192-194, 196-197, 210, 217, 230, 297, 299, 303, 312, 335-337, 340, 346-349, 351-353, 355, 403, 406, 415, 417, 420, 423

A

AAC 59, 67, 76-79, 81-83, 85
abstraction 361, 363, 377, 650, 654
academic literacy 298, 300, 313-314, 316
action research 194-197, 199-200, 202-203, 205, 207, 209-211, 222, 446, 451-452, 454, 466-468
active learning 63, 160, 220, 231, 278, 280, 282, 290, 292-295, 357, 536, 566, 626, 652-653
asynchronous teaching 631
attitudinal instruction 236-237, 239-240, 249, 253

B

best practices 2, 8, 11-12, 44, 47, 68-69, 79, 91, 95, 102, 110, 116, 122-123, 151, 153, 166-167, 188, 194-195, 207, 209, 213, 236, 239, 291, 299, 314, 332, 360, 406, 422, 424, 466-467, 495-496, 508, 534, 583-588, 590-591, 593, 600, 605-608, 610, 617-619, 624, 643-644, 658-659
Bitmoji classroom 194, 197, 207-210, 658
Blackboard Collaborate Ultra 480, 483, 492
Bridges in Mathematics 423-424, 428, 432, 443-445

C

case-based learning 379, 384, 390-391, 394-398
Children's Literature 363, 494
classroom environment 20, 29, 67, 72, 76, 272, 279, 405, 414, 447, 451, 562, 564, 570, 584-585, 594, 596, 617, 646, 654
classroom routines 403-404, 406, 585
Cognitive Task Analysis 540, 544, 547, 557

cohort model 617-618, 623
communities of practice 50, 60, 92, 362, 535-536, 641
Community of Inquiry 1, 6-8, 14, 17-18, 375, 532, 536, 538, 558, 658, 661-662
computational thinking 359-362, 366, 368, 373-375, 377, 580, 627
computer science 359, 361, 364, 366, 369, 371, 375, 377, 643-644, 646, 650
Connectivism 90, 101, 107, 151, 161, 167, 169, 534, 536, 559
constraints 12, 110, 113-114, 116, 119, 121, 125, 127, 132, 134, 196, 224, 239, 339, 347, 354, 366, 419, 421-422, 511, 517-518, 645
Constructivism 67-69, 81, 85, 90, 140, 144, 167, 169, 193, 278, 280, 534-535
conteXtual knowledge (XK) 177, 188-189, 193, 648, 655
continued learning 67, 72
COVID teaching 612, 614
COVID-19 2, 19-21, 23-25, 30-31, 34-41, 61, 63, 65, 67-69, 75-76, 82-86, 88, 98, 127, 149, 171, 189-190, 193-194, 197, 200, 202, 212-215, 221, 230, 232-233, 236, 255, 259-260, 263, 265, 272, 277, 279, 291, 293-294, 297-298, 313, 324-326, 330-332, 335, 337-338, 350, 355-357, 360, 362-364, 374-375, 377, 404, 425, 434, 443-444, 453, 490-491, 494-495, 497, 500, 509, 511-512, 519, 531-532, 535, 538, 562-563, 565, 567, 570, 573, 576-577, 579, 583-584, 587, 594, 597-598, 604, 606, 618-622, 624-625, 627-629, 637-638, 641, 643-644, 648, 650
creative problem-solving 126-127, 130, 146-147, 278, 291, 373
Creative teaching 137, 294
critical thinking 14, 91, 121, 161, 170, 172, 176-177, 180, 183, 185, 189, 193-195, 197-198, 200-202, 204-205, 207-212, 217-218, 230-231, 235, 243, 248-250, 278, 297, 299-301, 303, 306, 309, 312-313, 335-336, 339, 346, 350-354, 360-362,

366, 384, 389, 395, 398, 402, 406, 415, 418-421, 423-424, 428, 471-472, 474
culturally and linguistically diverse students 84, 297-298, 312, 316
curriculum design 56, 89-91, 94, 105, 107, 174, 472

D

debugging 360, 363, 366-367, 370, 377
decomposition 363, 377
deep learning 89, 149, 151, 153, 157, 160-162, 167, 404
deepening understandings 17, 659
Design Thinking 43, 126, 130-131, 141, 143, 145-147, 524, 526
Desmos 100, 282, 286-287, 448-449, 451-463, 465, 467-469, 549, 563, 566
Developmentally Appropriate Practice 72, 83-84, 212-213, 233-234
DGBL 236-237, 239-242, 246-247, 249, 256
differentiated instruction 212-213, 234, 260, 265, 271, 274, 323, 330, 549
digital accessibility 42, 53, 58
digital game-based learning 236-237, 239, 249-251, 254, 256
digital interactive notebook (dINB) 470, 472, 492
digital social platforms 624, 626-632, 634-635, 637-639
digital tools 48, 60, 93, 100-101, 103, 109-112, 114-116, 119-123, 125, 171, 178-179, 193, 237, 297, 299, 301, 303-304, 307, 311-313, 327-328, 330, 361-362, 379-382, 385, 396, 403, 407, 474-475, 519-520, 522, 524-528, 563, 584, 593, 600, 602
DisCrit 67-68, 70-72, 81-82

E

Early Childhood Education 16, 67-69, 81, 233
early elementary 215, 318-320, 330-331, 369
Ecological Systems 67, 70
eDelphi 149-150, 165
educational design 516-517, 519-532
educational reform 64
Educational Technology 15, 19, 32-35, 37, 41, 47, 65, 85, 90, 105-106, 123, 144, 171, 174, 190-193, 232, 236, 239, 251, 255-256, 274-276, 293-294, 316, 356-357, 376, 397, 444, 446, 448, 488, 490-491, 532-533, 559, 580, 587, 663
effect size 99, 534, 540, 546
Emergent Writing Instruction 334
environmental sustainability 236-239, 241, 248, 251, 253, 257-258
Equity in science 380

Evidence-Based Practices 19, 29, 41, 54, 76, 600
executive function 42, 46, 54-55, 61-62, 64, 66

F

feedback 8, 24, 31-32, 48, 50, 55, 60, 69, 72, 89, 115, 117, 119-120, 125, 127-128, 134-136, 139, 160, 196, 203, 205, 214, 218, 231, 241, 246, 264-266, 270, 302-303, 309-312, 325-326, 339, 351, 354, 364, 369, 382, 392-393, 411, 416, 426, 434-435, 442, 444, 447-448, 451, 454-457, 459, 467, 470-481, 484-492, 500, 504, 524-525, 527, 539-540, 545, 547, 550-551, 553-556, 558, 562, 567-568, 570, 593, 595, 603, 606-609, 615-616, 621-622, 626, 637, 658
feedback strategies 540, 553-554
five-A framework for creativity 126, 129
Flipgrid 120, 135-136, 164, 194-195, 197, 204-210, 305, 312-313, 325, 329, 379-380, 382-383, 390, 392-393, 395-398, 414-415, 417-419, 607, 658
formative assessment 123, 306, 386, 389, 434, 459, 470, 472-476, 478-481, 484-486, 489-490, 492, 518, 525, 539, 551-553, 555-557, 600
Four C Framework for Creativity 126

G

Gen Z 149-169
GeoGebra 448-449, 451, 453-454, 457-458, 460, 463-465, 467-469, 563, 566, 568
Google Slides 207, 209, 222, 229, 282-285, 288, 290, 324, 352, 367, 371-372, 379, 382-383, 386-388, 390, 396, 407, 430-431, 434-435, 437, 460, 476, 480, 498, 502, 504, 506, 548-550, 633-634, 658
Google Suite 382, 423, 425, 427, 443, 445, 447
growth mindset 475, 561-564, 566-569, 576-578, 580-581

H

hands-on learning 94, 212, 230, 234, 367
high school science 259, 386, 390, 548
humanizing 270, 275, 491

I

IAED framework 516-531
Inclusion Classroom 19
Inclusion classrooms 41
in-service teacher 404, 420, 482, 623, 660
instructional design 43, 45, 52, 54, 57-58, 60, 65, 72, 90,

106, 115, 124, 193, 243, 252-253, 262, 277, 390, 484, 488, 496, 498, 510-513, 557, 559, 586, 662
instructional planning 44-45, 49, 54, 61, 109-111, 113-117, 125, 407
instructional technology 39, 105, 107, 169, 298, 312-315, 449, 534-535, 538, 540, 554, 556, 559, 587
Interactive Mathematical Classroom Builder 446
ipsative assessment 470, 472, 474-476, 480-482, 487-488, 490, 492

J

Jamboard 194-195, 197-199, 201, 208-210, 337, 440-441, 447-448, 451, 460, 462, 465, 467, 476, 658

K

K-12 education 12, 31, 126, 149, 236, 314, 316, 471, 486, 494
K-3 Literacy 494

L

learner variability 42-43, 45, 48, 52-53, 57, 60, 66
Learning Disability 19, 35-38, 40-41, 64, 85
learning environment 5, 10-11, 16, 18-19, 21, 23, 28-34, 41-42, 45, 49, 52-55, 57-59, 62, 66, 68, 71, 89, 95, 110, 112, 116, 130, 133, 136, 143, 147, 168, 171, 174, 178, 189, 195, 197, 207, 210, 213-214, 218, 230, 238-239, 242, 246-247, 256, 260, 262, 266, 271, 274, 278, 281, 292, 295-296, 337, 380-381, 397, 447, 449, 451, 453, 467, 471-472, 496, 501, 504, 507, 509, 516, 520, 522, 535, 540, 543, 548, 556-558, 583, 585, 588, 590-595, 597-598, 602-603, 607
learning management system (LMS) 52, 259-260, 380
learning preferences 149, 153-154, 162, 165
learning sciences 86-87, 89, 91, 94, 102-103, 105-107, 252-253
learning space 52, 71, 157, 159, 161-162, 175, 178, 189, 193, 410, 422, 540
Legitimate peripheral participation 220, 222, 228, 232, 235, 376, 533, 558
literacy processing theory 323, 327, 329-330, 332, 334
little-c 126, 136-137, 139, 147

M

Making CT 359-360, 362, 364-366, 370-371, 373-374
Math Learning Center 423-424, 426, 434, 443-445
mathematics education 123, 144, 280, 294, 420, 468-469, 474, 477, 488-490, 561, 577, 579-580, 599
mathematics teacher education 407, 411, 489-490
mathematics teacher educators 420-421, 467, 470, 487
mathematics teaching and learning 402, 406, 424, 432, 468, 491, 579
meaning-making 18, 337, 373, 659, 661
Mentimeter 194-195, 197, 202-205, 208-210, 658
micro level factors 170-171, 175-176, 189
Micro-Level Context 175, 193, 643, 648
mini-c 137-138, 140, 147

N

Number Talks 402-411, 413-422

O

online education 3, 10, 12, 16, 81, 157, 212-214, 231, 332, 335-336, 350, 491, 519, 535-536, 539, 556, 559, 585, 598
online environment 2, 10-11, 28, 102, 164, 213-214, 280, 295-296, 348, 352, 398, 414, 416, 466, 534-535, 537-538, 540, 545, 556, 562, 567-568, 584, 596
online learning 1-3, 7, 9-11, 14-16, 18, 20-21, 23, 29-32, 34-37, 39, 58, 62-66, 69, 72, 86-88, 95, 98, 100-104, 106, 108, 123-124, 140, 143, 149-150, 152, 154, 156-159, 162-166, 168-169, 194, 196-197, 204, 209, 212, 214, 216-218, 221-222, 230-233, 235-236, 247-248, 259-260, 270-272, 277-281, 293-294, 318, 336, 348, 356, 360, 379, 398-399, 403-404, 447, 451, 470-477, 487, 489-490, 492-494, 501, 507, 509, 516-517, 526, 529, 531-532, 534, 536, 538, 555, 557, 559, 584, 594, 596, 599-600, 604, 609, 611, 616-617, 619-620, 624-625, 629, 631, 639, 663
online pedagogy 169, 194, 209, 337, 340, 352, 447, 465-466
online teaching 10, 38, 86, 93, 97, 102, 124, 149-150, 167, 169, 213-214, 216-217, 230, 236, 279, 336-337, 350, 403, 406, 416, 421-422, 446, 453, 460, 464-466, 470, 475, 483, 487, 516-519, 523, 526, 532, 534-536, 541, 553, 556-557, 565, 576, 591, 600, 604-606, 608-610, 619-620, 622, 624-627, 633, 635, 638-639, 661

P

Padlet 117-118, 194-195, 197, 200-202, 207, 209-210, 218, 305-307, 309, 312-313, 379-380, 382-383, 390-393, 395-396, 399-401, 652-653, 658

Pair Programming 378
pandemic 1-2, 12-13, 20-21, 23-25, 28, 31-32, 34, 36-38, 40-41, 61, 63, 68, 75, 86-88, 93, 95, 97-98, 100-102, 126-128, 131, 133, 140, 149, 151-152, 171, 176, 189-190, 193-194, 196-197, 200, 202, 209-210, 212-213, 221, 230-231, 233, 236, 259-260, 263, 272, 277, 279, 291, 297-299, 313, 332, 335, 337-338, 350-351, 354, 357, 360, 362, 364, 366, 374-375, 377, 380, 382, 391-392, 396, 403, 406, 411, 443, 447, 451, 453, 458, 471, 486-487, 491, 494-495, 497, 500, 503, 509, 513, 519, 531-532, 535, 538, 556, 563, 576-577, 579, 584-585, 587, 594, 597-598, 600, 605-606, 609, 618-622, 624-631, 633-634, 636-637, 641, 643-644, 648, 650, 657-659, 661
PDS 610, 616, 618, 623
pedagogical practices 37, 86-88, 92, 101-102, 139, 149-151, 154, 157, 161-162, 165-166, 171, 190, 207, 336, 339, 373, 534-535, 540-541, 543, 556-557, 583, 606, 608-609, 615, 617-618, 637, 660
pedagogical reasoning 68, 86-88, 95, 101-102, 110, 127, 131, 143-144, 172, 192, 195, 209, 236, 239, 278-279, 290-291, 294-295, 379, 382, 385, 444, 491, 516-517, 519-520, 522-524, 526-528, 531-532, 584, 587, 604, 643-645, 650-651, 661
peer support 231, 504, 564, 568, 570, 574
Performance-Based Assessment (PBA) 493
Planning Cycle 109-111, 122-123
PLS-SEM 239, 256
prepared speech 311, 316
pre-service 85, 91, 109-110, 113-114, 116, 122, 124, 192-193, 277, 355, 357, 407, 420, 469, 561-562, 579-580, 583-588, 590-595, 598-619, 621-623, 644, 660, 662
Preservice and Inservice Teacher Training 402
pre-service teacher 91, 193, 590, 599-600, 605, 609-610, 612-616, 618, 623, 662
Preservice Teachers 48, 69, 85, 109, 113-114, 116, 122-123, 154, 191-193, 207, 277, 315, 331, 358, 469, 510, 534-535, 558, 561-562, 579-581, 583-588, 590-595, 598, 600, 602-619, 621-622, 662
primary grades 212-214, 216-217, 222, 230-231, 235, 331
problem solving 4, 22, 91, 131, 142, 145, 151, 191-192, 237, 243, 280, 291, 293, 295, 301, 337, 384, 395, 404, 414-415, 418, 459, 465, 471, 474, 479, 482, 484-486, 492, 540, 577
problem statement 134-138, 147
pro-c 136-139, 147
productive struggle 404, 561-564, 569-572, 576-577, 579, 581

professional development 19, 64, 68-69, 82, 84, 86, 88-89, 91-106, 109-110, 114-115, 123-124, 140-142, 144-146, 154, 171, 179, 193, 256, 259, 303, 305, 312-313, 324, 333, 335, 337, 350-351, 359-360, 363, 374, 376-377, 384, 400, 403-404, 407, 411, 413, 445, 449, 451, 458, 466-468, 484, 496-497, 507-509, 513, 522, 559, 576, 584-587, 595, 610, 619, 623, 625-626, 628-630, 632, 634, 638, 640-641, 660

R

Reading Development 320, 322, 334
reading instruction 109, 116, 119, 325-327, 485, 608
referent group 3, 6, 10-11, 18
Reggio Emilia 217-218, 230-232, 235
relationship building 165, 592, 604-606, 614, 616-617
remote instruction 98, 302, 305, 404, 425, 435, 437, 445, 495, 502-503, 508, 567, 574
remote learning 28, 31, 86, 95, 97, 100, 102, 170-171, 174, 176-177, 179, 183, 185-188, 190, 214, 280, 282, 295-296, 298, 305, 382, 418, 424, 427, 434, 444, 450, 471, 494, 497, 500, 507-508, 517
Remote science teaching 379
remote teaching 28, 39, 63, 98, 100, 102, 150, 152, 154, 279, 294, 297, 299, 301-304, 313, 377, 398, 427, 446, 454, 457, 462, 464-465, 490, 500, 502, 508, 519, 532-533, 641
researcher-practitioner partnership 362, 378, 650

S

SAMR 318, 323, 325-329, 333-334, 404, 422, 443-444, 449, 469
Seesaw 24-26, 34, 38, 215, 233, 370, 423, 425, 427, 442-443, 445, 476, 658
self-directed learning 68, 149, 157-158, 162, 165, 167, 169
self-regulation 7, 11, 16, 42, 46, 54-55, 60, 62, 65-66, 271-272, 274, 399, 472, 474, 540, 551, 558
sense of belonging 1-18, 394, 600, 643, 654, 659-661, 663-664
social climate 261, 271, 275
Social Constructivism 67-69, 81, 140, 534-535
social interaction 34, 259-260, 262, 264, 268-273, 294, 300, 305, 446, 450, 453, 458-460, 532, 535, 641, 658
social presence 1-2, 6-8, 10-11, 13-18, 143, 365, 375, 383-384, 399, 643, 658-661
socio-scientific topics 236-242, 245-250
special education 22-23, 37, 55, 57, 63-65, 70-71, 76,

Index

82-85, 105, 122, 312, 357, 630
Structured Online Discussions 297
student engagement 9, 14-15, 19, 32-33, 39, 41, 88, 103, 109, 127, 131, 159, 177, 196-197, 208, 213, 221, 223, 230, 271, 277, 280, 282, 293, 296, 303, 312, 362, 365, 367-368, 379-380, 383-384, 395, 406, 445, 473-474, 539, 542, 548, 585, 592, 608-609, 616-618, 631, 634, 636, 649, 652, 658-659
Student Role 14-15
student-centered 9, 88-89, 93, 98-99, 101-102, 127, 150, 154-155, 161-162, 165, 214, 223, 280, 298-300, 303, 308, 312-313, 316, 338, 384, 429, 467, 471, 487, 534-535, 543, 554, 556, 587, 652-653, 659, 661
summative assessment 386-387, 389, 392, 470, 472-477, 482, 486-487, 489, 491, 493, 539
SWOC analysis 32-33, 39, 41
synchronous online learning 472, 477, 489, 493

T

tactile activity 278, 281
TACTivity 280-292, 296
task scaffolding 564, 570, 573
Teacher challenges 41
teacher change 51, 92, 128, 132, 139, 142, 578
teacher creativity 126-134, 136-140, 146-147
Teacher Education 38-39, 63, 81-83, 122-124, 140-143, 190-193, 210, 232-233, 251, 275, 294, 331-334, 338, 355, 357-358, 374-377, 396, 404, 407, 410-411, 422, 449, 472, 487-491, 510, 513, 516, 519, 523-524, 526-527, 529, 531-533, 538, 558-559, 580, 585, 587, 592, 594, 599, 604-605, 614, 617-618, 621, 623, 640-641, 645, 660, 662-663
teacher educator 71, 477, 523-525, 527, 533, 561, 563, 586, 594, 613
teacher learning 104, 107, 193, 359-360, 362-363, 377, 402, 404, 407, 410, 412, 482, 624-630, 638-639
Teacher Learning Cycle 402, 404, 407, 410, 412
teacher motivation 564, 570, 572-573
teacher preparation 84, 122, 171, 195, 403-404, 407, 411, 559, 583-584, 588-589, 591-594, 598, 601, 605-606, 613, 644, 648, 657, 660-661
Teaching Mathematics Online 443, 561
teaching modalities 171, 360, 367
Technoethics 121, 123, 125
technological content knowledge 171, 432, 445, 447-448, 561, 563, 566, 645
Technological Pedagogical Content Knowledge 111, 116, 123, 143, 171, 190-192, 295, 323, 333, 382, 422-424, 426, 432-433, 444-445, 447, 469-470, 489-490, 518, 533-535, 556, 558, 563, 565, 578-580, 643-645, 663
Technological Pedagogical Knowledge (TPK) 170-171, 176-179, 188-189, 191, 193, 430, 432, 445, 447-448, 566, 645
Technological Solution 147
technology integration 39, 67-68, 88, 92-93, 105, 109-111, 122-125, 132, 142, 144, 172, 174-176, 190, 193, 298, 312, 314-315, 376, 382, 447, 476, 538, 577, 579-580, 583-585, 587, 590-591, 593-595, 597-598, 602, 640, 648, 663
Technology-Enhanced Activities 423-425, 433, 443, 445
theoretical framework 70, 104, 111, 152, 339, 558, 562, 584
thought experiment 265-266, 269-270
TPACK 111, 114, 132, 140, 143, 171-173, 175-176, 191-192, 295, 318, 323, 325, 327-328, 334, 382, 423, 432-433, 440, 444, 447-449, 458-459, 464-466, 469-470, 472, 475-477, 487-489, 518-519, 534-538, 541, 543-544, 546, 548, 550-551, 555-559, 561, 563, 565, 568, 577-578, 580-581, 644-651, 654-657, 659, 663
transactional distance 259-262, 264, 268-277
trusting 10, 18, 659
tutor presence 17-18
twenty-first century learning 87, 200, 202, 207, 212-213, 235, 297, 395
twenty-first century skills 195-196, 297, 299, 301, 406

U

Universal Design of/for Learning 24, 28, 35, 41-46, 63-66, 70, 84

V

Virtual collaboration 379
virtual environment 11, 20, 28, 31, 33, 44, 111, 140, 179, 188, 200, 209, 240, 246, 266, 280-282, 291, 295-296, 329, 364, 418, 420, 447, 449, 487, 494-498, 500-502, 507-509, 517, 535-536, 543, 547, 551, 555-556, 583-584, 590, 594-595, 602, 644, 653-654, 656, 658, 660, 662
virtual instruction 44, 54, 58, 109, 111, 114, 121, 177, 302, 318, 321, 323, 326-328, 330, 334, 387, 415, 421, 500, 508-509, 583-585, 587, 591, 594, 643-644, 651, 653-655, 657-661
virtual learning 4, 19-21, 23-24, 28-34, 36, 41-44, 48-49, 52-53, 55, 58-59, 61-62, 68, 72, 109-112, 116, 121, 126-127, 130, 135, 147, 150, 162-163,

179, 189-190, 194-195, 197, 199, 202, 204, 207, 209-210, 233, 242, 247-248, 250, 264, 278, 282, 292, 319, 322, 325, 327, 337, 359-360, 366, 373, 380-387, 389-390, 392, 395-396, 401-402, 413, 418-419, 470, 474, 488, 495-496, 504, 507, 509, 535, 538, 540, 543, 556-558, 583-584, 588, 590-595, 597-598, 601-604, 607, 643, 648, 652, 658, 661

virtual learning environments 24, 28, 42-43, 48-49, 52, 55, 110-111, 121, 126-127, 194, 202, 209, 319, 359-360, 538, 540, 591, 593-595, 604

Virtual Reality (VR) 517, 529

virtual students 197-198, 210, 623

virtual teaching 30-31, 44, 95, 109, 207, 209, 355, 359-360, 373, 403-404, 407, 419, 482, 509, 607, 611, 617-618, 643-644, 650-651, 654, 656, 660-662

W

writing development 322, 327-328, 331, 334, 609

writing instruction 26, 39, 109, 116, 119, 121, 124, 323, 325-327, 332, 334, 562

Recommended Reference Books

IGI Global's reference books are available in three unique pricing formats:
Print Only, E-Book Only, or Print + E-Book.

Shipping fees may apply.

www.igi-global.com

ISBN: 978-1-7998-0420-8
EISBN: 978-1-7998-0421-5
© 2020; 1,757 pp.
List Price: US$ **1,975**

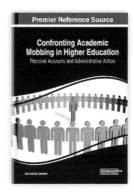

ISBN: 978-1-5225-9485-7
EISBN: 978-1-5225-9487-1
© 2020; 301 pp.
List Price: US$ **195**

ISBN: 978-1-5225-9631-8
EISBN: 978-1-5225-9637-0
© 2020; 379 pp.
List Price: US$ **195**

ISBN: 978-1-7998-0004-0
EISBN: 978-1-7998-0006-4
© 2020; 337 pp.
List Price: US$ **195**

ISBN: 978-1-5225-9833-6
EISBN: 978-1-5225-9835-0
© 2020; 203 pp.
List Price: US$ **155**

ISBN: 978-1-7998-1001-8
EISBN: 978-1-7998-1003-2
© 2020; 330 pp.
List Price: US$ **195**

Do you want to stay current on the latest research trends, product announcements, news, and special offers?
Join IGI Global's mailing list to receive customized recommendations, exclusive discounts, and more.
Sign up at: **www.igi-global.com/newsletters**.

Publisher of Peer-Reviewed, Timely, and Innovative Academic Research

www.igi-global.com   Sign up at www.igi-global.com/newsletters   facebook.com/igiglobal   twitter.com/igiglobal   linkedin.com/igiglobal

Ensure Quality Research is Introduced to the Academic Community

Become an Evaluator for IGI Global Authored Book Projects

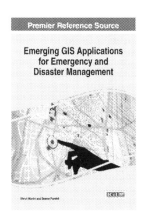   

The overall success of an authored book project is dependent on quality and timely manuscript evaluations.

Applications and Inquiries may be sent to:
development@igi-global.com

Applicants must have a doctorate (or equivalent degree) as well as publishing, research, and reviewing experience. Authored Book Evaluators are appointed for one-year terms and are expected to complete at least three evaluations per term. Upon successful completion of this term, evaluators can be considered for an additional term.

If you have a colleague that may be interested in this opportunity, we encourage you to share this information with them.

IGI Global Author Services

Providing a high-quality, affordable, and expeditious service, IGI Global's Author Services enable authors to streamline their publishing process, increase chance of acceptance, and adhere to IGI Global's publication standards.

Benefits of Author Services:

- **Professional Service:** All our editors, designers, and translators are experts in their field with years of experience and professional certifications.
- **Quality Guarantee & Certificate:** Each order is returned with a quality guarantee and certificate of professional completion.
- **Timeliness:** All editorial orders have a guaranteed return timeframe of 3-5 business days and translation orders are guaranteed in 7-10 business days.
- **Affordable Pricing:** IGI Global Author Services are competitively priced compared to other industry service providers.
- **APC Reimbursement:** IGI Global authors publishing Open Access (OA) will be able to deduct the cost of editing and other IGI Global author services from their OA APC publishing fee.

Author Services Offered:

English Language Copy Editing
Professional, native English language copy editors improve your manuscript's grammar, spelling, punctuation, terminology, semantics, consistency, flow, formatting, and more.

Scientific & Scholarly Editing
A Ph.D. level review for qualities such as originality and significance, interest to researchers, level of methodology and analysis, coverage of literature, organization, quality of writing, and strengths and weaknesses.

Figure, Table, Chart & Equation Conversions
Work with IGI Global's graphic designers before submission to enhance and design all figures and charts to IGI Global's specific standards for clarity.

Translation
Providing 70 language options, including Simplified and Traditional Chinese, Spanish, Arabic, German, French, and more.

Hear What the Experts Are Saying About IGI Global's Author Services

"Publishing with IGI Global has been an amazing experience for me for sharing my research. The strong academic production support ensures quality and timely completion." – **Prof. Margaret Niess, Oregon State University, USA**

"The service was very fast, very thorough, and very helpful in ensuring our chapter meets the criteria and requirements of the book's editors. I was quite impressed and happy with your service." – **Prof. Tom Brinthaupt, Middle Tennessee State University, USA**

Learn More or Get Started Here: For Questions, Contact IGI Global's Customer Service Team at cust@igi-global.com or 717-533-8845

www.igi-global.com

Celebrating Over 30 Years of Scholarly Knowledge Creation & Dissemination

InfoSci®-Books

A Database of Nearly 6,000 Reference Books Containing Over 105,000+ Chapters Focusing on Emerging Research

GAIN ACCESS TO **THOUSANDS** OF REFERENCE BOOKS AT **A FRACTION** OF THEIR INDIVIDUAL LIST **PRICE**.

InfoSci®-Books Database

The **InfoSci®-Books** is a database of nearly 6,000 IGI Global single and multi-volume reference books, handbooks of research, and encyclopedias, encompassing groundbreaking research from prominent experts worldwide that spans over 350+ topics in 11 core subject areas including business, computer science, education, science and engineering, social sciences, and more.

Open Access Fee Waiver (Read & Publish) Initiative

For any library that invests in IGI Global's InfoSci-Books and/or InfoSci-Journals (175+ scholarly journals) databases, IGI Global will match the library's investment with a fund of equal value to go toward **subsidizing the OA article processing charges (APCs) for their students, faculty, and staff** at that institution when their work is submitted and accepted under OA into an IGI Global journal.*

INFOSCI® PLATFORM FEATURES

- Unlimited Simultaneous Access
- No DRM
- No Set-Up or Maintenance Fees
- A Guarantee of No More Than a 5% Annual Increase for Subscriptions
- Full-Text HTML and PDF Viewing Options
- Downloadable MARC Records
- COUNTER 5 Compliant Reports
- Formatted Citations With Ability to Export to RefWorks and EasyBib
- No Embargo of Content (Research is Available Months in Advance of the Print Release)

*The fund will be offered on an annual basis and expire at the end of the subscription period. The fund would renew as the subscription is renewed for each year thereafter. The open access fees will be waived after the student, faculty, or staff's paper has been vetted and accepted into an IGI Global journal and the fund can only be used toward publishing OA in an IGI Global journal. Libraries in developing countries will have the match on their investment doubled.

To Recommend or Request a Free Trial:
www.igi-global.com/infosci-books

eresources@igi-global.com • Toll Free: 1-866-342-6657 ext. 100 • Phone: 717-533-8845 x100

www.igi-global.com

Publisher of Peer-Reviewed, Timely, and Innovative Academic Research Since 1988

www.igi-global.com

IGI Global's Transformative Open Access (OA) Model:
How to Turn Your University Library's Database Acquisitions Into a Source of OA Funding

Well in advance of Plan S, IGI Global unveiled their OA Fee Waiver (Read & Publish) Initiative. Under this initiative, librarians who invest in IGI Global's InfoSci-Books and/or InfoSci-Journals databases will be able to subsidize their patrons' OA article processing charges (APCs) when their work is submitted and accepted (after the peer review process) into an IGI Global journal.

How Does it Work?

Step 1: **Library Invests in the InfoSci-Databases:** A library perpetually purchases or subscribes to the InfoSci-Books, InfoSci-Journals, or discipline/subject databases.

Step 2: **IGI Global Matches the Library Investment with OA Subsidies Fund:** IGI Global provides a fund to go towards subsidizing the OA APCs for the library's patrons.

Step 3: **Patron of the Library is Accepted into IGI Global Journal (After Peer Review):** When a patron's paper is accepted into an IGI Global journal, they option to have their paper published under a traditional publishing model or as OA.

Step 4: **IGI Global Will Deduct APC Cost from OA Subsidies Fund:** If the author decides to publish under OA, the OA APC fee will be deducted from the OA subsidies fund.

Step 5: **Author's Work Becomes Freely Available:** The patron's work will be freely available under CC BY copyright license, enabling them to share it freely with the academic community.

Note: This fund will be offered on an annual basis and will renew as the subscription is renewed for each year thereafter. IGI Global will manage the fund and award the APC waivers unless the librarian has a preference as to how the funds should be managed.

Hear From the Experts on This Initiative:

"I'm very happy to have been able to make one of my recent research contributions *freely available* along with having access to the *valuable resources* found within IGI Global's InfoSci-Journals database."

– **Prof. Stuart Palmer**, Deakin University, Australia

"Receiving the support from IGI Global's OA Fee Waiver Initiative *encourages me to continue my research work without any hesitation*."

– **Prof. Wenlong Liu**, College of Economics and Management at Nanjing University of Aeronautics & Astronautics, China

For More Information, Scan the QR Code or Contact:
IGI Global's Digital Resources Team at eresources@igi-global.com.

Printed in the United States
by Baker & Taylor Publisher Services